american sociological association

the **contexts** reader

second edition

edited by DOUGLAS HARTMANN, *University of Minnesota*
and CHRISTOPHER UGGEN, *University of Minnesota*

W. W. NORTON & COMPANY • NEW YORK LONDON

W. W. Norton & Company has been independent since its founding in 1923, when William Warder Norton and Mary D. Herter Norton first published lectures delivered at the People's Institute, the adult education division of New York City's Cooper Union. The Nortons soon expanded their program beyond the Institute, publishing books by celebrated academics from America and abroad. By mid-century, the two major pillars of Norton's publishing program—trade books and college texts—were firmly established. In the 1950s, the Norton family transferred control of the company to its employees, and today—with a staff of four hundred and a comparable number of trade, college, and professional titles published each year—W. W. Norton & Company stands as the largest and oldest publishing house owned wholly by its employees.

Every effort has been made to contact the copyright holders of each of the selections. Rights holders of any selections not credited should contact W. W. Norton & Company, Inc. for a correction to be made in the next printing of our work.

The text of this book is composed in Sabon with the display set in Futura.
Editor: Karl Bakeman
Production manager: Eric Pier-Hocking
Editorial assistant: Rebecca Charney
Manufacturing by Quad Graphics, Fairfield
Book design by Joan Greenfield

Library of Congress Cataloging-in-Publication Data

The contexts reader / edited by Douglas Hartmann and Christopher Uggen.—2nd ed.
    p. cm.
    At head of title: American Sociological Association.
    Includes bibliographical references.
    ISBN 978-0-393-91232-6 (pbk.)
    1. Social problems.   I. Hartmann, Douglas.   II. Uggen, Christopher.   III. American Sociological Association.
    HN16.C674 2012
    301—dc22

                                        2010045514

W. W. Norton & Company, Inc., 500 Fifth Avenue,
New York, N.Y. 10110
www.wwnorton.com

W. W. Norton & Company Ltd., Castle House,
75/76 Wells Street, London W1T 3QT

1 2 3 4 5 6 7 8 9 0

contents

preface

Contexts magazine is one of the most ambitious, exciting, and important sociological publications in the field, if not the entire academic world—at least, that's what we told ourselves when we first came on board as editors. Such grand, optimistic visions can be difficult to sustain over time and in the face of the daily rigors of actually doing the work. Fortunately, however, our time at the editor's desk has done nothing to dampen our enthusiasm for *Contexts*—and indeed, has done much to confirm and intensify it, often in ways we couldn't anticipate or didn't even realize at the time. One of the most inspiring parts of the job is watching teachers bring sociology classrooms to life with *Contexts*.

When we took over, we were convinced that *Contexts* could bring sociology to a broader public audience (and help reinvigorate sociology in the process). What we didn't yet grasp was how teachers and students are a huge part of this public. By putting together the first edition of *The Contexts Reader*, James Jasper and Jeff Goodwin made it plain. Pitched to a general, nonacademic readership, *Contexts* articles seem to be just the right length and tone for students. But they're also rigorous—each *Contexts* feature has been peer reviewed by real experts who are passionate about both the quality and the readability of the work we're publishing in their fields of expertise. The finished product is a great quarterly magazine and a wide-ranging, accessible introduction to sociology.

We're happy to report this new edition maintains that tradition. We've kept the best, most relevant, and most popular pieces from the first edition and added some excellent and timely articles that have appeared over the past four volumes. Though we've moved a few pieces around, we've kept the basic, fourteen-section structure that corresponds with the organization of many sociology courses and texts. We've also created a new section on Aging and the Lifecourse.

Before letting the articles take center stage, we would be remiss if we didn't offer a few acknowledgments. Our thanks go, first of all, to our *Contexts* authors: obviously there would not be a magazine without you, much less this *Reader*. We also want to thank our predecessors Claude Fischer, the visionary founding editor of *Contexts*, and (again) James Jasper and Jeff Goodwin, who handed off the baton to us. Thanks, too, to the American Sociological Association's Karen Edwards, Sally Hillsman, and Janine Chiappa McKenna as well as the ASA Executive Council and Publications Committee members who have championed *Contexts* over the years. And we must recognize the incredible efforts of the University of California Press in launching and establishing the magazine in its first decade. All of the content in this *Reader* originally appeared under their imprint.

Editing is key to the *Contexts* mission, and the magazine has had several great managing editors over the years—ours at Minnesota have been Amy Johnson and Letta Page, and we cannot thank them enough for their efforts and total commitment to the project. We also want to celebrate the students in the University of Minnesota Department of Sociology who have contributed to *Contexts* over the years. Although they are simply too many to name, we do want to single out those who worked most directly with us on this *Reader*: Alex Casey, Kia Heise, Wes Longhofer, Hollie Nyseth, Jon Smajda, and Dan Winchester.

And one final thank you to our editor at Norton, Karl Bakeman. Without his energy, enthusiasm, and vision, neither this edition nor the previous one would have been possible.

Doug Hartmann
Chris Uggen

the **contexts** reader

part 1

Self and Community

bonnie erickson

social networks: the value of variety

winter 2003

people are healthier and happier when they have intimates who care about and for them. but they also do better when they know many different people casually.

aving close kin and intimate friends helps with many things, from coping with everyday problems to living longer. But what about the hundreds of more casual connections individuals have? What of acquaintances, workmates, and neighbors? We tend to make such fast friends easily and lose them without noticing. Nonetheless, these seemingly thin social bonds are quite valuable when they are diverse.

Variety is the key. Knowing many kinds of people in many social contexts improves one's chances of getting a good job, developing a range of cultural interests, feeling in control of one's life, and being healthy. Sometimes knowing many kinds of people is helpful because it improves the chances of having the right contact for some purpose: hearing of an attractive job opening, borrowing a lawnmower, getting the home cleaned.

Network variety can also be useful in itself, for example in jobs that call for diverse contacts. Either way, the critical matter is the variety of acquaintances and not the mere number.

understanding acquaintanceship

Sociologists have measured acquaintance networks by focusing on occupations. People in different occupations differ from each other in many important ways. The work we do reflects much of our pasts, such as schooling and family background, and shapes the ways we live, such as tastes and lifestyles. Generally, someone who knows people in diverse kinds of jobs will thereby know people who are diverse in many respects. The standard strategy is to present a respondent with a list of occupations that range from very high to very low in prestige, and ask whether the respondent knows anyone in each.

> Knowing many kinds of people in many social contexts improves one's chances of getting a good job, developing a range of cultural interests, feeling in control of one's life, and being healthy.

The greater the number of occupations within which a respondent has a contact, the more the variety in the respondent's social network.

Researchers using this measure have found interesting differences between respondents in different nations. For example, a study in Albany, New York, and a study in East Germany before the fall of the Communist regime each asked respondents about the same 10 occupations: Did they know anyone who was a lawyer, small business owner, teacher, engineer, motor mechanic, secretary, bookkeeper/office clerk, salesperson, porter/janitor, or waiter?

The average respondent in Albany knew someone in 4.5 of these occupations, compared to an average of 3.8 for East Germans, so the American networks were about 20 percent

One resource for keeping track of diverse acquaintances. (Courtesy of Jon Wagner)

more diverse. This is not surprising given that East Germans were wary of strangers in a totalitarian society in which about one in ten people in every work group was an informant for the secret police.

Such acquaintances are a more diverse set than are the few people to whom we feel really close—both because weak ties greatly outnumber strong ones, and because our close ties are usually limited to people very much like ourselves. For example, when I studied the private security industry in Toronto I asked whether people knew close friends, relatives, or anyone at all in each of 19 occupations. My respondents knew relatives, on average, in about two of these occupations, close friends in about half a dozen and anyone at all in about a dozen.

In every country that has been studied in this way, being of higher status goes with having a wider variety of acquaintances. In the Toronto security industry, business owners had contacts in 15 occupations, managers in 13, supervisors 10, and mere employees 9. In Hungary, before and even more so after the end of Communism, wealthier people had more diverse networks than the less wealthy. In Taiwan, more highly educated people have more diverse acquaintances than the less educated, and men have more diverse acquaintances than women do. In general, every kind of social advantage tends to generate a network advantage, which in turn helps the socially advantaged to stay ahead.

networks and jobs

Diverse networks can help people to get good jobs. Having a variety of acquaintances improves a jobseeker's chances of having one really useful contact, and variety itself is a qualification for some upper-end jobs.

People in North America find their jobs with the help of a contact roughly half the time. We might assume that such helpers must be close friends and relatives willing to work hard for the job hunter. But this is not the usual story in Western nations. Close friends and kin want to help, but often cannot do very much because they are too much alike: they move in the same social circles and share information and influence, so they can do little for the candidate beyond what he or she can do alone. But acquaintances are more varied, less like each other, more likely to have new information and more likely to include people highly placed enough to influence hiring. Thus family and close friends provide fewer jobs (and often worse jobs) than do people outside the intimate circle. This is the surprising finding that Mark Granovetter called "the strength of weak ties" (the title of one of the most frequently cited articles in social science).

The strength of strong ties applies best to the few people at the top, because they have highly placed kin and friends who collect a lot of information and can exert a lot of influence. In general, more highly placed people can connect a jobseeker to more highly placed jobs, and one big advantage of having a diverse network is the improved chance of knowing such a useful contact. The Albany study found that people with more diversified acquaintances were more likely to get help from contacts holding more prestigious jobs, which led in turn to getting a job with higher prestige. On the other hand, for most people, using a friend or relative as a contact meant using someone with a lower-ranking job, and hence getting a worse job. For the few who came from privileged backgrounds, all kinds of helpers—friends, relatives, or acquaintances—were in high-status positions on average, and all those kinds of contacts helped them get good jobs.

Having a diverse set of acquaintances matters where there is a fairly free market in jobs and a fairly rich supply of jobs. If jobs are scarce, those in the know will hoard access to good ones for people they care about the most, so strong ties are more valuable in these circumstances. In non-market systems run by the state, the private use of personal contacts to get jobs may be risky: networking subverts state power and policy, and influential people may not want to be responsible for the occupational or political errors of acquaintances whom they help. Well-placed people still provide personal help, but mainly to jobseekers or intermediaries whom they know well and can trust. Thus studies show that both the Chinese and the East Germans (before the change of regime) used strong ties the most, far more often than in the West.

Diversified acquaintances are valuable as an ensemble when employers want to recruit both a person and the person's contacts, to make his or her network work for the organization. This is especially true for higher-level jobs because it is only higher-level jobs that include consequen-

Diverse acquaintance networks help individuals locate health services and assistance. (Courtesy of Jon Wagner)

tial responsibility for the "foreign affairs" of the organization. For example, in my study of the private security industry in Toronto, I asked employers how they hired for jobs from security guard up to manager and asked whether the employer required "good contacts" for these positions. For lower-level jobs, they did not. But for upper-level jobs, employers often did want people with contacts they could use to monitor the industry and its environment, to get information, to recruit new customers, and to maintain good relationships with powerful outsiders such as the police.

When employers think of good contacts, what do they mean? In a word, variety. Employers named desirable contacts of many kinds (in their own industry, government, the police, senior management, etc.) and sometimes explicitly wanted variety as such ("all available"). The more varied a person's network, the more that network can do for the organization.

Employees with more network variety got jobs with higher rank and higher income. This was true whether or not people got those jobs through someone they knew. Again, a network of acquaintances is more useful than one of intimates, because acquaintances have the diversity employers seek.

Does all this add up to "it's not what you know, but who you know?" Not really. Sometimes what you know is critical. Even in the security industry, which has no formal certifications, employers often want to hire people with contacts and skills, not contacts instead of skills. Because employers look for both, using personal connections helps most to get a job at the top or bottom of the ladder, not in the middle. At the bottom, skill requirements are modest. Employers just want a reliable employee and jobseekers just want an adequate job. Using contacts is one cheap way to make this match.

> People with wider networks are better informed about most things, but they may not realize how many of their good health practices go back to a thousand tiny nudges from casual conversations.

At the top, skill requirements are important but also hard to measure (how do you know whether someone will be a dynamic manager with current knowledge of the market, for example?) so employers look for prospects they know or candidates recommended by people they trust. In the middle, skill requirements are serious and fairly easy to measure through credentials (like a recent computer programming degree from a good school) or experience (like a strong track record in sales), so who the candidate knows matters less.

networks and health

Knowing people is important in getting a job, but it also matters for other areas of our lives that are less obvious, such as good health. Research has long shown that having close friends and family is good for a person's health. People who say they have someone they can count on feel less depressed, get less physically ill and live longer than those who do not. The newer news is that having a variety of acquaintances also improves health. In a study of a Toronto social movement, I asked people about both the diversity of their contacts outside the group and the diversity of their contacts within the group. I found that people with more diversified general networks were less depressed, and people with more diverse contacts in the group more often felt that participation had improved their health. Such findings may seem odd, because our intimates play a more obvious role in our health. We discuss our health concerns with those we trust and get care from those who care about us.

Acquaintances make more subtle contributions in small, invisible increments over the long run. One such contribution is a sense of control over one's life, a well-documented source of good health. People who feel more in control are less depressed just because of that, since feeling pushed around is a miserable and unwelcome experience. Moreover, having a sense of control encourages people to tackle problems they encounter, so they cope better with stress. This valuable sense of control grows with the diversity of acquaintances.

People with diverse contacts consciously adapt to different situations and manage conflicting obligations. They have to decide whom to see, how to act appropriately with others differing in their expectations, how to balance sometimes conflicting demands. As they navigate their intricate options, they develop a well-grounded sense of control over their lives. Thus I found that members with more diversified acquaintances outside the Toronto movement felt more in control of their lives overall, and members with more diversified acquaintances within the group more often felt that participation had empowered them.

Acquaintance diversity also contributes to being better informed about health. People with wider networks are better informed about most things, but they may not realize how many of their good health practices go back to a thousand tiny nudges from casual conversations. They may know that they are committed to pushing down the broccoli and getting some exercise, while forgetting how many acquaintances mentioned the importance of such healthy habits. My study of the security industry shows a clear link between diversity and information flow, not only about health, but on a variety of topics. People with more varied connections knew more about each of several different kinds of things: the arts (books and artists), popular culture (sports stars), and business culture (business magazines and restaurants suited to power dining).

Feeling in control and being well-informed both flow from the diversity of the whole ensemble of acquaintances. But health, like work, sometimes benefits from a varied network because varied connections are more likely to include particular useful ones. For example, people who knew many kinds of people in the social movement group were much more likely to get some help with health (from organic vegetables to massage) from associates in the group. They knew what to look for and whom to trust to provide it.

Diverse networks also improve people's health indirectly, by helping them get ahead economically, and wealthier people tend to be healthier people. But the connection between wealth and health might suggest that all these benefits of having a variety of acquaintances might really just reflect the advantages of high social position. People with more network variety, better jobs, more feelings of control and better health may be that way because they come from more privileged circumstances. It is important to note, therefore, that all the studies that I have described have taken into account other characteristics of individuals, such as educational attainment and gender. Nonetheless, the diversity of acquaintanceship itself improves health and happiness.

what next?

Other possible benefits of network variety are yet to be studied. Students of politics have speculated that interacting with a range of people expands one's sources of political information and activity, and increases tolerance for others different from oneself—but this is only speculation at present because political research has focused exclusively on close relationships such as the handful of people with whom a person discusses important matters.

Another critical avenue for future work is the way in which we think about and measure network diversity. At present, almost all studies focus on the variety of occupations within which a respondent knows someone. This works very well, because occupation goes with so many important differences of resources, views, lifestyles and so on. But occupation is not the only way in which the social world is carved up into different kinds of people—gender and ethnicity also shape networks.

For instance, men occupy more powerful positions in organizations, so knowing a variety of men may help one's job search more than knowing a wide variety of women. But women take more responsibility for health, including the health of others, so knowing a good range of women may be better for one's health than knowing many kinds of men. In countries like the United States or Canada, ethnic groups have distinctive cultures and, sometimes, even labor markets. Knowing a variety of people in an ethnic group may lead to better jobs within the ethnic economy, to richer knowledge of the ethnic culture, to better access to alternative medicines, and to feeling better about the group. At the same time, having acquaintances exclusively in an ethnic group may cut one off from broader social benefits.

Indeed, there are many kinds of network variety: variety of occupation, gender, ethnicity, and much more. Each probably goes with a somewhat different menu of benefits. Future research should elaborate on the finding that, not only is knowing people good for you, but knowing many different kinds of people is especially good for you.

RECOMMENDED RESOURCES

Rose Laub Coser. "The Complexity of Roles as a Seedbed of Individual Autonomy." In Louis A. Coser (ed.), *The Idea of Social Structure: Papers in Honor of Robert K. Merton* (Harcourt Brace Jovanovich, 1975).

> Explains why acquaintance variety should lead to a greater sense of control over one's life and to more sophisticated language and more abstract thinking as well.

Bonnie H. Erickson. "Culture, Class, and Connections." *American Journal of Sociology* 102 (1996): 217–51.

> Shows that knowing many kinds of people goes with knowing a lot about many kinds of culture—and how knowing about culture matters at work.

Claude S. Fischer. *To Dwell Among Friends* (University of California Press, 1982).

> Strong ties matter too. This book describes their benefits and the kinds of people who benefit more or less.

Mark Granovetter. "The Strength of Weak Ties." *American Journal of Sociology* 78 (1973): 1360–80.

> Enormously influential, this essay concerns the advantages of acquaintances both for individuals and for communities.

Nan Lin. "Social Networks and Status Attainment." *Annual Review of Sociology* 25 (1999): 467–87.

> Authoritative review of research on networks and getting a job. It includes references to the Albany, East Germany, and China studies discussed in this article.

Nan Lin, Karen Cook, and Ronald S. Burt (eds.). *Social Capital: Theory and Research* (Aldine de Gruyter, 2001).

> Includes a number of recent, high quality theoretical discussions and research reports concerning the benefits of social networks, including a chapter on the Toronto security industry study.

Barry Wellman (ed.). *Networks in the Global Village* (Westview, 1999).

> A wide-ranging collection of studies on strong ties and weak ties, around the world and on the Internet.

REVIEW QUESTIONS

1. Sociologists have found that having diverse social connections is important for finding out about job opportunities. Once someone applies for a job, however, do you think knowing someone influential is enough to get the person hired? Why or why not? What other factors might be involved?

2. Erickson adds interesting elements to the discussion of mental health. What two things does she think healthy people develop in order to have a varied network?

3. Besides occupational diversity, what other forms of diversity exist in your own social networks? Do you think other forms of diversity might have effects similar to occupational diversity? Why or why not?

4. Activity: Use your cell phone or address book as the basis for a chart of your own social network. What are the broad categories that define your interactions with them? What are the overlapping social spheres? How are your acquaintances connected to each other?

barry wellman

connecting communities: on and offline

2

fall 2004

the internet is no longer a separate world for the techno-savvy. tens of millions of people around the world now go online daily. rather than isolating users in a virtual world, the internet extends communities in the real world. people use it to connect in individualized and flexible social networks rather than in fixed and grounded groups.

The 2004 documentary film *Almost Real* tells true-life Internet stories. For some characters, the Internet provides an escape from human interaction. A recluse living alone on an abandoned North Sea oil rig runs a data storage haven supposedly free of government interference. An antisocial eight-year-old boy hides from his schoolmates through home schooling and the Web. Meanwhile, the Internet brings other people together. A man and woman in a bondage and domination relationship communicate daily over Webcams thousands of miles apart. And teenagers socialize by incessantly playing a cooperative online game.

These stories are fascinating but misleading because they describe people whose social lives are wholly online. Few people dedicate most of their waking lives to the Internet. The Internet usually supplants solitary activities, like watching television, rather than other forms of social life. Most uses of the Internet are not "almost real," but are actual, quite normal interactions. The Internet has become an ordinary part of life.

Consider my own use. I have received several e-mail messages in the past hour. Friends confirm dinner for tonight. Even though it is the weekend, a student sends a question and expects a quick answer. So does a graduate student from Europe, with an urgent request for a letter of recommendation. Cousin Larry shares some political thoughts from Los Angeles. I arrange to meet friends at a local pub later in the week. My teenage niece avoids e-mail as "for adults," so I send her an instant message. And one of my most frequent correspondents writes twice: Ms. Miriam Abacha from Nigeria, wanting yet again to share her millions with me.

In addition to communication, the Internet has become an important source of information. To check facts for this article, I use Google to search the Web. It is too rainy to go out and buy a newspaper, so I skim my personalized Yahoo! News instead. My friend Joe is driving to my house for the first time and gets his directions online from MapQuest.

The Internet has burrowed into my life, but is not separate from the rest of it. I integrate offline and online activities. I e-mail, chat, Web search, and instant message—but I also walk, drive, bike, bus, fly, phone, and send an occasional greeting card. I am not unique. Both the exotic aura of the Internet in the 1990s and the fear that it would undermine "community" have faded. The reality is that using the Internet both expands community and changes it in subtle ways.

digital divides

Between 1997 and 2001, the number of Americans using computers increased by 27 percent—from 137 million to 174 million—while the

An 18-year-old girl uses her laptop and an Internet connection to create a personalized music CD for a close friend. She and her acquaintances tie their Internet shopping and browsing to local friendships through online messaging, phone calls, and meeting in person. (Courtesy of Jon Wagner)

online population rose by 152 percent. Nielsen NetRatings reported in March 2004 that three-quarters of Americans over the age of two had accessed the Internet. Many used the Internet both at home and at work, and about half went online daily. Instant messaging (IM) has spread from teenagers to adults in growing popularity, with more than one-third of all American adults now IM-ing.

A decade ago, the Internet was mainly North American, and largely the domain of young, educated, urban, white men. It has since become widely used. About one-third of users live in North America, one-third in Europe and Japan, and one-third elsewhere. India and China host many users, although the percentages of their population who are online remain small. China now has the second largest number of Internet users, growing from half a million in 1997 to 80 million in January 2004. Although the proliferation of computers is no longer headline news, 41 million PCs were shipped to retailers and customers worldwide in the first quarter of 2004.

As more people go online, the digital divide recedes. Yet even as the overall percentage of people online rises, differences in usage rates persist: between affluent and poor, young and old, men and women, more and less educated, urban and rural, and English and non-English readers. Moreover, there are substantial international differences, even among developed countries. For instance, the digital divide between high-income households and low-income households ranges from a gap of more than 60 percentage points in the United Kingdom to less than 20 percentage points in Denmark. In the United States, 79 percent of relatively affluent people (family income of $75,000 or more) were Internet users in September 2001, when just 25 percent of poor people (family income of less than $15,000) were online. And while the gender gap is shrinking in many developed countries, it is increasing in Italy and Germany as men get connected at a higher rate than women. Moreover, the digital divide cuts several ways. For instance, even among affluent Americans, there was a 31 percentage point gap in Internet access between those with a university education (82 percent) and those with less than a high school education (51 percent).

Digital divides are particularly wide in developing countries, where users tend to be wealthy, students, employees of large corporations, or people with easy access to cybercafes. The risk of a "digital penalty" grows as Internet use among organizations and individuals becomes routine. Those without access to the Internet will increasingly miss out on information and communication about jobs, social and political news, and community events.

The many who are using the Internet and the many more who will eventually use it face the question of how the experience might affect their lives. Fast messages, quick shopping, and instant reference works aside, widespread concerns focus on the deeper social and psychological implications of a brave new computer-mediated world.

hopes, fears, and possibilities

Just a few years ago, hope for the Internet was utopian. Entrepreneurs saw it as a way to get rich, policy makers thought it could remake society, and business people hoped that online sales would make stock prices soar. Pundits preached the gospel of the new Internet millennium. For example, in 1995, John Perry Barlow, co-leader of the Electronic Frontier Foundation, said, "We are in the midst of the most transforming technological event since the capture of fire. I used to think that it was just the biggest thing since Gutenberg, but now I think you have to go back farther."

The media generally saw the Internet as a weird, wonderful, and sometimes scary thing. The cover of the December 1999 issue of *Wired* depicted a lithesome cyber-angel leaping off a cliff into the glorious unknown. Major newspapers unveiled special Internet sections, and new computer magazines became fat with ads, advice, and influence. The meltdown of the dot-com boom in March 2000 snuffed out many dreams of a radiant Internet future. The pages of *Wired* magazine shrank by 25 percent from September 1996 to September 2001 and another 22 percent by September 2003. Revenue and subscription rates also plummeted. The editors ruefully noted in February 2004 that their magazine "used to be as thick as a phone book."

The advent of the Internet also provoked fears of personal danger and the loss of community. News media warned of men posing as women online, cyber-stalking, identity theft, and dangerous cyber-addiction. As recently as March 2004, computer scientist John Messerly warned that "computer and video games . . . ruin the social and scholastic lives of many students."

Much of the hype and fear about the Internet has been both *presentist*—thinking that the world started anew with its advent—and *parochial*—thinking that only things that happened on the Internet were relevant to understanding it. Yet, sociologists have long known that technology by itself does not determine anything. Rather, people take technology and use it (or discard it) in ways its developers never dreamed. For example, the early telephone industry marketed its technology simply as a tool for practical business and spurned the notion that it could be a device for sociability. Indeed, telephones, airplanes, and automobiles enabled far-flung communities to flourish well before the coming of the Internet.

Technologies themselves neither make nor break communities. Rather, they create possibilities, opportunities, challenges, and constraints for what people and organizations can do. For example, automobiles and expressways make it possible for people to live in sprawling suburbs, but they do not determine that people will do so. Compare the sprawl of American cities with the more compact suburbs of neighboring Canada. The Internet's low cost, widespread use, asynchronicity (people do not have to be connected simultaneously), global connectivity, and attachments (pictures, music, text) make it possible to communicate quickly and cheaply across continents and oceans. For example, emigrants use e-mail to chat with family and friends back home and visit Web sites to learn home news. *Yahoo! India Matrimonial* links brides and grooms in India, Europe, and North America. In countries with official censorship, emigrants use e-mail to gather news from back home and post it on Web sites for information hungry readers. Thus, the Internet allows mobile people to maintain community ties to distant places and also supports face-to-face ties closer to home.

community online and offline

Online communication—e-mail, instant messaging, and chat rooms—does not replace more traditional offline forms of contact—face-to-face and telephone. Instead, it complements them, increasing the overall volume of contact. Where some had feared that involvement in the Internet would detract from "real life" ties with friends and relatives, intensive users of e-mail contact others in person or by phone at least as frequently as those who rarely or never use the Internet. People who frequently use the Internet to contact others also tend to be in frequent contact with people in other ways (even after taking into account differences of age, gender, and education). Extroverts especially benefit from its use, simply adding another means of communication to their contact repertoire. For example, a 2001 National Geographic survey reports that North Americans who use e-mail to discuss important matters do so an average of 41 times per month, in addition to having an average of 84 face-to-face discussions and 58 phone discussions. Those who do not use e-mail to discuss important matters have about the same number of monthly face-to-face discussions, 83, but only 36 phone discussions. Thus, those who use e-mail report 183 significant discussions per month, 54 percent more than for those who do not use e-mail. The result: the more e-mail, the more overall communication.

This is not surprising, because the Internet is not a separate world. When we talk to people about what they do on the Internet, we find out that the great majority of the people they e-mail are people they know already. They are keeping in touch between visits, often by exchanging jokes, sharing gossip, or arranging to get together. If they e-mail someone they have not already met in person, they are frequently arranging a face-to-face meeting. Telephone calls also get intermixed with e-mails, because phone chats better convey nuances, provide more intrinsic enjoyment, and better accommodate complex discussions. Andrea Baker's book *Double-Click* reports that few cyber-dates stay online; they either proceed to in-person meetings or fade away. People also bring to their online interactions such offline baggage as their gender, age, family situation, lifestyle, ethnicity, jobs, wealth, and education.

E-mail is not inherently better or worse than other modes of communication. It is just different. E-mails are less intrusive than visits or phone calls and often come with useful attachments, be they baby pictures or maps to someone's home. The spread of high-speed ("broadband") Internet access makes it easier for people to integrate the Internet into the rest of their lives without long waits. By April 2004, 39 percent of U.S. Internet users had broadband at home and 55 percent either at work or home. Broadband means that people can always leave their Internet connection on so that they can spontaneously send e-mails

This neighborhood protest against the United States' military campaign in Iraq was one of many organized by both word-of-mouth and Internet communication. (Courtesy of Jon Wagner)

and search Web sites. Broadband connections also make it easier to surf the Web and download large image, music, and video files.

The longer people have been on the Internet, the more they use it. Most Americans—and many in the developed world—have online experience. According to the Pew Internet and American Life study, by February 2004 the average American had been using the Internet for six years. Internet use is becoming even more widespread as home users get access to broadband networks and as access proliferates from desk-bound computers to small portable devices such as "third-generation" mobile phones and personal digital assistants (Palm, Pocket PC). Yet, these small-screen, small-keyboard, lower-speed instruments are used differently than computers: to contact a small number of close friends or relatives or to coordinate in-person meetings. Far from homogenizing people's communications, Internet technology is used in different ways by different people.

the internet globally and locally

A decade ago analysts believed that as the rest of the world caught up to the United States in Internet use, they would use it in similar ways. Experience shows that this is not always so. For example, in Scandinavia and Japan, people frequently use advanced mobile phones to exchange e-mail and short text messages. Their Internet use is much less desktop-bound than that of Americans. Teens and young adults are especially heavy users of e-mail on their Internet-connected mobile telephones. Time will tell whether young people continue their heavy mobile use as they get older. Manuel Castells and his associates have shown that people in Catalonia, Spain, use the Internet more for information and services than for communication. They extensively search the Web to answer questions and book tickets, but they are much less likely to exchange e-mails. This may be because many Catalans live near each other and prefer to meet in cafés at night. Mobile phones sit beside them, ready to incorporate other close friends and relatives into conversations via short text messages. Many developing countries exhibit a different mode of use. Even if people can afford to connect to the Internet from their homes, they often do not have reliable electrical, telephone, or broadband service. In such situations, they often use public access points such as Internet cafés or schools. They are connecting to the Internet while their neighbors sit next to them in person.

Such complexities illuminate the role the Internet can play in specifically local communities. The issue is whether the Internet has fostered a "global village," to use Marshall McLuhan's phrase, and thereby weakened local community. Some intensive and engrossing online communities do exist, such as the "BlueSky" group of young male friends who appear to live online, as described by Lori Kendall in her book *Hanging Out in the Virtual Pub*. Yet, they are a small minority. Despite the Internet's ability to connect continents at a single bound, it does not appear to be destroying local community.

For example, in the late 1990s Keith Hampton and I studied "Netville" near Toronto, a suburban housing tract of middle-priced single-family homes. The teachers, social workers, police officers, and technicians who lived there were typical people buying homes to raise young families. The community was exceptional in one important way: As part of an experiment by the telephone company, many residents were given free, high-speed Internet access and became members of a neighborhood e-mail discussion group.

When we compared those who were given this Internet access with those who did not receive it, we found that those on the Internet knew the names of three times as many neighbors as those without Internet access. The "wired" residents had been invited into the homes of an average of 4 neighbors, compared to 2.5 for the unwired, and they regularly talked with twice as many neighbors. The Internet gave wired residents opportunities to identify others in the neighborhood whom they might want to know better. E-mail and the discussion group made it easier for them to meet fellow residents who were not their immediate neighbors: the wired residents' local friends were more widely dispersed throughout Netville than those of the unwired. The e-mail discussion group was frequently used to discuss common concerns. These included household matters such as plumbing and yardwork, advice on setting up home computer networks, finding a local doctor, and skills for hire such as those of a tax accountant or carpenter. As one resident commented on the discussion group: "I have walked around the neighborhood a lot lately and I have noticed a few things. I have noticed neighbors talking to each other like they have been friends for a long time. I have noticed a closeness that you don't see in many communities."

Not only did these wired residents talk to and meet one another more, they did most of Netville's civic organizing online, for example, by warning neighbors about suspicious cars in the development and inviting neighbors to social events such as barbeques and block parties. One typical message read: "For anybody interested there is a Sunday night bowling league looking for new people to join. It's lots of fun with prizes, playoffs, and more. For both ladies and gents. If interested e-mail me back or give me a call."

These community activities built bonds for political action. When irate Netville residents protested at City Hall against the developer's plans to build more houses, it was the wired Internet members who organized the protest and showed up to make their voices heard. Others grumbled, just like new residents of housing developments have often grumbled, but the Internet supplied the social bonds and tools for organizing, for telling residents what the issues were, who the key players were, and when the protest would be.

The Netville experience suggests that when people are offered an easier way of networking with the Internet, the scope and amount of neighborly contact can increase. Evidence from other studies also shows that the Internet supports nearby relationships. For example, the National Geographic Society asked visitors to its Web site about their communication with friends and relatives living within a distance of 30 miles. Daily Internet users contacted nearby friends and relatives 73 percent more often per year than they contacted those living further away.

At the same time, the Internet helped Netville's wired residents to maintain good ties with, and get help from, friends and relatives who lived in their former neighborhoods. The evidence shows that Internet users are becoming "glocalized," heavily involved in both local and long-distance relationships. They make neighborly contacts—on- and offline—and they connect with far-flung friends and relatives—mostly online.

"networked individualism"

As the Internet has been incorporated into everyday life, it has fostered subtle changes in community. In the old days, before the 1990s, places were largely connected—by telephone, cars, planes, and railroads. Now with the Internet (and mobile phones), people are connected. Where before each household had a telephone number, now each person has a unique e-mail address. Many have several, in order to keep different parts of their lives separate online. This change from place-based community to person-based community had started before the Internet, but the developing personalization, portability and ubiquitous connectivity of the Internet are facilitating the change. By April 2004, 17 percent of American users could access the Internet wirelessly from their laptop computers and the percentage is growing rapidly. As wireless portability develops from desktops to laptops and handheld devices, an individual's whereabouts become less important for contact with friends and relatives.

The Internet and other new communication technologies are facilitating a basic change in the nature of community—from physically fixed and bounded groups to social networks, which I call "networked individualism." These technologies are helping people to personalize their own communities. Instead of being rooted in homes, cafés, and workplaces, people are becoming connected as individuals, available for contact anywhere and at any time. Instead of being bound up in a neighborhood community where all know all, each person is becoming an individualized switchboard, linking a unique set of ties and networks. In a society where people rarely know friends of friends, there is more uncertainty about who will be supportive under what circumstances, more need to navigate among partial social networks, and more opportunity to access a variety of resources. The Internet provides communication and information resources to keep in closer touch with loved ones—from new friends to family members left behind in international migrations.

RECOMMENDED RESOURCES

Manuel Castells. *The Rise of the Network Society* (Blackwell, 2000).

> An insightful account of the transformation of societies into social networks.

Steve Jones and Philip Howard, eds. *Society Online: The Internet in Context* (Sage Publications, 2003).

> An important compendium of research, with much representation from the authoritative Pew Internet in American Life studies.

Howard Rheingold. *The Virtual Community: Homesteading on the Electronic Frontier* (MIT Press, 2000).

> A popular and sound account of life online.

Barry Wellman and Caroline Haythornthwaite, eds. *The Internet in Everyday Life* (Blackwell, 2000).

> A score of original research articles documenting many of the ideas presented in this article.

www.pewinternet.org

> The Pew Internet in American Life studies have carried out a large number of surveys on Internet use in American life.

http://virtualsociety.sbs.ox.ac.uk

> A British scholarly network doing a variety of mostly qualitative analyses of Internet and society.

www.webuse.umd.edu

> An interactive statistical database that makes it relatively easy to analyze a variety of surveys about the Internet and American life.

www.worldinternetproject.net

> Contains the reports of survey researchers in many nations on the nature of the Internet and society.

REVIEW QUESTIONS

1. Explain the "digital divide." What are three of the factors Wellman uses to describe it? Who is on either side of it?
2. Debate the "presentist" and "parochial" ways of thinking about the Internet. How does sociological thinking differ from those beliefs?
3. Using the example of Netville, wherein technology and geographic proximity combined to develop stronger ties between neighbors as compared to those who did not have Internet access, what do you hypothesize are the unseen consequences of these linkages? Can you think of any negative effects?

4. Activity: Keep an Internet journal for three days, recording how long you were online, what Web sites you visited (you can use the history function to make it easier), and what sorts of interactions you had with others online (how many times you instant messaged, how many e-mails you sent, how many e-mails you received, what you purchased online, etc.). Then estimate the time you spent face-to-face with people in those three days. Are there any friends you interact with solely on the Internet? If so, how do your Internet-only relationships differ from those that involve face-to-face contact? Prepare a synopsis of your activities to discuss in class.

joel best

sociologists as outliers

3

spring 2009

to regain their place in the public consciousness, sociologists can learn from the remarkable public resurgence of economics and from malcolm gladwell's ability to translate sociological findings into popular books.

Malcolm Gladwell's *Outliers: The Story of Success* (2008) was itself marketed to succeed. Gladwell appeared in numerous television interviews. *Outliers* was immediately reviewed by major newspapers in the United States, England, Canada, and Australia. Leading bookstore chains discounted the book and displayed it prominently. When I checked the day after it was released in November 2008, it was already fourth in Amazon.com's rankings.

Gladwell is the 21st century's preeminent popularizer of sociological research. He won the American Sociological Association's first Excellence in Reporting of Social Issues Award in 2007. Well-known for his earlier bestsellers *The Tipping Point* and *Blink*, he has been contributing articles (archived at www.gladwell.com) to *The New Yorker* since 1996. He specializes in provocative interpretations of work by social scientists, including psychologists, economists, anthropologists, and—yes—sociologists. *Outliers* is Gladwell's most sociological—and in my view his best—book. His theme is that success is socially patterned, often in subtle ways.

Why, for instance, do a disproportionate share of hockey players have birthdays in January, February, and March? Answer: Canadian youth hockey programs are organized by age cohorts,

> Gladwell is the 21st century's preeminent popularizer of sociological research. *Outliers* is his most sociological—and in my view, best—book.

and each cohort contains kids born in the same calendar year. Thus, a boy born in January will be placed in the same program as a boy born in December of the same year—they are, for organizational purposes, considered to be the same age. But of course, just by virtue of being older, one boy is likely to be bigger, faster, stronger, and better coordinated.

Children start playing on hockey teams before entering elementary school—young enough that being a few months older can make a real difference. So, when the best players are picked for all-star teams, the kids born early in the year have an advantage. And, being on an all-star team means kids get more coaching, more practice, and more experience playing, so they become increasingly better players than those not selected for all-stars. So they begin to accumulate advantages.

The irony is clear: social arrangements designed to make youth hockey fair—by having kids compete with others of the same age—actually work to the advantage of those kids who have the earliest birthdays.

Americans tend to attribute success to the personal qualities of individuals. They think of those who make it to the top as having worked especially hard, as having sacrificed, as being determined, dedicated, and therefore deserving. That is, they view success as a product of good character, of particular personality types—the result of psychological differences among people.

This makes intuitive sense. Ask successful people—and this certainly includes successful sociologists—what it takes to succeed and they will almost invariably talk about the importance of working hard. Success, whether in ice hockey or academia, rarely comes to those who don't work for it.

But, Gladwell argues, hard work isn't the whole story. Timing matters. It turns out that Bill Gates, Steve Jobs, and a large share of the other people who amassed vast fortunes when microcomputing began were all born around 1955. That meant they were about 20 years old in 1975 when microcomputers first emerged—old enough to have acquired considerable experience as teenage hobbyists working with computers, but not yet old enough to have completed college and taken jobs with IBM or other "real" computer companies. Being born in 1955 meant they were at the right age to take advantage of the historical moment when it became possible to build careers and make real money in microcomputing.

In other words, Gladwell argues, success isn't simply a product of individual character, it also depends on social context—the eligibility rules for youth hockey participation, technological developments in microcomputing, and so on. Reviews of *Outliers* often invoke the notion of luck (for example, the *Newsweek* review was titled "Maybe Geniuses Just Got Lucky"). But invoking luck, like emphasizing hard work, invites us to view success as a product of individual differences. Just as some people work harder, some people have more luck.

However in Gladwell's universe, luck isn't some random outcome. Rather, luck takes the

> In Gladwell's universe, luck isn't some random outcome. Rather, luck takes the form of social arrangements that work to the advantage of some more than others.

form of social arrangements—including cultural legacies and historical circumstances—that work to the advantage of some more than others. These may not seem advantageous on the surface. Gladwell shows, for example, how the anti-Semitism rampant in mid-century New York's leading law firms forced Jewish lawyers to join newer, far more marginal firms that practiced the sorts of law elite, white-shoe firms spurned, such as proxy fights. This turned into an advantage, though, when the business environment changed and hostile take-overs became commonplace. Those new firms and their partners, with their suddenly invaluable expertise, wound up making colossal fortunes.

In the course of this well-written book, Gladwell frequently refers to sociologists. Robert Merton, C. Wright Mills, Pitirim Sorokin, Annette Lareau, Erwin Smigel, Stephen Steinberg, Louise Farkas, Charles Perrow, Karl Alexander, Orlando Patterson, and Fernando Henriques are all mentioned in *Outliers,* and not just in the endnotes. How often does a best-selling author invoke sociology, let alone name sociologists?

These days, when the public wants to understand social behavior, they seem to turn to economists. Consider the remarkable number of recent successful trade books extolling the value of economics for understanding the social order, books such as Steven D. Levitt's and Stephen J. Dubner's *Freakonomics,* Tim Harford's *The Undercover Economist,* Stephen E. Landsburg's *More Sex Is Safer Sex,* Nassim Nicholas Taleb's *Fooled by Randomness,* and James Surowiecki's *The Wisdom of Crowds.* Meanwhile, the sociology sections in many bookstores seem to be shrinking.

Explanations for sociology's low status often mention its fondness for jargon, for using an unnecessarily pompous vocabulary to describe the everyday world. And no doubt sociologists often commit the sin of jargon. But that hardly explains the vogue for economics. Does anyone believe the typical economist's prose is clearer, more readily comprehensible, or less jargon-ridden than most sociologists' work? Nor should we blame sociology's growing dependence on abstruse statistics. If anything, economics is far more quantitative, and less readily accessible, to non-specialists.

Well, perhaps economics is seen as more practical, as linked to business and making money. Certainly Gladwell writes books considered relevant to business; *The Tipping Point* and *Blink* both seem to offer insights for marketing, while the examples chosen to illustrate success in *Outliers* often involve business careers. But *Freakonomics* and other economics-based bestsellers draw many of their examples from social behavior and public policy in order to show how rational choices and markets influence many aspects of our lives. The economists who write for the public certainly don't restrict their focus to moneymaking.

What both Gladwell and the pop-star economists share is a fondness for surprise, for the unexpected revelation. For example, economists favor a plot line that goes something like this: although at first glance some aspect of the world may seem confusing, even chaotic, once we understand that the people involved are making calculated choices in their own self-interest, we can recognize how their individual choices create consequential, often unexpected, patterns in behavior. Thus, the most notorious section in *Freakonomics* argues that the declining crime rates in the 1990s were an unanticipated byproduct of liberalized abortion policies, which led to fewer unwanted children being born and going on to become delinquents.

> Does anyone believe the typical economist's prose is clearer, more readily comprehensible, or less jargon-ridden than most sociologists' work?

"Ahh," the reader is supposed to exclaim, "now I understand!"

Sociologists used to be in the surprise business, and we used to attract our fair share of public attention. Back in 1937, Robert and Helen Lynd made a splash with *Middletown in Transition*. *Life* covered the study with photos showing the distinctive lifestyles of different social classes expressed in, for example, living room decor. In the aftermath of the Second World War, David Riesman published *The Lonely Crowd* (the all-time bestseller by an American sociologist), which argued the United States had experienced a profound cultural change.

By the late 1950s, Vance Packard was preceding Gladwell as an author who translated sociology into the best-selling *The Status Seekers*. Just a few years later, Tom Wolfe was making frequent references to sociologists while showing the importance of status for everyone from car customizers to modern artists to astronauts. In each case, sociology seemed to shed new light on the everyday and, in the process, offer surprising revelations. Sociology was entertaining.

It's worth appreciating that sociology has had a noticeable effect on Americans' thinking. A remarkable number of sociological terms have crept into everyday speech: lifestyle; upper-, middle-, and lower-class; charisma; status symbol; gender; self-fulfilling prophecy; role model; even significant other. It isn't clear that economics has had such a favorable reception. Still, sociology doesn't get much credit for these contributions. Once its concepts enter common parlance, their sociological origins tend to be forgotten.

Contemporary sociologists in particular seem to have trouble getting noticed, probably because they sound self-righteous. Economics may be the dismal science, but today's sociologists often describe a grim world governed by cruel, grinding inequalities of race, class, and gender. They portray a world of alienation, of lonely people living meaningless lives. Their idea of surprise is to expose the sexist imagery in advertisements and music videos. They seem to scold. The arguments seem familiar, predictable. Not surprisingly, they go over about as well as scolding usually does.

It isn't that inequality is unimportant, or that sociologists need to communicate via some sort of happy-talk. After all, much of *Outliers* concerns how social arrangements foster unequal outcomes. But Gladwell directs our focus toward success, rather than failure. The cover of the British hardcover edition of *Outliers* describes him as an "inspirational bestselling author." Rather than issuing blanket indictments of the social system, he identifies other non-utopian arrangements that might offer more equal opportunities: "We could set up two or even three hockey leagues, divided up by month of birth. Let the players develop on separate tracks and then pick all-star teams."

Later in the book he praises the KIPP schools, which give low-income middle-school children intensive training that boosts their math skills and opens doors to better high school and college opportunities. Success—even among those who seem predestined to fail—can, in Gladwell's view, be fostered by being alert to how social institutions work. In the chapter titled "The Ethnic Theory of Plane Crashes," he points to the once-alarming tendency of Korean Air jets to crash because their cultural obligations to be deferential kept Korean first officers and flight engineers from bluntly warning pilots about hazards. After Korean Air instituted a training program designed to change communication patterns among cockpit crews, the airline achieved an admirable safety record. Still, one can imagine some sociologists squirming at this exam-

ple, explaining that we need to appreciate—not judge—diverse communication styles.

But of course it does matter if some cultures are ill-suited to producing the sorts of quick, appropriate decisions among cockpit crew members needed to keep airliners from crashing. And not all the patterns identified by Gladwell are subject to social engineering. Doubling or tripling the number of youth hockey leagues in Canada may give more kids with late-in-the-year birthdays a better shot at developing their skills, but it won't change the size of NHL rosters. Lest this example seem a little arcane, Gladwell reminds us that U.S. schools are also age-graded (so that school districts define one-year spans of birth dates that make students eligible to enter kindergarten), and those with earlier birthdays prove to have an advantage of maturity that carries right through college admissions. We might reduce the impact of age differences by placing students with similar birthdates in the same classroom. And perhaps schooling isn't a zero-sum game. Perhaps more students would excel if they learned alongside others of comparable maturity, so that more would take to school and seek higher education.

Social arrangements and historical processes shape individual's prospects for success, but they can't tell the whole story. Those born in big, baby-boomer birth cohorts find themselves in tougher competition than those born in birth-dearth years, just as those who enter the workforce in good economic times have better career prospects than those who look for work when jobs are scarce. We can't choose our birth cohort or our society's economic circumstances. Yet, within those larger arrangements, people do make consequential choices that also affect their prospects for succeeding.

Sociologists often call for appreciation of diversity, for recognition of the talent, skills, and resilience demanded to live in disadvantaged circumstances, and for understanding why some people make choices others condemn. They invite us to understand why some youths leave school, why some people act violently, and so on. They have a point. People have their reasons for doing things, and not everyone has the same reasons.

But sociology has to do more than endorse differences. Maybe we ought to appreciate different modes of communication, but also that all modes are not equally useful for, say, landing an airliner safely. Understanding the range of human behavior doesn't require that we endorse the full range.

In order to regain their place in the public consciousness, sociologists could do worse than learn from the remarkable resurgence of economics, and from Gladwell's ability to translate sociological findings into popular books. We can't expect to influence public debate if we can't get people to listen to us. Contemporary sociology has become all too predictable; successful bids for public attention require arguments that are themselves outliers—surprising, interesting, and compelling.

RECOMMENDED RESOURCE

Malcolm Gladwell. *Outliers: The Story of Success* (Little, Brown, and Company, 2008).

REVIEW QUESTIONS

1. Pick a success in your life and identify the social factors that played a role in the chain of events that helped you achieve this outcome.
2. The hockey league example shows how circumstances can change outcomes. Think of another example where structural forces obviously shape individual outcomes and describe it briefly.
3. Activity: Find a news article on the Web that quotes a sociologist. (Sites might include: Contexts.org; thesocietypages.org; or wwnorton.com/college/soc/news). Why was a sociologist particularly well suited to comment on the topic of the article? What did sociology bring to the discussion that another field might not?

robert j. brym

six lessons of suicide bombers

4

fall 2007

much of what researchers have learned about suicide bombing is at odds with conventional wisdom and the thinking of policymakers.

In October 1983, Shi'a militants attacked the military barracks of American and French troops in Beirut, killing nearly 300 people. Today the number of suicide attacks worldwide has passed 1,000, with almost all the attacks concentrated in just nine countries: Lebanon, Sri Lanka, Israel, Turkey, India (Kashmir), Russia (Chechnya), Afghanistan, Iraq, and Pakistan. Israel, for example, experienced a wave of suicide attacks in the mid-1990s when Hamas and the Palestinian Islamic Jihad (PIJ) sought to undermine peace talks between Israel and the Palestinian Authority. A far deadlier wave of attacks began in Israel in October 2000 after all hope of a negotiated settlement collapsed. Altogether, between 1993 and 2005, 158 suicide attacks took place in Israel and the occupied Palestinian territories, killing more than 800 people and injuring more than 4,600.

Over the past quarter century, researchers have learned much about the motivations of suicide bombers, the rationales of the organizations that support them, their modus operandi, the precipitants of suicide attacks, and the effects of counterterrorism on insurgent behavior. Much of what they have learned is at odds with conventional wisdom and the thinking of policymakers who guide counterterrorist strategy. This paper draws on that research, but I focus mainly on the Israeli/Palestinian case to draw six lessons from the carnage wrought by suicide bombers. In brief, I argue that (1) suicide bombers are not crazy, (2) nor are they motivated principally by religious zeal. It is possible to discern (3) a strategic logic and (4) a social logic underlying their actions. Targeted states typically react by repressing organizations that mount suicide attacks, but (5) this repression often makes matters worse. (6) Only by first taking an imaginative leap and understanding the world from the assailant's point of view can hope to develop a workable strategy for minimizing suicide attacks. Let us examine each of these lessons in turn.

lesson 1: suicide bombers are not crazy

Lance Corporal Eddie DiFranco was the only survivor of the 1983 suicide attack on the U.S. Marine barracks in Beirut who saw the face of the bomber. DiFranco was on watch when he noticed the attacker speeding his truck full of explosives toward the main building on the marine base. "He looked right at me [and] smiled," DiFranco later recalled.

Was the bomber insane? Some Western observers thought so. Several psychologists characterized the Beirut bombers as "unstable individuals with a death wish." Government and media sources made similar assertions in the immediate aftermath of the suicide attacks on the United States on September 11, 2001. Yet these claims were purely speculative. Subsequent interviews with prospective suicide bombers and reconstructions of the biographies of successful suicide attackers revealed few psychological abnormalities. In fact, after examining many hundreds of cases for evidence of depression, psychosis, past suicide attempts, and so on, Robert Pape discovered only a single person who could be classified as having a psychological problem (a Chechen woman who may have been mentally retarded).

On reflection, it is not difficult to understand why virtually all suicide bombers are psychologically stable. The organizers of suicide attacks do not want to jeopardize their missions by recruiting unreliable people. A research report prepared for the Danish government a few years ago noted, "Recruits who display signs of pathological behaviour are automatically weeded out for reasons of organizational security." It may be that some psychologically unstable people want to become suicide bombers, but insurgent organizations strongly prefer their cannons fixed.

lesson 2: it's mainly about politics, not religion

In May 1972, three Japanese men in business suits boarded a flight from Paris to Tel Aviv. They were members of the Japanese Red Army, an affiliate of the Popular Front for the Liberation of Palestine. Eager to help their Palestinian comrades liberate Israel from Jewish rule, they had packed their carry-on bags with machine guns and hand grenades. After disembarking at Lod Airport near Tel Aviv, they began an armed assault on everyone in sight. When the dust settled, 26 people lay dead, nearly half of them Puerto Rican Catholics on a pilgrimage to the Holy Land.

Israeli guards killed one of the attackers. A second blew himself up, thus becoming the first suicide bomber in modern Middle Eastern history. The Israelis captured the third assailant, Kozo Okamoto.

Okamato languished in an Israeli prison until the mid-1980s, when he was handed over to Palestinian militants in Lebanon's Beka'a Valley in a prisoner exchange. Then, in 2000, something unexpected happened. Okamoto apparently abandoned or at least ignored his secular faith in the theories of Bakunin and Trotsky, and converted to Islam. For Okamoto, politics came first, then religion.

A similar evolution occurs in the lives of many people. Any political conflict makes people look for ways to explain the dispute and imagine a strategy for resolving it; they adopt or formulate an ideology. If the conflict is deep and the ideology proves inadequate, people modify the ideology or reject it for an alternative. Religious themes often tinge political ideologies, and the importance of the religious component may increase if analyses and strategies based on secular reasoning fail. When religious elements predominate, they may intensify the conflict.

For example, the Palestinians have turned to one ideology after another to explain their loss of land to Jewish settlers and military forces and to formulate a plan for regaining territorial control. Especially after 1952, when Gamal Abdel Nasser took office in Egypt, many Palestinians turned to Pan-Arabism, the belief that the Arab countries would unify and force Israel to cede territory. But wars failed to dislodge the Israelis. Particularly after the Six-Day War in 1967, many Palestinians turned to nationalism, which placed the responsibility for regaining control of lost territory on the Palestinians themselves. Others became Marxists, identifying wage-workers (and, in some cases, peasants) as the engines of national liberation. The Palestinians used plane hijackings to draw the world's attention to their cause, launched wave upon wave of guerilla attacks against Israel, and in the 1990s entered into negotiations to create a sovereign Palestinian homeland.

Yet Islamic fundamentalism had been growing in popularity among Palestinians since the late 1980s—ironically, without opposition from the Israeli authorities, who saw it as a conservative counterweight to Palestinian nationalism. When negotiations with Israel to establish a Palestinian state broke down in 2000, many Palestinians saw the secularist approach as bankrupt and turned to Islamic fundamentalism for political answers. In January 2006, the Islamic fundamentalist party, Hamas, was democratically elected to form the Palestinian government, winning 44 percent of the popular vote and 56 percent of the parliamentary seats. In this case, as in many others, secular politics came first. When secularism failed, notions of "martyrdom" and "holy war" gained in importance.

In Lebanon, Israel, the West Bank, and Gaza between 1981 and 2003, fewer than half of suicide bombers had discernible religious inclinations.

This does not mean that most modern suicide bombers are deeply religious, either among the Palestinians or other groups. Among the 83 percent of suicide attackers worldwide between 1980 and 2003 for whom Robert Pape found data on ideological background, only a minority—43 percent—were identifiably religious. In Lebanon, Israel, the West Bank, and Gaza between 1981 and 2003, fewer than half of suicide bombers had discernible religious inclinations. In its origins and at its core, the Israeli-Palestinian conflict is not religiously inspired, and suicide bombing, despite its frequent religious trappings, is fundamentally the expression of a territorial dispute. In this conflict, many members of the dominant group—Jewish Israelis—use religion as a central marker of identity. It is hardly surprising, therefore, that many Palestinian militants also view the struggle in starkly religious terms.

The same holds for contemporary Iraq. As Mohammed Hafez has recently shown, 443 suicide missions took place in Iraq between March 2003 and February 2006. Seventy-one percent of the identifiable attackers belonged to al-Qaeda in Iraq. To be sure, they justified their actions in religious terms. Members of al-Qaeda in Iraq view the Shi'a who control the Iraqi state as apostates. They want to establish fundamentalist, Sunni-controlled states in Iraq and other Middle Eastern countries. Suicide attacks against the Iraqi regime and its American and British supporters are seen as a means to that end.

But it is only within a particular political context that these ambitions first arose. After all, suicide attacks began with the American and British invasion of Iraq and the installation of a Shi'a-controlled regime. And it is only under certain political conditions that these ambitions are acted upon. Thus, Hafez's analysis shows that suicide bombings spike (1) in retaliation for big counterinsurgency operations and (2) as a strategic response to institutional developments which suggest that Shi'a-controlled Iraq is about to become more stable. So although communal identity has come to be religiously demarcated in Iraq, this does not mean that religion per se initiated suicide bombing or that it drives the outbreak of suicide bombing campaigns.

lesson 3: sometimes it's strategic

Suicide bombing often has a political logic. In many cases, it is used as a tactic of last resort undertaken by the weak to help them restore control over territory they perceive as theirs. This political logic is clear in statements routinely released by leaders of organizations that launch suicide attacks. Characteristically, the first communiqué issued by Hamas in 1987 stated that martyrdom is the appropriate response to occupation, and the 1988 Hamas charter says that jihad is the duty of every Muslim whose territory is invaded by an enemy.

The political logic of suicide bombing is also evident when suicide bombings occur in clusters as part of an organized campaign, often timed to maximize strategic gains. A classic example is the campaign launched by Hamas and the PIJ in the mid-90s. Fearing that a settlement between Israel and the Palestinian Authority would prevent the Palestinians from gaining control over all of Israel, Hamas and the PIJ aimed to scuttle peace negotiations by unleashing a small army of suicide bombers.

Notwithstanding the strategic basis of many suicide attacks, we cannot conclude that strategic reasoning governs them all. More often than not, suicide bombing campaigns fail to achieve their territorial aims. Campaigns may occur without apparent strategic justification, as did the campaign that erupted in Israel after negotiations between Israel and the Palestinian Authority broke down in 2000. A social logic often overlays the political logic of suicide bombing.

lesson 4: sometimes it's retaliatory

On October 4, 2003, a 29-year-old lawyer entered Maxim restaurant in Haifa and detonated her belt of plastic explosives. In addition to taking her own life, Hanadi Jaradat killed 20 people and wounded dozens of others. When her relatives were later interviewed in the Arab press, they explained her motives as follows: "She carried out the attack in revenge for the killing of her brother and her cousin [to whom she had been engaged] by the Israeli security forces and in revenge for all the crimes Israel is perpetrating in the West Bank by killing Palestinians and expropriating their land." Strategic calculation did not inform Jaradat's attack.

Research I conducted with Bader Araj shows that, like a majority of Palestinian suicide bombers between 2000 and 2005, Jaradat was motivated by the desire for revenge and retaliation.

Before people act, they sometimes weigh the costs and benefits of different courses of action and choose the one that appears to cost the least and offer the most benefits. But people are not calculating machines. Sometimes they just don't add up. Among other emotions, feelings of anger and humiliation can trump rational strategic calculation in human affairs. Economists have conducted experiments called "the ultimatum game," in which the experimenter places two people in a room, gives one of them $20, and tells the recipient that she must give some of the money—as much or as little as she wants—to the other person. If the other person refuses the offer, neither gets to keep any money. Significantly, in four out of five cases, the other person refuses to accept the money if she is offered less than $5. Although she will gain materially if she accepts any offer, she is highly likely to turn down a low offer so as to punish her partner for stinginess. This outcome suggests that emotions can easily override the rational desire for material gain. (Researchers at the University of Zürich have recently demonstrated the physiological basis of this override function by using MRI brain scans on people playing the ultimatum game.) At the political level, research I conducted with Bader Araj on the events precipitating suicide bombings, the motivations of suicide bombers, and the rationales of the organizations that support suicide bombings shows that Palestinian suicide missions are in most cases prompted less by strategic cost-benefit calculations than by such human emotions as revenge and retaliation. The existence of these deeply human emotions also helps to explain why attempts to suppress suicide bombing campaigns sometimes do not have the predicted results.

insurgency, repression, and perceptions by party

	HAMAS/PIJ	FATAH/Other
Number of successful suicide attackers, 2005–5	85	48
Number of attempted state assassinations, 2000–5	124	82
Percentage of leaders never willing to recognize Israel	100%	10%
How has Israel's assassination policy affected the ability of your organization to conduct suicide bombing operations?	Increased 33% Not affected 42% Decreased 25%	Increased 9% Not affected 5% Decreased 86%
In comparison with other tactics used by your organization, how costly has suicide bombing been in terms of the human and material resources used, damage to your organization, etc.?	As or less costly 53% More costly 20% Don't know 27%	As or less costly 11% More costly 86% Don't know 4%

The first two rows of data in this table were calculated from a systematic analysis of newspapers (the New York Times, ha-Aretz, al-Quds and al-'Arabi) by Robert Brym and Bader Araj. The remainder of the data are based on a survey of 45 Palestinian insurgent leaders conducted by Bader Araj in the West Bank and Gaza during the spring and summer of 2006.

lesson 5: repression is a boomerang

Major General Doron Almog commanded the Israel Defense Forces Southern Command from 2000 to 2003. He tells the story of how, in early 2003, a wealthy Palestinian merchant in Gaza received a phone call from an Israeli agent. The caller said that the merchant's son was preparing a suicide mission, and that if he went through with it, the family home would be demolished, Israel would sever all commercial ties with the family, and its members would never be allowed to visit Israel again. The merchant prevailed upon his son to reconsider, and the attack was averted.

Exactly how many suicide bombers have been similarly deterred is unknown. We do know that of the nearly 600 suicide missions launched in Israel and its occupied territories between 2000 and 2005, fewer than 25 percent succeeded in reaching their targets. Israeli counterterrorist efforts thwarted three-quarters of them using violent means. In addition, Israel preempted an incalculable number of attacks by assassinating militants involved in planning them. More than 200 Israeli assassination attempts took place between 2000 and 2005, 80 percent of which succeeded in killing their main target, sometimes with considerable "collateral damage."

Common sense suggests that repression should dampen insurgency by increasing its cost. By this logic, when state organizations eliminate the people who plan suicide bombings, destroy their bomb-making facilities, intercept their agents, and punish the people who support them, they erode the insurgents' capabilities for mounting suicide attacks. But this commonsense approach to counterinsurgency overlooks two complicating factors. First, harsh repression may reinforce radical opposition and even intensify it. Second, insurgents may turn to alternative and perhaps more lethal methods to achieve their aims.

Consider the Palestinian case (see "insurgency, repression, and perceptions by party"). Bader Araj and I were able to identify the organizational affiliation of 133 Palestinian suicide bombers between September 2000 and July 2005. Eighty-five of them (64 percent) were affiliated with the Islamic fundamentalist groups Hamas and the PIJ, while the rest were affiliated with secular Palestinian groups such as Fatah. Not surprisingly, given this distribution, Israeli repression was harshest against the Islamic fundamentalists, who were the targets of 124 Israeli assassination attempts (more than 60 percent of the total).

Yet after nearly five years of harsh Israeli repression—involving not just the assassination of leaders but also numerous arrests, raids on bomb-making facilities, the demolition of houses belonging to family members of suicide bombers, and so on—Hamas and PIJ leaders remained adamant in their resolve and much more radical than Palestinian secularist leaders. When 45 insurgent leaders representing all major Palestinian factions were interviewed in depth in the summer of 2006, 100 percent of those associated with Hamas and PIJ (compared to just 10 percent of secularist leaders) said they would never be willing to recognize the legitimacy of the state of Israel. That is, the notion of Israel as a Jewish state was still entirely unacceptable to each and every one of them. When asked how Israel's assassination policy had affected the ability of their organization to conduct suicide bombing operations, 42 percent of Hamas and PIJ respondents said that the policy had had no effect, while one-third said the policy had increased their organization's capabilities (the corresponding figures for secularist leaders were 5 percent and 9 percent, respectively).

And when asked how costly suicide bombing had been in terms of human and organizational resources, organizational damage, and so on, 53 percent of Hamas and PIJ leaders (compared to just 11 percent of secularist leaders) said that suicide bombing was less costly or at least no more costly than the alternatives. Responses to such questions probably tell us more about the persistent resolve of the Islamic fundamentalists than their actual capabilities. And that is just the point. Harsh Israeli repression over an extended period apparently reinforced the anti-Israel sentiments of Islamic fundamentalists.

Some counterterrorist experts say that motivations count for little if capabilities are destroyed. And they would be right if it were not for the substitutability of methods: increase the cost of one method of attack, and highly motivated insurgents typically substitute another. So, for example, Israel's late prime minister, Yitzhak Rabin, ordered troops to "break the bones" of Palestinians who engaged in mass demonstrations, rock throwing, and other nonlethal forms of protest in the late 1980s and early 1990s. The Palestinians responded with more violent attacks, including suicide missions. Similarly, after Israel began to crack down ruthlessly on suicide bombing operations in 2002, rocket attacks against

> Severe repression can work for a while, but a sufficiently determined mass opposition can always design new tactics to surmount new obstacles, especially if its existence as a group is visibly threatened.

Israeli civilians sharply increased in frequency. In general, severe repression can work for a while, but a sufficiently determined mass opposition can always design new tactics to surmount new obstacles, especially if its existence as a group is visibly threatened (and unless, of course, the mass opposition is exterminated in its entirety). One kind of "success" usually breeds another kind of "failure" if the motivation of insurgents is high.

lesson 6: empathize with your enemy

In October 2003, Israeli Chief of Staff Moshe Ya'alon explicitly recognized this conundrum when he stated that Israel's tactics against the Palestinians had become too repressive and were stirring up potentially uncontrollable levels of hatred and terrorism. "In our tactical decisions, we are operating contrary to our strategic interests," he told reporters. Ya'alon went on to claim that the Israeli government was unwilling to make concessions that could bolster the authority of moderate Palestinian Prime Minister Mahmoud Abbas, and he expressed the fear that by continuing its policy of harsh repression, Israel would bring about the collapse of the Palestinian Authority, the silencing of Palestinian moderates, and the popularization of more radical voices like that of Hamas. The head of the General Security Service (Shabak), the defense minister, and Prime Minister Ariel Sharon opposed Ya'alon. Consequently, his term as chief of staff was not renewed, and his military career ended in 2005. A year later, all of Ya'alon's predictions proved accurate.

Ya'alon was no dove. From the time he became chief of staff in July 2002, he had been in charge of ruthlessly putting down the Palestinian uprising. He had authorized assassinations, house demolitions, and all the rest. But 15 months into the job, Ya'alon had learned much from his experience, and it seems that what he learned above all else was to empathize with the enemy—not to have warm and fuzzy feelings about the Palestinians, but to see things from their point of view in order to improve his ability to further Israel's chief strategic interest, namely, to live in peace with its neighbors.

As odd as it may sound at first, and as difficult as it may be to apply in practice, exercising empathy with one's enemy is the key to an effective counterterrorist strategy. Seeing the enemy's point of view increases one's understanding of the minimum conditions that would allow the enemy to put down arms. An empathic understanding of the enemy discourages counterproductive actions such as excessive repression, and it encourages tactical moves that further one's strategic aims. As Ya'alon suggested, in the Israeli case such tactical moves might include (1) offering meaningful rewards—for instance, releasing hundreds of millions of Palestinian tax dollars held in escrow by Israel, freeing selected Palestinians from Israeli prisons, and shutting down remote and costly Israeli settlements in the northern West Bank—in exchange for the renunciation of suicide bombing, and (2) attributing the deal to the intercession of moderate Palestinian forces so as to buttress their popularity and authority. (From this point of view, Israel framed its unilateral 2005 withdrawal from Gaza poorly because most Palestinians saw it as a concession foisted on Israel by Hamas.) Once higher levels of trust and stability are established by such counterterrorist tactics, they can serve as the foundation for negotiations leading to a permanent settlement. Radical elements would inevitably try to jeopardize negotiations, as they have in the past, but Israel resisted the temptation to shut down peace talks during the suicide bombing campaign of the mid-1990s, and it could do so again. Empathizing with the enemy would also help prevent the breakdown of negotiations, as happened in 2000; a clear sense of the minimally acceptable conditions for peace can come only from an empathic understanding of the enemy.

conclusion

Political conflict over territory is the main reason for suicide bombing, although religious justifications for suicide missions are likely to become more important when secular ideologies fail to bring about desired results. Suicide bombing may also occur for strategic or retaliatory reasons—to further insurgent aims or in response to repressive state actions.

Cases vary in the degree to which suicide bombers are motivated by (1) political or religious and (2) strategic or retaliatory aims. For example, research to date suggests that suicide bombing is more retaliatory in Israel than in Iraq, and more religiously motivated in Iraq than in Israel. But in any case, repression (short of a policy approaching genocide) cannot solve the territorial disputes that lie at the root of suicide bombing campaigns. As Zbigniew Brzezinski, President Jimmy Carter's national security adviser, wrote a few years ago in the *New York Times*, "to win the war on terrorism, one must . . . begin a political effort that focuses on the conditions that brought about [the terrorists'] emergence." These are wise words that Israel—and the United States in its own "war on terror"—would do well to heed.

RECOMMENDED RESOURCES

Hany Abu-Hassad. *Paradise Now.*

> This movie sketches the circumstances that shape the lives of two Palestinian suicide bombers, showing that they are a lot like us and that if we found ourselves in similar circumstances, we might turn out to be a lot like them. (Nominated for the 2005 Oscar for best foreign-language film.)

Robert J. Brym and Bader Araj. "Suicide Bombing as Strategy and Interaction: The Case of the Second Intifada." *Social Forces* 84 (2006): 1965–82.

> Explains suicide bombing as the outcome of structured interactions among conflicting and cooperating parties and organizations.

Mohammed M. Hafez. "Suicide Terrorism in Iraq: A Preliminary Assessment of the Quantitative Data and Documentary Evidence." *Studies in Conflict and Terrorism* 29 (2006): 591–619.

> The first systematic analysis of suicide bombing in Iraq demonstrates the strategic and retaliatory aims of the assailants.

Errol Morris. *The Fog of War.*

> Robert McNamara's extraordinarily frank assessment of his career as secretary of defense in the Kennedy and Johnson administrations. This film is a profound introduction to strategic thinking and a valuable lesson on how to learn from one's mistakes. His first lesson: empathize with your enemy. (Winner of the 2003 Oscar for best documentary.)

Robert A. Pape. *Dying to Win: The Strategic Logic of Suicide Terrorism* (Random House, 2005).

> In support of the view that suicide bombing takes place mainly for rational, strategic reasons, Pape analyzes all suicide attacks worldwide from 1980 to 2003.

Christoph Reuter. *My Life Is a Weapon: A Modern History of Suicide Bombing.* Trans. H. Ragg-Kirkby (Princeton University Press, 2004).

> A succinct overview of the past 25 years of suicide attacks.

REVIEW QUESTIONS

1. Did it surprise you that suicide bombers tend not to be psychologically unstable or that they are not mainly motivated by religion? How do the facts and findings reported in this article

conflict with our usual cultural understanding of terrorists and suicide bombers?

2. According to this article, why don't terrorist organizations recruit "crazy" people for suicide attacks?

3. Many countries refuse to negotiate with terrorists, stating that negotiation validates terrorism as a form of international relations.

On the basis of this article, do you think such policies reduce the "boomerang effect"? Or do they make matters worse? Explain your answer.

4. Activity: Imagine you are the head of an antiterrorism advisory board for the United Nations. Using Brym's six lessons, devise a strategic action plan for combating and reducing instances of suicide bombing.

nicole martinrogers, ela rausch, and paul mattessich

communities that don't bowl in the fog

5

winter 2009

community indicators measure opinions, attitudes, demographics, and trends to reflect life in a community. projects to compile and make them more publicly accessible are sociology in action.

Early one morning, members of a Santa Cruz business owners' association discussed a request for a contribution to an affordable housing development. They considered making the donation, but couldn't agree about the need for this type of housing in their community.

Later that afternoon, the director of a Boston nonprofit searched for information about labor market conditions in her agency's service area. She wanted to demonstrate the need for more employment training in a grant proposal.

The same day in St. Paul, city council members struggled to prioritize funding for a ride share initiative, a crime prevention program, and a teen center's homework help program. Each had different perceptions of the needs for these services and thus advocated different priorities.

What do these people have in common? They all need objective information on conditions in their communities so they can make informed decisions about policies, programs, emerging problems, and new initiatives. That, and they all live in areas with a community indicators project that can provide it.

At the first annual meeting of our own community indicators project in Minneapolis–St.

Paul, Peter Hutchinson, president of the Bush Foundation, offered a metaphor that illustrates the basic principle of community indicators projects.

When you bowl in fog, he explained, you throw the ball down the lane and quickly hear it hit the pins, but you don't really know how well you've done or have any information on how to improve your game. Eliminate the fog, however, and you suddenly have data to work with, data that can help you better evaluate your performance and help you improve.

So, too, with public policies and social problems, Hutchinson continued. Without empirical data and information, we have no idea where we really stand or what we can do to improve our situation. It's like bowling in fog.

> By pulling together a variety of measures, community indicators projects serve as a barometer of a community's overall well-being.

a brief primer

A community indicators project compiles and presents up-to-date information on various aspects of community life in a given locale. Community indicators are simply measures—usually survey results and other compendia of social statistics—of opinions, attitudes, demographics, and trends that reflect the characteristics of and quality of life in a community.

(Courtesy of Lumaxart.com)

For example, the four-year high school graduation rate might be one measure of a community's educational performance. Change in the graduation rate over time represents a trend—or, we might say, is an indicator—that can be related to other social changes and, in some cases, to interventions that grow directly out of an indicators project itself.

The obesity rate would be another example. Important because it relates to other aspects of health such as heart disease and diabetes, the obesity rate is an "indicator" of a community's overall physical health, or lack thereof.

Some projects focus strictly on "objective" indicators such as high school graduation rates or obesity rates, whereas others also incorporate "subjective" indicators, such as residents' ratings of how safe they feel in their neighborhood. Some collect original data while others rely entirely on data collected by other organizations, typically governments.

By pulling together a variety of measures, community indicators projects serve as a barom-

eter of a community's overall well-being. They provide a tool that concerned citizens, local governments, service providers, advocates, and funders can use to examine the trends in their communities, evaluate the success of various initiatives and policy changes in a particular area, and recognize needs and opportunities in others.

Oriented toward public policy but wary of politics and partisanship, community indicators proponents believe in the need to bring concrete, objective data and information to the public debate and decision-making. A common theme across all community indicators projects is an emphasis on measurable outcomes so that empirical data, rather than conjecture, can be used to assess community well-being.

If these projects sound sociological, that's because they are—both in terms of their commitment to empirical research and in the actual methods (like surveys and mapping) used to assemble this information. Indeed, the roots of community indicators projects extend back to the University of Chicago's pioneering urban sociology of the early 20th century.

sociological roots

Chief architects of the Chicago School, Robert Park and Ernest Burgess developed the theory of urban ecology, called Concentric Zone Theory, in 1925. It argues that urban spaces are divided into niches in which the residents share certain social characteristics through exposure to similar environmental pressures.

Community indicators projects have a similar premise: residents within geographic regions form networks with common social, economic, and environmental interdependencies. Individual residents' characteristics shape, and are shaped by, regional trends. Park and Burgess discovered that mapping the incidence of these social characteristics provided a useful tool for geographic comparison and identifying "problem" areas.

In the 1960s, the term "social indicators" was coined by the American Academy of Arts and Sciences. Frustrated by the lack of available data and tools for charting social change, scientists at the academy attempted to develop a system that would allow them to anticipate change and assess the impact and value of their programs. They defined social indicators as "statistics, statistical series, and all other forms of evidence that enable us to assess where we stand and are going with respect to our values and goals . . ." This definition was first published in a volume entitled *Social Indicators*, edited by R. A. Bauer in 1966.

In 1976, two other important developments occurred in social indicators research that advanced the notion that a few carefully selected variables measured using scientifically sound methods can provide a brief overview of the well-being of the community. First, social psychologists Angus Campbell, Philip E. Converse, and Willard L. Rodgers published *The Quality of American Life: Perceptions, Evaluations, and Satisfactions*, in which they proposed to monitor quality of life by measuring Americans' satisfaction with different life "domains." As well that year, in *Social Indicators of Well-Being: Americans' Perceptions of Life Quality*, Frank A. Andrews and Stephen B. Withey introduced the use of public attitudes, called perceptual indicators, to measure community well-being.

In more recent years, Stephen Raudenbush and Rob Sampson improved social indicators methodology through what they termed "econometrics." Using data gathered through scientific observation and community-level surveys, they created scales to measure the level of social dys-

function and cohesion in neighborhoods. Their work supported the use of social surveys for measuring community well-being. It also supplemented official sources of neighborhood-level data, which are often limited in frequency and scope, with additional information about existing neighborhood conditions gathered through first-hand, scientific observation.

types of projects

During the past 20 years, foundations and nonprofits (with local governmental support in some cases) have initiated a new generation of community indicators projects in cities across the United States. Increased emphasis on evaluation, outcomes, and results-oriented decision-making in government funding and public policy are all responsible for the increased interest in these projects.

The City of Portland and Multnomah County in Oregon initiated a community indicators project in response to the call for more accountability in government. The Jacksonville Community Council in Florida started its indicators project to improve planning that would guide economic development and re-energize business activity. Sustainable Seattle sought to create concrete, understandable benchmarks for progress toward sustainability in the region.

There are broader uses for indicators, too. Researchers at Child Trends, a Washington, D.C.–based non-partisan research firm, suggest that social indicators can be used for description, monitoring, goal setting, increasing accountability, and reflective practice. Baltimore Vital Sign offers ". . . a common way of understanding how our neighborhoods and overall quality of life are changing over time . . ."

If these projects sound sociological, that's because they are—both in terms of their commitment to empirical research and in their methods.

Most generalized community indicators projects have goals similar to these, whereas specialized projects may have narrower goals, such as environmental preservation, healthy children, or a competitive regional economy. All, though, share the belief that empirical data and information are crucial to public planning and civic discourse.

As these examples suggest, however, indicators projects vary in terms of their goals and approaches to selection of indicators, their organizational structure, and in their methods of disseminating information.

David Swain, a founder of Jacksonville's project, categorized contemporary indicators projects into four primary types: healthy community, sustainability, government performance, and quality of life.

The first area, healthy community, originated with a strict public health focus but has expanded over time to include issues such as public safety, civic engagement, and other aspects of social well-being. Sustainability is characterized by a focus on ecological systems. These projects usually include environment, social, and economic indicators, but present information from an environmentally sensitive perspective. Government performance focuses on measures of efficiency and productivity, such as gross domestic product (GDP). Finally, quality of life includes both traditional economic indicators and healthy community indicators. This type of project is perhaps the broadest in its orientation and recognizes the importance of cost-benefit analysis in policy decision-making and allows users to draw the basic connections between social, physical, and economic well-being. Moreover, this method of presenting information can encourage the development of cross-sector approaches to problem-solving.

Our own project, Twin Cities Compass, best fits this last type because it provides a common foundation for identifying and understanding key issues that impact well-being in the Minneapolis–St. Paul metropolitan region. In terms of breadth of topics, Twin Cities Compass addresses nine areas deemed critical for the region's overall success (civic engagement, early childhood, economy, education, environment, health, housing, public safety, and transportation). We also monitor disparities in the well-being of different demographic groups. Twin Cities Compass balances the issue of breadth and depth by limiting each topic to four or fewer key indicators.

collaborative efforts

Because of the many options for consideration and interests involved, community indicators projects typically identify a leader to implement the selection, development, and publication of indicators as well as a host for sponsorship, guidance, and governance, which can be nonprofit foundations, online newspapers, local governments, or community collaboratives. Some projects have research staff in-house, others hire it out to consultants. A single organization can serve in both capacities, but most indicators projects have an oversight committee to coordinate all these functions.

The Amherst H. Wilder Foundation in St. Paul, where we work, operates Twin Cities Compass while a governance committee composed of the project's funders (nine major foundations in the region) and other community leaders provide oversight.

The governance committee, multiple advisory committees, and partner organizations provide a bridge between data and community engagement; they facilitate a bottom-up style of management and decision-making. The governance committee contributes to this bridge by ensuring the project shapes its activities and products in ways that will appeal to all constituencies in the region.

Indicators projects usually select variables that reflect community priorities, such as health care coverage for all residents, or current community concerns such as diabetes or crime rates. Twin Cities Compass worked with "topic advisory groups" composed of local leaders and experts to select the key indicators, with the intent of increasing community buy-in. Participants were carefully selected to ensure a broad range of perspectives, including representatives of local government, academia, advocacy, and business.

Besides being available and cost-effective (most indicators projects assemble and organize existing data rather than collect new information), indicators also need to be easily understandable and resonate with the general public. Most importantly, they should be indicative of broader trends in a given area. Finally, our project prefers indicators be focused on or tied to issues amenable to public policy or concrete social change.

It's anticipated that partner organizations will use the project's data for planning purposes and for promoting community action—for example, by means of task forces organized to recommend policies.

Similar to many other indicators projects across the country, Twin Cities Compass engages stakeholders—community leaders, nonprofit administrators, policy makers, and legislators— and invests them in the process of indicator development. This helps engender a sense of ownership among those stakeholders and maximizes the likelihood effective, broad-based action will follow from the information made available by the project. The easily accessible format of the Internet, used by most contemporary indicators projects as the primary method of information distribution, makes getting up-

to-date and reliable data possible for most in a community.

project must-dos

Our own preparation for the design of Twin Cities Compass helped us identify the key challenges all indicators projects must address. The decisions groups make about these issues are likely to have a significant impact on a project's long-term success.

purpose and scope

Projects need to address scope, in terms of both geographic coverage and breadth and depth of topics. Twin Cities Compass provides data for Minnesota's seven-county metropolitan area, home to nearly half of the state's residents, many of whom share similar social and economic development concerns because of their geographic proximity. A regional-level analysis like this is particularly useful for policy and planning purposes and is common among indicators projects across the country. A citywide or statewide focus is another common approach used by developers of contemporary indicators projects.

community engagement

Community stakeholders must be involved to create a sense of ownership and, thereby, maximize the likelihood the selected indicators will be widely accepted and used. Several indicators project leaders we interviewed said sustaining the interest of diverse stakeholders is a major challenge—some recommended new projects make it the top priority. Ongoing community engagement can be facilitated with regular meetings with key stakeholders; presentations to committees, boards, and associations; regional dialogues; maintaining an up-to-date, user-friendly Web site; and seeking out opportunities to talk about the project in the media.

dissemination and use

Projects must be accessible and widely distributed if they're to be used. Like many contemporary indicators projects, Twin Cities Compass is an online tool. By connecting users to a shared base of knowledge, Twin Cities Compass can answer the "what," "where," and "who," questions so policymakers and concerned citizens can focus on solutions.

Two other successful dissemination strategies Twin Cities Compass used were cross-promotion with a public television station and an annual "pocket report." Project staff partnered with Twin Cities Public Television (TPT) to raise awareness of regional disparities by holding a data seminar in conjunction with TPT's broadcast of a multi-part series that examined the widening gap in well-being among Minnesota residents. To pique stakeholder interest at the time of the annual review, staff released a print piece with dashboard information on regional trends in the form of an easy-to-read brochure.

> As they continue to grow and become more sophisticated, professional and academic sociologists may well find community indicators projects increasingly interesting and useful.

new uses for indicators projects

An exercise in applied sociology, community indicators projects enrich our understanding of community and society by enabling residents of a region to see and act upon the social, economic, and environmental issues affecting their lives. The core of contemporary community indicators work is applying scientific tools—that is, using valid, reliable indicators to create an ongoing portrayal of the dynamics of life in a region and its communities—in concert with public discussion to interpret the meaning of those indicators, and democratic decision-making from which public action evolves to solve or prevent social problems.

But as they continue to grow and become more sophisticated, professional and academic sociologists may well find community indicators projects increasingly interesting and useful as well. This development would not be unprecedented. Although the Chicago School originally informed the development of indicators research, this work on indicators also contributed to theoretical developments in the field.

For example, Clifford Shaw and Henry McKay, criminologists from the University of Chicago and the Illinois Institute for Social Research, developed the theory of social disorganization to explain why criminal behavior occurs more frequently in some areas than others, and why crime is a normal human response to adverse social conditions. Building on the work of Park and Burgess, Shaw and McKay mapped official, community-level delinquency data to illustrate the strong relationship between crime rates and census tracts. They looked at trends in these data over time to explain individual behavior by mapping and analyzing community-level delinquency rates.

It's these kinds of dialogues we believe community indicators projects, properly appreciated and understood, can help promote.

RECOMMENDED RESOURCES

M. Dluhy and N. Swartz. "Connecting Knowledge and Policy: The Promise of Community Indicators in the United States." *Social Indicators Research* (2006) 79 (1): 1–23.

Outlines factors that contribute to the success (or failure) of community indicator projects and offers advice for communities seeking to launch their own indicators projects.

K. C. Land, V. L. Lamb, S. O. Meadows, and A. Taylor. "Measuring Trends in Child Well-Being: An Evidence-Based Approach." *Social Indicators Research* (2007) 80 (1): 105–32.

A review of the goals of the social indicators and quality-of-life movements of the 1960s and 1970s, and newer methods of measuring child and youth well-being.

K. A. Moore, B. V. Brown, and H. H. Scarupa. "The Uses (and Misuses) of Social Indicators: Implications for Public Policy." Child Trends Research Brief #2003-01.

Describes five basic functions of social indicators—description, monitoring, setting goals, increasing accountability, and internal evaluation—as well as selected misuses.

S. Raudenbush and R. J. Sampson. "'Ecometrics': Toward a Science of Assessing Ecological Settings, with Application to the Systematic Social Observation of Neighborhoods." *Sociological Methodology* (1999) 29: 1–41.

Two academic sociologists demonstrate how information can be obtained from surveys and observational studies for the assessment of neighborhoods, schools, and other ecological settings.

D. Swain and D. Hollar. "Measuring Progress: Community Indicators and the Quality of Life." *International Journal of Public Administration* (2003) 26 (7): 789–814.

Summarizes four major approaches to community-indicators work, with detailed attention to the "quality of life" frame pioneered in Jacksonville, Florida.

REVIEW QUESTIONS

1. Community indicators summarize important information in a single statistic. Can you think of other statistics that are commonly used to represent aspects of individuals or nations? What information is conveyed in these statistics? What is left out?

2. What are the benefits of viewing an entire community as a whole? Are there drawbacks as well?

3. The authors mention "community well-being" often. In your opinion, what indicators should be included in the definition of community well-being? Are some more important than others?

4. Activity: Information needs to be both relevant and implementable for communities and their leaders. Find information from one of the projects mentioned in the article, then put together a one-page advisory memo on people in that community for one of the following groups: activists calling for a Hispanic community clinic; a multinational company thinking of moving its headquarters to the city; or a school district considering a proposal for a new elementary school for students with disabilities.

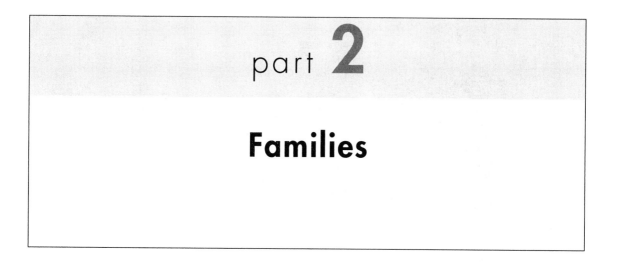

part **2**

Families

robin w. simon

the joys of parenthood, reconsidered

spring 2008

sociologists have found parents in the united states experience depression and emotional distress more often than their childless counterparts.

Hallmark stores stock baby cards filled with happy wishes for new parents, acknowledging and celebrating their long-awaited and precious bundle of joy. Too bad their selection doesn't include cards that recognize the negative emotions that often accompany parenthood.

Perhaps they should. Sociologists find that as a group, parents in the United States experience depression and emotional distress more often than their childless adult counterparts. Parents of young children report far more depression, emotional distress, and other negative emotions

(Courtesy of Anne Taintor)

than non-parents, and parents of grown children have no better well-being than adults who never had children.

That last finding contradicts the conventional wisdom that empty-nest parents derive all the emotional rewards of parenthood because they're done with the financially and psychologically taxing aspects of raising young kids.

These research findings, of course, fly in the face of our cultural dogma that proclaims it impossible for people to achieve an emotionally fulfilling and healthy life unless they become parents. And that's a problem, because the vast majority of American men and women eventually have children, yet conditions in our society make it nearly impossible for them to reap all the emotional benefits of doing so.

the greatest gift life has to offer

Americans harbor a widespread, deeply held belief that no adult can be happy without becoming a parent. Parenthood, we think, is pivotal for developing and maintaining emotional well-being, and children are an essential ingredient for a life filled with positive emotions like happiness, joy, excitement, contentment, satisfaction, and pride. Even more than marriage and employment, our culture promotes the idea that parenthood provides a sense of purpose and meaning in life, which are essential for good mental health.

As a result, we encourage men and women to have children in a variety of subtle and not so subtle ways. Then, we congratulate them when they become parents with baby showers, flowers, balloons, and cigars. These and other cultural celebrations of the transition to parenthood reflect, reinforce, and perpetuate Americans' beliefs that there's no better guarantee of achieving an emotionally fulfilling and healthy life than having children.

And most fall right in step. The vast majority of men and women in the United States become parents either through birth, adoption, or marriage. The 20th century witnessed important changes in the timing of parenthood (men and women are now deferring it until they're older, compared to previous generations), yet demographers have found that sooner or later about 80 percent of the adult population has biological children. Nothing indicates a decline in the near future as cohorts of young adults who are currently childless are still in their childbearing years.

These cultural beliefs about the importance of parenthood for achieving a happy and emotionally healthy adulthood extend to the way we respond to adults who either can't or choose not to have children. Because our culture equates childlessness with feelings of sadness, loneliness, emptiness, purposelessness, and meaninglessness—particularly as men and women approach the golden years, when the emotional rewards of parenthood are assumed to be at their peak—we feel sorry for and pity childless adults. We assume it's difficult, if not impossible, for them to have an emotionally fulfilling life without offspring. We also assume that those who are voluntarily child-free are selfish, unhappy, and will regret their decision after it's too late.

In her 1995 book on childlessness and the pursuit of happiness, Elaine Tyler May writes that in light of our cultural idealization of children, many reproductively challenged Americans subject themselves to expensive and invasive medical procedures in order to procreate. Heterosexual women and lesbians are increasingly conceiving offspring through in vitro fertilization, while heterosexual couples and gay men often turn to adoption and sometimes surrogacy to become parents. Culturally, we encourage those who can't have biological children to adopt—an idea buttressed by the highly publicized recent overseas adoptions among the Hollywood elite. There are no reliable estimates of the percentage of conceptions through artificial insemination or surrogacy, but between 2 percent and 4 percent of adults in the United States adopt children at some point in their lives.

Only in recent years have the media provided an alternative to the idealized portrayal of parenthood that has dominated the cultural landscape since the 1950s—a period marked by a strong, positive outlook on having children. Television shows like *Roseanne* and films like *Parenthood* that appeared in the 1980s debunked the overly romanticized conceptions of parenthood that had loomed large in our culture, portraying parents of young children as exhausted, frustrated, and at their wits end. Some recent films like *Meet the Parents* and television shows like *Everyone Loves Raymond* and *Brothers and Sisters* also depict strained relationships between empty-nest parents and their adult children.

But we're not deterred. These darker, though perhaps more realistic, portrayals of parenthood notwithstanding, most of us still adhere to the cultural belief that there's no better guarantee of a happy, healthy, and emotionally rich and

> Most of us adhere to the cultural belief that there's no better guarantee of a happy, healthy, and emotionally rich and rewarding life than having children.

rewarding life than having children, who are presumed to be "worth" the financial and psychological costs associated with raising them. Although most people today would probably agree that parenthood is often challenging, sometimes difficult, and involves continual self-sacrifice, periodic disaster, and occasional heartache— particularly when children enter the tumultuous adolescent years—our culture continues to promote the idea that the emotional rewards associated with parenthood far outweigh the personal costs.

numbers show otherwise

Sociological research finds an association between parenthood and depression.

Contrary to all of this, sociological research based on national surveys of American adults finds an association between parenthood and depression, emotional distress, and other negative emotions. While studies indicate parents derive more purpose, more meaning, and greater satisfaction from life than non-parents, they also reveal parents experience lower levels of emotional well-being, less frequent positive emotions, and more frequent negative emotions than their childless peers. Sara McLanahan and Julia Adams first summarized the evidence on parental status differences in mental health 20 years ago, but similar findings are evident in more recent research.

For example, a recent study I conducted with Ranae J. Evenson based on the National Survey of Families and Households—which includes a nationally representative sample of more than 10,000 adults in the United States—revealed that parents report significantly more symptoms of depression (feelings of sadness, loneliness, restlessness, and fear) than non-parents their own age. Several other studies based on different national surveys of adults also indicate that parents currently raising children are significantly more depressed and emotionally distressed than childless adults. Many others have found that living with minor children is associated with significantly lower levels of psychological well-being. The details of these studies can be found in a 2005 *Journal of Health and Social Behavior* article I wrote with Evenson, as well as McLanahan and Adam's 1987 *Annual Review of Sociology* article.

Additionally, Leda Nath and I studied Americans' everyday emotional experiences as reported on the General Social Survey, a nationally representative sample of more than 1,400 adults. It revealed that parents residing with minor children report significantly less frequent positive feelings (calm, contentment) but significantly more frequent negative feelings (fear, anxiety, worry, anger) than adults not living with young children. We further found that full-nest parents don't report more frequent feelings of happiness, excitement, joy, and pride than adults not residing with dependent offspring. Based on another national survey, Catherine E. Ross and Marieke Van Willigen also found that parents

because I'm the mother... that's why

(Courtesy of Anne Taintor)

the joys of parenthood, reconsidered **43**

with young children in the home are angrier than adults not living with kids.

Conventional wisdom tells us the emotional rewards of having children are fewest during the "full-nest" stage and greatest during the "empty-nest" stage of parenthood. Free of the onerous financial and psychological responsibilities associated with raising young offspring, empty-nest parents are ostensibly able to focus on the love, friendship, companionship, emotional support, and all sorts of assistance they receive from their adult children. Indeed, Debra Umberson's research on parent-adult child interaction in the United States indicates that most parents have frequent contact with their non-resident adult children, often speaking with them at least once a week.

However, studies based on recent national surveys indicate that empty-nest parents report similar levels of well-being as childless adults their own age. As a matter of fact, Evenson and I found no group of parents that reports significantly greater emotional well-being than people who never had children. This goes for married parents, cohabiting parents, single parents, noncustodial parents, and stepparents, as well as for fathers versus mothers, despite the fact that epidemiological research documents women's less frequent positive emotions, more frequent negative emotions, and higher levels of depression and emotional distress than men in general.

It's important to emphasize that while parents aren't any emotionally better off than their childless counterparts, parents' other social statuses—particularly their marital, employment, and socioeconomic status—influence the association between parenthood and mental health.

> Parents experience lower levels of emotional well-being, less frequent positive emotions, and more frequent negative emotions than their childless peers.

(Courtesy of Anne Taintor)

(Courtesy of Anne Taintor)

For example, research finds that single parents report higher levels of depression and emotional distress than married and cohabiting parents. Unemployment exacerbates the negative emotional effects of parenthood involving young children, particularly for men. Parents with lower levels of education and household income also experience higher levels of depression and emotional distress than their more advantaged peers. And, not surprisingly, parents who enjoy satisfying relationships with their children report greater emotional well-being than parents who have unsatisfying relationships with their offspring.

But, while these social characteristics influence or moderate the association between parenthood and mental health, little evidence exists that parenthood actually improves adults' emotional well-being. In fact, most evidence seems to point to the contrary.

the stresses of parenthood

Why doesn't parenthood have the positive emotional effects on adults that our cultural beliefs suggest? The answer to this question lies in the social conditions in which Americans today parent—they're far from ideal for allowing them to reap the full emotional benefits of having children. Parents are exposed to a number of different stressors that cancel out and often exceed the emotional rewards of having children. Making matters worse, parents and others perceive this stress as a private matter and reflective of their inability to cope with the "normal" demands of having children.

In their research examining change in the association between parenthood and psychological well-being from the 1950s to the 1970s, McLanahan and Adams found parenthood was perceived as more stressful and was more closely associated with emotional distress in the 1970s than in the 1950s. Much of this trend was due to changes in the employment and marital status of parents, they said.

A significant source of parental stress stems from the extraordinarily high financial cost of raising a child to adulthood these days. Even the basics such as food, clothing, and (for those who have it) healthcare are expensive, not to mention extracurricular activities parents feel compelled to provide their kids. Although the figures vary depending on parents' household income, the U.S. Department of Agriculture estimates families spend anywhere from $134,370 to $269,520 raising a child from birth through age 17. These figures don't include the astronomical cost of a college education; the College Board reports tuition alone is presently more than $20,000 at state universities, more than $80,000 at private universities, and continues to rise by an average of 6 percent to 7 percent each year.

Indeed, the increasing cost of raising kids is one factor that contributed to the large number of mothers who joined the labor force in the second half of the 20th century. Demographers estimate 70 percent of children in the United States are currently being raised in households in which all adults work outside the home. However, as Jennifer Glass and others point out, there's a fundamental incompatibility between employment and raising children, which makes juggling parenthood and paid work highly stressful.

Arlie Hochschild was the first to document that the lack of flexible work schedules, high-quality and affordable child care for preschool-aged children, and after-school care for elementary-aged children all contribute to stress from what's now commonly referred to as the "second shift" for employed parents, particularly employed mothers, who leave their jobs at 5 o'clock only to start another job caring for children at home. However, there are few policies or programs to alleviate the stress. In the end, our collective response to "stressed out" employed parents is that they need to become better organized.

Although financial stress and the stress of the second shift subside as children age and become independent, the majority of parents continue to be involved in their adult offspring's lives and worry about them. Among other things, parents worry about their grown children's financial well-being, their social relationships, their happiness, and both their mental and physical health. These observations have led sociologists to conclude that parenthood is the quintessential job that never ends.

Parents also shoulder the daunting responsibility for the development and well-being of another person, and our culture places high expectations on them for the way children "turn out." Irrespective of their children's age, we question parents' childrearing skills when they have problems. In fact, the way children turn out seems to be the only measure our culture offers for assessing whether men and women are "good" parents.

Alice S. Rossi has argued that unlike other societies, Americans receive relatively little preparation for parenthood and most parents raise their children in relative social isolation with little assistance from extended family members, friends, neighbors, and the larger community. At the same time, parents alone are accountable for raising children to be moral, responsible, intelligent, happy, healthy, and well-adjusted adults, and this awesome responsibility doesn't end when children are grown.

shifting the reward-cost analysis

Children provide parents with a sense of immortality, an important social identity, and emotional connections to extended family members and people in their communities. Children fulfill some basic human desires—including having someone to love and nurture, carrying on family traditions, and allowing us to become grandparents. Watching children grow and develop is enjoyable and parents feel comforted by the perception that they won't be alone to fend for themselves in old age. The parent-child relationship is perhaps the most important and enduring social bond in the lives of individuals, which is probably why parents derive more purpose and meaning in life than adults who never had children.

At the same time, the emotional benefits of having children are often overshadowed by the onerous demands and stressors associated with the role. Although experienced by mothers and fathers at a deeply personal level, the stressfulness of contemporary parenthood is firmly rooted in the social conditions in which people parent as well as our current social, economic, and cultural institutions.

> We need to reevaluate existing cultural beliefs that children improve the emotional health and well-being of adults.

(Courtesy of Anne Taintor)

In America we lack institutional supports that would help ease the social and economic burdens—and subsequent stressfulness and emotional disadvantages—associated with parenthood. Instituting better tax credits, developing more and better day care and after school options, as well as offering flexible work schedules for employed mothers and fathers would go far toward alleviating some of the stress for parents raising children.

However, providing these forms of assistance is only part of the solution, since parents whose children are grown don't report higher levels of emotional well-being than childless adults their own age. Affordable health care would insure individuals' basic health needs are met and would, therefore, lessen this lingering source of stress for all parents—irrespective of their children's age. Although there are no existing studies that systematically compare the mental health of parents and childless adults in other countries, it's likely that parents residing in societies with family-friendly and other social welfare policies enjoy better mental health than parents in the United States.

Of equal importance is the need to take stock of and reevaluate existing cultural beliefs that children improve the emotional health and well-being of adults. These cultural beliefs—and our expectations that children guarantee a life filled with happiness, joy, excitement, contentment, satisfaction, and pride—are an additional, though hidden, source of stress for all parents. Indeed, the feelings of depression, emotional distress, and other negative emotions parents experience on a daily basis may cause them to question what they're doing wrong. These negative emotions may also lead parents with children of all ages, especially mothers, to perceive themselves as inadequate since their feelings aren't consistent with our cultural ideal.

To this end, reducing the enormous and unrealistic cultural expectations we have for parenthood is as important as greater cultural recognition of the unrelenting challenges and difficulties associated with having children of all ages. Although there's no guarantee these changes would drastically improve the emotional lives of American mothers and fathers, at least they would help minimize the emotional costs and maximize the emotional benefits of parenthood in the United States today.

RECOMMENDED RESOURCES

Jennifer Glass. "Envisioning the Integration of Family and Work: Toward a Kinder, Gentler Workplace." *Contemporary Sociology* 29 (2000): 129–43.

> A provocative discussion of the incompatibility between raising children and women's success at work in the United States and factors underlying it.

Elaine Tyler May. *Barren in the Promised Land: Childless Americans and the Pursuit of Happiness* (Harvard University Press, 1995).

> An engaging historical analysis of public attitudes about the link between happiness and parenthood.

Sara McLanahan and Julia Adams. "The Effects of Children on Adults' Psychological Well-Being: 1957–1976." *Social Forces* 68 (1989): 124–46.

> A classic study comparing the mental health of parents between the 1950s and 1970s.

Kei M. Nomaguchi and Melissa A. Milkie. "Costs and Rewards of Children: The Effects of Becoming a Parent on Adults' Lives." *Journal of Marriage and the Family* 65 (2003): 356–74.

> A comparison of six dimensions of adults' lives between childless adults and adults who transitioned to parenthood.

Catherine E. Ross and Marieke Van Willigen. "Gender, Parenthood, and Anger." *Journal of Marriage and the Family* 58 (1996): 572–84.

A study showing that economic stress and stress associated with child care increase feelings of anger among parents—particularly among mothers.

Viviana A. Zelizer. *Pricing the Priceless Child: The Changing Social Value of Children* (Basic Books, 1985).

The seminal historical account of change in the value of children to parents from being economic assets to being emotionally priceless.

REVIEW QUESTIONS

1. Do you agree with the author that our society values having children so much that childless adults are either pitied or considered selfish? If so, why do you think this cultural belief is so strong? If not, why not?

2. Do you think having children will make/makes your life complete? How have the cultural beliefs about parenthood described in this article affected your personal desire (or lack thereof) for children?

3. Brainstorm about why these ideas about parenthood persist even if they are not statistically "true"? Who might have a vested interest in maintaining these beliefs?

ashley e. frost and f. nii-amoo dodoo

men are missing from african family planning 7

winter 2009

fertility programs in africa fail to understand that men, not women, have the most power over fertility decisions in their families.

Roughly 50 years ago it became clear that women across the developing world were bearing more children than they wanted. Poor access to modern contraception meant women couldn't properly plan their families or prevent unwanted pregnancies. Demographers and policy makers foresaw a potentially catastrophic global population explosion, and significant financial investments in family planning programs in Africa, Asia, and Latin America followed.

While global investments in family planning generally succeeded in Latin America and Asia—places where the average number of births per woman has fallen from six to two-and-a-half since the 1960s—these programs in sub-Saharan Africa haven't yielded similar results. Women in this part of the world continue to bear, on average, more than five children.

Obviously family planning programs in this vast region have missed the mark. From our vantage point as demographers who examine gender inequality in the region, it's clear these programs have compromised their chances of success by consistently disregarding a central driver of high fertility: men, who have significant control over childbearing in Africa.

It may seem counterintuitive to suggest that women, who bear the primary biological role in childbearing, aren't largely in control of decisions surrounding their own fertility. However—

and our research with teens in Ghana recently reinforced this for us—the marriage process itself, in which men give gifts and money to the families of their future wives through bridewealth payments, fundamentally shapes gender norms and determines the power relations between men and women.

Although Africa is an extremely diverse continent, these cultural norms and gender relations are remarkably widespread. Fertility programs in Africa fail because they target women as primary beneficiaries, and consider men, their preferences, and Africa's patriarchal culture only tangentially. The two predominant family

Women wait in an East African clinic for prenatal care, family planning, and basic ob-gyn services. (Advencap via Creative Commons)

planning policies—providing contraceptives and expanding girls' education—underestimate that men, not women, have the most power over fertility decisions in their families. As a result, efforts to curb population growth on the continent are severely handicapped.

the problem of population growth

Despite five decades of international investments in family planning in Africa, the continent continues to see fertility rates much higher than any other region in the world. Women in Western and Eastern Africa average more than five births each, and their counterparts in Middle Africa bear more than six, and this has actually shown signs of increase since 1990, according to the nonprofit Population Reference Bureau (PRB) in Washington, D.C.

Among the few African countries that experienced some fertility decline in the early 1990s (places like Kenya, Ghana, and Cameroon), none currently have fertility rates below four births per woman. While Eastern and Southern Africa have experienced improvements in modern contraceptive use in recent decades, only 8.6 percent of married women in Western Africa and 5.9 percent of married women in Middle Africa use modern forms of contraception such as condoms and hormonal birth control.

Across Africa, women bear more than double the number of children needed to replace the existing generation—for every two parents who grow old and die, approximately five children are left behind, most of whom will also have large families. When we compound this phenomenon across the continent, the result is immense population growth. At current rates, the population of 900 million in Africa will swell to 1.8 billion in just 28 years.

> Fertility programs in Africa fail because they consider men only tangentially.

Africa faces additional population challenges that compound the effects of high fertility. Since the explosion of development initiatives post–World War II, the continent has experienced fewer and fewer deaths (although the drop in the death rate has slowed somewhat because of the HIV/AIDS epidemic). This means more women are surviving to adulthood and are better able to conceive children because they're healthier. According to PRB, the number of women in their childbearing years will rise from 52 million to 151 million in West Africa alone between 2000 and 2059. This means that even if women have no more than two children and fertility rates decline drastically, the inbuilt momentum stemming from the large population base guarantees the population will continue to grow.

Although population growth isn't necessarily detrimental to development, the rapid upsurge of African populations clearly increases competition for limited resources that must be shared among more people. Social infrastructures like schools, health systems, clean water supplies, and waste management are severely

A billboard targeted at men in Zambia. (Matt Corks via Creative Commons)

strained by population growth, and governments struggle to keep up with the demands of their growing populations.

Individual families are also affected. In families with large numbers of children, parents ration money spent on health care and education. Inevitably, some children die from preventable disease and others can't attend school. Maternal mortality and morbidity increase with higher fertility because women bear children earlier and have less time between births, which puts them at greater risk for medical complications. Without sustained economic growth, rising populations can also mean greater unemployment as competition for jobs increases.

African men generally don't have positive attitudes about contraception, partly because it threatens their culturally supported right to control women's reproduction.

the failure of providing contraception

The 1994 International Conference on Population and Development, adopted by 179 countries worldwide, deems access to adequate reproductive services an inherent right of all women. Yet, despite the fact that African women want fewer children, they haven't been able to exercise that desire over many decades.

A cornerstone of current family planning strategies in Africa is the expansion of contraceptive and other reproductive health services to women. True, women can't fully implement their fertility choices without access to affordable modern methods, but, when they receive these services they inevitably go home to men, and it's here that most fertility decisions are made.

African men's attitudes vary, but they generally don't have positive attitudes about contraception, in part because it threatens their culturally supported right to control women's reproduction. Methods like hormonal birth control, which women can use without their husbands' knowledge, cause men particular anxiety, as they feel stripped of control over their wives' fertility.

Yet, women who want to space their births may have no other option but to use these forms of contraception secretly. A woman explained to demographer Ayaga Bawah and his colleagues in Ghana, "[E]ven when you tell your husband that you would not like to have another child (yet), he will tell you that he paid the bridewealth, so that he can have children with you and that you have no right to tell him not to have sex with you. If you still insist, he beats you up. But would you allow him to continue beating you every day? No. You will go and use a method, so that he can have sex with you while you plan your family." Women can't refuse sex for fear of violent retaliation, and those who use contraception in secret are also vulnerable to violence and divorce if their husbands find out.

In contrast, men have nearly full control over the use of condoms, and that provides them the opportunity to exercise greater control over women's fertility than contraceptive methods women can use in secret. But men are highly reluctant to use them. Sayings such as "you wouldn't eat a banana with the peel on, or candy with the wrapper on" have become familiar across much of Africa; our research teams have heard men use these anti-condom arguments in Ghana, Benin, and Kenya, and we have read of their prevalence in Malawi and South Africa.

While condom use in some countries has risen in recent years, much of this increase is within "risky" sexual relationships—among partners who aren't married or living together. In other words, men are likely using condoms to

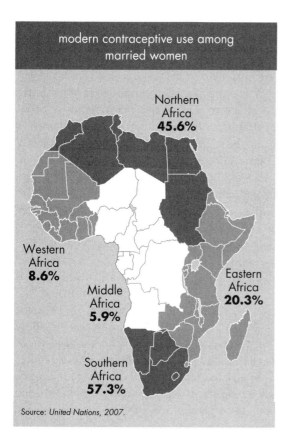

modern contraceptive use among married women

Northern Africa **45.6%**

Western Africa **8.6%**

Middle Africa **5.9%**

Eastern Africa **20.3%**

Southern Africa **57.3%**

Source: *United Nations, 2007.*

over the radio, he gets so angry and even wishes he could lay a hand on the person speaking. He fumes and shouts, cursing under his breath, that no one can ever tell him to practice family planning because nobody is taking care of his children for him," she said.

the masculine interest in fertility

The source of men's opposition to family planning may be that many men experience a net benefit from childbearing and thus continue to want large families (although, there's some evidence that men's support for large families is diminishing in urban areas and among highly educated populations).

Socially, fatherhood is essential to defining one's manhood in much of Africa. In fact, it's not unheard of for young unmarried men to try to father children prior to marriage to mark their entry into adulthood. Infertile men are pitied even more so than women who can't conceive. In a cultural context where family and lineage is so important, men (particularly those who belong to patrilineal ethnic groups) feel a deep sense of obligation to contribute to their family line, and a grave sense of failure when they can't.

In contrast to the many social benefits of fatherhood, there are very few costs of childbearing to men. Traditionally, African men and women divide childrearing responsibilities— women tend to care for the "daily needs" of children such as food and health care, while men are traditionally responsible for one-time large expenses, such as school fees. Ironically, recent attempts to provide free primary education for all children in Africa may actually bolster men's desires for large families because the costs of fatherhood decrease even further. Moreover, men who don't take on their paternal responsibility for their offspring—in contrast to women who do the same—typically experience

protect themselves from sexually transmitted infections and HIV/AIDS, but not to prevent pregnancy. As of 2002, only Botswana and Gabon reported rates of condom use among married women higher than 3.5 percent, according to PRB. In comparison, 13.3 percent of American women and 18 percent of British women who are married use condoms as their method of contraception, according to the bureau.

Men's opposition to family planning programs remains an insurmountable obstacle to wives and partners who want to use contraception. One older woman told Bawah and his colleagues that her husband is enraged at even the idea of family planning. "Every morning, whenever he hears people discussing family planning

few negative consequences, thus fostering men's carefree attitude toward pregnancy.

If there's a single cultural practice that reinforces these attitudes and the gender inequality in African marriages, it's the payment of bridewealth.

controlling fertility

Anthropologists explain bridewealth as reimbursement for the resources and energies parents invest in raising their daughters. But, in actual cultural practice, once husbands pay it, bridewealth gives them jurisdiction over their wives' sexual and reproductive practices.

Unlike the dowry system of South Asia, where brides bring financial resources to husbands and their families at marriage, in sub-Saharan Africa men and their families give bridewealth payments to women's families. Bridewealth payments can take many forms. Livestock and cattle, large and small sums of cash, and token gifts such as fabrics, kola nuts, and local alcoholic brews are all part of regional and ethnic bridewealth practices. Bridewealth can be a small gift-giving gesture between families or a significant financial exchange that impacts local economies.

In some circumstances men withhold the final bridewealth payment until their first child is born so they can confirm their wives' reproductive capacity. Among patrilineal ethnic groups where inheritance is passed through men—the predominant type in Africa—men's rights extend over offspring from the marriage, and children belong to the husband's lineage once bridewealth is paid. In fact, in many instances if women are unable to reproduce, the marriage itself is terminated and bridewealth payments must be returned in full. The pressure to do this is strong. One Ghanaian man, who stayed with his wife of 15 years despite her inability to conceive, explained to us that he didn't attend family functions because of the social pressure to end his marriage.

In the most extreme examples, bridewealth payments are cited as evidence of a husband's right to domineer his wife. In fact, one young boy we interviewed in Ghana explained that while boyfriends can't hit or beat their girlfriends under any circumstances, violence is fully acceptable after "you have paid so much for her to be your wife." Many of the young girls we interviewed agreed; one told us that while boyfriends have "no control over" a woman they have not married, she agreed that "they can do whatever they like" to their wives.

However practiced, bridewealth is a symbol that formalizes cultural norms in marriage in a way that uniformly gives power to men. While the extent of that power varies tremendously across Africa, the practice consistently establishes gender relationships in which men experience at least some sense of increased power, while women experience greater obligation. This has real and lasting consequences for the number of children couples conceive over the course of their lifetimes.

A fisherman and his seven children in Cameroon. (Teseum via Creative Commons)

female education inadequate

Like efforts to increase access to contraceptives, in recent decades large investments have been made to improve girls' education in Africa—the Millennium Development Goals and UNESCO's Education for All Initiative are multi-million dollar projects aimed at, among other goals, closing educational gaps between boys and girls in Africa. Advocates argue that not only does girls' education delay childbearing, but it alters the nature of gendered relationships. Educated women are more empowered and better able to negotiate their preferences, including the number of children they bear, with their spouses.

But no existing studies prove either of those goals are being achieved. While educated women are more likely to use contraception, it's unclear whether they're actually able to better negotiate their contraceptive preferences with their partners, or that they are more likely to select partners amenable to contraception.

In a recent study of girls' gender attitudes in Kenya, Francis Obare and colleagues dishearteningly found that in-school girls between ages 12 and 15 were significantly less likely to say that "a woman needs her husband's permission for everything" than their 16- to 19-year-old educated peers, regardless of their education level. Perhaps, because the older group of girls is closer to marriage, they more readily recognize the unequal gender dynamics that await them as wives. But, as the study suggests, instead of becoming more empowered as they grow older, girls may become less so, despite their school attendance.

We must also consider why girls who stay in school delay childbearing. As Barbara Mensch and her research team found in rural schools in Kenya, the nature of the schooling environment is critical to delaying sexual activity and childbearing. Girls who attend schools with high levels of gender inequality—sexual harassment by teachers and peers, sexist curricula, and few women role models—have sex at the same rate as girls who are out of school. Girls delay childbearing beyond their out-of-school peers only when their schooling environments are more gender equitable. Unfortunately, because schools reflect their surrounding communities, the same gender inequality students learn at home is frequently present at school.

> Unless men are integrated into reproductive health services, women will meet strong resistance to contraceptive use.

While education is clearly critical for broader economic and social development in Africa, we can't assume education, just as we can't assume access to contraceptives, will inevitably reduce fertility.

bringing men in

Some of our arguments here could be considered an unflattering portrayal of African men and boys. But gender inequality in Africa, just as in the United States and other developed nations, occurs within a particular social, historical, and cultural context.

A sociological approach to fertility decisions needs to be more concerned with understanding how existing gender and power structures in sub-Saharan Africa affect family planning failures rather than worried about assigning blame to individual men or boys. And the fact of the matter is, demographers believe that the two central population control strategies—access to contraception and better girls' education—are unlikely to deter population growth without changes in male attitudes.

Unless men's preferences change and they're better integrated into reproductive health services, women are likely to meet strong resistance to contraceptive use from their husbands and partners.

Without massive investment efforts it will be extremely difficult—perhaps impossible—to better incorporate men into family planning initiatives and still provide the existing level of services to women. That is, if men are better integrated into reproductive health services in Africa, it's possible fewer women overall will have access to these services because finite financial resources are deflected away from women to include men.

However, programs that address men's reproductive needs ultimately benefit women more than women-focused services alone. These needs may be partially addressed by training service providers to use male-friendly approaches, improving access to underused methods such as vasectomy, and creating more opportunities for men and women to discuss contraceptive use jointly with health practitioners.

Giving men some of the burden of pregnancy prevention can actually encourage greater gender equality by improving marital communication and empowering men with a deeper knowledge of and empathy for their wives' experiences. While women-centered approaches treat men as barriers, family planning programs that recognize men's central role may ultimately reduce both fertility and longstanding gender inequalities on the continent.

RECOMMENDED RESOURCES

Ayaga Agula Bawah, Patricia Akweongo, Ruth Simmons, and James F. Phillips. "Women's Fears and Men's Anxieties: The Impact of Family Planning on Gender Relations in Northern Ghana." *Studies in Family Planning* (1999) 30: 54–66.

Using data from focus groups, this paper highlights tensions between men and women over family planning.

F. Nii-Amoo Dodoo and Ashley E. Frost. "Gender in African Population Research: The Fertility/Reproductive Health Example." *Annual Review of Sociology* (2008) 34: 431–52.

The authors trace the history of mainstream fertility theories and examine how well they apply to the highly gendered context of sub-Saharan Africa.

Meyer Fortes. *Marriage in Tribal Societies* (Cambridge University Press, 1962).

A classic anthropological volume on the process of marriage bridewealth exchange in Africa.

Population Reference Bureau. *2008 World Population Data Sheet* (PRB, 2008).

Provides demographic data, including fertility and contraceptive use rates for the countries and regions of the world.

REVIEW QUESTIONS

1. Outline the main reasons the authors give for the high fertility rates among African women. In a nutshell, why aren't current planning policies working?
2. Using what you learned in the article as your guide, explain how gender roles and ideologies within different cultures can influence fertility rates. Compare the African example to another community that you are familiar with.
3. Activity: Imagine that you are a public health official working with the UN on overpopulation in Africa. Given what you learned from this article, create a plan for a program that would be more successful in reducing fertility rates among women in Africa.

kathleen e. hull, ann meier, and timothy ortyl

the changing landscape of love and marriage **8**

spring 2010

american norms about love and marriage are in transition—complicated by the paradoxical embrace of individualism and commitment.

Celebrities breaking up, making up, and having kids out of wedlock. Politicians confessing to extramarital affairs and visits to prostitutes. Same-sex couples pushing for, and sometimes getting, legal recognition for their committed relationships. Today's news provides a steady stream of stories that seem to suggest that lifelong love and (heterosexual) marriage are about as dated as a horse and carriage. Social conservatives continue sounding the alarm about the consequences of the decline of marriage and the rise of unwed parenting for children and for society at large. Are we really leaving behind the old model of intimacy, or are these changes significant but not radical? And what are the driving forces behind the changes?

In the United States, marriage historically has been an important and esteemed social institution. Historian Nancy Cott argues that, since colonial times, Americans have viewed marriage as the bedrock of healthy families and communities, vital to the functioning of democracy itself. But today, nearly half of all marriages end in divorce. People are getting married later than they used to; the median age at first marriage is now 28 for men and 26 for women, compared to 23 and 20 in 1960. The proportion of adults who never marry remains low but is climbing; in 2006, 19 percent of men and 13 percent of women aged 40–44 had never married. Roughly one-third of all births are to unmarried parents, and unmarried cohabitation has gone from a socially stigmatized practice to a normal stage in the adult lifecourse (more than half of all American marriages now begin as cohabitations). Many of the same patterns are seen in Europe, although divorce is lower there.

These demographic trends raise two seemingly undeniable conclusions: marriage has lost its taken-for-granted, nearly compulsory status as a feature of adult life, and, as a result, both adults and children are experiencing more change and upheaval in their personal lives than in the past. Sociologists have entered the fray to try to make sense of these trends, both by offering causal explanations and by predicting the depth and future direction of changes in intimacy.

rethinking commitment

Prominent sociologists offer two different but related theories about what is happening to intimacy in modern Western nations today. The British theorist Anthony Giddens argues that we are witnessing a "transformation of intimacy," while the American family scholar Andrew Cherlin suggests that we are witnessing the "deinstitutionalization" of marriage.

In his 1992 book *The Transformation of Intimacy*, Giddens observes that intimacy is undergoing radical change in contemporary Western societies. The romantic love model, which emphasizes relationship permanence ("till death do us part") and complementary gender roles, is being displaced by what Giddens calls "confluent love." The confluent love model features the ideal of the "pure relationship," one that's entered into for its own sake and maintained only as long as both partners get enough satisfaction from it to stick around. Partners in a pure relationship establish trust through intense communication, yet the possibility of breakup always looms. Giddens sees the rise of confluent love resulting from modernization and globalization. As family and religious traditions lose influence, people craft their own biographies through highly individualized choices, including choice of intimate partners, with the overarching goal of continuous self-development. Giddens argues that pure relationships are more egalitarian than traditional romantic relationships, produce greater happiness for partners, and foster a greater sense of autonomy. At the same time, the contingent nature of the relationship commitment breeds psychological insecurity, which manifests in higher levels of anxiety and addiction.

Cherlin's deinstitutionalization argument focuses more specifically on marriage now and in the future. The social norms that define and guide people's behavior within the institution of marriage are weakening, he writes. There's greater freedom to choose how to be married and when and whether to marry at all. The

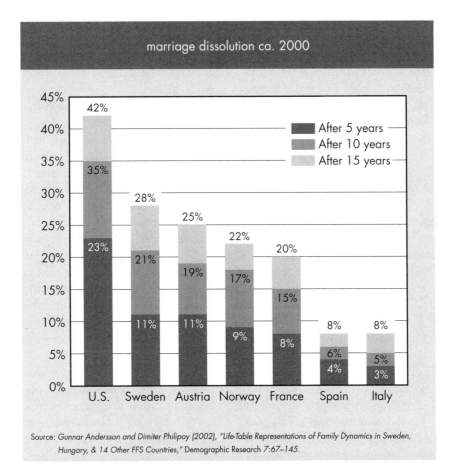

marriage dissolution ca. 2000

Legend:
- After 5 years
- After 10 years
- After 15 years

Country	After 5 years	After 10 years	After 15 years	Total
U.S.	23%	35%	42%	42%
Sweden	11%	21%	28%	28%
Austria	11%	19%	25%	25%
Norway	9%	17%	22%	22%
France	8%	15%	20%	20%
Spain	4%	6%	8%	8%
Italy	3%	5%	8%	8%

Source: Gunnar Andersson and Dimiter Philipov (2002), "Life-Table Representations of Family Dynamics in Sweden, Hungary, & 14 Other FFS Countries," Demographic Research 7:67–145.

deinstitutionalization of marriage can be traced to factors like the rise of unmarried childbearing, the changing division of labor in the home, the growth of unmarried cohabitation, and the emergence of same-sex marriage. These large-scale trends create a context in which people actively question the link between marriage and parenting, the idea of complementary gender roles, and even the connection between marriage and heterosexuality. Under such conditions, Cherlin argues, people feel freer to marry later, to end unhappy marriages, and to forgo marriage altogether, although marriage stills holds powerful symbolic significance for many people, partly as a marker of achievement and prestige. The future of marriage is hard to predict, but Cherlin argues it is unlikely to regain its former status; rather, it will either persist as an important but no longer dominant relationship form or it will fade into the background as just one of many relationship options.

Sociologist Andrew Cherlin concludes that a "carousel of intimate partnerships" results from the embrace of two contradictory American ideals: marriage and individualism.

marriage's persistent pull

Recent empirical studies suggest that the transformation of intimacy predicted by Giddens is far from complete, and the deinstitutionalization of marriage described by Cherlin faces some powerful countervailing forces, at least in the U.S. In her interview study of middle-class Americans, sociologist Ann Swidler found that people talking about love and relationships oscillated between two seemingly contradictory visions of intimacy. They often spoke about love and relationships as being hard work, and they acknowledged that relationship permanence is never a given, even in strong marriages. This way of talking about intimacy reflects the confluent love Giddens describes. But the same people who articulated pragmatic and realistic visions of intimacy also sometimes invoked elements of romantic love ideology, such as the idea that true love lasts forever and can overcome any obstacles.

Swidler speculates that people go back and forth between these two contradictory visions of love because the pragmatic vision matches their everyday experience but the romantic love myth corresponds to important elements in the institution of marriage. In other words, the ongoing influence of marriage as a social institution keeps the romantic model of intimacy culturally relevant, despite the emergence of a newer model of intimacy that sees love very differently. Swidler's findings at least partially contradict the idea of a wholesale transformation of intimacy, as well as the idea that marriage has lost much of its influence as a cultural model for intimate relationships.

Other studies have also challenged Giddens's ideas about the nature and extent of change occurring in intimate relationships. A 2002 study by Neil Gross and Solon Simmons used data from a national survey of American adults to test Giddens's predictions about the effects of "pure relationships" on their participants. They found support for some of the positive effects described by Giddens: people in pure relationships appear to have a greater sense of autonomy and higher relationship satisfaction. But the survey results did not support the idea that pure relationships lead to higher levels of anxiety and addiction. A 2004 British interview study of members of transnational families (that is, people with one or more close family members living in another country) found that people often strike a balance between individualistic approaches to marriage and attention to the marriage values of their home countries, families and religions.

Study authors Carol Smart and Beccy Shipman conclude that Giddens's theory of a radical transformation of intimacy overlooks the rich diversity of cultural values and practices that exists even in highly modernized Western nations. And sociologist Lynn Jamieson has critiqued Giddens's theory for ignoring the vast body of feminist research that documents ongoing gender inequalities, such as in housework, even among heterosexual couples who consider their relationships to be highly egalitarian.

In his recent book *The Marriage-Go-Round*, even Cherlin acknowledges the fact that the deinstitutionalization of marriage has not gone as far in the United States as in many other Western countries. Americans have established a pattern of high marriage and remarriage rates, frequent divorce and separation, and more short-lived cohabitations, relative to other comparable countries. The end result is what Cherlin calls a "carousel of intimate partnerships," leading American adults, and any children they have, to face more transition and upheaval in their personal lives. Cherlin concludes that this unique American pattern results from the embrace of two contradictory cultural ideals: marriage and individualism.

The differing importance placed on marriage is obvious in the realm of electoral politics, for example. The current leaders of France and Italy, President Nicolas Sarkozy and Prime Minister Silvio Berlusconi, have weathered divorces and allegations of extramarital affairs without any discernible effect on their political viability. In the U.S., by contrast, the revelations of extramarital dalliances by South Carolina governor Mark Sanford and former North Carolina senator John Edwards were widely viewed as destroying their prospects as future presidential candidates.

> Americans still place a high value on traditional, romantic love ideals like lifelong marriage. Yet, all evidence suggests that many of us do not follow through.

broader horizons

Mainstream media paints a picture of different generations holding substantially different attitudes toward intimacy. In some ways, young people's attitudes toward relationships today are quite similar to the attitudes of their parents. A 2001 study by sociologist Arland Thornton and survey researcher Linda Young–DeMarco compares the attitudes of high school students from the late 1970s to the late 1990s. They find strong support for marriage among all students across the two-decade period. The percentage of female students who rated "having a good marriage and family life" extremely important was roughly 80 percent throughout this time period, while for males, it hovered around 70 percent.

Some studies track changes in young people's specific expectations regarding intimate partnerships. For example, a study by psychologist David Buss and colleagues examined college students' preferences for mate characteristics over a period of several decades. They found that both male and female students rank mutual love and attraction as more important today than in earlier decades. Changing gender roles also translated into changes in mate preferences across the decades, with women's financial prospects becoming more important to men and men's ambition and industriousness becoming less important to women. Overall, differences in the qualities men and women are looking for in a mate declined in the second half of the 20th century, suggesting that being male or remale has become a less important factor in determining what young people look for in intimate partnerships.

We compared the relationship attitudes and values of lesbian/gay, bisexual, and heterosexual

18–28 year olds in a recent study published in the *Journal of Marriage and Family*. Notably, people in all of these groups were highly likely to consider love, faithfulness, and lifelong commitment as extremely important values in an intimate relationship. Romantic love seems to be widely embraced by most young adults, regardless of sexual orientation, which contests stereotypes and contrary reports that sexual minorities have radically different aspirations for intimacy. Yet, we also found modest differences that indicate that straight women are especially enthusiastic about these relationship attributes. They are more likely to rate faithfulness and lifelong commitment as extremely important compared to straight men and sexual minorities. Our findings are similar to other studies that consistently show that while both men and women highly value love, affection, and lifelong marriage, women assign greater value to these attributes than men.

Sociologist Michael Rosenfeld argues in *The Age of Independence* that both same-sex relationships and interracial relationships have become more common and visible in the last few decades in large part because of the same social phenomenon: young people today are less constrained by the watchful eyes and wishes of their parents. Unmarried young adults are much less likely to be living with their parents than in generations past, giving them more freedom to make less traditional life choices. And making unconventional choices along one dimension may make people more willing to make unconventional choices along other dimensions. Thus, while people's aspirations for romantic love may not be changing substantially, partner choice may be changing over time as taboos surrounding a broader range of relationships erode. In our study, we find that sexual-minority young adults report being more willing to date someone of a different race or enter into less financially secure relationships than heterosexual young adults, lending support to Rosenfeld's claim.

> Americans value the security of a lifelong partner, but we also want the option of an exit.

weighing our options

If the ideas of today's young adults are any indication, Americans still place a high value on traditional, romantic love ideals for their relationships, including the ideal of lifelong marriage. Yet, all evidence suggests that many of us do not follow through.

In 2004, sociologist Paul Amato outlined the typical positions on whether that shift matters. The marital decline position argues that changes in intimacy are a significant cause for concern. From this perspective, the current decline in lifelong marriage and the corresponding increase in single-parent and disrupted families are a key culprit in other social ills like poverty, delinquency, and poor academic performance among children. This is because stable marriages promote a culture in which people accept responsibility for others, and families watch over their own to

(Mark K. Mabos via Creative Commons)

protect against falling prey to social ills. In short, marriage helps keep our societal house in order.

The marital resilience perspective, in contrast, contends that changes in family life have actually strengthened the quality of intimate relationships, including marriages. From this perspective, in the past many people stayed in bad marriages because of strong social norms and legal obstacles to exit. Today, however, no-fault divorce provides an opportunity to correct past mistakes and try again at happiness with new partners. This is a triumph for individual freedom of choice and opportunities for equality within intimate relationships.

Perhaps today's intimacy norms dictate more individualism and a corresponding reduction in the responsibility we take for those we love or loved. Maybe we are better for it because we have more freedom of choice—after all, freedom is one of America's most cherished values. Americans in general seem willing to live with mixed feelings on the new norms for intimacy. Most of us value the commitment and security of a lifelong partner, but we also want the option of exit (tellingly, almost half of people who marry use this option).

Some evidence does suggest, though, that the "carousel of intimate relationships" may be taking its toll. Sociologists Mary Elizabeth

Hughes and Linda Waite recently compared the health of middle-aged Americans who were married once and still with their partner to those who were never married, those who were married then divorced and remarried, and those who were married, divorced, and not remarried. They found that those who experienced divorce reported more chronic conditions, mobility limitations, and depression years later, and remarriage boosted health some (particularly mental health), but not to the level of those who never divorced in the first place. Those who divorced and did not remarry had the worst health, even after accounting for many factors that may make one more likely both to have poor health and to divorce. Having loved and lost appears to have lasting consequences.

Academic and policy debates, as well as conversations among friends and neighbors, often hinge not on adults, but on what's best for children. A fair amount of research suggests that kids are more likely to avoid most social ills and develop into competent, successful adults if they are raised by two happily and continuously married parents. But marital happiness is key. A number of studies have found that frequently quarrelling parents who stay married aren't doing their kids many favors. Children of these types of marriages have an elevated risk of emotional and behavioral problems. But with the notable exception of parents in high-conflict marriages, most children who are raised by caring parents—one or two of them, married or not—end up just fine. Further, if our social policies provided greater support to all varieties of families, not just those characterized by lifelong heterosexual marriage, we might erase the association between growing up with happily married parents and children's well-being. More family supports, such as childcare subsidies, might translate into happily-ever-after for most kids regardless of family form.

(Philippe Leroyer via Creative Commons)

the changing landscape of love and marriage   61

Finally, the new rules of relationships have societal implications that go well beyond family life. If social order is substantially buttressed by traditional marriage, and a new model of intimacy is weakening the norm of lifelong, heterosexual marriage, logic suggests that we're eroding social cohesion and stability. If we think this is a threat, it seems a few policy adjustments could help to promote social order. For example, if marriage has the benefits of status, institutional support, and legitimacy, granting the right to marry to same-sex couples should bolster their relationships, making them more stable and long-lasting. Therefore, same-sex marriage would

bring some Americans into the marital fold, benefiting the adults and children in these families and society more generally.

In the meantime, there'd still be legions of those who already have access to the rights and protections of marriage, and either choose to divorce or never marry at all. Without reinforcing marriage as the ideal family form, some question whether healthy, well-functioning societies can be maintained. Evidence from other Western nations does suggest that different models of intimacy are compatible with societal well-being, but they also show that social policy must be aligned with the types of relationships that individuals choose to form. Many comparable coun-

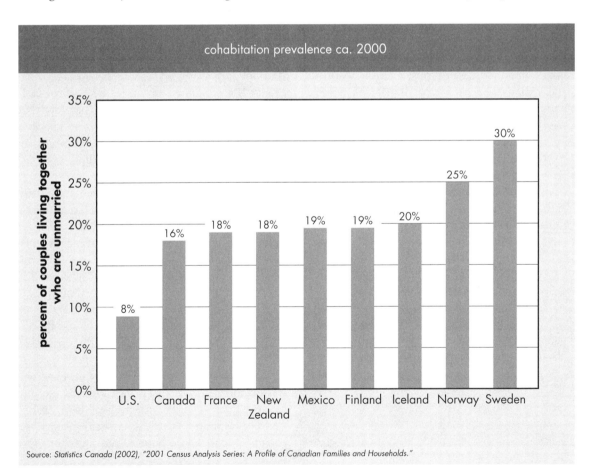

cohabitation prevalence ca. 2000

Source: *Statistics Canada (2002), "2001 Census Analysis Series: A Profile of Canadian Families and Households."*

tries have lower marriage rates and higher cohabitation rates than the U.S.

Those that extend significant legal protection and recognition to nonmarital relationships seem to do as well as, or sometimes better than, the U.S. on key measures of social and familial well-being. For example, Swedish children who live with only one parent do better, on average, than American children in the same circumstance, possibly because of Sweden's pro-family policies including long periods of paid maternity and sick leave and government-subsidized, high-quality childcare. Since all Swedes are eligible for these family supports, the differences in care received by children across family types are minimized.

In the end, current research suggests a paradox. Most people, including young adults, say things to researchers that suggest they hold fast to the ideal of an exclusive, lifelong intimate partnership, most commonly a marriage. Yet often people behave in ways more aligned with the "pure relationship" Giddens argues is the ascendant model of intimacy. Perhaps it's harder than ever for people to live out their aspirations in the area of intimacy. Or perhaps we are indeed in the midst of a transition to a brave new world of intimacy, and people's willingness or ability to articulate new relationship values has not yet caught up with their behavior.

RECOMMENDED RESOURCES

Andrew J. Cherlin. *The Marriage-Go-Round: The State of Marriage and the Family in America Today* (Alfred A. Knopf, 2009).

> Describes how Americans' simultaneous embrace of marital commitment and individual freedom has resulted in a "carousel of intimate partnerships."

Stephanie Coontz. *Marriage, a History: From Obedience to Intimacy, or How Love Conquered Marriage* (Viking, 2005).

> Offers a historical look at the linking of marriage and romantic intimacy.

Anthony Giddens. *The Transformation of Intimacy: Sexuality, Love and Eroticism in Modern Societies* (Stanford University Press, 1992).

> Argues that romantic love is being replaced by the ideal of the "pure relationship."

Judith Stacey. *In the Name of the Family: Rethinking Family Values in the Postmodern Age* (Beacon Press, 1996).

> Examines the fluid and contested nature of the "postmodern family condition," arguing that most contemporary social problems are not the result of innovations in family form.

Ann Swidler. *Talk of Love: How Culture Matters* (University of Chicago Press, 2001).

> Uses interviews with middle-class Americans to show that people oscillate between a romantic love ideology and a more pragmatic, contingent vision.

REVIEW QUESTIONS

1. The authors outline many changes in love and marriage in the United States. List several of the changes they discuss and then decide if you believe these changes are a problem for society or not.
2. The article broadly discussed romantic and confluent love. List the main features of each type. To what extent are they mirror images of one another?
3. Activity: Make a list of what you think are the five most important elements for a successful serious relationship. Compare your list with those of your classmates. Explain the differences that emerge. Also, what items did other students include that you would now think about adding to your list?

kathryn edin and maria kefalas

unmarried with children

9

spring 2005

have poor, unmarried mothers given up on marriage, as middle-class observers often conclude? to the contrary, most of the time they are simply waiting for the right partner and situation to make it work.

Jen Burke, a white tenth-grade dropout who is 17 years old, lives with her stepmother, her sister, and her 16-month-old son in a cramped but tidy row home in Philadelphia's beleaguered Kensington neighborhood. She is broke, on welfare, and struggling to complete her GED. Wouldn't she and her son have been better off if she had finished high school, found a job, and married her son's father first?

In 1950, when Jen's grandmother came of age, only 1 in 20 American children was born to an unmarried mother. Today, that rate is 1 in 3—and they are usually born to those least likely to be able to support a child on their own. In our book, *Promises I Can Keep: Why Poor Women Put Motherhood Before Marriage*, we discuss the lives of 162 white, African-American, and Puerto Rican low-income single mothers living in eight destitute neighborhoods across Philadelphia and its poorest industrial suburb, Camden. We spent five years chatting over kitchen tables and on front stoops, giving mothers like Jen the opportunity to speak to the question so many affluent Americans ask about them: Why do they have children while still young and unmarried when they will face such an uphill struggle to support them?

romance at lightning speed

Jen started having sex with her 20-year-old boyfriend Rick just before her 15th birthday. A month and a half later, she was pregnant. "I didn't want to get pregnant," she claims. "*He wanted me to get pregnant.*" "As soon as he met me, he wanted to have a kid with me," she explains. Though Jen's college-bound suburban peers would be appalled by such a declaration, on the streets of Jen's neighborhood, it is something of a badge of honor. "All those other girls he was with, he didn't want to have a baby with any of them," Jen boasts. "I asked him, 'Why did you choose me to have a kid when you could have a kid with any one of them?' He was like, 'I want to have a kid with *you*.'" Looking back, Jen says she now believes that the reason "he wanted me to have a kid that early is so that I didn't leave him."

In inner-city neighborhoods like Kensington, where childbearing within marriage has become rare, romantic relationships like Jen and Rick's proceed at lightning speed. A young man's avowal, "I want to have a baby by you," is often part of the courtship ritual from the beginning. This is more than idle talk, as their first child is typically conceived within a year from the time a couple begins "kicking it." Yet while poor couples' pillow talk often revolves around dreams of shared children, the news of a pregnancy—the first indelible sign of the huge changes to come—puts these still-new relationships into overdrive. Suddenly, the would-be mother begins to scrutinize her mate as never before, wondering whether he can "get himself together"—find a job, settle down, and become a family man—in time. Jen began pestering Rick to get a real job instead of picking up day-labor jobs at nearby construction sites. She also wanted him to stop hanging out with his ne'er-do-well friends, who had been getting him into serious trouble for more than a decade. Most of all, she wanted Rick to shed what she calls his "kiddie mentality"— his habit of spending money on alcohol and drugs rather than recognizing his growing financial obligations at home.

Rick did not try to deny paternity, as many would-be fathers do. Nor did he abandon or mistreat Jen, at least intentionally. But Rick, who had been in and out of juvenile detention since he was eight years old for everything from stealing cars to selling drugs, proved unable to stay away from his unsavory friends. At the beginning of her seventh month of pregnancy, an escapade that began as a drunken lark landed Rick in jail on a carjacking charge. Jen moved back home with her stepmother, applied for welfare, and spent the last two-and-a-half months of her pregnancy without Rick.

Rick sent penitent letters from jail. "I thought he changed by the letters he wrote me. I thought he changed a lot," she says. "He used to tell me that he loved me when he was in jail. . . . It was always gonna be me and him and the baby when he got out." Thus, when Rick's alleged victim failed to appear to testify and he was released just days before Colin's birth, the couple's reunion was a happy one. Often, the magic moment of childbirth calms the troubled waters of such relationships. New parents typically make amends and resolve to stay together for the sake of their child. When surveyed just after a child's birth, eight in ten unmarried parents say they are still together, and most plan to stay together and raise the child.

Promoting marriage among the poor has become the new war on poverty, Bush style. And it is true that the correlation between marital status and child poverty is strong. But poor single mothers already believe in marriage. Jen insists that she will walk down the aisle one day, though she admits it might not be with Rick. And demographers still project that more than seven in ten women who had a child outside of marriage will eventually wed someone. First, though, Jen wants to get a good job, finish school, and get her son out of Kensington.

> . . . more than seven in ten women who had a child outside of marriage will eventually wed someone.

Most poor, unmarried mothers and fathers readily admit that bearing children while poor and unmarried is not the ideal way to do things. Jen believes the best time to become a mother is "after you're out of school and you got a job, at least, when you're like 21. . . . When you're ready to have kids, you should have everything ready, have your house, have a job, so when that baby comes, the baby can have its own room." Yet given their already limited economic prospects, the poor have little motivation to time their births as precisely as their middle-class counterparts do. The dreams of young people like Jen and Rick center on children at a time of life when their more affluent peers plan for college and careers. Poor girls coming of age in the inner city value children highly, anticipate them eagerly, and believe strongly that they are up to the job of mothering—even in difficult circumstances. Jen, for example, tells us, "People outside the neighborhood, they're like, 'You're 15! You're pregnant?' I'm like, it's not none of their business. I'm gonna be able to take care of my kid. They have nothing to worry about." Jen says she has concluded that "some people . . . are better at having kids at a younger age. . . . I think it's better for some people to have kids younger."

when i became a mom

When we asked mothers like Jen what their lives would be like if they had not had children, we expected them to express regret over foregone opportunities for school and careers. Instead, most believe their children "saved" them. They describe their lives as spinning out of control before becoming pregnant—struggles with parents and peers, "wild," risky behavior, depression, and school failure. Jen speaks to this poignantly. "I was just real bad. I hung with a real bad crowd. I was doing pills. I was really depressed. . . . I was drinking. That was before I was pregnant." "I think," she reflects, "if I never had a baby or anything, . . . I would still be doing the things I was doing. I would probably still be doing drugs. I'd probably still be drinking." Jen admits that when she first became pregnant, she was angry that she "couldn't be out no more. Couldn't be out with my friends. Couldn't do nothing." Now, though, she says, "I'm glad I have a son . . . because I would still be doing all that stuff."

Children offer poor youth like Jen a compelling sense of purpose. Jen paints a before-and-after picture of her life that was common among the mothers we interviewed. "Before, I didn't have nobody to take care of. I didn't have nothing left to go home for. . . . Now I have my son to take care of. I have him to go home for. . . . I don't have to go buy weed or drugs with my money. I could buy my son stuff with my money! . . . I have something to look up to now." Children also are a crucial source of relational intimacy, a self-made community of care. After a nasty fight with Rick, Jen recalls, "I was crying. My son came in the room. He was hugging me. He's 16 months and he was hugging me with his little arms. He was really cute and happy, so I got happy. That's one of the good things. When you're sad, the baby's always gonna be there for you no matter what." Lately she has been thinking a lot about what her life was like back then, before the baby. "I thought about the stuff before I became a mom, what my life was like back then. I used to see pictures of me, and I would hide in every picture. This baby did so much for me. My son did a lot for me. He helped me a lot. I'm thankful that I had my baby."

Around the time of the birth, most unmarried parents claim they plan to get married eventually. Rick did not propose marriage when Jen's first child was born, but when she conceived a second time, at 17, Rick informed his dad, "It's time for me to get married. It's time for me to straighten up. This is the one I wanna be with. I had a baby with her, I'm gonna have another baby with her." Yet despite their intentions, few of these couples actually marry. Indeed, most break up well before their child enters preschool.

i'd like to get married, but . . .

The sharp decline in marriage in impoverished urban areas has led some to charge that the poor have abandoned the marriage norm. Yet we found few who had given up on the idea of marriage. But like their elite counterparts, disadvantaged women set a high financial bar for marriage. For the poor, marriage has become an elusive goal—one they feel ought to be reserved for those who can support a "white picket fence" lifestyle: a mortgage on a modest row home, a car and some furniture, some savings in the bank, and enough money left over to pay for a "decent" wedding. Jen's views on marriage provide a perfect case in point. "If I was gonna get married, I would want to be married like my Aunt Nancy and my Uncle Pat. They live in the mountains. She has a job. My Uncle Pat is a state trooper; he has lots of money. They live in the [Poconos]. It's real nice out there. Her kids go to Catholic school. . . . That's the kind of life I would want to have. If I get married, I would have a life like [theirs]." She adds, "And I would wanna have a big wedding, a real nice wedding."

Unlike the women of their mothers' and grandmothers' generations, young women like Jen are not merely content to rely on a man's earnings. Instead, they insist on being economically "set" in their own right before taking marriage vows. This is partly because they want a partnership of equals, and they believe money buys say-so in a relationship. Jen explains, "I'm not gonna just get into marrying him and not have my own house! Not have a job! I still wanna do a lot of things before I get married. He [already] tells me I can't do nothing. I can't go out. What's gonna happen when I marry him? He's gonna say he owns me!"

Economic independence is also insurance against a marriage gone bad. Jen explains, "I want to have everything ready, in case something goes wrong. . . . If we got a divorce, that would be my house. I bought that house, he can't kick me out or he can't take my kids from me." "That's what I want in case that ever happens. I know a lot of people that happened to. I don't want it to happen to me." These statements reveal that despite her desire to marry, Rick's role in the family's future is provisional at best. "We get along, but we fight a lot. If he's there, he's there, but if he's not, that's why I want a job . . . a job with computers . . . so I could afford my kids, could afford the house. . . . I don't want to be living off him. I want my kids to be living off me."

Why is Jen, who describes Rick as "the love of my life," so insistent on planning an exit strategy before she is willing to take the vows she firmly believes ought to last "forever?" If love is so sure, why does mistrust seem so palpable and strong? In relationships among poor couples like Jen and

Rick, mistrust is often spawned by chronic violence and infidelity, drug and alcohol abuse, criminal activity, and the threat of imprisonment. In these tarnished corners of urban America, the stigma of a failed marriage is far worse than an out-of-wedlock birth. New mothers like Jen feel they must test the relationship over three, four, even five years' time. This is the only way, they believe, to insure that their marriages will last.

Trust has been an enormous issue in Jen's relationship with Rick. "My son was born December 23rd, and [Rick] started cheating on me again . . . in March. He started cheating on me with some girl—Amanda. . . . Then it was another girl, another girl, another girl after. I didn't wanna believe it. My friends would come up to me and be like, 'Oh yeah, your boyfriend's cheating on you with this person.' I wouldn't believe it. . . . I would see him with them. He used to have hickies. He used to make up some excuse that he was drunk—that was always his excuse for everything." Things finally came to a head when Rick got another girl pregnant. "For a while, I forgave him for everything. Now, I don't forgive him for nothing." Now we begin to understand the source of Jen's hesitancy. "He wants me to marry him, [but] I'm not really sure. . . . If I can't trust him, I can't marry him, 'cause we would get a divorce. If you're gonna get married, you're supposed to be faithful!" she insists. To Jen and her peers, the worst thing that could happen is "to get married just to get divorced."

Given the economic challenges and often perilously low quality of the romantic relationships among unmarried parents, poor women may be right to be cautious about marriage. Five years after we first spoke with her, we met with Jen again. We learned that Jen's second pregnancy ended in a miscarriage. We also learned that

> . . . children, far from being liabilities, provide crucial social-psychological resources—a strong sense of purpose and a profound source of intimacy.

Rick was out of the picture—apparently for good. "You know that bar [down the street?] It happened in that bar. . . . They were in the bar, and this guy was like badmouthing [Rick's friend] Mikey, talking stuff to him or whatever. So Rick had to go get involved in it and start with this guy. . . . Then he goes outside and fights the guy [and] the guy dies of head trauma. They were all on drugs, they were all drinking, and things just got out of control, and that's what happened. He got fourteen to thirty years."

these are cards i dealt myself

Jen stuck with Rick for the first two and a half years of his prison sentence, but when another girl's name replaced her own on the visitors' list, Jen decided she was finished with him once and for all. Readers might be asking what Jen ever saw in a man like Rick. But Jen and Rick operate in a partner market where the better-off men go to the better-off women. The only way for someone like Jen to forge a satisfying relationship with a man is to find a diamond in the rough or improve her own economic position so that she can realistically compete for more upwardly mobile partners, which is what Jen is trying to do now. "There's this kid, Donny, he works at my job. He works on C shift. He's supervisor! He's funny, three years older, and he's not a geek or anything, but he's not a real preppy good boy either. But he's not [a player like Rick] and them. He has a job, you know, so that's good. He doesn't do drugs or anything. And he asked my dad if he could take me out!"

These days, there is a new air of determination, even pride, about Jen. The aimless high school dropout pulls ten-hour shifts entering data at a warehouse distribution center Monday through Thursday. She has held the job for three years, and her aptitude and hard work have earned her a series of raises. Her current salary is higher than anyone in her household commands—$10.25 per hour, and she now gets two weeks of paid vacation, four personal days, 60 hours of sick time, and medical benefits. She has saved up the necessary $400 in tuition for a high school completion program that offers evening and weekend classes. Now all that stands between her and a diploma is a passing grade in mathematics, her least favorite subject. "My plan is to start college in January. [This month] I take my math test . . . so I can get my diploma," she confides.

Jen clearly sees how her life has improved since Rick's dramatic exit from the scene. "That's when I really started [to get better] because I didn't have to worry about what *he* was doing, didn't have to worry about him cheating on me, all this stuff. [It was] then I realized that I had to do what I had to do to take care of my son. . . . When he was there, I think that my whole life revolved around him, you know, so I always messed up somehow because I was so busy worrying about what *he* was doing. Like I would leave the [GED] programs I was in just to go home and see what he was doing. My mind was never concentrating." Now, she says, "a lot of people in my family look up to me now, because all my sisters dropped out from school, you know, nobody went back to school. I went back to school, you know? . . . I went back to school, and I plan to go to college, and a lot of people look up to me for that, you know? So that makes me happy . . . because five years ago nobody looked up to me. I was just like everybody else."

Yet the journey has not been easy. "Being a young mom, being 15, it's hard, hard, hard, you know." She says, "I have no life. . . . I work from 6:30 in the morning until 5:00 at night. I leave here at 5:30 in the morning. I don't get home until about 6:00 at night." Yet she measures her worth as a mother by the fact that she has managed to provide for her son largely on her own. "I don't depend on nobody. I might live with my dad and them, but I don't depend on them, you know." She continues, "There [used to] be days when I'd be so stressed out, like, 'I can't do this!' And I would just cry and cry and cry. . . . Then I look at Colin, and he'll be sleeping, and I'll just look at him and think I don't have no [reason to feel sorry for myself]. The cards I have I've dealt myself so I have to deal with it now. I'm older. I can't change anything. He's my responsibility—he's nobody else's but mine—so I have to deal with that."

Becoming a mother transformed Jen's point of view on just about everything. She says, "I thought hanging on the corner drinking, getting high—I thought that was a good life, and I thought I could live that way for eternity, like sitting out with my friends. But it's not as fun once you have your own kid. . . . I think it changes [you]. I think, 'Would I want Colin to do that? Would I want my son to be like that . . . ?' It was fun to me but it's not fun anymore. Half the people I hung with are either . . . Some have died from drug overdoses, some are in jail, and some people are just out there living the same life that they always lived, and they don't look really good. They look really bad." In the end, Jen believes, Colin's birth has brought far more good into her life than bad. "I know I could have waited [to have a child], but in a way I think Colin's the best thing that could have happened to me. . . . So I think I had my son for a purpose because I think Colin changed my life. He saved my life, really. My whole life revolves around Colin!"

> Given the economic challenges and often perilously low quality of the romantic relationships among unmarried parents, poor women may be right to be cautious about marriage.

promises i can keep

There are unique themes in Jen's story—most fathers are only one or two, not five years older than the mothers of their children, and few fathers have as many glaring problems as Rick—but we heard most of these themes repeatedly in the stories of the 161 other poor, single mothers we came to know. Notably, poor women do not reject marriage; they revere it. Indeed, it is the conviction that marriage is forever that makes them think that divorce is worse than having a baby outside of marriage. Their children, far from being liabilities, provide crucial social-psychological resources—a strong sense of purpose and a profound source of intimacy. Jen and the other mothers we came to know are coming of age in an America that is profoundly unequal—where the gap between rich and poor continues to grow. This economic reality has convinced them that they have little to lose and, perhaps, something to gain by a seemingly "ill-timed" birth.

The lesson one draws from stories like Jen's is quite simple: Until poor young women have more access to jobs that lead to financial independence—until there is reason to hope for the rewarding life pathways that their privileged peers pursue—the poor will continue to have children far sooner than most Americans think they should, while still deferring marriage. Marital standards have risen for all Americans, and the poor want the same things that everyone now wants out of marriage. The poor want to marry too, but they insist on marrying well. This, in their view, is the only way to avoid an almost certain divorce. Like Jen, they are simply not willing to make promises they are not sure they can keep.

RECOMMENDED RESOURCES

Kathryn Edin and Maria Kefalas. *Promises I Can Keep: Why Poor Women Put Motherhood Before Marriage* (University of California Press, 2005).

How low-income women make sense of their choices about marriage and motherhood.

Christina Gibson, Kathryn Edin, and Sara McLanahan. "High Hopes but Even Higher Expectations: A Qualitative and Quantitative Analysis of the Marriage Plans of Unmarried Couples Who Are New Parents." Working Paper 03-06-FF, Center for Research on Child Wellbeing, Princeton University, 2004. Online at http://crcw.princeton.edu/workingpapers/WP03-06-FF-Gibson.pdf

The authors examine the rising expectations for marriage among unmarried parents.

Sharon Hays. *Flat Broke with Children: Women in the Age of Welfare Reform* (Oxford University Press, 2003).

How welfare reform has affected the lives of poor moms.

Annette Lareau. *Unequal Childhoods: Class, Race, and Family Life* (University of California Press, 2003).

A fascinating discussion of different childrearing strategies among low-income, working-class, and middle-class parents.

Timothy J. Nelson, Susan Clampet-Lundquist, and Kathryn Edin. "Fragile Fatherhood: How Low-Income, Non-Custodial Fathers in Philadelphia Talk About Their Families." In *The Handbook of Father Involvement: Multidisciplinary Perspectives*, eds. Catherine Tamis-LeMonda and Natasha Cabrera (Lawrence Earlbaum Associates, 2002).

What poor, single men think about fatherhood.

REVIEW QUESTIONS

1. What does *family* mean? Discuss the prevailing myths surrounding this term, and whether or not we commonly use an adequate definition. Then discuss how social scientists make a distinction between *family* and *household*.
2. Edin and Kefalas reject the notion that impoverished mothers have "abandoned the marriage norm." Why? Can you identify the factors that hamstring these mothers as compared to their richer counterparts?
3. The authors use the story of Jen as a window through which we can see the broader issues that confront the other 161 poor mothers in their study. What do you think are the advantages and disadvantages of this form of representing research?
4. This essay does not mention the increase in cohabitation in American society. Can you think of how this might challenge some of the authors' findings? Why or why not?

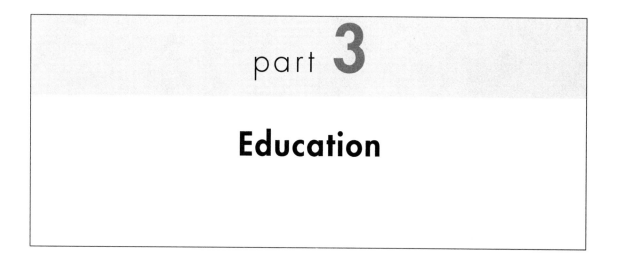

part **3**

Education

meika loe

the prescription of a new generation

10

spring 2008

psychostimulant use in conjunction with adhd raises questions about health, fairness, and identity.

U.S. college students today are among the first to be raised in a society where prescription drugs are an everyday commodity—socially branded and advertised directly to consumers—not unlike cars and blue jeans. These students are also the products of the most intense competition ever for college admission.

It's no wonder, then, some are tempted to enhance their academic performance with psychostimulant medications like Ritalin and Adderall, with or without a doctor's diagnosis of Attention Deficit/Hyperactivity Disorder (ADHD), the condition the drugs are most often prescribed to treat.

And it's also no wonder that, among some of their peers, this is generally acceptable behavior—even when obtained illegally from friends, family, or Internet pharmacies. Nearly one in four college students nationwide have reported doing so.

Psychostimulant use in conjunction with ADHD raises important questions about health, fairness, and the development of a person's identity, as well as safety, artificiality, and dependency.

When we analyzed students' experiences with prescription stimulants like Ritalin at a university in the northeastern United States, we gained a clearer picture of how and why students incorporate prescription medicine into their lives and identities, as well as the costs and benefits of the prescription of this generation.

medication everywhere

In *Running on Ritalin*, Lawrence Diller chronicled "a white middleclass suburban phenomenon" as psychostimulant medication became one answer to behavior problems in the classroom. In 1998, more than 5 million children had prescriptions for Ritalin, a five-fold increase from eight years before, according to Diller. Its use continues as students age: National surveys report an increased prevalence of psychotropic medication—with and without a prescription—among contemporary high school and college students.

ADHD, previously known as Attention Deficit Disorder (ADD), is the most commonly diagnosed and treated childhood psychiatric problem in the United States, according to Diller. Nearly 8 million children have been diagnosed with ADHD, according to the Centers for Disease Control and Prevention (CDC). As of 2003, 2.5 million children between ages 4 and 17 were being medicated for it, the centers have reported.

> Nearly 8 million children have been diagnosed with ADHD. As of 2003, 2.5 million children between ages 4 and 17 were being medicated for it.

White, insured children between ages 9 and 12 make up the highest prevalence group currently using psychostimulant medication in the United States, according to CDC. The picture is clearly gendered, as nearly 10 percent of 10-year-old boys in the United States use medication to treat ADHD while only roughly 5 percent of 10-year-old girls do, the centers have reported. In general, children are the largest market for these drugs, although this may change as the adult ADHD market expands.

While the phenomenon is increasingly global, the United States consumes between 80 percent and 90 percent of the Ritalin prescribed today, according to Richard Degrandpre, author of *Ritalin Nation: Rapid-Fire Culture and the Transformation of Human Consciousness*.

A psychostimulant "gray market" exists at secondary schools and colleges, where students can buy these drugs from peers. Up to 25 percent of college students on any given campus have used psychostimulants without a prescription, according to national research conducted by public health researchers at the University of Michigan. They found rates were highest at colleges in the northeastern United States and colleges with more competitive admission standards.

Social scientists have identified a variety of social circumstances that paved the way for medicine to solve a wide range of troubles. Managed health care, pharmaceutical consolidation and de-regulation, scientific and technological innovation, and a quick-fix pill culture that normalizes prescription drugs for lifestyle and identity choices are just some of them.

Sociologists have explored how the "Prozac era" and the "Viagra phenomenon," for example, have emerged out of these circumstances. These and other case studies address the double-edged sword of medicalization—a social process in which a problem becomes defined and treated as a medical issue. While prescription drugs may offer the promise of enhanced quality of life and shift blame away from the individual to the body, a focus on bodies obscures social context. In other words, the emphasis becomes individual students' bodies rather than the student body at large and the culture that surrounds it. What follows, then, is a Ritalin generation that associates medicine with academic success.

In separate studies, medical sociologists Peter Conrad and Adam Rafalovich have shown that what we now call ADHD has had a host of labels throughout the 20th century, many of which were coined when research on this and related behavioral disorders increased in the 1960s. As the scope of the disorder has expanded, a growing number of children, adolescents, and more recently adults in the United States have been diagnosed with ADHD and prescribed psychostimulants.

In this way, ADHD is a case study of expanding medicalization in American society today. While behavior modification through medication isn't new, sociologists have shown how, largely through the efforts of advocacy groups and pharmaceutical companies and with the assistance of popular media, diagnoses such as ADHD now address a wider range of troubles. Hyperactivity, general inattentiveness, and underperformance across a wider age range and in a variety of social arenas are now treated under the ADHD umbrella.

Medical professionals may see these numbers as representative of a growing clinical problem in our society. But sociologists see a social crisis and an opportunity to raise important questions about how medicine, the pharmaceutical industry, schools, and families define "normal" childhood behavior and academic achievement.

Parents, doctors, educators, and students play a major role in creating and maintaining—but also resisting—social expectations. In general, social scientists have expressed concern that medicalization, with its focus on the individual and the organic body, obscures the complex social forces that contribute to health and well-being. For example, a lack of hands-on learning opportunities and narrow definitions of academic success, part of an increasingly competitive academic ethic, in American classrooms may be just as central as physiological factors in contributing to behavioral issues.

the spectrum of use

Over the past several years I've worked with undergraduates to collect and understand data on the medicalization of student life. Drawn to the research because we were troubled and intrigued by patterns of pharmaceutical use—particularly psychostimulant use and abuse—we wanted to know more about scope, social meanings, and identity.

As we conducted our surveys and interviews, national surveys conducted by the University of Michigan exposed the scope of prescription drug use and abuse on college campuses. Our and the Michigan data revealed that for a generation coming of age in the pharmaceutical era, prescription drug use can be acceptable and even strategic in a competitive academic environment. But we also found that fears of dependency, loss of "authentic" identity, and implications for post-college career planning may motivate students to renegotiate their relationship with medication at some point in their college years.

In general, four types of experiences represent a spectrum of college-student stimulant users. They have in common that they use prescription drugs to enhance, fix, and/or normalize. One way they differ is in how they got to that point.

One group of students have been on a daily regimen of medication for the majority of their lives, having been diagnosed with ADHD by a professional. For them, stimulants are for treating their learning disorders. On the other end of the spectrum are students who have self-administered psychostimulant medication (many times without a prescription) intermittently during their college years. They may turn to ADHD meds to smooth the transition from high school to college or manage stress during their college years. These students represent the new and growing "adult ADHD" market.

In the middle of the spectrum are students who approached doctors for prescriptions as they transitioned into high school or boarding school. Some of these students, who in essence self-administered medication, soon faced problems with drug addiction or worse; others were closely monitored by a doctor and the drugs became a regular part of their identities or sense of personal potential.

For all these students, "pharming to get by" as some characterized it to us, is generally accepted and approached strategically. They diagnosed their failings and administered their own medications, and many believe that with the help of prescription stimulants they

Students turning to ADHD meds to smooth the transition from high school to college or manage stress during college represent the growing "adult ADHD" market. (Courtesy of Jon Smajda)

can block out distractions to concentrate on academic performance and become smart and studious on demand.

However, they also admit that medically managed bodies can have social, psychological, and physiological costs. For those college students asking themselves, "who am I?" medications can complicate the answer. Students said they prefer the "natural" over the "artificial," or the "real" person over the medicated self, and that Ritalin is central to their ability to focus and perform in school, but it blunts their personalities. Some complain that stimulants make them anxious or overly thin, or transform them and their peers into out-of-control busybodies.

For example, while most students report using psychostimulants for enhanced academic performance, some women, including one profiled on the 2005 MTV documentary program *True Life*, also use these drugs as an appetite suppressant. One female athlete we spoke with described using Adderall as a way to feel confident and in control in the classroom, on the sports field, and in managing her weight. It wasn't until this weight loss affected her athletic performance that she realized the drug might have unhealthy consequences.

Men also develop eating disorders as a result of psychostimulant use and overdosing. On the verge of a nervous breakdown in response to poor academic performance, a male student described turning to Adderall to help him concentrate and perform. However, on the drugs he found himself increasingly anxious and obsessive. The drugs made him feel like he could "do eight things at once, like on speed." As a result, he spent hours writing the perfect sentence, folding his roommates' laundry, even masturbating. He skipped meals and soon found himself emaciated, shaky, and addicted to Adderall. After taking time off school to regain his health, this student told us he has sworn off all drugs.

Such student accounts reveal the high social price of a medically managed body; besides concentrated weight loss, stimulant users report difficulty relaxing and sleeping, drug dependency, perfectionism gone too far, heightened social anxiety, and negative health effects. Some students decide to stop using prescription stimulants once they perceive their medicated bodies as out of control or unnatural. Others moderate their drug use, rationalizing stimulant use only in situations they perceive as urgent.

managing medical ambivalence

New college students who were diagnosed with ADHD as children or teens have had years to construct a personal identity that incorporates their medication use. However, by their junior and senior years many wonder whether their daily prescriptions are truly necessary, and some experiment with stopping the medication.

Looking back on 14 years of medication use, one student said: "I think it's messed up and twisted that I've been on study medications since first grade . . . but there's no way I'd be at [this college] without it." She said the pills made her more efficient with work, but she still spent long hours writing papers and wondered whether the pills were slowing her down or creating an obsessive degree of focus on detail. This type of internal debate is not uncommon, we found.

The majority of students we interviewed who had stimulant prescriptions chose not to take their medication over the summer, for example, preferring to be "themselves," instead of feeling "fake" when on medication. Besides disliking the transformative effect on their personalities, students expressed fear of dependency or reliance. Some expressed discomfort with the fact that their daily sense of who they are is achieved through "unnatural" chemicals and medication. Because of this discomfort, many students diagnosed with ADHD choose to take their prescription drugs only in cases of academic necessity; they don't feel like they're "better people" on the drugs.

A small but committed group of college students with ADHD take psychostimulants daily, even during school breaks, and have incorporated them into their sense of identity and potential, appreciating the seamless role medicine plays in their everyday lives. However, even these students report experimenting with going off their drugs simply out of curiosity, in order to assert control over what can be perceived as drug dependency during their school-aged years, or to prepare themselves for their post-school lives without the medication. After years of medicating in the context of academic pressures, taking schooling out of the equation may mean attempting everyday life without the drugs.

For many, these short experimental periods off stimulants end up reinforcing the need for medication and complicating perceptions of self in disturbing ways. One student's "interesting experiment" without his daily Adderall led him to feel more in control, but less motivated, like he "couldn't do anything." Other students reported that, off Adderall, all they wanted to do was sleep.

A similarly small group of students have instead chosen alternative, non-medical strategies for managing performance and avoiding failure. That meant scaling down aspirations or taking on less challenging courses. They have trained themselves to reverse ADHD symptoms by using study skills and concentration techniques like taking breaks, underlining while reading, and keeping reading notes to increase retention.

> A student said he doesn't really "believe in ADHD" because drugs like Adderall "help everyone."

imagining medication-free, post-college lives

Far more effort in our society is placed on getting patients on drugs than off them. This is particularly salient for members of the Ritalin generation. As they look ahead to their post-college futures and imagine life without the daily medicine they associate with academic performance, they wonder if their sense of self can be extricated from the effects of their medication.

Some are looking for careers and lifestyles that suit their unique attributes. One student said a fast-paced lifestyle in a large city might suit him best. Another described her ADHD not as a "deficit" but an ambitious drive to multitask—this, she feels, is a perfect fit for a career as an emergency room physician. On the other hand, another believes choosing a routinized, structured job will eliminate his need for a stimulant. Yet another said the goal of being an educator will take as much concentration and focus as being a student, so she thinks she'll stay on her pills.

A recent *New York Times* article estimated that a quarter of children attending summer overnight camps in 2006 were medicated for ADHD, psychiatric problems, or mood disorders. Beyond the growing numbers of children diagnosed with ADHD, prescriptions for ADHD drugs tripled between 2000 and 2004 for adults between ages 20 and 30 as drug marketing budgets have quadrupled and physicians remain uncertain about how to adequately diagnose ADHD.

Amidst the expansion of drug marketing budgets, the disorder, and the correspondingly "disordered" populace, debate about over-diagnosis and expanding psychostimulant use is still brewing in the medical field, in our education system, and among students on college campuses.

The college campus is a good place to begin a discussion about it. Students situate their own perceived need for stimulants within a larger social context, where, as some students explain, success is defined by unrealistic performance standards in every arena of life.

For example, one student commented: "I wonder, if so many people have ADD, at what level is this just because of the standards we hold over everyone and the expectations of the school system and the work world?" Another said he doesn't really "believe in ADHD" because drugs like Adderall "help everyone" and only become necessary in the context of academic performance pressures. Maybe, he concluded, "people are situationally ADD."

Contemporary students' life experiences allow them to think critically about the social construction of medicine and the effects of psychostimulant drugs on society. They should be leading this discussion. At the same time, rather than treating social problems solely with prescriptions, individuals and educational institutions must begin to rethink how they "do" education and define success. Now is the time to critically engage in these topics, before more individuals embrace prescription drugs as a "normal" part of their academic life and the net effect ends up disciplining society at large, becoming a self-perpetuating cycle.

RECOMMENDED RESOURCES

Adele E. Clarke, Janet K. Shim, Laura Mamo, Jennifer Ruth Fosket, and Jennifer R. Fishman.

"Biomedicalization: Technoscientific Transformations of Health, Illness, and U.S. Biomedicine." *American Sociological Review* 68 (2003): 161–94.

Contemporary context and working definitions for biomedicalization.

Peter Conrad and Deborah Potter. "From Hyperactive Children to ADHD Adults: Observations on the Expansion of Medical Categories." *Social Problems* 47 (2000): 559–82.

Introduces and explores medical diagnostic expansion in the case of ADHD.

Richard DeGrandpre. *Ritalin Nation: Rapid-Fire Culture and the Transformation of Human Consciousness* (W. W. Norton & Company, 1999).

An early socio-cultural analysis of Ritalin use, and an argument about over-diagnosis.

David E. Karp. *Is It Me or My Meds? Living with Anti-Depressants* (Harvard University Press, 2006).

Qualitative analysis exploring the relationship between medicine and identity.

Adam Rafalovich. "Exploring Clinician Uncertainty in the Diagnosis and Treatment of Attention Deficit Hyperactivity Disorder." *Sociology of Health and Illness* 27 (2005): 305–23.

Physicians' relationships to medical ambivalence and uncertainty in treating ADHD.

REVIEW QUESTIONS

1. Discuss how medical "breakthroughs" like the anti-depressants described in this article or the introduction of a drug like Latisse (which is supposed to treat short eyelashes) are changing ideas of normality and self-identity. Is there a stigma attached to either taking such medications or seeking alternative treatments?
2. The article states that we spend more time and effort getting people onto medications than off

them. What social functions do medications serve?

3. Near the end of the article, a student questions whether ADD and ADHD are actual problems or normal responses to the increasing—and sometimes overwhelming—demands of work and school. What do you think?

4. Activity: Find online examples or in the mainstream media where drugs or medications are being advertised. How do these ads explain and promote their products? To what extent do you think pharmaceutical companies help define "normal" behaviors and states?

douglas b. downey and benjamin g. gibbs

how schools really matter

11

spring 2010

emphasizing social context, the authors show how classroom time actually does foster equality among kids.

There's an old joke about a man on a street corner, down on his hands and knees searching for his lost wallet. A passerby stops to help, asking, "So you lost it right around here?" "Oh no," the man replies, "I lost the wallet several blocks ago. I'm just looking on this street corner because this is where the lighting is good."

It's tempting to look for the source of a problem in places where the lighting is good even if we're not in the right place. When we hear about high dropout rates; persistent black/white gaps in test scores; low American reading, math, and science scores; dramatic differences in resources among schools; and even growing childhood obesity, it's sort of easy to ascribe these negative outcomes to schools. In fact, this is the "traditional" story we hear about American schools.

the traditional tale of schools

The tendency to view schools as the source of so many problems is especially true when we consider equality of opportunity, an important American value. There are many good reasons to believe that schools are the primary engines of inequality. First, children attending schools with lots of high-income children tend to perform better on standardized tests than kids at schools with lots of low-income children. Second, there are clear resource differences between these schools, rooted in the fact that, in most

states, local tax revenues constitute a significant portion of the school's budget. For example, Ohio's local taxes constitute about half of a school's budget (state taxes constitute 43 percent and federal taxes about 7 percent). As a result of the heavy emphasis on local taxes, some schools are able to spend substantially more money per student than others. This means schools located in areas with expensive houses and successful businesses can spend more on new textbooks, teacher pay, recreational facilities, extracurricular activities, and help for students with special needs. Third, in high-resource schools, teachers encounter fewer children with behavioral problems and more parents engaged in their children's education, factors that can attract and retain better teachers. Based on these patterns, it seems obvious that if we want to improve the quality of life for the disadvantaged in the U.S., the best place to start is schools.

But this traditional story has developed largely without understanding the way in which children's academic outcomes are shaped by many factors outside of schools. Simply look at the amount of time children spend outside of school. If we focus on the 9-month academic year only, the proportion of time children spend in school is about one-third. And if we include the non-school summer, children spend just one-quarter of their waking hours in school each year. Now if we also include the years before kindergarten—which certainly affect children—we find that the typical 18-year-old American has spent just 13 percent of his or her waking hours in school. For most of us, it's surprising to learn that such a large percentage of children's time is spent outside of school, but it's important to keep in mind if we're serious about understanding how schools really matter.

A contextual perspective reminds us to look at the rest of kids' lives. For instance, not every student comes to school with the same economic, social, or cultural resources. Even with the same educational opportunities, some students benefit from home environments that prepare them for school work and so they are better able to take advantage of education.

> The typical 18-year-old American has spent just 13 percent of his or her waking hours in school.

Moving away from the traditional, narrow view of schools that forgets the importance of children's time outside the classroom, we endorse adopting a contextualized (or impact) view of schools. This new emphasis can really change how we think about what schools can—and can't—do for our kids.

pianos and parents

Imagine that we want to compare the effectiveness of two piano instructors who will both teach 10-week piano classes for beginners. We flip a coin and assign one instructor to place A and the other to place B. Our goal is complicated, however, by the fact that in place B, due to cost, almost no students come from a home with a piano, whereas in place A, whose parents have more disposable income, most students have a piano at home. As a result, place A's students have already had some practice time on a piano, whereas place B's students have had little to none. In addition, while both instructors teach a session once a week, place A's students practice on their own several times

a week, whereas in place B—where few have pianos at home—students have a much harder time finding a way to practice.

Obviously, if we just compared the piano students' skills at the end of the 10-week program we couldn't accurately assess the quality of the two instructors—the two groups' skills differed before the lessons began. And if we compared how much the students' skills improved during the instructional period, it would still be hard to know which instructor was more effective because place A's students practiced more often than place B's students did. Given that these two instructors face different challenges, is there a way to evaluate them fairly? Can we isolate how the piano teachers really mattered?

This is the quandary we have when trying to understand how schools (or teachers) matter for children's lives; the same kinds of complicating factors are at work. First, children begin schooling with very different levels of academic skills. For example, the black/white gap in math and reading skills is roughly a standard deviation at

As sociologist Annette Lareau describes, some home environments complement what happens at school. (Woodley Wonderworks via Creative Commons)

(Scott Feldstein via Creative Commons)

the end of high school, but half of this gap is evident at the beginning of kindergarten, before schools have had a chance to matter. And the differences in skills between high- and low-socioeconomic status (SES) students at the start of kindergarten are even larger. Obviously, these variations aren't a consequence of differences in school quality, but of the different kinds of students schools serve.

High- and low-socioeconomic status students gain academic skills at about the same rate during the school year. The gaps in their skills develop during the summer.

Thinking contextually, some home environments complement what occurs at school as parents help with homework, communicate with teachers, reinforce school concepts, provide a safe and stable environment for study, and attend to children's medical needs (by, for instance, providing consistent visits to doctors and dentists). In her book *Home Advantage*, sociologist Annette Lareau gives a poignant description of just how important parents can be, getting involved in their child's coursework and with their teachers in ways that promote academic success and instilling in their children a kind of academic entitlement. She wrote that these parents "made an effort to integrate educational goals into family life including teaching children new words when driving by billboards, having children practice penmanship and vocabulary by writing out shopping lists, practicing mathematics during baking projects, and practicing vocabulary during breakfast time." Interacting with instructors, the upper-middle-class parents Lareau observed requested specific classroom teach

ers or asked that their child be placed in school programs for the gifted, for speech therapy, or with the learning resource center. In contrast, low-SES parents tended to have less time for involvement with their children's schoolwork, leaving educational experiences in the hands of the "experts." Much like having a piano at home, these contexts of advantage and disadvantage play a critical role in shaping how children gain academic skills during their school years.

bringing in context

By using a contextual perspective, sociologists have contributed considerably to our understanding of how schools matter. One of the most influential studies was the 1966 *Coleman Report*, a massive analysis of American schools that was commissioned by the Federal Department of Education. James Coleman, the lead author of the report, directed the collection of data from 4,000 schools and more than 645,000 American school children in the early 1960s. The researchers were interested in why some children had high math and reading skills and others did not. They measured many characteristics of schools (including school curriculum, facilities, teacher qualities, and student body characteristics) and many characteristics of children's home lives (like parents' SES—education, income, and occupation level) to see which were more closely related to academic skills. Surprisingly, school characteristics were only weakly related to academic skills. It turned out that differences between schools in terms of quality played only a small role in understanding the variation in students' academic skills while home life (parents' SES showed the strongest relationship) mattered much more. Skeptics of this conclusion, such as sociologist Christopher Jencks, re-evaluated Coleman's conclusion with new data, but ended up finding similar patterns.

Of course, one limitation of this approach is that it depends heavily on whether Coleman and Jencks were measuring the right things about schools. Maybe they were missing what really mattered. While they were measuring per pupil expenditures, teacher/student ratios, and racial composition, they missed critical factors like teacher quality. If they failed to measure a lot of important things about schools, then their conclusions that schools play only a minor role in explaining inequality of skills might be wrong.

seasonal comparison research

What researchers need is a way to untangle the role of school and non-school influences. Observing student learning during the school year tells us little about how schools matter because students are exposed to both school and non-school environments. When we compare annually collected test scores, for example, it becomes very difficult to know why some students fall behind and some get ahead. Sociologist Barbara Heyns pointed out that during the summer children are influenced by non-school factors only. The best way to understand how schools matter, she reasoned, was to observe how things change between the non-school period (summer) and the school period. This strategy works like a natural experiment, separating the "treatment" from the treated. Knowing what happens to group-level differences in achievement by race, class, or gender when school is in session (the treatment) compared to when it is not (the control) is a good way to know if schools make educational gaps bigger or smaller.

This important insight led Heyns to collect a different kind of data. She evaluated fifth, sixth, and seventh grade students at the beginning and end of the academic years in Atlanta. By testing them both in the fall and spring, she was able to tell how much they learned during the summer, when school was out. This study design allowed her to uncover a provocative pattern—high- and low-SES students gained academic skills at about the same rate during the nine-month academic year. Gaps in skills developed during the summers. Although schools did not close achievement gaps between groups, these results bolstered Coleman and Jencks's initial conclusions that schools were not the primary reason for group-level inequalities. Heyns's provocative findings were replicated by sociologists Doris Entwisle and Karl Alexander in Baltimore and, more recently, by myself with colleagues at Ohio State. With nationally representative data, we found that low- and high-SES children learned math and reading at similar rates during the 9-month kindergarten and first grade periods, but that gaps in skills grew quickly during the summer in between, when school was out.

Taken together, the overall pattern from this seasonal research supports Coleman's conclusion: schools are not the source of inequality. The seasonal approach to understanding schools gives us a much more accurate understanding of how schools influence inequality. This research consistently produces an unconventional conclusion—if we lived in a world with no schools at

> When it comes to inequality, schools are more the solution than the problem.

all, inequality would be much worse. In other words, when it comes to inequality, schools are more part of the solution than the problem.

This contextual way of thinking about schools and inequality is difficult to reconcile, however, with the "traditional" story—that wide variations in school quality are the engine of inequality. By adopting a more contextual perspective on schools, we can understand this counterintuitive claim: despite the fact that some schools have more resources than others, schools end up being an equalizing force. The key is that the inequalities that exist outside of school are considerably larger than the ones students experience in school.

A contextual approach to schools recognizes that some schools and teachers face very different challenges than others.

schools, context, and policy

At the beginning of this article, we pointed out that it's natural to look to schools for the source of many of our kids' problems—they're the corner with the best "lighting." The often-unexplored terrain outside of schools, though, remains shadowy and seemingly inaccessible. This doesn't need to be the case. And, though extending the light beyond schools reveals that group-level inequality would be much worse if not for schools, it doesn't mean that schools are off the hook. In fact, using school impact as a guide, many "successful" schools in the traditional view are revealed as low-impact—good students don't always signal good instructors. In these schools, children pass proficiency exams, but since they started off in a better position, it's arguable that the schools didn't actually serve their students.

Clearly, when we employ a contextual perspective, we think about school policy, child development, and social problems in a new light. A contextual approach to schools promotes sensible policy, efficiently targeted resources, and reasonable assessment tools that recognize that some schools and teachers face very different challenges than others.

For example, a tremendous amount of energy and money is directed toward developing accountability systems for schools. But recall the analogy of the two piano instructors. It's difficult to determine which instructor is best, given that place A has students that start with more skills and practice more outside of instruction. Now suppose that we knew one more piece of information: how fast each group of piano players gained skills when not taking lessons. Suddenly, we could compare the rate of improvement outside of instruction with the rate observed during the instructional period. We could see how much instruction mattered.

This "impact" view has recently been applied to schools. In 2008, with fellow sociologists Paul T. von Hippel and Melanie Hughes, I constructed impact measures by taking a school's average difference between its students' first-grade learning rate and the learning rate observed in the summer prior to first grade. The key finding was that not all the schools deemed as "failing" under traditional criteria were really failing. Indeed, three out of four schools had been incorrectly evaluated. That's not to say that there were no variations in school quality, but many schools did much better than expected when we took a contextual approach to measurement. And some did much worse. If impact evaluations are more accurate, then teachers serving disadvantaged children are doing a better job than previously thought and current methods of school evaluation are producing substantial errors.

With its contextual orientation, seasonal research has also provided insights into other ways that schools matter. For example, researchers have considered whether "summer setback" can be avoided by modifying the school year so that there is no long gap in school exposure. Von Hippel has compared math and reading learning in schools with year-long calendars versus those with traditional school-year/summer break calendars. In both conditions, children attended school for about 180 days a year, but the timing of those days was spread more evenly in year-round schools. It turned out that, once a calendar year was up, both groups had learned about the same. The policy lesson is that increasing school exposure is probably more important than fiddling with how school days are distributed across the year.

Given that school exposure appears critical, many have viewed summer school (restricted to academically struggling children) as an attractive option for reducing inequality. It turns out, though, that children attending summer school gain fewer academic skills than we would expect. This may be because the academic programs in the summer are of lower quality, but it may also be because the kinds of students who typically attend summer school are also the kind who would typically suffer a "summer setback" without it. Viewed in this light, just treading water or maintaining the same academic skills during the summer could be viewed as a positive outcome.

And in other research employing seasonal comparisons, researchers have shown that children gain body mass index (BMI) three times faster during the summer than during the school year. Obviously, schools shouldn't abandon attempts to improve the quality of lunches or the schooling environment, but research suggests that attention should be paid to non-school factors as the primary sources of childhood obesity.

In the end, looking at schools through a contextual lens provides exciting insights. When we forget how other aspects of children's lives figure into their development, we create a distorted

Students play during recess. (Visual.dichotomy via Creative Commons)

view of schools. The contextual perspective corrects this error and produces a more accurate understanding of how schools really matter. It suggests that if we are serious about improving American children's school performance, we will need to take a broader view of education policy. In addition to school reform, we must also aim to improve children's lives where they spend the vast majority of their time—with their families and in their neighborhoods.

RECOMMENDED RESOURCES

James S. Coleman. "Equality of Educational Opportunity." United States Office of Education and National Center for Education Statistics (1966).

> The classic large-scale study of American schools and factors related to test score performance.

Douglas B. Downey, Paul T. von Hippel, and Melanie Hughes. "Are 'Failing' Schools Really Failing? Using Seasonal Comparisons to Evaluate School Effectiveness." *Sociology of Education* (2008), 81(3):242–70.

> Introduces impact evaluation, which isolates school from non-school factors in child achievement via seasonal comparisons.

Doris R. Entwisle, Karl L. Alexander, and Linda S. Olson. *Children, Schools and Inequality* (Westview Press, 1997).

> Uses data from Baltimore to show how social context shapes children's early schooling experiences.

Barbara Heyns. *Summer Learning and the Effects of Schooling* (Academic Press, 1978).

> Describes the seminal use of "seasonal comparisons" to report the results of summer versus school-time learning.

Annette Lareau. *Home Advantage: Social Class and Parental Intervention in Elementary Education* (Rowman & Littlefield, 2000).

> A vivid ethnographic account of the different ways working and middle-class families prepare their children for school and interact with teachers.

REVIEW QUESTIONS

1. Using "impact" measurements, sociologists have found that up to 75 percent of "failing" schools aren't actually failing their students. How does an impact measure differ from more traditional measures of school success? Can you think of other ways to measure the educational value of a school?

2. What do the authors suggest about the educational benefits of year-round schooling?

3. What are some mechanisms by which schools mitigate inequalities found outside the classroom? What, if any, policy implications might you derive from these findings?

4. Activity: The authors state that the typical 18-year-old has spent just 13 percent of his or her waking hours in school. Use the most recent American Time Use Survey, available from the Bureau of Labor Statistics (online at www.bls.gov/tus), to see how Americans are using the rest of their time. Although the survey doesn't present data for children, use the charts for college students, leisure time, and so on to discuss your priorities.

william beaver

a matter of degrees

12

spring 2009

americans value few things more than a college degree. but what exactly does a degree do for people? although college graduates do have higher incomes, the reasons why, and our ever-increasing need to acquire educational credentials, are tied to larger social forces.

Americans value few things more than college degrees. Right now, 29 percent of adults over age 25 have a bachelor's or higher. That figure has more than doubled since the 1970s, and many within the educational establishment argue it will have to increase significantly for the United States to remain globally competitive.

The number of graduate degrees also continues to rise—masters' have doubled since 1980 and record numbers are enrolled in master's programs, a recent article in *The New York Times* reported.

In many ways these numbers aren't surprising. Early on, students learn that a college degree is the starting point to making it in American society. Indeed, both the Clinton and Bush Administrations touted a college degree as the most expedient way to ensure economic well-being.

Media reports periodically reinforce such beliefs, reminding us that degree-holders have important income advantages. A recent news story in *The Washington Post* reported that in tough economic times, those with college degrees are much more likely to avoid lay-offs and maintain their incomes than those with high school diplomas or less.

But what exactly do degrees do for people? The conventional wisdom holds that college graduates acquire skills that better prepare them for the world of work, which makes them more attractive to employers. Thus, students and parents are willing to pay the continually rising costs of higher education, assuming the pay-off will be worth it.

Although college graduates do have higher incomes, the reasons why, and our ever-increasing need to acquire educational credentials, are tied to larger social forces that sociologists have explored—forces that will continue to impact all those trying to climb the ladder of success.

> Few college students learn job skills. In the business curriculum, not all areas focus on acquiring specific skills. In the social sciences and liberal arts, there is little or no skill-training.

the purpose of degrees

The most popular view on the purpose of a college degree is known as the human capital model, which argues students attend college to acquire the knowledge and skills modern societies require, and that this allows them to obtain meaningful employment.

It's the model most students seem to accept, too. For example, surveys conducted by UCLA's Higher Education Research Institute found that

72 percent of college freshmen cite "to get a better job" as the major reason for going to college.

However, if the human capital model is correct, it must be assumed students acquire skills in the classroom that are directly transferable to the job. One can certainly argue certain majors like accounting and computer science offer more skill-training than others, and research indicates that with these types of majors, employers do tend to hire on the basis of perceived skills.

The fact of the matter is, though, most college students don't major in areas that teach job skills. Some 22 percent of students currently major in business, but even within the business curriculum not all areas of study focus on acquiring specific skills. Moreover, many students continue to major in the social sciences and liberal arts, where there is little or no skill-training.

Along these lines, it would be logical to assume those possessing the necessary job skills, as indicated by their college major, would be more productive. Yet, the research that does exist on this idea suggests job productivity isn't significantly related to major.

Perhaps a more important question is, how much do students actually learn in college that could be applied to their job? In this regard, the Major Field Tests administered by the Educational Testing Service are designed to assess student learning by college major. Approximately 700 colleges use the tests, and on average, students answer slightly more than half the questions correctly, indicating that although some learning does occur, it doesn't appear to be substantial. Thus, although the human capital model tells us something about the purpose of degrees, there's certainly much more involved.

Another prominent theory holds that degrees are screening and sorting devices for employers,

> The fact that employers use degrees as screening devices raises questions about their real meaning, and this is where sociological research can provide valuable insights.

and this is supported by the work of organizational theorists like Herbert Simon. He argues human beings possess limited information processing abilities, which he calls bounded rationality. Due to these limitations, we use various techniques to make things simpler. One technique is to apply heuristics, or "rules of thumb," rather than more complex decision-making processes that would require substantial amounts of time and effort, to say nothing of the costs involved.

For example, it isn't unusual for employers to receive many more job applications than they can reasonably handle. To ease the process, employers limit the applications they'll seriously consider to those who hold a college degree, or a degree in a certain major, or even require a graduate degree.

It does seem obvious that employers use degrees as screening devices. Yet, the fact that degrees are used in this way raises questions about their real meaning to employers, and this is where sociological research can provide valuable insights.

why we credential

Max Weber is credited with being the first sociologist to closely examine the function of degrees. He concluded educational credentials had much less to do with acquiring job skills than providing occupational and professional groups with a way of excluding certain individuals. The ability to exclude not only gives these groups power but helps ensure those hired will be loyal to the organization.

Weber's basic insights provided the foundation for modern credentialing theory, the most important work about which remains Randall

Collins's *The Credentialed Society*. His detailed historical and social analysis supported Weber's contention that degrees allow certain occupational groups to exclude individuals, and that even business degrees seldom provide actual job training but do serve as indicators that a potential employee possesses the correct values that make compliance with organizational standards more likely.

There are always uncertainties about how new hires will adjust. The last thing most employers want is for them to "rock the boat," which could threaten stability within the organization. It's assumed individuals with the appropriate college degree will be more likely to fit in, but why? Part of the answer is self-selection. That is, students choose a college major that appeals to them, hoping to land a job and the start of a career, and hence are more than willing to conform. On the other hand, it's also likely that being exposed to a curriculum socializes students to acquire values associated with a profession. For years sociologists have investigated this so-called "hidden curriculum."

For example, prospective managers are taught that their interests and the interests of workers are often in conflict and that their loyalties should be tied to management. Credentialing theorists have also suggested possessing the appropriate values is particularly important in higher-level positions, where individuals are often given more autonomy and are less likely to be closely monitored. So perhaps it isn't surprising that business researchers Nasrollah Ahadiat and Kenneth Smith discovered employers considered "professional conduct" the most important attribute when hiring accounting graduates.

Besides conformity and control, credentialing theory emphasizes that degrees also confer status on those who hold them. Along these lines, sociologist David K. Brown traced the development of the credentialing system to the late 19th century and the rise of large-scale bureaucratic organizations where individuals with management skills were needed.

It was assumed college graduates possessed the cognitive and verbal abilities good managers needed, which also reduced the uncertainty associated with hiring. Interestingly, studies do show college tends to increase cognitive abilities, so in many cases these assumptions weren't unfounded. Nonetheless, degrees provided a claim of competence or status that came to be taken for granted.

Thus credentials, as David Labaree points out in his book *How to Succeed in College Without Really Learning*, have exchange value because they allow students to obtain employment based largely on the status a degree confers. However, much less use value is apparent because the connection between degrees and actual job performance is questionable.

the pay gap

Many students pursue a degree to position themselves to earn a higher income, and it has been well established that college graduates earn more. In fact, four-year degree holders earn nearly 45 percent more per year than high school graduates, according to the U.S. Census Bureau.

Indeed, the pay gap is one of the strongest arguments for the conventional wisdom of the human capital model, because it seems to demonstrate that employers are willing to pay for the skills college graduates possess. On the other hand, it's difficult to know exactly how much degrees are really worth because the most capable students go to college. As a result, there's no control group of equally capable, non-degree students available for comparison.

Nonetheless, credentialing theorists would agree that income and degrees are clearly related. Research by Ross Boylan found the largest gains in income occur soon after obtaining a degree. In this regard, reports from the Bureau of Labor Statistics show income gains for students are small unless they obtain a credential, even though students could certainly acquire job skills without earning a degree.

Consider that the median weekly income of individuals with some college but no degree in 2004 was $574, compared to $916 for those with a bachelor's. This suggests degrees do serve as status indicators. Just as important, Boylan found income gains experienced by degree holders are often relative. That is, as the number of people with degrees increase, degree holders take jobs formerly held by high school graduates. Hence, the relative value of a degree actually increases because non-degree holders are forced into even lower-paying jobs.

One result, according to D. W. Livingstone in his book *The Education-Jobs Gap*, is that workers are often underemployed, because employers have increased the educational requirements for jobs whose basic content hasn't changed. Research by Stephen Vaisey discovered that nearly 55 percent of workers are overqualified, which has produced increasing levels of job dissatisfaction, to say nothing of the fact that workers are forced to pursue even higher, increasingly expensive credentials (which is particularly burdensome to lower income groups) if they want a chance to be hired.

This phenomenon has been termed "defensive credentialing," where students attend college to keep from losing ground to degree holders. As one student recently put it, "I don't like college much, but what kind of job can I get without a degree?" Similarly, as the number of bachelor's degrees climbs, more have pursued graduate degrees, hoping to gain some advantage. This also helps explain the increase in the number of master's degrees.

credentialing and higher education

The role of higher education in a credentialing system seems obvious—to grant degrees to those who earn them. But there's still more involved. Although higher education certainly responds to the demands of industry and students for credentials, colleges haven't just been passive participants waiting for students to enroll. They've used the credentialing system to their advantage, having relied on demographic changes.

By the late 1970s, higher education faced a troubling reality. The education of the baby boom generation that had produced the so-called "golden years" of higher education, when enrollments tripled, was coming to an end. The last of the boomers would be graduating in a few years and the future looked grim. The Carnegie Council warned enrollments could decline by as much as 50 percent, while others predicted 30 percent of colleges might have to close or merge. To survive, they would have to recruit more students from a dwindling pool.

Hence, colleges began to enroll a more academically diverse group of students and recruit more women and minorities, many of whom represented first-generation college students. To a lesser extent, the situation was helped by the fact that more students were completing high school. According to the U.S. Department of Education, between 1972 and 1985 high school completion rates increased by roughly 2.6 percent, and then climbed by about 3 percent by 1999.

Moreover, the curriculum, particularly at less prestigious institutions, was expanded and further vocationalized. In fact, W. Norton Grubb and Marvin Lazerson in their book *The Education Gospel and the Economic Power of Schooling* maintain that expansion in higher education has only occurred when more occupational majors have been added to the curriculum.

In the early 1970s, 58 percent of majors were considered occupational and by the late 1980s that figure had climbed to 65 percent. These types of degrees can be particularly appealing to first-generation college students, who often come from working- and lower-class backgrounds and want a degree that seems to improve their chances for employment and justifies the considerable investment.

New degree programs were often in subject areas that in the past hadn't required a bachelor's degree for employment. For example, females who might have needed a certificate or an associate degree to secure work as a secretary could now earn a four-year degree in office management. Such was also true for other areas, ranging from various medical technologies to the performing arts, which reinforced the credentialing system in two significant ways. First, a more diverse group of students earned degrees, many of whom might not have obtained them in the past. Second, by creating new majors, credentialing was expanded into vocational areas not traditionally associated with a four-year degree, while at the same time reinforcing the notion that a college degree imparts job skills.

The efforts to enroll more students clearly succeeded. In the early 1980s, one-half of high school graduates attended two- and four-year colleges, and by the mid-1990s that number had climbed to two-thirds. In addition to attracting more traditional-aged students, major efforts were successfully undertaken to recruit older adults. By 2000, adult students represented 43 percent of all those enrolled in degree-granting institutions, a nearly three-fold increase since the 1970s.

Similar to trends in traditional undergraduate education, many of the new adult students were females, to the point that 57 percent of all college students now are women. A number of older students also returned to college to complete degrees they had started earlier in their lives. According to the U.S. Department of Education, 52.5 percent of adults over 25 have some college but no degree. These students also tend to be attracted to more occupational majors, and perhaps came to the realization that without a degree their incomes wouldn't increase much, which is consistent with the research findings. This trend, along with a growing number of graduate students, further boosted enrollments. Thus, the predicted declines in enrollments never happened, and attendance increased over the years.

Why? Obviously, factors like a more vocationalized curriculum and the willingness of colleges to enroll a more diverse group of students played a role. Yet, a purely economic explanation can't entirely explain the increases. If this were the case, enrollments should have declined at some point because the value of degrees diminishes as their numbers increase.

The most plausible explanation is that the relative (if not absolute) value of a credential rose, providing degree holders with an income advantage. Interestingly, researchers at the Economic Policy Institute found that during the 1990s, the pay gap between college graduates and those with less education could largely be explained by the decline in wages of those without degrees, not increases for those with them. Thus, it seems likely many new college students were simply protecting their own interests,

> For the foreseeable future, there appears to be few alternatives to a credentialing system that dates back more than a century.

fearing they would fall further behind without a degree. All of which created a momentum of its own that allowed higher education to expand.

For the foreseeable future, there appears to be few alternatives to a credentialing system that dates back more than a century. Indeed, Collins has speculated that such systems can last 200 years. Thus, higher education as we know it will obviously continue and college graduates will enjoy income advantages.

However, this isn't to say the system may not weaken. It appears, in fact, the pay gap between four-year degree holders and high school graduates is beginning to narrow, which could dissuade some from attending college, particularly if tuitions continue to rise. Although the reasons for this aren't entirely clear, some hypothesize that secondary education has improved, making high school graduates more attractive to employers. Other research indicates there's little, if any, monetary advantage to obtaining an MBA (the most valued of master's degrees), unless it's from a prestigious school.

If this sort of information ever becomes widely known, graduate enrollments could be negatively impacted. Moreover, how individuals are hired could be altered. Employers could begin to put less emphasis on degrees and more on other criteria, including job performance tests, experience, and motivation. However, such changes have been discussed for years but have never been widely implemented.

RECOMMENDED RESOURCES

Ross D. Boylan. "The Effect of the Number of Diplomas on Their Value." *Sociology of Education* (1993) 66: 206–21.

> Shows how the relative value of college degrees has increased while their absolute value has not.

David K. Brown. *Degrees of Control: A Sociology of Educational Expansion and Occupational Credentialism* (Teachers College Press, 1995.)

> Documents the development of the credentialing system to the late 19th century and how it came to be assumed that degree holders had certain traits that made them more attractive to employers.

Randall Collins. *The Credential Society: An Historical Sociology of Education and Stratification* (Academic Press, 1979).

> A detailed historical account of the credentialing system and its implications for American society.

W. Norton Grubb and Marvin Lazerson. *The Education Gospel and the Economic Power of Schooling* (Harvard University Press, 2004).

> Discusses the rise of vocationalism and its continuing impacts on higher education.

D. W. Livingstone. *The Education-Jobs Gap: Underemployment or Economic Democracy* (Westview Press, 1998).

> Suggests workers are increasingly underemployed because the educational credentials required for jobs has risen even though the content of most jobs has not essentially changed.

Eric Margolis, ed. *The Hidden Curriculum in Higher Education* (Routledge, 2001).

> One of the first attempts to describe and analyze the hidden curriculum at colleges and universities.

REVIEW QUESTIONS

1. In what ways is higher education more than a skill-training effort? What other important functions do the college years serve? How might these impacts and outcomes vary by institution or student?

2. The authors talk about "capable" students. Give examples from your own experience of how educational achievement (or failure) is used to make assumptions about a person's character.

3. Define "defensive credentialing." What impact might an economic recession and a tight labor market have on this rationale for education?

4. Activity: List five reasons you are in college and compare them with a classmate's. How do you think your reasons compare with those of the majority of the U.S. college population?

george farkas

the black-white test score gap

spring 2004

the supreme court's 2003 decision to uphold affirmative action in college admissions suggests that special treatment may be unnecessary in 25 years. but achieving equality without affirmative action will require overcoming a black-white test score gap that appears as early as preschool and is rooted in child-rearing practices.

When Supreme Court Justice Sandra Day O'Connor cast the deciding vote upholding affirmative action at the University of Michigan in 2003, she also suggested an expiration date for this policy. "We expect that 25 years from now the use of racial preferences will no longer be necessary" for racial balance, she wrote in her 5-4 majority opinion. Many consider this 25-year time-span to be overly optimistic because the black-white gap in standardized test scores of the sort used to decide college admissions is very large and has not changed since 1990. The average score for African-American 12th graders on the National Assessment of Educational Progress (NAEP) reading test matches the average score for white eighth graders. In a Washington, D.C., school district with mostly black students, 7 in 10 of all fourth graders recently scored below "basic" in mathematics and 6 in 10 scored below basic in reading.

Some commentators attribute the black-white test score gap to culturally biased tests rather than cognitive skills. In fact, black children perform at lower levels than white children due to experiences early in life. It may take longer than a quarter century before black students applying for college have the same average skills and test scores as white applicants.

is the gap real?

Research shows that when blacks and whites attend school together, black students typically get lower grades. For example, a recent study of the upper-middle-class community of Shaker Heights, Ohio, found that almost 80 percent of white students but fewer than 3 percent of black students graduated with honors (which required a grade-point average of at least 3.0). Grades may be poor indicators of ability because grading standards vary across classes, schools, and districts. Teachers may also be biased. Nationally standardized, computer-graded tests provide more reliable and comparable measures of academic performance. Over the past 10 years, research projects employing a variety of such tests have found the black-white gap in every age group.

Questions on these examinations are not esoteric. Tests for preschool and elementary school-age children ask students to name and write down letters of the alphabet, test oral vocabulary, assess the ability to read simple words and sentences, and test knowledge of numbers, counting, shapes, and simple mathematical operations. Tests for older elementary-school children include grade-appropriate problem solving and mathematical operations (e.g., the multiplication table up to 10×10), vocabulary, and reading and writing about passages on social studies and science. For middle and high school students, the tests focus on vocabulary, grammar, reading comprehension, writing simple essays, and solving basic geometry and algebra problems. These skills are required for high school graduation, college attendance, and military service. They are needed for most jobs, particularly those paying above the minimum wage. Thus, being able to perform these tasks and demonstrate these skills on tests is important. In this sense, the black-white test score gap is very real, with substantial consequences for the life chances of African-American students.

As large as the black-white test-score gap is, it used to be larger. It decreased by about 40 percent from 1970 to 1990, but has held steady since then. Researchers are unsure why the gap stopped narrowing at that time. Each of the following explanations has its proponents: biased testing, discrimination by teachers, test anxiety among black students, disparities between blacks and whites in income or family structure, and genetic and cultural differences between blacks and whites. Before evaluating these explanations, consider recent research.

recent evidence

Much of the latest research focuses on "culture," broadly defined as the skills, knowledge, habits, and behaviors parents, caretakers, and peers teach students. Child-rearing cultures vary strongly by class and race because residential segregation keeps these groups separate. The story of Eliza Doolittle in *My Fair Lady,* whose distinctively working-class vocabulary and dialect are remade by Professor Higgins, illustrates class differences. It is not just that poor children learn to speak with a different accent than middle-class children. Rather, parents with lower education and income tend to talk less and use a smaller vocabulary with their children than do middle-class parents. Lower-class parents typically teach their children fewer of the skills and behaviors that schools and teachers expect and that test scores measure.

Developmental psychologists Betty Hart and Todd Risley had their research team spend one hour every month in the homes of 42 families, as the child in the family grew from one to three years old. The families ranged across three economic levels—professionals, middle- and working-class, and low-income—and were both black and white. During each hour, the researchers recorded every word spoken between parent and child. The researchers found striking differences across the three groups in the amount of verbal interaction and the number of different words parents used (see figure 1). By the age of three, the professional parents had spoken 35 million words to their children, the middle- and working-class parents had spoken 20 million words to their children, and the lower-class parents had spoken only 10 million words to their children.

Due to these parents' verbal styles, the children of professionals added words to their vocabulary at a much higher rate than did the middle- and working-class children, and these in turn had much higher vocabulary growth rates than did the poorer children (see figure 2). By 18 to 20 months, the professional-class children's vocabulary growth trajectories accelerated away from those of the other children, and by two years, the middle- and working-class children's vocabulary had separated from that of the lower-class children. By 36 months of age, the professional-class children had a vocabulary more than double that of the poorest children. Hart and Risley concluded that by three years of age children have internalized the "conversational culture" of their family. And because these cultures vary by the educational and income

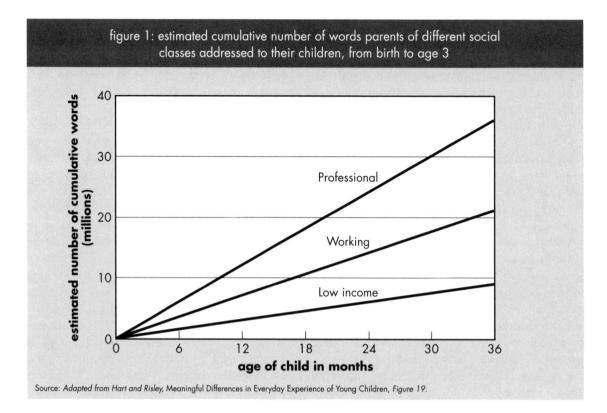

figure 1: estimated cumulative number of words parents of different social classes addressed to their children, from birth to age 3

Source: *Adapted from Hart and Risley,* Meaningful Differences in Everyday Experience of Young Children, *Figure 19.*

levels of the parents, the children learn to understand the world and to interact with others using the linguistic tools characteristic of those class levels. Consequently, children from high, middle, and low social class families begin school with very different bases upon which to build success in reading and mathematics.

Christopher Jencks and Meredith Phillips pursued the question of preschoolers' vocabularies into the arena of race, using a large national survey that measured the spoken vocabularies of thousands of children. (In the Peabody Picture Vocabulary Test used in this survey, interviewers read words to children, who then choose one of four pictures that best represents their meaning.) Jencks and Phillips found that among children aged three to six, the vocabulary knowl-

edge of black children lags behind that of white children by about a year. Although the educational and income levels of the parents also strongly affect vocabulary knowledge, taking these into account still leaves a significant portion of the black-white vocabulary gap unexplained. That is, black children from the same class backgrounds as white children typically have smaller vocabularies than their white counterparts. Kurt Beron and I have further analyzed these data, extending them to 13 years of age. Our findings are illustrated in figure 3. Again, race and class separately influence children's oral vocabulary, with white children from lower-class families having about the same vocabulary knowledge as black children from upper-class families. These differences already

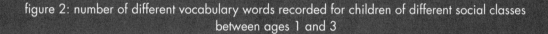

figure 2: number of different vocabulary words recorded for children of different social classes between ages 1 and 3

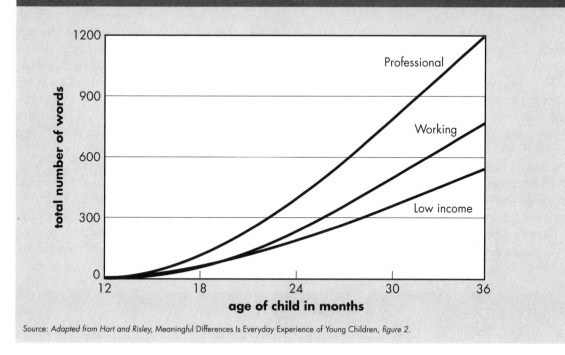

Source: *Adapted from Hart and Risley,* Meaningful Differences Is Everyday Experience of Young Children, *figure 2.*

exist by 36 months of age, and the class and race gaps persist into adolescence.

The newest research from the Early Childhood Longitudinal Study of Kindergarten (ECLS-K) also supports these findings. Researchers measured pre-reading and pre-mathematics knowledge and skills for a national sample of approximately 20,000 students when they entered kindergarten in 1998, and have continued to follow these students as they progress up the grades. These data show large black-white gaps in pre-reading and pre-mathematics skills at kindergarten entry. They also show these gaps widening over the school years.

The ECLS-K interviewers also asked teachers how engaged their students were in class instruc-

tion. Typically, teachers believed that black students were less likely than white students to persist at tasks, be eager to learn, or pay attention, and more likely to argue, fight, or get angry with others. These patterns were found even when the black children came from similar social class backgrounds as the white children, and when the teacher doing the rating was black. Persistence, paying attention, and other forms of school engagement help determine how much each student learns. Further, since they often start with weaker skills and are less engaged in school, black students are less likely than white students to be placed in higher ability groups or classes where more material is taught and learning proceeds faster. Taken together, the initial disadvantage, the weaker school engagement, and the lower track placement explains most of the widening in the black-white test score gap that occurs as students grow up.

which explanations are best supported?

The most popular explanation for the black-white test score gap is bias. Indeed, all standardized tests *are* biased, as are all textbooks, if "bias" means that they focus on skills involving Standard English vocabulary and grammar, abstract thought and argument, and mathematics concepts more commonly taught and learned in white than in black families. But since these skills are required to succeed in K-12 schooling, to attend college, and to get jobs paying middle-class wages, test makers and school personnel can hardly be accused of bias for requiring them. The issue is not so-called "intelligence," but the skills demanded by the job market.

Discrimination by teachers no doubt exists, but it is unlikely to account for much of the test score gap. A large portion of the gap is already present before schooling begins. Furthermore, about one in three African-American kindergarten and first-grade students have an African-American teacher, and studies show that black students do not achieve higher test scores when their teachers are black.

Experiments by social psychologist Claude Steele have found that black students suffer from race-related test anxiety—sensitivity that their performance will be weighed as a measure of inherent black ability—and that this distraction lowers their performance (see part 15: methods,

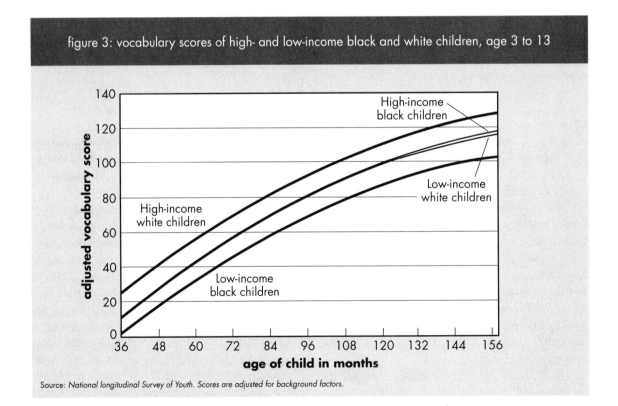

figure 3: vocabulary scores of high- and low-income black and white children, age 3 to 13

Source: *National longitudinal Survey of Youth. Scores are adjusted for background factors.*

The Zoo

I like to go the zoo with my family.

We all like to see the hippos, tigers, and monkeys.

When I go to the zoo, I like to eat cotton candy and corndogs and peanuts.

I like to ride the train that goes around the zoo.

I like to go to the zoo with my class. We ride the bus.

We have so much fun!

Teacher: Mrs. Clowers   Tutor: Pat Rigdon
Student: Devron Snead   1st grade

John Everett's Family

I live in a house with my mother and father. My room is decorated with Star Wars.

Sometimes I go out to my sister's house, and I play with my niece, and we go to the beach too.

I have a dog. He is a puppy and he is messy. He likes to dig and tear up paper.

My family enjoys fishing. My family also enjoys going to church.

I have many friends like Bryan and Mrs. Pat.

At school I learn reading, writing and spelling.

Mrs. Pat   John Everett fourth grade/ Ms Davis
Tutor: Pat Rigdon

Illustrated essays produced by black students working with individual reading tutors. The work of a first-grade student is on the left, that of a fourth-grade student on the right. In supplementing the efforts of parents and teachers, college students and paraprofessional tutors can help children regain the academic ground they lost from starting school without adequate pre-reading and pre-mathematics skills. The black-white test score gap used to be larger than it is now, and without continuing intervention, it could increase yet again. (Reading One-to-One Program, Duval County Public Schools, Florida)

"from summer camps to glass ceilings"). Related experiments by Michael Lovaglia find that black students not only worry about doing badly on standardized tests, but also worry about doing too well and thus being accused of "acting white." However, these findings apply in special circumstances: small groups of older students sensitive to racial issues who are taking tests within a manipulated experiment. Again, the fact that the test score gap is found even among very young children, including those in all-black neighborhoods, casts doubt on the likelihood that test anxiety arising from race awareness explains more than a modest portion of the gap.

Research supports the idea that black-white differences in social class, family structures, and child-rearing behaviors explain much of the test score gap. Despite economic progress, black parents still lag behind white ones in employment and income. Black families therefore have fewer resources, a situation that is exacerbated by the high percentage of black children raised in single-parent households. Financial and parenting resources improve children's school engagement, course grades and test scores. Significant portions—but usually not all—of the black-white test score gap disappear once social class differences between the groups are adjusted for. When one compares black and white children who come from similar economic and family circumstances, their test scores are typically closer than when one compares all black and white children. The percentage of the overall test score gap that can be explained by background varies greatly across studies depending on the study design, the year, and the test used. Most show that differences in children's class and family backgrounds explain about half of the black-white test score gap; fewer studies find that these background differences explain most or even all the gap. The latter studies suggest that, so long as blacks continue to close the economic gap with whites, successive generations of black students will narrow and eventually eliminate the test-score gap with whites.

However, there is also reason to be less optimistic. The black-white gaps in education and income (among adults) have narrowed significantly since 1990, yet the test score gap has remained unchanged. Further, SAT scores show a significant black-white gap within every family income level. This gap is so large that, in 2002, the average SAT score for blacks from families earning $80,000 to $100,000 per year was substantially lower than the average for whites from families earning $20,000 to $30,000 per year. Clearly, more than class background is involved.

What about a genetic basis for the test score gap? This suggestion, made by Richard Herrnstein and Charles Murray in their 1994 book, *The Bell Curve,* created a storm of controversy. Psychologist Richard Nisbett recently reviewed the research on this question and concluded that there is no evidence for the genetic superiority of individuals with either African or European ancestry. Instead, there is strong evidence for a significant effect of the mother's child-raising practices on the black-white test score gap. For example, he points to the fact that mixed-race children with a white mother show significantly higher IQ test scores than those with a black mother, even though the race mixture of their genetic inheritance is similar. By contrast, mixed-race children fathered by black GIs in Germany (with German women) had identical IQ scores to those fathered by white GIs with German women. (And this despite the fact that the black-white test score gap among GIs is similar to that in the population as a whole.)

This brings us back to differences in home environment. Much of these differences originate in the distinct child-rearing resources and styles of white and black mothers and caregivers even within the same class. Nisbett draws on an ethnographic study by Shirley Brice Heath of class and race differences in child-rearing to conclude that "systematic differences between the socialization of black and white children begin in the cradle." Such differences probably affect later cognitive skills. For example, parents of poor black children tend not to read to them, or train them in abstractions such as the form and color of objects, or teach them how to take information learned in one area and apply it to another. Other researchers, such as Hart and Risley, document both class and race differences in the verbal responses parents give to young children, with middle-class and white parents more likely to be encouraging and positive, and lower-income and black parents more likely to be discouraging and punitive. The large differences in skills and habits that appear by school age set the stage for continuing racial differences in cognitive performance and learning styles. Thus, culture and child-rearing, differing by class and by race, and operating from birth to adulthood, complete the explanation for the black-white test score gap.

how can the gap be closed?

The national trend toward smaller class sizes in school may help close the gap because smaller classes have been shown to disproportionately benefit African-American students. So will the current emphasis on phonics instruction for beginning readers, since this too particularly helps African-American students. However, the black-white school achievement gap will never be closed as long as African-American students continue to have lower pre-reading and pre-mathematics skills when they enter kindergarten and first grade.

We must work to increase the oral vocabulary and early alphabetic and phonemic (letter-sound linkage) awareness of African-American children during their preschool years. Research has shown that these skills best predict success in learning to read by first grade. We must also strive to increase preschool instruction in numbers, counting, shapes, and other prerequisites of elementary school mathematics because the kindergarten pre-mathematics gap is as large as the pre-reading gap.

We must also insure that most African-American children attend preschool, and we must strive to improve the quality and quantity of instruction provided by Head Start and similar preschool programs. Despite more than 30 years of existence, Head Start has no national instructional curriculum in pre-reading and pre-mathematics skills. Instead, the program tends to focus on social skills, based on the mistaken belief that young children are not "developmentally ready" to learn letters, shapes, and advanced vocabulary. Meanwhile, white middle-class mothers continue teaching these skills and knowledge to their children, who enter kindergarten better prepared to succeed than black and poor children. In low-income neighborhoods, Head Start teachers often have only a high school diploma, and often learned their own skills at the same low-performing schools that the children will soon be entering. The recent *No Child Left Behind* initiative of the U.S. Department of Education emphasizes training preschool and day care providers to offer better instruction to low-income children. Unfortunately, this initiative has been caught up in ideological struggles, and success is uncertain.

More generally, African-American parents (particularly those with limited schooling) must interact more with their children in ways that will better prepare them for school. Some intervention programs seek to help them do so. However, these have shown at best mixed success in reaching those low-income households that are most in need.

Potentially more promising is a new program, Early Head Start, which attempts to work with children prior to the usual Head Start ages. Low-income parents bring children as young as 12 months of age to a preschool center, where trained caregivers provide the stimulation the children may not otherwise receive at home. This and related initiatives offer some hope of progress in increasing the school readiness levels of black children by the time they reach first grade. However, even if these programs are successful, follow-up will be necessary to insure that these children do not fall behind later. My own contribution has been to develop a one-to-one tutoring program in reading, using low-cost college students and other paraprofessionals. This has been implemented in a large number of locations, and shows promise of helping children who have fallen behind during early elementary school.

the clock is ticking

The black-white test score gap is both real and consequential for the life chances of African-American students. Recent research has clearly demonstrated that this gap begins in the home at very early ages, and increases further during the school years. The nation is beginning to confront this issue, but it is difficult to improve the skills and knowledge that so many children bring to kindergarten, particularly when these are strongly determined by parenting styles, which in turn are rooted in class- and race-based experience. Nor will it be possible to substantially improve the middle and high school performance of African-American students if, as is now the case, they start school with reading and mathematics skills substantially below grade-level.

Justice O'Connor suggested a 25-year delay before ending affirmative action in college admissions. To ensure continuing equality of opportunity, the 18 year old African Americans taking the SAT that year will have to be better prepared than the 18 year olds of today. We have seven years before those children will be born. We had better get busy.

RECOMMENDED RESOURCES

Jonathan Crane., ed. *Social Programs That Work* (Russell Sage Foundation Press, 1998).

> This anthology evaluates successful intervention programs for low-income children.

George Farkas. *Human Capital or Cultural Capital? Ethnicity and Poverty Groups in an Urban School District* (Aldine de Gruyter, 1996).

> Explains how early skills and student behavior gaps lead to ethnic achievement gaps in urban school districts.

George Farkas. "Racial Disparities and Discrimination in Education: What Do We Know, How Do We Know It, and What Do We Need to Know?" *Teachers College Record* 105 (2003): 1157–88.

> Reviews the research literature on racial gaps in education.

Ronald Ferguson. "A Diagnostic Analysis of Black-White GPA Disparities in Shaker Heights, Ohio." *Brookings Papers on Education Policy 2001.* (The Brookings Institution, 2001).

> Investigates the black-white achievement gap in one affluent suburban school district.

Betty Hart and Todd Risley. *Meaningful Differences in Everyday Experience of Young Children* (Paul Brookes Publishing Co., 1995).

> Includes detailed evidence on how social class determines parents' conversations with preschool children, leading to differences in the children's vocabulary.

Christopher Jencks and Meredith Phillips, eds. *The Black-White Test Score Gap* (Brookings, 1998).

> One of the best collections of research papers on the nature, history, and causes of the test score gap; it includes Richard Nisbett's review of the evidence on racial differences in IQ scores.

Catherine Snow, M. Susan Burns, and Peg Griffin, eds. *Preventing Reading Difficulties in Young Children* (National Academy Press, 1998).

> Explains what research has taught us about effective reading instruction, particularly at young ages and for at-risk students.

REVIEW QUESTIONS

1. Farkas mentions several possible explanations for why the test gap between blacks and whites has held steady since 1990. Identify them.

2. Restate the author's explanation for how race and class affect differently the oral vocabulary of black and white children.

3. Because Farkas states that a "large portion of the gap is already present before schooling begins," there is a danger in misreading this as "blaming the victim." What would you identify as the larger structural reasons that could explain preschooling differences rather than "individualistic" reasons? Defend your position.

4. Activity: The author mentions that there are other aspects to a broad definition of "culture" that can be examined in relation to educational achievement. Write a short essay on other life skills that differentiate white and black child rearing (e.g., artistic expression, nurturing one's siblings, being encouraged to lead a group), and hypothesize why some skill sets are highly valued in school whereas others are not.

part **4**

Culture and Media

joshua gamson and pearl latteier

do media monsters devour diversity?

14

summer 2004

politicians and critics have long lamented that the rise of huge media conglomerates means the death of diversity in newspapers and on the airwaves. but research suggests that media conglomeration, however distasteful, does not necessarily reduce diversity.

Something odd is going on when Ted Turner, Trent Lott, Al Franken, the National Rifle Association, Jesse Jackson, and Walter Cronkite agree. Opposition to media consolidation has turned these adversaries on most issues into bedfellows. When the Federal Communications Commission (FCC) prepared to further loosen restrictions on media ownership—a move approved by the FCC in June 2003 and then blocked by a circuit court three months later—the decision was met with a motley chorus of criticism. FCC commissioner Jonathan Adelstein called the problem "the McDonaldization of American media." Former Senator Carol Moseley-Braun stated that "we have to ensure that there is a diversity of ownership, a diversity of voice." And Cronkite, the veteran and widely respected news anchor, declared concentration "an impediment to a free and independent press." The new rules would "stifle debate, inhibit new ideas, and shut out smaller businesses trying to compete," said Turner, whose vast holdings include CNN, TBS, and Hanna-Barbera cartoons, and who is a major shareholder in parent company Time Warner AOL. "There are really five companies that control 90 percent of what we read, see and hear. It's not healthy," Turner added.

Critics and policy makers have long been troubled by consolidation among America's mainstream media. Opponents of the Communications Act of 1934—which established the FCC and allocated the majority of the airwaves to commercial broadcasters—warned that commercial, network-dominated radio would squelch, as the ACLU director then put it, the few small stations that "voice critical or radical views." And in 1978, the Supreme Court ruled "it is unrealistic to expect true diversity from a commonly owned station-newspaper combination." Nonetheless, during the past two decades—and with a big boost from the Telecommunications Act of 1996—media ownership has become increasingly concentrated in fewer and fewer hands. Time and Warner Brothers merged into the world's biggest media company in 1989. A decade later, Viacom and CBS set a new record for the largest corporate merger ever. And the 2000 AOL-TimeWarner merger was several times bigger than that.

The critics' logic is this: Citizens need access to diverse sources of news and opinions to make well-informed decisions about how to vote and live. Also, media should address the needs and interests of America's diverse population, and not just those of its elite. When a small group of "gatekeepers" controls how information circulates, the spectrum of available ideas, images, and opinions narrows. Big media companies prefer programming and voices that conform to

Offices in Berkeley, California, for KPFA, the flagship radio station of the independent Pacifica Broadcasting Network. Consolidated ownership of many local radio stations, most notably by Clear Channel Communications, has dramatically decreased local programming while increasing the number of syndicated shows that air simultaneously in multiple markets. (Courtesy of Jon Wagner)

their own financial interests, and they make it nearly impossible for smaller, independent companies to offer alternatives.

This frightening vision is intuitively reasonable. But a close look at decades of scholarship on the relationship between media ownership and content diversity uncovers a surprising story—one much more complicated than the vision of media monsters gobbling up diversity.

Scholars have zeroed in on three broadly defined types of diversity in media: format diversity, demographic diversity, and idea diversity. The research suggests that when it comes to "diversity," media-consolidation critics are, if not barking up the wrong tree, at least in need of a more nuanced, sharper, more carefully directed bark. Indeed, effective opposition to media ownership consolidation may require, ironically, acknowledging the ways media giants sometimes promote diverse content.

format diversity

Suppose you turn on your TV after dinner, and every single channel is broadcasting either an *American Idol* spin-off or a makeover show. That would mean the after-dinner time slot in your area lacks "format diversity"—or variety in programming—turning everything into, as FCC commissioner Adelstein describes it, "Big Mac, fries and a Coke." In particular, observers worry that consolidation undercuts local content. Most experts agree that this has happened to radio since the late 1990s, as Clear Channel Communications has gobbled up stations throughout the country. Programming that was once determined locally is now overseen by Clear Channel programmers headquartered elsewhere, and local disc jockeys have been replaced by a single show that plays simultaneously in multiple markets. Consolidation of radio ownership encourages this centralized, cost-cutting format. The same logic would be expected in newspapers and television; running wire service copy is cheaper than employing staff reporters, and standardized production is less expensive than hiring a team of local broadcasters.

Of course, because different audiences are attracted to different content and format types, it also makes business sense for a conglomerate to maintain different sorts of programming—including locally produced content—just as General Motors produces lines of cars for different types of customers. This can actually promote format diversity. In a market with three competing stations, argues communications law expert Edwin Baker, each station will try to attract the largest possible audience by providing fare that the majority prefers. The stations will wind up sounding pretty similar. In contrast, if all three stations are owned by the same company, ownership has no incentive to compete against itself, and will try to make the stations dissimilar in order to attract different audiences. Similarly, it makes sense for entertainment conglomerates to make their various holdings more rather than less distinct in format, and to build a "diverse portfolio" of media properties. Viacom does not want its UPN (*America's Next Top Model, The Parkers, WWE Smackdown*) to be like its CBS (*CSI, Judging Amy, Late Show with David Letterman*), its Sundance Channel (documentaries on HIV/AIDS, the films of Patrice Chereau) to air the same kind of material as its Spike TV (*Sports Illustrated's 40th Anniversary Swimsuit Special*), or its Downtown Press ("chick-lit" like Alexandra Potter's *Calling Romeo*) to publish what its Atria Press does ("academic" titles like bell hooks' *The Will to Change*). This multiple-brand logic promotes rather than reduces format diversity.

Research suggests that media consolidation does not simply increase or decrease format diversity. Some studies compare the fate of local or public-affairs programming in independent versus conglomerated companies. Others look for shifts in content after a publication is bought by a bigger company. The results are tellingly mixed. Some find big differences between the offerings of independent and corporate-owned outlets, but ambiguous effects on format diversity. Others find little or no difference at all. For example, a 1995 study found that two years after Gannett—owner of *USA Today*, among many other papers—bought the *Louisville Courier-Journal*, the paper devoted almost 30 percent more space to news than it had before, and 7 percent less space to advertising. On the other hand, the average story became shorter, the percentage of hard-news stories smaller, and wire stories came to outnumber staff-written ones. Within the expanded news reporting, the proportions of local, national, and international news changed little. The paper became more like *USA Today*, but simultaneously the "news hole"—the amount of content consisting of news reporting—increased from when it was independently owned. Other studies of Gannett-bought papers—in Arkansas and Florida—found that international and national news decreased after the company took over. Local news, often in the form of crime or disaster stories, actually increased after consolidation.

A recent large-scale, five-year study by the Project for Excellence in Journalism also found mixed results. The researchers asked who produces "higher-quality" local television news, which they defined as news that "covers the whole community," is "significant and informative," demonstrates "enterprise and courage," and is "fair, balanced, and accurate," "authoritative," and "highly local." Although they did not isolate "format diversity" in their study, they nonetheless offer some clues about the relationship between ownership and formats. On the one hand, just as anti-consolidation critics would predict, of 172 newscasts and 23,000 stories, researchers found the "best" programs overall tended to come from smaller station groups or from stations affiliated with but not owned by networks. On the other hand, they also found that "local ownership offered little protection against newscasts being very poor." As an evening's cursory viewing might confirm, local news is weak regardless of whether or not it is part of a conglomerate. Even more to the point, the researchers found that stations whose parent companies owned a newspaper in the same market—exactly the kind of "cross-ownership" that consolidation critics worry about— produced "higher-quality" newscasts, including more locally relevant content. They ran more stories on "important community issues" and fewer celebrity and human-interest stories. Cross-ownership shifted the types of programming provided, but in the direction most critics of cross-ownership seem to favor. Moreover, being owned by a small company, while an advantage when it came to "quality," was certainly no guarantee of a diverse mix of local and nonlocal content.

For a glimpse of how big media corporations— aided by government deregulation—sometimes do reduce format diversity, look at the current state of commercial radio. In a series of scathing articles for Salon, Eric Boehlert exposed Clear Channel as "radio's big bully," known for "allowing animals to be killed live on the air, severing long-standing ties with community and charity events, laying off thousands of workers, homogenizing playlists, and a corporate culture in which dirty tricks are a way of life." Concentrated, conglomerate ownership is certainly a prerequisite for being a big bully, and Clear Channel has used its power to undercut local programming and standardize rather than diversity both music and talk on radio. But radio's striking homogeneity is not just the result of concentrated ownership. As Boehlert wrote in 2001, radio "sucks" (similar-sounding songs, cookie-cutter stars) because record companies, through independent promoters, pay radio stations huge amounts to get their songs on playlists. With or without Clear Channel, material without money behind it—alternative styles of music, music by artists who do not fit the standard celebrity model, innovative and therefore risky formats— does not get airplay. It is not that ownership has no effect on format diversity, only that the impact is neither uniform nor inevitable. It is instead influenced by particular corporate strategies and the inner workings of particular media industries.

demographic diversity

In everyday conversations, diversity usually refers to demographics: whether a workplace employs or a school enrolls people of various racial, ethnic, gender, and economic categories. How the media represents and addresses the interests of America's diverse populations—who gets seen and heard—is, appropriately, often in question. Studies routinely find that the individuals appearing in mass media are disproportionately white, middle-class men between the ages of 20 and 60. But they have not figured out how, if at all, concentrated corporate ownership affects representation. This should not be surprising. A gap between the diversity of the population and media images of that population existed long before the rise of the media giants. And it clearly cuts across commercial and noncommercial media: studies of public broadcasting's guests show little demographic diversity, while daytime talk shows produced by for-profit conglomerates—however tawdry—offer some of the greatest demographic diversity on television.

Both government agencies and scholars have assumed that the key to ensuring demographically diverse content is demographically diverse ownership. Until recently, the FCC and the courts attempted to promote this kind of diversity by giving licensing preferences to minority-owned (and sometimes female-owned) broadcast stations. The FCC halted the licensing preferences in 1995, and the rapid consolidation of deregulated media companies makes it even less likely that companies and stations will be minority-owned today. Although it might seem reasonable to think that fewer minority-owned companies will mean less demographically diverse content—in surveys, minority owners do report being more likely to produce "minority" programming—studies of content do not back up such claims. Two studies comparing minority-owned (African American and Latino) radio stations to white-owned stations in the 1980s found that owners' ethnic backgrounds did not significantly affect demographic representation in their programming. There are many good reasons to pursue affirmative action in media ownership and employment, but ensuring diversity in media content is not one of them.

If anything has promoted demographic diversity in media content, it is the rise of niche-marketing and narrow-casting, which target previously excluded demographic groups with images of themselves. Although minority owners often typically start that process—gay marketers tapping the gay niche, Latino publishers targeting Latino readers—it proceeds regardless of whether they remain owners. Indeed, niche marketing has become a media-giant staple: Time Warner AOL started the highly successful *People en Español* in 1996, NBC-owned Bravo produced the summer 2003 hit *Queer Eye for the Straight Guy*. Robert Johnson became the first African-American billionaire when he sold Black Entertainment Television to Viacom in 2002, and the largest shareholder of radio's Hispanic Broadcasting Corporation is Clear Channel. Multicultural content and oligopoly media ownership are clearly not incompatible.

idea diversity

Almost everyone pays lip service to the notion that citizenship thrives when people are exposed to a variety of contending viewpoints. As the number of owners decreases, critics of media conglomeration argue, so does the number of voices contributing to the "marketplace of ideas." Media conglomerates with holdings in all kinds of other media and nonmedia industries have the power to censor the news in accordance with their interests. There is plenty of anecdotal evidence that consolidation tips content against ideas critical of the corporate owners. The *Los Angeles Times*, for example, failed in 1980 to cover a taxpayer-funded $2 billion water project that stood to benefit the Times-Mirror Company. Likewise, NBC remained silent on the 1990 boycott of their owner GE. And CBS's *America Tonight* show had a pro-tobacco bias in the mid-1990s, when the Loews Corporation, owner of Lorillard Tobacco, held a controlling interest in CBS. Disney-owned ABC News even cancelled an investigative report about sloppy background checks at Disney-world. A recent study also found a "synergy bias" among media giants, in which media companies slip unannounced promotions of their other products and services into newscasts—as when ABC devoted two hours of *Good Morning America* to Disneyworld's 25th Anniversary. In short, media corporations act in their own special interests, promote ideas that suit those interests, and sometimes "spike" stories through self-censorship.

Beyond these forms of direct self-interest, though, the connection between ownership concentration and idea diversity is harder to discern. Generally speaking, one might observe that the American media environment has been an inhospitable place for radical, dissenting voices before, during, and after the rise of media giants. More specifically, scholars have found that viewpoint diversity does not line up neatly with particular ownership structures. For example, the recent Project for Excellence in Journalism study of local television measured how many sources were cited in a story and how many points of view were represented in stories involving a dispute or controversy. Locally owned stations presented no more viewpoint diversity than nonlocally owned ones, and small companies no more than big ones. Network-owned-and-operated stations did better than smaller, less well-funded affiliates. The weak connection between viewpoint diversity and monopoly ownership is actually old news. In a classic 1985 study, Robert Entman examined the first page and editorial section of 91 newspapers in three types of markets: competitive local markets with multiple, separately owned papers; monopolistic markets with only one local newspaper; and "quasi-monopolies," where joint-owned or joint-operated papers share a market. He measured diversity as the number of people or organizations mentioned in each story, and the number of stories that presented conflicting opinions. The study found that on no measure did independent papers present more diversity than papers in monopoly or quasi-monopoly situations. In all of the papers, more than half the stories involved fewer than two actors, and less than one-tenth presented conflicting opinions. In other words, regardless of who owned them or how competitive their markets were, the papers were not exactly brimming with lively debate and diverse ideas.

the challenge for media reformers

The radical concentration of global media ownership has spawned at least one excellent, rebellious child: a vibrant, smart, broad-based media reform movement. Groups like Fairness & Accuracy in Reporting, the Media Alliance, the Center for Digital Democracy, Independent Media Centers, the People's Communication Charter, and many others, are growing in strength, alliance, and effectiveness. There are many reasons to object to media oligopolies that research on diversity does not speak to: the concentration of private power over a public resource in a democracy is wrong in principle; standardized media are part of a distasteful, branded, chainstore life of Barnes and Noble, Starbucks, and Disney; corporate, multinational media are increasingly unaccountable to the public; and a corporate press is probably a less adversarial press. But the research on media concentration should challenge this reform movement to relinquish at least one sacrosanct belief. If our goal is vibrant, diverse media content—what the People's Communication Charter, an international activist group, refers to as the "plurality of opinions and the diversity of cultural expressions and languages necessary for democracy"—then research suggests that concentrated ownership is not equivalent to reduced diversity. Sometimes corporate media giants homogenize, and sometimes they do not. Sometimes they shut people up and stifle dissent, and sometimes they open up extra space for new people to be visible and vocal. That they do so not because they are committed to the public good but because diversity sometimes serves their interests does not negate the outcome. And, romantic notions notwithstanding, independently owned and noncommercial media hardly guarantee diverse content.

Just as there are different kinds of diversity, there are also different kinds of ownership concentration. A single corporation might own all the major outlets in a single market, or a chain of newspapers, or a film production company and a theater chain, or music, television, and book companies. These different kinds of concentration promote and inhibit different kinds of content diversity. Researchers, activists, and policy makers must identify the conditions under which concentrated, conglomerated media ownership facilitates diverse media formats, opinions, and demographic representations. A genuine commitment to diverse media content may require an unsettling task: encouraging those conditions even while opposing the corporate domination of media, feeding the giants while trying to topple them.

RECOMMENDED RESOURCES

Ben H. Bagdikian. *The Media Monopoly,* 6th ed. (Beacon Press, 2000).

> In this new edition of a now classic book, Bagdikian presents an impassioned argument against media concentration.

C. Edwin Baker. *Media, Markets, and Democracy* (Cambridge University Press, 2002).

> Demonstrates that media products are not like other commodities, and he argues that market competition alone fails to give media audiences what they want.

Columbia Journalism Review. Who Owns What? www.cjr.org/tools/owners

> This informative Web site lists the holdings of approximately 50 major media companies.

Benjamin M. Compaine and Douglas Gomery. *Who Owns the Media? Competition and Concentration in the Mass Media Industry* (Lawrence Erlbaum Associates, 2000).

> Provides a detailed look at the current media industry and challenges common assumptions about the dangers of ownership concentration.

David Croteau and William Hoynes. *The Business of Media: Corporate Media and the Public Interest* (Pine Forge Press, 2001).

> Contrasts two different views of media conglomeration: the market model, which regards people as consumers, and the public-interest model, which regards people as citizens.

Robert M. Entman. "Newspaper Competition and First Amendment Ideals: Does Monopoly Matter?" *Journal of Communication* 35 (1985): 147–65.

> This study of newspapers in competitive and noncompetitive markets concludes that market competition does not guarantee content diversity.

Robert Horwitz. "On Media Concentration and the Diversity Question," Department of Communication, University of California, San Diego, 2003. http://communication.ucsd.edu/people/ConcentrationpaperICA.htm

> A careful discussion of the media ownership debate, empirical research and the virtues of a "mixed media system."

Philip M. Napoli. "Deconstructing the Diversity Principle." *Journal of Communication* 49 (1999): 7–34.

> Argues that the FCC policies on media ownership have long been based on unproven assumptions about the relationship between ownership diversity and content diversity.

REVIEW QUESTIONS

1. This essay describes a "weak connection" between idea diversity and ownership concentration. Although this seems counterintuitive, identify the evidence Gamson and Latteier use to support this idea.
2. "Niche marketing" and "narrowcasting" appear to promote diversity in the cultural industries, but discuss the effects of what might be considered a "ghettoization" or marginalization of representations of particular social groups and ideas.
3. Gamson and Latteier begin by identifying three types of diversity, and end with a puzzle: How does monopolist "corporate domination" foster the very diversity that it seems to hide? How do you see this conundrum affecting each type of diversity? How does media consolidation play a part?

4. Activity: Watchdog groups, such as F.A.I.R. (Fairness and Accuracy in Reporting) and Media Matters for America, worry that the control of news programming by corporations is not primarily driven by profits, but that it does lead to censorship of political and social ideas. Drawing from the extensive online reporting of these two watchdog organizations, use examples to write a paragraph on a potential conflict of interest for Viacom or AOL-Time Warner's news operations.

douglas hartmann

the sanctity of sunday football: why men love sports

15

fall 2003

the american male's obsession with sports seems to suggest that the love affair is a natural expression of masculinity. but sociologists have found that, conversely, sports teach men how to be manly, and studying sports reveals much about masculinity in contemporary america.

My father, a no-nonsense grade school principal, had little time for small talk, contemplation, or leisure—with one major exception: sports. He spent Sunday afternoons watching football games on television, passed summer evenings listening to Jack Buck announce St. Louis Cardinals baseball games, and took me to every sporting event in town. He coached all the youth sports his children played, and spent hours calculating team statistics, diagramming new plays, and crafting locker room pep talks. Though never a great athlete, his high school varsity letters were displayed in his basement work area; just about the only surefire way to drag Dad out of the house after a long day at work was to play "a little catch." Sports were one of the few topics he ever joked about with other men.

My father's fascination with sports was not unique. Though women are increasingly visible throughout the sporting world, more men than women play sports, watch sports, and care about sports. Is it any wonder that corporate advertising campaigns, drinking establishments, and movements such as the Promise Keepers all use sports to appeal to men? Or that sports figures so prominently in many books and movies dealing with men and masculinity in America?

Nevertheless, there is surprisingly little serious reflection about why this is the case. When asked why so many men are so obsessed with sports, most people—regardless of their gender or their attitudes about sports—say something to the effect that men are naturally physical and competitive, and that sports simply provide an outlet for these inherently masculine traits.

To sociologists, however, men love playing, watching, and talking sports because modern, Western sports—dominated as they are by men and by values and behaviors that are traditionally regarded as masculine—provide a unique place for men to think about and develop their masculinity, to make themselves men, or at least one specific kind of man.

where boys become men

Ask sports enthusiasts why they participate in sports and you are likely to get a wide variety of answers. "Because it is fun and exciting," some respond. Others say it is because they need the exercise and want to stay physically fit. Still others talk about sports providing them a way to relax and unwind, or about the thrill of competition—these responses are especially common for that large percentage of sports lovers whose "participation" mainly takes the form of being a fan or watching sports on television. These are important parts of sports' value, but they do not really explain why men are, on average, more likely to be involved in sports than women.

For many men, the love of sports goes back to childhood. Sports provided them, as young boys and teens, with a reason to get together, to engage with other boys (and men), and in doing so to begin defining what separates boys from girls: how to act like men. Barrie Thorne's study of grammar school playgrounds illustrates the phenomenon. Thorne finds that preadolescent boys and girls use recreation on the schoolyard to divide themselves along gender lines. How they play—for example, running around or quiet games—Thorne suggests, distinguishes male and female child behavior. As they get older, kids become more aware of these distinctions and increasingly use sex-segregated athletics to discuss and act out gender differences. Gary Alan Fine, in *With the Boys,* describes how much of the learning that happens in Little League baseball involves being tough and aggressive and dealing with injuries and other setbacks; and in off-the-field conversations young ballplayers learn about sex and about what it means to be a man as opposed to a "dork," a "sissy," or a "fag."

When Michael Messner interviewed retired athletes and asked them how they initially got involved with sports, they told him it had little to do with any immediate or natural attraction to athletics and was really based upon connecting to other boys and men. "The most important thing was just being out there with the rest of the guys—being friends," said one. Sports, according to Messner, "was something 'fun' to do with fathers, older brothers, uncles and eventually with same-aged peers."

Girls start playing sports for similar reasons, and children of both genders join in other activities, such as choir or community service, for social purposes, too. (Many boys and girls start to drop out of sports at about ages 9 or 10—when the sports they play become increasingly competitive and require them to think of themselves primarily as athletes.) What is distinctive about the experience of boys and young men in sports, however, is that the sporting world is organized and run primarily by men, and that athletic activities require attitudes and behaviors that are typically understood to be masculine.

Of course, not all boys play sports, and boyhood and adolescent experiences in sports are not uniformly positive. A great deal of the sociological research in this area focuses on the downside of youth sports participation. Donald Sabo, for example, has written extensively about the pain and violence, both physical and psychological, experienced by many boys who compete in athletics. And Harry Edwards has long argued that over-investing in sports can divert poor and minority youth from more promising avenues of upward mobility. But, despite the harsh realities, sports remains one of the few socially approved settings in which boys and men, and fathers and sons, can express themselves and bond with each other.

sport as a masculine enterprise

Once boys and girls separate in physical play, it does not take long for gendered styles of play to emerge. Study after study confirms what most soccer moms and dads already know:

When Michael Messner interviewed retired athletes and asked them how they initially got involved with sports, they told him it had little to do with any immediate or natural attraction to athletics and was really about connecting to other boys and men.

boys' athletics tend to be more physical and aggressive and put more emphasis on winning, being tough in the face of adversity, and dealing with injuries and pain. Even in elementary school, Thorne finds boys take up far more of the physical space of the playground with their activities than girls, who tend to play (and talk about their play) in smaller spaces and clusters.

People debate whether there is a physiological component to these differences, but two points are clear. First, parents, coaches, and peers routinely encourage such intensity among boys in youth sports. More than a few single mothers bring their boys to the teams I coach out of concern that their sons are insufficiently tough or physical because they lack a male influence. Messner writes about how he learned—against his inclinations—to throw a ball overhand with his elbow tucked in because his father did not want him to "throw like a girl." Stories about overly competitive, physically abusive coaches may be overplayed in the American media, but in many ways they are the inevitable consequence of the emphases many parents express.

Second, the behaviors and attitudes valued in men's and boys' athletics are not just about sports, but about masculinity more generally. The inherent connection of sports to the body, physical activity and material results, the emphasis on the merit of competing and winning, the attention to rules, sportsmanship and team play, on the one hand, and gamesmanship, outcomes and risk, on the other, are not just the defining aspects of male youth sport culture, but conform to what many men (and women) believe is the essence and value of masculinity. Female reporters, homosexual athletes, and men who challenge the dominant culture of men's sports—especially in the sacred space of the locker room—quickly learn that sports are not just dominated by men but also dominated by thinking and habits understood to be masculine (in opposition to the more nurturing values of compromise, cooperation, sympathy, understanding, and sharing typically associated with femininity). If the military is the quintessential institution of Western masculinity, then sports is surely a close second.

The notion that sports is a masculine enterprise is closely connected with the development of modern Western sports. As historians have detailed, middle- and upper-class men used sports in the nineteenth and early twentieth centuries to present and protect their particular notions of masculinity in both schools and popular culture (the classic literary expression being *Tom Brown's School Days*, a nineteenth-century English story of boarding school boys' maturation through hard-nosed sports). The media is a critical part of perpetuating sports' masculine ethos today, because most adults participate in sports as spectators and consumers. Not only are female athletes and women's sports downplayed by most sports coverage, but the media accentuates the masculinity of male athletes. For example, Hall of Fame pitcher Nolan Ryan's media coverage, according to a study by Nick Trujillo, consistently described him in terms of the stereotypical American man: powerful, hard-working, family patriarch, a cowboy, and a symbol of heterosexual virility. Such images not only define an athlete's personal qualities but legitimate a particular vision of masculinity.

The authority of the masculine ethos is underlined by the fact that so many female athletes

> Study after study confirms what most soccer moms and dads already know: boys' athletics tend to be more physical and aggressive and put more emphasis on winning, being tough in the face of adversity, and dealing with injuries and pain.

believe they can receive no higher compliment than to be told they "play like a man." Many feminists cringe at the irony of such sentiments. But they also realize that, while the explosion of women in sports has challenged their male dominance (2.5 million girls and young women participated in interscholastic sport in 2003, up from 300,000 in 1972—before Title IX's federal mandate for gender equality), women's sports have essentially been based upon the same single-minded, hypercompetitive masculine model. Not surprisingly, they are witnessing the emergence of the same kinds of problems—cheating, physical and emotional stress, homophobia, eating disorders—that have long plagued men's sports.

sports and maintaining masculinity

As the men Messner interviewed became more committed to being athletes, they began to construct identities and relationships that conformed to—and thus perpetuated—sport's masculine values. Athletes are so bound up with being men that when, in his initial interviews, Messner inadvertently referred to them as "ex-athletes," his interviewees responded as if he were taking away their identities, their very manhood. A professional baseball player expressed a similar sentiment when I asked how he dealt with his time on the disabled list last summer because of a serious arm injury: "I'd throw wiffle balls left-handed to my eight-year-old son—and I had to get him out! Just so I could feel like a man again."

Of course, few men participate in sports with the intensity of professional athletes. Those who cannot move up the competitive ladder can still participate in other ways—in recreational sports, in coaching, and perhaps, most of all, in attending sporting events, watching sports on television, and buying athletic gear and apparel. Indeed, it is in being a fan (derived from *fanatic*)

that the male slant of sports is clearest. While women often follow sports, their interest tends to be driven by social ends, such as being with family or friends. Male spectators are far more likely to watch events by themselves, follow sports closely, and be affected by the outcomes of games and the performance of their favored teams and athletes. The basic explanation is similar to the one developed out of sports activity studies: Just as playing sports provides many boys and young men with a space to become men, watching sports serves many men as a way to reinforce, rework, and maintain their masculinity—in these cases, through vicarious identification with masculine pursuits and idealized men. Writing of his obsession with 1950s football star Frank Gifford in *A Fan's Notes*, novelist Fredrick Exley explained: "Where I could not, with syntax, give shape to my fantasies, Gifford could with his superb timing, his uncanny faking, give shape to his." "I cheered for him with inordinate enthusiasm," Exley wrote, because he helped me find "my place in the competitive world of men . . . each time I heard the roar of the crowd, it roared in my ears as much for me as for him."

It was no accident that Exley chose to write about football. With its explicit appropriation of the rhetoric and tactics of combat, the sport supplanted baseball as the most popular spectator sport in the United States in the 1970s. Football's primary ideological salience, according to Messner, "lies in its ability . . . to symbolically link men of diverse ages and socioeconomic backgrounds. . . . Interacting with other men and interacting with them in this male-dominated space . . . [is] a way to assert and confirm one's own maleness. . . ." Being with other men allows males to affirm their masculine identity. Listen to today's sports talk radio. These programs are not only sophomorically masculine, many of them serve as little men's communities unto themselves: Tiger fan Jack; Mike from Modesto;

Jay the Packer's guy—even teams' announcers have unique personalities and identities, fostering the impression that this is an actual club where all the guys know each other.

The salience of sports as a medium to validate masculinity may be best illustrated when it is taken away. Journalist Susan Faludi reported on what happened when the original Cleveland Browns football team left town to become the Baltimore Ravens. The mostly working-class men who occupied the section of seats in Cleveland called the "Dawg Pound" talked about the team's departure with an overwhelming sense of loss and powerlessness. As it often is for former athletes, it was as if they'd had their manhood taken from them. In tearful media interviews, John "Big Dawg" Thompson compared the team's departure to witnessing his best friend die in the hospital.

sports as "contested terrain"

Critics of sports' heavy masculinity (most scholars doing work in this area are critics) have focused on its neglect or even exclusion of women. The way that golf outings perpetuate the privileges men enjoy in the corporate world is a frequent example. Others have gone so far as to suggest that the powerful appeal of sports for men arises because sports provide them at least symbolic superiority in a world in which men's real authority is in decline. As columnist and former professional basketball player Mariah Burton Nelson put it in the deliberately provocative title of her popular 1994 book, "The stronger women get, the more men love football."

In recent years, sociologists of sports have also begun to identify tensions within the masculine culture of athletics. Looking at Great Britain's soccer stars, for example, Garry Whannel has studied how the hedonism of the "new lad lifestyle" (as represented by players like David Beckham) rubs up against the disciplined masculinity traditionalists perceive to be necessary for international football success. Messner, for his part, has shown how "high status" men (white and from middle-class backgrounds) and "low status" men differently understood themselves as athletes. The former tended to transfer what they learned in sports about being men to pursuing success in other spheres, such as education and career. Men from lower status backgrounds saw sports as their only hope for success as a man—an accomplishment that the higher status men looked down upon as a narrow, atavistic type of masculinity. Expanding from this, some scholars have demonstrated that in popular culture the masculinity of African-American athletes is often exaggerated and linked to racial stereotypes about violence, risk, and threat. Basketball star Dennis Rodman, for example, gained notoriety by playing on his persona as a "bad" ball player. While problematic in many respects, these images of black masculinity can also provide African-American men with unique opportunities for personal advancement and broader political visibility (as I have suggested in my work on the 1968 black Olympics protest movement).

Such research has led many scholars to see sports not only as a place where mainstream masculine culture is perpetuated, but also a place where it is challenged and possibly changed. These issues have played out clearly in the debates over the implementation of Title IX legislation for women's equal access to sports. While still hotly contested (as evidenced by the recent controversy surrounding the all-male Augusta National Golf Club, as well as speculation that the legislation may be challenged in court by the Bush administration), Title IX has transformed men's relationship to sports, to women, and even to masculinity itself. Sports' most vital social function with respect to masculinity is to provide a separate space for men to discuss—often indirectly, through evaluations of favorite players or controversial incidents—what it is to be a real man. And that space is increasingly shared with women.

Some scholars envision new, more humane or even feminine sports—marked less by an emphasis on winning, record-setting, and spectatorship, and more by open participation, enjoyment, and fitness. Cross-cultural studies of sports show that these are real possibilities, that sports are not "naturally" and inherently masculine as Americans have long assumed. Sexism and homophobia, for example, have never been a real problem in Chinese sports, anthropologist Susan Brownell explains, because sports emerged there as a low-status activity that more powerful men felt no special compulsion to control or participate in. As a consequence, it is widely believed that a skilled female practitioner of kung fu should be able to defeat stronger but less-skilled men. At the same time, Brownell points out, the current proliferation of Western, Olympic-style sports in China seems to be contributing to the redefinition of gender roles there nearer the pattern of Western sports and masculinity.

playing deeply

In a famous paper on cockfighting in Bali, American anthropologist Clifford Geertz used the term "deep play" to capture the way fans make sense of such competitions as the cockfight, cricket, or American football. As passionate and articulate as they may be, these enthusiasts generally do not attempt to justify their pursuits. Instead, they downplay the significance of sports as separate from the serious concerns of real life. We can learn a great deal from such play, Geertz said, if we think about it as an "art form" which helps us figure out who people really are and what they really care about. Similarly, American men who love sports

may not be able to fully articulate and understand how it is part of their being men, but their passion for sports can certainly help us understand them and their masculinity.

This peculiar, "deep play" understanding of sports makes it difficult for most men to recognize or confront the costs and consequences that may come with their sports obsessions. But in many ways isn't this true of masculine culture in general? It makes male advantages and masculine values appear so normal and "natural" that they can hardly be questioned. Therein may lie the key to the puzzle connecting men and the seemingly innocent world of sports: they fit together so tightly, so seamlessly that they achieve their effects—learning to be a man, male bonding, male authority, and the like—without seeming to be doing anything more than tossing a ball or watching a Sunday afternoon game.

RECOMMENDED RESOURCES

Susan Birrell and Cheryl L. Cole, eds. *Women, Sport and Culture* (Human Kinetics, 1994).

> A collection of feminist critiques of sport that includes several influential contributions on men and masculinity.

Susan Brownell. *Training the Body for China: Sports in the Moral Order of the People's Republic* (University of Chicago Press, 1995).

> The chapters on sex, gender, and the body offer a fascinating cross-cultural contrast, and provide an introduction to sports in the nation that hosted the 2008 Olympics.

Varda Burstyn. *The Rites of Men: Manhood, Politics and the Culture of Sport* (University of Toronto Press, 1999).

> The most comprehensive treatment of the social, cultural, and historical forces that account for the relationship between men and sports in modern society.

Gary Alan Fine. *With the Boys: Little League Baseball and Preadolescent Culture* (University of Chicago Press, 1987).

> A pioneering field study from a noted sociologist of culture.

Robin D. G. Kelley. "Playing for Keeps: Pleasure and Profit on the Postindustrial Playground." In *The House that Race Built*. ed. Wahneema Lubiano (Pantheon, 1997).

> An ethnographically informed treatment of the opportunities basketball presents to inner-city African-American men produced by the country's preeminent historian of black popular culture.

Alan M. Klein. *Little Big Men: Bodybuilding Subculture and Gender Construction* (State University of New York Press, 1993).

> A vivid ethnography of competitive body builders on the West Coast that draws upon Robert Connell's seminal critique of the intersection of men's bodies, identities, and sexualities in masculine culture.

Michael Messner. *Taking the Field: Women, Men, and Sports* (University of Minnesota Press, 2002).

> The latest book from the leading scholar in the field. It exposes the ways in which men and women together use sports to define gender differences.

Brian Pronger. *The Arena of Masculinity: Sports, Homosexuality and the Meaning of Sex* (St. Martin's Press, 1990).

> Pronger explores the problematic connections between gender and sexuality in sport, highlighting its libidinal dimensions.

REVIEW QUESTIONS

1. Before reading this article, how might you have explained why men love sports? How would you explain it now?
2. The article doesn't mention the critical issue of class. How do you think social class affects perceptions of sports and participation in it?
3. It is interesting that two of the four stars mentioned in Hartmann's article—Dennis Rodman and David Beckham—have been just as noted for playing with gender roles as they are for playing their sport. Both are known as tough competitors, but are also known to wear eyeliner, pink nail polish, and feather boas. Do you think such infusions of complexity in the tight interplay of masculinity and sports affect the spectator's perception of gender roles? How do you feel these actions are judged as compared to, for example, the stereotypes surrounding a female softball player?
4. Activity: Research the sports programs at your campus. What are the facilities like? Do you find any inequalities in resources based on gender?

andrew m. lindner

controlling the media in iraq

16

spring 2008

the pentagon's embedded media program dramatically inhibited journalists' coverage of iraqi civilians' war experiences.

In 2003, nearly 600 journalists working for news agencies from around the world traveled along-side U.S. and coalition forces as they invaded Iraq. The Pentagon's embedded journalists program allowed reporters for the first time to attach themselves to military units. While Bush Administration officials hailed it for its intimate access to soldiers' lives, media watchdogs criticized its often restrictive nature and publicly worried reporters would do little more than serve up rosy stories about soldiers' courage and homesickness.

Critics also argued the embedding program was essential to the administration's attempt to build popular support for the war in Iraq. Several influential members of the Pentagon leadership and the administration believed the media contributed to defeat in the Vietnam War by demoralizing the American public with coverage of atrocities and seemingly futile guerilla warfare. They hoped to avoid a similar result in Iraq by limiting journalists' coverage of darker stories on combat, the deaths of Iraqi civilians, and property damage. As media commentator Marvin Kalb noted, the embedding program was "part of the massive, White House–run strategy to sell . . . the American mission in this war."

While anecdotal examples of the worst excesses of embedded reporters abound, only a few studies have systematically considered news coverage by embedded reporters. Those studies show the program provided reporters with an insider's view of the military experience, but also

essentially blocked them from providing much coverage of the Iraqi experience of the war.

By examining the content of articles rather than the tone, and comparing embedded and non-embedded journalists' articles, it becomes clear that the physical, and perhaps psychological, constraints of the embedding program dramatically inhibited a journalist's ability to cover civilians' war experiences. While most embedded reporters didn't shy away from describing the horrors of war, the structural conditions of the embedded program kept them focused on the horrors facing the troops, rather than upon the thousands of Iraqis who died.

By comparison, independent reporters who were free to roam successfully interviewed coalition soldiers and Iraqi civilians alike, covering both the major events of the war and the human-interest stories of civilians.

But given the far greater frequency and prominence of published articles penned by embedded journalists, ultimately the embedding program proved a victory for the armed services in the historical tug-of-war between the press and military over journalistic freedom during wartime.

war reporting in perspective

From the Pentagon's perspective, the embedding program represented a potential compromise in a long-standing conflict between the press and the military over journalistic free-

William Howard Russell is considered the first modern war reporter. In 1853 the London Times *dispatched him to Malta to cover English support for Russian troops in the Crimean War. (Library of Congress)*

doms in a war zone. In the past 150 years, with the growth of both contemporary warfare and the modern media apparatus, the armed forces and the press have often been at odds in a battle to control information dissemination.

While accounts of warfare go back as far as cave paintings, most war historians mark William Howard Russell, an Irish special correspondent for the *London Times*, as the first modern war reporter. In 1853, Russell was dispatched to Malta to cover English support for Russian troops in the Crimean War. His first-hand reports from the front lines, often criticizing British military leadership, were unique at the time and stirred up much controversy back in England, both rallying support from some quarters and scandalizing military leaders and

the royal family. Bending under political pressure, the *Times* agreed to a degree of self-censorship, but a precedent had been set and news consumers would continue to expect the same caliber of war coverage in the future.

Since Russell's time, the relationship between the media and military has undergone many transformations. During World War II, American military and political leaders carefully noted the morally reprehensible yet highly effective propaganda of the Nazi party, most notably Leni Riefenstahl's *Triumph of the Will*. They responded with their own propaganda series, *Why We Fight*, created through the combined talents of director Frank Capra and Disney's animation staff.

In terms of frontline coverage, the United States military exercised limited censorship with a largely cooperative and nationalistic press, yielding what military scholar Brendan McLane called, "from the military perspective . . . a golden age of war reporting." Even independently minded reporter Edward R. Murrow, later a hero to many journalists for his bold castigation of the McCarthy hearings, provided assurances of the moral righteousness of the American military campaign alongside vivid descriptions of Allied bombing raids.

By contrast, the low levels of censorship, convenient transportation, and the significant technological advancement of television made coverage of the conflict in Vietnam the ideal of war coverage for much of the press. Lyndon B. Johnson's administration policy of "minimum candor" with the press as well as the military's efforts to push only those stories that emphasized progress led to the widespread belief in a "credibility gap" between what government officials claimed and the reality of the situation.

However, even if military and political leaders were successful in obstructing journalists in the White House pressroom, the very nature of a guerilla conflict with an ever-shifting frontline gave journalists in Vietnam excellent access to soldiers and civilians alike. In addition, with the advent of television and advancements in the portability of TV cameras, reporters were able to transmit powerful images of the conflict into living rooms, censored only by editors' sense of propriety and Federal Communications Commission (FCC) regulations.

While collective memory of the journalism during the Vietnam War today tends to be of the courageous release of the Pentagon papers by *New York Times* reporters or the image of the free-roaming photojournalist played by Dennis Hopper in *Apocalypse Now*, it's worth noting that, for more than 10 years until the late 1960s, the majority of the press corps complacently accepted the official story. Nonetheless, the important distinction between the modes of war reporting in World War II and Vietnam is that war correspondents in Vietnam—David Halberstam, Stanley Karnow, and Peter Arnett among them—always had the opportunity to roam and report on the story they chose.

> The distinction between war reporting in World War II and Vietnam is that in Vietnam, journalists had the opportunity to roam and report on the story they chose.

More than three decades later, it has become axiomatic that most military leaders and many among the political right believe a liberal-leaning press corps "lost" the Vietnam War by demoralizing the public with horrific images and accounts of atrocities. And, indeed, this simmering resentment has made military-media relations since Vietnam incredibly tense. During the first Gulf War, the media furiously complained about the infamous "press pools" that forced journalists into parroting official press releases from military headquarters in Kuwait. On occasion, selected journalists were allowed to ride with military minders on a tour of the battlefield after the struggle had ended and the bodies were removed. In the mid-1990s, the military was left similarly fuming as journalists arrived in Somalia before the troops.

Pentagon leadership, well aware that an ongoing feud with the press was not in its best interests, formed two workgroups to study the issue of how better to manage the press in wartime. In 1984, under the leadership of Brigadier General Winant Sidle, a military panel was charged to examine how to conduct military operations while protecting military lives and the security of the operation but also keeping the American public informed through the media. In the wake of complaints about the Desert Storm press pools, military and media leaders met for the Pentagon-Media Conference in 1992 and agreed on several principles of news coverage in a combat zone.

In the intervening years prior to the embedding program, technological changes once again altered the nature of war reporting. As satellite phones became more portable journalists became more self-sufficient, able to coordinate with newsrooms and feed reports, images, and video instantaneously. The newfound capacity of journalists to transmit information on the spot presented a new set of threats to operational security. Without the traditional lag-time of war reporting, even well-intentioned journalists might accidentally reveal information of strategic significance, such as locations or troop levels. Based on the recommendations of the various workgroups and the practical consequences of technological innovation, Pentagon officials began to develop training programs and other provisions for embedding in the next major conflict.

into the fray

In 2002, as the specter of conflict with Iraq began to loom larger, Pentagon officials announced a week-long "Embed Boot Camp" for journalists hoping to participate in the program. Reporters were outfitted with Kevlar helmets and military garb, slept in barracks bunks, and ate military grub in the mess hall aboard the USS *Iwo Jima*. Marines trained them in military jargon, tactical marches, direct fire, nuclear-biological-chemical attacks, and combat first aid.

Perhaps more significantly, embedded reporters were forced to sign a contract and agree to the "ground rules"—allow their reports to be reviewed by military officials prior to release, to be escorted at all times by military personnel, and to allow the government to dismiss them at any time for any reason.

Before a single word was printed, many speculated that embedded reporters would fall victim to Stockholm Syndrome, the condition, named after a notorious 1973 incident in the Swedish city, in which hostages begin to identify with their captors. Media commentators like Andrew Jacobs at *The New York Times*, Richard Leiby at *The Washington Post*, and Carol Brightman at *The Nation* argued that as embedded journalists became socialized into military culture, they would develop relationships with the soldiers and start reporting from the military point of view.

While labeling this condition Stockholm Syndrome is perhaps slightly inflammatory, much sociological research suggests socialization is one of the military's greatest strengths. In his classic collection of essays, *Asylums*, Erving Goffman noted the military is a total institution that not only controls all an individual's activities, but also informs the construction of identity and relationships. In total institutions, such as the military, prison, or mental institutions, Goffman argued, the individual must go through a process of mortification that undercuts the individual's civilian identity and constructs a new identity as a member of the institution. In such a communal culture, individuality is constantly repressed in the name of the institution's larger values and goals.

In the case of embedded journalists, it's easy to imagine how they might have come to identify with the military mission or, at the very least, the other members of their units. In addition to wearing military-issue camouflage uniforms, embedded journalists had to share living and sleeping space as well as food and water with their units. If embedded reporters ended up telling the story of the war from the soldiers' point of view, as so many critics charged, it would simply be the natural and expected result of a process of re-socialization.

However, a different, and arguably more compelling, explanation exists for why embedded reporters might depict the war in a military-centric manner: they didn't have the freedom to roam. George C. Wilson, for example, embedded for *National Journal*, compared it to being the second dog on a dogsled team, writing, "You see and hear a lot of the dog directly in front of you, and you see what is passing by on the left and right, but you cannot get out of the traces to explore intriguing sights you pass, without losing your spot on the moving team."

Many sociological studies have observed that journalists, whether reporting from a newsroom in New York or a bunker in Baghdad, encounter what Mark Fishman has called a "bureaucratically constructed universe." The constraints of journalists' "universes" lead them to make certain assumptions, engage in specific practices, and only pursue particular types of stories. For example, a typical beat reporter is constrained by technical requirements such as word counts, the publication's ideological commitments, and professional ideas about what is and isn't newsworthy.

Several commentators, notably Michael Massing in the *New York Review of Books*, argued that in addition to these common limitations, the embedding program made covering soldiers' experiences easy, while covering the experiences of Iraqi civilians was difficult, if not impossible. From the Pentagon's perspective, the ease of access to soldiers was the essential strength of the embedding program. As Deputy Assistant Secretary of Defense for Public Affairs Bryan Whitman told *The Nation*, "you get extremely deep, rich coverage of what's going on in a particular unit."

alternatives to embedding

Although the embedding program was the dominant form of reporting during the early days of Operation Iraqi Freedom, two alternatives did exist. Though slightly more expensive than embedding, some news organizations opted to station a reporter in Baghdad. These journalists bunkered down at the Sheraton Ishtar or the Palestine Hotel in central Baghdad and watched as the American "shock and awe" bombing raid wrought death and destruction on the city.

During the first few weeks of the war, many Baghdad-stationed journalists attended briefing sessions led by Iraqi government officials and were escorted on tours of the city by official Iraqi minders. As Saddam Hussein's government collapsed, Baghdad-stationed reporters took to the streets to cover the conflict and its consequences, either alone or with hired bodyguards.

The second alternative—funding an independent reporter with the freedom to roam—was far more costly and largely the province of elite news sources, particularly *The New York Times* and other national newspapers and wire services. In the weeks and months before the conflict began, many of these independent reporters traveled through Iran or Turkey into Iraqi Kurdistan and followed the slow advance of Kurdish forces and U.S. Special Forces toward Kirkuk and Mosul. Other independent reporters, after hiring a four-wheel-drive vehicle and private security team, fanned out across the country,

often buckling down in potential battlegrounds like Fallujah and Basrah. While ground commanders interacted positively with independent reporters, on several occasions Pentagon officials criticized what they called "four-wheel-drive" and "cowboy" journalists for operating outside of the embedding program.

Like the embedded reporters, the other two arrangements for reporting from Iraq—being stationed in Baghdad or independent—represent distinct journalistic social locations (often defined in sociology as sets of rules, expectations, and relations based on status) that channeled journalists toward producing certain types of content and limited access to other types.

While embedded reporters had nearly unlimited access to coalition soldiers, Baghdad-stationed reporters would seem to have the most extensive access to Iraqi civilians. Although media accounts have suggested both embedded and Baghdad-stationed reporters presented a narrow view of the war, we would expect independent reporters, with the freedom and resources to roam at will were the least constrained of the three types of journalists, and, therefore, most likely to produce articles that balanced the Iraqi and the military experiences of the war.

Nonetheless, given that embedded reporting was the dominant form of reporting from Iraq (both in sheer numbers and in prominence), if the claims regarding embedding are true, then the vast majority of the news coming out of Iraq may have emphasized military successes and the heroics of soldiers, rather than the consequences of the invasion for the Iraqi people.

the embedding effect

Much of the existing systematic research on the embedding program has focused on the issue of rhetorical tone. Adopting an approach similar to the Stockholm Syndrome explanation, these researchers have argued that embedded reporters tend to sympathize with the soldiers they cover and adopt a more supportive tone when describing the mission in Iraq.

For example, a 2005 cross-cultural study of various network and cable television news programs found 9 percent of embedded reporters adopted a supportive tone as opposed to only 5.6 percent of "unilateral" reporters. Another 2006 study of 452 articles from American national daily newspapers found that compared to non-embedded reporters, embedded reporters produced coverage significantly more positive about the military and "implied a greater trust toward military personnel." Research by the same group of scholars found similar results in broadcast news. These studies clearly suggest the embed-

ding program encourages journalists to adopt a positive outlook on both the soldiers with whom they live and the military mission as a whole.

While these findings tell us much about the social psychological consequences of embedding, without considering the actual content of news reports it's difficult to answer the more sociological question of how the various journalistic social locations inhibited or enabled journalists' access to various types of stories. The only research to address the substantive content of embedded reporting is a 2004 Project for Excellence in Journalism (PEJ) study that examined 108 embedded reports from 10 different television programs. Among the results, PEJ found 61 percent of reports were live and

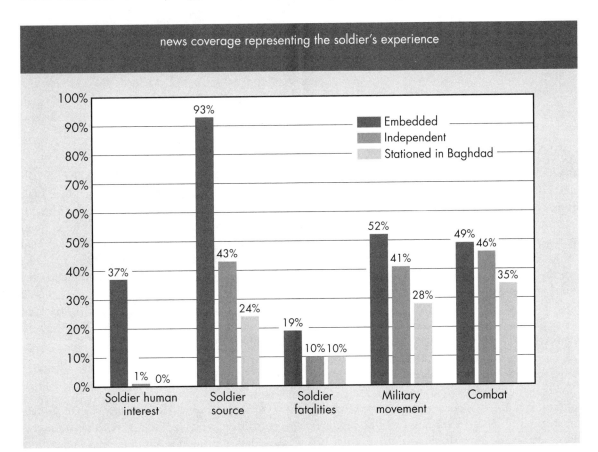

news coverage representing the soldier's experience

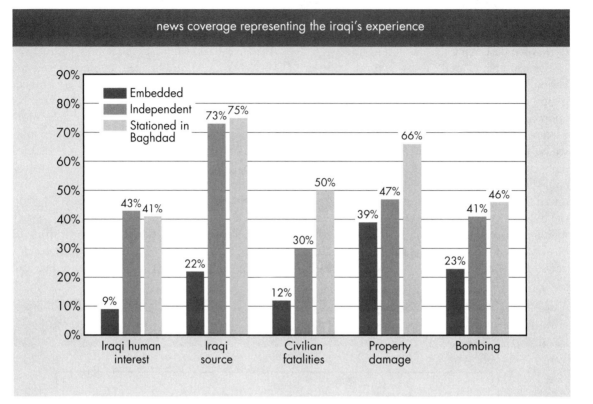

news coverage representing the iraqi's experience

Embedded
Independent
Stationed in Baghdad

Iraqi human interest: 9%, 43%, 41%
Iraqi source: 22%, 73%, 75%
Civilian fatalities: 12%, 30%, 50%
Property damage: 39%, 47%, 66%
Bombing: 23%, 41%, 46%

unedited, 21.3 percent showed weapons fired, and combat was the most commonly discussed topic, covered in 41 percent of stories. Unfortunately, the PEJ study didn't incorporate a comparison group of non-embedded journalists. Without such a group, we can't compare the effects of various journalistic contexts on cultural production.

A study of the substantive content produced by embedded reporters and both types of non-embedded reporters would allow us to consider two questions of considerable sociological interest. First, we can better understand how institutional contexts in a war zone can shape the ability of journalists to report on various types of stories (or speak to varying types of people). By contrast, while a study of tone can tell us

about how context shapes affective dispositions and/or ideological commitments, it does little to answer more concerning questions of limitations of access. Second, by focusing on content rather than tone, we learn more about what kind of information news consumers received. The capacity of governments to influence the types of information citizens have access to is an enduring theme of sociology, harking back to preeminent social thinkers from Karl Marx to C. Wright Mills.

a soldier's eye view

To consider how the context of the embedding program may have limited journalists' access and, thus, information about the war to the wider public, two research assistants and I studied five articles by each of the English-language print reporters in Iraq during the first six weeks of the war. We coded 742 articles by 156 journalists for five types of news coverage representing the soldier's experience of the war and five types representing the Iraqi civilians' experience. By comparing the differences in news coverage among embedded, independent, and Baghdad-stationed journalists, we are better able to understand how these different journalistic social locations may have limited reporters' ability to present a balanced portrayal of the war.

To capture the extent to which journalists depicted the soldier's experience in Iraq, we recorded the frequency of news coverage of combat, military movement, soldier fatalities, the use of a soldier as a source, and the inclusion of a soldier human interest story. As the results dramatically demonstrate, embedded reporters provided the most extensive coverage in all five categories representing the soldier's experience of the war. Such thorough coverage of military happenings is perhaps unsurprising, considering embedded journalists used a soldier as a source in 93 percent of all articles, more than twice as frequently as independent journalists.

More remarkable in light of much of the criticism of the embedding program is the fact that embedded reporters wrote about technical and often gritty subjects like combat and military movement in about half the articles. Clearly the common claim that embedded reporters wrote only "fluff pieces" about homesick soldiers is patently false (although soldier human interest stories were fairly common, appearing in 37 percent of all articles by embedded reporters).

Nonetheless, it's worth noting that Baghdad-stationed reporters, and in particular independent reporters, were fairly effective at portraying the military perspective of the war. Though both types of non-embedded reporters rarely covered soldier human interest stories, they both used soldiers as sources and covered combat and military movement in a quarter or more of the articles. In fact, independent reporters covered the "hard facts" of the war (like combat and military movement) nearly as frequently as embedded reporters.

To document the extent of news coverage of the Iraqi civilian experience of the war, we noted the frequency of coverage of bombings, property damage, civilian fatalities, the use of an Iraqi civilian as a source, and the inclusion of an Iraqi human interest story. The results show embedded reporters put forward a highly military-focused vision of the war, covering bombing and civilian fatalities and using Iraqis as a source far less frequently than either independents or reporters stationed in Baghdad.

Baghdad-stationed reporters provided the most extensive coverage of the consequences of the invasion, reporting on bombing, property damage, and/or civilian fatalities in half the articles. While independent reporters didn't conduct all types of coverage as well as Baghdad-stationed reporters, they used an Iraqi source in nearly three quarters of the articles and covered Iraqi human interest stories in 43 percent of their articles.

Most troubling of all the disparities among embedded, Baghdad-stationed, and independent journalists is in their respective coverage of civilian fatalities. While estimates of Iraqi civilian fatalities during this period of the war vary widely, at least 2,100 civilians died during the first six weeks of the invasion. Though civilian deaths were acknowledged in half the

> Civilian deaths were acknowledged in half the articles by Baghdad-stationed reporters, 30 percent of articles by independent reporters, and only 12 percent of articles by embedded reporters.

articles by Baghdad-stationed reporters and 30 percent of articles by independent reporters, only 12 percent of articles by embedded reporters noted the human toll of the war on the Iraqi people.

These findings strongly suggest the Pentagon's embedding program—the dominant journalistic arrangement during the Iraq War—channeled reporters toward producing war coverage from the soldier's point of view. While Baghdad-stationed reporters were similarly narrow in covering the Iraqi civilian experience of the war, independent reporters, who had freedom to roam and chose their sources and topics, produced the greatest balance between depicting the military and the Iraqi experience of the war.

Although the embedding program didn't print only good news, it did tend to emphasize military successes while downplaying the war's consequences. With upwards of 90 percent of articles by embeds using soldiers as a source, as long as the soldiers stayed positive, the story stayed positive. And thus, an administration that hoped to build support for the war by depicting it as a successful mission with limited costs was able to do so through the embed program and without some of the more heavy-handed propaganda efforts of Operation Desert Storm.

It's important to remember the embedding program was the only officially sanctioned mode of reporting, so we can't say the three arrangements for journalists painted a complete portrait of the war. A full 64 percent of print journalists in Iraq were embedded (the figure is even higher among TV journalists). In terms of visibility, the imbalance toward embedded coverage is even more striking—of the 186 articles in the sample that ultimately appeared on the front page of a newspaper, 71 percent were written by embedded reporters. Based on the content of articles by embedded journalists and the overwhelming dominance of the embedding program, it seems clear that, in the aggregate, the majority of the news coverage of the war was skewed toward the soldier's experience and failed to fully recognize the extent of the human and material costs.

embedding, then and now

The embedding program—the dominant journalistic arrangement during the Iraq War—channeled reporters toward producing war coverage from the soldier's point of view.

Shortly after President George W. Bush declared an end to "major combat" in Iraq in 2003, most embedding terms came to an end. For a time, Iraq was considered safe enough by most Western media outlets that journalists rented houses in Baghdad or freely traveled throughout the country. By September 2006 only 11 journalists were embedded with units in Iraq. However, as insurgent resistance grew many were forced to retreat to the safety of hotels protected by blast walls, occasionally taking excursions in armored cars with Iraqi bodyguards.

Today, a variation on the original embedding program exists, with journalists "embedding" with units on a particular mission or for shorter periods of time. Even journalists committed to depicting the Iraqi experience of the ongoing conflict, such as Jon Lee Anderson of *The New Yorker*, have traveled on brief stints with Army units because it's one of the least dangerous ways to cover the insurgency.

At the same time, the rules of the embedding contract have become more restrictive. In June 2007, The *New York Times* reported that embedded reporters would now be required to obtain signatures of consent before mentioning the names of soldiers used in moving or still images as well as in audio recordings. Some journalists have contended the new rules further enhance the military's ability to limit the release of undesirable news.

In the case of a future large-scale invasion (in Iran or Somalia, for example), both Pentagon officials and media industry leaders have indicated an interest in reviving the full embedding program. Should this happen, both sides must reconsider the nature of the embedding program, given its well documented pattern of leading journalists to produce reports that present the military in a more positive and less objective light.

RECOMMENDED RESOURCES

Jon Lee Anderson. *The Fall of Baghdad* (Penguin Press, 2004).

> A beautifully written and vivid portrait of the first six weeks of the war by a Baghdad-stationed reporter.

Department of Defense. "Pentagon Embedding Agreement." February 23, 2003.

> The contract journalists must sign before embedding with a military unit.

Department of Defense. "CJCS Media-Military Relations Panel (Sidle Panel)." August 23, 1984.

> The report of the findings of the Sidle Panel, which led to the development of the embedding program.

Mark Fishman. *Manufacturing the News* (University of Texas Press, 1980).

> An excellent sociological account of the journalistic process.

Andrew Jacobs. "My Week At Embed Boot Camp." *The New York Times Magazine*, February 3, 2003.

> A fascinating description of the activities at embed boot camp and the enthusiasm of military officials and journalists alike about the program.

REVIEW QUESTIONS

1. How has this article influenced your understanding of the relationship between journalism and war?
2. The author offers two ideas of how embedded reporters come to write from a military point of view. Discuss the theories of empathy through socialization (at the extreme, Stockholm Syndrome) versus boundaries and limitations imposed by the military.
3. What do you make of the findings that embedded journalists reported more frequently from a soldier's point of view?
4. Activity: Find a news story on military conflict in Iraq or Afghanistan (or some other location of your own choosing). Read the story and try to figure out whether the author was embedded, independent, or stationed. What are some of the clues you found in the story? How might the story be different if it had been written by one of the other types of reporters?

geoff harkness

hip hop culture and america's most taboo word

summer 2008

long used by african american artists, "the n-word" is increasingly employed by latino rappers as well. context and history are paramount to its acceptability.

When Sonny Black raps, the words sound like gunfire. This could have something to do with the fact that Black was shot twice by rival gang members last year, or that he hails from Logan Square, one of the grittier neighborhoods on the north side of Chicago. It certainly has something to do with his membership in 108, a hardcore rap outfit that's created a buzz in the city's hip hop underworld.

But there's also something about Black's lyrics and inflection that set him apart. While his bandmates rap with ironic winks of the eye, Black delivers every line at face value. His rhymes are gleefully violent and willfully aggressive, with nary a sense of humor to temper the savage images.

Tonight Black and 108 are performing at Club Capitol, a former strip joint that still features a dancer's pole running through its tiny stage. 108 enter from the wings, 10 members strong, and the crowd erupts, pushing forward to get a closer look. Superfans in the front row cheer and raise their hands toward the ceiling, exposing a series of forearm-length "108" tattoos of various design.

Black steps forward for a solo number and the place goes berserk. He performs a song titled "Watch Yo' Mouth," and in less than 90 seconds covers a range of topics including drug dealing, gangbanging, shooting cops, having sex, and boasts of being a "career criminal." He punctuates each stanza with a warning that sounds more like a threat.

Watch yo' mouth, nigga, watch yo' mouth, nigga.

Sonny Black is Latino.

taboo for whom?

The n-word was part of "street" language long before hip hop ever existed. Given sociologist Charis Kubrin's finding that commercial rappers inject linguistic cues from street language into mainstream rap songs, it's not unusual to hear black and Latino rappers utter the n-word onstage, in the studio, and in conversation. They apply the word to people of all races, including whites, most of whom are reluctant to use it themselves.

Urban scholar Alejandro Alonso has argued that non-blacks who use the n-word should "expect a certain level of backlash regardless of context," but this doesn't seem to prove true for Latino rappers. Acts such as Fat Joe, Cypress Hill, and Cuban Link are among those who use the word in standard vernacular; their works are evidence of how the word has filtered into Latinos' music.

Specifically in Chicago, the site of research that inspires this article, use of "nigga" by

Latinos and blacks is commonplace. Not every Latino or black rapper says it—the term appears more frequently in "gangsta" rap circles than other forms of the genre—but many do. Despite its widespread use by Latino hip hoppers, Latinos have been largely absent from the ongoing debate over who—if anyone—is "allowed" to say America's most taboo word.

In *The N Word: Who Can Say It, Who Shouldn't, and Why*, Jabari Asim notes that "most whites now adhere to post–civil rights notions of public decorum," and avoid voicing the term publicly. When someone violates this norm it can make the evening news. Former *Seinfeld* actor Michael Richards torpedoed his career in late 2006 during an n-word laced altercation with hecklers in a Los Angeles nightclub. In 2007, Duane "Dog" Chapman, star of the popular TV show *Dog the Bounty Hunter*, found himself in hot water after a recording of him using the term surfaced. Chapman issued a formal apology and confessed to talk show host Larry King, but the A&E network placed his top-rated show on hiatus and said it hoped Chapman would continue "the healing process that he has begun." (Satisfied he had done so, the network resurrected the show earlier this year.)

Rap's close relationship with the n-word has raised hackles in Washington, D.C., particularly as hip hop culture has become increasingly synonymous with youth culture. In September 2007 the House Energy and Commerce subcommittee held hearings over the negative language, violent images, and misogyny found in rap music. The hearings weren't the first time rap music was singled out for the proliferation of the n-word, and some critics have linked its increased use to larger social declines within the black community.

Actor/comedian Bill Cosby raised eyebrows during a 2004 speech in which he condemned gangsta rap music and culture, blaming it for the suffusion of the n-word.

Frank Nit believes African Americans and Puerto Ricans have biological and socioeconomic bonds that make it okay for Puerto Ricans to use the n-word. (Courtesy of Frank Nit)

"When you put on a record, and that record is yelling 'nigger this' and 'nigger that' and cursing all over the thing and you got your little 6-year-old and 7-year-old sitting in the back seat of the car . . . what are you saying to your children?" he asked the audience, which roundly applauded the diatribe.

Black scholar Michael Eric Dyson fired back the following year with the retort *Is Bill Cosby Right? (Or Has The Black Middle Class Lost Its Mind?)*. Dyson affirmed the latter question, castigating the elite black "Afristocracy" for its attacks on the "Ghettocracy," or black poor. In a 2005 interview, Dyson "retired" his own use of the word, but said that he had "no problem with its use by hip hoppers who continue to use it with verve, color, imagination, love and affection."

Harvard professor Randall L. Kennedy disagreed, blaming hip hop culture for an increase dissemination of the n-word but conceding that rappers eschew "nigger" in favor of the somewhat softer "nigga," and that the term is an important aspect of hip hop identity. In a 2007 interview, scholar Cornel West enjoined rappers to be "more sensitive to the vicious history of the n-word. I know that 'nigga' as opposed to 'nigger' is a term of endearment for some young people[But the history of 'nigger' with its connotation of self-hatred and self-disrespect needs to be acknowledged."]

Alonso asserts that a common belief in the black community is that the n-word should be used exclusively by blacks. This perspective, he writes, has resulted in a double standard—blacks can say it, non-blacks can't.

> A common belief in the black community is that the n-word should be used exclusively by blacks. This perspective has resulted in a double standard—blacks can say it, non-blacks can't.

Perhaps a better understanding, though, lies in looking beyond the notion of a double standard to examine how hip hop has blurred existing racial distinctions.

In hip hop culture, differing sets of norms regulate use of the n-word. These rules are dependent upon context as well as one's position in the racial hierarchy. At the top are blacks, who are "allowed" use the word freely and without penalty; for whites, at the bottom, the word remains largely taboo. The rules are less concrete, however, for non-black ethnic minorities, who fall somewhere between blacks and whites in hip hop's racial stratification.

In particular, Latinos (especially Puerto Ricans) are exempt from n-word regulation under many contexts. It's not a double standard, but a lack of an agreed-upon set of standards—even within ethnic groups—that underscores the fluid, socially constructed nature of race and authenticity. This serves as a powerful example of how people of all ethnicities contribute to and reshape the meaning of hip hop culture.

In his book *Colored White*, David Roediger details the black community's long-standing derision of Caucasians who try to act "too black" or adopt black culture falsely, invoking one of hip hop's more frequent issues: authenticity or "keeping it real."

Authenticity is that which is deemed to be genuine, original, and representing some sort of inherent or pure quality. Kembrew McLeod further argues that hip hop authenticity can be defined along six dimensions, one of which is this [contrast between black "realness" and white "fakeness."]

Drawing upon these notions, use of the n-word by black rappers might function as a means of preserving hip hop culture's "pure" or authentic black core, a symbolic boundary that creates ingroup-outgroup distinctions between "real" rappers who can use the term and "fake" rappers who can't.

do the white thing

Within subcultures, however, boundaries can be flexible. Sociologist Andy Bennett argues that hip hop culture—and its accompanying themes of authenticity—is under constant revision as various youth groups throughout the world adopt it. This notion of cross-cultural pollination is hardly new. In his famous 1957 essay "The White Negro," Norman Mailer describes "urban adventurers who drifted out at night looking for action with a black man's code to fit their facts. The hipster had absorbed the existentialist synapses of the Negro, and for practical purposes could be considered a white Negro." White negros, Mailer wrote, resist mainstream "white" society, and immerse themselves in black culture, taking cues from its linguistic, stylistic, and musical practices.

Mailer's hipsters reverberate in contemporary studies of whites who submerge themselves in hip hop culture. In her ethnography of British "wiggers" ("white niggers") Anoop Nayak suggests that white appropriation of hip hop culture has led to a sort of racial hybridity that bodes well for race relations. This cultural adaptation, she writes, "may be seen as postcolonial forms of mimicry that subvert, parody and reconfigure whiteness, race and nationhood, setting it free from any a priori sense of biological origins." In *Why White Kids Love Hip Hop*, Bakari Kitwana goes so far as to say that we live in an "age of appropriation," where black styles are assumed with progressive frequency by others. "Hip hop, for today's average kid—black or white—is just another part of growing up," pop-culture maven Charles Aaron writes.

> The rules are less concrete for non-black ethnic minorities, who fall somewhere between blacks and whites in hip hop's racial stratification.

Latino rapper Eoshel thinks the "n-word" will remain part of rap parlance. (Courtesy of Geoff Harkness)

There are limits, however, to racial hybridity. Kennedy explains that white use of the n-word is taboo because it's understood to be negative and racist, but black use of the term is construed in a positive manner.

"I would never say that word," avows T-Scar, a white rapper from the Chicago suburbs. "Hip hop was started by black people, so for me to say the n-word would just be disrespectful to everybody that built this culture strong enough so that I could participate in it."

For T-Scar and his like-minded white peers, using the word is dishonest—they don't employ it in their everyday speech, and so to use it onstage or in the studio would mean commiting hip hop's deadliest sin of being inauthentic, or untrue to their social lives. Others sidestep the word out of very real fears for their physical safety. "I don't use it 'cause I don't want to get my ass kicked," says white rapper Mike Don.

Sociologists Michele Lamont and Virag Molnar note that boundaries "separate people into groups and generate feelings of similarity and group membership. They are an essential medium through which people acquire status and monopolize resources." In this sense, "nigga" is hip hop's most powerful word, as a valuable status symbol and resource for those who are "allowed" to use it and a means of both dividing "authentic" rappers from fake and creating race-based distinctions between different groups of rappers.

latino roots and contours

So long as it isn't used pejoratively toward African Americans (including its "er" form), the word seems to be acceptable for Latino rappers in most situations, because contexts and history are paramount.

African Americans commonly invoke images of historical slavery and the general struggle for civil rights in the United States to explain why the boundary exists for whites but not Latinos. "If some Spanish dude is like 'nigga this,' 'nigga that,' I don't think he's thinking, 'You a nigga, and I'm a higher species,'" Wondur, a Chicago-based black rapper, explains. "Whereas you hear that shit out of a white dude's mouth, it goes right back to where it came from," meaning slavery and notions of white superiority.

"I can understand why the Latinos can do it, but the white people can't," says QT, a black rapper who uses the term frequently. "They can use it cause they ain't nothing but us, man. They do the same shit we do. They trapped, they grinding, they hard. Plus, they weren't the people that enslaved us. I'm keepin' it real, man. The Caucasian folks enslaved us. So when they say the word nigger, of course it would offend us."

Like blacks, Latinos also invoke historical images and lineages when explaining why they get an n-word pass, although this often occurs within a context of the Latino contribution to hip hop culture. Though hip hop is sometimes portrayed as having grown strictly out of African American culture, in reality it was the product of black interaction with a variety of ethnic groups, including large numbers of Latinos, particularly those of Puerto Rican descent. In *Puerto Rocks: Rap, Roots, and Amnesia*, Juan Flores argues that Latinos have been sorely overlooked in hip hop history and writes of the sense of "instant amnesia" that occurred as rap become increasingly commercial.

"When the media puts a face on hip hop, automatically the first face they put on it is a black face. But we all know that hip hop was started by blacks and Latinos. This was put on it when capitalism came into this music," says O-Zone, a Dominican DJ and producer.

In 2001, Latina actress/singer Jennifer Lopez caused a minor scandal when she dropped an n-bomb in her song "Jenny From the Block." Some media pundits took her to task for it, but the controversy blew over quickly. Black comedian Paul Mooney defended her right to use the term based on her Puerto Rican heritage: "Puerto Ricans and Cubans, aren't they black?" he asked. "I just thought they were niggas that could swim."

Kidding aside, many Chicago hip hoppers share the perception that African Americans and Puerto Ricans have a unique relationship. Rapper Frank Nit believes the two communities have biological and socioeconomic bonds that exempt Puerto Ricans from regulation of the n-word. Thus, it's a word he uses frequently, both onstage and in his everyday speech. Unlike some Latinos, who are cautious not to use the word in certain contexts (as an insult, for example), Nit uses it without restraint.

"Black people consider me to be black," he insists. "They understand that as Puerto Ricans, we've had it bad, too. I could say 'nigga' a thousand times and no one would care."

Pinqy Ring, who bills herself as the Puerto Rican Princess of Chicago and who uses the n-word onstage and in her everyday speech, also draws upon historical and biological connotations that link blacks and Puerto Ricans. These associations give Puerto Ricans a unique claim to "authentic" hip hop culture that isn't shared by whites—or perhaps other Latinos.

"Puerto Ricans were oppressed and the African Americans were oppressed," Ring explains. "Puerto Ricans have Taino Indian and African

> Though hip hop is sometimes portrayed as having grown strictly out of African American culture, in reality it was the product of black interaction with a variety of ethnic groups, including large numbers of Latinos, particularly Puerto Ricans.

in our blood. We can all appreciate the struggle that our families have been through, take it and make it something beautiful, make it something that we can call our own."

unattended funeral

Not everyone in Chicago believes it's a good idea for Latino rappers to say the n-word. Some disparage its use by people of any race, while others think African Americans, but no one else, should be able to use it. Alo is one of the few rappers to denounce its use by his fellow Latinos.

"I can't stand it when Latino people use that term," he says, adding that he doesn't have a problem with blacks using it. "It's just not cool. I know a lot of cats that use it and stuff, but that just ain't my thing. Call me old fashioned."

That probably wouldn't faze Sonny Black, the Latino rapper from 108, who believes the word is no longer a simple racial construct. Black asserts that anyone who comes from an impoverished community has a legitimate claim to the word's use, a perspective shared by many Chicago hip hoppers.

"If you 'hood,' you can say it," he insists. "I know white niggas that are hood, and they can say 'nigga' cause they in the hood. They hood niggas, plain and simple. That's how it is. If you hood, you got passes." None other than Bill Cosby expressed similar sentiments in a 1971 speech delivered to the Congressional Black Congress. "Niggas come in all colors," he told the audience.

The impact of hip hop and the n-word on racial relations and cultural practices remains to be seen. During its annual convention in July 2007, the National Association for the Advancement of Colored People held a mock funeral for the term, calling upon the rap community in particular to end its use. But apparently none of these musicians attended, or even read the n-word's obit.

"Until they outlaw the word, people are gonna use it," says Esohel, a Latino rapper who plans to continue using the term in his music. "For the better or for the worse."

RECOMMENDED RESOURCES

Jabari Asim. *The N Word: Who Can Say It, Who Shouldn't and Why* (Houghton Mifflin, 2007).

> A historical look at the lengthy history of the n-word, with the author concluding the term helps keep blacks at the lowest rungs of society, regardless of context.

Murray Forman and Mark Anthony Neal, eds. *That's the Joint! The Hip Hop Studies Reader* (Routledge, 2004).

> An excellent selection of articles that examine hip hop culture from a variety of perspectives.

John L. Jackson. *Real Black: Adventures in Racial Sincerity* (University of Chicago Press, 2005).

> A kaleidoscopic ethnography of New York City, with the author concluding racial sincerity trumps racial authenticity.

Bakari Kitwana. *Why White Kids Love Hip Hop: Wankstas, Wiggers, Wannabes, and the New Reality of Race in America* (Basic Books, 2005).

> A cogent analysis of the conditions that lead whites to embrace hip hop culture, underscoring the new forms of racial hybridity that have stemmed from the dissemination of hip hop culture.

REVIEW QUESTIONS

1. What social factors and cultural ties help explain the bonds Latino and black hip-hoppers express in this article?
2. As its music and culture has become more mainstream and moved across class and racial boundaries, how has hip hop changed?

3. As with the "n-words," groups sometimes "reclaim" words that are used as slurs to turn them into points of pride. Discuss the history and evolution of such words as *ghetto, redneck, queer, faggot,* and *bitch.* Why have people sometimes chosen to reclaim derogatory terms such as these?
4. Some words are loaded even if they seem neutral. Consider words such as *feminist, patriot, communist.* What meanings and implications are built into these words? Can you think of similar words that evoke strong feelings?
5. Activity: Form a small group and discuss whether, on the basis of what you read in this article, you think the "n-word" should be acceptable for anyone to use.

part **5**

Poverty and Inequality

kate ledger

the moynihan report, a retrospective   **18**

fall 2009

"the moynihan report revisited" illuminates how the much-maligned author turned out to be prescient about the effects of poverty and institutionalized oppression.

It doesn't take a sociologist to know that American society has long been plagued by problems of race and inequality. But knowing race is a problem and knowing how to think about that problem (much less what to do about it) are two very different things.

This, of course, is where sociologists come into play—or at least should. Yet, in an era where many are calling for colorblindness or even proclaiming the United States a post-racial society, sociological analysis and perspective is all too often ignored or dismissed.

Princeton sociologist Douglas Massey, who's long studied segregation and poverty, is well aware of these challenges. However, Massey also knows a thing or two about how to engage the public more effectively, having contributed to national legislative debates and public policy on matters ranging from housing to immigration. And recently Massey, who is also president of the American Association for Political and Social Science, had an idea, inspired by a moment in history and yet rooted in the present day, about how to make sociologists part of the ongoing national conversation on race.

Along with Harvard sociologist Robert Sampson, he organized a conference that prompted researchers to consider modern issues facing black Americans through the lens of the Moynihan Report, the White House document produced by a social scientist that lit the world afire with controversy in 1965 and altered discussions of race and inequality for decades.

The studies from the conference, compiled as "The Moynihan Report Revisited" and published in January as a special volume of *The Annals of the American Association for Political and Social Science*, return to the memo that embroiled the nation. With quantitative and qualitative studies, researchers re-examine some of the same issues and problems Moynihan described more than 40 years ago. Many of the studies in the volume point out marked changes in practices and attitudes since Moynihan's ill-received report. They also point out how its much-maligned author turned out to be prescient about the effects of poverty and the damage of institutionalized oppression.

When the collaboration got underway, no one knew its publication would coincide with the inauguration of the country's first African American president—an executive whose own family has been celebrated as a role model for all American families. But what the studies clearly show is that sociologists have more than ever to say about race and poverty in the United States, and that issues of class, culture, and family life are once again at the center of their conversations and contributions.

Any scholar studying race in America in the late 1960s knew about the Moynihan Report. The document, officially titled "The Negro Family: The Case for National Action," was written by Daniel Patrick Moynihan, who was then assistant secretary of labor under President Lyndon B. Johnson. Moynihan's task, in the year following the Civil Rights Act of 1964, was to write a persuasive memorandum to inspire the president to create jobs and programs to improve social and economic opportunities for impoverished African Africans.

A sociologist and researcher who had published on race issues, Moynihan described a desperate scenario facing poor inner-city blacks, a legacy of problems stemming from slavery and perpetuated by structural elements of society like segregation and institutionalized discrimination. "Moynihan was largely viewed as a thoughtful, somewhat progressive, if iconoclastic, irreverent figure, and he was not afraid to take a strong stand about things," says University of Pennsylvania sociologist Frank Furstenberg, another contributor to the volume.

Drawing on decades of demographic and sociological studies, the memo famously focused on the state of the black family. "[F]or vast numbers of the unskilled, poorly educated city working class, the fabric of conventional social relationships has all but disintegrated," Moynihan wrote. As long as the family remained in crisis, he added, the cycle of poverty would repeat itself. He advocated federal policy that would "bring the Negro American to full and equal sharing in the responsibilities and rewards of citizenship . . . [by] enhancing the stability and resources of the Negro American family."

But his report, intended as an internal memo with fewer than 100 copies printed, was leaked to the press. A firestorm followed. Black and white critics homed in on Moynihan's depiction of crumbling low-income African American families. They cried foul about couching the

argument in cultural issues—"divorce, separation, desertion, female family head, children in broken homes and illegitimacy"—accusing Moynihan of blaming the victim. They took issue with his description of the deeply entrenched problems of black families as a "tangle of pathologies." Massey points out that "people focused on the language and on the rhetorical flourishes." Few critics actually read the report, which wasn't released in its entirety until months after the press leak and the public outcry, but blacks and whites united in the opinion that Moynihan himself was a racist.

Even more remarkable, perhaps, was the afterlife of the document and what happened in the wake of the controversy. The very argument Moynihan had crafted to prompt federal policy became fodder over the years for conservative rhetoric that argued to reduce investment. Terms from the Moynihan Report, like "underclass," were used in conservative arguments "to enforce good behavior, get tough with the poor, stop handing out goodies from the state," says University of Minnesota political scientist and poverty scholar Joe Soss. Even in academia, the report continued to reverberate, having a stultifying effect on social research on race and inequality. "Social scientists avoided portrayals of the lives of African Americans," says Furstenberg. The result, he adds, was a several-decade void of forthright discussion about blacks and poverty. Paradoxically, the unpublished report became one of the most influential social science publications of the last 50 years.

Doug Massey was 13 years old when the Moynihan Report first exploded into the media, and he was aware of the controversy long before he ever read the document in the early 1980s as a young assistant professor at the Uni-

> A sociologist and researcher who had published on race issues, Moynihan described a desperate scenario facing poor inner-city blacks.

versity of Pennsylvania. When he perused it, however, he found it to be more perceptive and constructive than he'd expected. "I thought that it had been unfairly characterized and misconstrued," he says, "and that a lot of what [Moynihan] had predicted in 1965 had come to pass over the decades." As the 40th anniversary of the document rolled around, Massey thought it was high time to revisit it intellectually, think about it in its context and why it was so controversial, and consider what's changed over the years and what's stayed the same.

There are obvious indications society has changed, point out sociologists Lawrence Bobo, at Harvard, and Camille Charles, at the University of Pennsylvania, who noted signs of great improvement in public spheres, like the integration of neighborhoods and public schools. Looking at how white and black Americans "think and feel about the matter of race," they note that in polls most whites approve of integration and equality. But racial stereotyping and negative biases remain unconscious undercurrents in people's daily lives. These attitudes continue to influence group relations and opportunities. When it comes to housing, black homeseekers are still steered away at alarming rates from white communities. And today, Charles says, the middle-class blacks are "being devastated right now because they were disproportionately offered subprime mortgages, and they were targeted because of their race."

Negative stereotypes continue to play a role when it comes to hiring practices. In interviews with white employers, Princeton sociologist Devah Pager found that many held negative preconceptions of black job applicants for entry-level positions, even though they described having experienced blacks as better workers than whites. In fact, Pager's research has shown,

---

On its 40th anniversary, Massey thought it was high time to revisit the Moynihan report intellectually.

---

being black sooner disqualified an applicant from a job than having committed a crime. What Moynihan had described as "the racist virus in the American blood stream" appears to have persisted.

One trend Moynihan couldn't have foreseen was the "prison boom," the astronomical swell in the 1990s of black men serving time. Harvard sociologist Bruce Western describes the current phenomenon of mass incarceration as "a new stage in the history of American racial inequality." As conservative politics of the 1980s pushed for law and order, and public policy of the 1990s devoted money to prison construction, incarceration has become more than punitive, Western argues. It's become a people-managing tool in urban poor neighborhoods. The United States incarcerates at a rate more than seven times that of Europe, and black men in America are eight times more likely to be locked up than whites. It's a disparity "unmatched by most other social indicators" like wages, military enlistment, or college degrees.

There's no doubt entire families suffer the consequences of prison sentences. Far more men than women go to jail. Once they're released, men tend not to marry, so they don't get the stabilizing benefits of family networks. They become less likely to find jobs and to keep them. At the same time, they tend to have children at the same rate as non-incarcerated men. Regrettably, "men behind bars cannot fully play the role of father and husband," Western finds. Future studies may determine the financial consequences of incarceration on poor families and the effects on children, but the data "adds another chapter to Moynihan's original analysis of urban poverty and its social correlates."

Moynihan didn't investigate characteristics of black fathers, but when sociologists Kathryn

Edin, at Harvard, and Ronald Mincy, at Columbia, looked at fathers' roles in families, they discovered that the predominant image of the non-participatory, grudgingly involved, stereotypical so-called hit-and-run father didn't hold true. In fact, data from interviews and the Fragile Families Survey, a national longitudinal study of non-marital births in American cities, show that lack of interest wasn't what kept poor, unmarried African American men from being involved with their children. On the contrary, men were eager to be involved with their children, and intent on having lasting relationships with them, "even though sometimes they were immature in their conception of what fatherhood means," says Edin. The studies showed African American unmarried men living with their girlfriends tend to be present and participatory at their children's birth; that involvement diminishes, however, as the children get older and the relationship with the mother breaks up. Despite the men's intentions, complex family dynamics, jealousies, lack of money, and poor communication get in the way of steady parenting.

It's class culture—not race, as Moynihan suggested—that's come to characterize patterns of partnering and childbearing in today's families, Edin says. The habit of unmarried childbearing and "rapid repartnering" has grown common in lower-class families. In fact, had Moynihan focused on class differences, he would have come to different conclusions about black families, Penn's Furstenberg asserts in another study in the volume. Moynihan pointed to teenage and non-marital childbearing as a sign of decay in black culture. Today, Furstenberg shows, the rate of teen childbearing among blacks has decreased, and in fact is lower than when Moynihan wrote his report. Meanwhile,

> It's class culture, according to many sociologists, that has come to characterize patterns of partnering and childbearing in today's black families.

the rate of white teenage childbearing has risen among lower-class families. The converging figures suggest that class is the essential determinant. Overall, both studies show, the perception of marriage as an economically and socially stabilizing concept has changed.

For lower class families, the trends are sobering, Edin says. As children grow up with a string of uncommitted parent figures, greater exposure to abuse and sexual predators, and diminished access to steady financial support and educational opportunity, they have different characteristics from children of other social classes. On a large scale, Edin says, these disparities are becoming more pronounced. Moynihan, in the end, appears to have been right on about where attention ought to be focused. "When you're talking about the intergenerational transmission of poverty," she says, "the primary mechanism is the family."

The range of studies in "The Moynihan Report Revisited" reveal a society still struggling with racial disparities, despite a larger black middle class than ever before and despite highly visible and respected black figures in public arenas, says Charles. "There's a growing number of successful African Americans who are pointed to as proof that everything is okay . . . What [most people] are not seeing is blacks who are not okay and the systematic disadvantage they face."

But the collection appears to have emerged at an opportune time. "With the change in administrations," Massey says, "now there's a whole new interest in rethinking approaches to public policy." And with an African American at the pinnacle of American politics, there's a new opportunity to put the topic of race on the table, points out Furstenberg: "We now have somebody in a position who can talk about these issues comfortably."

As a tool to inform new policies for families, the studies offer a new perspective on disadvantaged families, particularly "why this might be so consequential for kids and what . . . policymakers should and shouldn't be focused on," says Edin. For instance, as lower-class families experience astronomically high divorce rates, policies like the Bush Healthy Marriage Initiative, intended to teach about and encourage marriage, only partially addresses the issue of creating a solid family unit. "If we don't figure out real ways to help couples build satisfying relationships," she says, "we're not going to solve anything by putting on the Band-Aid of a marriage certificate." Ultimately, she adds, teaching people "how to relate is a public health issue."

Just as importantly, the new scholarship affirms a willingness of social scientists to talk openly about race and poverty. The effect of the Moynihan Report was to bestow "a persistent taboo on cultural explanations to help explain social problems," sociologist William Julius Wilson explains in the volume. Over the years, that taboo took its toll. Research about family, race, and inequality in the ensuing decades happened "under the radar," says Edin, and scholars worried whether their conclusions from data sounded too much like Moynihan, or could be similarly misconstrued.

Another lesson from the Moynihan Report—not to mention from Moynihan himself, who went on to a long and distinguished career in public service—has been about how to communicate research on race and poverty to lay readers. When Charles published work recently on differences between recent-immigrant blacks and native blacks at top-notch universities, the media demanded to know whether the study showed immigrants were unduly benefiting from affirmative action. "It was not at all what

we were trying to say," she states. Moynihan's legacy is a reminder to "be cautious about what I'm writing, and how I'm writing it, and how people might take what I write and twist it for whatever purpose they're trying to fulfill," she says. "I think it helps me be more clear." Massey recalls when he began studying segregation at the beginning of his career, Moynihan's experience had already informed him: "If you're going to write on issues of race, you'd better have thick skin."

What the new volume shows is that conversations about race—and about class and also about fragmented families—are more complex than ever. Immigration, which took off in the late 1960s and swelled in the 1980s, added increasing populations of Latinos and Asians into the mix, and the studies in the collection touch on some of the changing trends of communities that present new class issues. Though it may not be the much-touted "post-racial moment," now may be just the time for what Massey calls "level-headed" discussion. His goal for the volume was to "try to start a new conversation about these terribly important but difficult issues." He adds, "time will tell."

REVIEW QUESTIONS

1. The Moynihan Report is available online at www.dol.gov/oasam/programs/history/ webid-moynihan.htm. Read the introduction and describe how it compares with the image you had after reading the *Contexts* article. Which analysis do you find more compelling and/or enlightening?

2. According to this article, a number of sociologists think Moynihan would have had different ideas about black families had he studied class instead of race. Why would this be true?

3. When the Moynihan Report was leaked to the press 45 years ago, there was an outcry and,

the article states, social science about family, race, and inequality started to happen "under the radar." What do you think this phrase refers to? How can the media help or hinder social science research?

4. Activity: Use www.eurekalert.org to find a press release on a social scientific study that sounds interesting. Read the press release and the original article (your school's library Web site will help you find the original) and compare them. Does the press release do the article justice? What parts of the original research seem overlooked? Do any seem overhyped?

javier auyero and debora swistun

amidst garbage and poison: an essay on polluted peoples and places

19

spring 2007

the world's poor often live with terrible pollution—but that doesn't mean they like it.

"This is my backyard" (Maria). (Courtesy of Javier Auyero and Debora Swistun)

Kids are sometimes more perceptive than anthropologists and sociologists. That's what we thought as we left the local school in Flammable shantytown (Dock Sud, Buenos Aires). We had just spent three hours talking with a group of middle school students (ranging from 13 to 17 years old) about the photographs they had taken of their barrio with the portable cameras we gave them. They see things about themselves and about their place that we keep ignoring, we realized. With a few exceptions, ethnographies of poverty and marginality in Latin America ignore something that school kids in Flammable shantytown know full well: the poor do not breathe the same air, drink the same water, or play on the same ground as others. Theirs is a poisoned environment with dire consequences for their present health and future capabilities.

This essay is part of a collaborative ethnography that examines the diverse ways in which shanty dwellers understand and explain (to outsiders and to themselves) the surrounding contamination. Flammable shantytown (its actual name!) is a poverty enclave adjacent to one of the largest petrochemical compounds in Argentina, the site of Shell's only oil refinery in South America.

We asked the 13 students in the ninth grade to work in teams, and we gave them disposable, 27-exposure cameras. We told them to take half the pictures of things they liked about the neighborhood and half of things they did not like. We gave them no further instructions. They all returned the cameras, providing a total of 134 pictures. For this essay, we selected the pictures that best show the group's recurrent themes. As we will see, they agreed on the things they like and the things they do not.

After a brief description of the community, its history (profoundly entangled with the growth of the adjacent petrochemical compound), and its present predicament, we turn to the images and voices of the students. The message conveyed in these voices and images is simple: where poisonous fumes, polluted waters and contaminated ground are concerned, habitat does not necessarily generate habituation.

Exposure to (or socialization in) a dirty and polluted environment does not accustom these youngsters to dirt and pollution. Even after years of living in it, they profoundly dislike what they are forced to see, touch, and smell.

an organic relationship

Flammable shantytown is located in the district of Avellaneda, on the southeastern border of Buenos Aires. The name "Flammable" is quite recent. On June 28, 1984, there was a fire in the *Perito Moreno*, an oil ship harbored in the nearby canal. The ship exploded and produced, in the words of an old resident, the "highest flames I've ever seen." After the accident, remembered by everyone as a traumatic experience, companies in the compound built a new (and according to experts, safer) dock exclusively for flammable products, which gave a new name to the adjacent community—formerly known simply as "the coast."

According to the latest available figures, in 2000 there were 679 households in Flammable. It is a fairly new population: 75 percent of the residents have lived in the area for less than 15 years. Although there is no exact count, municipal authorities, community leaders, and people who live or work in the area (in the petrochemical compound, the school, and health center) told us that in the past decade the population had increased at least fourfold—fed by shantytown removal in the city of Buenos Aires and by immigration from other provinces and nearby countries (Peru, Bolivia, and Paraguay). Internal differences separate a small sector composed of old-time, lower-middle-class residents from the majority of newer, low-income dwellers. Scavenging, state welfare programs, and part-time manual jobs in one of the companies in the compound are the main sources of subsistence.

Flammable shantytown is, in many ways, similar to other poverty enclaves in urban Argentina, deeply affected by the explosion of unemployment and the ensuing misery of the 1990s. What distinguishes this poor neighborhood from others, however, is its relationship with the compound's main company, Shell-Capsa, and the extent of the contamination that affects the area and its residents.

The brick walls and guarded gates that separate the compound (the site of six major petrochemical companies and numerous small ones) betray the organic connection that, for more than 70 years, Shell-Capsa has had with the community. The first Shell Oil refinery opened in 1931. Since then, together with the other chemical, oil, and electrical companies in the compound (notably YPF, Meranol, Central Dock Sud, and now Petrobras), it has attracted eager workers who came from the provinces to look for work in Buenos Aires. In the life stories we collected, older residents remember an abundance of work in the area. They also recall the lack of housing close to the compound and their efforts to build what initially were shacks in the middle of swamps (still, today, there are lowlands in the center of the neighborhood—many of the pictures taken by the students portray small lagoons in their backyards). Filling in the surroundings appears in old-timers' narra-

"This is the street where Yesica lives." (Courtesy of Javier Auyero and Debora Swistun)

tives as an important joint activity of those early days—and it still is, according to our interviews with middle-aged residents. Health practitioners in the area claim that one source of local contamination might be the materials, often loaded with toxic waste, that people in the neighborhood use to level their plots.

There are several main elements of the material and symbolic entanglement between the neighborhood and Shell, or *la empresa*, as residents call it. Historically, Shell provided formal and informal jobs for men (who worked in the refinery) and women (who did domestic work such as cleaning and baby-sitting for the professional workforce within the compound). Old-timers remember not only working for Shell, but also going to the health center located on the company's premises, obtaining drinkable water from the company, and receiving pipes and other building material from the company. Less than a decade ago, Shell funded the construction of the health center in the neighborhood (a center that employs seven doctors and two nurses and has a 24-hour guard and an ambulance, something quite uncommon in poor neighborhoods throughout the country). Having automated many of its operations, Shell is no longer the main employer in the community, but it still provides jobs to residents, young and old.

Furthermore, Shell routinely grants funds to the local school in what a company engineer we interviewed defined as a "social performance plan." Among the services the company funds are a nutritional program for poor mothers that includes the distribution of food; computing classes for school students (held inside Shell's compound); windows, paint, and heaters for the school building; the end-of-the-year trip for graduating classes; T-shirts with the Shell logo

for student soccer, volleyball, and handball teams; and toys for the students during the celebration of Children's Day. Through its community relations division, the company tries to follow what a former municipal official calls a "good neighbor policy." Shell's presence undoubtedly distinguishes Flammable from other poor communities.

Flammable is also different from other destitute neighborhoods throughout Buenos Aires in the extent (and known effects) of its air, water, and soil pollution. Experts (from both the local government and Shell) agree that the air quality associated with the compound's industrial activities makes the area unsuitable for human residence. The place has also been used as a dumping ground by many nearby companies. It is still used as an open-air waste disposal site by subcontractors who illegally dump garbage in the area (we witnessed several instances of this during our fieldwork). Many of the pipes that connect homes to the city water supply are plastic; breaks and defects in the joints allow the toxins in the soil to enter the stream of the officially defined "potable water." A nauseating stench often comes from these garbage disposal sites, from putrid waters filled with this same garbage, and from the chemicals stored and processed in the compound.

One epidemiological study compared a sample of children between seven and eleven years old living in Flammable with a control population living in another shantytown with similar socioeconomic characteristics but lower levels of exposure to industrial activities. In both neighborhoods, the study found, children are exposed to chromium and benzene (known carcinogens) and to toluene. But lead distinguishes the children of Flammable from the rest. Fifty percent of the children tested in this neighbor-

> It is still used as an open-air waste disposal site by subcontractors who illegally dump garbage in the area (we witnessed several instances of this during our fieldwork).

hood had higher-than-normal blood levels of lead (against 17 percent in the control population). Not surprisingly, given what we know about the effects of lead in children, the study found lower-than-average IQs among Flammable children and a higher percentage of neurobehavioral problems. The study also found strong statistical associations between frequent headaches and neurological symptoms, learning problems, and hyperactivity in school. Flammable children also reported more dermatological problems (eye irritation, skin infections, eruptions, and allergies), respiratory problems (coughs and bronco-spasms), neurological problems (hyperactivity), and sore throats and headaches.

Where does the lead come from? The study is inconclusive. Lead in the air of Flammable is two and a half times higher than the state threshold. The small river that borders the shantytown is also contaminated with lead (and chromium). Experts point to the material buried in the ground on which the children play as another possible source of lead poisoning. They also told us that, long before laws regulating toxic waste disposal existed, the companies within the compound used Flammable as a free dumping zone. Lead, in other words, might be coming from everywhere.

the "good" pictures

To see how the young think and feel about this poisoned place, we consider the pictures they took and what they told us about the images. We did not provide any training in the art of photography, and the cameras we supplied were basic.

Although a few stated that it was difficult to take pictures of the things they liked ("because there's nothing nice here"; "How can we take photos of the things we like if there's nothing pretty here?"), the concurrence among the teams

was striking: among the things they liked were people (most of the pictures classified as "good" portrayed friends and family—not included here) and traditionally beneficial institutions (the church, the school, the health center). Yet, even when they placed the school among the "good" pictures, they did not fail to notice the terrible condition of the school building. Many took pictures of the health center and included them among the "good" pictures for unfortunate reasons: they routinely use the center when they get

(Courtesy of Javier Auyero and Debora Swistun)

The Health Center. "There's an ambulance there, and they take good care of you." "If something happens, you can go there, and they treat you very well." (Courtesy of Javier Auyero and Debora Swistun)

sick or when there is an emergency. Those who photographed the center stressed how well they are treated.

the "bad" pictures

Among the things they dislike: the ubiquitous garbage and debris, the stagnant and filthy waters, the smokestacks, and the Shell-Capsa building. When speaking about the pictures, their agreement was overwhelming: there is a single viewpoint about their surroundings. The kids all abhor the contamination of the water, the soil, and the air, and they emphasize that pollution is the only reason they consider leaving the neighborhood. "The school building is falling apart. It's damned cold in the winter, we can't attend classes because of the cold. If you turn the [electric] heating on, the lights go off. And in our classroom there's a broken window, and it's very cold (*nos recagamos del frio*)."

Overall, students stressed that they did not like the "bad" pictures because they show how dirty and contaminated their barrio is: "We don't like any of these pictures because there's a lot of pollution, a lot of garbage"; "I like the

"This is my aunt's backyard." (Courtesy of Javier Auyero and Debora Swistun)

neighborhood, all my friends are here. But I don't like pollution." In their minds pollution is associated with smoke (represented in the pictures of smokestacks, most of them taken at night when the smoke could be better seen—not included here because they are difficult to reproduce), garbage, mud, and debris (shown in the photos of the fronts of their houses, their backyards, and the streets they travel daily). Pollution is also associated with Shell-Capsa

"This is right in front of our house. There's a man living there, poor guy. . . . You feel sorry for him. The rats are all around." (Courtesy of Javier Auyero and Debora Swistun)

"When you walk by, the stench kills you. . . . You can see the rats there, they are huge, like monsters." "Look at the river. . . . It is all contaminated. . . . I wish the neighborhood were cleaner." (Courtesy of Javier Auyero and Debora Swistun)

and particularly with the coke-processing plant that was installed a decade ago (environmental organizations and some community activists tried unsuccessfully to stop this, arguing that the plant was potentially carcinogenic).

All of them see themselves living in the midst of waste and debris, *en el medio de la basura*, surrounded by stagnant, stinking water and by refuse that feeds huge and menacing rats. In several conversations during our fieldwork, mothers of small babies told us that they feared their babies would be eaten by rats "which are this big!"

One of the most revealing dialogues was with Manuela (now 16). One of her photos shows the site where trucks illegally dump garbage (not included here because of poor quality). Many neighbors scavenge in the garbage and, according to Manuela, "They make a lot of money." In another picture, probably the one that best realizes students' concerns about their dirty surroundings, Manuela caught a cat eating from the garbage. She used the same word for the cat that she had used to refer to her neighbors (*ciruja*, scavenger): "Check out this cat

> Manuela caught a cat eating from the garbage. She used the same word for the cat that she had used to refer to her neighbors (*ciruja*, scavenger).

looking over the garbage. He is looking for something to eat. He is a scavenger cat (*un gato ciruja*)." In their survival strategies in the surrounding dirt, neighbors and animals are, in Manuela's eyes, clearly similar.

Pollution is not only "out there"—in dirty streets, backyards, and playgrounds; it is also inside their own bodies where "contamination" has, in their view, a very precise name: lead. The epidemiological study received a lot of media attention—in the press (which they do not read) and on TV (which they do watch). Teachers also informed their students about lead, and some of them or their relatives were actually tested for the study. When speaking about pollution in the neighborhood, the kids used the interviews and the pictures to talk about their loved ones and themselves as poisoned persons: "I would like to leave because everything is contaminated here. I don't know

(Courtesy of Javier Auyero and Debora Swistun)

"*We don't like the factories because of all the smoke.*"
"*This is all polluted. It's all coming from Shell.*"
"*I don't like Shell because it brings pollution. . . . I don't know how much lead we have in our blood.*"
(Courtesy of Javier Auyero and Debora Swistun)

how much lead my cousin has in his blood . . . all of my cousins have lead inside." (Laura) "I have lead inside . . . I had my blood tested because some lawyers said they were going to eradicate us." (Manuela).

Many of the students have visited the plant. Miguel liked it; as he puts it, "It's really cool . . . full of trucks." Carolina, who took a two-week-long computing course inside the company's premises, says, "It is ugly inside, machines, smoke, lots of smoke." Romina tells us that "We don't like it (Shell-Capsa) because at night there's a lot of smoke coming out. We once went to visit. They treated us really well, but they contaminate everything . . . (pointing to the coke plant). In front of my place there's a woman who came to live in the neighborhood with her daughter. After a couple of years, they were all contaminated because of the coke . . . most people are contaminated by that." And Samantha adds, "There's a lot of disease here (*aca hay mucha enfermedad*)." The pictures they took and their comments make it clear that, for these youngsters, Shell (and the petrochemical compound by extension) is associated with the smoke and the lead that affect their health. Shell is, for them, the source of their (and their neighbors') sickness.

lives exposed, minds unused

Where does this visual journey leave us? In speaking so adamantly about their surroundings, these youngsters remind us of a simple truth: poor people's lives do not unfold neatly but rather messily in polluted waters, poisoned soils, and contaminated air, surrounded by garbage where the rats, as one of the students put it, invoking his worst nightmares, "look like monsters."

Poor people's lives unfold badly in polluted environments. How do the poor experience this situation? In an effort to answer this question, we gave cameras to school students, interviewed them, and found they were highly critical of their surroundings. Despite being regularly exposed to (and endangered by) contamination, they are not "used" to what they routinely see and smell. They cannot stop thinking about their environment, and they were eager to talk about it in the interviews. Why? Why can't they simply "forget about" contamination? First, their aching, itching (and, in many cases, lead-poisoned) bodies and their nervous minds constantly remind them that something is not right with themselves and their setting. Their suffering prevents forgetfulness. Second, the words and actions of teachers, lawyers, activists, and journalists also thwart habituation. Youngsters' critical views are shaped by teachers who educate them on a daily basis, lawyers who frequently come to the neighborhood in search of (sick or potentially sick) clients on whose behalf they might sue one or more companies in the compound, activists (like those of Greenpeace) who occasionally organize protests against some of the adjoining companies, and journalists who report the (mostly bad) news about the neighborhood. All these influence how youngsters think and

(Courtesy of Javier Auyero and Debora Swistun)

feel about their lives in the midst of garbage and poison.

shaky grounds

Many students took pictures of Dock Oil, an abandoned factory that was the site of the most recent community tragedy. On May 16, 2005, three youngsters, one of them a classmate of the students we interviewed, broke into the premises of the abandoned building to scavenge for iron bars. Apparently, a wall fell down after one of the teenagers pulled the wrong beam. Two were injured, and the third died. When we asked the students why they included so many pictures of Dock Oil among the "disliked" aspects of their neighborhood, they all said, "Because that's where one of our classmates died." As we looked at the pictures and transcribed these youngsters' voices, we felt that the reason they included so many pictures of that ugly building was related to the shaky ground on which they live—both literally and figuratively. No image, and certainly no words, can better convey the sense of existential insecurity among these youngsters. In this dangerous context where their bodies and minds are under constant (visible and invisible) attack, giving them cameras so that they could photograph their space and themselves was our way to better grasp their lived experiences of space and place. It was also our way of telling them that we were concerned about them, we were listening to their stories, and we would testify to what they were living through.

RECOMMENDED RESOURCES

Pierre Bourdieu and Marie-Claire Bourdieu. "The Peasant and Photography." *Ethnography* 5 (2004):601–16.

An insightful analysis of the meanings and social uses of photography in the peasant society of Bearn in the early 1960s.

Wendy Ewald. *Secret Games: Collaborative Works with Children 1969–1999* (Scalo, 2000).

Children from around the globe, trained by an award-winning photographer, portray their social worlds.

Jim Hubbard. *Shooting Back from the Reservation* (New Press, 1994).

A moving reconstruction of Native American life as seen through the cameras of Native American children and teenagers.

Steve Kroll-Smith, Phil Brown, and Valerie J. Gunter, eds. *Illness and the Environment: A Reader in Contested Medicine* (New York University Press, 2000).

A comprehensive and informative collection of articles on the (contested) relationships between health, illness, and the environment.

Jon Wagner. "Constructing Credible Images: Documentary Studies, Social Research, and Visual Studies." *American Behavioral Scientist* 47 (2004):1477–1506.

An illustrative piece on the challenges faced by documentary photographers and visual social researchers with useful lessons for empirical investigators.

REVIEW QUESTIONS

1. What was your reaction to learning about how the people in Flammable live? What do you think could be done to improve their situation?
2. Describe how capitalism in the United States affects people in Flammable. Do

you think that Shell-Capsa has a responsibility to the people of Flammable? Why or why not?

3. Research and define the terms *environmental justice* and *environmental racism*. How do they relate to the case of Flammable?

4. Activity: Take three photographs of sites in your neighborhood or city that you think exemplify environmental inequality and share them with the class. Why did you choose these sites? What do you think they say about your city?

lane kenworthy

is equality feasible?

summer 2007

is income equality possible in modern capitalism? yes. would it hurt the economy? no.

The principal argument for equality is that it is fair. Much of what determines people's earnings and income—intelligence, creativity, physical and social skills, motivation, persistence, confidence, inherited wealth, discrimination—is a product of genetics, parents' assets and traits, and the quality of one's childhood neighborhood and schools. For the most part, these factors are a matter of luck. A large portion of earnings and income inequality is therefore undeserved, which makes institutions and policies that can reduce inequality attractive. While few egalitarians favor complete equality of incomes, most would prefer less inequality than exists in the contemporary United States.

In the view of many economic analysts, equality comes at a cost. A high minimum wage reduces jobs. Generous government benefits discourage job searching. High taxes reduce incentives for saving, investment, and entrepreneurship. The result is low employment, stagnation, and mediocre living standards.

Are these claims true? Each of them is plausible, but we can also argue that equality might contribute to a healthier economy: it might boost consumer demand, spur productivity by enhancing perceptions of fairness, encourage the development of new skills by facilitating investments in college education by the poor, increase trust, and reduce crime and political conflict. Ultimately, the question of equality's effects can only be answered empirically.

the new economic environment

In some countries, such as Sweden and Denmark, many employees are unionized, and unions have strongly influenced wage patterns and government policy. Governments have enacted generous benefits to cover risks that individuals and households face in a market economy—low income, unemployment, sickness, disability, poor health, old age. In other countries, such as the United States and Canada, unions have been smaller, less cohesive, and less influential. Less of these nations' incomes is taxed from the wealthy and transferred to the poor.

Through the 1970s, comparatively equal countries grew just as rapidly as less equal ones, and employment tended to be higher in the former. Looking across these nations, we see no indication of a trade-off between equality and economic dynamism.

Then the economic environment changed. Heightened competition in various industries, a result of globalization and domestic developments such as deregulation, encouraged firms to become more cost-conscious and thus to reduce pay levels. Enhanced ability to hire foreign workers and to automate low-skilled tasks has given employers additional leverage. Declining unionization and decentralization of wage-setting have weakened the major institutional forces supporting decent wages for the less-skilled. Immigrant job-seekers have also put downward pressure on wages at the low end of the labor market. The shift of employment from manufacturing to services has reduced the share of jobs in the sector where pay traditionally has been most equal and increased the share in the sector where it tends to be most unequal. With later marriage and increased divorce, more households have just one adult and therefore only one potential earner. Because firms and investors can more easily move their plants or their money to other countries, governments feel pressure to reduce tax rates.

These changes threaten both the viability and the desirability of pursuing equality. The new environment has made it more difficult for countries to reduce income inequality, and many fear that there may be greater costs to doing so.

While I do not pretend to know what will happen in the next several decades, it is worth examining what has occurred so far. I focus on the experiences since the late 1970s of nineteen affluent countries: Australia, Austria, Belgium, Canada, Denmark, Finland, France, Germany, Ireland, Italy, Japan, the Netherlands, New Zealand, Norway, Spain, Sweden, Switzerland, the United Kingdom, and the United States.

the end of equality?

Although most research has focused on unequal earnings among employed individuals ("pay inequality"), the inequality of income among households is more important because households typically pool their earnings. The amount of income inequality in a country is commonly measured using the Gini coefficient, which indicates the proportion of a country's income that would have to be redistributed in order to achieve perfect equality among households. It ranges from 0 to 1, with larger numbers indicating greater inequality. As of 2000, the most recent year for which data are available for many countries, the Gini coefficient ranged

from .25 in Sweden, Norway, Finland, and the Netherlands to .37 in the United States.

Since the late 1970s, household inequality has increased in the most affluent countries. But the increase has been small, as government taxes and transfers have helped to offset rising market inequality. Only in the United States and the United Kingdom has the jump in income inequality been substantial.

an equality/incomes trade-off?

Even if equality remains viable, is it compatible with other desirable social and economic outcomes? Hard-core advocates of free markets have long argued against "excessive" pursuit of equality. In recent years even scholars with egalitarian sympathies have expressed skepticism about the degree to which countries can effectively combine low inequality and a strong economy.

Debate about whether equality is compatible with a dynamic, productive economy has a long history. Much of it has focused on the relationship between inequality and economic growth. The traditional view of this relationship, outlined in Arthur Okun's 1975 book *Equality and Efficiency: The Big Tradeoff*, holds that inequality contributes to growth. Those with higher incomes tend to save more of their income than do those with moderate or low incomes. The wealthy are thus the principal source of investment in a capitalist economy. Consequently, the smaller the income share of the rich (i.e., the less inequality), the less investment there is. Compressed earnings distributions and high taxes reduce the financial gain from hard work and skill development. This may cause people to reduce their work effort and investment in skills. And those with limited labor market prospects may be tempted to live off government benefits rather than work.

On the other hand, we can argue that income inequality may be bad for growth. Since the wealthy tend to save more of their income, greater inequality may weaken consumer demand, which can be as debilitating for the economy as low investment. Those in the middle and lower classes may regard high inequality as excessively unfair, reducing employee motivation and workplace cooperation. High inequality may also reduce the share of the population that is able to invest in higher education. And the financial constraints and frustration created by high inequality may decrease trust, cooperation, civic engagement, and other growth-enhancing forms of social support.

What does the comparative evidence suggest? Figure 1 plots levels of per capita gross

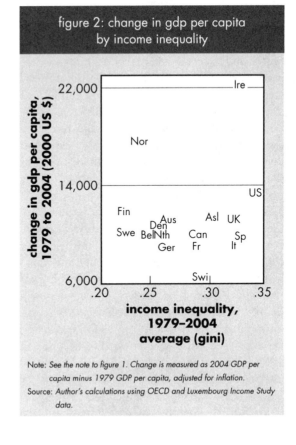

figure 2: change in gdp per capita by income inequality

Note: See the note to figure 1. Change is measured as 2004 GDP per capita minus 1979 GDP per capita, adjusted for inflation.
Source: Author's calculations using OECD and Luxembourg Income Study data.

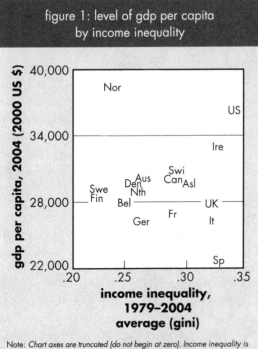

figure 1: level of gdp per capita by income inequality

Note: Chart axes are truncated (do not begin at zero). Income inequality is for posttax-posttransfer household income, with income adjusted for household size. GDP per capita is converted into U.S. dollars using purchasing power parities.
Source: Author's calculations using OECD and Luxembourg Income Study data.

domestic product (GDP) in 2004 (the most recent year for which data are available) by the average level of income inequality since the late 1970s. We see no indication that income inequality contributes to economic affluence. Figure 2 shows change in per capital GDP between 1979 and 2004 on the vertical axis. Here too the pattern does not support the view that high inequality is beneficial.

A thorough analysis of the impact of income inequality on economic affluence and growth would go well beyond the simple bivariate patterns shown in figures 1 and 2. It would be helpful to control for other factors. We might wish to measure economic growth in other ways—as change in GDP per employed person rather than per population, or as percentage change rather than absolute change. We might want to use the level of inequality at the beginning of the 1980s, rather than an average for the period, to ensure that there is no reverse causality. We might also change the starting and ending points or break this period into smaller subperiods. None of this, however, alters the conclusion that cross-country patterns since the late 1970s do not support the idea that pursuit of low income inequality impedes economic growth. There surely is some point at which the distribution of income in a country might be too egalitarian to be compatible with a desirable rate of growth. But the experience of the past two decades suggests that none of these countries has reached that point.

GDP per capita is thought to be a good indicator of a country's living standards. Across the affluent countries, GDP per capita is indeed strongly correlated with median household income—that is, with the income level of households in the middle (50th percentile) of the income distribution. But it is less useful as an indicator of living standards for households at the low end fo the distribution. A better indicator is the income level at the 10th percentile of the distribution (below the 10th percentile there is more reason to worry about measurement error). These data suggest the same conclusion as those in figures 1 and 2: there is no apparent trade-off between low income inequality and high incomes at the bottom of the distribution or rapid growth of these incomes.

an equality/jobs trade-off?

In the past decade much of the debate about the effects of egalitarianism has centered on jobs. Here the concern is about pay equality rather than income equality—specifically, about the impact of high wages for those at the low end of the labor market. The equality/jobs trade-off view runs as follows. In many affluent nations the fastest-growing job sector, and the likely locus of future employment growth, is consumer-related services such as restaurants, hotels, retail trade, cleaning, and child care. In many consumer-service jobs, productivity levels are low and difficult to increase. In order to pay high wages, firms would have to pass the cost on to customers. But if the market is reasonably competitive, customers will refuse to pay a higher price. Unless wages for these consumer service jobs are low—which implies a high level of earnings inequality—the jobs will not exist.

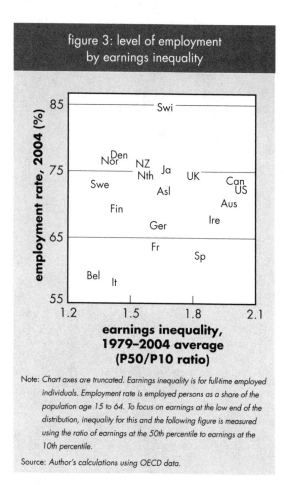

figure 3: level of employment by earnings inequality

Note: Chart axes are truncated. Earnings inequality is for full-time employed individuals. Employment rate is employed persons as a share of the population age 15 to 64. To focus on earnings at the low end of the distribution, inequality for this and the following figure is measured using the ratio of earnings at the 50th percentile to earnings at the 10th percentile.

Source: Author's calculations using OECD data.

Here too we need to look at the evidence. Figure 3 plots employment rates (employed persons as a share of the population age 15–64) in 2004 by the average level of earnings inequality among full-time employees since the late 1970s. There is no association. However, that could be a function of the period preceding the 1980s. Suppose that countries with less earnings inequality tended to have higher employment through the end of the 1970s (they did), but then around 1980 the economic environment changed so that low inequality began to harm employment. This development might take a long time to show up in an analysis of cross-country variation in employment levels. The sensible way to address this possibility is to look at change in employment, rather than levels of employment.

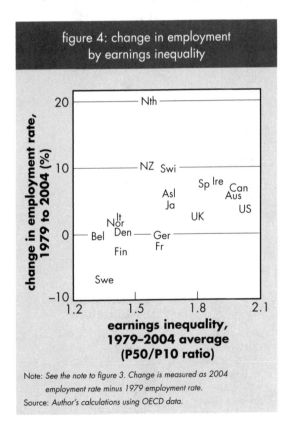

figure 4: change in employment by earnings inequality

Note: *See the note to figure 3. Change is measured as 2004 employment rate minus 1979 employment rate.*
Source: *Author's calculations using OECD data.*

Figure 4 does that. It shows change in the employment rate between 1979 and 2004. Except for the Netherlands, there is a positive association between earnings inequality and employment growth. With the Netherlands excluded, the correlation between the two is .58.

Is the positive association between earnings inequality and employment growth spurious? A variety of labor market policies and institutions—including government benefit levels and their duration, tax structures, employment protection regulations, and wage-setting arrangements—tend to correlate fairly closely with levels of earnings equality across these countries. One or more of these might be the true obstacle to employment growth. My attempts to disentangle the effects of these various factors suggest that the adverse impact of low earnings inequality on employment growth has been smaller than suggested in figure 4, but very likely real.

Is this apparent trade-off a cause for concern? Yes, for several reasons. Employment has intrinsic merits. With heightened geographical mobility, later marriage, and increased divorce, neighborhood and family ties have dissipated somewhat. As a result, work is an increasingly important site of social interaction. Employment also brings regularity and discipline to people's lives. It can be a source of mental stimulation. It helps fulfill the desire to contribute to and be integrated with the larger society. For many people, employment is inextricably bound up with identity and self-esteem.

Of perhaps greater importance for egalitarians, a high employment rate may increasingly be a prerequisite for greater household income equality. Higher employment can help to reduce market income inequality among households and to facilitate government redistribution.

How does it reduce market income inequality? Half a century ago it was common for many working-age adults to be out of the labor force.

They were mainly women, and their husbands were employed. The fact that some adults were employed and others were not had little impact on the distribution of income among households because inequality of employment occurred mainly within, rather than between, households. That is no longer the case. As more women enter the labor market, inequality of employment occurs more and more between households.

In other words, instead of having many households with one (usually male) earner and one (usually female) non-earner, a country with a low or moderate employment rate is now more likely to have many households with two earners and some with no earners. This increases inequality of earnings and incomes between households. To the extent that it reduced the number of zero-earner households, high employment helps to counteract this development and reduce income inequality.

How does high employment facilitate government redistribution? The aging population will soon force a larger share of government revenues to go to the elderly. The ability of firms and investors to move funds across national borders makes it difficult for governments to increase tax rates in order to maintain or increase the generosity of redistributive programs for the non-elderly population. This poses a challenge for a government committed to equality. A rising employment rate increases tax revenues without an increase in tax rates. And to the extend that it moves some current recipients of government benefits into the work force, it reduces welfare cost.

Is it possible for countries to combine high employment with low pay inequality? Yes. Denmark, Norway, and Sweden have been able to do so by relying on high levels of public employment to offset deficits in private-sector, consumer-service jobs. Unlike most private firm, governments can pay wages that exceed productivity levels without having to raise prices. Employ-

ment rates in the Nordic countries continue to be high (figure 3). The question is whether this strategy is sustainable. Increasing capital mobility is a threat, but the main determinant will be whether citizens in these countries remain willing ot be taxed at comparatively high rates.

Even if the Nordic approach proves to be sustainable, it is unlikely to be an option for countries that historically have had lower tax burdens. An alternative strategy is to allow relatively low wages at the bottom of the earnings distribution in order to stimulate private-sector employment. This implies more earnings inequality than there is in Sweden, though not as much as in the United States. However, it need not imply greater inequality of *household incomes*, which I suggested earlier should be of greater concern for egalitarians. To the extent that those who move into such jobs come from zero- or single-earner households at the low end of the distribution, the new earnings, even though relatively low, will pull up the income of the household. This will have the effect of reducing income inequality across households.

Moreover, low-income households can supplement their earnings with an employment-conditional earnings subsidy, along the lines of the Earned Income Tax Credit (EITC) in the United States and the Working Tax Credit in the United Kingdom. These programs provide a tax refund to households with low earnings. If (as often happens) the refund is greater than the amount the household owes in income taxes, the household receives the difference as a cash benefit. In order to encourage employment, the amount of the credit increases with earnings up to a point, then begins to decrease. The EITC has existed since the mid-1970s, and most studies conclude that it heightens labor force participation, effectively boosts the incomes of households most in need, creates minimal stigma, and has low administrative costs.

what to do?

Despite profound changes in the economic environment since the 1970s, affluent countries with egalitarian institutions and policies have so far been fairly successful at maintaining relatively high levels of income equality. And that success does not appear to have come at the expense of income growth for the middle class or the poor.

There may be a trade-off between earnings equality and job growth, but its magnitude appears to be modest. In any event, the existence of such a trade-off does not mean that high employment is incompatible with low income inequality. Countries unwilling or unable to collect sufficient tax revenues to pursue the Nordic strategy of extensive public employment may find it useful to allow more wage inequality than Sweden or Denmark. But the resulting higher employment can help to reduce income inequality among households, both by boosting the incomes of formerly zero- or one-earner households and by facilitating generous government benefits.

RECOMMENDED RESOURCES

Francine D. Blau and Lawrence M. Kahn. *At Home and Abroad: U.S. Labor Market Performance in international Perspective* (Russell Sage Foundation, 2002).

> A useful statement and empirical assessment of the view that high wages at the low end of the earnings distribution are an impediment to high employment.

Robert E. Goodin, Bruce Headey, Ruud Muffels, and Henk-Jan Dirven. *The Real Worlds of Welfare Capitalism* (Cambridge University Press, 1999).

> Examines the impact of social policies on economic growth, inequality, poverty, and other outcomes in the United States, Germany, and the Netherlands.

Lane Kenworthy. *Egalitarian Capitalism* (Russell Sage Foundation, 2004).

> Assesses the causes and consequences of inequality in affluent nations in the 1980s and 1990s.

Lane Kenworthy. *Jobs with Equality* (Russell Sage Foundation, forthcoming 2007).

> Argues that high employment is crucial to the sustainability of generous redistributive programs and therefore to low income inequality, and analyzes the effects of institutions and policies on employment in affluent countries.

Fritz W. Scharpf and Vivien A. Schmidt, eds. *Welfare and Work in the Open Economy*, 2 vols. (Oxford University Press, 2000).

> Case studies and comparative analyses of what determines employment performance in rich nations.

REVIEW QUESTIONS

1. What is the Gini coefficient? How can it be used to influence social policy?
2. Summarize the argument that inequality contributes to affluence in a given country. What is the equality/jobs trade-off?
3. The author talks about the non-pay benefits of employment. Can these benefits be achieved in other ways? What are some possible consequences of not having access to these benefits (for both individuals and society)?
4. How does unemployment affect societies beyond simple poverty?
5. Activity: Using online resources, look up the most recent Gini coefficients for the five countries with the highest levels of inequality and the five countries with the lowest levels of inequality. Does the presence of any countries on these lists surprise you?

stephen j. scanlan, j. craig jenkins, and lindsey peterson

the scarcity fallacy

21

winter 2010

most policies aiming to feed the world's one billion hungry people assume a limited food supply is the only problem. sociologists argue that affordability and accessibility are the bigger barriers to solving hunger.

For the first time in human history, the world is home to more than one billion hungry people. New data from the United Nations suggest that a higher proportion of the Earth's people are hungry now than just a decade ago, the reverse of a long and otherwise positive trend.

The conventional wisdom is that world hunger exists primarily because of natural disasters, population pressure, and shortfalls in food production. These problems are compounded, it is believed, by ecological crises and global warming, which together result in further food scarcity. Ergo, hunger exists simply because there isn't enough food to go around. Increase the food supply, and we will solve the problem of hunger on a global scale.

Scarcity is a compelling, common-sense perspective that dominates both popular perceptions and public policy. But, while food concerns may start with limited supply, there's much more to world hunger than that.

A good deal of thinking and research in sociology, building off the ideas of Nobel laureate economist Amartya Sen, suggests that world hunger has less to do with the shortage of food than with a shortage of affordable or accessible food.

Sociologists have found that social inequalities, distribution systems, and other economic and political factors create barriers to food access. Hunger, in this sociological conception, is part of the broader concept of "food security," which the World Bank describes as the inability to acquire the food necessary to sustain an active and healthy life. A central sociological element of this is "food poverty."

the (recycled) rhetoric of scarcity

The idea that hunger is due to scarcity has roots in Thomas Malthus's classic 1798 book *An Essay on the Principle of Population*. Malthus predicted widespread suffering and death from famine would result from the planet's inability to feed itself, stemming from its failure to cope with exponential population growth. Malthus turned out to be wrong—food production grew much faster than population–but his arguments have been recycled over generations, and today, especially with ongoing threats to Earth's carrying capacity, they have come to define conventional wisdom on hunger in the mainstream media and general public as well as for policymakers.

> The challenge is to create a more equitable and just society in which food access is ensured for all.

Food scarcity has long been the focus of agencies such as the UN Food and Agriculture Organization (FAO), the U.S. Department of Agriculture, and the U.S. Agency for International Development. Each uses some version of the scarcity argument to shape food security and development policies in collaboration with global agribusiness and food scientists. In such arrangements, concerns about hunger are viewed as production, marketing, and logistics problems that have solutions in the market-based policies of the global food system.

Fighting hunger from this approach means the top priority is reducing scarcity. This is most often addressed by increasing food yields with new technologies and by shipping food to more places more efficiently. The underlying goal in this approach is to facilitate what has been called the "supermarket revolution"—a term used by the World Bank to describe the growing reliance of global citizens on large-scale agricultural industries and commodity chains to obtain their food.

This supermarket model has created steady growth in the global import and export of food. But it can also produce its own problems and be counterproductive. What's worse is that the increased prices that often accompany market-based production make food less affordable for those in need. Furthermore, increased production may do nothing at all to guarantee more food. For example, the market model has increased use of crops for biofuel, which shifts agriculture away from producing food. In an oft-cited *Washington Post* editorial, Earth Policy Institute president Lester R. Brown noted that the same amount of grain needed to fill an SUV's 25-gallon gas tank with ethanol could feed a single person for a whole year.

The bigger problem with emphasizing food supply as the problem, however, is that scarcity is largely a myth. On a per capita basis, food is more plentiful today than any other time in human history. Figures on the next pages reveal that over the last several decades food production (represented here in a common staple, cereals) and the average daily food availability per capita have grown, outpacing what has been the most rapid expansion of human population ever. Data such as these from the FAO reveal that even in times of localized production shortfalls or regional famines there has long been a global food surplus.

The problem is ensuring access to this food and distributing it more equitably. A 2002 *New*

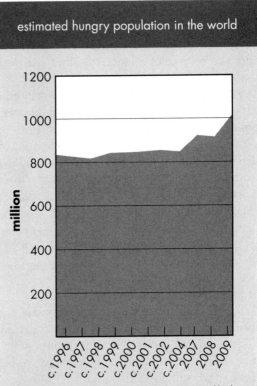

The time periods are three-year reporting periods as presented by the U.N. Food and Agriculture Organization's State of Food Insecurity (SOFI) from various years, with the exception of 2007–2009, which are from press releases specific to those years. The trend line is a two-year moving average for these figures. Missing years indicate periods where SOFI didn't report clear estimates.
Source: U.N. Food & Agriculture.

York Times headline proclaiming "India's Poor Starve as Wheat Rots" dramatically, if tragically, illustrates this point. Starvation amidst plenty has occurred in many a famine, as in Bangladesh in 1974 or Ethiopia in the 1980s. Even Ireland during the Great Famine exported vast quantities of food. Hunger in contemporary world societies is often no different. Markets are overflowing and even when shortfalls occur in emergencies, the global surplus is more than adequate to address such concerns.

Crop science can produce more food, and transportation and storage improvements can distribute greater amounts of it, but these

> Scarcity, in short, isn't the problem. Giving it undue attention reinforces myths that get in the way of understanding hunger.

don't guarantee access for all—a scenario that became quite evident with the 2007 global food crisis and spikes in food prices. Indeed, the global supermarket revolution can actually be devastating and counterproductive on the local level when prices increase and make food unaffordable for hundreds of millions of people.

Scarcity, in short, isn't the problem, and giving it undue attention reinforces many of the myths that get in the way of understanding hunger. In *World Hunger: Twelve Myths*, food scholars Frances Moore Lappé, Joseph Collins, and Peter Rosset have elaborated on this, addressing the problems of misplaced focus. Blaming population growth, food shortages, or natural disasters sidetracks attention from the challenges of the global food distribution system, the authors argue. They warn that free markets, free trade, food aid, or even green revolution technologies, for example, can all be barriers to obtaining food when inequalities are deeply ingrained. Rather than food scarcity, then, we should focus our attention on the persistent inequalities that often accompany the growth in food supply.

beyond scarcity

The basic statistics about world hunger are staggering—and revealing. Some 96 percent of hungry people live in developing countries and according to Unicef nearly a quarter of them are children. The UN World Food Programme notes that in developing countries, the poorest citizens spend upwards of 60 percent of their income on food. By way of contrast, according to a *New York Times* editorial the poorest Americans only spend between 15 percent and 20 percent on food. With declining disposable income, those who already may eat only two

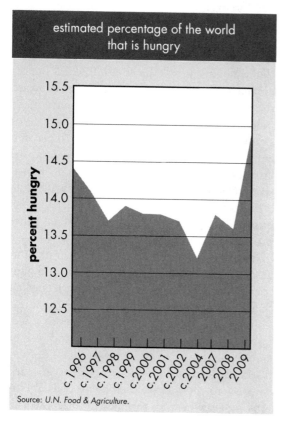

estimated percentage of the world that is hungry

Source: U.N. Food & Agriculture.

very simple meals each day now may have to cut back to one.

These statistics reveal a clear link between poverty and hunger. Two-thirds of the countries in the world with the most severe extreme poverty—rates greater than 35 percent—also have child hunger rates of 35 percent or more. As evidenced by the prevalence of hunger in the world's 77 low-income food deficit countries (LIFDCs) as designated by the FAO, poverty is inseparable from hunger and should thus be considered its primary root cause. No wonder the 2000 UN Millennium Summit concluded that the most serious problem confronting the world is persistent poverty and its connection to hunger. The prevalence of hunger in LIFDCs is particularly important because these countries are not only among the world's poorest by World Bank classification standards but are also net importers of basic foodstuffs because they are unable to produce amounts to meet their own needs. This makes them more at risk in that they lack sufficient foreign exchange in the international marketplace, something further exacerbated by global price spikes like those experienced in 2007. As evidence of the prevalence of food insecurity in LIFDCs, 23 of the 25 countries with the highest rates of child hunger in the world are also designated as LIFDCs (the exceptions being Burma and Maldives) and they continue to be predominant well down this list. Without guaranteed entitlements or other assistance, hunger is certain to persist among these most vulnerable nations, where addressing it is least affordable.

Moreover, most of the LIFDCs are in sub-Saharan Africa, where very little progress on hunger has been made over the last couple of decades—children, for example, fare only slightly better now than in 1990, child hunger having declined only 0.5 percent. In contrast, the remaining regions of the world have made much larger gains; East Asia and the Pacific, for example, have reduced child hunger 16 percent. Stagnation in the African subcontinent can be attributed directly to its persistent and pervasive poverty and underdevelopment, which creates further problems with conflict, health crises, and political instability, among other problems that contribute to hunger.

The developing world isn't alone in its hunger and poverty, though. Demand on food pantries in the United States is increasing according to a 2009 survey of food banks by the organization Feeding America (formerly America's Second Harvest). Evidence of poverty and loss of employment income as a primary cause of food insecurity can be even more evident in stark contrast to the relative well-being of U.S. citizens or elsewhere in the industrialized world.

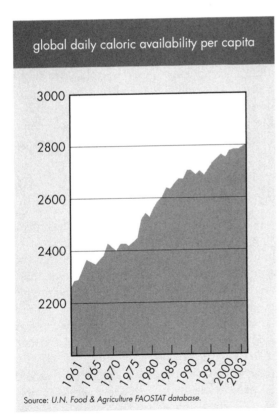

global daily caloric availability per capita

Source: U.N. Food & Agriculture FAOSTAT database.

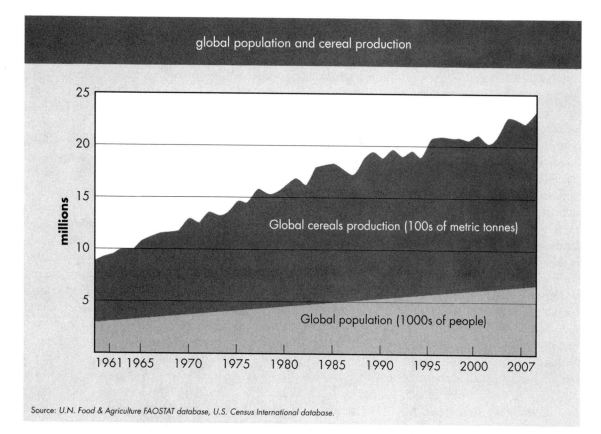

global population and cereal production

millions

Global cereals production (100s of metric tonnes)

Global population (1000s of people)

1961 1965   1970   1975   1980   1985   1990   1995   2000   2007

Source: U.N. Food & Agriculture FAOSTAT database, U.S. Census International database.

Here, food scarcity isn't even (or shouldn't be) a consideration. In difficult times and tight budgets, as freelance journalist and senior fellow at the policy and advocacy organization Demos, Sasha Abramsky, found in *Breadline U.S.A.*, families keep gas in the car to get to work, prescriptions filled, and the heat and lights turned on but often cut their food budgets, with the hope public or private assistance will help put dinner on the table.

Poverty, though, is only one form of inequality. Gender, ethnic, and other types of stratification have contributed considerably to hunger as well. Women are disproportionately likely to suffer from hunger, and in fact constitute approximately 60 percent of the world's hungry. This is particularly troubling given that

women do as much as 80 percent of the world's agricultural labor, working land that in more than a few places they may not be legally entitled to own.

As we have found in our own work, countries with more gender inequality (especially in education) have the greatest degree of child hunger. Gender inequality also influences women's health and access to contraception as well as limits their opportunities in society, potentially condemning them to lives where childrearing is their only opportunity for social status. In this context, large numbers of children may not be a cause of scarcity so much as a consequence of poverty and powerlessness.

Ethnic inequality can also contribute significantly to world hunger, especially in countries with marginalized minorities and a history or present situation of ethnic violence. Such "minorities at risk," as social movements scholar Ted Gurr calls them in *People versus States*, have long been threatened with hunger. Eritrea, Indonesia, Rwanda, Sri Lanka, and the Sudan are among many such places. While contributing to rampant militarism and armed conflicts, ethnic discrimination also silently marginalizes minorities to less desirable lands and occupations. The effects of ethnic discrimination then go beyond immediate violence, creating market disruptions, dispersed labor, and land degradation that destroys what for many is their only chance to produce or earn money for food.

Further exacerbating the effects of these social inequalities, international food aid—initiated by the U.S. government in the 1960s to remove surplus grain from domestic markets and assist military allies—has long been ineffective and misdirected. According to Public Law 480, U.S. aid must travel in U.S.-flagged vessels and depends on market surpluses. The results, critics contend, is that the major beneficiaries are not those in need of food but U.S. shipping companies, agri-business, and countries with geopolitical value for the United States.

Studies of who gets food aid partially support this criticism. In an article in *Food Policy* aid specialists Daniel C. Clay, Daniel Molla, and Debebe Habtewold, for example, found no relationship between need and food aid in Ethiopia. Food aid was instead allocated to areas where organizations had stable operations, to favored ethnicities, and to female and aged heads of households regardless of need. Tina Kassebaum, a senior research scientist at Strategic Research Group, has found that program aid (bilateral U.S. donations) is unrelated to a country's share of child hunger, while emergency/project aid (multilateral World Food Programme donations) is targeted at needy countries.

Making matters worse, emergency food delivery, which has become one of the most visible forms of assistance to those in need of food, has been corrupt on many fronts in recent years. According to Michael Slackman at the *New York Times*, in Egypt, the government subsidizes flour so that it can be baked into bread and sold cheaply to the population. However, the aid is routinely diverted into the black market and sold at a much greater profit while corrupt inspectors are bribed to certify that it has gone to assist the hungry. In the Democratic Republic of Congo, a 15-year civil war has been fought between the remnants of the Hutu guerrilla force that perpetrated the 1994 Rwandan genocide and other parties. In refugee camps, food is often used as a weapon—camp guards allocate it to those who will keep order, not to those most in need, while also having connections to widespread use of rape. Grim reports such as these have appeared in media outlets such as *The Guardian*, *The Gazette* (Montréal), and the *New York Times* who further note a key tactic in this battle has been attacking food aid and relief convoys, leading to threat and withdrawal of relief agencies, thus further compounding hunger as refugees and internally displaced persons flee for safety, left to fend for themselves. Similar patterns have occurred in Darfur and other conflict-ridden zones.

Some argue that corruption is a product of scarcity, and that if food did not have to be delivered to areas where it was in short supply such fraud would not exist. This argument is true to a point, but such disruptions in the food distribution chain are much more attributable to conflict and inequality, with power and powerlessness at the core of the problem. Corruption is simply another barrier to access—especially in times of acute conflict. Indeed, the poor and powerless are ultimately those most affected by these failures in the systems designed to help them.

Poverty, inequality, conflict, and corruption are all crucial contributors to world hunger, then. But what may be even more important and difficult to understand is how these can all fit together, reinforce one another, and even intensify the impacts of more basic food crises or the limits of various natural resources—that is, of scarcity itself. Environmental scarcity can, for example, be both a cause and a consequence of the inequalities associated with hunger. Entrenched poverty can contribute to further conflict and environmental destruction. This limits food access and reinforces a feedback cycle causing more conflict, which in turn creates more scarcity, and so on. As we've learned from Oxford economist Paul Collier's *The Bottom Billion*, hunger can be a product of a vicious cycle in which violent conflicts borne of corrupt and repressive government, poverty, and ethnic marginalization reinforce one another.

addressing hunger

Addressing world hunger is difficult and complex. To do it properly, we must get beyond the limited rhetoric of scarcity and instead focus on the inequalities, social conflicts, and organizational deficiencies at its roots.

To get at inequality, policy must give attention to democratic governance and human rights, fixing the politics of food aid, and tending to the challenges posed by the global political economy. At the very least, food must be upheld as a human right. In *Freedom from Want*, for example, political scientist George Kent places hunger squarely in the discussion of politics and the global human rights system. In his view, for hunger to be adequately addressed there must be worldwide recognition of food as a fundamental human right bound up in inter-

national law. It is only in this way that that both moral and legal accountability for failing to meet the needs of those not empowered to ensure their own food security can be established. Connecting this to our own work, we have found that democratization and increased protection of political rights reduces child hunger, paralleling a reduction of ethnic and gender inequality. Recognition of this fundamental human rights premise could elevate hunger to a higher level in international discussions and ultimately render it a non-issue, safeguarding it from the negative impacts of inequality, conflict, and politics.

Upholding this principle would also protect vulnerable citizens in industrialized countries who are finding it increasingly difficult to afford food as prices increase, real wages decline, and unemployment grows. Moreover, plans emphasizing nutrition and health, such as school feeding programs or those that target women, infants, and children, could be justified on the grounds of human rights and equal protection for the deserving poor entitled to assistance.

A second focus should be ensuring that international food aid actually gets to those in need, overcoming the problems of inefficiency and corruption that have long plagued such efforts. Fortunately, the news here is not all negative. Over the last decade international aid has moved toward less politicized emergency/project aid. Studies of the impact of this kind of food aid have revealed a relatively favorable picture. Still, this kind of aid, at best a temporary corrective, can be improved by attending more directly to the underlying conditions of poverty and inequality.

There is, for example, a longstanding debate over in-kind aid versus cash assistance. Oxfam International argues that the developed world should not dump cheap, subsidized food aid that

> At the very least, food must be upheld as a human right.

undermines local food production and markets in the developing economies it purports to help. A better solution would be to provide direct cash assistance to promote food purchases in local or regional economies. Recognizing that many poor depend on land for their income, such an approach would channel money to those who need it most, rather than to global agri-business and shipping companies profiting from food aid politics (this is a more ecologically sound practice as well). If reformed and effectively managed with minimal corruption, this approach could have a huge impact at minimal cost.

Leading up to the 2009 G-20 meetings in London, World Bank president Robert Zoellick noted that it would cost less than one percent of the current U.S. stimulus package to save a generation around the world from poverty and its consequences, including hunger. An influx of money could stabilize hundreds of countries throughout the world, not just with regard to hunger but politics and social conditions as well.

Fiscal challenges are further complicated by the fact that they are intricately connected with the global political economy, a third focus area. A number of ideas exist for making the globalized world more equitable so that ending hunger is a significant positive outcome. Strategies should empower societies and individuals to become more food-sovereign (able to exercise power over their food decisions).

Promoting sustainable agriculture with an emphasis on local food systems and empowering farmers to compete in their own markets is one such dimension. It will reduce ecological scarcity and go far toward ensuring food security, and ultimately food sovereignty, while having the added benefit of injecting additional money into local communities.

Effective long-term solutions through development of production capabilities, however, won't succeed unless ethnic and gender inequality are reduced or better yet, eliminated. Freeing ethnic minorities from the fear they will face violence if they come to aid distribution stations or, better yet, providing them with the tools to produce their own food and economic sustenance, will contribute greatly to reducing hunger. Too, providing women with control over childbearing, giving them access to education, allowing them the right to own land and businesses, and facilitating their economic activities with micro-credit and other innovations will significantly reduce hunger. Investing in the well-being of women and reducing gender inequality not only can improve their lives but benefit entire countries.

The challenge, in short, is to create a more equitable and just society in which food access is ensured for all. Food scarcity matters. However, it is rooted in social conditions and institutional dynamics that must be the focus of any policy innovations that might make a real difference.

RECOMMENDED RESOURCES

Laurie DeRose, Ellen Messer, and Sara Millman, eds. *Who's Hungry? And How Do We Know?* (United Nations University, 1998).

> A social scientific treatment of the causes and conceptualization of hunger as well as appropriate responses to it.

Food and Agricultural Organization of the UN. *The State of Food Insecurity in the World* (FAO, various years).

> An annual assessment of world hunger, including the latest figures and most recent policy discussions.

Amartya Senn. *Poverty and Famines: An Essay on Entitlement and Deprivation* (Oxford University Press, 1981).

A presentation of "entitlement failure," the seminal theory for understanding global hunger as connected problems of distribution, access, and the human causes of famine.

James Vernon. *Hunger: A Modern History* (Belknap Press, 2007).

A useful historical account of evolving conceptions of world hunger.

REVIEW QUESTIONS

1. Why is food scarcity a fallacy? What do the authors suggest that we focus on instead?

2. The authors assert that food must be upheld as a human right. Do you agree? How might this be enforced?

3. Activity: At the start of the new millennium, the United Nations set eight Millennium Development Goals for all member nations to achieve by 2015. Goal 1 is to eradicate extreme poverty and hunger. Visit www.un.org/millenniumgoals/poverty.shtml and read the specific targets associated with Goal 1. How could policymakers use what you have learned from this the article to achieve these objectives?

mark r. rank

as american as apple pie: poverty and welfare

22

summer 2003

few americans see poverty as a normal state of affairs. yet most will experience poverty and will use welfare at some point in their lives. how can this be, and how does (or should) it change the way we look at poverty in the united states?

For many Americans, the words "poverty" and "welfare" conjure images of people on the fringes of society: unwed mothers raising several children, inner-city black men, high school dropouts, the homeless, and so on. The media, political rhetoric, and often even the research of social scientists depict the poor as alien and often undeserving of help. In short, being poor and using welfare are perceived as outside the American mainstream.

Yet, poverty and welfare use are as American as apple pie. Most of us will experience poverty during our lives. Even more surprising, most Americans will turn to public assistance at least once during adulthood. Rather than poverty and welfare use being an issue of *them*, it is more an issue of *us*.

By the time Americans have reached the age of 75, 59 percent will have spent at least a year below the poverty line during their adulthood, while 68 percent will have faced at least a year in near poverty.

---

the risk of poverty and drawing on welfare

Our understanding about the extent of poverty comes mostly from annual surveys conducted by the Census Bureau. Over the past three decades, between 11 and 15 percent of Americans have lived below the poverty line in any given year. Some people are at greater risk than others, depending on age, race, gender, family structure, community of residence, education, work skills, and physical disabilities. (See sidebar, "counting the poor.")

Studies that follow particular families over time—in particular, the Panel Study of Income Dynamics (PSID), the National Longitudinal Survey (NLS), and the Survey of Income and Program Participation (SIPP)—have given us a further understanding of year-to-year changes in poverty. They show that most people are poor for only a short time. Typically, households are impoverished for one, two, or three years, then manage to get above the poverty line. They may stay above the line for a while, only to fall into poverty again later. Events triggering these spells of poverty frequently involve the loss of a job and its pay, family changes such as divorce, or both.

There is, however, an alternative way to estimate the scope of poverty. Specifically, how many Americans experience poverty at some point during adulthood? Counting the number of people who are ever touched by poverty, rather than those who are poor in any given year, gives us a better sense of the scope of the problem. Put another way, to what extent is poverty a "normal" part of the life cycle?

My colleague Tom Hirschl and I have constructed a series of "life tables" built from PSID data following families for over 25 years. The life table is a technique for counting how often specific events occur in specific periods of time, and is frequently used by demographers and medical researchers to assess risk, say, the risk of contracting breast cancer after menopause. It allows us to estimate the percentage of the American population that will experience poverty at some point during adulthood. We also calculated the percentage of the population that will use a social safety net program—programs such as food stamps or Aid to Families with Dependent Children (AFDC, now replaced by the Temporary Assistance for Needy Families [TANF] program)—sometime during adulthood. Our results suggest that a serious reconsideration of who experiences poverty is in order.

Figure 1 shows the percentage of Americans spending at least one year living below the official poverty line during adulthood. It also graphs the percentage who have lived between the poverty line and just 25 percent above it—what scholars consider "near poverty."

By the age of 30, 27 percent of Americans will have experienced at least one year in poverty and 34 percent will have fallen below the near-poverty line. By the age of 50, the percentages will have risen to 42 and 50 percent, respectively. And finally by the time Americans have reached the age of 75, 59 percent will have spent at least a year below the poverty line during their adulthood, while 68 percent will have faced at least a year in near poverty.

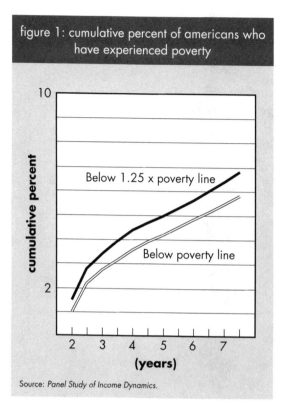

figure 1: cumulative percent of americans who have experienced poverty

Below 1.25 x poverty line

Below poverty line

cumulative percent

(years)

Source: *Panel Study of Income Dynamics.*

If we included experiences of poverty in childhood, these percentages would be even higher. Rather than an isolated event that occurs only among the so-called "underclass," poverty is a reality that a clear majority of Americans will experience during their lifetimes.

Measuring impoverishment as the use of social safety net programs produces even more startling results. Figure 2 draws on the same PSID survey to show the proportion of people between the ages of 20 and 65 who will use one of the major need-based welfare programs in the United States, including food stamps, Medicaid, AFDC, Supplemental Security Income, and other cash subsidies such as general assistance. By the time Americans reach the age of 65, approximately two-thirds will have, as adults, received

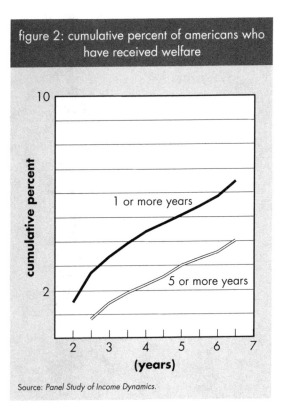

figure 2: cumulative percent of americans who have received welfare

cumulative percent

1 or more years

5 or more years

(years)

Source: *Panel Study of Income Dynamics.*

The life table techniques employed in figures 1 and 2 are based upon assessing the risk of poverty across a lifetime, more than 50 years. Over so many years, individuals face many unanticipated events—households split up, workers lose their jobs, family members become sick, and so on—that become financial emergencies. The familiar saying of being "one paycheck away from poverty" is particularly apt. For example, it is estimated that families with average incomes have enough assets to maintain their standards of living for just over one month.

the safety net

A second reason poverty rates are so high is that there is little government help to tide households over during financial emergencies. Although most Americans will eventually rely on need-based government aid (as shown in figure 2), that assistance often fails to save them from poverty. Contrary to the rhetoric about vast sums being spent on public assistance, the American welfare system can be more accurately described as minimal. Compared to other Western industrialized countries, the United States devotes far fewer resources to assisting the economically vulnerable.

Most European countries provide a wide range of social and insurance programs that effectively keep families from falling into poverty. These include substantial cash payments to families with children. Unemployment assistance is far more generous in these countries than in the United States, often providing support for more than a year following the loss of a job. Furthermore, universal health coverage is routinely provided along with considerable support for child care.

These social policies substantially reduce the risk of poverty in Europe and Canada, while U.S. social policies—aside from programs specifically directed to aid the elderly—have

assistance for at least a year, while 40 percent will have used a welfare program in at least five separate years. (Again, adding childhood experiences would only raise the rates.) Contrary to stereotypes, relying on America's social safety net is widespread and far-reaching.

Of course, people with disadvantages such as single parents or those with fewer skills will have even higher cumulative rates of poverty and welfare use than those shown in figures 1 and 2. Yet to portray poverty as an issue affecting only marginalized groups is clearly a mistake.

why is the risk of poverty so high?

time

First, most discussions of poverty look at single years, or five or ten years at a stretch.

When President Johnson declared his War on Poverty in 1964, the United States had no official measure of the number of people who were poor. The official poverty line that was subsequently developed estimated the minimum amount of income necessary in order to purchase a basic "basket" of goods and services. If a family's income falls below that level, members in the household are counted as poor. The poverty line is adjusted for the size of the family and increased each year to keep up with the cost of living. For example, in 2001 the poverty line for a household of one was $9,039, for a household of four, $18,104, while for a household of nine or more it was $36,286.

reduced poverty modestly at best. As economist Rebecca Blank notes in *It Takes a Nation*, "the national choice in the United States to provide relatively less generous transfers to low-income families has meant higher relative poverty rates in the country. While low-income families in the United States work more than in many other countries, they are not able to make up for lower governmental income support relative to their European counterparts" (pp. 141–142).

Scholars who have used the Luxembourg Income Study (LIS), an international collection of economic surveys, have documented the inability of the American safety net to reduce the risk of poverty. For example, Finnish social scientist Veli-Matti Ritakallio has examined the extent to which cash assistance reduces poverty across eight European countries, Canada, and the United States. European and Canadian programs reduce rates of poverty by an average of 79 percent from what they would have been absent the assistance. Finland, for instance, reduced the percentage of its residents who would have been poor from 33 percent down to

> Contrary to the rhetoric about vast sums being spent on public assistance, the American welfare system can be more accurately described as minimal. Compared to other Western industrialized countries, the United States devotes far fewer resources to assisting the economically vulnerable.

4 percent. In contrast, the United States was only able to reduce its percentage in poverty at any given time from 29 percent to 18 percent. As a result, the current rates of U.S. poverty are among the highest in the industrialized world.

the labor market

A third factor elevating the risk of American poverty across the lifecourse is the failure of the labor market to provide enough jobs that pay well enough. During the past 30 years, the U.S. economy has produced increasing numbers of low-paying jobs, part-time jobs, and jobs without benefits. For example, the Census Bureau estimated that the median earnings of workers who were paid hourly wages in 2000 was $9.91. At the same time, approximately 3 million Americans were working part-time because of a shortage of full-time jobs. As journalist Barbara Ehrenreich and others have shown, these jobs simply do not support a family.

A higher percentage of the U.S. workforce falls into this low-wage sector than is true in comparable developed countries. For example, economist Timothy Smeeding and his colleagues have found that 25 percent of all American full-time workers could be classified as being in low-wage work (defined as earning less than 65 percent of the national median for full-time jobs). This was by far the highest percentage of the countries analyzed, with the overall average of non-U.S. countries falling at 12 percent.

In addition, there are simply not enough jobs to go around. Labor economist Timothy Bartik used several different approaches to estimate the number of jobs that would be needed to significantly reduce poverty in the United States. Even in the booming economy of the late 1990s, between 5 and 9 million more jobs were needed in order to meet the needs of the poor and disadvantaged.

To use an analogy, the demand for labor versus the supply of decent paying jobs might be thought of as an ongoing game of musical chairs. That is, the number of workers in the labor market is far greater than the number of jobs that pay a living wage. Using SIPP data for 1999, I estimated this imbalance as ranging between 9 percent and 33 percent, depending upon how poverty and labor market participation were defined. Consequently, between 9 and 33 percent of American household heads were either in nonliving-wage jobs or looking for work. The very structure of the labor market ensures that some families will lose out at this musical chairs game and consequently will run a significant risk of poverty.

Some may point out that U.S. rates of unemployment are fairly low when compared to European levels. Yet Bruce Western and Katherine Beckett demonstrate that these lower rates are largely a result of extremely high rates of incarceration. By removing large numbers of American men from the labor force and placing them into the penal system (thus out of our musical chairs analogy altogether), unemployment rates are kept artificially low. When this factor is taken into account and adjusted for, U.S. unemployment rates fall more into line with those of Europe.

changing the poverty paradigm

A lifecourse perspective shows us that Americans are highly susceptible to experiencing poverty first-hand. Understanding the normality of poverty requires us to rethink several of our most enduring myths. Assuming that most Americans would rather avoid such an experience, it becomes in our enlightened self-interest to ensure that we reduce poverty and establish an effective safety net. This risk-sharing argument has been articulated most notably by the philosopher John Rawls. As well as being charitable, improving the plight of those in poverty is an issue of common concern.

We are also beginning to recognize that, as a nation, we pay a high price for our excessive rates of poverty. Research shows that poverty impairs the nation's health, the quality of its workforce, race relations, and, of course, its future generations. Understanding the commonality of poverty shifts how we choose to think about the issue—from a distant concept of *them*, to an active reality of *us*. In addition, much of the public's resistance to assisting the poor and particularly those on welfare is the perception that the poor are often undeserving of assistance, that their poverty arises from a lack of motivation, questionable morals, and so on. Yet my analysis suggests that, given its pervasiveness, poverty appears systemic to our economic structure. In short, we have met the enemy, and they are us. C. Wright Mills made a similar point about unemployment:

When, in a city of 100,000, only one man is unemployed, that is his personal trouble, and for its relief we properly look to the character of the man, his skills, and his immediate opportunities. But when in a nation of 50 million employees, 15 million men are unemployed, that is an issue, and we may not hope to find its solution within the range of opportunities open to any one individual. The very structure of opportunities open to any one individual. The very structure of opportunities has collapsed. Both the correct statement of the problem and the range of possible solutions require us to consider the economic and political institutions of the society, and not merely the personal situation and character of a scatter of individuals.

So too with poverty. That America has the highest poverty rates in the Western industrialized world and that most Americans will experience poverty during their lifetimes has little to do with individual motivation or attitudes. Rather, it has much to do with a labor market that fails to produce enough decent paying jobs, and social policies that are unable to pull individuals and families out of poverty when unforeseen events occur. The United States has the means to alleviate poverty, and a range of models from other countries to borrow from. Allowing our policies to be mired in self-righteous moralism while millions of citizens suffer is unconscionable. It is time to shift the debate from one of blame, to one of justice and common concern.

RECOMMENDED RESOURCES

Timothy H. Bartik. "Poverty, Jobs, and Subsidized Employment." *Challenge* 45 (2002): 100–11.

An argument for the importance of labor demand policies that encourage job growth and improved wages for low-income workers.

Rebecca Blank. *It Takes a Nation: A New Agenda for Fighting Poverty* (Russell Sage Foundation, 1997).

A review of the characteristics, nature, and current strategies for addressing American poverty.

Barbara Ehrenreich. *Nickel and Dimed: On (Not) Getting By in America* (Henry Holt and Company, 2001).

A first-hand account of trying to survive on low-wage work in three different settings.

Alice O'Connor. *Poverty Knowledge: Social Science, Social Policy, and the Poor in Twentieth-Century U.S. History* (Princeton University Press, 2001).

O'Connor critiques the dominant social science emphasis in the past 40 years on analyzing individual attributes as the primary cause of poverty.

James T. Patterson. *America's Struggle Against Poverty in the Twentieth Century* (Harvard University Press, 2000).

An historical overview of American social policy directed at the alleviation of poverty.

Mark R. Rank. *One Nation Underprivileged: How American Poverty Affects Us All* (Oxford University Press, 2004).

A new perspective on understanding and addressing U.S. poverty.

Mark R. Rank and Thomas A. Hirschl. "Rags or Riches? Estimating the Probabilities of Poverty and Affluence Across the Adult American Life Span." *Social Science Quarterly* 82 (2001): 651–69.

An examination of the likelihood that Americans will experience poverty or affluence at some point during their adulthood, which suggests a new conceptualization of social stratification.

Veli-Matti Ritakallio. "Trends of Poverty and Income Inequality in Cross-national Comparison." from *Luxembourg Income Study Working Paper* no. 272 (Maxwell School of Citizenship and Public Affairs, Syracuse University, 2001).

Uses the Luxembourg Income Study to assess the effectiveness of government policy in reducing poverty among nine developed countries.

Timothy M. Smeeding, Lee Rainwater, and Gary Burtless. "U.S. Poverty in a Cross-national Context." In *Understanding Poverty*, eds. Sheldon H. Danziger and Robert H. Haveman (Harvard University Press, 2001).

> The authors compare the extent of poverty in the United States and other developed countries.

Bruce Western and Katherine Beckett. "How Unregulated Is the U.S. Market? The Penal System as a Labor Market Institution." *American Journal of Sociology* 104 (1999): 1030–60.

> Shows the role that incarceration plays in lowering overall U.S. unemployment rates.

REVIEW QUESTIONS

1. Identify and describe three factors that make the risk of poverty so high in the United States.

2. Throughout the essay, Rank compares and contrasts the differences between European and U.S. models for combating poverty. Discuss two of those differences and what they say about our society.

3. Toward the end of the essay, Rank uses a quote from C. Wright Mills to describe the sociological perspective on unemployment. Describe that view in relation to other explanations of poverty (e.g., economic or psychological).

4. Activity: How do you think unemployment and poverty in the United States compares to those in other countries? First, rank what you feel the order is of the following countries on both variables: Costa Rica, Kenya, Russia, United States, France, and Malaysia. Second, find the C.I.A. World Factbook online (www.cia.gov/library/publications/the-world-factbook/index.html), and search the "Economy" section for each country. What do you find?

part **6**

Work and the Economy

pamela stone

the rhetoric and reality of "opting out"   **23**

fall 2007

professional women who leave the workforce may have fewer options than it seems. what does that tell us about work in america today?

As a senior publicist at a well-known media conglomerate, Regina Donofrio had one of the most coveted, glamorous jobs in New York. A typical workday might include "riding around Manhattan in limousines with movie stars." She loved her job, had worked "a long time," and felt "comfortable" in it. So when the time came to return to work after the birth of her first child, Regina did not hesitate. "I decided I would go back to work, because the job was great, basically," she told me.

Before long, Regina found herself "crying on the train," torn between wanting to be at home with her baby and wanting to keep up her successful, exciting career. She started feeling she was never in the right place at the right time. "When I was at work, I should have been at home. When I was at home, I felt guilty because I had left work a little early to see the baby, and I had maybe left some things undone." Ever resourceful, she devised a detailed job-share plan with a colleague who was also a first-time mother. But their proposal was denied. Instead, Regina's employer offered her more money to stay and work full time, and Regina left in a huff, incensed that her employer, with whom she had a great track record, would block her from doing what she wanted to do—continue with her career and combine it with family.

Despite mainstream media portrayals to the contrary, Regina's reasons for quitting are all too typical of what I found in my study of high-achieving, former professionals who are now at-home moms. While Regina did, in fact, feel a strong urge to care for her baby, she decided to quit because of an inflexible workplace, not because of her attraction to home and hearth. She gave up her high-powered career as a last resort, after agonized soul-searching and exhausting her options. Her story differs from the popular depiction of similar, high-achieving, professional women who have headed home. Media stories typically frame these women's decisions as choices about family and see them as symptomatic of a kind of sea-change among the daughters of the feminist revolution, a return to traditionalism and the resurgence of a new feminine mystique.

The quintessential article in this prevailing story line (and the one that gave the phenomenon its name) was published in 2003 by the *New York Times's* work-life columnist, Lisa Belkin, titled "The Opt-Out Revolution." "Opting out" is redolent with overtones of lifestyle preference and discretion, but Regina's experience counters this characterization; her decision to quit was not a lifestyle preference, nor a change in aspirations, nor a desire to return to the 1950s family. Regina did not "opt out" of the workplace because she chose to, but for precisely the opposite reason: because she had no real options and no choice.

High-achieving women's reasons for heading home are multilayered and complex, and generally counter the common view that they quit because of babies and family. This is what I found when I spoke to scores of women like Regina: highly educated, affluent, mostly white, married women with children who had previously worked as professionals or managers and whose husbands could support their being at home. Although many of these women speak the language of choice and privilege, their stories reveal a choice gap—the disjuncture between the rhetoric of choice and the reality of constraints like those Regina encountered. The choice gap reflects the extent to which high-achieving women like Regina are caught in a double bind: spiraling parenting (read "mothering") demands on the homefront collide with the increasing pace of work in the gilded cages of elite professions.

some skepticism

I approached these interviews with skepticism tempered by a recognition that there might be some truth to the popular image of the "new traditionalist." But to get beyond the predictable "family" explanation and the media drumbeat of choice, I thought it was important to interview women in some depth and to study women who, at least theoretically, could exercise choice. I also gave women full anonymity, creating fictitious names for them so that they would speak to me as candidly as possible. The women I interviewed had outstanding educational credentials; more than half had graduate degrees in business, law, medicine, and other professions, and had once had thriving careers in which they had worked about a decade. By any measure, these were work-committed women, with strong reasons to continue with the careers in which they had invested so much.

Moreover, they were in high-status fields where they had more control over their jobs and enjoyed (at least relative to workers in other fields) more family-friendly benefits.

While these women had compelling reasons to stay on the job, they also had the option not to, by virtue of their own past earnings and because their husbands were also high earners. To counter the potential criticism that they were quitting or being let go because they were not competent or up to the job, I expressly chose to study women with impeccable educational credentials, women who had navigated elite environments with competitive entry requirements. To ensure a diversity of perspectives, I conducted extensive, in-depth interviews with 54 women in a variety of professions—law, medicine, business, publishing, management consulting, nonprofit administration, and the like—living in major metropolitan areas across the country, roughly half of them in their 30s, half in their 40s.

To be sure, at-home moms are a distinct minority. Despite the many articles proclaiming a trend of women going home, among the demographic of media scrutiny—white, college-educated women, 30–54 years old—fully 84 percent are now in the workforce, up from 82 percent 20 years ago. And the much-discussed dip in the labor-force participation of mothers of young children, while real, appears to be largely a function of an economic downturn, which depresses employment for all workers.

Nevertheless, these women are important to study. Elite, educated, high-achieving women have historically been cultural arbiters, defining what is acceptable for all women in their work and family roles. This group's entrance into high-status, formerly male professions has been crucial to advancing gender parity and narrowing the wage gap, which stubbornly persists to this day. At home, moreover, they are rendered silent and invisible, so that it is easy to project and speculate about them. We can see in them whatever we want to, and perhaps that is why they have been the subject of endless speculation—about mommy wars, a return to traditionalism, and the like. While they do not represent all women, elite women's experiences provide a glimpse into the work-family negotiations that all women face. And their stories lead us to ask, "If the most privileged women of society cannot successfully combine work and family, who can?"

motherhood pulls

When Regina initially went back to work, she had "no clue" that she would feel so torn. She advises women not to set "too much in stone," because "you just don't know, when a human being comes out of your body, how you're going to feel." For some women, the pull of children was immediate and strong. Lauren Quattrone, a lawyer, found herself "absolutely besotted with this baby. . . . I realized that I just couldn't bear to leave him." Women such as Lauren tended to quit fairly soon after their first child was born. For others, like Diane Childs, formerly a nonprofit executive, the desire to be home with the kids came later. "I felt that it was easy to leave a baby for twelve hours a day. That I could do. But to leave a six-year-old, I just thought, was a whole different thing."

But none of these women made their decisions to quit in a vacuum. In fact, they did so during a cultural moment when norms and practices for parents—mothers—are very demanding. These women realized they would rear children very differently from the way their own mothers raised them, feeling an external, almost competitive pressure to do so. Middle- and upper-middle-class women tend to be particularly mindful of expert advice, and these women

were acutely aware of a well-documented intensification in raising children, which sociologist Sharon Hays calls an "ideology of intensive mothering." This cultural imperative, felt by women of all kinds, "advises mothers to expend a tremendous amount of time, energy, and money in raising their children."

A corollary is what Annette Lareau terms "concerted cultivation," a nonstop pace of organized activities scheduled by parents for school-age children. Among the women I spoke to, some, like Diane, felt the urgency of "concerted cultivation" and reevaluated their childcare as the more sophisticated needs of their older children superseded the simpler, more straightforward babysitting and physical care required for younger children. Marina Isherwood, a former executive in the health care industry, with children in the second and fourth grades, became convinced that caregivers could not replace her own parental influence:

There isn't a substitute, no matter how good the childcare. When they're little, the fact that someone else is doing the stuff with them is fine. It wasn't the part that I loved anyway. But when they start asking you questions about values, you don't want your babysitter telling them. . . . Our children come home, and they have all this homework to do, and piano lessons and this and this, and it's all a complicated schedule. And, yes, you could get an au pair to do that, to balance it all, but they're not going to necessarily teach how to think about math. Or help you come up with mnemonic devices to memorize all of the countries [sic] in Spain or whatever.

Because academic credentials were so important to these women's (and their husband's) career opportunities, formal schooling was a critical factor in their decisions to quit. For some, the premium they placed on education and values widened the gap between themselves and their less educated caregivers.

Depending on the woman, motherhood played a larger or smaller role in her decision whether and when to quit. Children were the main focus of women's caregiving, but other family members needed care as well, for which women felt responsible. About 10 percent of the women spoke of significant elder-care responsibilities, the need for which was especially unpredictable. This type of caregiving and mothering made up half of the family/career double bind. More important, though, motherhood influenced women's decision to quit as they came to see the rhythms and values of the workplace as antagonistic to family life.

workplace pushes

On top of their demanding mothering regime, these women received mixed messages from both their husbands and their employers. Husbands offered emotional support to wives who were juggling career and family. Emily Mitchell, an accountant, described her marriage to a CPA as "a pretty equal partnership," but when his career became more demanding, requiring long hours and Saturdays at work, he saw the downside of egalitarianism:

I think he never minded taking my daughter to the sitter, that was never an issue, and when he would come home, we have a pretty equal relationship on that stuff. But getting her up, getting her ready, getting himself ready to go into work, me coming home, getting her, getting her to bed, getting unwound from work, and then he would come home, we'd try to do something for dinner, and then there was always something else to do—laundry, cleaning, whatever—I think he was feeling too much on a treadmill.

But husbands did little to share family responsibilities, instead maintaining their own demanding careers full-speed ahead.

Similarly, many workplaces claimed to be "family friendly" and offered a variety of supports. But for women who could take advantage of them, flexible work schedules (which usually meant working part-time) carried significant penalties. Women who shifted to part-time work typically saw their jobs gutted of significant responsibilities and their once-flourishing careers derailed. Worse, part-time hours often crept up to the equivalent of full time. When Diane Childs had children, she scaled back to part-time and began to feel the pointlessness of continuing:

And I'm never going to get anywhere—you have the feeling that you just plateaued professionally because you can't take on extra projects; you can't travel at a moment's notice; you can't stay late; you're not flexible on the Friday thing because that could mean finding someone to take your kids. You really plateau for a much longer period of time than you ever realize when you first have a baby. It's like you're going to be plateaued for thirteen to fifteen years.

Lynn Hamilton, an M.D., first met her husband at Princeton, where they were both undergraduates. Her story illustrates how family pulls and workplace pushes (from both her career and her husband's) interacted in a marriage that was founded on professional equality but then devolved to the detriment of her career:

We met when we were 19 years old, and so, there I was, so naïve, I thought, well, here we are, we have virtually identical credentials and comparable income earnings. There's an opportunity. And, in fact, I think our incomes were identical at the time I quit. To the extent to which we have articulated it, it was always understood, well, with both of us working, neither of us would have to be working these killer jobs. So, what was happening was, instead, we were both working these killer jobs. And I kept saying, "We need to reconfigure this." And what I realized was, he wasn't going to.

Meanwhile, her young daughter was having behavioral problems at school, and her job as a medical director for a biomedical start-up company had "the fax machine going, the three phone lines upstairs, they were going." Lynn slowly realized that the only reconfiguration possible, in the face of her husband's absence, was for her to quit.

Over half (60 percent) of the women I spoke to mentioned their husband as one of the key reasons why they quit. That not all women talked about their husbands' involvement, or lack thereof, reveals the degree to which they perceived the work-family balancing act to be their responsibility alone. But women seldom mentioned their husbands for another reason: they were, quite literally, absent.

Helena Norton, an educational administrator who characterized her husband as a "workaholic," poignantly described a scenario that many others took for granted and which illustrates a pattern typical of many of these women's lives: "He was leaving early mornings; 6:00 or 6:30 before anyone was up, and then he was coming home late at night. So I felt this real emptiness, getting up in the morning to, not necessarily an empty house, because my children were there, but I did, I felt empty, and then going to bed, and he wasn't there."

In not being there to pick up the slack, many husbands had an important indirect impact on their wives' decisions to quit. Deferring to their husbands' careers and exempting them from household chores, these women tended to accept this situation. Indeed, privileging their husbands' careers was a pervasive, almost tacit undercurrent of their stories.

When talking about their husbands, women said the same things: variations on "he's supportive," and that he gave them a "choice." But this hands-off approach revealed husbands to be bystanders, not participants, in the work-family bind. "It's your choice" was code for "it's your problem." And husbands' absences, a direct result of their own high-powered careers, put a great deal of pressure on women to do it all, thus undermining the façade of egalitarianism.

Family pulls—from children and, as a result of their own long work hours, their husbands— exacerbated workplace pushes; and all but seven women cited features of their jobs—the long hours, the travel—as another major motivation in quitting. Marketing executive Nathalie Everett spoke for many women when she remarked that her full-time workweek was "really 60 hours, not 40. Nobody works nine-to-five anymore."

Surprisingly, the women I interviewed, like Nathalie, neither questioned nor showed much resentment toward the features of their jobs that kept them from fully integrating work and family. They routinely described their jobs as "all or nothing" and appeared to internalize what sociologists call the "ideal worker" model of a (typically male) worker unencumbered by family demands. This model was so influential that those working part time or in other flexible arrangements often felt stigmatized. Christine Thomas, a marketing executive and job-sharer, used imagery reminiscent of *The Scarlet Letter* to describe her experience: "When you job share, you have 'MOMMY' stamped in huge letters on your forehead."

While some women's decisions could be attributed to their unquestioning acceptance of the status quo or a lack of imagination, the unsuccessful attempts of others who tried to make it work by pursuing alternatives to full-time, like Diane, serve as cautionary tales. Women who made arrangements with bosses felt like they were being given special favors.

Their part-time schedules were privately negotiated, hence fragile and unstable, and were especially vulnerable in the context of any kind of organizational restructuring such as mergers.

the choice gap

Given the incongruity of these women's experiences—they felt supported by "supportive" yet passive husbands and pushed out by workplaces that once prized their expertise—how did these women understand their situations? How did they make sense of professions that, on the one hand, gave them considerable status and rewards, and, on the other hand, seemed to marginalize them and force them to compromise their identity as mothers?

The overwhelming majority felt the same way as Melissa Wyatt, the 34-year-old who gave up a job as a fund-raiser: "I think today it's all about choices, and the choices we want to make. And I think that's great. I think it just depends on where you want to spend your time." But a few shared the outlook of Olivia Pastore, a 42-year-old ex-lawyer:

I've had a lot of women say to me, "Boy, if I had the choice of, if I could balance, if I could work part-time, if I could keep doing it." And there are some women who are going to stay home full-time no matter what and that's fine. But there are a number of women, I think, who are home because they're caught between a rock and a hard place. . . . There's a lot of talk about the individual decisions of individual women. "Is it good? Is it bad? She gave it up. She couldn't hack it." . . . And there's not enough blame, if you will, being laid at the feet of the culture, the jobs, society.

My findings show that Olivia's comments—about the disjuncture between the rhetoric of choice and the reality of constraint that shapes women's decisions to go home—are closer to the mark. Between trying to be the ideal mother (in an era of intensive mothering) and the ideal worker (a model based on a man with a stay-at-home wife), these high-flying women faced a double bind. Indeed, their options were much more limited than they seemed. Fundamentally, they faced a "choice gap": the difference between the decisions women could have made about their careers if they were not mothers or caregivers and the decisions they had to make in their circumstances as mothers married to high-octane husbands in ultimately unyielding professions. This choice gap obscures individual preferences, and thus reveals the things Olivia railed against—culture, jobs, society— the kinds of things sociologists call "structure."

Overall, women based their decisions on mutually reinforcing and interlocking factors. They confronted, for instance, two sets of trade-offs: kids versus careers, and their own careers versus those of their husbands. For many, circumstances beyond their control strongly influenced their decision to quit. On the family site of the equation, for example, women had to deal with caregiving for sick children and elderly parents, children's developmental problems, and special care needs. Such reasons figured in one-third of the sample. On the work side, women were denied part-time arrangements, and some had to relocate for their own careers or their husbands'. A total of 30 women, a little more than half the sample, mentioned at least one forced-choice consideration.

But even before women had children, the prospect of pregnancy loomed in the background, making women feel that they were perceived as flight risks. In her first day on the job as a marketing executive, for example, Patricia Lambert's boss asked her: "So, are you going to have kids?" And once women did get pregnant, they reported that they were often the first in their office, which made them feel more like outsiders. Some remarked that a dearth of role models created an atmosphere unsympathetic to work-family needs. And as these women navigated pregnancy and their lives beyond, their stories revealed a latent bias against mothers in their workplaces. What some women took from this was that pregnancy was a dirty little secret not to be openly discussed. The private nature of pregnancy thus complicated women's decisions regarding their careers once they became mothers, which is why they often waited until the last minute to figure out their next steps. Their experiences contrasted with the formal policies of their workplaces, which touted themselves as "family friendly."

the rhetoric of choice

Given the indisputable obstacles—hostile workplaces and absentee husbands—that stymied a full integration of work and family, it was ironic that most of the women invoked "choice" when relating the events surrounding their decision to exit their careers. Why were there not more women like Olivia, railing against the tyranny of an outmoded workplace that favored a 1950s-era employee or bemoaning their husbands' drive for achievement at the expense of their own?

I found that these women tended to use the rhetoric of choice in the service of their exceptionality. Women associated choice with privilege, feminism, and personal agency, and internalized it as a reflection of their own perfectionism. This was an unattractive combination that played to their drive for achievement and also served to compensate for their loss of the careers they loved and the professional identities they valued. Some of these women bought into the media message that being an at-home mom was a status symbol, promoted by such

cultural arbiters as *New York Magazine* and the *Wall Street Journal*. Their ability to go home reflected their husbands' career success, in which they and their children basked. Living out the traditional lifestyle, male breadwinner and stay-at-home mom, which they were fortunate to be able to choose, they saw themselves as realizing the dreams of third-wave feminism. The goals of earlier, second-wave feminism, economic independence and gender equality, took a back seat, at least temporarily.

> When women quit, not wanting to burn bridges, they cited family obligations as the reason, not their dissatisfaction with work, in accordance with social expectations. Their own explanations endorsed the prevalent idea that quitting to go home is a choice.

challenging the myth

These strategies and rhetoric, and the apparent invisibility of the choice gap, reveal how fully these high-achieving women internalized the double bind and the intensive-mothering and ideal-workers models on which it rests. The downside, of course, is that they blamed themselves for failing to "have it all" rather than any actual structural constraints. That work and family were incompatible was the overwhelming message they took from their experiences. And when they quit, not wanting to burn bridges, they cited family obligations as the reason, not their dissatisfaction with work, in accordance with social expectations. By adopting the socially desirable and gender-consistent explanation of "family," women often contributed to the larger misunderstanding surrounding their decision. Their own explanations endorsed the prevalent idea that quitting to go home is a choice. Employers rarely challenged women's explanations. Nor did they try to convince them to stay, thus reinforcing women's perception that their decision was the right thing to do as mothers and perpetuating the reigning media image of these women as traditionalists.

Taken at face value, these women do seem to be traditional. But by rejecting an intransigent workplace, their quitting signifies a kind of salient strike. They were not acquiescing to traditional gender roles by quitting, but voting with their feet against an outdated model of work. When women are not posing for the camera or worried about offending former employers (from whom they may need future references), they are able to share their stories candidly. From what I found, the truth is far different and certainly more nuanced than the media depiction.

The vast majority of the type of women I studied do not want to choose between career and family. The demanding nature of today's parenting puts added pressure on women. Women do indeed need to learn to be "good enough" mothers, and their husbands need to engage more equally in parenting. But on the basis of what they told me, women today "choose" to be home full-time not as much because of parenting overload as because of work overload, specifically long hours and the lack of flexible options in their high-status jobs. The popular media depiction of a return to traditionalism is wrong and misleading. Women are trying to achieve the feminist vision of a fully integrated life combining family and work. That so many attempt to remain in their careers when they do not "have to work" testifies strongly to their commitment to their careers, as does the difficulty they experience over their subsequent loss of identity. Their attempts at juggling and their plans to return to work in the future also indicate that their careers were not meant to be ephemeral and should not be treated as such. Rather, we should regard their exits as the miner's canary—a frontline indication that something is seriously amiss in many workplaces. Signs of toxic work environments and white-collar sweatshops are ubiquitous. We can glean from these women's experiences the true cost of these work conditions, which are personal and professional, and, ultimately, societal and economic.

Our current understanding of why high-achieving women quit—based as it is on choice and separate spheres—seriously undermines the will to change the contemporary workplace. The myth of opting out returns us to the days when educated women were barred from entering elite professions because "they'll only leave anyway." To the extent that elite women are arbiters of shifting gender norms, the opting out myth also has the potential to curtail women's aspirations and stigmatize those who challenge the separate-spheres ideology on which it is based. Current demographics make it clear that employers can hardly afford to lose the talents of high-achieving women. They can take a cue from at-home moms like the ones I studied: Forget opting out; the key to keeping professional women on the job is to create better, more flexible ways to work.

RECOMMENDED RESOURCES

Mary Blair-Loy. *Competing Devotions: Career and Family among Women Executives* (Harvard University Press, 2003).

> Argues for a cultural, less materialist, understanding of contemporary work-family conflict among high-achieiving working wormen.

Sharon Hays. *The Cultural Contradictions of Motherhood* (Yale University Press, 1995).

> Describes the historical emergence and contemporary internalization of motherhood norms that are at odds with the realities of women's changing lives, with powerful theorizing as to why.

Arlie Hochschild. *The Second Shift* (Viking, 1989).

> Still the defining classic of the work-family field, identifying in women's work at home another problem that had no name.

Jerry A. Jacobs and Kathleen Gerson. *The Time Divide: Work, Family and Gender Inequality* (Harvard University Press, 2004).

> Makes the case for time as the newly emerging basis of gender and class inequality, with lots of hard-to-find facts and good policy prescriptions.

Phyllis Moen and Patricia Roehling. *The Career Mystique: Cracks in the American Dream* (Rowman and Littlefield, 2005).

> A masterful exploration of the creation, maintenance, and consequences of the high-demand, all-consuming workplace, whose title consciously echoes Friedan's *The Feminine Mystique*.

REVIEW QUESTIONS

1. How does your generation view mothers who stay at home? Do you think these perceptions have changed from your parents' and grandparents' generations? Is this positive or problematic?

2. According to Stone, what is the real reason behind more and more mothers dropping out of the workforce? What are some underlying problems with many "family-friendly" work arrangements?

3. Activity: Assume you've been given the task of redesigning your company's workplace environment and scheduling norms so they are better suited for the types of working parents highlighted in this article. How could you change the work culture so mothers weren't penalized for taking advantage of flexible work arrangements? Could any other problems result from your solutions?

cedric herring

is job discrimination dead?

24

summer 2002

political and legal debate in recent years has focused on whether discrimination in favor of african americans is justified. what receives less attention is that employment discrimination against african americans, though illegal, is still alive and well in america.

In November 1996, Texaco settled a case for $176 million with African-American employees who charged that the company systematically denied them promotions. Texaco originally vowed to fight the charges. When irrefutable evidence surfaced, however, Texaco changed its position. The *New York Times* released a tape recording of several Texaco executives referring to black employees as "niggers" and "black jelly beans" who would stay stuck at the bottom of the bag. Texaco also ultimately acknowledged that they used two promotion lists—a public one that included the names of blacks and a secret one that excluded all black employee names. The $176 million settlement was at the time the largest amount ever awarded in a discrimination suit.

Much has changed in American race relations over the past 50 years. In the old days, job discrimination against African Americans was clear, pervasive, and undeniable. There were "white jobs" for which blacks need not apply, and there were "Negro jobs" in which no self-respecting white person would be found. No laws prohibited racial discrimination in employment. Indeed, in several states laws required separation of blacks and whites in virtually every public realm. Not only was racial discrimination the reality of the day, but also many whites supported the idea that job discrimination against blacks was appropriate. In 1944, 55 percent of whites admitted to interviewers that they thought whites should receive preference over blacks in access to jobs, compared with only 3 percent who offered such opinions in 1972.

Many blatant forms of racism have disappeared. Civil rights laws make overt and covert acts of discrimination illegal. Also, fewer Americans admit to traditional racist beliefs than ever before. Such changes have inspired many scholars and social commentators to herald the "end of racism" and to declare that we have created a color-blind society. They point to declines in prejudice, growth in the proportion of blacks who hold positions of responsibility, a closing of the earnings gap between young blacks and young whites, and other evidence of "racial progress."

However, racial discrimination in employment is still widespread; it has just gone underground and become more sophisticated. Many citizens, especially whites who have never experienced such treatment, find it hard to believe

> Racial discrimination in employment is still widespread; It has just gone underground and become more sophisticated.

that such discriminatory behavior by employers exists. Indeed, 75 percent of whites in a 1994 survey said that whites were likely to lose a job to a less-qualified black. Nevertheless, clear and convincing evidence of discriminatory patterns against black job seekers exists.

In addition to the landmark Texaco case, other corporate giants have made the dishonor roll in recent years. In 2000, a court ordered Ford Motor Company to pay $9 million to victims of sexual and racial harassment. Ford also agreed to pay $3.8 million to settle another suit with the U.S. Labor Department involving discrimination in hiring women and minorities at seven of the company's plants. Similarly in 1999, Boeing agreed to pay $82 million to end racially based pay disparities at its plants. In April 2000, Amtrak paid $16 million to settle a race discrimination lawsuit that alleged Amtrak had discriminated against black employees in hiring, promotion, discipline, and training. And in November 2000, the Coca-Cola Company settled a federal lawsuit brought by black employees for more than $190 million. These employees accused Coca-Cola of erecting a corporate hierarchy in which black employees were clustered at the bottom of the pay scale, averaging $26,000 a year less than white workers.

The list of companies engaged in discrimination against black workers is long and includes many pillars of American industry, not just marginal or maverick firms. Yet when incidents of discrimination come into public view, many of us are still mystified and hard-pressed for explanations. This is so, in part, because discrimination has become so illegitimate that companies expend millions of dollars to conceal it. They have managed to discriminate without using the blatant racism of the old days. While still common, job discrimination against blacks has become more elusive and less apparent.

how common?

Most whites think that discriminatory acts are rare and sensationalized by a few high-profile cases and that the nation is well on its way to becoming a color-blind society. According to a 2001 Gallup survey, nearly 7 in 10 whites (69 percent) said that blacks are treated "the same as whites" in their local communities. The numbers, however, tell a different story. Annually, the federal government receives about 80,000 complaints of employment discrimination, and another 60,000 cases are filed with state and local fair employment practices commissions. One recent study found that about 60 percent of blacks reported racial barriers in their workplace in the last year, and a 1997 Gallup survey found that one in five reported workplace discrimination in the previous month.

The results of "social audits" suggest that the actual frequency of job discrimination against blacks is even higher than blacks themselves realize. Audit studies test for discrimination by sending white and minority "job seekers" with comparable résumés and skills to the same hiring firms to apply for the same job. The differential treatment they receive provides a measure of discrimination. These audits consistently find that employers are less likely to interview or offer jobs to minority applicants. For example, studies by the Fair Employment Practices Commission of Washington, D.C., found that blacks face discrimination in one out of every five job interviews and that they are denied job offers 20 percent of the time. A similar study by the Urban Institute matched equally qualified white and black testers who applied for the same jobs in Chicago. About 38 percent of the time, white applicants advanced further in the hiring process than equally qualified blacks. Similarly, a General Accounting Office audit study uncovered significant discrimination against black and Latino testers. In comparison with whites, black and Latino candidates with equal credentials received 25 percent fewer job interviews and 34 percent fewer job offers.

These audit studies suggest that present-day discrimination is more sophisticated than in the old days. For example, discriminating employers do not explicitly deny jobs to blacks; rather, they use the different phases of the hiring process to discriminate in ways that are difficult to detect. In particular, when comparable résumés of black and white testers are sent to firms, discriminatory firms systematically call whites first and repeatedly until they exhaust their list of white applicants before they approach their black prospects. They offer whites jobs on the spot but tell blacks that they will give them a call back in a few weeks. These mechanisms mean that white applicants go through the hiring process before any qualified blacks are even considered.

Discriminatory employers also offer higher salaries and higher-status positions to white applicants. For example, audit studies have documented that discriminatory employment agencies often note race in the files of black applicants and steer them away from desirable and lucrative positions. A Fair Employment Practices Commission study found that these agencies, which control much of the applicant flow into white-collar jobs, discriminate against black applicants more than 60 percent of the time.

Surprisingly, many employers are willing to detail (in confidence to researchers) how they discriminate against black job seekers. Some admit refusing to consider any black applicants. Many others admit to engaging in recruitment practices that artificially reduce the number of black applicants who know about and apply for entry-level jobs in their firms. One effective way is to avoid ads in mainstream newspapers. In one Chicago study, more than 40 percent of the employers from firms within the city did not advertise their entry-level job openings in mainstream newspapers. Instead, they advertised job vacancies in neighborhood or ethnic newspapers that targeted particular groups, mainly Hispanics or white East European immigrants. For the employer who wants to avoid blacks, this strategy can be quite effective when employment ads are written in languages other than English, or when the circulation of such newspapers is through channels that usually do not reach many blacks.

Employers described recruiting young workers largely from Catholic schools or schools in white areas. Besides avoiding public schools, these employers also avoided recruiting from job-training, welfare, and state employment service programs. Consequently, some job-training programs have had unanticipated negative effects on the incomes and employment prospects of their African-American enrollees. For instance, research on the effect of such training programs on the earnings and employability of black inner-city residents found that those who participated in various job-training programs earned less per month and had higher unemployment rates than their counterparts who had not participated in such programs.

who suffers?

Generally, no black person is immune from discriminatory treatment. A few factors make some even more vulnerable to discrimination than others. In particular, research has shown that African Americans with dark complexions are likelier to report discrimination—one-half do—than those with lighter complexions. Job discrimination is also associated with education in a peculiar fashion: Those blacks with more education report more discrimination. For example, in a Los Angeles study, more than 80 percent of black workers with college degrees and more than 90 percent of those with graduate-level educations reported facing workplace discrimination. Black immigrants are more likely than nonimmigrants to report discrimination experiences, residents of smaller communities report more than those of larger ones, and younger African Americans report more than older ones. Rates of job discrimination are lower among those who are married than among those who are not wed. Research also shows that some employment characteristics also appear to make a difference: African Americans who are hired through personal contacts report discrimination less often, as do those who work in the manufacturing sector and those who work for larger firms.

Discrimination exacts a financial cost. African Americans interviewed in the General Social Survey in 1991 who reported discrimination in the prior year earned $6,200 less than those who reported none. (In addition, blacks earn $3,800 less than whites because of differences in educational attainment, occupation, age, and other factors.) A one-time survey cannot determine whether experiences of discrimination lead to low income or whether low income leads to feeling discriminated against. Multivariate research based on data from the Census Bureau, which controls for education and other wage-related factors, shows that the white-black wage gap (i.e., "the cost of being black") has continued to be more than 10 percent—about the same as in the mid 1970s. Moreover, research looking at the effects of discrimination over the lifecourse suggests a cumulative effect of discrimination on wages such that the earnings gap between young blacks and whites becomes greater as both groups age.

how can there be discrimination?

Many economists who study employment suggest that job discrimination against blacks cannot (long) exist in a rational market economy because jobs are allocated based on ability and earnings maximization. Discrimination, they argue, cannot play a major role in the rational employer's efforts to hire the most productive worker at the lowest price. If employers bypass productive workers to satisfy their racism, competitors will hire these workers at lower-than-market wages and offer their goods and services at lower prices, undercutting discriminatory employers. When presented with evidence that discrimination does occur, many economists point to discriminators' market monopoly: Some firms, they argue, are shielded from competition and that allows them to act on their "taste for discrimination." These economists, however, do not explain why employers would prefer to discriminate in the first place. Other economists suggest that employers may rationally rely on "statistical discrimination." Lacking sufficient information about would-be employees, employers use presumed "average" productivity characteristics of the groups to which the potential employees belong to predict who will make the best workers. In other words, stereotypes about black workers (on average) being worse than whites make it "justifiable" for employers to bypass qualified black individuals. In these ways, those economists who acknowledge racial discrimination explain it as a "rational" response to imperfect information and imperfect markets.

In contrast, most sociologists point to prejudice and group conflict over scarce resources as reasons for job discrimination. For example, racial groups create and preserve their identities and advantages by reserving opportunities for their own members. Racially based labor queues and differential terms of employment allow members to allocate work according to criteria that have little to do with productivity or earnings maximization. Those who discriminate against blacks often use negative stereotypes to rationalize their behavior after the fact, which, in turn, reinforces racism, negative stereotypes, and caricatures of blacks.

In particular, labor market segregation theory suggests that the U.S. labor market is divided into two fundamentally different sectors: (1) the primary sector and (2) the secondary sector. The primary sector is composed of jobs that offer job security, work rules that define job responsibilities and duties, upward mobility, and higher incomes and earnings. These jobs allow incumbents to accumulate skills that lead to progressively more responsibility and higher pay. In contrast, secondary sector jobs tend to be low-paying, dead-end jobs with few benefits, arbitrary work rules, and pay structures that are not related to job tenure. Workers in such jobs have less motivation to develop attachments to their firms or to perform their jobs well. Thus, it is mostly workers who cannot gain employment in the primary sector who work in the secondary sector. Race discrimination—sometimes by employers but at times by restrictive unions and professional associations fearful that the inclusion of blacks may drive down their overall wages or prestige—plays a role in determining who gets access to jobs in the primary sector. As a consequence, African Americans are locked out of jobs in the primary labor market, where they would receive higher pay and better treatment, and they tend to be crowded into the secondary sector. And these disparities compound over time as primary sector workers enhance their skills and advance while secondary sector workers stay mired in dead-end jobs.

An alternative sociological explanation of African-American disadvantage in the U.S. labor market is what can be referred to as "structural discrimination." In this view, African Americans are denied access to good jobs through practices that appear to be race-neutral but that work to the detriment of African Americans. Examples of such seemingly race-neutral practices include seniority rules, employers' plant location decisions, policy makers' public transit decisions, funding of public education, economic recessions, and immigration and trade policies.

In the seniority rules example, if blacks are hired later than whites because they are later in the employers' employment queue (for whatever reason), operating strictly by traditional seniority rules will ensure greater job security and higher pay to whites than to African Americans. Such rules virtually guarantee that blacks, who were the last hired, will be the "first fired" and the worst paid. The more general point is that employers do not have to be prejudiced in implementing their seniority rules for the rules to have the effects of structural discrimination on African Americans. Unequal outcomes are built into the rules themselves.

These same dynamics apply when (1) companies decide to locate away from urban areas with high concentrations of black residents; (2) policy makers decide to build public transit that provides easy access from the suburbs to central city job sites but not from the inner city to central city job sites or to suburban job sites; (3) public education is funded through local property tax revenues that may be lower in inner-city communities where property values are depressed and higher in suburban areas where property values are higher and where tax revenues are supplemented by corporations that have fled the inner city; (4) policy makers attempt to blunt the effects of inflation and high interest rates by allowing unemployment rates to climb, especially when they climb more rapidly in African-American communities; and (5) policy makers negotiate immigration and trade agreements that may lead to lower employer costs but may also lead to a reduction in the number of jobs available to African Americans in the industries affected by such agreements. Again, in none of these cases do decision makers need to be racially prejudiced for their decisions to have disproportionately negative effects on the job prospects or life chances of African Americans.

what can be done?

Employment discrimination, overt or covert, is against the law, yet it clearly happens. Discrimination still damages the lives of African Americans. Therefore, policies designed to reduce discrimination should be strengthened and expanded rather than reduced or eliminated, as has recently occurred. Light must be shed on the practice, and heat must be applied to those who engage in it. Some modest steps can be taken to reduce the incidence and costs of racial discrimination:

conduct more social audits of employers in various industries of varying sizes and locations

In 2000, the courts upheld the right of testers (working with the Legal Assistance Foundation of Chicago) to sue discriminatory employers. Expanded use of evidence from social audits in lawsuits against discriminatory employers provides more information about discriminatory processes, arms black applicants more effectively, and provides greater deterrence to would-be discriminators who do not want to be exposed. Even when prevention is not successful, documentation from social audits makes it easier to prosecute illegal discrimination. As in the Texaco case, it has often been through exposure and successful litigation that discriminatory employers mended their ways.

restrict government funding to and public contracts with firms that have records of repeated discrimination against black applicants and black employees

The government needs to ensure that discriminatory employers do not use taxpayer money to carry out their unfair treatment of African Americans. Firms that continue discriminating against blacks should have their funding and their reputations linked to their performance. Also, as lawsuits over this issue proliferate, defense of such practices becomes an expensive proposition. Again, those found guilty of such activities should have to rely on their own resources and not receive additional allocations from the state. Such monetary deterrence may act as a reminder that racial discrimination is costly.

redouble affirmative action efforts

Affirmative action consists of activities undertaken specifically to identify, recruit, promote, or retain qualified members of disadvantaged minority groups to overcome the results of past discrimination and to deter discriminatory practices in the present. It presumes that simply removing existing impediments is not sufficient for changing the relative positions of various groups. In addition, it is based on the premise that to truly affect unequal distribution of life chances, employers must take specific steps to remedy the consequences of discrimination.

speak out when episodes of discrimination occur

It is fairly clear that much discrimination against African Americans goes unreported because it occurs behind closed doors and in surreptitious ways. Often, it is only when some (white) insider provides irrefutable evidence that such incidents come to light. It is incumbent upon white Americans to do their part to help stamp out this malignancy.

Now that racial discrimination in employment is illegal, stamping it out should be eminently easier to accomplish. The irony is that because job discrimination against blacks has been driven underground, many people are willing to declare victory and thereby let this scourge continue to flourish in its camouflaged state. If we truly want to move toward a color-blind society, however, we must punish such hurtful discriminatory behaviors when they occur, and we should reward efforts by employers who seek to diversify their workforce by eliminating racial discrimination. This is precisely what happened in the landmark Texaco case, as well as the recent Coca-Cola settlement. In both cases, job discrimination against African Americans was driven above ground, made costly to those who practiced it and offset by policies that attempted to level the playing field.

RECOMMENDED RESOURCES

Katherine P. Dickinson, Terry R. Johnson, and Richard W. West. "An Analysis of the Impact of CETA Programs on Participants' Earnings." *Journal of Human Resources* 21 (1986): 64–91.

Joe Feagin. *Racist America: Roots, Current Realities, and Future Reparations* (Routledge, 2001).

Michael Fix and Raymond J. Struyk. *Clear and Convincing Evidence: Measurement of Discrimination in America* (Urban Institute, 1993).

Peter Gottschall. "Inequality, Income Growth, and Mobility: The Basic Facts." *Journal of Economic Perspectives* 11 (1997): 21–40.

Cedric Herring, ed. *African Americans and the Public Agenda: The Paradoxes of Public Policy* (Sage Publications, 1997).

Joleen Kirschenman and Kathryn M. Neckerman. "'We'd Love to Hire Them, But . . .': The Meaning of Race for Employers." In *The Urban Underclass*, eds. C. Jencks and P. Peterson (Brookings Institution, 1991).

Alice O'Connor, Chris Tilly, and Lawrence Bobo, eds. *Urban Inequality: Evidence from Four Cities* (Russell Sage Foundation, 2001).

Melvin Thomas, Cedric Herring, and Hayward Derrick Horton. "Discrimination over the Life Course: A Synthetic Cohort Analysis of Earnings Differences between Black and White Males, 1940–1990." *Social Problems* 41 (1994): 608–28.

William Julius Wilson. *When Work Disappears: The World of the New Urban Poor* (Vintage Books, 1997).

REVIEW QUESTIONS

1. Herring writes that racism is barely evident for most of us in our everyday experiences but has headed "underground." Discuss how this covert form of racism has affected popular perceptions of race. Has this approach to understanding racism become a challenge to social scientists? How?
2. How does "labor market theory" relate to issues of racism? What is the "structural discrimination" theory of racism? Which position do you find most compelling?
3. Affirmative action has been debated for years, and Herring claims that such programs are necessary to redress the consequences of discrimination. Discuss both the positive and negative consequences of affirmative action.

bruce g. carruthers

a sociology of bubbles

25

summer 2009

a re-examination of the recent economic meltdown reveals not only the roots of the collapse but the social and institutional foundations of markets themselves.

We have just lived through a classic market bubble. Asset prices climbed for many years, the good times rolled, and even those who knew better participated in the irrational exuberance. Then the bubble burst: housing prices dropped, banks became insolvent, and the stock market lost half its value. Market liquidity disappeared almost overnight as lenders stopped lending.

The current economic crisis has created tremendous uncertainty and huge social problems. And at an individual level, many Americans are suffering from job loss, shrinking home equity, a decline in the value of their pensions, and a substantial loss of wealth.

Disaster like this prompts (or at least should) a collective reflection on how we got into this mess in the first place—in particular, why the institutional foundations for markets stopped working. Today, the "real economy" is doing very poorly, but the problems seem to have started in the subprime mortgage market within the U.S. financial sector.

Three aspects of this situation seem particularly amenable to sociological analysis: bond-rating agencies and how they "know" what they think they know, the social networks and personal connections that encourage "herding" among financial elites, and the political consequences of recent transformations in investment. Striking in all this is the contrast between the massive scale of the crisis in the global finance system and the concentrated, tight-knit nature of the financial community that helped create it.

ratings, structured finance, and (misplaced) trust

After bubbles burst, the recriminations usually begin. Much of the finger-pointing over the collapse of the real estate market has been directed at the rating agencies, the best-known being Moody's Investors Service and Standard & Poor's.

Traditionally, these private firms rated corporate and government bonds by assessing the creditworthiness of the borrower. Good ratings were much sought after because highly rated borrowers paid less interest. Furthermore, various financial regulations used the ratings when telling banks how much capital they had to set aside to cover potential losses, or when constraining insurance companies not to make speculative investments.

Rating agencies were paid by the entity issuing the bonds (creating an obvious conflict of interest), and rating involved classification in terms of the well-known ordinal category system that ranged from "AAA" at the top down to "CA" at the bottom. The higher categories were known as "investment grade" and the lower categories as "junk." For a long time, the rating agencies generally did a decent job of assessing long-term risks, showing that the chances of default on an "AAA" corporate bond was indeed small, whereas the likelihood of default on a junk bond was much higher. In supplying critical information, they became central players in the operation of modern credit markets.

As a consequence of the deregulation that began in the 1980s, however, the separation between commercial banks and investment banks broke down. U.S. finance changed, and along with it the role of the rating agencies. The 1990s especially saw the growth of "structured finance," where instead of commercial banks taking deposits and making loans, and corporations issuing stocks or bonds to raise additional money, investment banks began to craft new kinds of financial instruments that attracted money from all over the world.

Structured finance became especially popular in the mortgage industry because it seemed to boost profits, steer more investment into housing, and increase homeownership. When applied to subprime mortgages, structured finance appeared to combine virtue with profitability because it helped people with otherwise poor credit records buy homes. It was also great business for the rating agencies because they earned a lot of money rating these new and complex instruments. But this system marked a significant departure from traditional home mortgages.

In the old days (recall Frank Capra's *It's a Wonderful Life*), mortgages were simple and boring. Bankers would make long-term loans to individuals they knew personally or knew a good deal about so those individuals could purchase homes. The house served as collateral for the loan, and the bank kept the loan on its books. The loans the bankers carried on their balance sheets were what's called "illiquid assets," basically because it was hard to pass on the idiosyncratic, local information on which the loan was based. If the individual successfully repaid the loan, the bank got a long-term income stream, paid in monthly installments.

But once bankers got the idea they could sell bundles of mortgages to investors, they shifted from being lenders to being originators. "Securitization" involved pooling thousands of mortgages together and then issuing securities against the cash flow that the mortgage payments collectively generated. Instead of holding a single illiquid home mortgage, the investor got a liquid and more diversified investment. A bank that made a mortgage loan could securitize it and sell it to an investor, and with its capital the bank could make another mortgage loan. Before long, the origination process itself became a separate business as mortgage brokers passed loans on to banks, and banks packaged, securitized, and passed them on to investors. Because originators no longer held on to their loans, they had less incentive to be diligent lenders. This is where the ratings agencies came into play in a whole new way.

> In the old days, mortgages were simple and boring. But once bankers got the idea they could sell bundles of mortgages to investors, they shifted from being lenders to being originators.

The problems in the U.S. financial sector seem to have started in the sub-prime mortgage market. (Andrew Ciscel via Creative Commons)

Investors who purchased mortgage-backed securities, and more complicated instruments, didn't have the detailed local knowledge about borrowers that a local bank possessed. They had to depend on the rating agencies to tell them about the riskiness of a particular investment to provide credible knowledge about the value of new financial products.

The problem is, the ratings agencies didn't create new rating systems to assess the risks and uncertainties of these complicated new securities. They simply folded their assessment of these new products into the rating system they had created for the traditional bond market. This offered a familiar, standardized, and legitimate type of "knowledge" about these new approaches to finance. However, it's now obvious the traditional rating system wasn't matched to the complexities of the new structured finance model.

levels of complexity and uncertainty

A mortgage-backed security is a relatively simple device (a "pass through" security), but financial wizards added another layer of complication and turned mid-rated (say, "BAA1") mortgage-backed securities into collateralized debt obligations (CDOs) with different ratings (many that were higher, "AAA," and some that were lower, "B1"). This operation is hard to understand, and that's one reason why investors and rating agencies didn't really grasp the risks involved with structured finance.

Creating CDOs involved establishing separate layers, called "tranches," and giving them different priority claims over the cash flow the mortgage-backed securities generated. The senior tranche had the highest priority and so got paid first. Then the mezzanine tranche was paid. And only if it were fully satisfied did income go to the lowest tranche (the equity tranche).

To appreciate the importance of priority, imagine a restaurant in which the chef cooked an amount of food that varied daily. Each day a fixed number of tickets were sold to diners, with each ticket entitling the diner to a meal. The tickets were numbered 1 through 100, and diners were seated in the same order as their number (1 ate first, 2 ate second, and so on). Because the amount of food varied, sometimes the chef didn't cook enough to feed everyone. When she didn't, the diners seated last wouldn't get full meals. In fact, they might get nothing at all.

Diners with low-number tickets are like the senior tranche in a CDO: they have the highest priority and are the first to consume. Diners with very high numbers eat last and are at the highest risk of not getting enough food. They're like the

The New York Stock Exchange building. Mass participation in the stock market enabled the contemporary finance system and all its foibles to emerge and evolve. (B. Tse via Creative Commons)

equity tranche in a CDO. Exposure to the risk of hunger is concentrated among low-priority diners. Because high-priority tickets are less risky, they command a higher price. Were rating agencies advising diners, they would give their highest ratings to the low-number meal tickets.

Creating a CDO allowed banks to extract more highly rated securities from the same underlying pool of home mortgages. Higher ratings attracted more investment and allowed for higher fees. The alchemical transformation was most impressive when financial wizards turned a pool of subprime mortgages into AAA-rated securities. In fact, some banks even applied the CDO operation (dividing cash flows into tranches with different priorities, and earmarking those cash flows to new securities) to CDOs themselves, creating the CDO2. Each additional layer of pooling, slicing, and dicing moved the investor farther away from the underlying assets and made the value of those assets increasingly harder to know.

More than ever investors depended on the rating agencies and their traditional rating system. By giving a "AAA" rating to a CDO or CDO2, raters implied that such an investment was similar to a AAA-rated corporate bond. Indeed, that was what helped lure investors into buying these otherwise opaque instruments, for the traditional rating system offered a familiar, standardized, and legitimate type of "knowledge."

These new instruments helped boost the rating agencies' revenues, but they posed a challenge. Unlike the "single-name" bonds Moody's and Standard & Poor's had been rating for a century, for CDOs there was no long-term baseline of data on which to estimate the probability of default. Wall Street firms hired lots of physicists and mathematicians to do their numbers, but the data they used covered a thin and atypi-

> The strangest thing about the financial community is that it's an actual community in the traditional, localized, sociological conception of the term.

cal slice of time. Specifically, estimates of the probabilities of default for subprime mortgages were calculated over a period (roughly the last 10 years) of rising home prices. As soon as home prices leveled and then dropped, defaults in subprime mortgages quickly climbed to much higher levels than anyone expected on the basis of their models.

The misplaced confidence in subprime-based mortgage-backed securities and CDOs was akin to concluding a home is earthquake-proof because it has remained intact over a period in which there were no earthquakes. No one factored in the effect of declining home prices, particularly on variable-rate subprime mortgages with "teaser" interest rates that floated after two years. In addition, the default estimates for CDOs were very sensitive to estimation errors—a small mistake in calculating the probability of default for an underlying asset was amplified many fold when estimating default probabilities for the CDO manufactured out of those assets. So if Moody's got it wrong for subprime mortgages, they really got it wrong for CDOs. Their sophisticated quantitative models were indeed "rocket science," but this created too much confidence in estimates that, in reality, weren't very robust.

"herding" in the financial community

Rating agencies are among the most high-profile culprits in the recent economic meltdown, but they're only one part of a much broader financial community. And the strangest thing about the financial community is that it's an actual community in the traditional, localized, sociological conception of the term.

Even at the global level, modern financial communities remain close-knit and geographically concentrated in small areas of New York City, London, and Tokyo. This concentration occurs despite the fact that electronic communications (think: Skype) can cheaply and instantaneously link people from around the world. Bankers and other financial elites are also embedded in multiple, interlocking networks, both informal and professional. (Indeed, the most formal and professional of these—the network of director "interlocks" where elites sit on each others' boards and participate in shared governance—help explain why corporate policies and innovations typically spread so quickly and thoroughly.) High finance is, in short, a very small world.

Many people have wondered why many financial institutions and professionals did things that in retrospect seem so stupid. Why was there a lemming-like rush into exotic derivatives that even Wall Street rocket scientists couldn't understand? These tight, close-knit communities and networks provide an important part of the answer.

Investment banks have well-defined peer groups, and if one bank is doing something that seems profitable, others will want to do it as well, and as soon as possible. Strong and dense interconnections within financial communities made it hard for even a skeptical financier to resist something when "everyone else" was doing it. After all, the imperative to emulate others was what allowed these innovations to diffuse throughout the financial system so quickly in the first place. This is what sociologists sometimes call "herding." This kind of situation offers advantages even when decisions turn out poorly: mistakes become forgivable if everyone else was doing the same thing.

What may have encouraged the stampede even further was the propensity for financial professionals and institutions to hire socially similar or "homophilous" individuals. For some decades, the financial sector of the U.S. econ-omy has been growing in relative size. Since financial markets were deregulated, investment banks and other elite financial institutions offered increasingly lucrative and high-status jobs to the best and brightest, so they could be very picky about hiring. But by favoring some groups in recruitment and by putting a premium on picking "team players," the financial community reproduced itself socially. When peers come from the same social background, with similar education, it's easy to embrace the kind of "me too" attitude that produced a great deal of imitation. When coupled with collective overconfidence, the result was little short of disastrous.

We also see the same herd-like behavior in the collapse of the subprime mortgage market and in the decline of structured finance. Once the financial world soured on subprimes and CDOs, the rush to escape was even faster than the rush to get in. Now, no financial institution wants to lend to anyone else (with the notable exception of the U.S. Treasury), and everyone is hoarding their cash. Liquidity has dried up. And as firms' financial situations worsen, they have to sell off assets, which drives down prices, which worsens their financial situation, and so on in a vicious downward circle.

Tight-knit communities may be interesting and harmless when located in small towns in southern France or midwest America. And herding can be quite entertaining to observe among peer-conscious teenagers. But the financial sector stuck together like a bunch of villagers, behaved like a crowd of college sophomores, and managed to endanger the world economy in the process.

political fallout

This bubble, like previous bubbles (e.g., the Tulip Bubble, the South Sea Bubble), will pass. But it will have consequences—as legislators and policy-makers well know. Indeed, the political reactions to the financial crisis have been as interesting as the collapse itself.

The recent explosion in the number of individuals who participate in stock market investment and own shares in the market has played a crucial role here. Over the past 30 years, individual share ownership, college savings funds, ownership of mutual funds, and participation in 401(k) or 403(b) pension funds have increased substantially. This mass participation enabled the contemporary finance system and all its foibles to emerge and evolve, at least as long as times were good. At the same time, though, many people now perceive a direct link between their personal financial well-being and the performance of the stock market. Ordinary citizens are more directly exposed to the vagaries of the stock market because more of them now have a stake.

Moreover, the growth of financial journalism makes it hard not to know about the market and news about those risks is now a daily staple. This all helped create a political incentive to react swiftly to the economic crisis. It has also led to some quite unexpected outcomes, like conservative Republicans in the White House spearheading a de facto nationalization of large portions of the banking system in the fall of 2008. (The recent collapse has also probably postponed, for at least a generation, the Republican dream of "privatizing" social security.)

The fact that today's crash was preceded by a long period of growing economic inequality is also politically significant. Disparities in household incomes are at a level not seen since the end of the Roaring '20s (or, more sobering, the start of the Great Depression). Political outrage against the huge bonuses paid to the financiers whose most recent accomplishment was to lose vast sums of money may signal the start of another populist moment in American politics.

Disaster creates a political opportunity not only for Congress to ritually disparage a few Wall Street plutocrats but also to rewrite the economic rules and more equitably distribute the economic surplus. The New Deal put in place institutions that led to long-term economic gains for middle- and working-class Americans, but those changes wouldn't have been possible without the discrediting (perhaps temporary) of corporate and financial elites.

> Future reforms will be shaped by the fact that the U.S. financial system is globally connected. Policies that may seem attractive for domestic political reasons will be judged by foreign investors.

no more wonderful life

The bankers in *It's a Wonderful Life* gave mortgages to people they knew well in a small, sleepy town. In the more recent past, mortgage lenders transformed themselves into high-powered sellers of exotic CDOs offered to a global market of investors. But even though the financial products left the small-town world behind long ago, the financial sector continued to act a lot like a small, close-knit community where people looked and thought and acted like the close neighbors they could trust if only because things weren't too complicated. The failure of the banking system and financial community to realize this mismatch has had nasty results on, unfortunately, a global scale.

At the very least, public oversight of the financial sector will be strengthened to compensate for the excesses of deregulation. However, future reforms will be also be shaped by the fact that the U.S. financial system is globally connected, and policies that may seem attractive for domestic political reasons will be judged by the foreign investors who currently fund the U.S. government's deficits. After the Asian financial crisis 10 years ago, East Asian leaders heard a lot of speeches from the International Monetary Fund and U.S. Treasury Department about the virtues of Anglo-Saxon capitalism. Clearly a lot has changed. We don't live in a wonderful-life world anymore.

RECOMMENDED RESOURCES

Greta R. Krippner. "The Financialization of the American Economy." *Socio-Economic Review* (2005) 3: 173–208.

An overview of the growing size and importance of the financial sector.

Donald MacKenzie. *An Engine, Not a Camera: How Financial Models Shape Markets* (MIT Press, 2006).

Illuminates the invention and diffusion of option-pricing models as a social process that helped remake financial markets.

Louise Marie Roth. "The Social Psychology of Tokenism: Status and Homophily Processes on Wall Street." *Sociological Perspectives* (2004) 47(2): 189–214.

Shows that despite its strong "bottom-line" orientation, Wall Street is not immune to various types of social preference.

Saskia Sassen. "The Embeddedness of Electronic Markets: The Case of Global Capital Markets." In *The Sociology of Financial Markets* (Oxford University Press, 2005).

Explains why contemporary financial communities are still very much communities.

Timothy J. Sinclair. *The New Masters of Capital: American Bond Rating Agencies and the Politics of Creditworthiness* (Cornell University Press, 2005).

One of the few social science books on credit-rating agencies.

REVIEW QUESTIONS

1. Do you have any experience with the finance system in the United States (e.g., the stock market, mortgages, school loans)? Has your experience been positive or negative? Explain. If you have no experience, how do you think you will in the future?

2. Has the economic recession changed your views of the financial system in this country? What consequences of the recession have you seen in your own life? Make a list and compare it with a partner's.

3. Why do you think so many people invest in the stock market or borrow from banks when the risks are so high? What do you think this says about our culture? What would a sociologist say?

4. The author writes that economic inequality in this country is at levels not seen since the Great Depression. On the basis of what you learned from this article and your own knowledge, what do you think are the social repercussions of such high economic inequality?

lane kenworthy

tax myths

26

summer 2009

taxation may be necessary to fund government services and redistribute wealth and resources. but do taxes really harm the economy? a sociological take on this and other puzzles.

Tax paradoxes abound. Taxation is a vital component of government policy, yet most citizens profess little understanding of the tax system. Many Americans wish taxes were lower, but they want to maintain or expand most of the government programs taxes fund. Policymakers regularly pledge to simplify the tax code, yet it grows ever more complicated.

Tax myths are equally common. In recent years, social scientists have devoted greater attention to empirical study of taxes—how they operate, what effects they have, how the public perceives them. As it turns out, a number of things—four in particular—citizens and policymakers think they know about taxation are wrong.

> Heavy taxation certainly doesn't ensure a competitive economy, but it appears to be perfectly compatible with one.

myth #1: heavy taxation reduces economic competitiveness

Taxes distort the market's ability to allocate resources toward their most productive use, and textbook economic theory tells us this is bad for the economy. Taxation may be necessary to fund government services and redistribution of wealth and resources in a way that conforms to the needs and norms of a modern society, but it's a necessary evil.

But do taxes really harm the economy? And if so, how much?

One way to think about this is in terms of economic competitiveness. In recent years the World Economic Forum has scored most of the world's countries on a competitiveness index that aims to assess the quality of nine components of a nation's economy: public and private institutions, infrastructure, macro-economic policy, health and primary education, higher education and training, market efficiency, technological readiness, business sophistication, and innovation. The scores range from a low of 1 to a high of 7.

As the chart suggests, as of 2007, the most recent year with available data, there's no association across the world's affluent countries between the level of taxation—the share of economic output (gross domestic product, or GDP) that passes through the government as taxes—and competitiveness.

How can this be? One hypothesis, suggested by economic historian Peter Lindert in his book *Growing Public*, is that high-tax countries such as Sweden, Denmark, and Finland rely heavily on consumption taxes, the burden of which is shared broadly across the citizenry rather than concentrated on firms and affluent individuals. Other analysts, though, contend that heavy consumption taxes weaken the economy, especially job creation, by raising the price of goods and services.

taxation and economic competitiveness in 2007

economic competitive score

5.7

United States
Switzerland

Germany   Finland   Denmark
                                  Sweden

Japan   United Kingdom
                 Netherlands
        Canada

                        Austria
                        Norway
Australia   France
                        Belgium

        Ireland
              New Zealand

              Spain

              Portugal

                        Italy

4.3

25 percent
of GDP   50

tax revenues

Source: OECD, World Economic Forum.

An alternative view is that the effect of taxation on economic health depends not on the level or type of taxation but instead on how tax revenues are used. Sociologist Gøsta Esping-Andersen has pointed out that at least some of the high-tax nations shown in "inne-quality reductions via taxation and transfers" devote a significant share of their revenues to providing public services and transfers—Social Security, Medicare and Medicaid, unemployment compensation, the Earned Income Tax Credit, Temporary Assistance to Needy Families, and food stamps, among others—that tend to boost, rather than impede, economic competitiveness.

For example, a schooling system that begins with affordable and high-quality child care ("early education"), includes good general education through high school for even the poorest, and offers broad access to university education is likely to facilitate innovation and flexibility in a globalized, knowledge-based economy. As well, universal access to health care and generous transfers to low-earning households improve the chances of building strong cognitive and social skills throughout the population. Government-provided or -subsidized child care and parental leave encourage women's employment, thereby boosting the economy's supply of ideas and creativity.

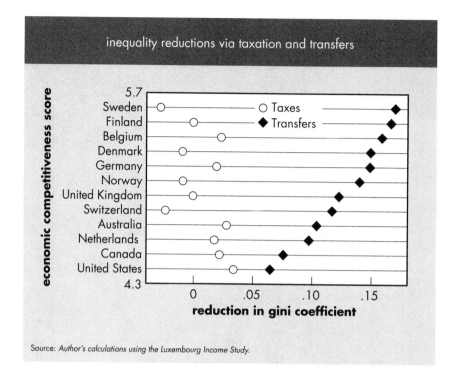

inequality reductions via taxation and transfers

economic competitiveness score

reduction in gini coefficient

Source: *Author's calculations using the Luxembourg Income Study.*

These are just some of the ways effective use of tax revenues can help offset whatever negative impact taxes may have on economic performance. Heavy taxation certainly doesn't ensure a competitive economy, but it appears to be perfectly compatible with one.

myth #2: republicans favor tax cuts because they believe they're good for the economy and key constituents

"The one thing that unites Republicans from Maine to Mississippi," Mitch McConnell, the current Republican leader in the Senate, told National Public Radio in January, "is tax cuts."

He's right. And it's been true for nearly three decades.

One reason why this may be true is many Republicans believe less taxation is good for the economy. Another is that tax reductions appeal to two of the party's core constituencies: businesses and people with high incomes. Both of these explanations have merit, but in his recent book *The Permanent Tax Revolt*, sociologist Isaac Martin offers an equally, if not more, compelling account.

It comes down to, Martin says, the legacy of Proposition 13's passage in California in 1978, similar victorious initiatives in other states, Ronald Reagan's presidential victories in 1980 and 1984, and the Reagan tax cuts of 1981.

Proposition 13 was a California referendum that restricted property tax increases. Movements for state and local property tax limits had existed for a number of years, but prior to the late 1970s they had enjoyed limited popularity and virtually no ballot success. The victory of Proposition 13, itself a product of a peculiar conjunction of circumstances, provided credibility and political momentum to the cause in other states and led to Reagan's conversion to tax cuts as a political strategy. Not long after there were several additional property tax cap wins at the state level in addition to Reagan's two election triumphs. In 1981, the Reagan administration successfully pushed a major tax reform, which included sharp reductions in income tax rates, through Congress.

These successes shaped the thinking of a new generation of Republican leaders, advisors, and voters. For many, they created an image of the modern Republican party as the party of tax cuts. Just as a generation of Democrats identified theirs as the party of the New Deal following Franklin D. Roosevelt's success and popularity in the 1930s and early 1940s, tax cuts became the core element of the political culture of the post-1980 generation of Republicans.

Moreover, for many Republicans the lesson of the late 1970s and early 1980s was that advocating tax reductions is the key to electoral success. Reversals by two key Republican presidential candidates in subsequent years are illustrative.

During the 1980 Republican primary, George H. W. Bush ridiculed Reagan's tax-cut proposals as "voodoo economics." Reagan won the primary and was then victorious in two presidential elections, continuing with his tax-cutting pledge throughout. When again campaigning for president in 1988, Bush switched his position—his mantra became "no new taxes," even though the federal government's debt had risen sharply during the eight years of Reagan's presidency.

This story replayed two decades later with Senator John McCain. In the early 2000s, McCain criticized president George W. Bush's proposed tax cuts as fiscally irresponsible. When running for president in 2008, however, McCain switched his stance and argued forcefully for further tax reductions, despite evidence that the tax cuts of the 1980s and 2000s had contributed to sizable budget deficits. The circumstances of these turnabouts suggest that both Bush and McCain were swayed mainly by a belief that tax cuts bring electoral victory, I would argue.

Republican candidates' and politicians' emphasis on tax cuts since the late 1970s has put taxes front and center in American political discourse. This is a marked change compared to earlier decades when taxes were much less prominent in political debate.

Using survey data going back to the 1940s, political scientist Andrea Louise Campbell has found that as politicians have devoted greater attention to taxation, public dissatisfaction with income taxes has tracked actual taxation levels much more closely than in the 1940s, 1950s, and 1960s. As a result, Campbell argues, when policymakers raise income tax rates, they're more likely now to encounter opposition not only from Republicans but from the citizenry as a whole. Though this doesn't render tax increases impossible, it surely makes them less likely.

myth #3: taxes reduce inequality

A good bit of the political debate about tax policy in the United States has to do with the tax system's progressivity—the degree to which it reduces income inequality. Most citizens and policymakers assume the tax system is progressive. Conservatives often think it's too progressive, while many liberals think it isn't progressive enough.

Taxes do help reduce income inequality, but not in the way many people think.

The U.S. tax system as a whole is essentially flat, rather than progressive. Individuals and households throughout the income distribution pay approximately the same share of their market incomes—earnings and other nongovernment sources such as investments, gifts from friends, alimony, and so on—in taxes. How can that be, when tax rates on income are higher for those with higher incomes?

Income taxes are indeed progressive, but that's offset by regressive payroll and consumption taxes. Payroll taxes, which fund Social Security and Medicare, are levied at a flat rate (7.65 percent) regardless of how much one earns. But earnings above a certain amount ($102,000 as of 2008) are exempt from the payroll tax, so the portion of earnings taxed is larger for low and middle earners than for high earners. Consumption is taxed via state and local sales taxes. These too are a flat rate, usually in the neighborhood of 4 percent to 8 percent. Yet, because those with lower incomes by necessity spend (rather than save) more of their incomes, a larger portion of their incomes is subject to consumption taxes.

In a report by the non-partisan educational nonprofit Tax Foundation, economists Andrew Chamberlain and Gerald Prante estimated the share of market incomes that each segment of the population paid in taxes to federal, state, and local governments in 2004. They divided households into five equally sized groups (called quintiles) based on their market income. The effective tax rate is roughly the same throughout the income distribution: households in the poorest quintile paid, on average, 31 percent of their market income in taxes, each of the next three quintiles paid approximately 28 percent, and the highest-income quintile paid 30 percent. Contrary to widespread opinion, then, taxes accomplish very little, if any, reduction of inequality.

This doesn't mean there's no redistributive effect of government policy. It simply tells us that taxes aren't the locus of redistribution. Instead, transfers are. Far more poor than rich receive cash and noncash government transfers.

The United States isn't exceptional in this regard. Transfers do most of the redistributive work in rich countries. The chart "taxation and inequality reduction via government transfers" illustrates this, showing the degree to which income inequality is reduced by taxes and government transfers in 12 countries. Larger numbers indicate greater reduction of inequality. In most of the countries, virtually all income redistribution occurs via transfers. Taxes do little or nothing to reduce income inequality, and in several countries they increase it.

Actually, these data overstate the degree of inequality reduction accomplished via taxes, because consumption taxes, which are always regressive, aren't included. Sociologists Monica Prasad and Yingying

> Taxes are quite important for inequality reduction, but what matters most is their quantity rather than their progressivity.

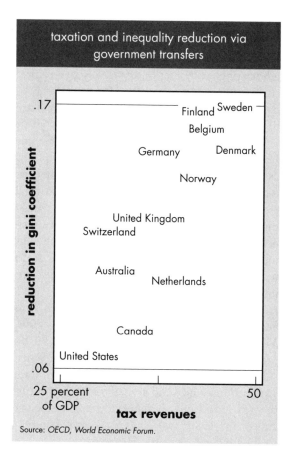

Source: OECD, World Economic Forum.

Deng have attempted to incorporate consumption taxes into calculations of tax progressivity. They've found that in the 1990s and 2000s none of the eight countries for which a calculation is possible have had a progressive tax system. All have been regressive.

However, taxes do play a vital role in reducing inequality. They fund the transfers and services that do the redistributive work. The chart "taxation and inequality reduction via government transfers" highlights a finding from my own research: countries that achieve more redistribution via transfers are able to do so because they collect more tax revenues. (The redistributive effect of services is very difficult to measure.) In other words, taxes are quite important for inequality reduction, but what matters most is their quantity rather than their progressivity.

myth #4: globalization makes heavy taxation impossible

Over the past two decades, a number of policymakers and social scientists have predicted that globalization and capital mobility would engender a "race to the bottom" in taxation. With

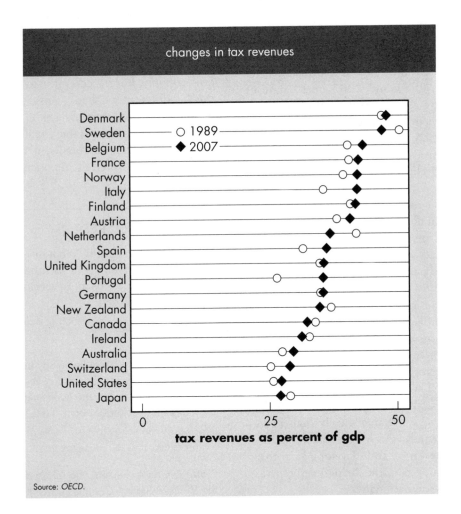

changes in tax revenues

○ 1989
◆ 2007

tax revenues as percent of gdp

Source: OECD.

firms and investors free to move to whatever country offers the lowest tax rates, governments have a strong incentive to reduce taxation in order to gain a competitive advantage. Others are then forced to follow suit.

This assumption is a perfectly reasonable one. Yet so far it's proved largely wrong.

Governments indeed feel heightened pressure to reduce tax rates, but while most countries have lowered statutory tax rates on investment income and corporate profits, such reductions have been mostly or fully offset by scaling back tax exemptions and deductions and, in some countries, by increasing the rates for other types of taxes, such as those on consumption and payroll.

The result has been little change in tax revenues as a share of GDP, as the chart "changes in tax revenues" indicates. It shows tax revenue levels in 1989 and 2007 in 20 nations (both years are business cycle peaks, so it's fair to compare them). In a few countries tax revenues decreased, but in others they increased. In most they stayed more or less the same.

Why no decline? Various hypotheses have been offered. A particularly compelling one is suggested by sociologist John Campbell, who points out that domestic institutions shape both the perceived interests of economists and politicians in the face of globalization pressures and their ability to pursue those interests. He writes:

Where labor is well organized and politically influential, unions and their political supporters are willing to support relatively high taxes because they expect it will help finance the programs from which they benefit. Similarly, where business is well organized, such as through business associations, firms tends to see that relatively high taxes support programs (health insurance, education, and research and development) that ensure social peace and help them remain competitive internationally.

Moreover, the manner in which politics is arranged institutionally affects tax policymaking. Countries with inclusive policymaking institutions, such as corporatism or electoral systems that yield coalition governments, tend to be less inclined to race toward the bottom because these institutional arrangements encourage compromises that mitigate such behavior.

Despite very real pressures favoring lower taxation, we therefore observe little or no movement toward a reduction of revenues in high-tax nations.

The stability of tax levels over the past few decades doesn't, of course, guarantee they won't fall in the future. But it does suggest heavy taxation is feasible in a globalized economy.

Taxation is an integral component of a modern economy. But it's complicated and operates much differently than most conventional assumptions and theorizing would have it. A better understanding of these realities not only makes manifest the necessity, it could lead to better, more informed fiscal policies.

RECOMMENDED RESOURCES

Andrea Louise Campbell. "What Americans Think of Taxes." In *The New Fiscal Sociology: Taxation in Comparative and Historical Perspective* (Cambridge University Press, 2009).

Examines U.S. public opinion on taxes from 1940 to the present.

John L. Campbell. "Fiscal Sociology in an Age of Globalization: Comparing Tax Regimes in Advanced Capitalist Countries." In *The Economic Sociology of Capitalism* (Princeton University Press, 2005).

Assesses the notion that economic globalization forces countries to reduce tax rates.

Gøsta Esping-Andersen. "Equal Opportunities and the Welfare State," *Contexts* (2007) 6(3): 23–27.

Highlights how government investment in cognitive and noncognitive skill development expands opportunity.

Isaac William Martin. *The Permanent Tax Revolt* (Stanford University Press, 2008).

Explores the causes and consequences of the property tax revolt of the 1970s.

Monica Prasad and Yingying Deng. "Taxation and the Worlds of Welfare." *Socio-Economic Review* (online release, April 2009).

Analyzes the progressivity of various types of taxes in rich countries.

REVIEW QUESTIONS

1. Choose one tax myth from the article that particularly surprised you. Why do you think that you, and many other Americans, believed it?
2. The author states that taxes don't directly reduce inequality. How might they indirectly affect levels of inequality?
3. Activity: Chart a day in your life and show where taxes affect your daily routine. For example, your taxes help pay to enforce environmental regulations that protect your drinking water.

stephen lerner

global corporations, global unions

27

summer 2007

as corporations extend their global reach, could they be making themselves more vulnerable to unions?

In November 2006 a group of Latino immigrant janitors won a historic strike in Houston, Texas—doubling their income, gaining health benefits, and securing a union contract for 5,300 workers with the Service Employees International Union (SEIU). At a critical moment in the strike, 1,000 janitors marched on the police station to protest the illegal arrests of two strikers. The next day, when the charges were dropped and the workers released, a local newspaper reported the crowd's chant as "*Arriba Revolución!*" The article got it wrong—workers were actually chanting "*Arriba La Unión!*" But it got the mood right. It looked and felt like a revolution in Houston. Thousands of immigrant workers and their supporters had successfully challenged the corporate power structure and its allies. They stood up to the police, blocked streets, garnered widespread support, and prevailed against enormous odds.

To many observers, a union fight in the heart of Texas seemed like a shot in the dark. But to workers toiling in poverty for the wealthiest corporations on earth, Houston was a shot heard around the world.

The SEIU janitors' month-long strike exposed a global economy addicted to cheap labor. Immigrant workers challenged a system that paid them $20 a night to clean toilets and vacuum the offices of global giants like Chevron and Shell Oil. They stood up to the global real estate interests that own and manage the office buildings where they work and the national cleaning companies that stay competitive by paying worker next to nothing.

Supported by activists from religious, civil rights, and community movements, janitors marched through Houston's most exclusive neighborhoods and shopping districts, into the lives of the rich and powerful. These disruptions forced Houston's elite, normally insulated from the workers who keep the city functioning, to face up to the human downside of the low-wage economy. Invoking the legacy of the civil rights movement, more than 80 union janitors and activists from around the country flew to Houston on "freedom flights" to support the strikers. They chained themselves to buildings, blocked streets, and were arrested for nonviolent acts of civil disobedience.

The city's corporate and political establishment tried to thwart the strikers. Twenty years ago they had successfully resisted an SEIU-led organizing drive among the city's janitors. So when workers took to the streets, the gloves came off again. Police helicopters circled, mounted police moved in, and protestors nursed broken bones in jail, while the district attorney demanded $40 million in combined bond, nearly $900,000 for each person arrested.

If the strike had been only a local affair, the civic elite would probably have won. But the campaign went global, arising in front of properties controlled by the same firms in cities around the world. As the strike spread, janitors in Chicago, New York, Washington, Mexico City, London, Berlin, and other cities honored picket lines or sponsored demonstrations. These protests and the negative publicity they drew put the struggle of 5,000 workers in Texas in the international spotlight. Houston's business leaders intervened to end the dispute, and the workers secured their historic victory. The strike, the tension and passion is generated, and the reaction of the power structure explain why a reporter hearing "*Arriba La Unión*" thought he heard "*Revolución.*"

Such a victory in anti-union Texas is worth attention. During the past four decades, union membership has steadily shrunk, first in the United States and now increasingly around the world. As unions have declined, we have seen greater inequality, cuts in social benefits, and a redistribution of wealth to giant multinational corporations around the globe. Trade unions, laws, and social policies that benefited workers have been gutted in country after country. Corporations and newly minted private-equity billionaires boast of their ability to operate anywhere in the world without challenges from workers, unions, or governments to their increasing dominance of the global economy.

Given these trends, many observers have written the labor movement's obituary. But the

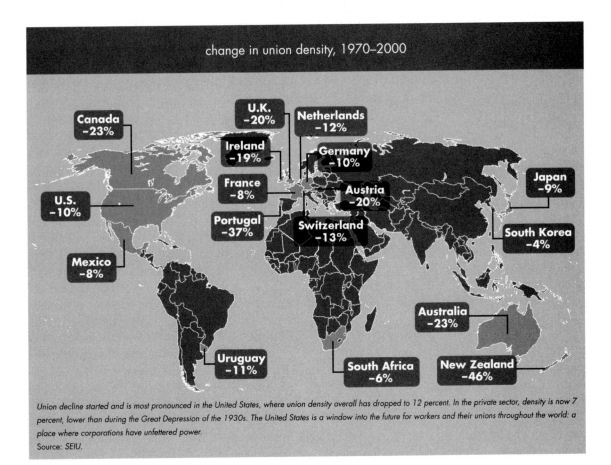

change in union density, 1970–2000

Canada −23%
U.K. −20%
Netherlands −12%
Ireland −19%
Germany −10%
France −8%
Austria −20%
Japan −9%
U.S. −10%
Portugal −37%
Switzerland −13%
South Korea −4%
Mexico −8%
Australia −23%
Uruguay −11%
South Africa −6%
New Zealand −46%

Union decline started and is most pronounced in the United States, where union density overall has dropped to 12 percent. In the private sector, density is now 7 percent, lower than during the Great Depression of the 1930s. The United States is a window into the future for workers and their unions throughout the world: a place where corporations have unfettered power.

Source: SEIU.

Houston victory and successes by janitors elsewhere around the world signal a new upsurge of labor activism in America and beyond. Contrary to conventional wisdom, the spread of multinational corporations and the increasing concentration of capital have created the conditions that can turn globalization on its head and lift people out of poverty.

a turning point

SEIU's Building Services Division, like many U.S. unions, declined dramatically in the 1970s and 1980s. It lost a quarter of its members, work was part-timed, and benefits were cut. Through its Justice for Janitors campaign in the 1980s and 1990s, the SEIU grappled with how to respond to outsourcing within the United States; as large-contract cleaning companies consolidated on a national basis, so too co-workers in far-flung cities consolidated their efforts to win campaigns and contracts. By 2006, the SEIU had figured out how to use this national scope for growth and power, and members around the country used their sway with national employers and building owners to help the Houston janitors win their strike. Cleaners across the globe bore witness to the struggle and put Houston's real estate leaders under an international microscope.

But the conditions that allowed for success in Houston are already changing. Again the ground is shifting under our feet as the service industry and its clients continue to globalize. Just as the SEIU moved from organizing in single buildings to organizing whole cities and extending that strength to new regions like the South, it must respond to these new changes by developing a deeper global strategy. The largest property owners and service contractors are becoming global companies that operate in dozens of countries and employ or control the employment conditions of hundreds of thousands of workers. Simple solidarity will no longer suffice. Without a global union that unites U.S. workers with their counterparts across the world, workers' power to influence these corporations will continue to wane. Such corporations may threaten workers' way of life, but they also present an opportunity.

It is ironic that a great opportunity to organize global unions comes among the poorest, least skilled workers in one of the least organized and wealthiest sectors of the world economy. Contract janitors, security officers, and others who clean, protect, and maintain commercial property (most of them immigrants) perform site-specific work that is local by nature; their jobs cannot be moved from country to country. Workers who follow global capital from country to country in search of jobs have the power to demand and win better working and living standards. It is among the most invisible and seemingly powerless workers—whose labor is nonetheless essential to the economic success of the most powerful corporations—that we can build a global movement to reinvigorate trade unions, stop the race to the bottom, and lift workers out of poverty. Far from an isolated event, the Houston strike demonstrates how the extraordinary reorganization and realignment of the world's economy has opened up the opportunity to unite workers around the globe in a movement to improve their lives by redistributing wealth and power.

> Contract janitors, security officers, and others who clean, protect, and maintain commercial property (most of them immigrants) perform site-specific work that is local by nature; their jobs cannot be moved from country to country.

understanding globalization

The world is tilting away from workers and unions and the traditional ways they have fought for and won justice—away from the power of national governments, national unions, and national solutions developed to facilitate and regulate globalization. It is tilting toward global trade, giant global corporations, global solutions, and toward Asia—especially China and India. We cannot depend on influencing bureaucratic global institutions, like the World Trade Organization. Workers and their unions need to use their still-formidable power to counter the power of global corporations before the world tilts so far that unions are washed away, impoverishing workers who currently have unions and trapping those who lack them in ever-deeper poverty. The power equation needs to be balanced before democratic institutions are destroyed.

As multinationals have grown, wealth and capital have become increasingly concentrated. Of the 100 largest economies in the world, 52 are not nations—they are global corporations. The top five companies, Wal-Mart, General Motors, Exxon Mobil, Royal Dutch/Shell, and BP, are each financially larger than all but 24 of the world's nations. The problem is not that corporations operate in more than one country—it is that multinational corporations are so powerful they increasingly dominate what happens in whole countries, hemispheres, and the entire globe.

As global corporations grow and state power declines, national unions are shrinking in membership and power. Union density is down across the globe. Though many countries experienced an increase in unionization during the 1970s and 1980s, density declines in the 1990s. From 1970 to 2000, 17 out of 20 wealthy countries surveyed by the Organisation for Economic Co-operation

and Development had a net decline in union density. While the specifics and timing are different in each country, what is remarkable over the last 30 years is the similarity of the results.

No country, no matter how strong its labor movement or progressive its history, is immune to these global trends. Density is starting to decline in Scandinavia, South Africa, Brazil, and South Korea, countries that until recently had stable or growing labor movements. In France, general strikes and mass worker and student mobilizations have slowed the rollback of workers' rights, but these are defensive strikes by workers desperately trying to maintain standards that those in surrounding countries are losing.

> Of the 100 largest economies in the world, 52 are not nations—they are global corporations.

the antidote: global unions

For 150 years the argument for global unions was abstract, theoretical, and ideological: in brief, capitalism is global, therefore worker organizations should be too. However, even though capitalism was global, most employers were not. Theoretically, workers were stronger if united worldwide, but the day-to-day reality of unionized workers enabled them to win through the power of national governments. Unionized workers saw workers in other countries as potential competition for their jobs rather than allies. There was no immediate, compelling reason to act beyond national boundaries.

Now, globalization itself is creating the conditions to organize global unions in the service economy. The infrastructure of the FIRE sector (finance, insurance, and real estate) and the millions of service jobs needed to support it are concentrated in some 40 global cities, while manufacturing and mobile jobs—aided by new technology—are being shifted and dispersed around the globe. Global unions could certainly be formed in manufacturing or other sectors characterized by mobile jobs, but right now the opportunity is greatest in service jobs concentrated in the cities that drive the world economy.

Global cities—like New York, Hong Kong, London, and São Paulo—are economic hubs that rely on service jobs to function. Multinational corporations and their executives increasingly depend on these cities because they physically work, live, and play in them. Deeply embedded in each of these cities are hundreds of thousands of janitors, security guards, maintenance, hotel, airport, and other service workers whose labor is essential and cannot be offshored. And, unlike the jobs in manufacturing and the garment industry, there is no threat of relocation.

The coexistence of immense wealth and low-wage service jobs concentrated in these global economic "engine rooms" dramatically increases the potential power of service workers to build a global movement.

the houston victory

Houston's janitors won because the five cleaning contractors that employ them clean more than 70 percent of the office space in the city and operate throughout the United States. Real estate companies like Hines and major tenants like Chevron and Shell operate around the world, allowing union allies to organize actions in places like Mexico City, Moscow, London, and Berlin. The unquenchable thirst of real estate companies for capital to finance their global expansion allowed pension funds like the California Public Employment Retirement fund to intervene, saying that conditions for janitors were both unacceptable and bad for their investment. If Houston's janitors had confronted a local oligarchy of cleaning contractors, building

owners, and corporations, they would likely have stood alone and again been crushed.

The union worked among janitors in downtown commercial office buildings in the major northern cities of the United States. But even as the SEIU expanded to organize service workers in other sectors, the gains among janitors were severely threatened by the wave of outsourcing in the 1970s and 1980s.

The union's own structure—dozens of local unions, often competing and undercutting each other in the same city—constrained its ability to fight back, and it needed to build strong local unions that could bargain across a geographic jurisdiction. The SEIU learned the hard way that it could not make gains by organizing building by building; even if a contractor allowed its workers to unionize, the union was likely to be undercut when the contract next went out to bid.

So the SEIU scaled its strategy upwards, reckoning that the resources needed to wage a fight in a single building could be more efficiently deployed in winning a contractor's entire portfolio across a city, and by doing this with multiple contractors in a citywide campaign, it could unionize the entire commercial office-cleaning industry. Crucial to this was developing the "trigger": after a contractor agreed to go union, SEIU would not raise wages until a majority of its competitors also went union, ensuring that no contractor was put at a competitive disadvantage. It began to untangle the complicated relationships between the janitors' direct employers—the contractors—and their secondary employers, the building owners. It also worked to understand the latter's financial, regulatory, political, and operational situation and their key relationships, especially with investors.

The union also learned that the janitors had hidden power: their critical—though invisible—position in the FIRE industry meant they could not be off-shored. As a result, powerful constituencies in these cities rallied to demand justice for janitors in their communities who earned poverty wages while cleaning the offices of multibillion-dollar companies.

These formed the core elements of an integrated strategy that allowed the Justice for Janitors campaign to reestablish or win master agreements for janitors in commercial office markets in the largest U.S. cities, bringing 100,000 new members into the union. In turn, that strength allowed the campaign to spread to cities such as Houston, where the same owners operated. Master agreements that included the right to honor picket lines meant that a contractor's unfair labor practices in one city could trigger strike action by SEIU locals in other cities.

There is no geographic limit to this strategy—as the key owners and contractors globalize, so do workers. Their victories demonstrate that in many ways multinationals are becoming more—not less—vulnerable as they spread across the globe.

global movement

In the face of the ascendancy of neoliberal policies, it may sound preposterous to argue that we are entering a moment of incredible opportunity for workers and their unions. But sometimes an unplanned combination of events may unleash social forces and contradictions that create the possibility—not the guarantee, the possibility—of creating a movement that lets us accomplish things we had never imagined possible. We are now in such a time.

How do we mount a campaign to organize workers into trade unions strong enough to raise wages and unite communities into organizations powerful enough to win decent housing, schools, and medical care? How do we build on the critical lessons and challenges of Houston, where janitors were far stronger than they would have been if they had focused their efforts on one building, company or group of workers?

1. organize globally

Most trade unions still focus their resources and activity in one country. Despite one hundred years of rhetoric about the need for workers to unite across borders, most global work is symbolic solidarity action and not part of a broader strategy. As the economy has become interrelated and global, organizing work must do the same.

2. corporations not countries

A campaign to change the world needs to focus on the corporations that increasingly dominate the global economy. To raise wages and living standards, we must force the largest corporations in the world to negotiate a new social compact that addresses human rights and labor rights in enforceable agreements that could lift tens of millions out of poverty. This campaign must be grounded in the work sites of the corporations that drive the economy and the cities in which they are located and from which they get much of their capital.

Unions as well as community, religious, and political leaders need to lead a campaign calling on the 300 largest pension funds in the world to adopt responsible investment policies covering their 6.9 trillion euros (U.S.$9 trillion) in capital. If corporations want access to the capital in workers' pension funds, they ought to develop responsible policies that govern how workers' money is to be invested and used.

3. global workers, global unions, global cities

We must create truly global unions, whose mission and focus is on the new global economy, spread across six continents. But they do not need to be in every country or major city in order to have the breadth and reach to tackle the largest global corporations. The challenge of building global unions is not to be everywhere in the world; rather, we need to determine the minimum number of countries and cities in which we must operate in order to exercise maximum power to persuade corporations to adopt a new social compact. This means organizing janitors, security, hotel, airport, and other service workers in some of the 40 or so global cities that are central to the operations of these corporations. Such organization must take place not only in individual work sites, but across cities, corporate groups, and industry sectors to improve immediate conditions and to build a union that organizes not only where workers labor but also in their neighborhoods and communities.

4. a moral and economic message

It is not enough to organize workers and their workplaces. The campaign needs a powerful message about the immorality of forcing workers to live in poverty amidst incredible wealth. Religious, community, and political leaders need to embrace and help lead the campaign because it highlights the moral issues of poverty, calls the corporations responsible for it to task, and offers solutions that are good for workers and the community as a whole. There are signs that elements of this campaign are becoming politically fashionable. Public-opinion polls suggest there is significant concern about the growing inequality between rich and poor. In a national *Los Angeles Times/Bloomberg* poll in December 2006, nearly three-quarters of respondents said they considered the income gap in America to be a serious problem.

To organize successfully at the work site and in communities, immigrants and migrant workers need to be brought out of the shadows of second-class status in the countries where they work. This campaign needs to take the lead in each country, and globally, to defend the rights of immigrant and migrant workers. It must promote laws that give immigrant and migrant workers full legal rights to that they can orga-

nize, unite with native-born workers, and help lead this fight.

5. disrupting—and galvanizing—the global city

It would be naïve to imagine that traditional union activity, moral persuasion, and responsible investment policies are enough to change corporate behavior or the world. These are starting points—small steps that allow workers and their allies to win victories, solidify organization, and increase the capacity to challenge corporate power. As activity and tension increase, the global business elite will go back and forth between making minor concessions to placate workers and attacking them at the workplace, in the media, and in political circles. But in the end, we only get real change by executing a two-part strategy: (1) galvanizing workers, community leaders, and the public to lift up our communities and (2) creating a crisis that threatens the existing order.

This is why this moment is so exciting and ripe with opportunity. In the last century industrial workers learned that increasingly coordinated industrial action could cripple national economies, topple governments, and win more just and humane societies. This strategy worked for more than 50 years. But production has been redesigned and shifted across the globe to disperse the power of workers and their unions. The rapid convergence of global corporations and workers in key cities around the world—where corporations are concentrating, not dispersing—has created the conditions and contradictions that allow us to encision how organized service workers can capture the imagination of people in their communities who are disturbed by poverty and income inequality while simultaneously learning how to disrupt the "engine rooms" in cities across the globe and so gain the leverage needed to start to tip the balance of economic power in the world.

In the same year as the Houston janitors' historic strike, the following occurred:

· A month after the Houston strike settlement, immigrant cleaners in London—from South America, East Asia, and Africa—scored a similar victory. They forced London's largest cleaning contractors to sign union contracts after they occupied the Goldman Sachs building.

· In Australia and New Zealand, janitors marched together in dozens of cities to launch the Clean Start campaign in both countries to negotiate agreements with the real estate industry and cleaning contractors.

· In Miami, Cuban and Haitian janitors at the University of Miami, whose jobs had been outsourced to a private company, struck for nine weeks, went on a 17-day hunger strike, and built a multiracial coalition to win health insurance and a union.

· In the Netherlands, immigrant cleaners in major office buildings and the airport have launched the Ten Euro Campaign, demanding higher pay and clearer respect for the country's 200,000 cleaners.

· In South Africa, security guards went back to work after winning a three-month national strike that gained 15,000 new members. Cleaners followed them in a general strike a few months later.

· In Jakarta, security officers occupied the offices of their employer, Group 4 Securicor, the largest private security guard company in the world, settling a year-long strike and winning a rare victory in the Indonesian Supreme Court.

· In Los Angeles, Boston, and Washington, D.C., thousands of mostly African-American security officers united and forced building owners and security contractors to accept unionization as part of a campaign that has successfully organized the first new, private-sector industry in the post–World War II era.

· In Germany, Poland, and India, security officers who earn poverty-level wages are starting campaigns to win justice from global security companies.

· In Luxemburg, representatives from security officers' unions in 19 countries joined together and agreed to unite workers in 104 countries in Africa, Asia, Europe, and the Americas in a global campaign to force Group 4 Securicor to respect the human and labor rights of its 400,000 workers in countries around the world.

Global capitalism operates smoothly in these cities because business leaders from around the world can fly in and out of their airports, stay in their hotels, and travel their streets to offices, banks, finance houses, and stock exchanges. Global cities and the multinational corporations that have centered the economic life of the world in them cannot operate without the global workers who literally feed, protect, and serve the richest and most powerful corporations and people in the world.

By learning how to disrupt these airports, offices, and hotels, service workers can exert their newly available and previously unimagined power—not for a day, but for weeks and months in an escalating campaign that demands decent wages and living conditions for workers and a stronger, more prosperous future for entire communities and cities. In using this power, they can take the lead in creating a new world where the incredible technological progress, wealth, and economic advances of the global economy lift up the poor, empower the powerless, and inspire all of us to fight for justice.

RECOMMENDED RESOURCES

For more information on global union organizing, see www.uniglobalunion.org. To learn about SEIU, go to www.seiu.org.

Dan Clawson. *The Next Upsurge: Labor and the New Social Movements* (Cornell University Press, 2003).

A progressive transformation, Clawson believes, will be difficult or impossible without the active involvement of the working class and its collective voice, the labor movement.

Rick Fantasia and Kim Voss. *Hard Work: Remaking the American Labor Movement* (University of California Press, 2004).

Fantasia and Voss examine the decline of the American labor movement and the emergence of a new kind of "social movement unionism" that suggests the potential revival of unionism in the United States.

Stephen Lerner. "An Immodest Proposal: A New Architecture for the House of Labor." *New Labor Forum* 12, no. 2 (Summer 2003):7039; and "A Winning Strategy to Do Justice." *Tikkun* (May/June 2005):50–51.

Drawing lessons from how SEIU remade itself so that workers could take on big, nonunion employers, Lerner argues that the labor movement's structure, culture, and priorities stand in the way of workers' gains and the need to change.

Ruth Milkman. *L.A. Story: Immigrant Workers and the Future of the U.S. Labor Movement* (Russell Sage Foundation, 2006).

Milkman explains how Los Angeles, once known as a company town hostile to labor, became a hotbed of unionism, and how immigrant service workers emerged as the unlikely leaders in the battle for workers' rights.

Ruth Milkman and Kim Voss, eds. *Rebuilding Labor: Organizing and Organizers in the New Union Movement* (Cornell University Press, 2004).

Milkman and Voss bring together established researchers and a new generation of labor scholars to assess the current state of labor organizing and its relationship to union revitalization.

Saskia Sassen. *Cities in a World Economy* (Pine Forge Press, 2006).

Sassen uses the term "global cities" to capture the growth of service firms under globalization and their concentration in a small number of cities, as well as discussing these firms' increasing dependence on low-paid service workers.

REVIEW QUESTIONS

1. What purposes do unions serve? What benefits do they bring to workers and employers? Can you think of any drawbacks to unions for workers or employers?
2. How is globalization both a threat and an opportunity for low-income workers?
3. What does the phrase "race to the bottom" refer to? How does it affect economic stability and working conditions at local, national, and international levels?
4. Activity: The author suggests that workers consider global unions. Why? Visit www.seiu.org and peruse the Web site. How does this union's organizing affect your understanding of the potential benefits and challenges of global unionizing?

part **7**

Gender and Sexualities

ronald weitzer

prostitution: facts and fictions

28

fall 2007

although sometimes romanticized in popular culture, prostitution is more often portrayed as intrinsically oppressive and harmful. how accurate is this image?

When I mentioned the topic of prostitution to a friend recently, he said, "How disgusting! How could anybody sell themselves?" A few weeks later an acquaintance told me she thought prostitution was a "woman's choice, and can be empowering." These opposing views reflect larger cultural perceptions of prostitution, as well as much academic writing on the topic.

A growing number of scholars regard prostitution, pornography, and stripping as "sex work" and study it as an occupation. Exploring all dimensions of the work, in different contexts, these studies document substantial variation in the way prostitution is organized and experienced by workers, clients, and managers. These studies undermine some deep-rooted myths about prostitution and challenge writers and activists who portray prostitution monolithically.

The most popular monolithic perspective is that prostitution is an unqualified evil. According to this *oppression model*, exploitation, abuse, and misery are intrinsic to the sex trade. In this view, most prostitutes were physically or sexually abused as children, which helps to explain their entry into prostitution; most enter the trade as adolescents, around 13–14 years of age; most are tricked or forced into the trade by pimps or sex traffickers; drug addiction is rampant; customer violence against workers is rou-

tine and pervasive; working conditions are abysmal; and legalization would only worsen the situation.

Some writers go further, characterizing the "essential" nature of prostitution. Because prostitution is defined as an institution of extreme male domination over women, these writers say that violence and exploitation are inherent and omnipresent—transcending historical time period, national context, and type of prostitution. As Sheila Jeffreys writes, "Prostitution constitutes sexual violence against women in and of itself"; and according to Melissa Farley, prostitution is a "vicious institution" that is "Intrinsically traumatizing to the person being prostituted." Many writers who subscribe to the oppression model use dramatic language ("sexual slavery," "paid rape," "survivors," and so on) and describe only the most disturbing cases, which they present at typical—rhetorical tricks designed to fuel public indignation.

The oppression model's images of victimhood erase workers' autonomy and agency, and preclude any possibility of organizing sex work in order to minimize harm and empower workers. This model holds that prostitution should be eradicated, not meliorated. But much research challenges the oppression model as well as some other popular fictions.

the street vs. indoors

Street prostitution differs sharply from *indoor prostitution*. Many of the problems associated with "prostitution" are actually concentrated in street prostitution and much less evident in the indoor sector.

Certainly many street prostitutes work under abysmal conditions and are involved in "survival sex," selling sex out of a dire necessity or to support a drug habit. Some are runaway youths with no other options. Many use addictive drugs; risk contracting and transmitting sexual diseases; are exploited and abused by pimps; are vulnerable to being assaulted, robbed, raped, or killed; and are socially isolated and disconnected from support services. This is the population best characterized by the oppression model.

Other street prostitutes are in less desperate straits. Some work independently, without pimps (a Miami study found that only 7 percent had pimps, but the percentage varies greatly by city). Regarding age of entry, the oppression model's claim of 13–14 years is clearly not the norm. A recent British study by Marianne Hester and Nicole Westmarland found that 20 percent of their sample had begun to sell sex before age 16 while almost half (48 percent) had begun after age 19. Childhood abuse (neglect, violence, incest) is indeed part of the biography of some prostitutes, but studies that compare matched samples of street prostitutes and nonprostitutes show mixed results; some find a statistically significant difference in experience of family abuse, while others find no difference. HIV infection rates are highest among street prostitutes who inject drugs and less common among others.

Different writers report very different rates of victimization. Scholar-activists and some "survivor organizations" (Breaking Free, Standing Against Global Exploitation, Council for Prostitution Alternatives) cite high levels of violence against prostitutes (70–100 percent). Samples

Amsterdam's Prostitution Information Center. (Courtesy of Ronald Weitzer)

drawn from the clients of social service agencies or from antiprostitution survivor groups yield a much higher level of victimization (their clients were desperate enough to seek help) than samples drawn from the wider population of street workers. A study by Stephanie Church and colleagues found that 27 percent of a sample of street prostitutes had been assaulted, 37 percent robbed, and 22 percent raped. Criminologists John Lowman and Laura Fraser reported similar results: 39 percent assaulted, 37 percent robbed, and 37 percent sexually assaulted. Since random sampling of this population is impossible, we must approach all victimization figures cautiously, but victimization is apparently not nearly as prevalent, even among street prostitutes, as the oppression model asserts.

Unfortunately, much popular discourse and some academic writing extrapolate from (a caricature of) street prostitution to prostitution in general. What gets less attention is the hidden world of indoor prostitution in venues such as bars, brothels, massage parlors, tanning salons, or in services provided by escort agencies or independent call girls. An estimated 20 percent of all prostitutes work on the streets in the United States. Although this number is hard to substantiate at the national level, some city-level studies support it. Regardless of the exact numbers, indoor sex work clearly accounts for a large share of the market.

Less research has been conducted on indoor prostitution, but available studies indicate that, compared to streetwalkers, indoor workers have lower rates of childhood abuse, enter prostitution at an older age, and have more education. They are less drug-dependent and more likely to use softer drugs (marijuana instead of crack or heroin). Moreover, they use drugs for difference reasons. Street workers consume drugs or alcohol to help them cope with the adversities of the job, whereas indoor workers use them both for coping and as part of their socializing with customers. Sexually transmitted diseases are fairly rare among call girls, escorts, and women who work in brothels where condom use is mandatory. Indoor workers tend to earn more money, are at lower risk of arrest, and are safer at work. They are in a better position to screen out dangerous customers (through a referral system for call girls and vetting by gatekeepers in brothels and massage parlors), and they have a higher proportion of low-risk, regular clients.

Studies conducted in a variety of countries have found that indoor sex workers are less likely to experience violence from customers than those who work on the streets. For example, Church found that few call girls and sauna workers had experienced violence (only 1 percent had ever been beaten, 2 percent raped, and 10 percent robbed). This and other studies support Lilly Plumridge and Gillian Abel's conclusion that "street workers are significantly more at risk of more violence and more serious violence than indoor workers." (Obviously, this does not apply to persons recruited by force or fraud and trafficked into brothels, who are at high risk for subsequent exploitation and abuse.)

Research finds that many indoor workers made conscious decisions to enter the trade; they do not see themselves as oppressed victims and do not feel that their work is degrading. Consequently, they express greater job satisfaction than their street-level counterparts. And they may differ little from nonprostitutes: A study by psychologist Sarah Romans and colleagues comparing indoor workers and an age-matched sample of nonprostitute women found no differences between the two groups in physical health, self-esteem, mental health, or the quality of their social networks.

Some prostitutes feel validated and empowered by their work. In some studies, a large percentage of indoor workers report an increase in self-esteem after they began working in prostitution, state that they are very satisfied with their work, or feel that their lives improved after entering prostitution. Escorts interviewed by sociologist Tanice Foltz took pride in their work and viewed themselves as morally superior to others: "They consider women who are not 'in the life' to be throwing away woman's major source of power and control, while they as prostitutes are using it to their own advantage as well as for the benefit of society." A study by the Australian government reported that half of the 82 call girls and 101 brothel workers interviewed felt that their work was a "major source of satisfaction" in their lives; two-thirds of the brothel workers and seven out of ten call girls said they would "definitely choose this work" if they had it to do over again; and 86 percent in the brothels and 79 percent of call girls said that "my daily work is always varied and interesting." Ann Lucas's interviews with escorts and call girls revealed that these women had the "financial, social, and emotional wherewithal to structure their work largely in ways that suited them and provided . . . the ability to maintain healthy self-images." Other studies indicate that such control over working conditions greatly enhances overall job satisfaction among these workers.

Indoor and street prostitutes also differ in whether they engage in "emotion work" (providing intimacy, emotional support) in addition to sexual services. Emotion work is rare among streetwalkers, whose encounters are limited to quick, mechanical sex. But call girls and escorts (and, to a lesser degree, brothel and massage parlor workers) are often expected to support and counsel clients, and their encounters may resemble dating experiences, including conversation, gifts, hugging, massage, and kissing. Janet Lever and Deanne Dolnick's comparative study of a large number of street and indoor workers in Los Angeles found striking differences between the two groups in the quantity and quality of their sexual and emotional interactions with clients. Emotion work is not necessarily easy; workers who feign intimacy or emotional support over an extended period of time may find the work quite draining.

Many customers are looking for more than sex from indoor workers. Reviews of several Web sites where customers discuss their preferences and experiences indicate that many seek women who are friendly, conversational, generous with time, and who engage in cuddling and foreplay. This has come to be known as a "girlfriend experience" (GFE), with elements of romance and intimacy in addition to sex. One client writing in the popular Punternet Web sites said that he had "a gentle GFE that was more lovemaking than sex," and another stated, "There was intimacy and sweat and grinding and laughter, and those moments that are sexy and funny and warm and leave you with a grin on your face the next day. Girlfriend sex." Escorts and call girls also contribute to these Web sites, and their comments make it clear that many do not believe the oppression model applies to them.

In sum, prostitution takes diverse forms and exists under varying conditions, a complexity that contradicts popular myths and sweeping generalizations. Plenty of evidence challenges the notion that prostitutes, across the board, are coerced into the sex trade, lead lives of misery, experience high levels of victimization, and want to be rescued. These patterns characterize one segment of the sex trade, *but they are not the defining features of prostitution*. Sex workers differ markedly in their autonomy, work experiences, job satisfaction, and self-esteem. It's time to replace the oppression model with a polymorphous model—a perspective that recognizes multiple structural and experiential realities.

> Prostitution takes diverse forms and exists under varying conditions, a complexity that contradicts popular myths and sweeping generalizations.

legalization?

According to the oppression model, legalization would only institutionalize exploitation and abuse. Antiprostitution groups insist that legalization is a recipe for misery and has a "corrosive effect on society as a whole," according to the Coalition Against Trafficking in Women. It is difficult to measure something as vague as a "corrosive effect," but it is possible to evaluate some other dimensions of legalization, including the effects on workers themselves. To address this question, we need to examine cases where prostitution is legal and regulated by the government. Brothels are legal in a number of places, including Nevada, the Netherlands, Australia, and New Zealand. Statutory regulations vary by country, but a com-

(Courtesy of Jacco J. Van Giessen)

mon objective is harm reduction. New Zealand's 2003 law, for instance, gives workers a litany of rights, provides for the licensing and taxing of brothels, and empowers local governments to determine where they can operate, limit their size, vet the owners, ban offensive signage, and impose safe-sex and other health requirements.

Research suggest that, under the right conditions, legal prostitution can be organized in a way that increases workers' health, safety, and job satisfaction. Mandatory condom use and other safe-sex practices are typical in legal brothels, and workers face much lower risk of abuse from customers. According to a 2004 report by the Ministry of Justice in the Netherlands, the "vast majority" of workers in Dutch brothels and window units report that they "often or always feel safe." Nevada's legal brothels "offer the safest environment available for women to sell consensual sex acts for money," according to a recent study by sociologists Barbara Brents and Kathryn Hausbeck. And a major evaluation of legal brothels in Queensland, Australia, by the government's Crime and Misconduct Commission concluded, "There is no doubt that licensed brothels provide the safest working environment for sex workers in Queensland. . . . Legal brothels now operating in Queensland provide a sustainable model for a healthy, crime-free, and safe legal licensed brothel industry." In each of these systems, elaborate safety measures (surveillance, panic buttons, listening devices) allow managers to respond to unruly customers quickly and effectively. These studies suggest that legal prostitution, while no panacea, is not inherently dangerous and can be structured to minimize risks and empower workers.

The question of whether legalization is preferable to criminalization—in terms of harm reduction—is one thing. The question of its feasibility in the United States is another. Today it is legal only in Nevada, where about 30 brothels exist in rural counties; it is prohibited in Las Vegas and Reno. According to a 2002 poll, 31 percent of Nevadans are opposed to the state's legal brothels while 52 percent support them. And a 2004 ballot measure to ban brothels in one of Nevada's rural counties was defeated: 63 percent voted to retain legal prostitution in Churchill county. Rural support comes largely from the tax revenues that counties derive from the brothels.

And the rest of the country? Although many Americans consider prostitution immoral or distasteful, a large minority disagrees. In the 1996 General Social Survey, 47 percent (52 percent of men, 43 percent of women) agreed that, "There is nothing inherently wrong with prostitution, so long as the health risks can be minimized. If consenting adults agree to exchange money for sex, that is their business."

Moreover, a sizeable number favor alternatives to criminalization. A 1991 Gallup poll found that 40 percent of the public thought that prostitution should be "legal and regulated by the government." Unfortunately, no American poll has specified the meaning of legalization, which could involve licensing, mandatory health exams, brothels, a designated zone of street prostitution, or other regulations.

A fair number of men have bought sex. According to the 2000 General Social Survey, 17 percent of American men have paid for sex at some time in their lives, and 3 percent have done so in the past year. Recent surveys indicate that 9 percent of British men and 16 percent of Australian men report paying for sex. The actual numbers are likely higher, given the stigma involved.

Despite the significant support for legalization and sizeable customer base, there has been almost no serious debate among American policymakers on alternatives to prohibition. As a 1999 task force in Buffalo, New York, reasoned, "Since it is unlikely that city or state officials could ever be convinced to decriminalize or legalize prostitution in Buffalo, there is nothing to be gained by debating the merits of either." This logic seems to put the cart before the horse, but on those rare occasions when policy alternatives have been floated in other cities, they have met with the same status-quo outcome. When a San Francisco task force boldly recommended decriminalization in 1996, the city's political leaders promptly rejected the idea. And in 2004 a Berkeley, California, ballot measure that called on police to refrain from enforcing prostitution laws was defeated: 64 percent voted against it. Opposition was likely due to the measure's laissez-faire approach; people are more inclined to support some kind of regulation, just as they are with regard to some other vices. Still, despite the substantial minority of Americans who support legaliza-

tion in principle, outside of Nevada, the idea has attracted little public attention.

increasing criminalization

Although the issue of legalization is dormant in the contemporary United States, prostitution policy has recently become a hot issue. An antiprostitution coalition has gathered steam, composed of the religious right and abolitionist feminists. Judging by their publications and pronouncements, the coalition not only accepts the myths I have described but actively perpetuates them.

During the Bush administration, this coalition has played a major role in redefining the issue and influencing public policy. Coalition views have been incorporated in key legislation and in the official policies of several federal agencies. What began (in the 1990s) as a campaign focused on international trafficking has morphed into a frontal assault on the domestic sex industry in America.

In 2001, the State Department created a new unit, the Office to Monitor and Combat Trafficking in Persons. This office has endorsed the same extraordinary claims that are made by the antiprostitution coalition. One example is the State Department's remarkable Web site, "The Link Between Prostitution and Sex Trafficking," which contains these nuggets: "Prostitution is inherently harmful. Few activities are as brutal and damaging to people as prostitution"; it "leaves women and children physically, mentally, emotionally, and spiritually devastated"; and "Prostitution is not the oldest profession, but the oldest form of oppression."

Similar claims appear in the Web sites and publications of some other government agencies—the Justice Department, Health and Human Services, United States Agency for International Development—and have been recapitulated by some members of Congress and by the president. In 2002, President Bush signed a Presidential Directive on trafficking that defines prostitution as "inherently harmful and dehumanizing," and in a 2003 speech at the United Nations he declared, "The victims of the sex trade see little of life before they see the very worst of life—an underground of brutality and lonely fear. . . . Those who patronize this industry debase themselves and deepen the misery of others."

The Bush administration has funneled more than $350 million into international and domestic organizations fighting prostitution, many of which are right-wing, faith-based, or abolitionist feminist in orientation. These groups have received funds to conduct "research," operate "rescue" missions, and engage in other interventions. Organizations that provide services to sex workers but do not formally condemn prostitution have been denied funding.

Criminalization of other sectors of the sex industry also appears to be on the American agenda. Activists have been pressing the government to criminalize the commercial sex trade as a whole, contending that the oppression model applies to all forms of sex work. For example, in a 2005 report funded by the State Department, scholar-activist Donna Hughes condemned both stripping and pornography. She claimed that women and girls are trafficked to perform at strip clubs (though she found only six cases of this in the United States during 1998–2005) and that the producers of pornography "often rely on trafficked victims," a charge made with no supporting evidence. Some government officials have echoed these claims.

In 2005, the Justice Department launched a new crackdown on adult pornography and obscenity. (Under the Clinton administration, child pornography was the main target.) The stated objective of the 2005 End Demand for Sex Trafficking bill was to "combat commercial sexual activities" in general. The rationale for this sweeping approach, according to the bill, is that "commercial sexual activities have a devastating impact on society. The sex trade has a dehumanizing effect on all involved." Commercial sex is defined remarkably broadly as "any sex act on account of which anything of value is given to, or received by, any person." The overall trend is clear: the Bush administration has embraced the oppression model as a rationale for its expanding, multifaceted crackdown on the sex industry.

Although the oppression framework dominates today, there is a diametrically opposed cultural representation that romanticizes prostitution. We see this in some rock and hip hop songs, films like *Pretty Woman* and *The Best Little Whorehouse in Texas*, novels like Tracy Quan's *Diary of a Married Call Girl*, television shows like HBO's *Cathouse*, and a handful of academic writings. Such representations portray prostitution as enjoyable, empowering, and lucrative work. In my view, this celebratory model is just as one-dimensional and empirically limited as the oppression model. The alternative, superior perspective recognizes that prostitution varies enormously across time, place, and sector—with important consequences for workers' health, safety, and job satisfaction.

RECOMMENDED RESOURCES

Elizabeth Bernstein. *Temporarily Yours: Intimacy, Authenticity, and the Commerce of Sex* (University of Chicago Press, 2007).

> Tracks trends in commercialized sex, focusing on the growing marketing of intimacy coupled with sexual services.

Wendy Chapkis. "Power and Control in the Commercial Sex Trade." In *Sex for Sale: Prostitution, Pornography, and the Sex Industry*, ed. Ronald Weitzer (Routledge, 2000).

> Identifies variables that shape worker experiences in different sectors of the sex industry.

Martin Monto. "Female Prostitution, Customers, and Violence." *Violence Against Women* 10 (2004): 160–68.

Exposes several myths regarding prostitutes' clients.

Ine Vanwesenbeeck. "Another Decade of Social Scientific Work on Prostitution." *Annual Review of Sex Research* 12 (2001): 242–89.

A comprehensive literature review, providing support for the polymorphous model.

Ronald Weitzer. "New Directions in Research on Prostitution." *Crime, Law, and Social Change* 43 (2005): 211–35.

Analysis of deficiencies in the research literature and some promising studies that help to address them.

Ronald Weitzer. "The Social Construction of Sex Trafficking: Ideology and Institutionalization of a Moral Crusade." *Politics & Society* 35 (2007): 447–75.

Critical evaluation of the claims of antitrafficking forces and their increasing endorsement in U.S. government policy.

REVIEW QUESTIONS

1. Define the oppression and celebratory models of prostitution. How would you characterize the alternative model proposed by the author?
2. What is your reaction to Weitzer's claim that some prostitutes are empowered by their jobs? Do you agree that sex work can be empowering for women? Or do you agree more with the oppression model?
3. The article states that 17 percent of American men have paid for sex at some point in their lives. Do you think this is a high or a low number? Why do you think there is a stigma against paying for sex?
4. Activity: Organize a class debate with one side arguing that prostitution should be legalized and regulated in the United States, and the other side arguing that it should remain illegal.

kathleen gerson and jerry a. jacobs

the work-home crunch

29

fall 2004

the decade-long debate over whether americans are working longer hours is misleading. indeed, while well-educated professionals are working more hours than they used to, others with less education are working fewer. and the people under the most pressure are not just overburdened at work. increasingly, these single parents and two-income couples find themselves in a time squeeze between home and work.

More than a decade has passed since the release of *The Overworked American*, a prominent 1991 book about the decline in Americans' leisure time, and the work pace in the United States only seems to have increased. From sleep-deprived parents to professionals who believe they must put in long hours to succeed at the office, the demands of work are colliding with family responsibilities and placing a tremendous time squeeze on many Americans.

Yet beyond the apparent growth in the time that many Americans spend on the job lies a more complex story. While many Americans are working more than ever, many others are working less. What is more, finding a balance between work and other obligations seems increasingly elusive to many workers—whether or not they are actually putting in more time at work than workers in earlier generations. The increase in harried workers and hurried families is a problem that demands solutions. But before we can resolve this increasingly difficult time squeeze we must first understand its root causes.

average working time and beyond

"There aren't enough hours in the day" is an increasingly resonant refrain. To most observers, including many experts, the main culprit appears to be overwork—our jobs just take up

too much of our time. Yet it is not clear that the average American is spending more time on the job. Although it may come as a surprise to those who feel overstressed, the average work week—that is, hours spent working for pay by the average employee—has hardly changed over the past 30 years. Census Bureau interviews show, for example, that the average male worked 43.5 hours a week in 1970 and 43.1 hours a week in 2000, while the average female worked 37.1 hours in 1970 and 37.0 hours in 2000.

Why, then, do more and more Americans feel so pressed for time? The answer is that averages can be misleading. Looking only at the average experience of American workers misses key parts of the story. From the perspective of individual workers, it turns out some Americans are working more than ever, while others are finding it harder to get as much work as they need or would like. To complicate matters further, American families are now more diverse than they were in the middle of the twentieth century, when male-breadwinner households predominated. Many more Americans now live in dual-earner or single-parent families where all the adults work.

These two trends—the growing split of the labor force and the transformation of family life—lie at the heart of the new time dilemmas facing an increasing number of Americans. But

Three businessmen in San Francisco's financial district walk briskly to lunch. More than one-third of male managers and professionals now work 50 hours or more per week, a substantial increase since 1970. (Courtesy of Jon Wagner)

more likely to be concentrated in the lower-paying jobs.

But the experiences of individuals does not tell the whole story. When we shift our focus to the family, it becomes clear that time squeezes are linked to the total working hours of family members in households. For this reason, two-job families and single parents face heightened challenges. Moreover, women continue to assume the lion's share of home and child care responsibilities and are thus especially likely to be squeezed for time. Changes in jobs and changes in families are putting overworked Americans and underemployed Americans on distinct paths, are separating the two-earner and single-parent households from the more traditional households, and are creating different futures for parents (especially mothers) than for workers without children at home. (On the issue of which specific schedules people work and the consequences of nonstandard shifts, see "The Economy that Never Sleeps," *Contexts*, Spring 2004.)

a growing divide in individual working time

In 1970, almost half of all employed men and women reported working 40 hours a week. By 2000, just 2 in 5 worked these "average" hours. Instead, workers are now far more likely to put in either very long or fairly short work weeks. The share of working men putting in 50 hours or more rose from 21 percent in 1970 to almost 27 percent in 2000, while the share of working women putting in these long work weeks rose from 5 to 11 percent.

At the other end of the spectrum, more workers are also putting in shorter weeks. In 1970, for example, 5 percent of men were employed for 30 or fewer hours a week, while 9 percent worked these shortened weeks in 2000. The share of employed women spending 30 or

they have not affected all workers and all families in the same way. Instead, these changes have divided Americans into those who feel squeezed between their work and the rest of their life, and those who have more time away from work than they need or would like. No one trend fits both groups.

So, who are the time-squeezed, and how do they differ from those with fewer time pressures but who may also have less work than they may want or need? To distinguish and describe the two sets of Americans, we need to look at the experiences of both individual workers and whole families. A focus on workers shows that they are increasingly divided between those who put in very long work weeks and who are concentrated in the better-paying jobs, and those who put in comparatively short work weeks, who are more likely to have fewer educational credentials and are

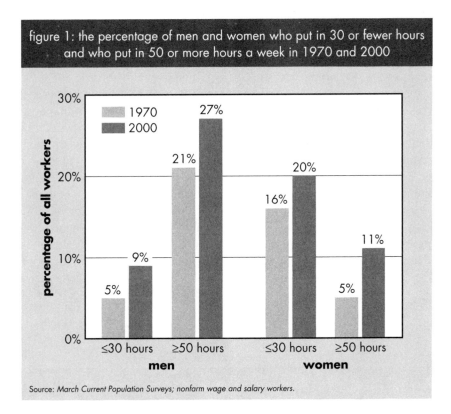

figure 1: the percentage of men and women who put in 30 or fewer hours and who put in 50 or more hours a week in 1970 and 2000

Source: *March Current Population Surveys; nonfarm wage and salary workers.*

fewer hours on the job also climbed from 16 percent to 20 percent (see figure 1). In total, 13 million Americans in 2000 worked either shorter or longer work weeks than they would have if the 1970s pattern had continued.

These changes in working time are not evenly distributed across occupations. Instead, they are strongly related to the kinds of jobs people hold. Managers and professionals, as one might expect, tend to put in the longest work weeks. More than 1 in 3 men in this category now work 50 hours or more per week, compared to only 1 in 5 for men in other occupations. For women, 1 in 6 professionals and managers work these long weeks, compared to fewer than 1 in 14 for women in all other occupations. And because jobs are closely linked to education, the gap in working time between the college educated and those with fewer edu-

cational credentials has also grown since 1970.

Thus, time at work is growing most among those Americans who are most likely to read articles and buy books about overwork in America. They may not be typical, but they are indeed working more than their peers in earlier generations. If leisure time once signaled an elite lifestyle, that no longer appears to be the case. Working relatively few hours is now more likely to be concentrated among those with less education and less elite jobs.

Workers do not necessarily prefer these new schedules. On the contrary, when workers are asked about their ideal amount of time at work, a very different picture emerges. For example, in a 1997 survey of workers conducted by the Families and Work Institute, 60 percent of both men and women responded that they would like to work less while 19 percent of men and women said that they would like to work more. Most workers—both women and men—aspire to work between 30 and 40 hours per week. Men generally express a desire to work about 38 hours a week while women would like to work about 32 hours. The small difference in the ideal working time of men and women is less significant than the shared preferences among them. However, whether their jobs require very long or comparatively short work weeks, this shared ideal does stand in sharp contrast to their job realities. As some workers are pressured to put in more time at work and others less, finding the right balance between work and the rest of life has become increasingly elusive.

overworked individuals or overworked families?

Fundamental shifts in family life exacerbate this growing division between the over- and under-worked. While most analyses of working time focus on individual workers, time squeezes are typically experienced by families, not isolated individuals. A 60-hour work week for a father means something different depending on whether the mother stays at home or also works a 60-hour week. Even a 40-hour work week can seem too long if both members of a married couple are juggling job demands with family responsibilities. And when a family depends on a single parent, the conflicts between home and work can be even greater. Even if the length of

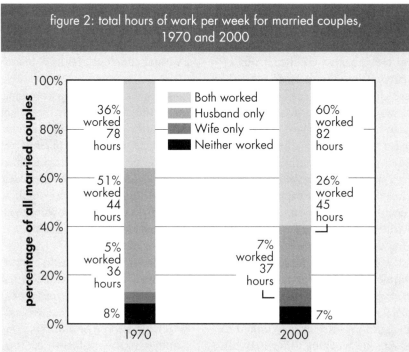

figure 2: total hours of work per week for married couples, 1970 and 2000

Source: March Current Population Surveys; nonfarm married couples aged 18–64.

the work week had not changed at all, the rise of families that depend on either two incomes or one parent would suffice to explain why Americans feel so pressed for time.

To understand how families experience time squeezes, we need to look at the combined working time of all family members. For example, how do married couples with two earners compare with those anchored by a sole, typically male, breadwinner? For all married couples, the work week has indeed increased from an average of about 53 hours in 1970 to 63 hours in 2000. Given that the average work week for individuals did not change, it may seem strange that the couples' family total grew so markedly. The explanation for this apparent paradox is both straightforward and crucial: married women are now far more likely to work. In 1970, half of all married-couple families had only male breadwinners. By 2000, this group had shrunk to one quarter (see figure 2). In 1970, one-third of all married-couple families had two wage-earners, but three-fifths did in 2000. In fact, two-earner families are more common today than male-breadwinner families were 30 years ago.

Each type of family is also working a little more each week, but this change is relatively modest and certainly not large enough to account for the larger shift in total household working time. Two-earner families put in close to 82 working hours in 2000 compared with 78 hours in 1970. Male-breadwinner couples worked 44 hours on average in 1970 and 45 hours in 2000. The vast majority of the change in working time over the past 30 years can thus be traced to changes in the kinds of families we live in rather than to changes in how much we work. Two-earner couples work about as much today as they did 30 years ago, but there are many more of them because more wives are working.

Single parents, who are overwhelmingly mothers, are another group who are truly caught in a time squeeze. They need to work as much as possible to support their family, and they are less likely to be able to count on a partner's help in meeting their children's daily needs. Although these households are not displayed in figure 2, Census Bureau data show that women headed one-fifth of all families in 2000, twice the share of female-headed households in 1970. Even though their average work week remained unchanged at 39 hours, the lack of child care and other support services leaves them facing time squeezes at least as sharp. Single fathers remain a much smaller group, but their ranks have also grown rapidly. Single dads work almost as much as single moms—37 hours per week in 2000. Even though this represents a drop of two hours since 1970, single fathers face time dilemmas as great as those facing single mothers. Being a single parent has always posed daunting challenges, and now there are more mothers and fathers than ever in this situation.

At the heart of these shifts is American families' growing reliance on a woman's earnings—whether or not they depend on a man's earnings as well. Women's strengthened commitment to paid employment has provided more economic resources to families and given couples more options for sharing the tasks of breadwinning and caretaking. Yet this revolution in women's work has not been complemented by an equal growth in the amount of time men spend away from the job or in the availability of organized child care. This limited change at the workplace and in men's lives has intensified the time pressures facing women.

dual-earner parents and working time

The expansion of working time is especially important for families with children, where work and family demands are most likely to conflict. Indeed, there is a persisting concern that in their desire for paid work, families with two earners are shortchanging their children in time and attention. A closer look reveals that even though parents face increased time pressure, they cope with these dilemmas by cutting back on their combined joint working time when they have children at home. For example, U.S. Census data show that parents in two-income families worked 3.3 fewer hours per week than spouses in two-income families without children, a slightly wider difference than the 2.6 hours separating them in 1970. Working hours also decline as the number of children increase. Couples with one child under 18 jointly averaged 81 hours per week in 2000, while couples with three or more children averaged 78 hours. Rather than forsaking their children, employed parents are taking steps to adjust their work schedules to make more time for the rest of life.

However, it is mothers, not fathers, who are cutting back. Fathers actually work more hours when they have children at home, and their working hours increase with the number of children. Thus, the drop in joint working time among couples with children reflects less working time among mothers. Figure 3 shows that in 2000, mothers worked almost 4 fewer hours per week than married women without children. This gap is not substantially different than in 1970.

This pattern of mothers reducing their hours while fathers increase them creates a larger gender gap in work participation among couples with children compared to the gender gap for childless couples. However, these differences are much smaller than the once predominant pattern in which many women stopped working for pay altogether when they bore children. While

A school district superintendent works at home. He spends 50 to 60 hours a week at his office, over an hour commuting each day, and like many professionals, another 5 to 10 hours a week working at home. The long hours are easier to manage now that his children have grown up and left home. (Courtesy of Jon Wagner)

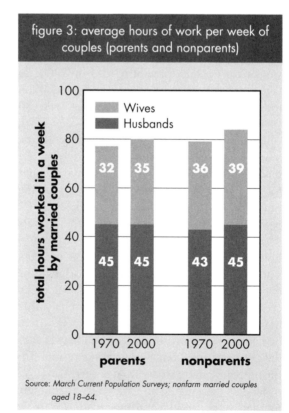

figure 3: average hours of work per week of couples (parents and nonparents)

Source: March Current Population Surveys; nonfarm married couples aged 18–64.

the transition to raising children continues to have different consequences for women and men, the size of this difference is diminishing.

It is also important to remember that the rise in working time among couples is not concentrated among those with children at home. Though Americans continue to worry about the consequences for children when both parents go to work, the move toward more work involvement does not reflect neglect on the part of either mothers or fathers. On the contrary, employed mothers continue to spend less time at the workplace than their childless peers, while employed fathers today do not spend substantially more time at work than men who are not fathers.

solving the time-pressure puzzle

Even though changes in the average working time of American workers are modest, many American families have good reason to feel overworked and time-deprived. The last several decades have witnessed the emergence of a group of workers who face very long work weeks and live in families that depend on either two incomes or one parent. And while parents are putting in less time at work than their peers without children at home, they shoulder domestic responsibilities that leave them facing clashes between work demands and family needs.

The future of family well-being and gender equality will depend on developing policies to help workers resolve the time pressures created by the widespread and deeply rooted social changes discussed above. The first step toward developing effective policy responses requires accepting the social transformations that sent women into the workplace and left Americans wishing for a balance between work and family that is difficult to achieve. Unfortunately, these changes in the lives of women and men continue to evoke ambivalence.

For example, mothers continue to face strong pressures to devote intensive time and attention to child rearing. Indeed, generally they want to, despite the rising economic and social pressure to hold a paid job as well. Even though most contemporary mothers are counted on to help support their families financially, the United States has yet to develop the child care services and flexible jobs that can help workers meet their families' needs. Whether or not mothers work outside the home, they face conflicting expectations that are difficult to meet. These social contradictions can be seen in the political push to require poor, single mothers to work at a paid job while middle-class mothers continue to be chastised for spending too much time on their jobs and away from home.

To a lesser but still important extent, fathers also face intensifying and competing pressures. Despite American families' increasing reliance on women's earnings, men face significant barriers to family involvement. Resistance from employers and coworkers continues to greet individual fathers who would like to spend less time at work to care for their children. For all the concern and attention focused on employed mothers, social policies that would help bring men more fully into the work of parenting get limited notice or support. New time squeezes can thus be better understood by comparing the large changes in women's lives with the relative lack of changes in the situation for men. The family time bind is an unbalanced one.

Even as family time has become squeezed, workers are also contending with changes in the options and expectations they face at work. Competitive workplaces appear to be creating rising pressures for some workers, especially professionals and managers, to devote an excessive amount of time to their jobs, while not offering enough work to others. In contrast to these bifurcating options, American workers increasingly express a desire to balance the important work of earning a living and caring for a new generation.

Finding solutions to these new time dilemmas will depend on developing large-scale policies that recognize and address the new needs of twenty-first-century workers and their families. As we suggest in our book, *The Time Divide*, these policies need to address the basic organization of American work and community institutions. This includes revising regulations on hours of work and providing benefit protections to more workers, moving toward the norm of a shorter work week, creating more family-supportive workplaces that offer both job flexibility and protections for employed parents, and developing a wider array of high-quality, affordable child care options.

Extending protections, such as proportional benefits and overtime pay, to workers in a wider range of jobs and occupations would reduce the built-in incentives employers have to extract as much work as possible from professionals and managers while offering less work to other employees. If professionals and managers were given overtime pay for overtime work, which wage workers are now guaranteed under the Fair Labor Standards Act, the pressures on these employees to put in endless workdays might lessen. Yet, the Bush administration recently revised these rules to move more employees into the category of those ineligible for overtime pay. Similarly, if part-time workers were offered fringe benefits proportional to the hours they work (such as partial pensions), there would be fewer reasons for employers to create jobs with work weeks so short that they do not provide the economic security all families need.

Reducing the average work week to 35 hours would also reduce the pressures on workers and help them find a better work-family balance. While this goal may seem utopian, it is important to remember that the 40-hour standard also seemed unimaginably idealistic before it was adopted in the early twentieth century. Other countries, most notably France, have adopted this standard without sacrificing economic well-being. A shorter work week still would allow for variation in work styles and commitments, but it would also create a new cultural standard that better reflects the needs and aspirations of most contemporary workers. It would also help single parents meet their dual obligations and allow couples to fashion greater equality in their work and caretaking responsibilities.

Time at work is clearly important, but it is not the whole story. The organization of the workplace and the structure of jobs also matters, especially for those whose jobs and occupations require intensive time at work. Among those putting in very long work weeks, we find that having job flexibility and autonomy help ease the perceived strains and conflicts. The work environment, especially in the form of support from supervisors and coworkers, also makes a difference. In addition, we find that workers with access to such family-friendly options as flexible work schedules are likely to use them, while workers without such benefits would like to have them.

Flexibility and autonomy are only useful if workers feel able to use them. Women and men both express concern that making use of "family-friendly" policies, such as extended parental leaves or nonstandard working hours, may endanger their future work prospects. Social policies need to protect the rights of workers to be involved parents without incurring excessive penalties at the workplace. Most Americans spend a portion of their work lives simultaneously immersed in work for pay and in parenting. Providing greater flexibility at the workplace will help workers develop both short- and longer-term strategies for integrating work and family life. However, even basic changes in the organization of work will not suffice to meet the needs of twenty-first-century families. We also need to join the ranks of virtually all other industrialized nations by creating widely available, high-quality, and affordable child care. In a world where mothers and fathers are at the workplace to stay, we need an expanded network of support to care for the next generation of workers.

These changes will not be easy to achieve. But in one form or another, they have been effectively adopted in other societies throughout the modern world. While no one policy is a cure-all, taken together they offer a comprehensive approach for creating genuine resolutions to the time pressures that confront growing numbers of American workers and their families. Ultimately, these new time dilemmas cannot be resolved by chastising workers (and, most often, mothers) for working too much. Rather, the time has come to create more flexible, family-supportive, and gender-equal workplaces and communities that complement the twenty-first-century forms of work and family life.

RECOMMENDED RESOURCES

James T. Bond. *Highlights of the National Study of the Changing Workforce* (Families and Work Institute, 2003).

Bond reports findings from a major national survey of contemporary American workers, workplace conditions, and work-family conflict.

Janet Gornick and Marcia Meyers. *Families that Work: Policies for Reconciling Parenthood and Employment* (Russell Sage Foundation, 2003).

This important study compares family-supportive policies in Europe and the United States.

Sharon Hays. *The Cultural Contradictions of Motherhood* (Yale University Press, 1997).

Hays examines how American mothers continue to face pressure to practice intensive parenting even as they increase their commitment to paid work.

Jody Heymann. *The Widening Gap: Why America's Working Families Are in Jeopardy and What Can Be Done About It* (Basic Books, 2000).

Drawing from a wide range of data, this study makes a compelling case for more flexible work structures.

Arlie Hochschild. *The Time Bind: When Home Becomes Work and Work Becomes Home* (Metropolitan Books, 1997).

A rich study of how employees in one company try to reconcile the tensions between spending time at work and caring for their families.

Jerry A. Jacobs and Kathleen Gerson. *The Time Divide: Work, Family and Gender Inequality* (Harvard University Press, 2004).

An overview of trends in working time, which shows why and how time pressures have emerged in America over the past three decades, how they are linked to gender inequality and family change and what we can do to alleviate them.

John P. Robinson and Geoffrey Godbey. *Time for Life: The Surprising Ways Americans Use Their Time* (Pennsylvania State University Press, 1999).

Drawing on time diaries, Robinson and Godbey conclude that Americans' leisure time has increased.

Juliet Schor. *The Overworked American: The Unexpected Decline of Leisure* (Basic Books, 1991).

This early and original analysis of how Americans are overworked sparked a national discussion on and concern for the problem.

REVIEW QUESTIONS

1. Although the average working week has shrunk over the last few decades, Gerson and Jacobs note that there have been a number of negative trends obscured by this fact. Summarize at least three significant changes.

2. According to Gerson and Jacobs, "If leisure time once signaled an elite lifestyle, that no longer appears to be the case." Some sociological research contradicts this argument. For example, lower-income families might have *more* time to raise their children than the upper classes. What do you think accounts for these shifts? What are the potential consequences?

3. What are the specific policies the authors argue are important for creating a more flexible, family-supportive, and gender-equal workplace and community? Discuss what you think of these recommendations, and whether or not they will be effective.

elizabeth a. armstrong, laura hamilton, and paula england

is hooking up bad for young women?

30

summer 2010

"hookup culture" is in the crossfire, but is casual college sex really so bad? as it turns out, women experience pleasures and pitfalls in both hookups and relationships.

Girls can't be guys in matters of the heart, even though they think they can," says "Laura Sessions Stepp, author of *Unhooked: How Young Women Pursue Sex, Delay Love, and Lose at Both,* published in 2007. In her view, "hooking up"—casual sexual activity ranging from kissing to intercourse—places women at risk of "low self-esteem, depression, alcoholism, and eating disorders." Stepp is only one of half a dozen journalists currently engaged in the business of detailing the dangers of casual sex.

On the other side, pop culture feminists such as Jessica Valenti, author of *The Purity Myth: How America's Obsession with Virginity is Hurting Young Women* (2010), argue that the problem isn't casual sex, but a "moral panic" over casual sex. And still a third set of writers like Ariel Levy, author of *Female Chauvinist Pigs: Women and the Rise of Raunch Culture* (2005), questions whether it's empowering for young women to show up at parties dressed to imitate porn stars or to strip in "Girls Gone Wild" fashion. Levy's concern isn't necessarily moral, but rather that these young women seem less focused on their own sexual pleasure and more worried about being seen as "hot" by men.

Following on the heels of the mass media obsession, sociologists and psychologists have begun to investigate adolescent and young adult hookups more systematically. In this essay, we draw on systematic data and studies of youth sexual practices over time to counter claims that hooking up represents a sudden and alarming change in youth sexual culture. The research shows that there is some truth to popular claims that hookups are bad for women. However, it also demonstrates that women's hookup experiences are quite varied and far from uniformly negative and that monogamous, long-term relationships are not an ideal alternative. Scholarship suggests that pop culture feminists have correctly zeroed in on sexual double standards as a key source of gender inequality in sexuality.

the rise of limited liability hedonism

Before examining the consequences of hooking up for girls and young women, we need to look more carefully at the facts. *Unhooked* author Stepp describes girls "stripping in the student center in front of dozens of boys they didn't know." She asserts that "young people have virtually abandoned dating" and that "relationships have been replaced by the casual sexual encounters known as hookups." Her sensationalist tone suggests that young people are having more sex at earlier ages in more casual contexts than their Baby Boomer parents.

This characterization is simply not true. Young people today are not having more sex at younger ages than their parents. The sexual practices of American youth changed in the 20th century, but the big change came with the Baby Boom cohort who came of age more than 40 years ago. The National Health and Social Life Survey—the gold standard of American sexual practice surveys—found that those born after 1942 were more sexually active at younger ages than those born from 1933–42. However, the trend toward greater sexual activity among young people appears to halt or reverse among the youngest cohort in the NHSLS, those born from 1963–72. Examining the National Survey of Family Growth, Lawrence B. Finer, Director of Domestic Research for the Guttmacher Institute, found that the percent of women who have had premarital sex by age 20 (65–76 percent) is roughly the same for all cohorts born after 1948. He also found that the women in the youngest cohort in this survey—those born from 1979–1984—were less likely to have premarital sex by age 20 than those born before them. The Centers for Disease Control, reporting on the results of the National Youth Risk Behavior Survey, report that rates of sexual intercourse among 9th–12th graders decreased from 1991–2007, as did numbers of partners. Reports of condom use increased. So what are young people doing to cause such angst among Boomers?

The pervasiveness of casual sexual activity among today's youth may be at the heart of Boomers' concerns. England surveyed more than 14,000 students from 19 universities and colleges about their hookup, dating, and relationship experiences. Seventy-two percent of both men and women participating in the survey reported at least one hookup by their senior year in college. What the Boomer panic may gloss over,

however, is the fact that college students don't, on average, hook up that much. By senior year, roughly 40 percent of those who ever hooked up had engaged in three or fewer hookups, 40 percent between four and nine hookups, and only 20 percent in ten or more hookups. About 80 percent of students hook up, on average, less than once per semester over the course of college.

Hooking up isn't the rampant, hedonistic free-for-all portrayed by the media.

In addition, the sexual activity in hookups is often relatively light. Only about one third engaged in intercourse in their most recent hookup. Another third had engaged in oral sex or manual stimulation of the genitals. The other third of hookups only involved kissing and non-genital touching. A full 20 percent of survey respondents in their fourth year of college had never had vaginal intercourse. In addition, hookups between total strangers are relatively uncommon, while hooking up with the same person multiple times is common. Ongoing sexual relationships without commitment are labeled as "repeat," "regular," or "continuing" hookups, and sometimes as "friends with benefits." Often there is friendship or socializing both before and after the hookup.

Hooking up hasn't replaced committed relationships. Students often participate in both at different times during college. By their senior year, 69 percent of heterosexual students had been in a college relationship of at least six months. Hookups sometimes became committed relationships and vice versa; generally the distinction revolved around the agreed upon level of exclusivity and the willingness to refer to each other as "girlfriend/boyfriend."

And, finally, hooking up isn't radically new. As suggested above, the big change in adolescent and young adult sexual behavior occurred with the Baby Boomers. This makes sense, as the forces giving rise to casual sexual activity among the young—the availability of [the] birth control pill, the women's and sexual liberation movements, and the decline of in loco parentis on college campuses—took hold in the 1960s. But changes in youth sexual culture did not stop with the major behavioral changes wrought by the Sexual Revolution.

Contemporary hookup culture among adolescents and young adults may rework aspects of the Sexual Revolution to get some of its pleasures while reducing its physical and emotional risks. Young people today—particularly young whites from affluent families—are expected to delay the commitments of adulthood while they invest in careers. They get the message that sex is okay, as long as it doesn't jeopardize their futures; STDs and early pregnancies are to be avoided. This generates a sort of limited liability hedonism. For instance, friendship is prioritized a bit more than romance, and oral sex appeals because of its relative safety. Hookups may be the most explicit example of a calculating approach to sexual exploration. They make it possible to be sexually active while avoiding behaviors with the highest physical and emotional risks (e.g., intercourse, intense relationships). Media panic over hooking up may be at least in part a result of adult confusion about youth sexual culture—that is, not understanding that oral sex and sexual experimentation with friends are actually some young people's ways of balancing fun and risk.

Even though hooking up in college isn't the rampant hedonistic free-for-all portrayed by the media, it does involve the movement of sexual activity outside of relationships. When *Contexts* addressed youth sex in 2002, Barbara Risman and Pepper Schwartz speculated that the slowdown in youth sexual activity in the 1990s might be a result of "girls' increasing control over the conditions of sexual intercourse," marked by the restriction of sex to relationships. They expressed optimism about gender equality in sexuality on the grounds that girls are more empowered in relationship sex than casual sex. It appears now that these scholars were overly optimistic about the progress of the gender revolution in sex. Not only is casual sex common, it seems that romantic relationships themselves are riddled with gender inequality.

hookup problems, relationship pleasures

Hookups are problematic for girls and young women for several related reasons. As many observers of American youth sexual culture have found, a sexual double standard continues to be pervasive. As one woman Hamilton interviewed explained, "Guys can have sex with all the girls and it makes them more of a man, but if a girl does then all of a sudden she's a 'ho' and she's not as quality of a person." Sexual labeling among adolescents and young adults may only loosely relate to actual sexual behavior; for example, one woman complained in her interview that she was a virgin the first time she was called a "slut." The lack of clear rules about what is "slutty" and what is not contribute to women's fears of stigma.

On college campuses, this sexual double standard often finds its most vociferous expression in the Greek scene. Fraternities are often the only venues where large groups of underage students can readily access alcohol. Consequently, one of the easiest places to find hookup partners is in a male-dominated party context. As a variety of scholars have observed, fraternity men often use their control of the situation to undermine women's ability to freely consent to sex (e.g., by pushing women to drink too heavily, barring their exit from private rooms, or refusing them rides home). Women report varying degrees of sexual disrespect in the fraternity culture, and the dynamics of this scene predictably produce some amount of sexual assault.

The most commonly encountered disadvantage of hookups, though, is that sex in relationships is far better for women. England's survey revealed that women orgasm more often and report higher levels of sexual satisfaction in relationship sex than in hookup sex. This is in part because sex in relationships is more likely to include sexual activities conducive to women's orgasm. In hookups, men are much more likely to receive fellatio than women are to receive cunnilingus. In relationships, oral sex is more likely to be reciprocal. In interviews conducted by England's research team, men report more concern with the sexual pleasure of girlfriends than hookup partners, while women seem equally invested in pleasing hookup partners and boyfriends.

The continuing salience of the sexual double standard mars women's hookup experiences. In contrast, relationships provide a context in which sex is viewed as acceptable for women, protecting them from stigma and establishing sexual reciprocity as a basic expectation. In addition, relationships offer love and companionship.

relationship problems, hookup pleasures

Relationships are good for sex but, unfortunately, they have a dark side as well. Relationships are "greedy," getting in the way of other things that young women want to be doing as adolescents and young adults, and they are often characterized by gender inequality—sometimes even violence.

Talking to young people, two of us (Hamilton and Armstrong) found that committed relationships detracted from what women saw as main tasks of college. The women we interviewed complained, for example, that relationships made it difficult to meet people. As a woman who had just ended a relationship explained:

I'm happy that I'm able to go out and meet new people . . . I feel like I'm doing what a college student should be doing. I don't need to be tied down to my high school boyfriend for two years when this is the time to be meeting people.

Women also complained that committed relationships competed with schoolwork. One woman remarked, "[My boyfriend] doesn't understand why I can't pick up and go see him all the time. But I have school . . . I just want to be a college kid." Another told one of us (Hamilton) that her major was not compatible with the demands of a boyfriend. She said, "I wouldn't mind having a boyfriend again, but it's a lot of work. Right now with [my major] and everything . . . I wouldn't have time even to see him." Women feared that they would be devoured by relationships and sometimes struggled to keep their self-development projects going when they did get involved.

Subjects told us that relationships were not only time-consuming, but also marked by power inequalities and abuse. Women reported that boyfriends tried to control their social lives, the time they spent with friends, and even what they wore. One woman described her boyfriend, saying, "He is a very controlling person . . . He's like, 'What are you wearing tonight?' . . . It's like a joke but serious at the same time." Women also became jealous. Coping with jealousy was painful and emotionally absorbing. One woman noted that she would

> The most commonly encountered disadvantage of hookups is that sex in relationships is far better for women.

"do anything to make this relationship work." She elaborated, "I was so nervous being with Dan because I knew he had cheated on his [prior] girlfriend . . . [but] I'm getting over it. When I go [to visit him] now . . . I let him go to the bar, whatever. I stayed in his apartment because there was nothing else to do." Other women changed the way they dressed, their friends, and where they went in the hope of keeping boyfriends.

When women attempted to end relationships, they often reported that men's efforts to control them escalated. In the course of interviewing 46 respondents, two of us (Hamilton and Armstrong) heard ten accounts of men using abuse to keep women in relationships. One woman spent months dealing with a boyfriend who accused her of cheating on him. When she tried to break up, he cut his wrist in her apartment. Another woman tried to end a relationship, but was forced to flee the state when her car windows were broken and her safety was threatened. And a third woman reported that her ex-boyfriend stalked her for months—even showing up at her workplace, showering her with flowers and gifts, and blocking her entry into her workplace until the police arrived. For most women, the costs of bad hookups tended to be less than costs of bad relationships. Bad hookups were isolated events, while bad relationships wreaked havoc with whole lives. Abusive relationships led to lost semesters, wrecked friendships, damaged property, aborted pregnancies, depression, and time-consuming involvement with police and courts.

The abuse that women reported to us is not unusual. Intimate partner violence among adolescents and young adults is common. In a survey of 15,000 adolescents conducted in 2007, the Centers for Disease Control found that 10 perecent of students had been "hit, slapped, or physically hurt on purpose by their boyfriend or girlfriend" in the last 12 months.

If relationships threaten academic achievement, get in the way of friendship, and can involve jealousy, manipulation, stalking, and abuse, it is no wonder that young women sometimes opt for casual sex. Being open to hooking up means being able to go out and fit into the social scene, get attention from young men, and learn about sexuality. Women we interviewed gushed about parties they attended and attention they received from boys. As one noted, "Everyone was so excited. It was a big fun party." They reported turning on their "make out radar," explaining that "it's fun to know that a guy's attracted to you and is willing to kiss you." Women reported enjoying hookups, and few reported regretting their last hookup. Over half the time women participating in England's survey reported no relational interest before or after

> The cost of bad hookups tend to be less than the costs of bad relationships: bad hookups are isolated events, but bad relationships wreak havoc with whole lives.

Problems posed by relationships range from time conflicts with schoolwork to the more serious issue of relationship violence. (Cyndy Andrews via Creative Commons)

their hookup, although more women than men showed interest in a relationship both before and after hookups. The gender gap in relationship interest is slightly larger after the hookup, with 48 percent of women and 36 percent of men reporting interest in a relationship.

toward gender equality in sex

Like others, Stepp, the author of *Unhooked*, suggests that restricting sex to relationships is the way to challenge gender inequality in youth sex. Certainly, sex in relationships is better for women than hookup sex. However, research suggests two reasons why Stepp's strategy won't work: first, relationships are also plagued by inequality. Second, valorizing relationships as the ideal context for women's sexual activity reinforces the notion that women shouldn't want sex outside of relationships and stigmatizes women who do. A better approach would challenge gender inequality in both relationships and hookups. It is critical to attack the tenacious sexual double standard that leads men to disrespect their hookup partners. Ironically, this could improve relationships because women would be less likely to tolerate "greedy" or abusive relationships if they were treated better in hookups. Fostering relationships among young adults should go hand-in-hand with efforts to decrease intimate partner violence and to build egalitarian relationships that allow more space for other aspects of life—such as school, work, and friendship.

RECOMMENDED RESOURCES

Kathleen A. Bogle. *Hooking Up: Sex, Dating, and Relationships on Campus* (New York University Press, 2008).

> A provocative investigation of college hookups based on 76 interviews.

Paula England, Emily Fitzgibbons Shafer, and Alison C. K. Fogarty. "Hooking Up and Forming Romantic Relationships on Today's College Campuses." In M. Kimmel and A. Aronson (eds.), *The Gendered Society Reader*, 3rd edition (Oxford University Press, 2008).

> Overview of the role of gender in the college hookup scene.

Norval Glenn and Elizabeth Marquardt. *Hooking Up, Hanging Out, and Hoping for Mr. Right: College Women on Mating and Dating Today* (Institute for American Values, 2001).

> One of the first empirical investigations of college hookups.

Laura Hamilton and Elizabeth A. Armstrong. "Double Binds and Flawed Options: Gendered Sexuality in Early Adulthood." *Gender & Sexuality* (2009) 23: 589–616.

> Provides methodological details of Hamilton and Armstrong's interview study and elaborates on costs and benefits of hookups and relationships for young women.

Derek A. Kreager and Jeremy Staff. "The Sexual Double Standard and Adolescent Peer Acceptance." *Social Psychology Quarterly* (2009) 72: 143–64.

> New empirical research confirming the continued existence of sexual double standards.

Wendy D. Manning, Peggy C. Giordano, and Monica A. Longmore. "Hooking Up: The Relationship Contexts of 'Nonrelationship' Sex." *Journal of Adolescent Research* (2006) 21: 459–83.

> Part of a series on sexual activity among younger adolescents.

REVIEW QUESTIONS

1. In this essay, the authors point out that the popular characterization of people having more sex at a younger age is statistically

untrue. Would you have assumed that young people are more sexually active now than ever before? What might that assumption say about popular culture?

2. How does public perception of hooking up vary by the gender of the participant? Have you witnessed, or even found yourself taking part in, the sexual double standard? Do you think this relates to other expectations about how different genders should act?

3. Activity: Create a lesson for a high school sex-education class based on the information and insights in this article.

sharon hays and jess butler

low-calorie feminism

31

spring 2008

in full frontal feminism, *author jessica valenti presents an updated, white-middle-class, hetero-friendly, do-it-yourself version of feminism for young women. hays and butler argue that this version of feminism is ultimately vacuous and reproduces the very problems valenti is trying to confront.*

Try feminism. It's cool! It's trendy! It's fun! It's easy! It isn't about fat, ugly, man-hating, hairy (gasp!) bra-burners. Feminism helps you feel good about yourself: "It's like self-help times one hundred," author Jessica Valenti tells us. Plus, she reveals, feminists have better sex! Phew.

It's the F-word, the Feminist Fear Factor (the terror that becoming a feminist would require you to throw away your romance novels and stilettos and stop having random sex), that Valenti aims to address in *Full Frontal Feminism.* Explicitly written to appeal to young women who find themselves saying, "I'm not a feminist, but . . . ," it surely takes on a noble cause. And there's good reason to expect Valenti—the founder and executive editor of the popular blog Feministing.com—is the right person for the job.

Feministing.com provides a useful (and fun) round-up of the latest news stories, Internet posts, cartoons, Web links, and YouTube videos dealing with issues of gender inequality across the nation and around the world, along with commentary from its staff and guest bloggers, and a regularly featured "Friday Feminist Fuck You" video. Feministing.com claims *The Nation* columnist Katha Pollit and comedienne Margaret Cho among its fans and brings in advertising dollars from the likes of Miller Beer, the American Automobile Association, Boden, and Hummer. It also sells t-shirts and tote bags.

Valenti's book uses similar techniques to sell feminism to young skeptics. The feminism of *Full Frontal* is pop feminism—dressed for sex and success. It's *The L Word* for heterosexuals. "Young women need to get past the bullshit, scoff at the shame tactics, and get back to the hard work of getting off," Valenti writes. You can be a "fuck you" feminist, she suggests, and still be sexy, hip, and popular.

Relative to the theory and reality of gender inequality, the 256 pages of this breezy read contain no new news. To be sure, the book covers a tremendous amount of ground—from sexual etiquette and pornographic pop culture to domestic violence and reproductive rights, from the glass ceiling and the mommy wage gap to abstinence education and parental consent laws, from sexist dating rituals and the oppressively rigid definition of "masculinity" to the underrepresentation of women in voting and political leadership, from the history of feminism to the academic theory of intersectionality. *Full Frontal,* in other words, touches upon virtually all the central issues in gender studies today.

Yet all this information is transmitted through sound bytes. Cryptic text messages. Truncated colloquialisms. Natch. Analysis is virtually nonexistent. The tone is simultaneously condescending, informal, bold, and bratty. This style, of course, is meant to appeal to young, white, middle-class heterosexual hipsters born in the U.S. of A.

Although Valenti references inequalities of class, race, and sexuality, these are implicitly presented as problems faced by others. Global inequalities are entirely absent. The feminization of poverty warrants only one paragraph of text and is rendered as "just something to think about." A list of racial stereotypes ("black women are bitchy," "Asian women are docile") is summed up with this analysis: "Puke." The only context in which Valenti focuses specifically on inequalities of sexuality, race, and class is a chapter titled "A Quick Academic Aside." And quick it is: this chapter, which begins with an apology for its academic tone, offers just two pages each for class, race, and sexuality, and has a grand total of seven pages.

It's hard to pin down Valenti's underlying theory of gender inequality. Depending on the context, she tells us that "pop culture" or "conservative pundits" or "men" or "society" or the "powers that be" or a mysterious "they" are responsible for discrimination against women. The (rare) analyses of specific issues one finds in these pages are similarly broad, fast, and loose. For instance, she explains the U.S. Food and Drug Administration's fear of "sex-based cults" is why women don't have access to safe, legal contraception. The "folks" promoting stay-at-home motherhood, she writes, are also responsible for women's poverty. The "real" foundation for the anti-abortion movement, according to Valenti, is the fact that pro-lifers "hate that women have sex."

In a similar vein (like many of us), Valenti often chooses outrageous, egregious examples of injustice—pharmacies refusing to dispense birth control, forced sterilization, mothers prosecuted for drinking a glass of wine, 9-year-olds on diets, vaginal rejuvenation surgery—to get her point across. Yet (unlike the rest of us, we hope), she rarely follows up on these examples with deeper analyses of their more subtle forms and broader causes. Instead, she simply concludes with trite condemnations: "Terrifying." "Beyond horrifying." "I shit you not." Or simply, "'nuff said."

Nowhere in the book does one find a consideration of the dynamics of power or the historically grounded institutional and structural forces that undergird gender inequality. Seldom does Valenti ask the reader to step outside her comfort zone and realize that feminism is no joke. When she does suggest activism, for instance, she prefaces it with an apology: "I know this is annoying," or "time to suck it up." She reassures her readers that feminism is not a full-time job: "You can be a feminist without making it your life's work." And the form of activism she recommends is often of the individualistic variety. The solution to the wage gap, for example, is to "climb the ranks."

Valenti ultimately buys right in to the very thing she's trying to combat: the primary reason young women are shying away from feminism today is it seems old-fashioned, un-cool, and might interfere with their chances of being attractive to men. Her solution? Present an updated, cool, white-middle-class-hetero-friendly—and completely vacant—do-it-yourself version of feminism for young women to turn to when feeling particularly rejected by their weekend booty call. But for those young, hip, and/or awake enough to understand that feminism isn't about dumbing down your politics and wagging your finger at those old-school feminists who are just sooooo depressing, well, we have a few sound bytes of our own.

> Get real. Look around. Feminism isn't about being easy and breezy, and it sure as hell isn't about being condescending and ethnocentric.

Get real.

Look around.

Feminism isn't about being easy and breezy, and it sure as hell isn't about being condescending and ethnocentric.

For all these reasons, this is not a text we would recommend to the readers of *Contexts*, social scientists, journalists, or any educated adult. Those scholars with a serious background in feminist theory would find this book an embarrassment. Actually, we'd like to go further and tell you that reading this book made our skin crawl. We became increasingly weary of its emptiness, its hip pajama-party style, and the author's self-indulgent and self-congratulatory tone. By page 30 it required a strong sense of professional obligation just to make us read on. We found it deeply condescending to treat young women as if they couldn't be required to think too deeply, or tackle abstract concepts, or consider forms of activism that might not be all that fun, or cool, or trendy. We have to think (hope and pray) that Valenti seriously underestimates the analytic abilities of her audience.

All that being said, we also found this book absolutely fascinating. We could hardly stop talking about it. We wanted to run right out and interview all its readers. While completely uninteresting as an introduction to gender studies, as a piece of popular culture, and a representation of Third Wave Feminism, *Full Frontal Feminism* is a bewitching curiosity, an alluring would-be window into the soul of (an imagined version of) contemporary white, middle-class, pop-culture-fetishizing American girlhood.

We weren't all that surprised to learn that plenty of 18-year-old undergraduates are eating this up. We had to wonder: even if we wouldn't recommend this book to grown-ups, do we think you should buy a copy for your teenage daughter? After all, an intro to feminism is good therapy and it is cool. We surely want young women to be able to recognize that they're not alone in their experiences of sexism, we're happy to see them ignore contemporary beauty standards, and we'd like them to enjoy sex, use condoms, and feel empowered. If *Full Frontal* can help our daughters feel good about themselves and embrace feminism as their own, then what's the problem? Are we just being prudish and narrow-minded, stuck in the Second Wave?

In many respects, an examination of *Full Frontal Feminism* offers us an almost caricatured rendering of the differences among and (alleged) rift between Second and Third Wave feminists. Compared to outdated ("1960s") Second Wave, Friedan- and National Organization for Women (NOW)–following feminists, Third Wavers represent the new, cool ("1990s") genre of celebratory grrrl power feminism—an explosive and free-wheeling world of zines, blogs, music, chat rooms, and all-inclusive activism.

In the (rarely explicit) debate, Second Wavers are accused of being rigid and anti-sex: they have sewn up their crotches and are demanding unified, politically correct behavior 24/7. No make-up, no clubbing, no fun. Third Wavers, on the other hand, love sex and have lots of fun; they get off on mascara, high heels, and lipstick just as they love pink hair, combat boots, and nose rings. They ignore the demand for unified activism—they're über-tolerant, multi-issue, multi-path.

Valenti exhorts her readers to "Mix it up. Create your own standards," because "at the end of the day, feminism is really something you define for yourself." She also lets us know that old feminists are "cliquey" and relatively

> Those scholars with a serious background in feminist theory would find this book an embarrassment. Reading this book made our skin crawl.

inept at recruiting young feminists. (NOW's Web site, she writes, uses "hackneyed 'young' language" and a "bad graffiti font." Humph.)

One of us—Sharon—is an old feminist, apparently stuck in the mud, wary of bloggers, blind to the wonders of lipstick, and zine illiterate. Hence, one shouldn't be surprised that she finds Valenti mind-numbingly tedious. But the other of us—Jess—is 25, has heels in her closet and loves Carrie Bradshaw as much as the next girl . . . and still finds *Full Frontal* deeply superficial.

For both of us, this multi-issue thing, this freedom to be whomever you want to be, may be fine on the face of it, but when applied to questions of social justice it ends up looking like a complete lack of commitment to anything that might actually require hard work and hard thinking. In fact, from where we sit Valenti's representation of the Third Wave looks like relentless individualism, a celebration of empty freedoms, a fetishizing of sex, and a blindness to the deeply distressing consequences of structural inequalities. Pick a cause like you pick your outfit. Obvi.

Although reading *Full Frontal* and writing this review may have stimulated our own "bratty" tone, we do think Valenti deserves serious credit for taking on the difficult task of convincing skeptical youth of the importance of feminism. We've met plenty of girls who say "I'm not a feminist, but . . ." and we know how hard it is to get them on board the F-word express. Academic sociology, after all, hasn't exactly been in the forefront of recruiting new feminists to the cause. Unfortunately, *Full Frontal* turns out to be recruitment "lite."

Do we think you should buy *Full Frontal Feminism* for the 16-year-olds you know? It's your call. It does make feminism seem sexy and accessible. But at the end of the day, we think it

translates into nothing more than the feminism of diary entries and lunchtime conversations about troubles with men, bosses, sex, and birth control. It's important to offer a context for thinking that you're not alone in your inability to achieve orgasm with misogynist men and dick-in-hole sex, but if this is all there is to feminism, we're in serious trouble. Although the perfect book has not yet been written, better primers for those young skeptics include Valenti's (useful) blog and the deeper and more diversity-sensitive books of other Third Wavers: *Colonize This!*, *Listen Up*, and *The Fire This Time*.

Beyond that, it's still our job to figure out a way to say that feminism is crucial, and it's more than fun, it's more than trendy, it can enrich your life in ways that go well beyond therapy. Moreover, feminism isn't a zero-sum game.

Jess says: Go ahead, watch *Sex and the City*, put on your make-up and heels, have a boyfriend or a girlfriend or a one-night-stand—hell, join a sorority if you want to—as long as you also always read books, think critically, organize feminist activities, protest sexism in public (yikes!), and realize that feminism is about challenging yourself and others to face gender inequality and then doing something about it.

Sharon says: A sorority?!? Well, okay.

Feminism isn't a luxury, it's not easy, and it requires something more than blithely saying, "fuck you!" to systematic oppression. Dedicating yourself to the hard thinking required to understand the historical, cross-cultural, structured, and constructed roots of gender inequality, and dedicating yourself to the hard work required to sustain collective and inclusive political activism, may not always make you particularly "happy," but it will make you a better person and a better citizen of the world.

> Feminism is crucial, and it's more than fun, it's more than trendy, it can enrich your life in ways that go well beyond therapy.

REVIEW QUESTIONS

1. The authors of this review criticize the book *Full Frontal Feminism* for placing the blame for gender inequality on ambiguous sources such as "pop culture," "the powers that be," and "they." What are some more concrete roots of gender inequality?

2. Why do you think the word *feminism* is often associated with negative connotations? What is your experience with feminism? Would you call yourself a feminist?

3. Activity: The history of feminism is often described as having three waves. Do some research and see if you can find out what these three waves are. What were the goals of each wave of feminism? Were these goals achieved? What aspects of gender equality, if any, do you think have yet to be achieved?

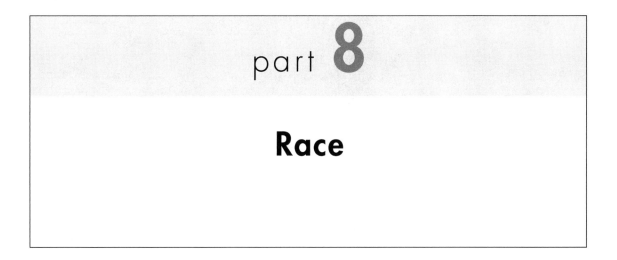

part **8**

Race

ellen berrey

sociology finds discrimination in the law

32

spring 2009

good sociology often complicates our understanding of important institutions and basic concepts. the recent discrimination research group conference showcased some of the best new research by social scientists that does just this for law and discrimination.

In 1988, Chris Burns, an African American man who built machinery for the military, injured his back on the job while carrying a heavy metal plate. He requested different work responsibilities and was fired soon after.

He first tried to find a lawyer, appealing to legal aid clinics, congressional representatives, even the President of the United States, all to no avail.

"I been searching for a lawyer to fight the government for 12 years, and there's no point," he said. With assistance from his wife and his uncle, Burns, who had only a high school diploma, filed a lawsuit. He claimed the military had discriminated against him based on his race, age, and physical handicap and had retaliated against him for seeking an accommodation.

The U.S. federal district court initially didn't consider Burns's arguments, citing his "failure to exhaust administrative remedies." While the court gave him 30 days to revise his original complaint, Burns didn't understand that part, he thought the case was over.

"I got so, you know, depressed. They send you through all this red tape gobbledy-goo, and they say these big 25-cents words. And you know without a lawyer degree that you don't understand a thing that they are telling you," he recalled.

Sociologist Laura Beth Nielsen told Burns's story at the Discoveries of the Discrimination Research Group conference last November. Held at Stanford Law School, the two-day conference showcased some of the latest research by social scientists who study employment discrimination and the law.

The findings spoke to why workplace inequalities persist despite the civil rights reforms enshrined in Title VII of the U.S. Civil Rights Act of 1964 and other subsequent laws. They reveal the complex nuances, challenges, and contradictions of the law and its implementation.

Good sociology often does this—it complicates our understanding of important institutions, such as law, and basic concepts, such as discrimination. It raises as many provocative questions as it answers.

Take Burns's experience. He was one of 41 plaintiffs interviewed for a study of employment discrimination litigation led by Nielsen and fellow sociologists Robert Nelson and Ryon Lancaster (I also collaborated with them). In interviews, plaintiffs recounted how they quickly found themselves in what seemed a maze of manipulative lawyers, judges in cahoots with employers, and unreasonable or mysterious rules that prevented them from ever telling their stories. For Burns and many others in similar situations, the law provides partial protection and inadequate recourse, and it can inflict its own harms.

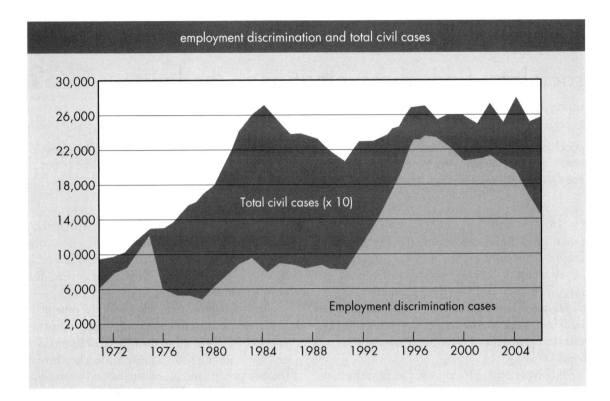

employment discrimination and total civil cases

Total civil cases (x 10)

Employment discrimination cases

We developed our study in conjunction with the Discrimination Research Group (DRG), a network of many of the top social scientists, lawyers, and policymakers who study the changing dynamics of employment discrimination. Legal studies is an interdisciplinary field, so although most DRG participants are sociologists, our projects often incorporate questions, concepts, and methods from outside sociology.

The panelists at this conference spoke on topics ranging from the effects of civil rights legislation to workplace strategies that increase equality to the insight social science can offer when drafting laws. The sociological findings highlighted tensions, exposed ironies, and posed new ways of thinking about the layers of contradictions operating in anti-discrimination initiatives.

unfairness in the workplace

While workplace discrimination is prevalent, white women and black, Latino, and Asian men and women have made some inroads into well-paying and high status jobs since 1966, when the U.S. government began to collect these data. Yet, most of these groups remain underrepresented (some grossly) in craft production, managerial, and professional jobs, according to a 2007 study by sociologists Donald Tomaskovic-Devey and Kevin Stainback.

The U.S. Current Population Census reveals that in 2006, white men still earned significantly more than white women, African Americans, and Latinos. White women had the closest parity, earning 73.5 percent of what white men earned that year, while Hispanic women had the greatest earnings gap, 51.7

percent. Although these figures don't control for significant factors that affect earnings, such as education, they nonetheless demonstrate the persistence of substantial economic inequity.

Sociological research on discrimination not only documents these patterns of inequality, it tries to explain them. And it shows that our explanations can't just point to sexism and racism in society at large. Rather, workplaces are a significant source of discrimination, which can take many forms.

Sometimes discrimination involves flagrant acts of racism or sexism. Employment law today is designed to adjudicate this intentional discrimination. Often, however, people discriminate unintentionally and unconsciously, or in ways that obscure their prejudice.

Sociologist and social psychologist Cecelia Ridgeway, one of the conference panelists, has shown in her research how unconscious bias operates. Popular gender stereotypes contain assumptions about people's status and competence. Such stereotypes may lead those making decisions to an "implicit bias" in their judgments and actions, such as their willingness to listen to another person's opinion. These biases tend to work to the disadvantage of women, people of color, and other marginalized groups.

Organizations' own practices also generate much inequity at work, especially when combined with widespread patterns of gender and racial bias. Many jobs continue to be segregated by race and gender, even though civil rights laws make it illegal for employers to consider race or sex when they assign positions and set wages. Employers who rely on their employees' networks to obtain applicants are more likely to

hire people of the same gender and ethnic characteristics of their current workforce.

Here, sociological research provides a compelling explanation for why the law fails to remedy much workplace inequality: the legal definition of intentional discrimination leaves out implicit bias, hiring by networks, and other influential organizational practices.

the litigation system

Under the current system, people who believe they have been targets of discrimination must file a complaint with the Equal Employment Opportunity Commission (EEOC), or a state or local agency, and then pursue litigation. Despite the challenges plaintiffs like Chris Burns face when pursuing a lawsuit, the volume of employment discrimination litigation ballooned in the 1990s, Nielsen and her colleagues have shown. The number of discrimination lawsuits filed in federal court tripled from 8,000 in 1990 to 23,000 in 1998, but then dropped to 15,000 by 2006.

Some of the rise in litigation can be explained by the 1991 Civil Rights Act and the 1992 Americans with Disabilities Act (ADA)—legislation whose track record of helping its intended beneficiaries is mixed, but which nonetheless spurred attention.

Law professors John Donohue and Peter Siegelman surveyed a wide range of social scientific studies and found the early federal employment discrimination laws of 1964 and 1972 generated significant benefits—African Americans and white women, for example, made inroads into jobs that previously had shut them out—but later interventions in the 1990s had less encouraging results.

> Employment law is designed to adjudicate intentional discrimination. Often, however, people discriminate unintentionally and unconsciously, or in ways that obscure their prejudice.

One study, by Donohue and colleagues, suggested the ADA didn't actually result in more people with disabilities becoming employed, nor did it stem the decline in their wages that had begun in 1986. This research raises a troubling possibility: in some cases, the newer extensions of employment discrimination law may have serious drawbacks, such as business costs for compliance, but no clear benefits. They may even harm the employment prospects of their intended beneficiaries.

If litigation is workers' primary option, how do they fare once they've filed suit? The literature on litigation (both civil in general and employment discrimination in particular) suggests the system of individual claims is inadequate. Most targets of discrimination won't pursue a claim. Many who do face the common

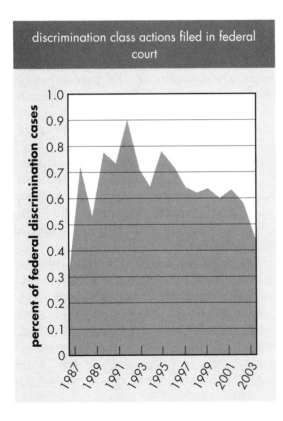

discrimination class actions filed in federal court

percent of federal discrimination cases

problems of inadequate legal representation, lack of knowledge, and lack of resources.

The law can lead to social change only when individuals choose to mobilize it, according to Nielsen and her colleagues. A group of plaintiffs can opt to file a class-action lawsuit, and these can have far-reaching consequences. Class actions are most likely to claim disparate impact—that an employment practice like a height requirement might seem neutral but, in fact, systematically hurts a protected group—so they're able to help far more people. Class actions also are more likely to succeed. Yet, they made up less than 1 percent of the federal cases between 1987 and 2003, Nielsen and her colleagues reported in their presentation.

Moreover, most litigation doesn't address systemic patterns of discrimination. The vast majority of cases—93 percent—consist of a single plaintiff. Many plaintiffs, especially those without a lawyer, are dismissed by the court or lose early in the process on summary judgment.

If we got our information on these discrimination cases from the news alone, we might conclude that all plaintiffs reap a windfall. Some 96 percent of media reports cover successful plaintiff wins at trial, but just 2 percent of cases filed actually result in a plaintiff win. As well, media reports tend to focus on big wins—more than $1 million—but the actual median award in these cases is just $150,000, Nielsen has also found. The litigation study shows plaintiffs are far more likely to settle, and for a median award of $30,000.

Although employers complain about the hassles of employee lawsuits, employment discrimination law favors employers in both overt and subtle ways. Since the inception of equal employment opportunity law, employers have created departments, positions, policies, and other programs that allegedly prevent or mitigate work place inequality. But, employers' willingness to follow formal and legal procedures when dealing with workers—what sociologist Lauren Edelman and her colleagues call the "legalization of the workplace"—doesn't necessarily translate into less workplace discrimination.

In fact, formal legality can make the law work to an employer's benefit. The courts have developed legal standards based on the very policies and programs employers have created to signal their workplaces are "fair," according to a study by Edelman, and law professors Catherine Albiston and Linda Krieger, sociologist Scott Eliason, and EEOC administrative judge Virginia Mellema.

Judges treat the mere existence of personnel practices, non-discrimination policies, and diversity programs as evidence discrimination hasn't been taking place. They fail to question whether these practices are really implemented or truly effective at protecting workers from discrimination.

promising alternatives

Social scientists are now beginning to identify systemic practices that can promote greater equality in organizations. Many are the reverse of the routine organizational practices that generate inequality. Job segregation, for example, can be mitigated when employers formalize their processes for posting job openings, establish clear criteria for selecting candidates, and hold administrators accountable for improving the representation of women and people of color.

Other effective practices may come as a surprise. After analyzing more than 800 private employers since the early 1970s, sociologist Alexandra Kalev has demonstrated that some employee involvement programs adopted by companies to increase worker efficiency actually end up helping white women, black women, and black men enter managerial ranks.

"Most women and minorities are channeled into low-visibility jobs with little opportunity for advancement. When companies create selfdirected work teams and cross-training programs, these women and minorities suddenly have more opportunities to demonstrate their skills and smarts," she said.

Sociological research also reveals the law can, in surprising ways, thwart organizational interventions. Sociologist Frank Dobbin presented new results from his study with Kalev showing that most corporate diversity programs fail to improve the numbers of female and African American managers.

Managers aren't persuaded by mandatory diversity trainings nor by company statements that justify support for women and people of color because of the risks of lawsuits or other legal issues. Diversity trainings can be effective, though. When training references the "business case" for cultural differences—that workplace diversity leads to better products and greater profits—and when it avoids any mention of the law, more women and African Americans move into management positions.

These findings are significant because the less effective diversity trainings are more popular: roughly 80 percent of companies make training mandatory and nearly 75 percent refer to law in their training curricula. These practices are a mainstay of the estimated $8 million diversity management industry.

Despite popular rhetoric about the business case for diversity, though, the number of racial minority corporate board members and senior executives still remains limited. This finding came from a study of corporate boardrooms by sociologists Clayton Rose and William Bielby. When large American companies systematically manage the racial composition of their boards, they focus on African Americans and ignore other groups. "Race is about black . . . all boards need an African American today," one white board member interviewed for their study said.

In even the best corporate diversity management programs, many workers fall through the cracks. In my own study of a Fortune 500 company, I've found the company measures "diversity" by the number of women and people of color who earn annual salaries more than $24,000 from non-unionized, non-hourly positions. The company's diversity networking groups are for senior managers and professionals, and they hold events during business hours, which means a worker who assembles products on a factory line can't attend. Such an approach assumes female and minority representation at the top will "trickle down" to benefit everyone else.

What this sociological research shows us, however, is that law has both real payoffs and serious limitations as a strategy for promoting equality.

the discrimination frame

With all these new employer interventions, it may seem like there's no reason to retain traditional concepts of discrimination. But participants in the final roundtable considered discrimination as an analytical and legal frame, suggesting different ways to think about it.

Since the 1950s, sociologist Sam Lucas explained, civil rights law and activism have renounced prejudice with considerable success. Discrimination, however, remains deeply entrenched.

"We should still care about the results of discrimination," he insisted. Moreover, the law focuses on assigning blame for discrimination, but blame "is not helping the social scientific analysis." Sociologists should instead analyze discrimination in terms of the conditions under which it tends to occur and the actual parties involved.

Some of those at the discussion fiercely defended the legal model of discrimination. Miranda Massie, a civil rights attorney, argued political activism and class-action lawsuits together can create disincentives for discrimination. One of her legal cases helped end sexual harassment in a car manufacturing plant where a male manager repeatedly revealed himself to female employees and abuse of women seemed to be a management perk. Their win created a better workplace for female employees in that factory, Massie said, and these legal victories must be continually reinforced.

Law professor Susan Sturm's current project examines institutional innovation, specifically initiatives that address structural inequalities and promote inclusion. She and her colleagues look at "institutional change on the cutting edge" in such areas as low-wage work, housing, and criminal justice to understand how change happens. They see success among institutions "that take up diversity as part of their core mission." In these models, legal action is just one of many possible strategies for achieving change, not the primary one.

The debate continued on the role law can, and should, play in achieving social change.

"Rights aren't only about litigation," Edelman argued. "And if you move too far away from rights, what do you lose?"

"This is not a move away from rights," Sturm replied. "It's about situating rights in a broader context, but people hear this as abandoning rights and litigation." She added that the risk comes from the current political context: "There are risks both in moving towards the innovation model and letting go of rights and in holding on to court-enforced rights and missing the train."

"All frames have costs and benefits," sociologist Robin Stryker interjected. "We need to ask: what do we get and what do we lose?"

social science and the law

A pressing question remained after two days of presentations and debate: can sociological findings like these improve the law? After all, the social sciences haven't gained authority within the law, which sometimes wholesale disregards an enormous body of published, refereed research. Judges, too, tend to minimize or ignore social scientific literature. And, many basic legal concepts are at odds with sociological findings on inequality, workplace discrimination, and effective solutions.

Scientific evidence doesn't always fit neatly within a legal framework. For example, in court, expert witnesses have cited research findings on implicit bias, but they rarely, if ever, can prove it exists in any particular workplace or that it produces the specific instances of discrimination an employee experiences. Social science can, however, influence the content, implementation, and effects of civil rights law, Stryker argued.

In the 1960s and 1970s, for example, industrial psychologists played a critical role in preventing employers, especially in the south, from discriminating against African American job applicants and workers. Many employers used general thinking tests to screen blue collar jobs, but to the disadvantage of people of color. Industrial psychologists were able to convince courts that these tests didn't predict job performance, and the EEOC and the Supreme Court adopted their scientific definitions as the basis of disparate impact, which is a very effective legal doctrine for ending workplace discrimination.

We still need a legal system that frees Chris Burns and others like him from discrimination in the jobs they need—a system that fully hears and fairly considers the cases of aggrieved parties and that ultimately brings greater parity in wages, career opportunities, and other key measures of social equality. Without such change, civil rights law will perpetuate, rather than remedy, workplace injustice.

What this sociological research shows us, however, is that law has both real payoffs and serious limitations as a strategy for promoting equality. We learn from sociology that discrimination is a tricky concept. Tools to combat it can be easily co-opted, and even good policies have limitations. Sociology reveals the subtleties, nuances, tensions, and contradictions that abound when law is put into practice in the real world. The value of sociology lies in its ability to complicate our assumptions about law and demonstrate both its promises and pitfalls.

RECOMMENDED RESOURCES

Lauren B. Edelman, Christopher Uggen, and Howard S. Erlanger. "The Endogeneity of Legal Regulation: Grievance Procedures as Rational Myth." *American Journal of Sociology* (1999) 105: 406–54.

> Shows how courts incorporate organizations' norms and ideas into legal rules.

Sam Lucas. *Theorizing Discrimination in an Era of Contested Prejudice* (Temple University Press, 2008).

> Draws on critical scholarship to explain racial and gender discrimination as an insidious social dynamic in many social contexts.

Robert L. Nelson, Ellen Berrey, and Laura Beth Nielsen. "Divergent Paths: Conflicting Conceptions of Employment Discrimination in Law and the Social Sciences." *Annual Review of Law and Social Science* (2008) 4: 103–22.

> An overview of socio-legal research on workplace discrimination.

Laura Beth Nielsen, Robert L. Nelson, Ryon Lancaster, and Nicholas Pedriana. *Contesting Workplace Discrimination in Court: Characteristics and Outcomes of Federal Employment Discrimination Litigation, 1987–2003* (American Bar Foundation, 2008).

Unique documentation of the latest trends in federal employment discrimination lawsuits and their outcomes in court.

Nicholas Pedriana and Robin Stryker. "The Strength of a Weak Agency: Early Enforcement of Title VII of the 1964 Civil Rights Act and the Expansion of State Capacity." *American Journal of Sociology* (2004) 110: 709–60.

Shows how the EEOC, in its early years, took advantage of broadly constructed legislation to expand and enforce civil rights law aggressively.

REVIEW QUESTIONS

1. How would you define discrimination? How does your definition compare with a more formal, legal definition?
2. The article states that sometimes people discriminate unintentionally. What are some examples of unintentional discrimination?
3. In your opinion, what should be done to rectify the effects of discrimination? Who should be responsible for taking action?
4. Activity: Research the Equal Employment Opportunity Commission (www.eeoc.gov). What type of authority does the commission have? How can employees utilize its services? Bonus: How have the bases for complaints changed over time?

donald tomaskovic-devey and patricia warren

explaining and eliminating racial profiling   **33**

spring 2009

racial profiling in law enforcement has been called biased and discriminatory. however, the same politics and practices that cause racial profiling are the tools communities can use to end it.

The emancipation of slaves is a century and a half in America's past. Many would consider it ancient history. Even the 1964 Civil Rights Act and the 1965 Voting Rights Act, which challenged the de facto racial apartheid of the post–Civil War period, are now well over 40 years old.

But even in the face of such well-established laws, racial inequalities in education, housing, employment, and law enforcement remain widespread in the United States.

Many Americans think these racial patterns stem primarily from individual prejudices or even racist attitudes. However, sociological research shows discrimination is more often the result of organizational practices that have unintentional racial effects or are based on cognitive biases linked to social stereotypes.

Racial profiling—stopping or searching cars and drivers based primarily on race, rather than any suspicion or observed violation of the law—is particularly problematic because it's a form of discrimination enacted and organized by federal and local governments.

In our research we've found that sometimes formal, institutionalized rules within law enforcement agencies encourage racial profiling. Routine patrol patterns and responses to calls for service, too, can produce racially biased policing. And, unconscious biases among individual police officers can encourage them to perceive some drivers as more threatening than others (of course, overt racism, although not widespread, among some police officers also contributes to racial profiling).

Racially biased policing is particularly troubling for police-community relations, as it unintentionally contributes to the mistrust of police in minority neighborhoods. But the same politics and organizational practices that produce racial profiling can be the tools communities use to confront and eliminate it.

> The same politics and practices that produce racial profiling can be the tools communities use to confront and eliminate it.

profiling and its problems

The modern story of racially biased policing begins with the Drug Enforcement Agency's (DEA) Operation Pipeline, which starting in 1984 trained 25,000 state and local police officers in 48 states to recognize, stop, and search potential drug couriers. Part of that training included considering the suspects' race.

Jurisdictions developed a variety of profiles in response to Operation Pipeline. For example, in Eagle County, Colorado, the sheriff's office profiled drug couriers as those who had fast-food wrappers strewn in their cars, out-of-state license plates, and dark skin, according to the book *Good Cop, Bad Cop* by Milton Heuman and Lance Cassak. As well, those authors wrote, Delaware's drug courier profile commonly targeted young minority men carrying pagers or wearing gold jewelry. And according to the American Civil Liberties Union (ACLU), the Florida Highway Patrol's profile included rental cars, scrupulous obedience to traffic laws, drivers wearing lots of gold or who don't "fit" the vehicle, and ethnic groups associated with the drug trade (meaning African Americans and Latinos).

In the 1990s, civil rights organizations challenged the use of racial profiles during routine traffic stops, calling them a form of discrimination. In response, the U.S. Department of Justice argued that using race as an explicit profile produced more efficient crime control than random stops. Over the past decade, however, basic social science research has called this claim into question.

> More stops and searches of minorities doesn't lead to more drug seizures than stops and searches of white drivers. In fact, the rates of contraband found in searches of minorities are typically lower.

The key indicator of efficiency in police searches is the percent that result in the discovery of something illegal. Recent research has shown repeatedly that increasing the number of stops and searches among minorities doesn't lead to more drug seizures than are found in routine traffic stops and searches among white drivers. In fact, the rates of contraband found in profiling-based drug searches of minorities are typically lower, suggesting racial profiling decreases police efficiency.

In addition to it being an inefficient police practice, Operation Pipeline violated the assumption of equal protection under the law guaranteed through civil rights laws as well as the 14th Amendment to the U.S. Constitution. It meant, in other words, that just as police forces across the country were learning to curb the egregious civil

rights violations of the 20th century, the federal government began training state and local police to target black and brown drivers for minor traffic violations in hopes of finding more severe criminal offending. The cruel irony is that it was exactly this type of flagrant, state-sanctioned racism the civil rights movement was so successful at outlawing barely a decade earlier.

Following notorious cases of violence against minorities perpetrated by police officers, such as the videotaped beating of Rodney King in Los Angeles in 1991 and the shooting of Amadou Diallo in New York in 1999, racially biased policing rose quickly on the national civil rights agenda. By the late 1990s, challenges to racial profiling became a key political goal in the more general movement for racial justice.

The National Association for the Advancement of Colored People (NAACP) and the ACLU brought lawsuits against law enforcement agencies across the United States for targeting minority drivers. As a result, many states passed legislation that banned the use of racial profiles and then required officers to record the race of drivers stopped in order to monitor and sanction those who were violating citizens' civil rights.

Today, many jurisdictions continue to collect information on the race composition of vehicle stops and searches to monitor and discourage racially biased policing. In places like New Jersey and North Carolina, where the national politics challenging racial profiling were reinforced by local efforts to monitor and sanction police, racial disparities in highway patrol stops and searches declined.

Our analysis of searches by the North Carolina Highway Patrol shows that these civil rights–based challenges, both national and local, quickly changed police behavior. In 1997, before racial profiling had come under attack, black drivers were four times as likely as white drivers to be subjected to a search by the North Carolina Highway Patrol. Confirming that the high rate of searches represented racial profiling, black drivers were 33 percent less likely to be found with contraband compared to white drivers. The next year, as the national and local politics of racial profiling accelerated, searches of black drivers plummeted in North Carolina. By 2000, racial disparities in searches had been cut in half and the recovery of contraband no longer differed by race, suggesting officers were no longer racially biased in their decisions to search cars.

This isn't to suggest lawyers' and activists' complaints have stopped profiling everywhere. For example, Missouri, which has been collecting data since 2000, still has large race disparities in searching practices among its police officers. The most recent data (for 2007) shows blacks were 78 percent more likely than whites to be searched. Hispanics were 118 percent more likely than whites to be searched. Compared to searches of white drivers, contraband was found 25 percent less often among black drivers and 38 percent less often among Hispanic drivers.

how bias is produced

Many police-citizen encounters aren't discretionary, therefore even if an officer harbors racial prejudice it won't influence the decision to stop a car. For example, highway patrol officers, concerned with traffic flow and public safety, spend a good deal of their time stopping speeders based on radar readings—they often don't even know the race of the driver until after they pull over the car. Still, a number of other factors can produce high rates of racially biased stops. The first has to do with police patrol patterns, which tend to vary widely by neighborhood.

Not unreasonably, communities suffering from higher rates of crime are often patrolled more aggressively than others. Because minorities more often live in these neighborhoods, the routine deployment of police in an effort to increase public safety will produce more police-citizen contacts and thus a higher rate of stops in those neighborhoods.

A recent study in Charlotte, North Carolina, confirmed that much of the race disparity in vehicle stops there can be explained in terms of patrol patterns and calls for service. Another recent study of pedestrian stops in New York yielded similar conclusions—but further estimated that police patrol patterns alone lead to African American pedestrians being stopped at three times the rate of whites. (And similar to the study of racial profiling of North Carolina motorists, contraband was recovered from white New Yorkers at twice the rate of African Americans.)

Police patrol patterns are, in fact, sometimes more obviously racially motivated. Targeting black bars, rather than white country clubs, for Saturday-night random alcohol checks has this character. This also happens when police stop minority drivers for being in white neighborhoods. This "out-of-place policing" is often a routine police practice, but can also arise from calls for service from white households suspicious of minorities in their otherwise segregated neighborhoods. In our conversations with African American drivers, many were quite conscious of the risk they took when walking or driving in white neighborhoods.

"My son . . . was working at the country club . . . He missed the bus and he said he was walking out Queens Road. After a while all the lights came popping on in every house. He guessed they called and . . . the police came and they questioned him, they wanted to know why was he walking through Queens Road [at] that time of day," one black respondent we talked to said.

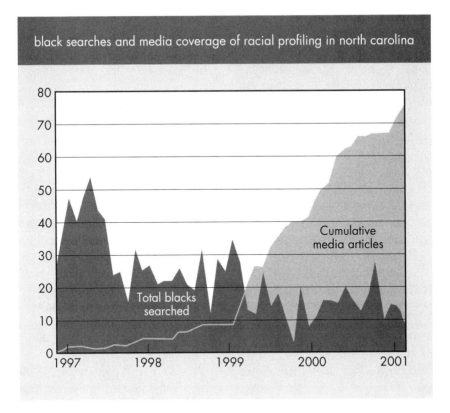

black searches and media coverage of racial profiling in north carolina

Cumulative media articles

Total blacks searched

The "wars" on drugs and crime of the 1980s and 1990s encouraged law enforcement to police minority neighborhoods aggressively and thus contributed significantly to these problematic patterns. In focus groups with African American drivers in North Carolina, we heard that many were well aware of these patterns and their sources. "I think sometimes they target . . . depending on where you live. I think if you live in a side of town . . . with maybe a lot of crime or maybe break-ins or drugs, . . . I think you are a target there," one respondent noted.

These stories are mirrored in data on police stops in a mid-size midwestern city reported in the figure "blacks stopped more in neighborhoods with few black drivers." Here, the fewer minorities there are in a neighborhood, the more often African Americans are stopped. In the whitest neighborhoods, African American drivers were stopped at three times the rate you'd expect given how many of them are on the road. In minority communities, minority drivers were still stopped disproportionally, but at rates much closer to their population as drivers in the neighborhood.

This isn't to say all racial inequities in policing originate with the rules organizations follow. Racial attitudes and biases among police officers are still a source of racial disparity in police vehicle stops. But even this is a more complicated story than personal prejudice and old-fashioned bigotry.

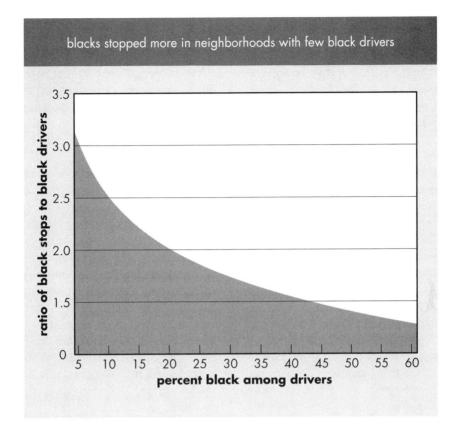

blacks stopped more in neighborhoods with few black drivers

bias among individual officers

The two most common sources of individual bias are conscious prejudice and unconscious cognitive bias. Conscious prejudice is typically, but incorrectly, thought of as the most common source of individuals' racist behavior. While some individual police officers, just like some employers or real estate agents, may be old-fashioned bigots, this isn't a widespread source of racial bias in police stops. Not only is prejudice against African Americans on the decline in the United States, but most police forces prohibit this kind of racism and reprimand or punish such officers when it's discovered. In these cases, in fact, organizational mechanisms prevent, or at least reduce, bigoted behavior.

Most social psychologists agree, however, that implicit biases against minorities are widespread in the population. While only about 10 percent of the white population will admit they have explicitly racist attitudes, more than three-quarters display implicit anti-black bias.

Studies of social cognition (or, how people think) show that people simplify and manage information by organizing it into social categories. By focusing on obvious status characteristics such as sex, race, or age, all of us tend to categorize ourselves and others into groups. Once people are racially categorized, stereotypes automatically, and often unconsciously, become activated and influence behavior. Given pervasive media images of African American men as dangerous and threatening, it shouldn't be surprising that when officers make decisions about whom to pull over or whom to search, unconscious bias may encourage them to focus more often on minorities.

These kinds of biases come into play especially for local police who, in contrast to highway patrol officers, do much more low-speed, routine patrolling of neighborhoods and business districts and thus have more discretion in making decisions about whom to stop.

In our research in North Carolina, for example, we found that while highway patrol officers weren't more likely to stop African American drivers than white drivers, local police stopped African Americans 70 percent more often than white drivers, even after statistically adjusting for driving behavior. Local officers were also more likely to stop men, younger drivers, and drivers in older cars, confirming this process was largely about unconscious bias rather than explicit racial profiles. Race, gender, age, class biases, and stereotypes about perceived dangerousness seem to explain this pattern of local police vehicle stops.

strategies for change

Unconscious biases are particularly difficult for an organization to address because offending individuals are typically unaware of them, and when confronted they may deny any racist intent.

There is increasing evidence that even deep-seated stereotypes and unconscious biases can be eroded through both education and expo-sure to minorities who don't fit common stereotypes, and that they can be contained when people are held accountable for their decisions. Indeed, it appears that acts of racial discrimination (as opposed to just prejudicial attitudes or beliefs) can be stopped through managerial authority, and prejudice itself seems to be reduced through both education and exposure to minorities.

For example, a 2006 study by sociologists Alexandra Kalev, Frank Dobbin, and Erin Kelly of race and gender employment bias in the private sector found that holding management accountable for equal employment opportunities is particularly efficient for reducing race and gender biases. Thus, the active monitoring and managing of police officers based on racial composition of their stops and searches holds much promise for mitigating this "invisible" prejudice.

Citizen and police review boards can play proactive and reactive roles in monitoring both individual police behavior as well as problematic organizational practices. Local police forces can use data they collect on racial disparity in police stops to identify problematic organizational behaviors such as intensively policing minority neighborhoods, targeting minorities in white neighborhoods, and racial profiling in searches.

Aggressive enforcement of civil rights laws will also play a key role in encouraging local police chiefs and employers to continue to monitor and address prejudice and discrimination inside their organizations. This is an area where the federal government has a clear role to play. Filing lawsuits against cities and states with persistent patterns of racially biased policing—whether based on the defense of segregated

> Unconscious biases can be eroded through education and exposure to minorities who don't fit common stereotypes. Biases can also be contained when people are held accountable for their decisions.

white neighborhoods or the routine patrolling of crime "hot spots"—would send a message to all police forces that the routine harassment of minority citizens is unacceptable in the United States.

justice in the obama era

Given the crucial role the federal justice department has played in both creating and confronting racial profiling, one may wonder whether the election of President Barack Obama will have any consequences for racially biased policing.

Obama certainly has personal reasons to challenge racist practices. And given the success of his presidential campaign, it would seem he has the political capital to address racial issues in a way and to an extent unlike any of his predecessors.

At the same time, the new president has vowed to continue to fight a war on terrorism, a war often understood and explicitly defined in religious and ethnic terms. In some ways, the threat of terrorism has replaced the threat of African Americans in the U.S. political lexicon. There's evidence as well that politicians, both Democrat [sic] and Republican, have increased their verbal attacks on illegal immigrants and in doing so may be providing a fertile ground for new rounds of profiling against Hispanics in this country. So, while the racial profiling of African Americans as explicit national policy is unlikely in the Obama Administration, other groups may not be so lucky.

Americans committed to racial justice and equality will likely take this as a cautionary tale. They will also likely hope the Obama Administration decides to take a national leadership role in ending racial profiling. But if it does, as sociologists we hope the administration won't make the all too common mistake of assuming racial profiling is primarily the result of racial prejudice or even the more widespread psychology of unconscious bias.

RECOMMENDED RESOURCES

American Civil Liberties Union. Campaign against Racial Profiling. www.aclu.org/racial-justice/racial-profiling/index.html

> The leading civil rights agency speaking out against racial profiling has actively challenged police departments across the United States on biased policing practices.

N. Dasgupta and Anthony Greenwald. 2001. "On the Malleability of Automatic Attitudes: Combating Automatic Prejudice with Images of Admired and Disliked Individuals." *Journal of Personality and Social Psychology* (2001) 81: 800–14.

> Shows unconscious cognitive biases can be countered by positive, stereotype-disrupting role models.

Alexandra Kalev, Frank Dobbin, and Erin Kelly. 2006. "Best Practices or Best Guesses? Assessing the Efficacy of Corporate Affirmative Action and Diversity Polices." *American Sociological Review* (2006) 71: 598–617.

> Shows that holding managers accountable for racial and gender bias leads to lower levels of discrimination.

Racial Profiling Data Collection Resource Center at Northeastern University. Legislation and Litigation. www.racialprofilinganalysis.neu.edu/legislation/

> Provides detailed information about racial profiling studies across the United States.

Patricia Warren, Donald Tomaskovic-Devey, William Smith, Matthew Zingraff, and Marcinda Mason. "Driving While Black: Bias Processes and Racial Disparity in Police Stops." *Criminology* (2006) 44: 709–38.

Uses survey data to identify the mechanisms that give rise to racial disparity in traffic stops.

REVIEW QUESTIONS

1. Have you experienced or seen racial profiling? How prevalent do you think it is in your area?
2. How are systematic, individual, and unconscious bias related? Is one type more damaging than another? Use an example other than racial profiling to discuss how all three types of bias might arise in a given situation.
3. How can sociological research help reduce racial profiling?
4. Activity: You are the chief of police. Design a five-point program for your department to help combat and eliminate racial profiling.

edward e. telles

mexican americans and immigrant incorporation

34

winter 2010

mexicans have been "coming to america" for over 150 years. their diverse experiences illustrate the complexities of integration.

Sociologists, public-policy makers, and the general public usually try to anticipate how modern immigrants and their descendants will become part of American society by comparing their experiences to those of European immigrants a century or more ago.

The European American experience of incorporation is often described using the language and framework of "assimilation," wherein immigrants or their descendants eventually become an indistinguishable part of the dominant or mainstream society. However, an increasing number of sociologists argue that this may not always be true: today's immigrants are far less homogenous and encounter distinct circumstances and conditions when they arrive in the United States and as they become part of its society. For example, unlike the immigration of predominately low-skilled Europeans in the late 19th and early 20th centuries, today's immigrants are mostly from Latin America and Asia, they have varied skills and educational backgrounds, and many work in labor markets that offer fewer opportunities than before. The experience of today's immigrants with American society and culture, in other words, is more varied and uncertain than the old models can allow.

At the extreme, pundits like political scientist Samuel Huntington have argued that some new immigrants have not assimilated (or will not assimilate) and so they are a threat to American national unity. Similar, though usually more muted, claims about immigrant assimilation often involve cultural, economic and political worries about the new immigrants, which incidentally were similar to those raised during previous cycles of immigration. In any case, a careful examination of the evidence is important in order to design appropriate immigration and immigrant incorporation policies.

For examining the full range and complexity of the contemporary incorporation process, Mexican Americans, with their history, size, and internal diversity, are a very useful group. Their multiple generations since immigration, variation in their class backgrounds, the kinds of cities and neighborhoods they grew up in, and their skin color may reveal much about diverse patterns of immigrant incorporation in American society today. Unlike the study of

> The experience of today's immigrants with American society and culture is more varied and uncertain than the old models can allow.

most other non-European groups, the study of Mexican Americans allows analysts to examine the sociological outcomes of adults into the third and fourth generations since immigration.

some history

According to the U.S. Census Bureau, about 30 million people of Mexican origin currently live in the United States, and 13 million of them are immigrants. Mexicans comprise the largest group of immigrants in the United States—28 percent—so what happens to them and their descendants largely reflects what will happen to today's immigrants in general.

Moreover, Mexicans have been "coming to America" for over 150 years (before Americans came to them), and so there are several generations of U.S.-born Mexican Americans for us to study. (Ironically, analysts have mostly overlooked the fact that Mexican immigration is part of the old, or classic, period of immigration—seen as primarily European—as well as the new.) Each of these generations, successively more removed from the first-generation immigrant experience, informs our understanding of incorporation.

But first, we must start with approximately 100,000 Mexicans who instantly became Americans following the annexation of nearly half of Mexico's one-time territory [in 1848]. Since that year, Mexican immigration has been continuous, with a spike from 1910 through 1930. A second peak, beginning in 1980, continues today.

Mexico shares a 2,000-mile border with the United States. Until recently, Mexican immigration has been largely seasonal or cyclical and largely undocumented. The relative ease of entry and tight restrictions set by the U.S. government on immigrant visas for Mexicans have created a steady undocumented flow, which has increased in recent years. Demographers estimate that 7 million undocumented Mexican immigrants now live in the United States.

The issue of race has also been important to the Mexican American experience throughout history. The United States based its conquest of the formerly Mexican territory (the current U.S. Southwest) on ideas of manifest destiny and the racial inferiority of the area's racially mixed inhabitants. Throughout the 19th and early 20th centuries, race-based reasoning was often used to segregate and limit Mexican American mobility. However, prior to the civil rights movement, Mexican American leaders strategically emphasized their Spanish roots and sought a white status for the group to diminish their racial stigma.

These leaders associated their belief in whiteness with the goal of middle-class assimilation, which they saw as possible for groups like southern and central Europeans, who were not considered fully white at the time. Indeed, historians like David Roediger show that European Americans were able to become white and thus fully included in American society through state benefits, such as homeownership subsidies, that were largely denied to African Americans.

Mexican Americans didn't, however, succeed in positioning themselves on the "white track." Jim Crow–like segregation persisted against them until the 1960s, when a Chicano movement in response to discrimination in education and other spaces emerged among young Mexican Americans. The movement encouraged ethnic and racial pride by opposing continued discrimination and exclusion and drew on symbols of historic colonization.

Only a few Mexican Americans today can trace their ancestry to the U.S. Southwest prior to 1848, when it was part of Mexico, but this experience arguably has implications for the Mexican-origin population overall. This history of colonization and subsequent immigration, the persistence of racial stigmatization by American society, and the particular demographics involved in Mexican immigration and settlement make the Mexican American case unique and informative.

the mexican american study project, 1965 to 2000

In 1993, my collaborator, Vilma Ortiz, and I stumbled upon several dusty boxes containing the questionnaires for a 1965 representative survey of Mexican Americans in Los Angeles and San Antonio. We believed that a follow up survey of these respondents and their children would provide a rare but much-needed understanding of the intergenerational incorporation experiences of the Mexican American population. Indeed, based upon this data set, we initiated a 35-year longitudinal study. In 2000, we set out to re-interview 684 of the surviving respondents and 758 of their children.

The original respondents were fairly evenly divided into three generations: immigrants (1st generation), the children of immigrants (2nd), and the grandchildren of immigrants (or later generations since immigration—the 3rd+). Their children, then, are of the 2nd, 3rd, and 4th+ generations. Using their responses from 2000, we examined change across these four generations regarding education, socioeconomic status, language, intermarriage, residential segregation, identity, and political participation.

We found that Mexican Americans experienced a diverse pattern of incorporation in the late 20th century. This included rapid assimilation on some dimensions, slower assimilation and even ethnic persistence on others, and persistent socioeconomic disadvantage across generations.

In terms of English language acquisition and development of strong American identities, these Mexican Americans generally exhibit rapid and complete assimilation by the second generation. They show slower rates of assimilation on language, religion, intermarriage, and residential

integration, although patterns can also indicate substantial ethnic persistence. For example, 36 percent of the 4th generation continues to speak Spanish fluently (although only 11 percent can read Spanish), and 55 percent feel their ethnicity is very important to them (but often also feel that "being American" is very important to them). Spanish fluency clearly erodes over each generation, but only slowly.

The results for education and socioeconomic status show far more incomplete assimilation. Schooling rapidly improves in the 2nd generation compared to the 1st but an educational gap with non-Hispanic whites remains in the 3rd and even by the 4th and 5th generation among Mexican Americans. (This stands in contrast to the European immigrants of the previous century who experienced full educational assimilation by the 3rd.) Although we see that conditions for Mexican Americans in 2000 have reportedly improved from their parents in 1965, the education and socioeconomic status gap with non-Hispanic white Americans remains large, regardless of how many generations they have been in the U.S. The 2000 U.S. Census showed that, among 35 to 54 year olds born in the in the United States, only 74 percent of Mexican Americans had completed high school compared to 90 percent of non-Hispanic whites, 84 percent of blacks, and 95 percent of Asians.

The graph "educational and linguistic incorporation in 2000" illustrates the contrasting incorporation trajectories for Mexican Americans on Spanish language retention and education. While we see a large gain in education between immigrants and their 2nd-generation children, there is a slight decline in education to the 3rd and 4th generation. [The figure] also reveals a slow but certain linear trend toward universal English monolingualism. In other words, educational assimilation remains elusive, but complete linguistic assimilation—or the loss

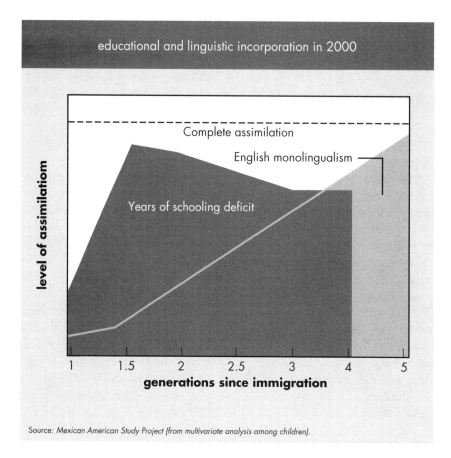

educational and linguistic incorporation in 2000

Complete assimilation

English monolingualism

level of assimilatiom

Years of schooling deficit

generations since immigration

1   1.5   2   2.5   3   4   5

Source: Mexican American Study Project (from multivariate analysis among children).

of Spanish bilingualism—is nearly reached by the 5th generation.

Indeed, consistent with at least a dozen other studies, our evidence suggests that when the education of parents and other factors are similar across generational groups, educational attainment actually decreases in each subsequent generation.

the continuing importance of race and ethnicity

A high percentage of the Mexican Americans in our study claim a non-white racial identity. Even into the 3rd and 4th generations, the major-

ity see themselves as non-white and believe they are stereotyped because of their ancestry. Nearly half report personal incidents of racial discrimination. Race continues to be important for them, and Mexican continues to be a race-like category in the popular imagination in much of the Southwest. In addition, the predominance and undocumented status of Mexican immigration coupled with large doses of anti-Mexican nativism may stigmatize all members of the group, whether immigrant or U.S.-born.

In many places, Mexican Americans are intermediate in the racial hierarchy, situated between whites and blacks (and newly arrived Mexican immigrants). Our survey did not directly examine the process through which race or racial stigma limits Mexican Americans. However, based on our in-depth interviews and other evidence, it seems that this occurs through both personal and institutional racial discrimination as well as through the internalization of a race-based stigma (which may affect life strategies and ambitions, especially during schooling). The geographical proximity of an underdeveloped and misunderstood Mexico and the persistent immigration of poorly educated (and often undocumented) Mexican workers may also reinforce the low status and the self-perceptions of Mexican Americans.

> The Mexican American experience in education is particularly problematic and leads to persistent socioeconomic disadvantage across generations.

Low levels of education across generations also slows assimilation on other dimensions. Less-educated Mexican Americans of all generations earn less, are in less prestigious occupations, and are less likely to own their home than if they had more education. They are also more likely to live among, befriend, and marry other Mexican Americans; tend to have more children than their more-educated counterparts; are less likely to strongly identify as American; are less likely to vote; and are more tied to the Democratic party.

Finally, the large size and urban concentration of this population facilitates in-group interaction and limits exposure to out-group members. It also provides a large market for Spanish language media. Along with these, the continuous flow of immigrants from Mexico reinforces Spanish language fluency and use and provides incentives for later generation Mexican Americans to continue speaking Spanish. Also, the common use of Spanish language may raise nativist ire, which, in turn, may sharpen ethnic and racial identities for later generation Mexican Americans.

lessons for immigrant incorporation

The Mexican American incorporation experience is not easy to sum up or generalize. But in many ways, that is precisely the point. The findings from the Mexican American Study Project demonstrate a range of outcomes and experiences. There are dimensions on which Mexican Americans assimilate as would be expected by the traditional (and most optimistic) theories. At the same time, there are other domains in which their experience is one of limited assimilation and even ethnic persistence. Particularly problematic is their experience in the educational realm, which leads to persistent socioeconomic disadvantage across generations. Racial differences and stigmas can further contribute to these disadvantages, though the persistence of linguistic and other ethnic differences may be beneficial in other ways.

Perhaps because of immigration's centrality to the economy and social policies regarding immigrant incorporation, the heated immigration debates today are largely about whether or how long it will take the descendants of immigrants to assimilate in terms of schooling and the job market. In framing the debates about immigrant incorporation simply in these terms, we have neglected other dimensions of that process. The Mexican American case clearly demonstrates the multifaceted nature of the incorporation experience. Moreover, it has clear implications for how Americans—scholars and policy makers as well as the lay public— think about the incorporation of new generations of immigrants in their midst.

For example, there is a tendency to exaggerate the consistency of assimilation across dimensions. While examining the heterogeneous Mexican American population, we have shown that incorporation on particular dimensions may directly affect others and that the speed and direction of these dimensions may vary in unexpected ways.

To be certain, we have found that education affects nearly all other dimensions of assimilation. Moreover, we have also found that residential integration is a key intermediate variable where low education impedes one's ability to afford housing in an integrated middle-class neighborhood, which in turn slows other dimensions such as intermarriage. A generation later, children who grew up in integrated neighborhoods and whose parents were intermarried are more likely to assimilate themselves. There may also be gradual assimilation on dimensions like retaining an ethnic language and increasing intermarriage, at the same time that there is rapid assimilation on learning English or no assimilation on educational attainment after the 2nd generation.

The study of Mexican Americans also points to the importance of looking at the diversity of the immigrant incorporation experience within groups. Previous findings mostly compare group averages or statistical distributions. We find, for example, that Mexican Americans in the 2nd generation and beyond have lower educational levels and are more likely to end up with working class jobs than other groups. But, we also found a diversity of economic experiences among Mexican Americans, ranging from a few who move into the middle class and fall out of the ethnic community to others who are poor and are strongly rooted in the ethnic community, even into the 4th generation.

We often forget about the importance of history. This is understandable since many immigrant groups arrived at a specific time point so most group members experienced the same historical events. Most Italians that came to the United States, for example, arrived in the first fifteen years of the 20th century and experienced World War I as immigrants, World War II as 2nd-generation ethnics, and as 3rd-generation Italian Americans fully integrated into the American mainstream by the 1970s.

For Mexican Americans, though, successive waves of immigrants have led to generations that experienced different historical events. We found that the experiences of incorporation for Mexican Americans depend largely on where they are inserted in history. The Mexican American Study Project disentangled generations-since-immigration from historical generations. By doing so, we found, for example, that the educational gap with whites has been narrowing for adults educated in the 1970s and 80s compared to those educated at mid-century. Spanish fluency has also diminished in recent decades for Mexican Americans of comparable generations-since-immigration. These are both indicators of group assimilation over historical time, though educational assimilation does not necessarily occur over generations-since-immigration.

Connected with this is the importance of examining multiple generations and at ages when they have completed their education and are well into their careers. Other empirical studies of incorporation have examined only the 2nd generation that are in their 20s at the oldest, compared to their immigrant parents. This is largely due to the policy-related concerns of funders and researchers about how the children of the current wave of immigrants are faring. Our respondents, though, include the 3rd and 4th generation as well and are in their

Americans like to repeat the American narrative of immigrant success and assimilation, but that story doesn't describe the experience of many of today's immigrants.

30s, 40s and 50s, ages when they are more likely to have formed families and to have already availed themselves of the second chances that American society often provides, including the GED and occupational skills training. This gives us a fuller picture of incorporation.

Previous studies of incorporation have also generally overlooked local context. We also showed substantial variation in how Mexican Americans growing up in Los Angeles and San Antonio were incorporated. Overall, Mexican Americans in San Antonio had more ethnic lifestyles and behaviors, including retaining Spanish fluency into the third and fourth generation, but they were more politically conservative and identified as white to a greater extent than their Angeleno counterparts. However, educational disadvantage was similar in the two urban areas. Variations in urban contexts are likely to affect how some immigrants or groups of immigrants and their descendants incorporate into society, especially as some areas place greater demographic or political pressures on assimilation. These factors may help account for differences in the incorporation of Mexican Americans compared to European Americans, whose ancestors arrived to New York and other east coast cities.

Finally, many previous studies of incorporation have emphasized a core to which immigrants and their descendants assimilate. But the case of Mexican Americans reminds us of the importance of a long-standing Mexican American core, which has arguably been a dominant model for assimilation for descendants of Mexican immigrants in many Southwest urban areas. This ethnic-based core represents models for Mexican American incorporation including acceptable occupations or class positions as well as cultural styles and models of political action.

Americans like to repeat the American narrative of immigrant success and assimilation, but that story doesn't describe the experience of many of today's immigrants. Even worse, to insist on the assimilation narrative as the story of all immigrants ignores the need for policies that address the specific needs and situations of different groups of immigrants. This neglect—born of a certain kind of historical optimism—comes at the peril of the lives of many Americans. But it also limits educational policies appropriate for the American economy, which increasingly requires an educated, employed, and integrated workforce and populace to maintain its international edge.

Perhaps the most basic and important lesson of the Mexican American incorporation experience, then, is the danger of trying to understand all immigrants with a single, one-size-fits-all model.

RECOMMENDED RESOURCES

Richard Alba and Victor Nee. *Remaking the American Mainstream: Assimilation and Contemporary Immigration* (Harvard University Press, 2003).

A modern theory of assimilation based on new immigrant realities and an analysis of official government data.

Brian Duncan, V. Joseph Hotz, and Stephen J. Trejo. "Hispanics in the U.S. Labor Market." In *Hispanics and the Future of America*, ed. Marta Tienda and Faith Mitchell. (National Academies Press, 2006).

Compares Mexican Americans to other Hispanic and non-Hispanic groups over three generations using recent government data.

Milton M. Gordon. *Assimilation in American Life: The Role of Race, Religion and National Origins* (Oxford University Press, 1964).

The classic statement on the many dimensions of assimilation in the United States.

Phillip Kasinitz, John Mollenkopf, Mary C. Waters, and Jennifer Holdaway. *Inheriting the City: Children of Immigrants Come of Age* (Russell Sage Foundation Press, 2008).

> A recent study of the children of immigrants in New York City that finds rapid assimilation for the second generation.

Alejandro Portes and Ruben Rumbaut. *Legacies: The Story of the Immigrant Second Generation.* (University of California Press, 2001).

> An analysis from the well-known Children of Immigrants Longitudinal Survey that shows various paths of incorporation for the second generation, including both upward and downward mobility.

David R. Roediger. *Working Toward Whiteness: How America's Immigrants Became White* (Basic Books, 2005).

> A historical work that shows how previously stigmatized European groups were accepted as part of the white majority in the United States.

REVIEW QUESTIONS

1. What are some societal factors that could explain why even fourth- and fifth-generation Mexican immigrants view themselves as "non-white," when other immigrant groups have historically seen themselves as white by the second or third generation?
2. The article talks about internalization of "race-based" stigma. What does this term mean? What factors help produce this stigma? What are some other examples of this trend?
3. What implications does this article have for U.S. immigration policy? If you were given the task of redesigning the immigration policy in the United States, what would you change?

herbert j. gans

race as class

fall 2005

why does the idea of race continue to exert so much influence in the united states? because the skin colors and other physical features used to define race were selected precisely because they mirror the country's socioeconomic pecking order.

Humans of all colors and shapes can make babies with each other. Consequently most biologists, who define races as subspecies that cannot interbreed, argue that scientifically there can be no human races. Nonetheless, lay people still see and distinguish between races. Thus, it is worth asking again why the lay notion of race continues to exist and to exert so much influence in human affairs.

Lay persons are not biologists, nor are they sociologists, who argue these days that race is a social construction arbitrary enough to be eliminated if "society" chose to do so. The laity operates with a very different definition of race. They see that humans vary, notably in skin color, the shape of the head, nose, and lips, and quality of hair, and they choose to define the variations as individual races.

More important, the lay public uses this definition of race to decide whether strangers (the so-called other) are to be treated as superior, inferior, or equal. Race is even more useful for deciding quickly whether strangers might be threatening and thus should be excluded. Whites often consider dark-skinned strangers threatening until they prove otherwise, and none more than African Americans.

Scholars believe the color differences in human skins can be traced to climatic adaptation. They argue that the high levels of melanin in dark skin originally protected people living outside in hot, sunny climates, notably in Africa and South Asia, from skin cancer. Conversely, in cold climates, the low amount of melanin in light skins enabled the early humans to soak up vitamin D from a sun often hidden behind clouds. These color differences were reinforced by millennia of inbreeding when humans lived in small groups that were geographically and socially isolated. This inbreeding also produced variations in head and nose shapes and other facial features so that Northern Europeans look different from people from the Mediterranean area, such as Italians and, long ago, Jews. Likewise, East African faces differ from West African ones, and Chinese faces from Japanese ones. (Presumably the inbreeding and isolation also produced the DNA patterns that geneticists refer to in the latest scientific revival and redefinition of race.)

Geographic and social isolation ended long ago, however, and human population movements, intermarriage, and other occasions for mixing are eroding physical differences in bodily features. Skin color stopped being adaptive too after people found ways to protect themselves from the sun and could get their vitamin D from the grocery or vitamin store. Even so, enough color variety persists to justify America's perception of white, yellow, red, brown, and black races.

Never mind for the moment that the skin of "whites," as well as many East Asians and Latinos is actually pink; that Native Americans are not red; that most African Americans come in various shades of brown; and that really black skin is rare. Never mind either that color differences within each of these populations are as great as the differences between them, and that, as DNA testing makes quite clear, most people are of racially mixed origins even if they do not know it. But remember that this color palette was invented by whites. Nonwhite people would probably divide the range of skin colors quite differently.

Advocates of racial equality use these contradictions to fight against racism. However, the general public also has other priorities. As long as people can roughly agree about who looks "white," "yellow," or "black" and find that their notion of race works for their purposes, they ignore its inaccuracies, inconsistencies, and other deficiencies.

Note, however, that only some facial and bodily features are selected for the lay definition of race. Some, like the color of women's nipples or the shape of toes (and male navels) cannot serve because they are kept covered. Most other visible ones, like height, weight, hairlines, ear lobes, finger or hand sizes—and even skin texture—vary too randomly and frequently to be useful for categorizing and ranking people or judging strangers. After all, your own child is apt to have the same stubby fingers as a child of another skin color or, what is equally important, a child from a very different income level.

race, class, and status

In fact, the skin colors and facial features commonly used to define race are selected precisely because, when arranged hierarchically,

they resemble the country's class-and-status hierarchy. Thus, whites are on top of the socioeconomic pecking order as they are on top of the racial one, while variously shaded nonwhites are below them in socioeconomic position (class) and prestige (status).

The darkest people are for the most part at the bottom of the class-status hierarchy. This is no accident, and Americans have therefore always used race as a marker or indicator of both class and status. Sometimes they also use it to enforce class position, to keep some people "in their place." Indeed, these uses are a major reason for its persistence.

Of course, race functions as more than a class marker, and the correlation between race and the socioeconomic pecking order is far from statistically perfect: All races can be found at every level of that order. Still, the race-class correlation is strong enough to utilize race for the general ranking of others. It also becomes more useful for ranking dark-skinned people as white poverty declines so much that whiteness becomes equivalent to being middle or upper class.

The relation between race and class is unmistakable. For example, the 1998–2000 median household income of non-Hispanic whites was $45,500; of Hispanics (currently seen by many as a race) as well as Native Americans, $32,000; and of African Americans, $29,000. The poverty rates for these same groups were 7.8 percent among whites, 23.1 among Hispanics, 23.9 among blacks, and 25.9 among Native Americans. (Asians' median income was $52,600—which does much to explain why we see them as a model minority.)

True, race is not the only indicator used as a clue to socioeconomic status. Others exist and are useful because they can also be applied to

> When the descendants of the European immigrants began to move up economically and socially, their skins apparently began to look lighter.

ranking co-racials. They include language (itself a rough indicator of education), dress, and various kinds of taste, from given names to cultural preferences, among others.

American English has no widely known working-class dialect like the English Cockney, although "Brooklynese" is a rough equivalent, as is "black vernacular." Most blue-collar people dress differently at work from white-collar, professional, and managerial workers. Although contemporary American leisure-time dress no longer signifies the wearer's class, middle-income Americans do not usually wear Armani suits or French haute couture, and the people who do can spot the knockoffs bought by the less affluent.

Actually, the cultural differences in language, dress, and so forth that were socially most noticeable are declining. Consequently, race could become yet more useful as a status marker, since it is so easily noticed and so hard to hide or change. And in a society that likes to see itself as classless, race comes in very handy as a substitute.

the historical background

Race became a marker of class and status almost with the first settling of the United States. The country's initial holders of cultural and political power were mostly WASPs (with a smattering of Dutch and Spanish in some parts of what later became the United States). They thus automatically assumed that their kind of whiteness marked the top of the class hierarchy. The bottom was assigned to the most powerless, who at first were Native Americans and slaves. However, even before the former had been virtually eradicated or pushed to the country's edges, the skin color and related facial features of the majority of colonial America's slaves had become the markers for the lowest class in the colonies.

Although dislike and fear of the dark are as old as the hills and found all over the world, the distinction between black and white skin became important in America only with slavery and was actually established only some decades after the first importation of black slaves. Originally, slave owners justified their enslavement of black Africans by their being heathens, not by their skin color.

In fact, early Southern plantation owners could have relied on white indentured servants to pick tobacco and cotton or purchased the white slaves that were available then, including the Slavs from whom the term *slave* is derived. They also had access to enslaved Native Americans. Blacks, however, were cheaper, more plentiful, more easily controlled, and physically more able to survive the intense heat and brutal working conditions of Southern plantations.

After slavery ended, blacks became farm laborers and sharecroppers, de facto indentured servants, really, and thus they remained at the bottom of the class hierarchy. When the pace of industrialization quickened, the country needed new sources of cheap labor. Northern industrialists, unable and unwilling to recruit southern African Americans, brought in very poor European immigrants, mostly peasants. Because these people were near the bottom of the class hierarchy, they were considered nonwhite and classified into races. Irish and Italian newcomers were sometimes even described as black (Italians as "guineas"), and the eastern and southern European immigrants were deemed "swarthy."

However, because skin color is socially constructed, it can also be reconstructed. Thus, when the descendants of the European immigrants began to move up economically and socially, their skins apparently began to look lighter to the whites who had come to America before them. When enough of these descendents became visibly middle class, their skin was seen as fully white. The biological skin color of the second and third generations had not changed, but it was socially blanched or whitened. The process probably began in earnest just before the Great Depression and resumed after World War II. As the cultural and other differences of the original European immigrants disappeared, their descendants became known as white ethnics.

This pattern is now repeating itself among the peoples of the post-1965 immigration. Many of the new immigrants came with money and higher education, and descriptions of their skin color have been shaped by their class position. Unlike the poor Chinese who were imported in the nineteenth century to build the West and who were hated and feared by whites as a "yellow horde," today's affluent Asian newcomers do not seem to look yellow. In fact, they are already sometimes thought of as honorary whites, and later in the twenty-first century they may well turn into a new set of white ethnics. Poor East and Southeast Asians may not be so privileged, however, although they are too few to be called a "yellow horde."

Hispanics are today's equivalent of a "swarthy" race. However, the children and grandchildren of immigrants among them will probably undergo "whitening" as they become middle class. Poor Mexicans, particularly in the Southwest, are less likely to be whitened, however. (Recently a WASP Harvard professor came close to describing these Mexican immigrants as a brown horde.)

Meanwhile, black Hispanics from Puerto Rico, the Dominican Republic, and other Caribbean countries may continue to be perceived, treated, and mistreated as if they were African American. One result of that mistreatment is their low median household income of $35,000, which was just $1,000 more than that of non-Hispanic blacks but $4,000 below that of so-called white Hispanics.

Perhaps South Asians provide the best example of how race correlates with class and how it is affected by class position. Although the highly educated Indians and Sri Lankans who started coming to America after 1965 were often darker than African Americans, whites only noticed their economic success. They have rarely been seen as nonwhites, and are also often praised as a model minority.

Of course, even favorable color perceptions have not ended racial discrimination against newcomers, including model minorities and other affluent ones. When they become competitors for valued resources such as highly paid jobs, top schools, housing, and the like, they also become a threat to whites. California's Japanese-Americans still suffer from discrimination and prejudice four generations after their ancestors arrived here.

african-american exceptionalism

The only population whose racial features are not automatically perceived differently with upward mobility are African Americans: Those who are affluent and well educated remain as visibly black to whites as before. Although a significant number of African Americans have become middle class since the civil rights legislation of the 1960s, they still suffer from far harsher and more pervasive discrimination and segregation than nonwhite immigrants of equivalent class position. This not only keeps whites and blacks apart but prevents blacks from moving toward equality with whites. In their case, race is used both as a marker of class and, by keeping blacks "in their place," an enforcer of class position and a brake on upward mobility.

In the white South of the past, African Americans were lynched for being "uppity." Today, the enforcement of class position is less deadly but, for example, the glass ceiling for professional and managerial African Americans is set lower than for Asian Americans, and on-the-job harassment remains routine.

Why African-American upward economic mobility is either blocked or, if allowed, not followed by public blanching of skin color remains a mystery. Many explanations have been proposed for the white exceptionalism with which African Americans are treated. The most common is "racism," an almost innate prejudice against people of different skin color that takes both personal and institutional forms. But this does not tell us why such prejudice toward African Americans remains stronger than that toward other nonwhites.

A second explanation is the previously mentioned white antipathy to blackness, with an allegedly primeval fear of darkness extrapolated into a primordial fear of dark-skinned people. But according to this explanation, dark-skinned immigrants such as South Asians should be treated much like African Americans.

A better explanation might focus on "Negroid" features. African as well as Caribbean immigrants with such features—for example, West Indians and Haitians—seem to be treated somewhat better than African Americans. But this remains true only for new immigrants; their children are generally treated like African Americans.

Two additional explanations are class-related. For generations, a majority or plurality of all African Americans were poor, and about a quarter still remain so. In addition, African Americans continue to commit a proportionally greater share of the street crime, especially street drug sales—often because legitimate job opportunities are scarce. African Americans are apparently also more often arrested without cause. As one result, poor African Americans are more often considered undeserving than are other poor people, although in some parts of America, poor Hispanics, especially those who are black, are similarly stigmatized.

The second class-based explanation proposes that white exceptionalist treatment of African Americans is a continuing effect of slavery: They are still perceived as ex-slaves. Many hateful stereotypes with which today's African Americans are demonized have changed little from those used to dehumanize the slaves. (Black Hispanics seem to be equally demonized, but then they were also slaves, if not on the North American continent.) Although slavery ended officially in 1864, ever since the end of Reconstruction subtle efforts to discourage African-American upward mobility have not abated, although these efforts are today much less pervasive or effective than earlier.

Some African Americans are now millionaires, but the gap in wealth between average African Americans and whites is much greater than the gap between incomes. The African-American middle class continues to grow, but many of its members barely have a toehold in it, and some are only a few paychecks away from a return to poverty. And the African-American poor still face the most formidable obstacles to upward mobility. Close to a majority of working-age African-American men are jobless or out of the labor force. Many women, including single mothers, now work in the low-wage economy, but they must do without most of the support systems that help middle-class working mothers. Both federal and state governments have been punitive, even in recent Democratic administrations, and the Republicans have cut back nearly every antipoverty program they cannot abolish.

Daily life in a white-dominated society reminds many African Americans that they are perceived as inferiors, and these reminders are louder and more relentless for the poor, especially young men. Regularly suspected of being criminals, they must constantly prove that they are worthy of equal access to the American Dream. For generations, African Americans have watched immigrants pass them in the class hierarchy, and those who are poor must continue to compete with current immigrants for the lowest-paying jobs. If unskilled African Americans reject such jobs or fail to act as deferentially as immigrants, they justify the white belief that they are less deserving than immigrants. Blacks' resentment of such treatment gives whites additional evidence of their unworthiness, thereby justifying another cycle of efforts to keep them from moving up in class and status.

Such practices raise the suspicion that the white political economy and white Americans may, with the help of nonwhites who are not black, use African Americans to anchor the American class structure with a permanently lower-class population. In effect, America, or those making decisions in its name, could be seeking, not necessarily consciously, to establish an undercaste that cannot move out and up. Such undercastes exist in other societies: the gypsies of Eastern Europe, India's untouchables, "indigenous people" and "aborigines" in yet other places. But these are far poorer countries than the United States.

some implications

The conventional wisdom and its accompanying morality treat racial prejudice, discrimination, and segregation as irrational social and individual evils that public policy can reduce but only changes in white behavior and values can eliminate. In fact, over the years, white prejudice as measured by attitude surveys has dramatically declined, far more dramatically than behavioral and institutional discrimination.

But what if discrimination and segregation are more than just a social evil? If they are used to keep African Americans down, then they also serve to eliminate or restrain competitors for valued or scarce resources, material and symbolic. Keeping African Americans from decent jobs and incomes as well as quality schools and housing makes more of these available to all the rest of the population. In that case, discrimination

and segregation may decline significantly only if the rules of the competition change or if scarce resources, such as decent jobs, become plentiful enough to relax the competition, so that the African-American population can become as predominantly middle class as the white population. Then the stigmas, the stereotypes inherited from slavery, and the social and other arrangements that maintain segregation and discrimination could begin to lose their credibility. Perhaps "black" skin would eventually become as invisible as "yellow" skin is becoming.

the multiracial future

One trend that encourages upward mobility is the rapid increase in interracial marriage that began about a quarter century ago. As the children born to parents of different races also intermarry, more and more Americans will be multiracial, so that at some point far in the future the current quintet of skin colors will be irrelevant. About 40 percent of young Hispanics and two-thirds of young Asians now "marry out," but only about 10 percent of blacks now marry nonblacks—yet another instance of the exceptionalism that differentiates blacks.

Moreover, if race remains a class marker, new variations in skin color and in other visible bodily features will be taken to indicate class position. Thus, multiracials with "Negroid" characteristics could still find themselves disproportionately at the bottom of the class hierarchy. But what if at some point in the future everyone's skin color varied by only a few shades of brown? At that point, the dominant American classes might have to invent some new class markers.

If in some utopian future the class hierarchy disappears, people will probably stop judging differences in skin color and other features. Then lay Americans would probably agree with biologists that race does not exist. They might even insist that race does not need to exist.

RECOMMENDED RESOURCES

David Brion Davis. *Challenging the Boundaries of Slavery* (Harvard University Press, 2001).

> A historical account of the relation between race and slavery.

Joe R. Feagin and Melvin P. Sikes. *Living with Racism: The Black Middle-Class Experience* (Beacon, 1994).

> Documents continuing discrimination against middle- and upper-middle-class African Americans.

Barbara Jeanne Fields. "Slavery, Race and Ideology in the United States of America." *New Left Review* 181 (May/June 1990): 95–118.

> A provocative analysis of the relations between class and race.

Marvin Harris. "How Our Skins Got Their Color." In *Who We Are, Where We Came From, and Where We Are Going* (HarperCollins, 1989).

> An anthropologist explains the origins of different skin colors.

Jennifer Lee and Frank D. Bean. "Beyond Black and White: Remaking Race in America." *Contexts* (Summer 2003): 26–33.

> A concise analysis of changing perceptions and realities of race in America.

REVIEW QUESTIONS

1. What does Gans mean when he conceptualizes "race as class"? How does he use South Asians as perhaps "the best example" of how race correlates with class?
2. Gans writes about how commonplace assumptions obscure particular instances that might conflict with our racial stereotypes (e.g., poor whites and wealthy African Americans), and he rejects psychological and physiological explanations of racism. In the place of such explanations he offers two class-based formulations. What are they?
3. Gans offers several possible solutions to the social problem of race. Which ones do you feel are the most persuasive? Discuss and defend your position.
4. Activity: The African-American feminist bell hooks writes about how multiple social systems intersect with each other to create multiple levels of oppression. In addition to racism, what other -isms can you list? How do these isms interact with one another?

min zhou

are asian americans becoming "white"?

36

winter 2004

asian americans have been labeled a "model minority" for their high rates of achievement, and some say they are on their way to becoming "white." but these expectations can be a burden, and the predictions are surely premature. even today, many americans see asians as "forever foreign."

"I never asked to be white. I am not literally white. That is, I do not have white skin or white ancestors. I have yellow skin and yellow ancestors, hundreds of generations of them. But like so many other Asian Americans of the second generation, I find myself now the bearer of a strange new status: white, by acclamation. Thus it is that I have been described as an 'honorary white,' by other whites, and as a 'banana' by other Asians . . . to the extent that I have moved away from the periphery and toward the center of American life, I have become white inside."

—Eric Liu, The Accidental Asian (p. 34)

Are Asian Americans becoming "white"? For many public officials the answer must be yes, because they classify Asian-origin Americans with European-origin Americans for equal opportunity programs. But this classification is premature and based on false premises. Although Asian Americans as a group have attained the career and financial success equated with being white, and although many have moved next to or have even married whites, they still remain culturally distinct and suspect in a white society.

At issue is how to define *Asian American* and *white*. The term *Asian American* was coined by the late historian and activist Yuji Ichioka during the ethnic consciousness movements of the late 1960s. To adopt this identity was to reject the Western-imposed label of "Oriental." Today,

"Asian American" is an umbrella category that includes both U.S. citizens and immigrants whose ancestors came from Asia, east of Iran. Although widely used in public discussions, most Asian-origin Americans are ambivalent about this label, reflecting the difficulty of being American and still keeping some ethnic identity: Is one, for example, Asian American or Japanese American?

Similarly, white is an arbitrary label having more to do with privilege than biology. In the United States, groups initially considered non-white, such as the Irish and Jews, have attained "white" membership by acquiring status and wealth. It is hardly surprising, then, that non-whites would aspire to becoming "white" as a mark of and a tool for material success. However, becoming white can mean distancing oneself from "people of color" or disowning one's ethnicity. Pan-ethnic identities—Asian American, African American, Hispanic American— are one way the politically vocal in any group try to stem defections. But these group identities may restrain individual members' aspirations for personal advancement.

varieties of asian americans

Privately, few Americans of Asian ancestry would spontaneously identify themselves as Asian, and fewer still as Asian American. They instead link their identities to specific countries of origin, such as China, Japan, Korea, the Philippines, India, or Vietnam. In a study of Vietnamese youth in San Diego, for example, 53 percent identified themselves as Vietnamese, 32 percent as Vietnamese American, and only 14 percent as Asian American. But they did not take these labels lightly; nearly 60 percent of these youth considered their chosen identity as very important to them.

Some Americans of Asian ancestry have family histories in the United States longer than many Americans of Eastern or Southern European origin. However, Asian-origin Americans became numerous only after 1970, rising from 1.4 million to 11.9 million (4 percent of the total U.S. population), in 2000. Before 1970, the Asian-origin population was largely made up of Japanese, Chinese, and Filipinos. Now, Americans of Chinese and Filipino ancestries are the largest subgroups (at 2.8 million and 2.4 million, respectively), followed by Indians, Koreans, Vietnamese, and Japanese (at more than one million). Some 20 other national-origin groups, such as Cambodians, Pakistanis, Laotians, Thai, Indonesians, and Bangladeshis, were officially counted in government statistics only after 1980; together they amounted to more than two million Americans in 2000.

The sevenfold growth of the Asian-origin population in the span of 30-odd years is primarily due to accelerated immigration following the Hart-Celler Act of 1965, which ended the national origins quota system, and the historic resettlement of Southeast Asian refugees after the Vietnam War. Currently, about 60 percent of the Asian-origin population is foreign-born (the first generation), another 28 percent are U.S.-born of foreign-born parents (the second generation), and just 12 percent were born to U.S.-born parents (the third generation and beyond).

Unlike earlier immigrants from Asia or Europe, who were mostly low-skilled laborers looking for work, today's immigrants from Asia have more varied backgrounds and come for many reasons, such as to join their families, to invest their money in the U.S. economy, to fill the demand for highly skilled labor, or to escape war, political or religious persecution, and economic hardship. For example, Chinese, Taiwanese, Indian, and Filipino Americans tend to be overrepresented among scientists, engineers, physicians, and other skilled professionals, but less-educated, low-skilled workers are more common among Vietnamese, Cambodian, Laotian, and Hmong Americans, most of whom entered the United States as refugees. While middle-class immigrants are able to start their American lives with high-paying professional careers and comfortable suburban lives, low-skilled immigrants and refugees often have to endure low-paying menial jobs and live in inner-city ghettos.

Asian Americans tend to settle in large metropolitan areas and concentrate in the West. California is home to 35 percent of all Asian Americans. But recently, other states such as Texas, Minnesota, and Wisconsin, which historically received few Asian immigrants, have become destinations for Asian American settlement. Traditional ethnic enclaves, such as Chinatown, Little Tokyo, Manilatown, Koreatown, Little Phnom Penh, and Thaitown, persist or have emerged in gateway cities, helping new arrivals to cope with cultural and linguistic difficulties. However, affluent and highly skilled immigrants tend to bypass inner-city enclaves and settle in suburbs upon arrival, belying the stereotype of the "unacculturated" immigrant. Today, more than half of the Asian-origin population is spreading out in suburbs surrounding traditional gateway cities, as well as in new urban centers of Asian settlement across the country.

Differences in national origins, timing of immigration, affluence, and settlement patterns profoundly inhibit the formation of a pan-ethnic identity. Recent arrivals are less likely than those born or raised in the United States to identify as Asian American. They are also so busy settling in that they have little time to think about being Asian or Asian American, or, for that matter, white. Their diverse origins include drastic differences in languages and dialects, religions, cuisines, and customs. Many national groups also bring to America their histories of conflict (such as the Japanese colonization of Korea and Taiwan, Japanese attacks on China, and the Chinese invasion of Vietnam).

Immigrants who are predominantly middle-class professionals, such as the Taiwanese and Indians, or predominantly small business owners, such as the Koreans, share few of the same concerns and priorities as those who are predominantly uneducated, low-skilled refugees, such as Cambodians and Hmong. Finally, Asian-origin people living in San Francisco or Los Angeles among many other Asians and self-conscious Asian Americans develop a stronger ethnic identity than those living in predominantly Latin Miami or predominantly European Minneapolis. A politician might get away with calling Asians "Oriental" in Miami but get into big trouble in San Francisco. All of these differences create obstacles to fostering a cohesive pan-Asian solidarity. As Yen Le Espiritu shows, pan-Asianism is primarily a political ideology of U.S.-born, American-educated, middle-class Asians rather than of Asian immigrants, who are conscious of their national origins and over-burdened with their daily struggles for survival.

underneath the model minority: "white" or "other"

The celebrated "model minority" image of Asian Americans appeared in the mid-1960s, at the peak of the civil rights and the ethnic consciousness movements, but before the rising waves of immigration and refugee influx from Asia. Two articles in 1966—"Success Story, Japanese-American Style," by William Petersen in the *New York Times Magazine*, and "Success of One Minority Group in U.S.," by the *U.S. News & World Report* staff—marked a significant departure from how Asian immigrants and their descendants had been traditionally depicted in the media. Both articles congratulated Japanese and Chinese Americans on their persistence in overcoming extreme hardships and discrimination to achieve success, unmatched even by U.S.-born whites, with "their own almost totally unaided effort" and "no help from anyone else." (The implicit contrast to other minorities was clear.) The press attributed their winning wealth and respect in American society to hard work, family solidarity, discipline, delayed gratification, nonconfrontation, and eschewing welfare.

This "model minority" image remains largely unchanged even in the face of new and diverse waves of immigration. The 2000 U.S. Census shows that Asian Americans continue to score remarkable economic and educational achievements. Their median household income in 1999 was more than $55,000—the highest of all racial groups, including whites—and their poverty rate was under 11 percent, the lowest of all racial groups. Moreover, 44 percent of all Asian Americans over 25 years of age had at least a bachelor's degree, 18 percentage points more than any other racial group. Strikingly, young Asian Americans, including both the children of foreign-born physicians, scientists, and professionals and those of uneducated and penniless refugees, repeatedly appear as high school valedictorians and academic decathlon winners. They also enroll in the freshman classes of prestigious universities in disproportionately large numbers. In 1998, Asian Americans, just 4 percent of the nation's population, made up more than 20 percent of the undergraduates at universities such as Berkeley, Stanford, MIT, and Cal Tech. Although some ethnic groups, such as Cambodians, Lao, and Hmong, still trail behind other East and South Asians in most indicators of achievement, they too show significant signs of upward mobility. Many in the media have dubbed Asian Americans the "new Jews." Like the second-generation Jews of the past, today's children of Asian immigrants are climbing up the ladder by way of extraordinary educational achievement.

One consequence of the model-minority stereotype is that it reinforces the myth that the United States is devoid of racism and accords equal opportunity to all, fostering the view that those who lag behind do so because of their own poor choices and inferior culture. Celebrating "model minorities" can help impede other racial minorities' demands for social justice by pitting minority groups against each other. It can also pit Asian Americans against whites. On the surface, Asian Americans seem to be on their way to becoming white, just like the offspring of earlier European immigrants. But the model-minority image implicitly casts Asian Americans as different from whites. By placing Asian Americans above whites, this image still sets them apart from other Americans, white or nonwhite, in the public mind.

There are two other less obvious effects. The model-minority stereotype holds Asian Americans to higher standards, distinguishing them from average Americans. "What's wrong with being a model minority?" a black student once asked, in a class I taught on race, "I'd rather be in the model minority than in the downtrodden minority that nobody respects." Whether people are in a model minority or a downtrodden minority, they are still judged by standards different from average Americans. Also, the model-minority stereotype places particular expectations on members of the group so labeled, channeling them to specific avenues of success, such as science and engineering. This, in turn, makes it harder for Asian Americans to pursue careers outside these designated fields. Falling into this trap, a Chinese immigrant father gets upset when his son tells him he has changed his major from engineering to English. Disregarding his son's talent for creative writing, such a father rationalizes his concern, "You have a 90 percent chance of getting a decent job with an engineering degree, but what chance would you have of earning income as a writer?" This thinking represents more than typical parental concern; it constitutes the self-fulfilling prophecy of a stereotype.

The celebration of Asian Americans rests on the perception that their success is unexpectedly high. The truth is that unusually many of them, particularly among the Chinese, Indians, and Koreans, arrive as middle-class or upper-middle-class immigrants. This makes it easier for them and their children to succeed and regain their middle-class status in their new homeland. The financial resources that these immigrants bring also subsidize ethnic businesses and services, such as private after-school programs. These, in turn, enable even the less fortunate members of the groups to move ahead more quickly than they would have otherwise.

not so much being "white" as being american

Most Asian Americans seem to accept that "white" is mainstream, average, and normal, and they look to whites as a frame of reference for attaining higher social positions. Similarly, researchers often use non-Hispanic whites as the standard against which other groups are compared, even though there is great diversity among whites, too. Like most immigrants to the United States, Asian immigrants tend to believe in the American Dream and measure their achievements materially. As a Chinese immigrant said to me in an interview, "I hope to accomplish nothing but three things: to own a home, to be my own boss, and to send my children to the Ivy League." Those with sufficient education, job skills, and money manage to move into white middle-class suburban neighborhoods immediately upon arrival, while others work intensively to accumulate enough savings to move their families up and out of inner-city ethnic enclaves. Consequently, many children of Asian ancestry have lived their entire childhood in white communities, made friends with mostly white peers, and grown up speaking only English. In fact, Asian Americans are the most acculturated non-European group in the United States. By the second generation, most have lost fluency in their parents' native languages (see "English-Only Triumphs, But the Costs Are High," *Contexts*, Spring 2002). David Lopez finds that in Los Angeles, more than three-quarters of second-generation Asian Americans (as opposed to one-quarter of second-generation Mexicans) speak only English at home. Asian Americans also intermarry extensively with whites and with members of other minority groups. Jennifer Lee and Frank Bean find that more than one-quarter of married Asian Americans have a partner of a different racial background, and 87 percent of those marry whites; they also find that 12 percent of all Asian Americans claim a multiracial background, compared to 2 percent of whites and 4 percent of blacks.

Even though U.S.-born or U.S.-raised Asian Americans are relatively acculturated and often intermarry with whites, they may be more ambivalent about becoming white than their immigrant parents. Many only cynically agree that "white" is synonymous with "American." A Vietnamese high school student in New Orleans told me in an interview, "An American is white. You often hear people say, hey, so-and-so is dating an 'American.' You know she's dating a white boy. If he were black, then people would say he's black." But while they recognize whites as a frame of reference, some reject the idea of becoming white themselves: "It's not so much being white as being American," commented a Korean-American student in my class on the new second generation. This aversion to becoming white is particularly common among second-generation college students who have taken ethnic studies courses, and among Asian-American community activists. However, most of the second generation continues to strive for the privileged status associated with whiteness, just like their parents. For example, most U.S.-born or U.S.-raised Chinese-American youth end up studying engineering, medicine, or law in college, believing that these areas of study guarantee a middle-class life.

Second-generation Asian Americans are also more conscious of the disadvantages associated with being nonwhite than their parents, who as immigrants tend to be optimistic about overcoming the disadvantages of this status. As a Chinese-American woman points out from her own experience, "The truth is, no matter how American you think you are or try to be, if you have almond-shaped eyes, straight black hair, and a yellow complexion, you are a foreigner by default . . . You can certainly be as good as or even better than whites, but you will never become accepted as white." This remark echoes a commonly held frustration among second-generation, U.S.-born Asians who detest being treated as immigrants or foreigners. Their experience suggests that whitening has more to do with the beliefs of white America than with the actual situation of Asian Americans. Speaking perfect English, adopting mainstream cultural values, and even intermarrying members of the dominant group may help reduce this "otherness" for particular individuals, but it has little effect on the group as a whole. New stereotypes can emerge and un-whiten Asian Americans, no matter how "successful" and "assimilated" they have become. For example, Congressman David Wu once was invited by the Asian-American employees of the U.S. Department of Energy to give a speech in celebration of Asian-American Heritage Month. Yet, he and his Asian-American staff were not allowed into the department building, even after presenting their congressional identification, and were repeatedly asked about their citizenship and country of origin. They were told that this was standard procedure for the Department of Energy and that a congressional ID card was not a reliable document. The next day, a congressman of Italian descent was allowed to enter the same building with his congressional ID, no questions asked.

The stereotype of the "honorary white" or model minority goes hand-in-hand with that of the "forever foreigner." Today, globalization and U.S.–Asia relations, combined with continually high rates of immigration, affect how Asian Americans are perceived in American society. Many historical stereotypes, such as the "yellow peril" and "Fu Manchu" still exist in contemporary American life, as revealed in such highly publicized incidents as the murder of Vincent Chin, a Chinese American mistaken for Japanese and beaten to death by a disgruntled white auto worker in the 1980s; the trial of Wen Ho Lee, a nuclear scientist suspected of spying for the Chinese government in the mid 1990s; the 1996 presidential campaign finance scandal, which implicated Asian Americans in funneling foreign contributions to the Clinton campaign; and most recently, in 2001, the Abercrombie & Fitch t-shirts that depicted Asian cartoon characters in stereotypically negative ways, with slanted eyes, thick glasses, and heavy Asian accents. Ironically, the ambivalent, conditional nature of their acceptance by whites prompts many Asian Americans to organize pan-ethnically to fight back—which consequently heightens their racial distinctiveness. So becoming white or not is beside the point. The bottom line is: Americans of Asian ancestry still have to constantly prove that they truly are loyal Americans.

RECOMMENDED RESOURCES

John Horton. *The Politics of Diversity: Immigration, Resistance, and Change in Monterey Park, California* (Temple University Press, 1995).

> This study of a Chinese immigrant community in an affluent Los Angeles suburb explores how new immigrants confront resistance from more established Anglo, Asian-American, and Latino neighbors.

Nazli Kibria. *Becoming Asian American: Second-Generation Chinese and Korean American Identities* (Johns Hopkins University Press, 2002).

> Depicts the challenges of migration and resettlement faced by Vietnamese immigrants in inner-city Philadelphia.

Eric Liu. *The Accidental Asian* (Random House, 1998).

> A thoughtful memoir of a second-generation Chinese American.

David Lopez and Yen Espiritu. "Panethnicity in the United States: A Theoretical Framework." *Ethnic and Racial Studies* 13 (1990): 198–224.

> Examines how diverse national-origin groups organize as pan-ethnic movements.

Mia Tuan. *Forever Foreign or Honorary White? The Asian Ethnic Experience Today* (Rutgers University Press, 1999).

> Tuan's account of West Coast Asian Americans reveals the hidden and not-so-hidden injuries of race suffered by the second and third generations.

Frank Wu. *Yellow: Race in America beyond Black and White* (Basic Books, 2002).

> This insightful book explores, among other topics, the model-minority myth and issues of racial diversity.

Henry Yu. *Thinking Orientals: Migration, Contact, and Exoticism in Modern America* (Oxford University Press, 2002).

> Details how social scientists at the University of Chicago addressed the "Oriental problem" during the first half of the twentieth century.

Min Zhou and James V. Gatewood, eds. *Contemporary Asian America: A Multidisciplinary Reader* (New York University Press, 2000).

> This collection shows how contemporary immigration from Asia creates issues of identity and assimilation for both native-born and foreign-born Asian Americans.

REVIEW QUESTIONS

1. Which stereotypes does the label "honorary white" reinforce?

2. Zhou identifies factors that affect whether groups develop a pan-ethnic identity (e.g., timing of immigration). What are they? Write a paragraph on how two of them might affect the formation of a pan-ethnic identity.

3. Zhou questions the popular view that the success of Japanese and Chinese Americans is due to hard work rather than governmental assistance, thus making them "model minorities." What are the implications of this label for both Asians and other minority groups?

4. Activity: After speaking with your parents, come to class prepared to talk about your ethnic background. Break into discussion groups to address the following questions: How many generations of your family have lived in the United States? Where did most of your ancestors settle? Did they live in a very diverse community like Los Angeles or New York City or in a very homogenous one? In what ways did various members of your family assimilate into American society? Did they, for example, insist upon only speaking English in the household? Did they maintain "traditional" customs?

part **9**

Religion

jen'nan ghazal read

muslims in america

37

fall 2008

recent research into the diverse opinions and demographics of muslim americans shows just how inaccurate the prevailing stereotypes really are.

Seven years after the terrorist attacks on U.S. soil catapulted Muslims into the American spotlight, concerns and fears over their presence and assimilation remain at an all-time high. Recent national polls find that four in 10 Americans have an unfavorable view of Islam, five in 10 believe Islam is more likely than other religions to encourage violence, and six in 10 believe Islam is very different from their own religion. All this despite the fact that seven in 10 admit they know very little about Islam. And yet Americans rank Muslims second only to atheists as a group that doesn't share their vision of American society.

These fears have had consequences. In 2001, the U.S. Department of Justice recorded a 1,600 percent increase in anti-Muslim hate crimes from the prior year, and these numbers rose 10 percent between 2005 and 2006. The Council on American-Islamic Relations processed 2,647 civil rights complaints in 2006, a 25 percent increase from the prior year and a 600 percent increase since 2000. The largest category involved complaints against U.S. government agencies (37 percent).

Clearly, many Americans are convinced Muslim Americans pose some kind of threat to American society.

> In 2001, the U.S. Department of Justice recorded a 1,600 percent increase in anti-Muslim hate crimes from the prior year. Most complaints involved U.S. government agencies.

Two widespread assumptions fuel these fears. First, that there's only one kind of Islam and one kind of Muslim, both characterized by violence and anti-democratic tendencies. Second, that being a Muslim is the most salient identity for Muslim Americans when it comes to their political attitudes and behaviors, that it trumps their social class position, national origin, racial/ethnic group membership, or gender—or worse, that it trumps their commitment to a secular democracy.

Research on Muslim Americans themselves supports neither of these assumptions. Interviews with 3,627 Muslim Americans in 2001 and 2004 by the Georgetown University Muslims in the American Public Square (MAPS) project and 1,050 Muslim Americans in 2007 by the Pew Research Center show that Muslim Americans are diverse, well-integrated, and largely mainstream in their attitudes, values, and behaviors.

The data also show that being a Muslim is less important for politics than how Muslim you are, how much money you make, whether you're an African-American Muslim or an Arab-American Muslim, and whether you're a man or a woman.

The notion that Muslims privilege their Muslim identity over their other interests and affiliations has been projected onto the group rather than emerged from the beliefs and practices of the group itself. It's what sociologists call a social construction, and it's one that has implications for how these Americans are included in the national dialog.

some basic demographics

Let's start with who Muslim Americans really are. While size estimates of the population range anywhere from 2 million to 8 million, there is general agreement on the social and demographic characteristics of the community.

Muslim Americans are the most ethnically diverse Muslim population in the world, originating from more than 80 countries on four continents. Contrary to popular belief, most are not Arab. Nearly one-third are South Asian, one-third are Arab, one-fifth are U.S.-born black Muslims (mainly converts), and a small but growing number are U.S.-born Anglo and Hispanic converts. Roughly two-thirds are immigrants to the United States, but an increasing segment is second- and third-generation, U.S.-born Americans. The vast majority of immigrants have lived in the United States for 10 or more years.

Muslim Americans also tend to be highly educated, politically conscious, and fluent in English, all of which reflects the restrictive immigration policies that limit who gains admission into the United States. On average, in fact, Muslim Americans share similar socioeconomic characteristics with the general U.S. population: one-fourth has a bachelor's degree or higher, one-fourth lives in households with incomes of

$75,000 per year or more, and the majority are employed. However, some Muslims do live in poverty and have poor English language skills and few resources to improve their situations.

One of the most important and overlooked facts about Muslim Americans is that they are not uniformly religious and devout. Some are religiously devout, some are religiously moderate, and some are non-practicing and secular, basically Muslim in name only, similar to a good proportion of U.S. Christians and Jews. Some attend a mosque on a weekly basis and pray every day, and others don't engage in either practice. Even among the more religiously devout, there is a sharp distinc-

> Muslim Americans also tend to be highly educated, politically conscious, and fluent in English. They are not, however, uniformly religious and devout.

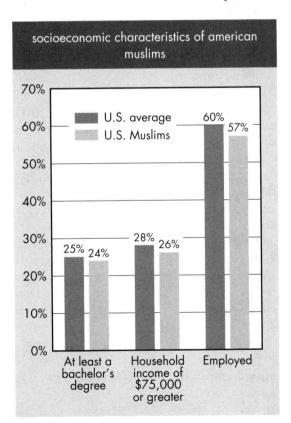

socioeconomic characteristics of american muslims

- U.S. average
- U.S. Muslims

At least a bachelor's degree: 25% (U.S. average), 24% (U.S. Muslims)
Household income of $75,000 or greater: 28% (U.S. average), 26% (U.S. Muslims)
Employed: 60% (U.S. average), 57% (U.S. Muslims)

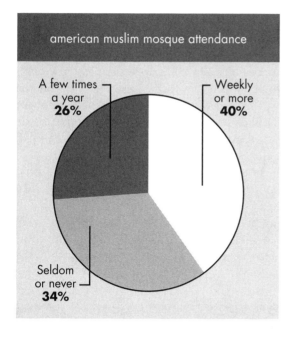

american muslim mosque attendance

A few times a year **26%**

Weekly or more **40%**

Seldom or never **34%**

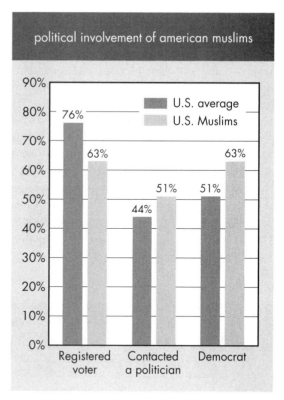

political involvement of american muslims

- U.S. average
- U.S. Muslims

Registered voter: 76%, 63%

Contacted a politician: 44%, 51%

Democrat: 51%, 63%

tion between being a good Muslim and being an Islamic extremist.

None of this should be surprising. Many Muslim Americans emigrated from countries in the Middle East (now targeted in the war on terror) in order to practice—or not practice—their religion and politics more freely in the United States. And their religion is diverse. There is no monolithic Islam that all Muslims adhere to. Just as Christianity has many different theologies, denominations, and sects, so does Islam. And just like Christianity, these theologies, denominations, and sects are often in conflict and disagreement over how to interpret and practice the faith tradition. This diversity mimics other ethnic and immigrant groups in the United States.

Evidence from the MAPS project, Pew Research Center, and General Social Survey demonstrates that Muslim Americans are much more politically integrated than the common stereotypes imply. Consider some common indicators of political involvement, such as party affiliation, voter registration, and contact with politicians. Compared to the general public, Muslim Americans are slightly less likely to be registered to vote, reflecting the immigrant composition and voter eligibility of this group (63 percent compared to 76 percent of the general population), slightly more likely to have contacted a politician (51 percent compared to 44 percent of the general population), and slightly more likely to affiliate with the Democratic Party, which falls in line with other racial and ethnic minorities (63 percent compared to 51 percent of the general population).

All these data demonstrate that, contrary to fears that Muslim Americans comprise a monolithic minority ill-suited to participation in American democracy, Muslim Americans are actually highly diverse and already politically integrated. They are also in step with the rest of the American public on today's most divisive political issues.

attitudes, values, and variation

The majority of both Muslim Americans (69 percent) and the general public (76 percent) oppose gay marriage, favor increased federal government spending to help the needy (73 percent and 63 percent, respectively), and disapprove of President George W. Bush's job performance (67 percent and 59 percent). Muslim Americans are slightly more conservative than the general public when it comes to abortion (56 percent oppose it, compared to 46 percent) as well as the federal government doing more to protect morality in society (59 percent compared to 37 percent).

The one area in which American Muslims are not entirely in step with the general public is foreign policy, especially having to do with the Middle East. In 2007, for example, the general public was nearly four times as likely to say the war in Iraq was the "right decision" and twice as likely to provide the same response to the war in Afghanistan (61 percent compared to 35 percent of Muslim Americans).

In short, these numbers tell us that Muslim Americans lean to the right on social issues (like most Americans), but to the left on foreign policy. But these generalizations don't tell the whole story—in particular, these averages don't demonstrate the diversity that exists within the

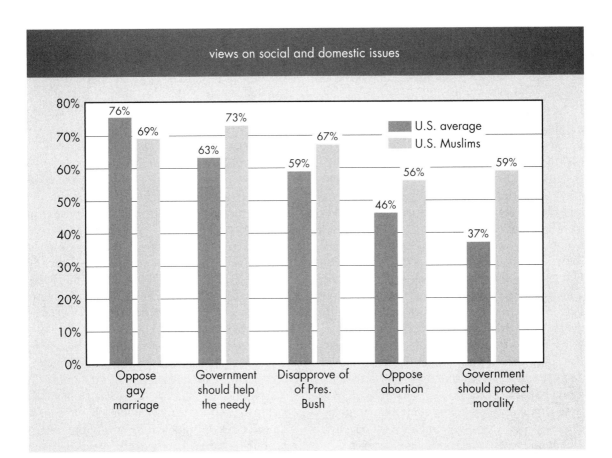

views on social and domestic issues

Muslim population by racial and ethnic group membership, national origin, socioeconomic status, degree of religiosity, or nativity and citizenship status.

Consider, for example, Muslim Americans' levels of satisfaction and feelings of inclusion (or exclusion) in American society—major building blocks of a liberal democracy. In examining how these perceptions vary by racial and ethnic group membership within the group, we see that African-American Muslims express more dissatisfaction and feel more excluded from American society than Arab or South Asian Muslims. They're more likely to feel the United States is fighting a war against

Islam, to believe Americans are intolerant of Islam and Muslims, and to have experienced discrimination in the past year (whether racial, religious, or both is unclear). South Asians feel the least marginalized, and Arab Muslims fall in between. These racial and ethnic differences reflect a host of factors, including the immigrant composition and higher socioeconomic status of the South Asian and Arab populations and the long-standing racialized and marginalized position of African-Americans. Indeed, many (though not all) African Americans converted to Islam seeking a form of religious inclusion they felt lacking in the largely white Judeo-Christian traditions.

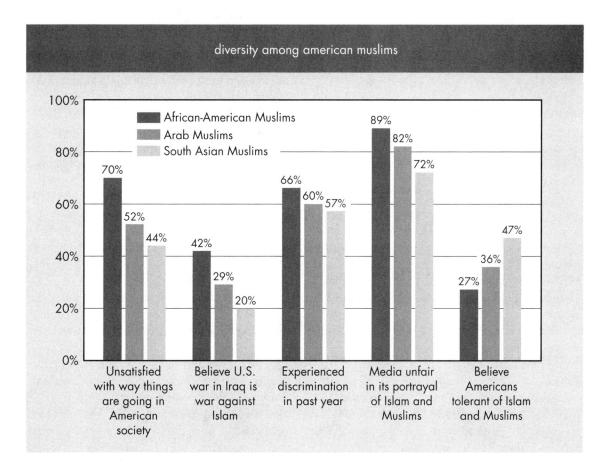

diversity among american muslims

- African-American Muslims
- Arab Muslims
- South Asian Muslims

	African-American Muslims	Arab Muslims	South Asian Muslims
Unsatisfied with way things are going in American society	70%	52%	44%
Believe U.S. war in Iraq is war against Islam	42%	29%	20%
Experienced discrimination in past year	66%	60%	57%
Media unfair in its portrayal of Islam and Muslims	89%	82%	72%
Believe Americans tolerant of Islam and Muslims	27%	36%	47%

(Incidentally, most African-American Muslims adhere to mainstream Islam [Sunni or Shi'a], similar to South Asian and Arab Muslim populations. They should not be confused with the Nation of Islam, a group that became popular during the civil rights era by providing a cultural identity that separated black Americans from mainstream Christianity. Indigenous Muslims have historically distanced themselves from the Nation of Islam in order to establish organizations that focus more on cultural and religious [rather than racial] oppression.)

Before we can determine whether religion is the driving force behind all Muslims' political opinions and behaviors—whether Islam, as is popularly assumed, trumps Muslim Americans' other commitments and relationships to nationality, ethnicity, race, and even democracy—let's step back and place Muslim Americans in a broader historical context of religion and American politics.

when religion matters, and doesn't

Muslim Americans aren't the first religious or ethnic group considered a threat to America's religious and cultural unity. At the turn of the 20th century, Jewish and Italian immigrants were vilified in the mainstream as racially inferior to other Americans. Of course today those same fears have been projected onto Hispanic, Asian, and Middle Eastern immigrants. The Muslim American case shares with these other immigrant experiences the fact that with a religion different from the mainstream comes the fear that it will dilute, possibly even sabotage, America's thriving religious landscape.

Yes, thriving. By all accounts, the United States is considerably more religious than any of its economically developed Western counterparts. In 2000, 93 percent of Americans said they believed in God or a universal spirit, 86 percent claimed affiliation with a specific religious denomination, and 67 percent reported membership in a church or synagogue. The vast majority of American adults identify themselves as Christian (56 percent Protestant and 25 percent Catholic), with Judaism claiming the second largest group of adherents (2 percent), giving America a decidedly Judeo-Christian face. There are an infinite number of denominations within these broad categories, ranging from the ultra-conservative to the ultra-liberal. And there is extensive diversity among individuals in their levels of religiosity within any given denomination, again ranging from those who are devout, practicing believers to those who are secular and non-practicing.

This diversity has sparked extensive debates among academics, policy-makers, and pundits over whether American politics is characterized by "culture wars," best summarized as the belief that Americans are polarized into two camps, one conservative and one liberal, on moral and ethical issues such as abortion and gay rights. Nowhere has the debate played out more vividly than the arena of religion and politics, where religiously based mobilization efforts by the Christian right helped defeat liberal-leaning candidates and secure President Bush's reelection in 2004. Electoral victories, however, haven't usually translated into policy victories, as evidenced by the continued legality of abortion and increasing protection of gay rights. So when does religion matter for politics and when doesn't it?

Here we come back to the Muslim American case. Like Muslim Americans, Americans generally have multiple, competing identities that shape their political attitudes and behaviors—93 percent of Americans may believe in God or a universal spirit but 93 percent of Americans don't base their politics on that belief alone. In other words, just because most Americans are religiously affiliated doesn't mean most Americans base their politics on religion. To put it somewhat differently, the same factors that influence other Americans' attitudes and behaviors influence Muslim Americans' attitudes and behaviors. Those who are more educated, have higher incomes, higher levels of group consciousness, and who feel more marginalized from mainstream society are more politically active than those without these characteristics. Similar to other Americans, these are individuals who feel they have more at stake in political outcomes, and thus are more motivated to try to influence such outcomes.

Muslims, on average, look like other Americans on social and domestic policies because, on average, they share the same social standing as other Americans, and on average, they are about as religious as other Americans. Consider two common indicators of religiosity, frequency of prayer and frequency of church attendance, and compare Muslim Americans to Christian Americans. Both groups are quite religious, with the majority praying every day (70 percent of Christians compared to 61 percent of Muslims) and a sizeable proportion attending services once a week or more (45 percent compared to 40 percent). And they look similar with respect to attitudes on gay rights and abortion, in part because Christian and Muslim theology take similar stances on procreation and gender roles.

Again, these numbers tell only part of the story. What's missing is that religion's relationship to politics is multidimensional. In more complex analyses it has become clear that the more personal dimensions of religious

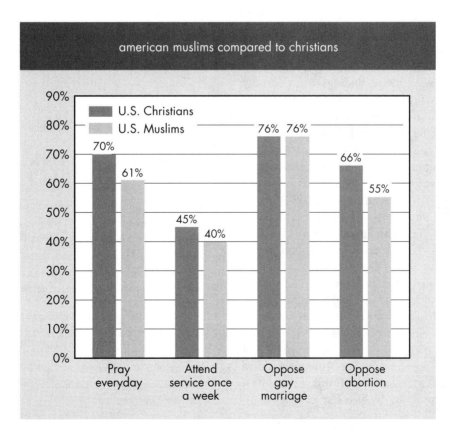

american muslims compared to christians

- U.S. Christians
- U.S. Muslims

	Pray everyday	Attend service once a week	Oppose gay marriage	Oppose abortion
U.S. Christians	70%	45%	76%	66%
U.S. Muslims	61%	40%	76%	55%

identity—or being a devout Muslim who prays every day—have little influence on political attitudes or behaviors, which runs counter to stereotypes that link Islamic devotion to political fanaticism.

In contrast, the more organized dimensions of Muslim identity, namely frequent mosque attendance, provide a collective identity that stimulates political activity. This is similar to what we know about the role of the church and synagogue for U.S. Christians and Jews. Congregations provide a collective environment that heightens group consciousness and awareness of issues that need to be addressed through political mobilization. Thus, it is somewhat ironic that one of the staunchest defenders of the war on terror—the Christian right—may be overlooking a potential ally in the culture wars—devout Muslim Americans.

an exceptional experience

In many ways these findings track closely with what we know about the religion-politics connection among other U.S. ethnic and religious groups, be they Evangelical Christians or African Americans. They also suggest that the Muslim experience may be less distinct than popular beliefs imply. In fact, Muslim Americans share much in common with earlier immigrant groups who were considered inassimilable even though they held mainstream American values (think Italian, Irish, and Polish immigrants).

At the same time, though, we can't deny that the Muslim American experience, particularly since 9/11, has been "exceptional" in a country marked by a declining salience of religious boundaries and increasing acceptance of religious difference. Muslim Americans have largely been excluded from this ecumenical trend. If we're going to face our nation's chal-lenges in a truly democratic way, we need to move past the fear that Muslim Americans are un-American so we can bring them into the national dialogue.

RECOMMENDED RESOURCES

Anny Bakalian and Mehdi Bozorgmehr. *Backlash 9/11: Middle Eastern and Muslim Americans Respond* (University of California Press, 2009).

> One of the comprehensive assessments of the experiences of Middle Eastern Americans in the aftermath of 9/11.

Clem Brooks and Jeff Manza. "Social Cleavages and Political Alignments: U.S. Presidential Elections, 1960 to 1992." *American Sociological Review* (1997) 62: 934–46.

> A sociological framework for understanding how social group memberships, such as gender and race, impact [sic] Americans in presidential elections.

Nancy Foner. *In a New Land: A Comparative View of Immigration* (New York University Press, 2005).

> A thorough historical, comparative account of immigration in the United States.

Gary Gerstle and John Mollenkopf, eds. *E Pluribus Unum? Contemporary and Historical Perspectives on Immigrant Political Incorporation* (Russell Sage Foundation, 2001).

> This edited volume places contemporary immigration politics in historical and comparative context.

Ted J. Jelen. "Religion and Politics in the United States: Persistence, Limitations, and the Prophetic Voice." *Social Compass* (2006) 53: 329–43.

> A useful overview of the U.S. religion-politics connection situated in comparison to other Western, industrialized nations.

REVIEW QUESTIONS

1. How do the political views of Muslim Americans compare with those of the rest of the American religious public?
2. Why might Muslims, who ideologically align with most of mainstream America, still be considered "outsiders"?
3. Are any other groups similarly considered "outsiders" in American society today? Why?

4. Activity: The author provides demographic information on Muslim Americans. Download the Pew Center Report (http://pewresearch.org/pubs/483/muslim-americans) used in the article. Write a paragraph about other surprising statistics you learn about Muslim Americans from this report.

elaine howard ecklund

religion and spirituality among scientists   **38**

winter 2008

scientists aren't as anti-religion as the conventional wisdom leads us to believe—a surprising number of believers teach at the nation's top academic institutions.

Religion and science face off over many of the most important issues our society faces. Authorities debate whether intelligent design should be taught alongside evolution in public schools, for example, and the stem cell research debate features both scientific advocacy and religious opposition.

The assumption is that scientists attack the religious aspects of these issues because they are, above all else, atheists and anti-religion. While highly influential scientists like Richard Dawkins and the Human Genome Project's Francis Collins have been publicly outspoken about their views on religion and science, we really know very little about what elite university scientists as a whole—what some would call the most influential sphere of science—think about matters of faith.

The study of Religion among Academic Scientists (RAAS) closes this gap in understanding. During 2005 and 2006 it examined the religious and spiritual beliefs and practices of academics in the natural and social sciences at 21 of the most influential research universities in the United States. Some 75 percent—1,646 individuals—responded to the survey. From among those participants 271 also took part in in-depth interviews.

These scientists revealed they are not as anti-religion as volumes like Dawkins' The God Delusion might lead us to believe. In fact, a surprising number of believers teach the sciences at the nation's top academic institutions. However, these scientists approach religion and spirituality in diverse ways—ways often different from the religiosity and spirituality of the general public. While scientists are indeed less religious in a traditional sense than the general public, the majority of scientists are interested in matters of spirituality and a significant minority is religious. These findings differ little between natural and social scientists.

Religion and science connect for university scientists in a range of ways. Some scientists see religion or spirituality enhancing their work. Propelled by recent public events, even those who previously had no interest in religion or spirituality are finding it necessary to involve students in discussions about these topics.

god and religion

When this research is presented in public settings, audiences inevitably ask, Do scientists believe in God? And when looking just at the measure of belief in God, it seems a large proportion of scientists confirm the conventional wisdom that scientific understanding and personal religious belief have a hard time coexisting. Nearly 34 percent of academic scientists identified themselves as atheists and almost 30 percent as agnostic in the RAAS study. In comparison, in the general U.S. population a mere 2 percent claimed to be atheist and roughly 4 percent claimed to be agnostic, according to the 2006 General Social Survey (GSS). A huge difference, for sure.

Consider beliefs about religion, however, and the picture becomes considerably less simple. Some 26 percent of elite natural and social scientists think most religions hold very little truth. In the general population, only 4 percent answer the same way. When compared to scientists, four times as many in the general population think only one religion holds the most truth. Such results indicate many scientists appear to discount religion altogether.

But when we look at the "religious relativist" position—those who think there are truths found in many religions—our understanding becomes even more nuanced. More than 70 percent of scientists think many religions hold basic truths. Nearly the same proportion of those surveyed in the general population agree. This suggests there may be much untapped common ground between scientists and the general public, as being a religious relativist and being outright hostile to religion are two very different things.

When examining affiliation with particular religions, academic scientists differ significantly from the general population. Roughly 53 percent of the scientists have no religious affiliation, compared to only 16 percent of those surveyed in the general population. While nearly 24 percent of the U.S. population identify with evangelical Protestant religious traditions, less than 2 percent of the scientists do, according to the 2000 GSS. The only religion more faculty in the natural and social sciences are affiliated with is Judaism. While in the GSS slightly less than 2 percent identify as Jewish, in comparison approximately 16 percent of the academic scientists identify as Jewish. Based on the broader RAAS data, it's clear many of those

who are Jewish would see themselves as Reform rather than Conservative or Orthodox.

In the midst of reports appearing in the *Chronicle of Higher Education* and the *New York Times* describing liberal political and anti-religious bias among many university professors, this lack of religiosity among top scientists begs the question, Are professors in the sciences less religious because they know more about science? The general tenor of previous research supports the perception that those who pursue science tend to abandon religion, either because of inherent conflict between the two or because scientific education exerts a secularizing force.

But just as what the general public grew up believing influences decisions to believe, the same follows for scientists. Rather than transitioning from faith to no faith upon learning more about science, a good proportion of non-believing scientists had very little experience with religion as children. Sometimes, for those scientists whose families were part of a religious tradition, membership was only significant as a label rather than a matter of regular practice. Consequently, these scientists didn't learn much about their tradition nor were they taught to see religion as an integral part of everyday life. Scientists who said religion wasn't important in their families while growing up are now less likely to believe in God or attend religious services.

A larger proportion of scientists compared to other Americans come from backgrounds without faith or where faith traditions were seldom practiced, making some of the differences between elite scientists and other Americans more clear. For example, only 8 percent of the general population were raised with no religion, compared to 13 percent of scientists. While 54 percent of the general population were raised Protestant, only 39 percent, a large difference in statistical terms, of scientists at elite universities

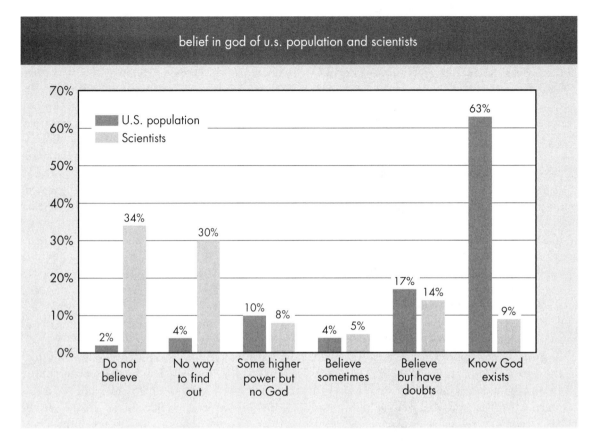

belief in god of u.s. population and scientists

- U.S. population
- Scientists

	Do not believe	No way to find out	Some higher power but no God	Believe sometimes	Believe but have doubts	Know God exists
U.S. population	2%	4%	10%	4%	17%	63%
Scientists	34%	30%	8%	5%	14%	9%

were raised in a Protestant tradition. Even those scientists raised in a religious tradition were often from homes where religion was practiced only occasionally, while nearly 40 percent of Americans attend religious services once a week.

Consider two sociologists who are similar in other respects. If one was raised in a Protestant tradition and religion was very important while growing up, and the other was raised without a religious tradition, the sociologist raised without a tradition is four times more likely to be an atheist. A striking difference. These findings point toward some reasons why university scientists may be less religious than the broader population. The idea that scientists simply drop their religious identities upon professional train-

ing isn't strongly supported by these data. If this were the case, then religious upbringing wouldn't be related to present religious identities for scientists. In other words, if religious upbringing didn't matter we would see even those scientists raised in religious homes losing religion once they enter the academy or receive scientific training.

the village spiritualist

These findings also cast doubt on the village atheist stereotype of the profession. As the scientists who work at the most elite universities in the United States, we might expect that, of any group, this population would have the most pervasive scientific worldview. As part of this worldview, scientists might reject most attempts at creating purpose that seem contradictory to science and scientific understanding. Given the large proportion of atheist or agnostic elite scientists and the proportion who have no religious affiliation, elite university scientists are surprisingly interested in spirituality.

Approximately 66 percent of natural scientists and nearly 69 percent of social scientists identified as spiritual. In fact, significant proportions of scientists who are atheist, agnostic, or without any religious tradition still see themselves as spiritual—more than 22 percent of the atheists and more than 27 percent of the agnostics. Some 39 percent of those who have no current religious affiliation identify as spiritual.

Findings from in-depth interviews with a systematically sampled portion of these scientists revealed their definitions of spirituality varied a great deal, from being a vague feeling of something outside themselves to a deep and compelling, other-centered worldview that directs how they conduct research and interactions with students. For the scientists who considered spirituality a daily part of their lives—more than 40 percent of those interviewed—their deepest sense of identity comes from being scientists and their spirituality flows from the same characteristics they value in their identities as scientists. This is a spirituality characterized by consistency.

These scientists don't want spirituality to be intellectually compartmentalized from the rest

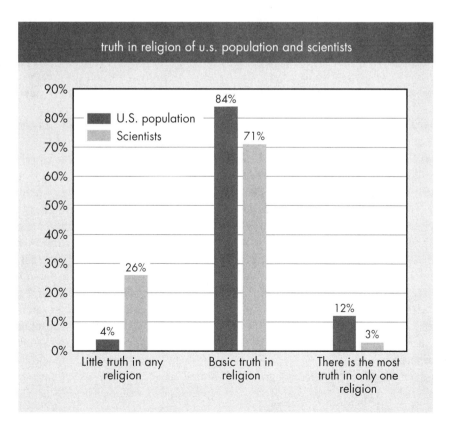

of their lives, but are seeking a core sense of truth through spirituality in much the same way they seek truth through their science. A small but important minority of this population perceive spirituality as consistent in so far as it suffuses their everyday lives and is instantiated in their practices as teachers, as citizens of the university, and as researchers.

Definitions of "religion" and "spirituality" weren't benign constructs. Among university scientists such distinctions often carried a moral weight. One chemistry professor described religion that doesn't work as "being a mechanism by which people's thoughts and lives are controlled or meant to be controlled." This same professor, when asked to compare religion and spirituality, said spirituality was "more flexible and personal and a lot less judgmental." In fact, the professor went on to explain, "when I think of a spiritual person, the word 'judgment' doesn't even pop into my mind."

Beyond personal practices and beliefs, it's vital to know what these scientists think about the place of religion in their specific fields and departments. Asked to respond to the following statement, "In general I feel that the scholars in my field have a positive attitude towards religion," roughly 23 percent agreed compared to 45 percent who disagreed (nearly 32 percent of the sample had no opinion). The in-depth interviews revealed that while natural and social scientists rarely think their colleagues are hostile toward religion, strong cultural barriers exist against discussing religion (especially traditional forms of religion, such as Catholicism) in academic settings. University scientists simply don't think it acceptable to discuss religion in their departments and many think it unacceptable to have such discussions even in informal university settings.

Sociologists are roughly split (45 percent) on the question of whether their spiritual or religious beliefs influence how they interact with colleagues or students (approximately 9 percent of the sociologists had no opinion). Among the broader sample, 39 percent said their religious or spiritual beliefs to some extent influence interactions with students or colleagues while 54 percent had some variation of disagreement with the statement (approximately 7 percent had no opinion).

Especially in light of recent public events surrounding intelligent design, as well as the religious involvements of students, there are faculty, even those who aren't personally religious, who think they need to interact with religion. The discussion about religion and science in the broader public is obviously of particular relevance for those in the natural sciences.

During the summer of 2005 the *New York Times* published a series of articles on religion and science, largely in response to the disputes over teaching intelligent design in Kansas and Pennsylvania. Although these cases were intentionally never mentioned by our interviewers, respondents consistently brought them up. We could imagine such events might have made scientists—especially natural scientists in the sample—respond negatively to religion. Rather, in many instances such events outside the university actually pushed scientists into the realm of religion, even those who otherwise seemed to have no previous interest in matters of faith.

For example, one respondent explained she hadn't thought much about religion. But the intelligent design debates meant students wanted to talk about religion in the science courses she taught at her university. To remain an effective teacher, she was actively searching religiously based Web sites to find any resources that dealt with the connection between religion and science in what she viewed as thoughtful ways. This respondent said that although she hasn't thought much about religion, "what is going on now is forcing [her] to think about religion and its relationship to science."

godless scientists?

Results from the RAAS study show some truth to the perception that scientists and the academy are "godless." Yet to see the academy only from this monolithic view would overlook the 48 percent of academic scientists who do identify with some form of religion and the nearly 68 percent interested in spirituality.

When we look at the religious backgrounds of scientists, the picture becomes more complicated. Scientists come disproportionately from liberal religious and irreligious backgrounds.

The question of why scientists come from these backgrounds will need further exploration beyond the findings presented here. One possible explanation is that there may indeed be tension between the religious tenets of some groups (such as those advocating young-earth creationism) and the theories and methods of particular sciences, making members of such religions less likely to pursue scientific careers. That few scientists subscribe to the more conservative or traditional strands of religion would seem to support this idea. Scientists raised in religious homes often remain religious.

Whatever the reason, these results show a more complex story than the simple "religion is contradictory to science and hence religious individuals don't go into science" argument.

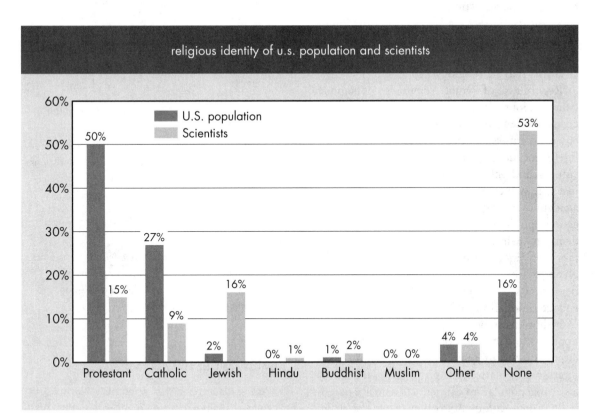

religious identity of u.s. population and scientists

If the goal is to increase dialogue between academics in science fields and different sectors of the American public, then we need to consider what these findings say about how academic scientists might contribute to that dialogue. There's no getting around the fact that many scientists at elite universities are less religious than individuals in the general population. These results point to a mismatch between the high religiosity of the American public and the comparatively low religiosity of scientists, a mismatch that may be a barrier to communication and understanding. This is a potentially serious problem in an era when, based on international comparisons, U.S. schoolchildren have poorer education in science than the other most industrialized nations, according to a report by the National Center for Education Statistics.

Scientists are right to lament scientific illiteracy among the U.S. population. But these findings also reveal that a portion of academic scientists may be religiously illiterate.

Regardless of what scientists personally believe about matters of faith, religion and science are often connected in a surrounding social environment—such as in public debates about intelligent design, stem cell research, human cloning, and public funding for science, to name just a few. Increasing communication between academics in various scientific fields and the general public (some of whom are the very students in their classes) may become an important goal indeed. More thought ought to be given to how those in the academy outside the fields that study religion could learn about and engage productively with religion.

It should also be emphasized that, whether or not academic scientists openly discuss religion, a large minority are religious and the majority are interested in matters of spirituality. This leaves a sizeable population of scientists who are potentially crucial commentators in the midst of an American public searching for a way to meaningfully understand the connections between religion and science. These are the prospective bridge-builders between scientists and the broader public. That these scientists are from elite universities makes them all the more poised to contribute to such a dialogue.

RECOMMENDED RESOURCES

Michael J. Behe. "Design for Living," *New York Times*, February 7, 2005.

> A professor of biological sciences at Lehigh University argues intelligent design has often been misconstrued in the media, and he attempts to correct some of the misconceptions about it.

Francis Collins. *The Language of God: A Scientist Presents Evidence for Belief* (Free Press, 2006).

> A personal overview of how the head of the Human Genome Project reconciles his evangelical Christianity with his work as one of the world's leading scientists.

Richard Dawkins. *The God Delusion* (Houghton Mifflin, 2006).

> A noted author, Oxford professor, and evolutionary biologist argues collective belief in God is responsible for many of the problems the world currently faces.

"Okay, We Give Up." *Scientific American*, April 1, 2005.

> In a sarcastic April Fool's Day editorial, the editors of *Scientific American*—a leading scientific journal—defend their exclusion of articles on creationism or intelligent design.

REVIEW QUESTIONS

1. Are you surprised that scientists often hold religious views? Have you ever thought about the religious beliefs of your professors? Based

on the article, would you assume that they are religious or not? How do you think it varies by discipline?

2. Why do you think a greater proportion of scientists than the general public are atheists?

3. Considering that 69 percent of social scientists surveyed identified themselves as spiritual, how might you explain a reluctance to discuss religion in an academic setting?

4. Activity: Interview one of your professors about her or his religious beliefs and how these relate (or not) to their academic work.

w. bradford wilcox

religion and the domestication of men

39

fall 2006

should we worry that evangelical protestantism turns men into abusive and insensitive patriarchs in the home? not exactly.

A wife should "submit herself graciously" to her husband's leadership, and a husband should "provide for, protect, and lead his family." So proclaimed the Southern Baptist Convention—the nation's largest evangelical Protestant denomination—in 1998. Statements like this, and religious support for gender traditionalism and antifeminist public policies more generally, indicate how conservative religious institutions have helped to stall the gender revolution of the last half century. The crucial role that Phyllis Schlafly's Eagle Forum played in defeating the ERA in the 1970s is but one example.

Beneath the politics, we know less about how religious institutions influence individual men. Journalists, academics, and feminists have been skeptical—to say the least—about the influence of religion on American family men. Journalists Steve and Cokie Roberts responded to the 1998 Southern Baptist statement, for instance, by writing that such thinking "can clearly lead to abuse, both physical and emotional." Similarly, sociologists Julia McQuillan and Myra Marx Ferree have argued that evangelical Protestantism is an influential force "pushing men toward authoritarian and stereotypical forms of masculinity and attempting to renew patriarchal relations."

Academics, journalists, and feminists raise an important question: Are religious institutions,

especially conservative ones such as evangelical Protestantism or Mormonism, a force for patriarchy?

Critics have yet to examine how religious institutions, particularly conservative ones, have also become deeply concerned about the family revolution of the last half century. Increases in divorce, nonmarital childbearing, and premarital sex in the society at large and in their own ranks have disturbed many conservative churches, organizations, and leaders. Partly as a consequence of this revolution, and partly because feminism has raised women's expectations of men in the society at large and within conservative churches, conservative religious institutions have turned their focus on men with the aim of encouraging them to devote more time, attention, and emotional energy to their families. They hope to strengthen families that seem increasingly vulnerable to fragmentation.

Does religion domesticate men in ways that make them more engaged and attentive husbands and fathers? To answer this question, I focus not only on white middle-class families, but also on the urban poor, who have borne the brunt of our nation's retreat from marriage.

a force for patriarchy?

So how do religious institutions affect men who are married with children? In my book,

Soft Patriarchs and New Men: How Christianity Shapes Fathers and Husbands, I find some evidence that religion is a force for patriarchy.

When it comes to work and family life, evangelical Protestantism (theologically conservative churches such as the Southern Baptist Church, Assemblies of God, the Presbyterian Church of America, and nondenominational evangelical churches) fosters gender inequality. Evangelical Protestant family men are more likely to endorse traditional gender attitudes than are other men. For instance, I found that 58 percent of churchgoing, evangelical men who are married with children believe that it is "much better for everyone if the man earns the main living and the woman takes care of the home and family," compared to only 44 percent of churchgoing, mainline Protestant men and 37 percent of unaffiliated men. (Mainline Protestantism encompasses the Episcopal Church, Presbyterian Church [USA], the Lutheran Church [ELCA], and the United Methodist Church.)

These attitudes, reinforced by church-based activities and social networks, matter. Evangelical Protestant husbands do an hour less housework per week than other American husbands; not surprisingly, the division of household labor is less equal in evangelical homes than in other American homes. Sociologists Jennifer Glass and Jerry Jacobs have shown that women raised in evangelical Protestant families are more likely to focus on motherhood than work: they marry earlier, bear children earlier, and work less than other women in the United States. So it is true that evangelical Protestantism—but not mainline Protestantism, Reform Judaism, and Roman Catholicism—appears to steer men (and women) toward gender inequality.

Evangelical Protestantism also steers fathers in a patriarchal direction when it comes to discipline. Drawing in part on their belief in original sin and on biblical passages that seem to promote a strict approach to discipline—"He who spares the rod hates his son, but he who loves him is careful to discipline him" (*Proverbs* 13:24)—evangelical Protestant leaders, such as Focus on the Family President James Dobson, stress the divine authority of parents and the need for parents to take a firm hand with their children. As Dobson writes, "If a little child is taught to disrespect the authority of his parents, systematically from the tender years of childhood—to mock their leadership, to 'sass' them and disobey their instructions, to exercise extreme self-will from the earliest moments of awareness—then it is most unlikely that this same child will turn his face up to God, about twenty years later, and say humbly, 'Here I am Lord; send me!'"

Many evangelical fathers take these views to heart. They are more likely to value obedience in their children. They are also more likely to spank their children when they do not get that obedience. Specifically, evangelical fathers are significantly more likely to use corporal punishment on their children than Catholic, Jewish, and unaffiliated fathers. In important respects, evangelical Protestantism appears to be a force for patriarchal authority and gender relations.

turning the hearts of men toward their families

But this is not the whole story about religion and men in the United States. Because they are worried about the social and religious consequences of divorce and nonmarital childbearing, and because they view the vocations of marriage and parenthood in a transcendent light, churches and family ministries have devoted countless radio broadcasts, books, and sermons to the task of encouraging Americans to make their marriages and children a top priority.

Conservative religious groups, such as Promise Keepers and the Southern Baptist Convention, have been particularly attentive to the family failures of men. Recognizing that men are often the weak link in families—because they fail to focus emotionally and practically on their wives and children, and because they are often absent, physically or financially—evangelical Protestant churches and ministries have generally taken the lead in the religious world in calling on men to put their families first. Drawing also on a therapeutic emphasis that entered evangelical Protestantism in the 1970s, evangelical elites urge men to be emotionally and practically engaged with their wives and children.

For instance, one popular book among evangelicals, *If Only He Knew: What No Woman Can Resist*, by therapist Gary Smalley, chides husbands for their insensitivity toward their wives. He lists 122 ways in which husbands are insufficiently attuned emotionally to their wives—from "not inviting her out on special romantic dates from time to time" to "being easily distracted when she is trying to talk"—and exhorts men to comfort, to listen, to praise, and to communicate with their wives. Likewise, popular Christian pastor Charles Swindoll urges men to model God's love to their children in the following way: "Your boy must be very aware that *you love him*. . . . When is the last time you took him in your arms and held him close so no one else could hear, and whispered to him how happy you are to have him as your son?"

Mainline Protestant, Catholic, and Reform Jewish congregations also encourage men to invest in their families, although they do it more in the context of encouraging both men and women to honor the Golden Rule by treating their spouses and especially their children with care and consideration. As sociologist Penny Edgell reports in her new book, *Religion and Family in a Changing Society*, moderate-to-liberal congregations in these traditions criticize lives centered around careers or materialism and stress the importance of putting family life first.

This emphasis on family seems to be bearing fruit. I found that men who are religious—especially evangelical fathers and husbands—are more involved and affectionate with their children and wives than are unaffiliated family men. As fathers, religious men spend more time in one-on-one activities like reading to their children, hug and praise their kids more often, and keep tabs on the children more than unaffiliated fathers do. For instance, churchgoing fathers spend 2.9 hours per week with their children in youth activities such as soccer, Boy Scouts, and religious youth groups, and churchgoing evangelical fathers spend 3.2 hours per week on these activities, compared to 1.6 hours for unaffiliated fathers.

As husbands, religious men are more affectionate and understanding with their wives, and they spend more time socializing with them, compared to husbands who are not regular churchgoers. I also found—contrary to the expectations of critics—that churchgoing, evangelical married men have the lowest rates of reported domestic violence of any major religious or secular group in the United States. (On the other hand, evangelical married men who do not attend church regularly have the highest rates of domestic violence.) Not surprisingly, wives of religious men report higher levels of marital happiness than wives of men who are not religious.

Religious family men—especially more conservative ones—combine elements of the new and the old in their approach to family life. They are more likely to have unequal marriages and to take a strict approach to discipline; but they are also more emotionally and practically engaged than the average secular or nominally religious family man. In a word, their approach to family life can be described as neotraditional.

faith and marriage in the city

In their recent book, *Promises I Can Keep: Why Poor Women Put Motherhood Before*

Marriage (and in their *Contexts* article, Spring 2005), Kathy Edin and Maria Kefalas argue that one important reason that poor women in urban America put motherhood before marriage is that they do not have ready access to a pool of "decent," marriageable men. They claim that most of the men whom these women encounter are unemployed or underemployed in the legal economy, are in and out of jail, are unfaithful, are violent, or cannot leave drugs and alcohol alone.

It is certainly true that many young urban men do not seem to be promising candidates for marriage. But my current research on religion and marriage in America's cities suggests that religious institutions play an important and understudied role in keeping marriage alive in poor and especially working-class urban communities— including African-American communities—where marriage is often comparatively fragile. They do so in part by supplying churchgoing women with churchgoing men who are responsible, faithful, and employed.

Marriage persists in American cities partly because the three largest religious traditions— Black Protestantism, Roman Catholicism, and evangelical Protestantism—depict marriage as a sacred institution that is the best context in which to have sex, raise children, and enjoy divine favor for an intimate relationship. As Wallace Charles Smith, pastor of Shiloh Baptist in Washington, D.C., has written, "God's revelation clearly points to male-female monogamous relationships as the gift by God to humankind for the purposes of procreation and nurturing. Even for people of African descent, this concept of monogamy must be at the heart of even the extended family structure."

In my ethnographic research in the Bronx and Harlem, I have found that many pastors and priests touch on the joys and challenges of married life, encouraging spouses to be kind and forgiving to one another; more conservative clergy also encourage their members to avoid nonmarital sex and, if they are cohabiting, to consider marriage. Married church members— especially married men—are usually given prominent roles as deacons, ushers, and Bible-study leaders. Marriage is depicted as the ideal in these churches, even when many, sometimes most, of the congregants are unmarried.

But churches do more than idealize marriage. They also encourage their members—male and female—to live "decent" lives. Decent or righteous living is exalted from the pulpit as divinely ordained, and it is reinforced by fellow believers who model decent behavior and sanction members who betray the church's code of decency. At a minimum, decency encompasses hard work, sexual fidelity, the Golden Rule, avoiding drug use and excessive drinking, and responsible parenting.

For instance, earlier this year at the Abyssinian Church in Harlem, Rev. Calvin Butts III delivered a sermon entitled, "The Recovery of Righteousness": "So, Beloved, I am suggesting to you that there is no greater need before us today than the recovery of plain old-fashioned righteousness. . . . who among us would . . . eschew drunkenness, idleness, and immorality? Who would dare to stand in the face of the onslaught of the culture of sin that has enveloped our nation and say, 'I refuse to succumb. I will not yield to the temptation. I will stand like a tree planted by the water. I will not move.'?"

By lifting up the ideal of marriage, and especially by encouraging their members to live decent lives, urban churches encourage marriage and help their members to have higher-quality

> Men who are religious—especially evangelical fathers and husbands—are more involved and affectionate with their children and wives than are unaffiliated family men.

relationships. The effects of church attendance are particularly strong among urban men. Using data from the Fragile Families and Child Wellbeing Study, demographer Nicholas Wolfinger and I found that urban couples are 40 percent more likely to bear a child in wedlock if the mother attends church on a regular basis (several times a month or more) and 95 percent more likely if the father also regularly attends church. The man's attendance is also a better predictor than the woman's of whether urban parents will marry after a nonmarital birth.

Wolfinger and I also found that couples with children in urban America report higher levels of marital happiness and supportive behavior (affection, compromise, and encouragement) from their partners when the father, but not necessarily the mother, regularly attends church. In other words, his church attendance seems to matter for the quality of both men's and women's marriages in urban America. We also find that male church attendance improves the quality of relationships among unmarried couples.

Why is his attendance so important? Because decent men are in relatively short supply in many urban communities, especially among African Americans, churches play a crucial role in enabling urban women to locate good men and in encouraging men to remain or become decent. (Many of the urban, churchgoing men I spoke with have overcome previous problems with the law, substance abuse, or sexual promiscuity.) Although these men are by no means perfect, they are regularly encouraged by their pastors and fellow congregants to avoid the siren calls of the street, to give God glory through righteous living, and to treat their wives and children with love and respect. Besides being more supportive than other husbands, churchgoing, urban fathers are also more likely to be employed full-time and to be clean and sober. As a result, urban women are more likely to marry, and be happy in their marriages, if they find a decent, churchgoing husband.

Religion also plays an important role in reducing the wide gap between white and black marriage rates. My research suggests that church attendance is as important in promoting marriage among African Americans as it is among other racial and ethnic groups in the United States. Indeed, were it not for higher-than-average levels of church attendance among African Americans, the racial gap in marriage rates between African Americans and whites in urban America would be even larger than it already is.

Let me be clear: religion is no magic bullet for strengthening family life in urban America. Slightly more than one-third of urban mothers attend church regularly, compared to about one-fifth of urban fathers. Most urban adults—especially men—are not exposed to the family message and focus, and the code of decency, found in churches. Even couples who attend church regularly experience nonmarital pregnancies, infidelity, and the larger forces of poverty, discrimination, unemployment that can throw their relationships and lives into a downward spiral. Thus, academics, religious leaders, and especially policy makers should not view religious institutions as a panacea for nonmarital childbearing, family instability, and relationship problems in urban America.

religion in men's lives

The United States has witnessed two distinct but related revolutions in the last half-century: a gender revolution marked by increased equality in the opportunities, rewards, and responsibilities that men and women face, and a family revolution marked by the weakening of marriage as the central institution for organizing sex, childbearing, childrearing, and adult life more generally. The gender revolution has not completely triumphed, in part because men have not taken up an equal share of housework and child care. My research and that of others suggests another reason: religious institutions—particularly more conservative ones like the Southern Baptist Convention—often lend ideological and practical support to traditional gender attitudes and family behaviors; thus, feminist, academic, and journalistic critics are rightly concerned about how some religious institutions reinforce gender inequality.

But critics miss how religious institutions—especially more conservative ones—also encourage men to put their families first. Most of the institutions that men encounter in their daily lives—work, popular culture, and sports, for instance—do not push men to invest in family life. But religious institutions—especially traditional ones worried about the well-being of the family in the modern world—do encourage men to focus on their families. They provide men with messages, rituals, and activities that help them to see their roles as husbands and fathers as meaningful and important, and to improve their performance of these roles.

Churchgoing family men in the United States are more involved and affectionate fathers and husbands, compared to their peers who are secular or just nominally religious. Their wives report greater marital happiness, and are therefore less likely to divorce them. At least in urban America, these men also appear more likely to engage in "decent" behavior—for example, holding regular jobs and avoiding drug and alcohol abuse—than their less religious peers.

This neotraditional approach to family life, combining a progressive insistence on men's active engagement in family life with a traditional insistence on some degree of gender complementarity in family life, has not received much scholarly attention. But if we seek to understand family pluralism and family change in the United States in all of its complexity, we must keep these neotraditional men and their families in our sociological imagination.

RECOMMENDED RESOURCES

John P. Bartkowski. *Remaking the Godly Marriage: Gender Negotiation in Evangelical Families* (Rutgers University Press, 2001).

> Evangelical Protestant couples draw selectively on both essentialist and feminist gender ideals in negotiating married life.

Penny Edgell. *Religion and Family in a Changing Society* (Princeton University Press, 2005).

> Men, more than women, attend church to socialize their children, and—as a consequence—are more likely than women to be attracted to churches that cater to traditional families.

Sally Gallagher. *Evangelical Identity and Gendered Family Life* (Rutgers University Press, 2003).

> The conventional critique of evangelical Protestant gender politics does not capture the ambiguities and heterogeneity of gender beliefs and behaviors in this subculture.

Jennifer Glass and Jerry Jacobs. "Childhood Religious Conservatism and Adult Attainment among Black and White Women." *Social Forces* (2005) 84: 555–79.

> Evangelical Protestantism puts many women on a trajectory toward early motherhood and marriage, and away from full-time employment.

W. Bradford Wilcox. *Soft Patriarchs, New Men: How Christianity Shapes Fathers and Husbands* (University of Chicago Press, 2004).

> The religious rituals, social networks, and ideas associated with evangelical Protestantism.

REVIEW QUESTIONS

1. Wilcox suggests that evangelical Protestantism fosters gender inequality. How so? Provide an example of the statistical evidence that Wilcox offers to support this assertion.
2. In poor and especially working-class urban communities, how do religious institutions play an important role in keeping marriage alive?
3. Why have conservative religious groups like Promise Keepers and the Southern Baptist Convention paid particular attention to the family failures of men as opposed to women? If one compares churchgoing fathers with unaffiliated dads, do these efforts seem to be successful?

mark chaves
photos by dianne hagaman

abiding faith

40

summer 2002

contrary to the popular impression that americans have become more secular, in some ways they are as religious as ever. but organized religion occupies less of americans' time, and exerts less influence on society as a whole than in the past.

God is dead—or God is taking over. Depending on the headlines of the day, soothsayers pronounce the end of religion or the ascendancy of religious extremists. What is really going on?

Taking stock of religion is almost as old as religion itself. Tracking religious trends is difficult, however, when religion means so many different things. Should we look at belief in the supernatural? Frequency of formal religious worship? The role of faith in major life decisions? The power of individual religious movements? These different dimensions of religion can change in different ways. Whether religion is declining or not depends on the definition of religion and what signifies a decline.

Perhaps the most basic manifestation of religious observance is piety: individual belief and participation in formal religious worship. Recent research on trends in American piety supports neither simple secularization nor staunch religious resilience in the face of modern life. Instead, Americans seem to believe as much but practice less.

religious belief

Conventional Judeo-Christian religious belief remains very high in the United States, and little evidence suggests it has declined in recent decades. Gallup polls and other surveys show that more than 90 percent of Americans believe in a higher power, and more than 60 percent are certain that God exists. Approximately 80 percent believe in miracles and in life after death, 70 percent believe in heaven, and 60 percent believe in hell. Far fewer Americans—from two in three in 1963 to one in three today—believe the Bible is the literal Word of God. The number who say the Bible is either the inerrant or the inspired Word of God is still impressively high, however—four of every five.

Religious faith in the United States is more broad than deep, and it has been for as long as it has been tracked. Of Americans who say the Bible is either the actual or the inspired Word of God, only half can name the first book in the Bible and only one-third can say who preached the Sermon on the Mount. More than 90 percent believe in a higher power, but only one-third say they rely more on that power than on themselves in overcoming adversity. People who claim to be born-again or evangelical Christians are no less likely than others to believe in ideas foreign to traditional Christianity, such as reincarnation (20 percent of all Americans), channeling (17 percent), or astrology (26 percent), and they are no less likely to have visited a fortune teller (16 percent).

Despite the superficiality of belief among many, the percentage of Americans expressing religious faith is still remarkably high. How should we understand this persistent religious belief? High levels of religious belief in the United States seem to show that, contrary to widespread expectations of many scholars, industrialization, urbanization, bureaucratization, advances in science and other developments associated with modern life do not automatically undermine religious belief. In part this is because modernization does not immunize people against the human experiences that inspire religious sentiment. As anthropologist Mary Douglas points out, scientific advances do not make us less likely to feel awe and wonder when we ponder the universe and its workings. For example, our feelings of deference to physicians, owing to their experience and somewhat mysterious scientific knowledge, may not be so different from the way other people feel about traditional healers—even if the outcomes of treatment are

indeed different. Likewise, bureaucracy does not demystify our world—on the contrary, it may make us feel more helpless and confused in the face of powers beyond our control. When confronted with large and complex bureaucracies, modern people may not feel any more in control of the world around them than a South Pacific Islander confronted with the prospect of deep-sea fishing for shark. Modern people still turn to religion in part because certain experiences—anthropologist Clifford Geertz emphasizes bafflement, pain, and moral dilemmas—remain part of the human condition.

> Conventional Judeo-Christian religious belief remains very high in the United States, and little evidence suggests it has declined in recent decades.

That condition cannot, however, completely explain the persistence of religious belief. It is clearly possible to respond in nonreligious ways to these universal human experiences, and many people do, suggesting that religiosity is a feature of some responses to these experiences, not an automatic consequence of the experiences themselves. From this perspective, attempting to explain religion's persistence by the persistence of bafflement, pain, and moral paradox sidesteps a key question: Why do so many people continue to respond to these experiences by turning to religion?

Another, more sociological explanation of the persistence of religious belief emphasizes the fact that religion—like language and ethnicity—is one of the main ways of delineating group boundaries and collective identities. As long as who we are and how we differ from others remains a salient organizing principle for social movements and institutions, religion can be expected to thrive. Indeed, this identity-marking aspect of religion may also explain why religious belief often seems more broad than deep. If affirming that the Bible is the inerrant Word of God serves in part to identify oneself as part of the community of Bible-believing Christians, it is

Mass broadcast from Rome is received at a church in Seattle, Washington. Televised images of Pope John Paul II are projected on screens beside the altar. (Photo by Dianne Hagaman)

not so important to know in much detail what the Bible actually says.

The modern world is not inherently inhospitable to religious belief, and many kinds of belief have not declined at all over the past several decades. Certain aspects of modernity, however, do seem to reduce levels of religious observance. In a recent study of 65 countries, Ronald Inglehart and Wayne Baker find that people in industrialized and wealthy nations are typically less religious than others. That said, among advanced industrial democracies the United States still stands out for its relatively high level of religious belief. When asked to rate the importance of God in their lives on a scale of 1 to 10, 50 percent of Americans say "10," far higher than the 28 percent in Canada, 26 percent in Spain, 21 percent in Australia, 16 percent in Great Britain and Germany, and 10 percent in France. Among advanced industrial democracies, only Ireland, at 40 percent, approaches the U.S. level of religious conviction.

religious participation

Cross-national comparisons also show that Americans participate in organized religion more often than do people in other affluent nations. In the United States, 55 percent of those who are asked say they attend religious services at least once a month, compared with 40 percent in Canada, 38 percent in Spain, 25 percent in Australia, Great Britain, and West Germany, and 17 percent in France.

The trends over time, however, are murkier. Roger Finke and Rodney Stark have argued that religious participation has increased over the course of American history. This claim is based mainly on increasing rates of church membership. In 1789 only 10 percent of Americans belonged to churches, with church membership rising to 22 percent in 1890 and reaching 50 to 60 percent in the 1950s. Today, about two-thirds of Americans say they are members of a church or a synagogue. These rising figures should not, however, be taken at face value, because churches have become less exclusive clubs than they were earlier in our history. Fewer people attend religious services today than claim formal membership in religious congregations, but the opposite was true in earlier times. The long-term trend in religious participation is difficult to discern.

Although we have much more evidence about recent trends in religious participation, it still is difficult to say definitively whether religious-service attendance—the main way Americans participate collectively in religion—has declined or remained stable in recent decades. The available evidence is conflicting. Surveys using the traditional approach of asking people directly about their attendance mainly show stability over time, confirming the consensus that attendance has not declined much.

New evidence, however, points toward decline. Drawing on time-use records, which ask individuals to report everything they do on a given day, Stanley Presser and Linda Stinson find that weekly religious-service attendance has declined over the past 30 years from about 40 percent in 1965 to about 25 percent in 1994. Sandra Hofferth and John Sandberg also find a decline in church attendance reported in children's time-use diaries. Time-use studies mitigate the over-reporting of religious-service attendance that occurs when people are asked directly whether or not they attend. Also, these time-use studies find the same lower attendance rates found by researchers who count the number of people who actually show up at church rather than take them at their word when they say they attend.

Additional evidence of declining activity comes from political scientist Robert Putnam's book on civic engagement in the United States, *Bowling Alone*. Combining survey data from five different sources, Putnam finds some decline in religious participation. Perhaps more important, because

Monthly women's Bible study group. (Photo by Dianne Hagaman)

of the context they provide, are Putnam's findings about a range of civic and voluntary association activities that are closely related to religious participation. Virtually every type of civic engagement declined in the last third of the twentieth century: voting, attending political, public, and club meetings, serving as officer or committee member in local clubs and organizations, belonging to national organizations, belonging to unions, playing sports and working on community projects. If religious participation has indeed remained constant, it would be virtually the only type of civic engagement that has not declined in recent decades. Nor did the events of September 11, 2001, alter attendance patterns. If there was a spike in religious service attendance immediately following September 11, it was short-lived.

Overall, the following picture emerges from recent research: Since the 1960s, Americans have engaged less frequently in religious activities, but they have continued to believe just as much in the supernatural and to be just as interested in spirituality. This pattern characterizes many other countries around the world as well. Inglehart and Baker's data suggest that American trends are similar to those in other advanced industrialized societies: declining religious activities, stability in religious belief and increasing interest in the meaning and purpose of life.

Important differences among subgroups remain nonetheless. Blacks are more religiously active than whites, and women are more active than men. There is little reason to think, however, that the recent declines in participation vary among subgroups.

New forms of religious participation are not replacing attendance at weekend worship services. When churchgoers are asked what day they attended a service, only 3 percent mention a day other than Sunday. Perhaps more telling, when those who say they did not attend a religious service in the past week are asked if they participated in some other type of religious event or meeting, such as a prayer or Bible study group, only 2 percent say yes (although 21 percent of nonattendees say they watched religious television or listened to religious radio). The vast majority of religious activity in the United States takes place at weekend religious services. If other forms of religious activity have increased, they have not displaced traditional weekend attendance.

Overall, the current knowledge of individual piety in the United States does not conform to expectations that modernity is fundamentally hostile to religion. Many conventional religious beliefs remain popular, showing no sign of decline. That said, research on individual piety neither points to stability on every dimension nor implies that social changes associated with modernity leave religious belief and practice unimpaired. The evidence supports neither a simple version of secularization nor a wholesale rejection of secularization. Moreover, focusing on levels of religious piety diverts attention from what may be more important: the social significance of religion.

religious piety in context

Focusing exclusively on levels of religious belief and practice overlooks something crucial about religion's social significance. Consider, for example, the difference between two charismatic worship services, complete with speaking in tongues, one occurring outside a village in colonial central Africa early in the twentieth century and the other occurring in an urban Pentecostal church on a Sunday morning in the contemporary United States. In the first case, described by anthropologist Karen Fields, charismatic religion—simply by encouraging baptism and speaking in tongues—challenged the traditional religious authority on which colonial rule was based; the American service plays no such political role. Similarly, consider the difference between two "new age" religious groups, both of which encourage certain kinds of physical exercise to achieve spiritual peace and growth, with one group meeting in a YMCA somewhere in New York City and the other meeting in a park somewhere in Beijing. In the two examples, the same religious action takes on dramatically different meanings that can lead to very different consequences depending on the institutional and political context. In some times and places, speaking in tongues or seeking health by stretching one's limbs shakes social institutions and provokes hostile reactions. In other times and places, such displays shake nothing but the bodies of the faithful, provoking little hostility or, indeed, any other reaction. The social significance of religious piety—its capacity to mean something beyond itself—depends on the context in which it occurs.

From this perspective, we can wonder how high levels of belief and practice are relevant to understanding the social importance of religion. Where people are interested in the spiritual and the supernatural, both traditional religions and new religious movements try to capture that interest. Some successfully bring people into the fold, energize members' beliefs and activities and build impressive organizations. But even a wildly successful religious movement does not expand

Interfaith Prayer Service for Peace, University of Washington, Seattle. (Photo by Dianne Hagaman)

religion's dominion if its success is limited to influencing how people spend an hour or two a week of their leisure time in a society where such activity only occasionally reverberates beyond the walls of the church. Increases in charismatic religion in the United States, for example, may be interesting to chart, but when religious institutions do not generally shape other important social institutions, like government or the market, such increases lack the consequences they have where speaking in tongues challenges a village leader's authority. The same can be said of ebbs and flows of any religious style.

Of course, when many people are religiously active, religion can have more social influence. A society like the United States, with more than 300,000 religious congregations, presents opportunities for political mobilization that do not exist in societies where religion is a less prominent part of society. Witness the Civil Rights Movement, the Religious Right, and other causes that mix religion and politics. Nonetheless, religion in the United States, as in most other advanced societies, is organizationally separate from (even if occasionally overlapping) government, the economy, and other parts of civil society. This limits a religion's capacity to change the world, even if it converts millions.

The social significance of religious belief and participation depends on the institutional settings in which they occur. This is why the religious movements of our day with the greatest potential for increasing religion's influence are not those that simply seek new converts or spur belief and practice, no matter how successful they may be. The movements with the greatest such potential are those that seek to expand religion's authority or influence in other domains. In some parts of the contemporary world, this has meant religious leaders seeking and sometimes achieving the power to veto legislation, dictate university curricula, exclude girls from schooling and women from working in certain jobs, and determine the kinds of art or literature offered to the public. In the United States, the most significant contemporary movement to expand religious influence probably is the effort to shape school curricula concerning evolution and creationism. Wherever they occur, when such movements succeed they change the meaning and significance of religious piety. Efforts like these reflect and shape the abiding role of religion in a society in ways that go beyond the percentages of people who believe in God, pray, or attend religious services.

RECOMMENDED RESOURCES

Mark Chaves. "Secularization as Declining Religious Authority." *Social Forces* 72 (1994): 749–74.

George Gallup, Jr. and D. Michael Lindsay. *Surveying the Religious Landscape* (Morehouse Publishing, 1999).

Sandra L. Hofferth and John F. Sandberg. "Children at the Millennium: Where Have We Come From, Where Are We Going?" In *Advances in Life Course Research*, eds. T. Owens and S. Hofferth. (Elsevier Science, 2001). Also available at www.ethno.isr.umich.edu/06papers/html.

Ronald Inglehart and Wayne E. Baker. "Modernization, Cultural Change, and the Persistence of Traditional Values." *American Sociological Review* 65 (2000): 19–51.

Stanley Presser and Linda Stinson. "Data Collection Mode and Social Desirability Bias in Self-Reported Religious Attendance." *American Sociological Review* 63 (1998): 134–45.

Robert Putnam. "Religious Participation." In *Bowling Alone: The Collapse and Revival of American Community* (Simon and Schuster, 2000).

REVIEW QUESTIONS

1. Might church membership or church attendance be problematic measures of religiosity? How else might we measure religiosity?

2. The essay notes that industrialization, urbanization, and bureaucratization "do not automatically undermine religious belief." How might one or more of these processes actually encourage religiosity?

3. Sociologist Emile Durkheim wrote that "we do not find religion without a church." Thinking about the relationship between ideas and practices, what do you think he was referring to? How does this statement relate to the essay?

4. The essay includes an image of a congregation in song. In this photo, there is a projected image on a screen. Perhaps this service is being televised. In what ways do you think technology may be changing American religiosity?

part **10**

Aging and the Lifecourse

frank f. furstenberg, jr., sheela kennedy, vonnie c. mcloyd, rubén g. rumbaut, and richard a. settersten, jr.

growing up is harder to do

41

summer 2004

in the past several decades, a new life stage has emerged: early adulthood. no longer adolescents, but not yet ready to assume the full responsibilities of an adult, many young people are caught between needing to learn advanced job skills and depending on their family to support them during the transition.

In the years after World War II, Americans typically assumed the full responsibilities of adulthood by their late teens or early 20s. Most young men had completed school and were working full-time, and most young women were married and raising children. People who grew up in this era of growing affluence—many of today's grandparents—were economically self-sufficient and able to care for others by the time they had weathered adolescence. Today, adulthood no longer begins when adolescence ends. Ask someone in their early 20s whether they consider themselves to be an adult, and you might get a laugh, a quizzical look, a shrug of the shoulders, or a response like that of a 24-year-old Californian: "Maybe next year. When I'm 25."

Social scientists are beginning to recognize a new phase of life: early adulthood. Some features of this stage resemble coming of age during the late nineteenth and early twentieth centuries, when youth lingered in a state of semi-autonomy, waiting until they were sufficiently well-off to marry, have children, and establish an independent household. However, there are important differences in how young people today define and achieve adulthood from those of both the recent and the more distant past.

This new stage is not merely an extension of adolescence, as has been maintained in the mass media. Young adults are physically mature and often possess impressive intellectual, social, and psychological skills. Nor are young people today reluctant to accept adult responsibilities. Instead, they are busy building up their educational credentials and practical skills in an ever more demanding labor market. Most are working or studying or both, and are developing romantic relationships. Yet, many have not become fully adult—traditionally defined as finishing school, landing a job with benefits, marrying and parenting—because they are not ready, or perhaps not permitted, to do so. For a growing number, this will not happen until their late 20s or even early 30s. In response, American society will have to revise upward the "normal" age of full adulthood, and develop ways to assist young people through the ever-lengthening transition.

Among the most privileged young adults—those who receive ample support from their parents—this is a time of unparalleled freedom from family responsibilities and an opportunity for self-exploration and development. For the less advantaged, early adulthood is a time of struggle to gain the skills and credentials required for a job that can support the family they wish to start (or perhaps have already started), and a struggle to feel in control of their lives. A 30-year-old single mother from Iowa laughed when asked whether she considered herself an adult: "I don't know if I'm an adult yet. I still don't feel quite grown up. Being an adult kind of sounds like having things, everything is kind of in a routine and on track, and I don't feel like I'm quite on track."

changing notions of adulthood

Traditionally, the transition to adulthood involves establishing emotional and economic independence from parents or, as historian John Modell described it, "coming into one's own." The life events that make up the transition to adulthood are accompanied by a sense of commitment, purpose, and identity. Although we lack systematic evidence on how adulthood was defined in the past, it appears that marriage and parenthood represented important benchmarks. Nineteenth-century American popular fiction, journalism, sermons, and self-help guides rarely referred to finishing school or getting a job, and only occasionally to leaving home or starting one's own household as the critical turning point. On the other hand, they often referred to marriage, suggesting that marriage was considered, at least by middle-class writers, as the critical touchstone of reaching adulthood.

By the 1950s and 1960s, most Americans viewed family roles and adult responsibilities as nearly synonymous. In that era, most women married before they were 21 and had at least one child before they were 23. For men, having the means to marry and support a family was the defining characteristic of adulthood, while for women, merely getting married and becoming a mother conferred adult status. As Alice Rossi explained in 1968: "On the level of cultural values, men have no freedom of choice where work is concerned: they must work to secure their status as adult men. The equivalent for women has been maternity. There is considerable pressure upon the growing girl and young woman to consider maternity necessary for a woman's fulfillment as an individual and to secure her status as an adult."

Research conducted during the late 1950s and early 1960s demonstrated widespread antipathy in America toward people who remained unmarried and toward couples who were childless by choice. However, these views began to shift in the late 1960s, rendering the transition to adulthood more ambiguous. Psychologists Joseph Veroff, Elizabeth Douvan, and Richard Kulka found that more than half of Americans interviewed in 1957 viewed someone who did not want to get married as selfish, immature, peculiar, or morally flawed. By 1976, fewer than one-third of a similar sample held such views. A 1962 study found that 85 percent of mothers believed that married couples should have children. Nearly 20 years later, just 40 percent of those women still agreed, and in 1993 only 1 in 5 of their daughters agreed. Arland Thornton and Linda Young-Demarco, who have studied attitudes toward family roles during the latter half of the twentieth century, conclude that "Americans increasingly value freedom and equality in their personal and family lives while at the same time maintaining their commitment to the ideals of marriage, family, and children." While still personally committed to family, Americans increasingly tolerate alternative life choices.

To understand how Americans today define adulthood, we developed a set of questions for the 2002 General Social Survey (GSS), an opinion poll administered to a nationally representative sample of Americans every two years by the National Opinion Research Center. The survey asked nearly 1,400 Americans aged 18 and older how important each of the following traditional benchmarks was to being an adult: leaving home, finishing school, getting a full-time job, becoming financially independent from one's parents, being able to support a family, marrying, and becoming a parent.

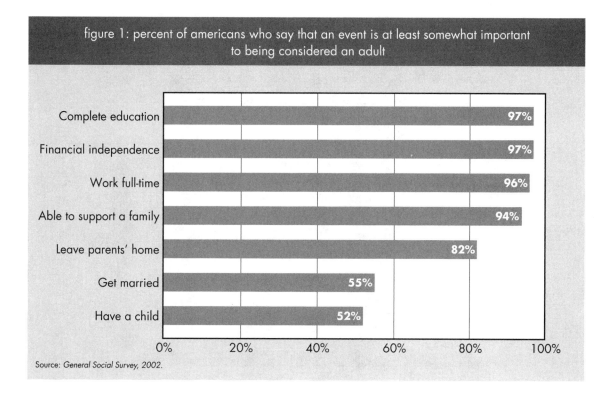

figure 1: percent of americans who say that an event is at least somewhat important to being considered an adult

Complete education	97%
Financial independence	97%
Work full-time	96%
Able to support a family	94%
Leave parents' home	82%
Get married	55%
Have a child	52%

Source: *General Social Survey, 2002.*

The definition of adulthood that emerges today does not necessarily include marriage and parenthood. As shown in figure 1, the most important milestones are completing school, establishing an independent household, and being employed full-time—concrete steps associated with the ability to support a family. Ninety-five percent of Americans surveyed consider education, employment, financial independence, and the ability to support a family to be key steps on the path to adulthood. Nonetheless, almost half of GSS respondents do not believe that it is necessary to actually marry or to have children to be considered an adult. As a young mother from San Diego explained, having a child did not make her an adult; instead she began to feel like an adult when she realized that "all of us make mistakes, but you can fix them and if you

keep yourself on track . . . everything will come out fine." Compared with their parents and grandparents, for whom marriage and parenthood were virtually a prerequisite for becoming an adult, young people today more often view these as life choices, not requirements.

the lengthening road to adulthood

Not only are the defining characteristics of adulthood changing, so is the time it takes to achieve them. To map the changing transitions to adulthood, we also examined several national surveys that contain information on young adults both in this country and abroad. Using U.S. Census data collected as far back as 1900, we compared the lives of young adults over time. We also conducted about 500 in-depth

figure 2: percent completing transition to adulthood in 1960 and 2000 using traditional benchmarks (leaving home, finishing school, getting married, having a child, and being financially independent)

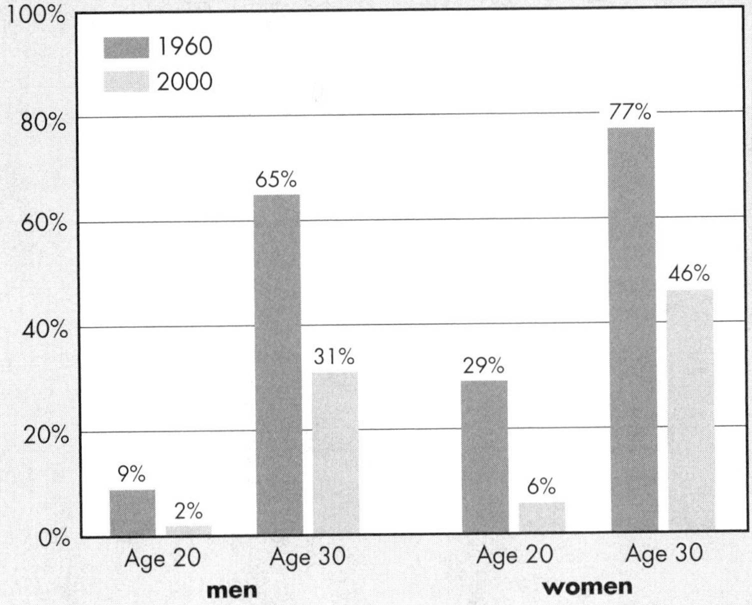

Source: Integrated Public Use Microdata Series extracts (IPUMS) of the 1960 and 2000 U.S Censuses.

interviews with young adults living in different parts of the United States, including many in recent immigrant groups.

Our findings, as well as the work of other scholars, confirm that it takes much longer to make the transition to adulthood today than decades ago, and arguably longer than it has at any time in America's history. Figure 2, based on the 1960 and 2000 U.S. censuses, illustrates the large decline in the percentage of young adults who, by age 20 or 30, have completed all of the traditionally defined major adult transitions (leaving home, finishing school, becoming financially independent, getting married, and having a child). We define financial indepen-

dence for both men and women as being in the labor force; however, because women in 1960 rarely combined work and motherhood, married full-time mothers are also counted as financially independent in both years. In 2000, just 46 percent of women and 31 percent of men aged 30 had completed all five transitions, compared with 77 percent of women and 65 percent of men at the same age in 1960.

Women—who have traditionally formed families at ages younger than men—show the most dramatic changes at early ages. Although almost 30 percent of 20-year-old women in 1960 had completed these transitions, just 6 percent had done so in 2000. Among 25-year-olds (not shown), the decrease is even more dramatic: 70 percent of 25-year-old women in 1960 had attained traditional adult status, in 2000 just 25 percent had done so. Yet, in 2000, even as they delayed traditional adulthood, 25-year-old women greatly increased their participation in the labor force to levels approaching those of 25-year-old men. The corresponding declines for men in the attainment of traditional adult status are less striking but nonetheless significant. For both men and women, these changes can largely be explained by the increasing proportion who go to college and graduate school, and also by the postponement of marriage and childbearing.

If we use the more contemporary definition of adulthood suggested in figure 1—one that excludes marriage and parenthood—then the contrasts are not as dramatic. In 2000, 70 percent of men aged 30 had left home, were financially independent, and had completed their schooling, just 12 points lower than was true of 30-year-old men in 1960. Nearly 75 percent of 30-year-old women in 2000 met this standard, compared to nearly 85 percent of women in 1960. Nonetheless, even these changes are historically substantial, and we are not even taking into account how many of these independent, working, highly educated young people still feel that they are not yet capable of supporting a family.

The reasons for this lengthening path to adulthood, John Modell has shown, range from shifting social policies to changing economic forces. The swift transition to adulthood typical after World War II was substantially assisted by the government. The GI Bill helped veterans return to school and subsidized the expansion of education. Similarly, government subsidies for affordable housing encouraged starting families earlier. At the same time, because Social Security was extended to cover more of the elderly, young people were no longer compelled

to support their parents. The disappearance or reduction of such subsidies during the past few decades may help to explain the prolongation of adult transitions for some Americans. The growing cost of college and housing forces many youth into a state of semi-autonomy, accepting some support from their parents while they establish themselves economically. When a job ends or they need additional schooling or a relationship dissolves, they increasingly turn to their family for assistance. Thus, the sequencing of adult transitions has become increasingly complicated and more reversible.

However, the primary reason for a prolonged early adulthood is that it now takes much longer to secure a full-time job that pays enough to support a family. Economists Timothy Smeeding and Katherin Ross Phillips found in the mid-1990s that just 70 percent of American men aged 24 to 28 earned enough to support themselves, while fewer than half earned enough to support a family of three. Attaining a decent standard of living today usually requires a college education, if not a professional degree. To enter or remain in the middle class, it is almost imperative to make an educational commitment that spans at least the early 20s. Not only are more Americans attending college than ever before, it takes longer to complete a degree than in years past. Census data reveal that from 1960 to 2000, the percentage of Americans aged 20, 25, and 30 who were enrolled in school more than doubled. Unlike during the 1960s, these educational and work investments are now required of women as well as men. It is little wonder then that many young people linger in early adulthood, delaying marriage and parenthood until their late 20s and early 30s.

Those who do not linger are likely those who cannot afford to and, perhaps as a result, views on how long it takes to achieve adulthood differ markedly by social class. Less-educated and less-affluent respondents—those

A faculty mentor helps a PhD student adjust her graduation hood. To earn credentials required for many middle-class jobs, students must invest in schooling throughout their 20s or even beyond. (Courtesy of Jon Wagner)

who did not attend college and those at the bottom one-third of the income ladder—have an earlier expected timetable for leaving home, completing school, obtaining full-time employment, marriage, and parenthood. Around 40 percent of the less well off in the GSS sample said that young adults should marry before they turn 25, and one-third said they should have children by this age. Far fewer of the better-off respondents pointed to the early 20s, and about one-third of them said that these events could be delayed until the 30s. These social class differences probably stem from the reality that young people with more limited means do not have the luxury of investing in school or experimenting with complex career paths.

new demands on families, schools, and government

The growing demands on young Americans to invest in the future have come at a time of curtailed government support, placing heavy demands on families. Growing inequality shapes very different futures for young Americans with more and less privileged parents.

Early adulthood is when people figure out what they want to do and how best to realize their goals. If they are lucky enough to have a family that can help out, they may proceed directly through college, travel or work for a few years, or perhaps participate in community service, and then enter graduate or professional school. However, relatively few Americans have this good fortune. Youth from less well-off families must shuttle back and forth between work and school or combine both while they gradually gain their credentials. In the meantime, they feel unprepared for marriage or parenting. If they do marry or parent during these years, they often find themselves trying to juggle too many responsibilities and unable to adequately invest in their future. Like the mother from Iowa, they do not feel "on track" or in control of their lives.

More than at any time in recent history, parents are being called on to provide financial assistance (either college tuition, living expenses, or other assistance) to their young adult children. Robert Schoeni and Karen Ross conservatively estimate that nearly one-quarter of the entire cost of raising children is incurred after they reach 17. Nearly two-thirds of young adults in their early 20s receive economic support from parents, while about 40 percent still receive some assistance in their late 20s.

A century ago, it was the other way around: young adults typically helped their parents when they first went to work, if (as was common) they still lived with their parents. Now, many young adults continue to receive support from their parents even after they begin working. The exceptions seem to be in immigrant families; there, young people more often help support their parents. A 27-year-old Chinese American from New York explained why he continued to live with his parents despite wanting to move out, saying that his parents "want me [to stay] and they need me. Financially, they need me to take care of them, pay the bills, stuff like that, which is fine."

As young people and their families struggle with the new reality that it takes longer to attain adulthood, Americans must recognize weaknesses in the primary institutions that facilitate this transition—schools and the military. For the fortunate few who achieve bachelor's degrees and perhaps go on to professional or graduate training, residential colleges and universities seem well designed. They offer everything from housing to health care while training young adults. Likewise, the military provides a similar milieu for those from less-privileged families. However, only about one in four young adults attend primarily residential colleges or join the military after high school. The other three-quarters look to their families for room and board while they attend school and enter the job market. Many of these youth enter community colleges or local universities that provide much less in the way of services and support.

The least privileged come from families that cannot offer much assistance. This vulnerable population—consisting of 10 to 15 percent of young adults—may come out of the foster care system, graduate from special education programs, or exit jails and prisons. These youth typically lack job skills and need help to secure a foothold in society. Efforts to increase educational opportunities, establish school-to-career paths, and help students who cannot afford postsecondary education must be given higher priority, even in a time of budget constraints. The United States, once a world leader in providing higher education to its citizens, now lags behind several other nations in the proportion of the population that completes college.

Expanding military and alternative national service programs also can help provide a bridge from secondary school to higher education or the labor force by providing financial credit to those who serve their country. Such programs also offer health insurance to young adults, who are often cut off from insurance by arbitrary age limits. Finally, programs for the vulnerable populations of youth coming out of foster care, special education, and mental health services must not assume that young people are fully able to become economically independent at age 18 or even 21. The timetable of the 1950s is no longer applicable. It is high time for policy makers and legislators to address the realities of the longer and more demanding transition to adulthood.

RECOMMENDED RESOURCES

Frank F. Furstenberg, Jr., Thomas D. Cook, Robert Sampson, and Gail Slap, eds. *Early Adulthood in Cross-National Perspective* (Sage Publications, 2002).

> The contributors describe the emergence of this life stage across countries and the wide variation between them in the patterns of adult transitions.

Reed W. Larson, Bradford B. Brown, and Jeylan T. Mortimer, eds. *Adolescents' Preparation for the Future: Perils and Promises* (The Society for Research on Adolescence, 2002).

> The articles in this interdisciplinary book consider how well adolescents in different societies are being prepared for adulthood in a rapidly changing and increasingly global world.

John Modell. *Into One's Own: From Youth to Adulthood in the United States 1920–1975* (University of California Press, 1989).

> Documents dramatic twentieth-century changes in the transition to adulthood and places these shifts within the context of larger economic, political, and technological changes.

Alejandro Portes and Rubén G. Rumbaut. *Legacies: The Story of the Immigrant Second Generation* (University of California Press, 2001).

Includes findings from the Children of Immigrants Longitudinal Study on the adaptation of second-generation immigrants during adolescence.

Robert Schoeni and Karen Ross. "Material Assistance Received from Families during the Transition to Adulthood." In *On the Frontier of Adulthood: Theory, Research, and Public Policy*, eds. Richard Settersten, Jr., Frank Furstenberg, Jr., and Rubén Rumbaut (University of Chicago Press, 2004).

Estimates the amount of financial assistance given to young adults by their families at different points during early adulthood.

Richard A. Settersten, Jr., Frank F. Furstenberg, Jr., and Rubén G. Rumbaut, eds. *On the Frontier of Adulthood: Theory, Research, and Public Policy* (University of Chicago Press, 2004).

Describes prolonged and complex patterns of school, work, and family transitions for young adults in America and Western Europe.

Timothy Smeeding and Katherin Ross Phillips. "Cross-National Differences in Employment and Economic Sufficiency." *Annals of the American Academy of Political and Social Science* 580 (2002): 103–33.

Examines the economic independence of young adults in seven industrialized countries.

Arland Thornton and Linda Young-DeMarco. "Four Decades of Trends in Attitudes Toward Family Issues in the United States: The 1960s Through the 1990s." *Journal of Marriage and the Family* 63 (2001): 1009–37.

The authors review survey data showing changes in Americans' attitudes toward the family.

REVIEW QUESTIONS

1. How do the authors define "early adulthood"? How do they explain the incidence of prolonged early adulthood in the United States?
2. Examine figure 2. How are the lives of young people in 2000 different from those in 1960? What do you think accounts for these differences?
3. Discuss positive and negative effects of postponing adulthood on parenting. How do you suspect this changes childrearing practices? How does having children change the careers of middle-aged workers?
4. Activity: C. Wright Mills describes the "sociological imagination" as the ability to connect "private troubles" with "public issues." Write a paragraph using your sociological imagination to examine how something you previously thought of as a private trouble in your own childhood education is connected to larger social issues.

macarthur foundation research network on an aging society

facts and fictions about an aging america 42

fall 2009

the realities of an aging society will require many adjustments in coming years. to develop sound policy, we must first unpack the myths that pass for knowledge about aging in america.

The dramatic increase in life expectancy in the United States and all other developed nations in the 20th century is one of the greatest cultural and scientific advances in our history. Yet we are woefully unprepared to address the challenges—such as potential conflicts aggravated by generational differences—and take advantage of the opportunities—unleashing the productivity inherent in a healthy elderly population, for example—that stand before us.

In this emerging "aging society," in which those over age 60 will outnumber those under 15, there remains substantial uncertainty about what life will be like for the elderly and, perhaps more importantly, for the middle-aged and younger generations that will follow in the footsteps of today's oldest Americans.

With these considerations in mind, in 2008 the MacArthur Foundation established a Research Network on an Aging Society, bringing together 12 scholars from the United States and Europe from a variety of relevant disciplines including economics, sociology, psychology, political science, medicine, public health, demography, and public policy. Our goal is to identify the changes that need to be made in many aspects of American life, including retirement, the workforce, education, and even the design of our future cities, that will enable us to deal with the challenges and take advantage of the opportunities posed by the aging of our society.

The task before us is to establish a secure infrastructure for such a society, a revised set of core elements—family, workforce, retirement, churches, political parties, communities, volunteer organizations, and financial entitlements, among others—that will be needed for our future society to function effectively. But first we must understand the realities of the current demographic transition in life expectancy and their implications for American society as a whole. Too much of what passes for knowledge and understanding of aging in America today are beliefs that are completely or partially false—myths, if you like—that must be recognized and unpacked.

> Too much of what passes for knowledge and understanding of aging in America today are myths.

myth #1: aging in america is a temporary phenomenon caused by the baby boom.

The aging world won't disappear once the baby boomers have passed on—we are well on our way toward a fundamentally new, permanent, and older age structure in our society. Yes the baby boom has contributed to the aging of American society, but so have rapid increases in life expectancy and reductions in birth rates.

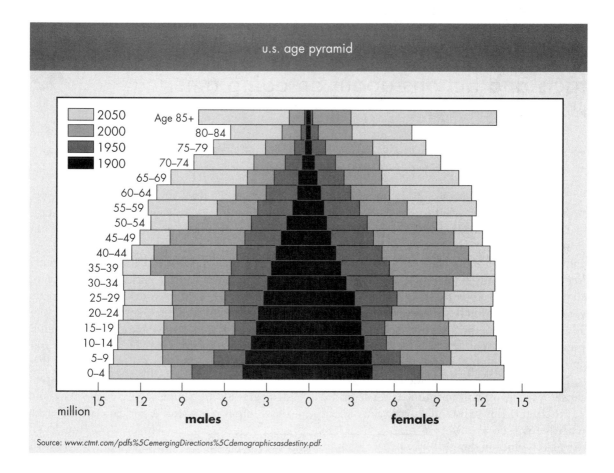

Source: www.ctmt.com/pdfs%5CemergingDirections%5Cdemographicsasdestiny.pdf.

The aging of our nation began early in the 20th century as advances in public health led to rapid reductions in infant, child, and maternal mortality. At that time, infectious diseases were the leading causes of death, as had been the case throughout human history. Because the risk of death was always high for younger ages, only a relatively small segment of every birth cohort prior to the 20th century had an opportunity to live to older ages. This characteristic pattern of mortality and survival, combined with high birth rates, produced an age distribution for America that took the shape of a pyramid—there were more younger people, situated at the bottom of the pyramid, than older people, situated at the top of the pyramid.

In the early 20th century, as young people lived longer and death rates declined further at the middle and older ages in the second half of the century, life expectancy at birth rose rapidly—by more than 30 years. For example, 42 percent of the babies born in 1900 were expected to survive past age 65, but by 2000 this rate had nearly doubled to 83 percent. The result is that death has been permanently shifted from a phenomenon among the young to one of the old. This critical component of the ongoing process of aging in America will likely remain an enduring part of our demographic destiny long after the baby boomers pass on.

Although, the baby boomers, who can first be detected at the base of the age pyramid in 1950 and by the year 2000 dominate the middle part of the age structure, are obviously important. When they were under age 65, their numbers postponed the emergence of an aging society despite increases in life expectancy, and as they cross into "old age" their vast numbers are accelerating it.

Uncertainty remains about how the health and longevity of future cohorts of older people will unfold. In recent years we've witnessed an increase in the proportion of the lifespan spent in good health and an extension of disability-free life expectancy, but this trend may not continue in the face of evidence suggesting that some younger generations are less healthy than those that preceded them into older ages. It's possible the recent increases in obesity and diabetes will actually lead to declines in life expectancy in this century. However, the quick pace of advances in biomedical technology makes scientists optimistic that advances in life expectancy in America will both accelerate and continue beyond the middle of this century.

myth #2: physical and mental capacity inevitably decline with biological aging.

Being old doesn't necessarily entail being frail. While normal human aging does involve progressively worse organ function compared to the peak in early adulthood, the impact of these physiological changes on the capacity of

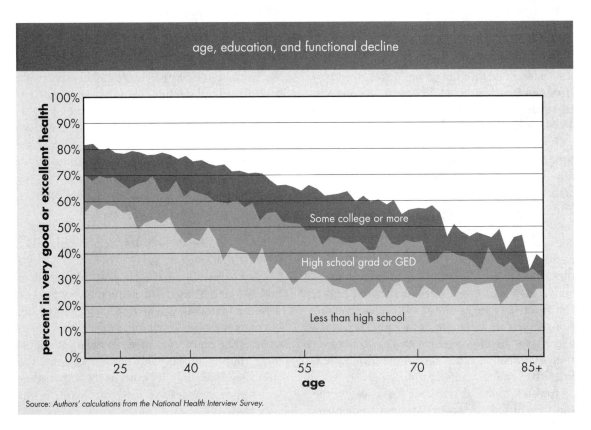

age, education, and functional decline

Source: Authors' calculations from the National Health Interview Survey.

individuals to function in society is quite modest. The exaggeration of the elderly's diminished function is due in part to archaic views that overlook the fact that people are becoming disabled later and later in their lives. Thus, not only are people living longer, but they're healthier and are disabled for fewer years of their lives than older people decades ago. This phenomenon of progressively pushing disability later and later in life is referred to as "compression of morbidity." As a result, active life span is increasing faster than total life span. The health and functional status of the elderly has been improving steadily since the early 1980s, much of it because of improvements in medical care. A landmark study published in 1994, and since confirmed by other research, found the number of elders unable to perform daily tasks decreased by 3.6 percentage points from 1982 to 1994 (from 24.9 percent to 21.3 percent). As a result, there were 1.2 million fewer disabled elders in 1994.

> The evidence doesn't show significant intergenerational conflict over old-age entitlements. In fact, quite the opposite appears to be true.

Interestingly, there's evidence from the same time period suggesting disability has increased among those younger than 65, thanks to substantial increases in rates of asthma, obesity, and diabetes. Very recent analyses show an increase in the need for personal assistance, such as help with bathing, dressing, or other basic activities of daily living among 59-year-olds. The trend, therefore, is toward a more active and healthier older population, and a less healthy younger and middle-aged population, which includes the early baby boomers. Clearly we are no longer a society with a functionally impaired older generation alongside a fit, active, younger population.

Another frame of reference for assessing the function of older people relates not to comparing them to young adults, focusing on how many health problems they have, or how they score on an individual test, but instead looking at their overall capacity to function. From this perspective, it's clear many people successfully adapt in ways that allow them to lead full, productive lives into their oldest ages. Such adaptations build on the fact that important abilities, such as perspective, experience, social values, emotional regulation, and wisdom, may all increase with age.

When it comes to functional capacity, it may be that factors other than age are driving the changes we're seeing. Some of the most important determinants of diminished capacity—cognitive and functional decline—are more closely related to socioeconomic factors including race, ethnicity, and educational attainment, than to age. As we can see in the figure "age, education, and functional decline", education in particular plays a prominent role in determining quality of life at older ages. This finding mirrors the role education plays in other social contexts. The economic returns from education in the labor market and the health benefits associated with additional years of schooling have both expanded sharply over time.

myth #3: aging mainly impacts the elderly.

That this statement appears self-evident makes it one of the most pernicious myths. The facts are that while population "aging" is driving our demographic transition, from a policy perspective the elderly are often not the most important group from the point of view of either the risks they face going forward or the impact they will feel as changes are made to adapt to our society's aging.

(MRBECK via Creative Commons)

For example, the young may lose support for education as expenditures for old-age entitlements grow, as has been the experience in some European countries. Or, perhaps the middle-aged will be strained by their responsibility to provide goods and services for a rapidly growing elderly population.

As we move ahead, the most productive strategy is not to focus on just one generation, such as the elderly, but to consider the entire society, and the interactions of the generations it includes. Only in this broader context can we consider the essential dynamics of the overall population and identify the key opportunities for meaningful change.

myth #4: in an aging society, the young and old are inevitably pitted against each other.

A number of pundits and doomsayers have long predicted that as aging baby boomers

vastly increase the ranks of older voters, class warfare in America will be fought not between the rich and poor, but between the old and young. This scenario presumes elders will be voting exclusively on the basis of their material self-interests to increase spending on Social Security, Medicare, and other old-age entitlements, thereby eroding support for educational and other programs critical to the future of younger generations. In response, the story goes, young and middle-aged voters will act out politically to reduce their "burden" of supporting elders by having their tax revenues allocated for other purposes.

It's true the number and percentage of older voters will increase substantially in the decades ahead. According to the Census Bureau, the number of voters age 65 and older is projected to increase from 40 million in 2010 to 72 million in 2030, and then to 89 million in 2050. Although people 65 and over are only 17 percent of the voting-age population today, they will be 25 percent in 2030 and stay at about that proportion until 2050.

Yet, the evidence to date doesn't show significant intergenerational conflict over old-age entitlements. In fact, quite the opposite appears to be true.

Throughout many decades of national elections (the arena most salient to Social Security and Medicare policies) there has been no credible evidence that older people vote as a unified bloc focusing only on old-age benefits. In fact, national exit polls and post-election surveys suggest the contrary. Like the overall electorate, older voters so far have differed in their political attachments, economic and social status, race and ethnicity, and many other characteristics that shape their preferences among candidates for office.

Moreover, surveys of public attitudes in the United States over the years show a surprising but consistent convergence of opinions across generations. Large, multigenerational majorities express strong support for programs directed at seniors—including both employer-based retirement benefits and Social Security—as well as educational programs for children and government assistance for the poor. Young and middle-aged adults recognize the financial relief old-age entitlements provide, and perhaps also see themselves as future beneficiaries of the programs. This finding is in line with European surveys of voting and attitudes among young and middle-aged generations. These surveys consistently show support for, rather than hostility toward, benefits for older generations.

Notwithstanding the absence of intergenerational conflict to date, it could be engendered by changes in the broader social and economic environment. Over the next several decades, for instance, younger people will be disproportionately minority—Hispanics, African Americans, and Asians—while older people remain disproportionately non-minority because 75 percent of baby boomers fall into that racial/ethnic category. Indicators such as educational attainment suggest that much of the young minority workforce over the next 30 years, like today, will be working in relatively low-wage jobs. Will a generally low-paid, young, minority population resent having to pay taxes to support entitlement programs that benefit a mostly white, relatively well-off, retired population? This potential conflict may be exacerbated if the already substantial income inequalities and access to health care keep increasing.

myth #5: policy-makers must choose between investments in youth or the elderly.

The transformation of America into an older society creates novel challenges for the Obama administration and raises questions about how to target new investments of precious public resources across the generations in education, training, and preventative health. As various advocacy groups vie for the attention of the new administration, some advocates for children's programs contend that youth are the only generation worthy of investment.

This approach views expenditures for children as investments with long-term returns for all of society and resources spent on the elderly as short-term benefits limited to the direct beneficiaries. This view belies the fact that many mid- and late-life interventions such as new skills training, efforts to enhance civic engagement and volunteerism, and programs to reduce health risks pay off. Their modest costs are more than offset by substantial intermediate and longer-term economic gains, including increased productivity and decreased health care expenditures.

It's well established that experiences and investments early in life have an important impact on later socioeconomic position, health, and well-being and that some childhood social programs, such as Head Start (pre-K) are valuable. Accumulating evidence indicates, however, that interventions spaced across an entire lifetime can have cumulative benefits better than the effects of interventions made in childhood alone.

Moreover, many programs that target the elderly have significant benefits for younger generations and should properly be seen as family programs. Social Security payments to older people relieve their middle-aged children of the economic burden of supporting their parents. But they also help the elderly support their children. European evidence shows that up to about age 80, parents continue to give their children financial and social support. And in South Africa, when older women living in extended families received a pension, granddaughters in those households were healthier over time. Such multigenerational win-win opportunities exist in many areas, including education, training and job flexibility, retirement, welfare, and health.

myth #6: the biggest public problems facing an aging america stem from social security and medicare/medicaid.

The (currently unfunded) future financial obligations of Social Security and especially Medicare and Medicaid are indeed staggering and threaten our nation's future financial stability. Nonetheless, while they're the elephant in the living room, the fact is that elephant isn't alone.

We've neglected more fundamental questions about the nature of life in an aging America, our commitments among generations, and the structure and function of our key institutions that might best allow us to achieve a productive and equitable society. As the age structure of our society changes we must reexamine the social compact between generations that has been the basis of many of our policies. What should a normal life look like in the future? Should there be more education interspersed throughout middle age so individuals will be prepared to cope productively with technological change and be able to continue to be productive later in life? Should employers have incentives to educate employees and keep them in the workforce longer? Can we develop more flexible approaches to work schedules and worksite design? Should efforts outside the workforce, such as volunteering, be encouraged in some way? Should win-win approaches that benefit multiple generations, like the South African pension example, be given special incentives? Lack of attention to these issues could prove, in the long run, to be just as damaging as the financial imbalances in entitlements.

myth #7: we can stabilize the age of our population by increasing immigration.

A couple specific issues are embedded within this myth. The first relates to the nature of the alleged problem. Many think our aging society won't have a workforce large enough because demographic shifts will increase the size of the older population relative to the young. They say we should increase immigration levels rather than or in addition to trying to keep older individuals working longer.

In truth, most estimates suggest the United States will have a sufficient overall number of workers in 2030 and 2050, assuming legal migration continues at current levels of approximately 1 million people annually. This is due in large part to the stable and relatively high total fertility rate (TFR) in the United States, which continues at or very close to the replacement rate (the rate needed to keep the population constant in size, or 2.1 births per woman). The TFR in the United States today is substantially higher than in many European countries and Japan. It's important to note, however, that while the size of the overall workforce may be sufficient for years

Being old doesn't necessarily entail being frail. The aging of America presents many opportunities. (Foreversouls via Creative Commons)

to come, it's highly likely skill gaps will emerge in particular areas, nursing and engineering among them.

A second way to look at this is that the "problem" is the result of an upward shift in the age structure of our future society, and we can "cure" this simply by importing more young people from other countries for awhile in order to mitigate the changes in our population pyramid. There are several difficulties with this approach.

First, it may seem that encouraging younger migrants to enter the country will immediately fix the problem, but the fact is, these immigrants will also grow older. A genuine fix of this kind would require a sustained stream of young immigrants entering the country every year; however, the number of immigrants we'd need to balance the age structure is very large, and may not be feasible either politically or because sufficient immigrants with the requisite capacity to participate productively in our society couldn't be identified. For example, the number of annual immigrants needed to keep the proportion of our population that is under 65 at the current level has been estimated at more than 11 million—a more than 1,000 percent increase from the current level of immigration, which is already unpopular in some circles.

The danger of myths is that they lull people into complacency. If the general public and our elected officials don't understand the reality of what's facing us, they'll essentially be in denial and unable to move forward to fix what's broken.

Our current approaches to the elderly were designed for a different society. They're based on a set of policies, like the formal and informal rules regarding work, retirement, and social security, that limit opportunities for the elderly to be productive.

If we don't change these approaches, we could end up with a dysfunctional society that will pit one generation against another, be unable to care for its citizens, provide equal opportunity for all, or be competitive in a global economy.

Some of the myths described here have proven quite durable and a significant effort will be required to educate our society with the facts about aging America. Only then can we start to develop and implement effective policies, at both the local and national levels, that will increase the likelihood that the America that emerges is productive and equitable.

In next quarter's *Contexts*, the MacArthur Aging Society Network will offer our perspectives on the major areas ripe for policy development and the key principles that should guide those efforts.

> Our current approaches to aging were designed for a different society and limit opportunities for the elderly to be productive.

RECOMMENDED RESOURCES

Dana Goldman, Jaoping Shang, Jayanta Bhattacharya, Alan M. Garber, Michael Hurd, Geoffrey F. Joyce, Darius N. Lakdawalla, Constantijn Panis, and Paul G. Shekelle. "Consequences of Health Trends and Medical Innovation for the Future Elderly." *Health Affairs* (2005) 24 Suppl 2: W5-R5–W5-R17.

> Examines how medical technology and declining health in younger generations affect the future health and medical spending of the elderly.

Robert B. Hudson, ed. *Boomer Bust? Economic and Political Issues of the Graying Society* (Vol. 1) and *The Boomers and Their Future* (Vol. 2) (Praeger, 2008).

> Provides dozens of perspectives from a multidisciplinary roster of authors on the implication of becoming an aging society.

Kenneth Manton, Larry Corder, and Eric Stallard. "Chronic Disability Trends in Elderly United States Populations: 1982–1994." *Proceedings of the National Academy of Sciences* (1997) 94: 2593–98.

Examines trends in the functional status of older generations.

Linda Martin, Vicki Freedman, Robert Schoeni, and Patricia Andrewski. "Health and Functioning among Baby Boomers Approaching 60." *Journal of Gerontology: Social Sciences* (2009) 64B(3): 369–77.

Recent evidence that the decades-long declines in disability rates in older people may be waning.

James H. Schulz and Robert H. Binstock. *Aging Nation: The Economics and Politics of Growing Older in America* (Johns Hopkins University Press, 2008).

Presents the arguments for and against the likelihood of "intergenerational warfare," proposing an alternative "family-based" perspective on entitlements.

REVIEW QUESTIONS

1. What were your preconceptions about the elderly in America before reading this article? Did the facts presented in this article debunk any of your beliefs?
2. Do you think we respect the elderly in our culture? Why or why not? Explain your opinion with examples from the article and from your own knowledge.
3. Activity: Pretend you are a policy-maker considering strategies to handle an aging population. On the basis of what you learned from this article, what should be the focus of your efforts? Now compare your ideas and speculations on this point with the next article, where the authors lay out some of their own ideas.

macarthur foundation research network on an aging society

policies and politics for an aging america   **43**

winter 2010

having previously addressed common myths about our "graying society," the authors explore long-term, multigenerational approaches to help america age gracefully.

In "Facts and Fictions About an Aging America" (*Contexts*, Fall 2009), our research group unpacked a series of widely held, interrelated misconceptions about our aging population and outlined the broad societal implications of the realities. With the realities articulated and myths exposed, we can start to explore how policy-makers can effectively invest across the lifecourse to create a successful aging society. We call for a new approach to aging—one that involves not only new policies, but also new ways to think about aging in America. Both our reframing and subsequent policy proposals will increase the likelihood that the United States, as it ages, will become a more productive and equitable society.

Over the coming decades, the age distribution of our population will shift to one that is older than it is young for the first time ever. By 2020, there will be more Americans over the age of 65 than under 15. In the United States and most developed and rapidly developing societies, this "graying" is not a transient phenomenon brought on by the baby boom. Nor is it feasible that increased immigration will mitigate the age shift. While the presence of the "baby boom" generation prevented the United States from becoming an aging society in the 20th century, as that large group now reaches 65, it will accelerate our demographic transformation, enhancing the urgency of putting the proper policies in place soon.

In our last article, we presented the facts regarding a number of ideas about aging: aging does not necessarily bring on a host of infirmities and disabilities, societal aging impacts [sic] all generations (not just the elderly), and despite the increased financial pressures of entitlements for a growing elderly population, the young and old are not inevitably pitted against each other.

Further, too many of the discussions about the "problem" of an aging America seem preoccupied with the solvency and sustainability of Social Security and Medicare. These issues must be effectively addressed, but they aren't our only, perhaps not even our biggest, challenges. And this narrow focus among policy-makers has led many to see older people as only consumers, and not producers, of resources. Understandably, young people with that outlook may begin to see their elders as competitors who consume too much of the "pie."

Finally, because we've been preoccupied by doomsday scenarios raised by the host of myths about aging, we haven't paid enough attention to tackling the very real future stresses on many of the country's core institutions and functions, like workforce participation, retirement, the family, housing, and the design of our communities. The fact is, many of these institutions weren't designed to support the needs and characteristics of the population we'll soon be. It's possible that we could solve the Social Security and Medicare crises, but without overhauling America's infrastructure, we'd still fail older and younger people alike.

long-term, multifaceted strategies

Since the aging of our society is not a temporary, baby boomer phenomenon, we must understand there will be no quick fix to solve the challenges it brings. As we move forward, we must develop long-view, intersecting policies with an understanding of the impact they will have across generations, including socioeconomic, racial, and ethnic inequalities that may actually grow during this demographic transition. No single short-term policy will save us.

> We could solve the Social Security and Medicare crises, but without overhauling America's infrastructure we'd still fail older and younger people alike.

We've learned from past policy changes that advance planning, gradual implementation, and attention to unintended societal side effects will be extremely valuable. This strategy allows adequate notice and time to citizens across the age range to plan for change. It also increases political feasibility because those citizens who are close to experiencing what might have been a radical short-term change don't have to adapt rapidly to a new, unforeseen situation.

A model example of successful advance planning and gradual implementation is the 1983 amendment to Social Security that raised the age of eligibility for full retirement benefits from 65 to 67. Under this legislation, the age of full eligibility didn't begin to change until 20 years later, in 2003, and won't become age 67 until 2027. The timing of this incremental policy change warded off any significant political opposition. Younger people had time to adjust their planning and saving for retirement over several decades. At the same time, those who had planned to retire between 1983 and 2003 were able to do so without being caught in a lurch.

The implementation has gone smoothly since the changes began in 2003.

It's also clear that we can't simply come up with a singular strategy for addressing aging. Despite the widely held belief that physical and mental capacity inevitably decline with biological aging, for instance, the overwhelming body of research demonstrates that many elderly people remain fit and highly functioning, physically and cognitively, until late in life. In fact, a large portion of the elderly are fit. The percentage of non-disabled people over age 85 in 1994 was 40.2 percent, a 5.4 percent increase from 1982 (compared with an increase of 2.6 percent for those ages 65 to 74, from 85.9 percent to 88.5 percent non-disabled). Concurrently, the percentage of highly disabled people over age 85 in 1994 was 52.7 percent, a 4.7 percent decrease over the same time period. The older people become, the less like each other they are. The fairly uniform functional status of younger groups evolves into a broad array of functional capabilities—and a broad array of needs and talents.

investing across generations

The three related misconceptions mentioned above—that societal aging mainly impacts the elderly, that in an aging society the young and old are inevitably pitted against each other, and that policy-makers must choose between investments in youth or the elderly—have led us to work under one guiding principle: we must adopt robust multigenerational and intergenerational perspectives on aging policies.

Older people are far from being the majority in an aging society. Most people in an aging society are under age 65, so we need to invest across the age spectrum. No single generation or age group should be thought of as the problematic creator of intergenerational tensions or political and policy struggles.

Moreover, many of the key determinants of successful aging are cumulative, occurring throughout the lifetime and, importantly, starting in early childhood. The people who will turn 65 between 2050 and 2070 have already been born. If we want to promote their health and well-being into old age, we need to begin now, when they are infants and children. Childhood and early adolescent experiences leave a footprint for many functions in older age. Failing to invest in education and health throughout childhood and young adulthood is shortsighted. Within a generation, the United States will reap what it has sown in this regard. Childhood social programs such as Head Start (pre-K) are valuable, and experts agree that the educational trajectory established early in life has an important impact on socioeconomic position, health, and well-being in early and late adulthood.

One study that followed individuals for 27 years after an educational intervention found that they experienced significant increases in high school graduation rates, employment, and home ownership and reductions in delinquency and teen pregnancy when compared to their peers. The wide range of abilities among older people and our understanding of the conditions that determine successful aging suggest that many such interventions across a lifetime, from early adulthood right into old age, may have a positive and lasting impact.

Prevention, including behavioral interventions, seems to offer definite benefits late in life. In a major and widely cited study of diabetes prevention, the benefits of an intensive lifestyle change (diet, exercise) were greater in the oldest age group (60–85 year olds) than for younger groups. The effect was so great that the rate of new onset of diabetes in the elders was lower (3.3 cases per 100 person years) than was seen for the 45–59 year olds and the 25–44 year olds (4.9 and 6.3 cases per 100 person years, respectively). The concept that it is ever too late for intervention is clearly false.

While early and lifelong prevention is still the optimal approach to a long and healthy life, it's important to integrate a lifelong approach to disease prevention. When it comes to health care, and many other areas, we must not choose between investments in the young or the old. We need to leverage and optimize policies that benefit people's well-being throughout their lifetimes. In fact, policies that can be leveraged to improve well-being throughout the lifetime should be optimized.

Effective policies embraced across many groups have two qualities that are especially worth noting in the context of an aging society: spillover and crossover effects. By spillover we mean that investment in one area (education, for example) affects another area in the same person (health, for example). Crossover effects are those that pass from one person to another, say from the parent to the child. Many investments in programs for the elderly benefit younger generations. For example, an important economic benefit of Social Security payments and Medicare coverage for older people is that they relieve many middle-aged children of some of the economic burden of taking care of their parents. This also leaves the adult children with more resources to support their own children.

Some policies adopted by other countries have shown crossover and spillover effects. In 1993, South Africa expanded its pension program to the black population. Roughly one-quarter of South African children lived with a pension recip-

> The aging of our society is not a temporary, baby boomer phenomenon, and no single short-term policy will save us.

ient. When older women living in extended families received a pension, their granddaughters had healthier weights and heights. This demonstrates that programs aimed at benefiting the elderly can positively affect their families, too.

Likewise, workplace flexibility and family-friendly work policies benefit those in the labor force with young children and child care responsibilities, but they're equally good for people with frail parents or partners. Flexibility in age at retirement, flex time, part-time work, and other forms of workplace consideration have obvious benefits to offer people at many stages in their lifetimes.

looking to the private sector

Regarding employment, progress is resisted by the presence of yet another myth, the belief that one must move older persons out of the workforce to make room for younger adults. Analyses in several countries have shown this to be a fallacy; and, in fact, higher older age employment rates are often associated with higher younger employment. It is important to note that not all the policies for our aging society must come from the public sector. Private sector policies regarding job flexibility, retirement, health insurance, and education over a lifetime all have the potential to create win-win situations and help multiple generations. Work-life balance policies in the corporate world have shown benefits to young and old employees alike as both confront the issues of providing care for children, parents, and other family members.

Such policies are already in place in a number of countries, and have been beneficial in terms of productivity and employee well-being.

Many private companies in Europe already realize the need for experienced staff. For example, companies value engineers who know how to repair older equipment and service personnel who know how to serve a range of customers. To help meet staffing needs and retain excellent employees, 45 percent of employers in the United Kingdom now provide job-sharing arrangements and 18 percent allow flexible work hours.

U.S. employers, who are much more likely than European firms to be privately, rather than publicly, owned are far more heterogeneous in their adoption and application of these kinds of policies. Work-life balance policies have not yet become the American norm. One reason is such policies have short-term costs including increased numbers of employees, more facilities and space requirements, and more intensive interactions between employees and human resources staff. But the long-term payoffs such as lower staff turnover and absenteeism, better recruitment possibilities, staff diversity, higher worker loyalty to the organization, and reduction in employee stress are all very attractive. We will need to be attentive to corporate needs as we consider these policies, but they certainly present one long-term policy shift that could have widespread positive impact across generations.

the societal benefits of aging

Central to our perspectives about aging and capacity is the notion that although disease and disabilities certainly increase in prevalence with advancing age, in today's and tomorrow's America older people have a wide array of capacities that are often underused. We must

> Bringing the talents of older people to disadvantaged children will not only use a pool of untapped resources, it will also build the foundation for coming generations of happy and healthy seniors.

find ways to use the abilities of older people. Moving forward we will have to create new institutions or revise our thinking about the limits and ranges we've set for work, education, housing, civic engagement, and other domains.

We need to foster the capacities of older adults. Sociologist Peter Uhlenberg outlines some scenarios for win-win policy options, prime among them is the employment of older men and women to serve as caretakers and guardians of the young, as either grandparents by kin or grandparents in a more functional sense.

In these and other roles that use the skills and abilities of older people, we see an interesting opportunity to reap a benefit from a possible challenge of aging. As discussed previously, some of the ways by which we can create a successful aging society actually start in childhood. Bringing the talents and experience of older people to bear on the problems facing disadvantaged children will not only wisely use a pool of untapped resources, it will also build the foundation for coming generations of happy and healthy seniors. Experience Corps, for example, deploys older people in public schools to help young children and adolescents, with demonstrable benefit for both groups. This program exemplifies the kinds of policies Uhlenberg suggests will be critical in confronting educational and health outcomes— essentially, performing the kinds of interventions we outlined above—among the coming generations of disadvantaged children.

Rather than allowing the devotion of increasing resources to older men and women to create divides between young and old and between the haves and have-nots, careful planning can actually bridge divides.

> Effective policies are intergenerational and equitable, emphasize new avenues to increase economic productivity, and embrace a long-term perspective.

inspiration from another sector

With these considerations in mind as we move to develop policies at many levels—from local, state, and federal public-sector policies, to those in the private sector (like those relating to work or housing)—we propose that our society look to environmental impact assessments for inspiration. In this case, however, such impacts will have to do with multigenerational investments.

We say this because in an aging society, it will be essential to maintain intergenerational equity and balance. Thus, we propose that virtually all policies for our aging society be evaluated for the impacts they have within each generation (the multigenerational perspective) and on the interactions between generations (the intergenerational effects). Environmental projects have been required to conduct impact statements like this for many years, and approximately 17 health impact assessments have been conducted across the country that evaluate the health effects of policies ranging from living-wage campaigns to housing redevelopment to the U.S. Federal Farm Bill. If by investing in the large number of older men and women we neglect younger generations, our nation will not be able to thrive, nor can our society be a successful one.

Over the next decades the United States may reap the benefits of immigration because many younger people will come seeking work, and they may have slightly higher fertility rates than the rest of our population (up to 30 percent higher, according to the U.S. Census). In the short run, the aging experiences of baby boomers may be bound to the recent waves of immigration. We should build on these joint demographic transitions to increase well-being for both boomers and recent immigrants. Yet, as we discussed in our last article, immigration won't solve all our problems.

While increasing immigration is not the answer, it will be important to invest in education and skills training for new immigrants so they can attain high-skill jobs and participate fully in our society. Increasing the underused potential of immigrants and their children is key. Offering educational opportunities and training for high-skill jobs to others in the United States who are not recent immigrants, but have historically lacked adequate resources, will also help us maintain a vibrant and diverse America as we age. Here again we see that policies for an aging society need to reinforce the goal of a more equitable distribution of resources across socioeconomic groups and the long-term integration of excluded groups from social participation.

As an interdisciplinary network we are developing specific policy recommendations for the national and local levels. Effective policies are intergenerational and multigenerational in the distribution of benefits, are oriented toward reducing disparities in health and well-being in current and future generations, emphasize new avenues to increase economic productivity, and embrace a long-term perspective. Our recommendations will be based on issues of intergenerational relations with regard to labor and educational policies, as well as on the value of advance planning and gradual implementation of policies.

With these principles in mind, we are moving to fashion a core set of strategies through which we can advocate for the healthy development of all generations of Americans, young and old alike. These strategies should include forming a coalition of stakeholders that will help design a future America that builds on the fact that we will be an aging society. It will also be essential to develop innovative approaches to work, family life, education, and civic participation.

Finally, when it comes to the challenge of planning for a successful aging society, we must remind ourselves what failure would look like. If we don't take concrete steps toward preparing our society for a steady transition into demographic change, our complacency will have created large gaps in opportunity, education, and wellness between the haves and have-nots. Society will struggle to cope with the demands for goods and services, including health care, from a large elderly population, while at the same time neglecting to take advantage of the potential productivity among the elderly.

RECOMMENDED RESOURCES

Jeremy S. Barron, Erwin J. Tan, Qilu Yu, Meilin Song, Sylvia McGill, and Linda P. Fried. "Potential for Intensive Volunteering to Promote the Health of Older Adults in Fair Health." *Journal of Urban Health* (2009), 86(4): 641–53.

> An ongoing study to improve opportunities for older Americans to volunteer, especially in intergenerational settings.

Lisa F. Berkman and M. Maria Glymour. "How Society Shapes Aging: The Centrality of Variability." *Daedalus* (2006), Winter: 105–14.

> Discusses how social and economic policies change how people and societies change.

Esther Duflo. "Grandmothers and Granddaughters: Old Age Pension and Intrahousehold Allocation in South Africa." National Bureau of Economic Research working paper 8061.

> An analysis of family effects of pension reform in South Africa.

Diabetes Prevention Program Research Group. "The Influence of Age on the Effects of Lifestyle

Modification and Metformin in the Prevention of Diabetes." *Journal of Gerontology: Medical Sciences* (2006), 61A(10): 1075–81.

Reports findings from a randomized clinical trial to prevent diabetes across age groups.

Kenneth Manton, Larry Corder, and Eric Stallard. "Chronic Disability Trends in Elderly United States Populations, 1982–1994." *Proceedings of the National Academy of Science* (1997), 94: 2593–98.

Documents disability prevalence among older Americans and the financial and policy consequences of these shifts.

Peter Uhlenberg. "Children in an Aging Society." *Journal of Gerontology Series B: Psychological Sciences and Social Sciences* (2009), 64B(4): 489–96.

Explores the impacts of an aging society on children and opportunities for intergenerational exchange and support.

REVIEW QUESTIONS

1. Which of the facts about older Americans presented in this article were most surprising to you? Explain.
2. On what grounds do the authors argue that Social Security and Medicare are not the biggest problems presented by an aging America?
3. The article states that policies to help the elderly often need to target young people in order to come to a long-term solution. Think of a problem faced by the elderly. What policies directed at children now might help alleviate that problem in the future?

vincent j. roscigno

ageism in the american workplace

44

winter 2010

a better understanding of the causes and costs of ageism, as well as the capabilities and rights of older workers, might let us overcome the "discrimination that nobody talks about."

When I wrote an article on age discrimination last year, I couldn't believe the response: countless emails and at least five phone calls a week for several months. These communications weren't coming from researchers in the field but from workers across the country, male and female, semi-skilled, skilled, and professional. They shared stories of age discrimination that they, a spouse, or a parent had experienced or were currently living through, asked for information about their rights and what could be done, and thanked me for bringing light to an issue that "nobody talks about."

They were and are correct about the neglect of age discrimination in public dialogue. There is remarkably little coverage in the popular press and, with a few exceptions, social scientists who study employment inequality often overlook ageism—a problem that Equal Employment Opportunity Commission statistics show is on the rise.

The increase in workplace ageism is due to a host of cultural, demographic, and structural factors: a society increasingly consumed by "youth," be it in culture, mass media or medicine; a large and aging baby boomer population, many of whom will remain in the workforce well into their 70s and 80s; and current corporate downsizing and globalization pressures that heighten worker insecurities and vulnerabilities. Social researchers are now documenting trends in aging workers' employment prospects and employer stereotyping and discrimination. Using both survey research and first-hand accounts by victims, they are uncovering the real social and human costs of age discrimination.

talking with victims

Almost all victims with whom I spoke related tangible costs to them or a loved one. Many conveyed fear of defaulting on mortgages or being unable to pay for their children's college after being pushed out of their current jobs. Others expressed anger and insecurity over the loss of affordable health insurance or pension benefits—benefits that they felt were both earned and owed. Just as prevalent and somewhat surprising to me in these discussions were the less-tangible, yet deeper social-psychological and emotional costs that social science research has established for racial discrimination or sexual harassment, for instance, but are only now being considered in relation to older workers.

The first-hand experiences of victims aligned closely with my own research on the topic. Karen, for instance, told me about her mother who, several months prior, was pushed out of her job of 20 years and replaced with a 25-year-old. Her mother felt isolated and helpless. She continues to cry at night, months later, due to the loss of a job, loss of friends she loved, and an overarching violation of trust by her employer. "She thought of her colleagues as

Skilled and dedicated workers, older people may be one asset employers overlook. (Bernard Pollack via Creative Commons)

her family," Karen noted, "but now it is her family that abandoned her like . . . like she just doesn't matter. It killed her inside . . . It's still killing her inside."

Violations of trust, despite a history of hard, dedicated work and good citizenship, seemed especially poignant. Joe, a committed maintenance worker, talked with me just as he was "being pushed out" after 23 years of work. He expressed anger—anger triggered by violations of a "normative social contract," wherein employee dedication and hard work are met with employer obligation and "making good" on past promises. "They now don't want to pay me my pension. I was a good worker for them and always did everything they asked. I went out of my way to help train people and make everything run smoothly, so everybody was happy and it was a good place to work. And now this is what I get, like I never really mattered to them. It's just not right."

age stereotypes at work

Stereotypes—negative generalizations about entire groups of people—indicate status and

inequality that can spur discriminatory behaviors and actions. Although employers may say they want long-term, experienced, dedicated workers, survey research tells us they tend to view older workers like Joe and Karen's mother as expensive, inflexible, possibly stubborn or forgetful, and bad for the company image. We also know from reports and surveys from organizations like the AARP that more than half of aging workers have either experienced age discrimination on their jobs or witnessed such discrimination toward others.

Erdman Palmore of the Duke University Center for the Study of Aging and Human Development reports that 84 percent of Americans over 60 years old report one or more incidents of ageism, including insulting jokes, disrespect, patronizing behavior, and assumptions about frailty or ailments. Such patterns are manifested by a culture consumed with "youth"—a culture passed to young people through socialization and then reproduced in institutions and organizations like the workplace.

Surveys, interviews, and experimental research all uncover ageism in employment. Classic work by Benson Rosen and Thomas Jerdee, for example, revealed perceptions of older workers as less responsive, if not resistant, to workplace changes. A more recent book by social psychologist Todd Nelson confirms this point, revealing how managers and younger coworkers tend to view older workers as inflexible, slow, unorganized, difficult, and expensive to train. Such stereotypes, which sometimes take a gender-specific character, are notable given that older workers often exhibit greater job commitment, less turnover, and lower rates of absenteeism than do younger workers.

No doubt some employers try to protect older workers from discriminatory treatment in an effort to maintain a well-trained, highly skilled labor force. Yet an emerging body of research is finding that employers invoke age stereotypes and discrimination to help justify cost savings for the business. This may be especially true for skilled workers, such as those in manufacturing, given recent trends in globalization, downsizing, and corporate restructuring. Indeed, such economic trends and employers' responses to them have created a structurally vulnerable, aging workforce or, as Arne Kalleberg described in his 2009 Presidential Address to the American Sociological Association, "precarious work" and "insecure workers."

economics and vulnerability

There is solid evidence of growing insecurity among all workers, but perhaps especially among aging workers, beginning in the 1990s and continuing to the present. The United States has witnessed mass layoffs, declining relative wages, the growth of part-time and temporary work, and what Robert Valletta of the Federal Reserve Bank of San Francisco describes as an "employer breach of implicit employment arrangements." Here, Valletta is referring to the "normative social contract" described earlier—the expectation that good workplace citizenship and tenure will be rewarded with security and job benefits.

In the face of corporate restructuring and downsizing, replacing older with younger workers may be seen by some employers as a cost-savings technique,

> An emerging body of research is finding that employers invoke age stereotypes and discrimination to help justify cost savings.

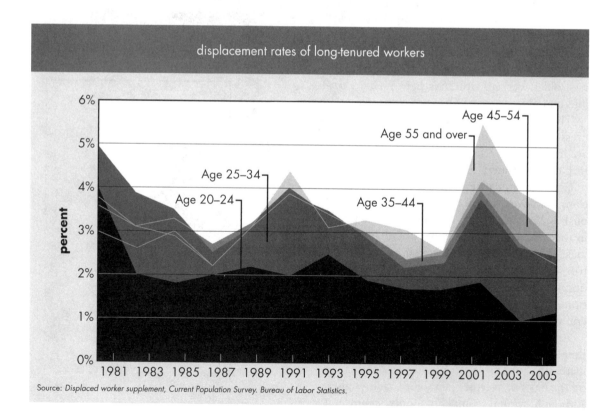

displacement rates of long-tenured workers

Source: Displaced worker supplement, Current Population Survey. Bureau of Labor Statistics.

insomuch as pension payouts can be circumvented and wages decreased. Moreover, health benefit payouts can be held in check, and promotions and on-the-job training opportunities can be reserved for younger workers who are often seen as cheaper and more worth the long-term investment. The consequences, particularly for higher skilled older workers, have included significant job displacement over the past twenty years, involuntary exit from the labor market, and downward mobility upon reemployment.

Research on long-term employment by Princeton economist Henry Farber corroborates such findings, reporting deterioration of jobs in the private sector from 1990 to 2006, with tenure declining substantially for workers over 40 years of age. What this means is that older workers are being "displaced" or pushed out of long-term employment at an even higher rate than younger workers. This occurs largely through plant closings and job elimination. Employers have some discretion in deciding which plants to close and jobs to eliminate, which can disadvantage older workers who may have higher earnings and more expensive benefits packages.

Though this sort of vulnerability to economic pressure is not the same as discrimination, there are important overlaps that suggest they are, in fact, closely related. First, as I found in my study of age discrimination suits, the very justifications employers use to discriminate against and push out aging workers are often "age-neutral" in tone, incorporating rhetoric about "cost savings," "downsizing," and "restructuring." This is true even when no such formal restructuring occurs. Second, the pattern of age discrimination suits nationally closely mirrors more general worker displacement trends.

Age discrimination complaints to the Equal Employment Opportunities Commission are increasing rapidly in proportion to complaints on the basis of race, sex, disability, and religion. Although formal complaints only capture a

sliver of the discriminatory acts occurring in the real world, the data point to an absolute as well as a relative increase in age discrimination. The raw number of case filings, monetary awards for damages, and percentage of cases settled in the employee's favor also show that age discrimination charges and their seriousness are on the rise, paralleling the broader trends in worker displacement. The costs are multidimensional and serious.

tangible costs, emotional scarring, and injustice

Much age discrimination in the American economy is linked to being fired, let go, or laid off, often preceded by a period of outright harassment or unequal terms and conditions of employ-

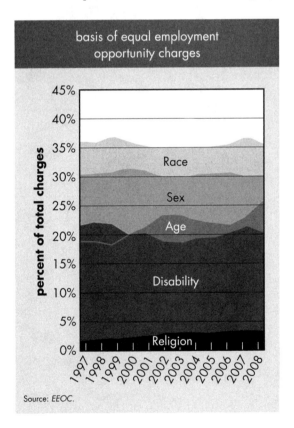

Source: EEOC.

ment (such as being asked to perform tasks other employees are not asked to do). The consequences can be numerous and wide-ranging.

There are immediate costs surrounding wage and benefits losses and the need to find new employment. With Sherry Mong, Reginald Byron, and Griff Tester, I studied both the age discrimination process and the resulting job security and financial hardships, based on 120 discrimination cases verified by state Civil Rights investigators. Consider, for example, the case of Jim Terry, a shift foreman who was terminated and replaced by a younger employee just 23 days prior to his 30-year anniversary with the company. Jim was cross-trained in several areas and could have easily performed any of the duties in his department. Yet he was terminated for minor "infractions" when other foremen were not. Consequently, his pension benefits were cut by about $300 per month, and his medical and life insurance were immediately shut off. Sarah Ray, an African American executive secretary for a government agency, was pushed into involuntary retirement after 21 years with her employer and, like Jim, received only a portion of her pension as a result: "At 59 years of age I felt desperate because of the financial situation in our home that I had to do something to keep money coming. So, at that choice—at that time, I retired even though that's not what I wanted to do . . ."

The push to create and maintain a young workforce due to stereotypes of aging workers and their assumed higher costs means that companies may feel pressure to both purge older workers from their ranks and hire younger rather than older workers. This two-pronged pressure—in employer biases about who to purge and who to hire—makes older workers vulnerable in both the hiring and firing process.

They are susceptible to being pushed out or laid off, to be sure. But once they are out, they will also expend disproportionate time and energy seeking reemployment elsewhere.

According to recent data from the Bureau of Labor Statistics, about 65 percent of all displaced workers find gainful employment within two years of the initial job loss. Workers 55 and older, however, encounter the greatest obstacles and worst prospects for reemployment. For them, reemployment often occurs in part-time or temporary work with lower wages and job benefits. And, as time passes, many give up job searches and take themselves out of the labor market altogether. As Sarah Rix of the AARP wrote in *Aging and Work: A View from the United States*, labor analysts and advocates for older workers have long been concerned with the extent to which older workers become discouraged.

Beyond the employment and wage toll, then, age discrimination also brings psychological, social, and emotional costs—costs that deserve attention. Aging research on employment disruptions, such as that by Victor Marshall and colleagues, shows how unplanned job losses bring adverse health effects for both men and women. My own conversations with victims also brought out such impacts, especially for social psychological well-being and depression. It began with 56-year-old Margaret, an administrative assistant, who was terminated without just cause several months earlier. She described herself as forever "emotionally scarred." Catching me somewhat off guard by that phrase, I asked what she meant, to which she replied, "I am drained. Besides having to start over and find a new job, I no longer know who to trust. I lost most of my friends. And I have little faith left to believe anything an employer might tell me."

> A two-pronged pressure makes older workers vulnerable in both the hiring and firing process.

An architect by trade, John Cuningham hopes to keep working—and contributing—for as long as possible. (Courtesy of by Bill Alkofer)

After our talk, I couldn't help but revisit the other phone conversations and e-mail communications I had been having, recognizing similar emotional currents running well beyond concerns about lost wages, benefits, and newly encountered economic insecurity. Like Margaret, Joe, and Karen's mother quoted earlier, many of those encountering age discrimination were clearly injured by the unexpected nature of what unfolded and what it meant for their friendships, sense of identity, and overall sense of fairness. Of course, some sought justice through the legal system. Many became even more cynical, however, about what had occurred and about the overarching power of employers. In an e-mail, Michael, an electrical engineer who recently went through litigation, wrote:

> That experience has taught me that the legal system is no deterrent to the workplace age discrimination that you have described in your paper. Litigation takes 4–7 years, the laws regarding age discrimination are weak, the state and federal agencies set up to protect older workers are effected [sic] by politics and the same cultural influences you describe, the legal process "rules" regarding permissible age discrimination "damages" claims do not provide adequate deterrence, and older workers making under $75k (median household income is ~$55k) do not have access to the legal system (on a "contingency fee" basis) because the possible returns to an attorney are not worth the time ("the business of law").

Importantly, the people making these comments considered themselves good, hard-working people and long-term dedicated employees. They believed, at some earlier point, what culture tells us about employment and effort: namely, that hard work, commitment, and dedication are reciprocated. And according to them, this is precisely what their employers claimed to have wanted in employees. Many were terminated, regardless. Others were harassed by supervisors and co-workers. And some were isolated or relegated to less-desirable, sometimes lower-paid positions.

That victims of age discrimination experience psychological stress and emotional scarring should not come as a surprise given what we know about the impact of race and sex discrimination on well-being and how harassment and bullying affect social and emotional health. What is unique about age discrimination, however, is the lack of attention to the psychological and emotional damage it may cause and the long-term sense of injustice and emotional turmoil, if not outrage, that victims experience when the "normative social contract" that bound them to employers is abridged. To the extent that such a contract still exists, it is being fundamentally altered if not altogether dismantled via globalization, restructuring, and corporate downsizing. This seems to be bolstered by employers' willingness to discriminate despite formal federal protections. Aging workers—all of us, eventually—are a major casualty.

fighting ageism

Current trends—in downsizing, in the aging baby boomer generation, and in rates of discrimination complaints—certainly suggest a growing problem. Yet growing recognition of the causes, costs, and legal status of age discrimination could alter this trajectory.

Understanding and appreciating the attitudinal and behavioral dimensions of ageism could well provide the knowledge base needed to sensitize public and human resource audiences to aging workers' true capabilities and their legal right to equitable treatment. Social science can play an important role in this regard by distilling the causes in digestable form and laying bare the human toll of age discrimination. Employers, for their part, need not only be held accountable for unfair treatment, but must also become better informed about the business costs of engaging in unfair treatment of older

> Social science can play an important role by distilling the causes and laying bare the human toll of age discrimination.

employees. Although employers may see the purging of older workers as a cost-saving technique, in the process they are losing talent, experience, and a stable and predictable workforce.

Workplace age discrimination is ultimately illegal, and perhaps that is where the greatest challenge lies. The Age Discrimination in Employment Act provides aging workers with federal legal protection against much of the conduct described in this article, yet age discrimination persists and is likely intensifying. Lack of knowledge about legal protections and avenues for recourse is partly to blame. More prominent, however, is limited corporate accountability and disparities in resources and power in the legal-judicial process. Such disparities make it difficult for victims to mount challenges, allowing age discrimination to go, for the most part, unchecked. Some recent and proposed changes to discrimination law and practice include time extensions to charge filing, greater resources and investigative oversight powers for the EEOC and state civil rights commissions, and the removal of damage caps for companies found guilty of violations. Such reforms would help bring older workers the protections already guaranteed in law—and bring to light the discrimination that "nobody talks about."

Employers of older workers benefit from the talent and experience of a stable workforce. (Courtesy of Bill Alkofer)

RECOMMENDED RESOURCES

Arne L. Kallenberg. "Precarious Work, Insecure Workers: Employment Relations in Transition." *American Sociological Review* (2007), 74:1–22.

> Addresses the implications of recent economic shifts for worker vulnerabilities and insecurities.

Todd Nelson. *Ageism: Stereotyping and Prejudice Against Older Persons* (MIT Press, 2004).

An examination of the manifestations of age stereotypes in our culture.

Erdman B. Palmore. "Research Note: Ageism in Canada and the United States." *Journal of Cross-Cultural Gerontology* (2004), 19:41–46.

Gives generalizeable statistical data, for both the United States and Canada, on attitudes toward older citizens and the experiences of older persons.

Vincent J. Roscigno, Sherry Mong, Reginald Byron, and Griff Tester. "Age Discrimination, Social Closure, and Employment." *Social Forces* (2007), 86:313–34.

Looks at the dynamics of age discrimination in employment, drawing on qualitative content from verified case files.

Robert G. Valetta. "Declining Job Security." *Journal of Labor Economics* (1999), 17:S170–97.

Provides an overview of increasing worker insecurity and the changing nature of the employer-employee relationship.

REVIEW QUESTIONS

1. Why is ageism the "discrimination that nobody talks about"?
2. What are some of the stereotypes about older people that lead to employment discrimination against them? Are there stereotypes about young people that could spur ageist discrimination? What can be done to dispel myths and reduce discrimination in either case?
3. How is discrimination related to economics? How might the current economic recession affect ageism in the workplace?

deborah carr

golden years? poverty among older americans **45**

winter 2010

since the 1970s, the elderly poverty rates have declined. however, deborah carr asks if this historical trend masks data about late-life poverty.

In the wake of the Bernard Madoff investment scandal, the television news broadcast heart-wrenching images of devastated older adults—many living in the tony enclaves of West Palm Beach, Florida—whose fortunes had evaporated in Madoff's Ponzi scheme. Although few of the victimized retirees are indigent, their declin-

ing fortunes did cast the spotlight on a social issue that has been largely neglected over the past several decades: the economic well-being of older adults.

The economic standing—and poverty levels, more specifically—of Americans ages 65 and older has fallen off the national radar, replaced

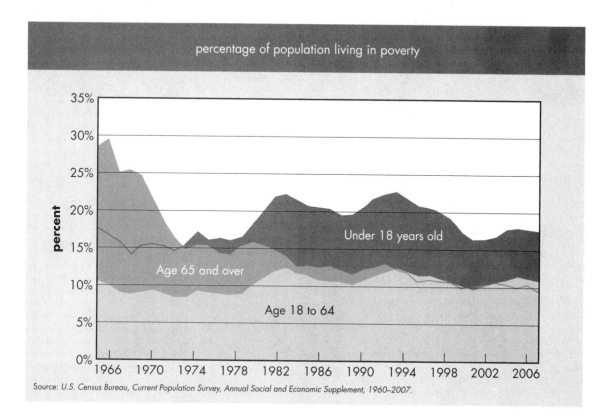

percentage of population living in poverty

Under 18 years old

Age 65 and over

Age 18 to 64

Source: U.S. Census Bureau, Current Population Survey, Annual Social and Economic Supplement, 1960–2007.

by widespread concerns over child poverty. A quick look at historical data might lead the casual observer to conclude that this shift in focus is justified. Elderly poverty rates declined sharply from 35 percent in 1959 to 15 percent by the 1970s. The proportion of older persons living in poverty has wavered between 10 and 12.5 percent since the 1980s. Child poverty rates, by contrast, climbed through the 1960s and 1970s, surpassed elderly poverty rates in 1974, and have fluctuated between 17 and 20 percent ever since.

But the decline and stabilization of overall poverty rates among older adults reveals an incomplete portrait of late-life poverty. Poverty rates among older adults range from just 3.1 percent among white married men to an astounding 37.5 percent for black women who

live alone and 40.5 percent for Hispanic women living alone. In other words, older women of color who live alone are more than ten times as likely as their white married male counterparts to be poor. Moreover, recent research by the National Academy of Sciences suggests that overall poverty rates among older adults may be severely underestimated because the current measure fails to consider the high (and rising) costs of medical care, which disproportionately strike older adults.

How can we make sense of the fact that overall elderly poverty levels have dropped precipitously over the past four decades, while some subgroups of older adults remain at great risk of impoverishment? The overall declines in elderly poverty rates are due to Social Security benefits, which remain the nation's largest

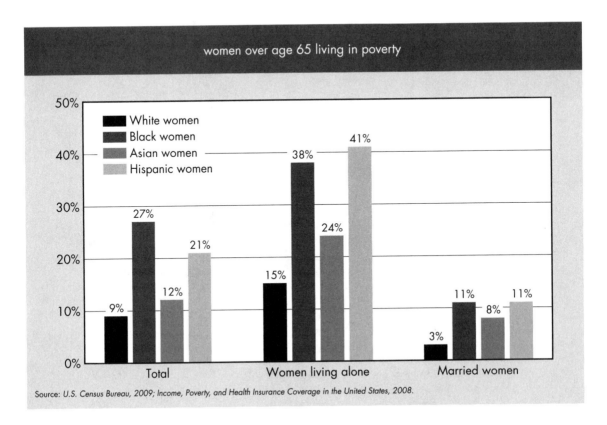

women over age 65 living in poverty

Legend: White women, Black women, Asian women, Hispanic women

Total: White women 9%, Black women 27%, Asian women 12%, Hispanic women 21%
Women living alone: White women 15%, Black women 38%, Asian women 24%, Hispanic women 41%
Married women: White women 3%, Black women 11%, Asian women 8%, Hispanic women 11%

Source: U.S. Census Bureau, 2009; Income, Poverty, and Health Insurance Coverage in the United States, 2008.

social welfare program. The Social Security Act was signed by President Franklin D. Roosevelt in 1935 as part of the New Deal. The intention was to provide "social insurance," or income protection, for older adults. During the program's first three decades, though, its benefits barely provided a minimum standard of living because monthly payments were not adjusted annually to offset inflation.

The first-ever beneficiary of Social Security, retired legal secretary Ida May Fuller, received a benefit of $22.54 in January 1940, and her monthly checks remained at that amount for more than a decade. In 1950, benefits were raised for the first time. In 1972, Congress enacted a law that allowed for annual and automatic Cost of Living Adjustments (COLAs). The current average monthly payment is $1,094. Econo-

mists estimate that without Social Security, the 2008 elderly poverty rate would be 40—rather than 9.4—percent.

Given these advances, why do poverty levels remain higher among women, especially unmarried women and persons of color? Experts point to three main explanations. First, most women have had lower-paying jobs, more sporadic employment, and more part-time work over the lifecourse than their male counterparts. Because of stark gender differences in lifetime earnings (on which Social Security benefits are based), women's own benefits are lower than those of their male peers. (Housework and childcare are unpaid activities and thus are not directly calculated into benefits levels.) Given the "double jeopardy" of being a woman and

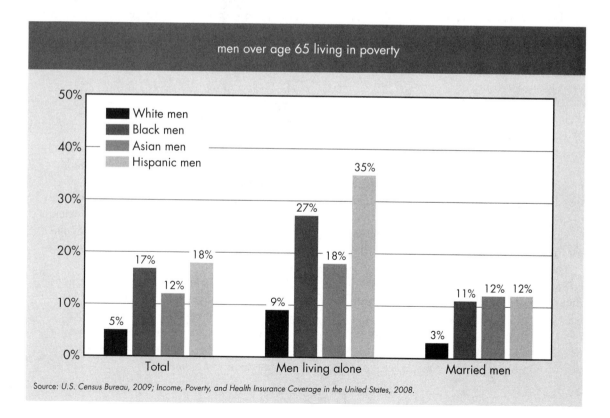

Source: U.S. Census Bureau, 2009; Income, Poverty, and Health Insurance Coverage in the United States, 2008.

an ethnic minority in the labor market, benefits are typically lower for blacks and Latinos than for whites, thus the particularly disadvantaged state of older women of color.

Second, women (and especially women of color) are less likely than men to receive private pensions. This is due to women's more discontinuous work histories and their tendency to work part-time or in occupations providing few benefits. This pattern contributes to late life poverty because private pension benefits are an important supplement to monthly Social Security benefits. While roughly one-third of older men receive a private pension, only 18 percent of women do so. Among those who receive a pension, men's pensions are nearly twice the size of women's. In 2000, the median private pension or annuity income for older women was $4,100 compared to men's $7,800.

Finally, women who have lost a husband to death forsake his employment income if he is working at the time of death or his pension income if he is retired at the time of death. Widows also must pay high end-of-life medical expenses and funeral bills that can overwhelm their already low income and savings. Further, married couples tend to underestimate the number of years that a widow will outlive her husband, so they may not plan their savings and investments accordingly. As a result, older widowed women, especially those who faced economic disadvantages earlier in life, are at an elevated risk of late-life poverty relative to their married male counterparts.

Despite tremendous improvements in overall economic well-being among older adults during the past half-century, the future looks bleak—at least for some elders. Some experts argue that the current government indicator of poverty does not adequately capture the economic realities of late life. The National Academy of Sci-

ences has proposed a new calculation that takes into account rising health care costs. Under this new formula, the proportion of older adults living in poverty would double from just over 9 percent to 18.6 percent. (By contrast, the overall U.S. poverty rate would increase only slightly from 12.5 to 15.3 percent).

To compound matters, for the first time since 1975, Social Security recipients won't get an automatic cost of living increase in their benefits in 2010. Increases are tied to inflation, and inflation was negative in 2009. To offset the flat payments, President Barack Obama vowed to send all seniors a one-time $250 payment. However, this payment may be little consolation to those older adults with declining assets and investment income due to the collapse of the housing bubble, failed investments, and falling stock prices. Fortunate older adults may find their retirement years to be "golden," while others may need to continue working far past age 65 just to maintain a minimum standard of living.

REVIEW QUESTIONS

1. The author notes that although adult poverty rates have dropped, they remain high for some groups. Which groups remain more disadvantaged? Why might this be the case?

2. If Social Security disappeared, how would it alter the landscape for retirees? What effects might a "Social Security crash" have on the American economy in general?

3. Activity: Interview your parents/guardians and grandparents about their retirement expectations. How do their hopes and expectations compare? Are your views for your own future similar? What about your future quality of life?

part 11

Medicine and Health

william marsiglio

healthy dads, healthy kids

46

fall 2009

body images and caregiving ideals make it difficult for men to prioritize health for themselves and their children. understanding those constraints is essential for cultivating a more engaged, health-conscious style of fathering.

Far too many babies and children in the United States today struggle with myriad conditions that negatively affect their emotional, mental, and physical health. We initially see this tragedy in the high rates of infant mortality and low-birth-weight babies and then in the discouragingly high numbers of youth who are obese, get pregnant, contract a sexually transmitted infection, smoke, binge drink, abuse drugs, develop an eating disorder, or attempt suicide. Sadly, when young people look at adult men they often find poor role models who are ill equipped to help them avoid or correct unhealthy behaviors.

One third of American men are obese and one in 10 will become an alcoholic in his lifetime. Men are more likely than women to smoke, eat fatty foods, drink and drive, use guns, play violent sports, and not get enough sleep, and they're less likely to use seatbelts. Men are also less likely than women to seek medical attention for either routine physicals or when more serious problems occur.

Many factors contribute to children's poor health, but one we hear little about is how fathers act and what they do and don't say about health. Indeed, what men say and do can help prevent or minimize some of their chil-

> Understanding how fathers make decisions is essential for cultivating a more engaged, health-conscious style of fathering.

dren's health problems and effectively manage the adverse effects when problems do arise.

However, social pressures and financial struggles limit the choices men can make to prioritize health for themselves and their children. Understanding how fathers make decisions, as well as their social networks and diverse experiences over their lifetimes, is essential for cultivating a more engaged, healthconscious style of fathering that will, in turn, positively affect their children's health.

The theory of "constrained choice," developed by health policy experts Chloe Bird and Patricia Rieker, can guide efforts to help fathers do a better job in this regard. Touted as a "platform for prevention," the theory suggests that individuals' opportunities to pursue healthy options are shaped by decision-making processes at multiple levels: nation/state, community, workplace, family, and individual. By paying attention to gender-based health disparities, this framework also highlights the diverse social forces that organize men's and women's lives differently. These conditions, along with biological processes and other social realities like socioeconomic status, expose men and women to specific stresses, burdens, and health risks. Consequently, men in general, and fathers in particular, face unique challenges to assert themselves as more positive role models for healthy behavior.

We're entering a propitious moment in history to foster real changes in how fathers perceive, practice, and promote health. President Barack Obama's commitment to reforming health care on multiple levels while promoting preventative care and wellness resonates with Bird's and Rieker's idea that individuals' health experiences are shaped by a multilayered social context and their call for prevention strategies. Indeed, as an outspoken public advocate of getting men to step up and become more involved fathers, Obama and his administration are poised to spearhead cultural, policy, and programmatic changes that could link health promotion with good fathering.

connecting fathers' and children's health

Since the 1980s scholars have explored extensively how fathers from all kinds of families are involved with their children and how that involvement affects their children. Currently, a nascent and promising multidisciplinary research agenda (involving sociologists, nurses, pediatric psychologists, and public health experts) considers how fathers' health consciousness, practices, and outcomes relate to their children's quality of health and care. Attention has even been given to how men's actions prior to a child's conception or birth can influence that child's health.

Political scientist Cynthia Daniels argues that men's behaviors can indeed make a difference. Prevailing cultural conceptions of how masculinity is related to reproduction, she observes, have compromised scientific assessments of how sperm damaged from toxicity at work and at war, as well as from men's smoking, drinking, and drug habits, produces negative outcomes for fetuses and infants. She also notes that scientists

and funding agencies apply a higher level of scrutiny when reviewing reproductive studies of male sperm compared to those examining female reproductive issues. Such scientific bias has perpetuated the public's disproportionate interest in how women's allegedly bad behavior increases fetal health risks while largely ignoring how men's preconception experiences can negatively contribute to fetal and children's health. Indeed, Daniels argues that many have resisted human and animal research that suggests connections between males and both birth defects and childhood diseases, in part because it "places men closer and closer to culpability for the health problems of their children."

In addition to direct biological influences, various studies show that fathers may indirectly affect children's health outcomes by influencing the mother's prenatal and early postnatal behavior and stress levels. Researchers can't say definitively whether and how men make a difference, but as sociologist Rachel Kimbro's work from the Fragile Families and Child Wellbeing study indicates, women in more stable and supportive relationships do exhibit more positive prenatal health behaviors. They're more apt to receive prenatal care and less likely to smoke, drink, or abuse drugs during pregnancy. Women with partners who have completed at least some college have lower odds of smoking and using drugs during pregnancy. (On the other hand, these women have higher odds of drinking occasionally during pregnancy and, surprisingly, fathers' education is not related to the women's inadequate prenatal care.)

Health policy researcher Laurie Martin and colleagues also show that fathers with at least a high school education, first-time fathers, and those who want a pregnancy are more likely to be involved prenatally. And health researchers Manoj Sharma and Rick Petosa argue that partners' views consistently play a major role in whether mothers start and sustain breastfeeding.

Finally, Craig Garfield, a pediatrician at the Evanston Northwestern Healthcare Research Institute, confirms that fathers' poor postnatal mental health brings on negative consequences for both children's developmental outcomes and maternal mental health.

Resident and nonresident fathers have many opportunities to affect their children's health beliefs and practices after the infant and toddler years as well. Though relatively few studies have explored these possible links, sociologist Chadwick Menning's longitudinal research with a national sample suggests that nonresident fathers' greater involvement with their adolescent children reduces the likelihood the children will begin smoking regularly. This outcome changes with fathers' level of involvement. Furthermore, children are more likely to smoke when their fathers smoke.

Menning's earlier research with family demographer Susan Stewart paints a similar portrait of resident and nonresident fathers' contributions to their children's obesity. Chil-

> How men see their own bodies and their role as caregivers shapes the role fathers play in their kids' health.

dren are more likely to be obese if their fathers (or mothers) are obese, they found. Among nonresident fathers, those more highly educated and more involved with their children tend to have children at lower risk for obesity. Similar trends are evident among white, rural families in Iowa, where fathers' lack of exercise, poor eating, excessive drinking, and smoking predicts the same behaviors among adolescents. Lower family social status, as measured by education, increases fathers' chances of exhibiting health-risk lifestyles, partly explaining the path of intergenerational transmission of poor health behaviors from fathers to adolescents.

Fathering may also have significant health consequences for fathers themselves. For example, Garfield, the Northwestern pediatrician, describes how stressful experiences associated with fathering can accumulate and debilitate fathers' health over time. Presumably, fathers at risk of experiencing this pattern include those frustrated by their inability to fulfill their breadwinning role because of low wages or job loss, as well as those working stressful, high-risk jobs for the money.

masculine body images, caregiving ideals

How men see their own bodies and their role as caregivers shapes the role fathers play in influencing their kids' health. Boys and men are regularly exposed to media, family, peers, and other sources that transmit messages about health. How they think about gender and social class, for example, affects how they construct images of manliness, perceive their own and others' bodies, manage friendships, and approach fathering.

Discussions about health are influenced by how males think about gender and their

Men who work at dangerous jobs may compromise their reproductive health as well as their safety and well-being. (Brian Del Vecchio via Creative Commons)

individual exposure to stress and risk, factors themselves that are affected by various social processes and limited—constrained—choices, be they cultural, structural, or interpersonal. For example, the messages permeating organized sports, friendships, and workplaces often encourage males to assert a stoic, risk-taking, and "hard" image that rejects expressions of vulnerability and femininity.

Sociologist Michael Messner asserts that contrary to popular wisdom, boys' and men's sports activity often breeds "unhealthy practices, drug and alcohol abuse, pain, injury, and (in some sports) low life expectancy." Referencing the "pain principle," Messner observes that if boys don't learn to "'shake it off,' ignore their own pain, and treat their bodies as instruments to be used—and used up—to get a job done . . . [then] they may lose their position on the team, or they may be labeled as 'women,' 'fags,' or 'pussies' for not being manly enough to play hurt."

The masculine ideology that perpetuates bodily harm extends well beyond the sports world, whether it's excessive drinking, drug use, fast driving, fighting, or some other display of a potentially self-destructive behavior. Much of this is tied to and supported by males having friends and acquaintances who take unnecessary risks.

For example, in his recent book *Guyland*, gender scholar Michael Kimmel discusses the disturbing way peer pressure fuels hazing rituals. In fraternities, young men seduced by the masculine status that flows from belonging to a tightly knit, all-male group, subject themselves to humiliation and sometimes untold health risks. A 2008 study of hazing in more than 50 schools found drinking was involved in the hazing of 31 percent of the men, and 17 percent "drank until they passed out."

Consistent with sociologist Erving Goffman's view that "men must be prepared to put up their lives to save their faces," men who work dangerous jobs as loggers, miners, construction workers, police officers, firefighters, EMTs, and the like are engulfed in an atmosphere that defines the drama of manhood as physical, fearless, and full of risk. Granted recent studies, such as the compelling ethnography of wildland firefighters by sociologist Matthew Desmond, suggest a much more complex picture, where the skills and dispositions children and adolescents acquire from their blue-collar upbringing prepare them to view as unthreatening the high-risk work many will perform as young men. What's fascinating, Desmond and others have observed, is that men don't avoid, but instead actively pursue, jobs that threaten their bodies and health.

In recent decades, diverse tactics have been used to persuade adult men to adopt a more attentive self-care philosophy. Men have been encouraged to become more body conscious, embrace healthier life practices, and develop closer ties with the health-care community. Magazines launched since the late 1980s like *Men's Health* found a niche among an expanding segment of professional men eager to learn the latest developments in nutrition, fitness training, and body care. Increasingly, too, a range of books, newsletters, magazines, websites, and other media outlets have driven the boom industries to educate men about a host of issues including prostate, colon, and heart care; testosterone therapy; hair replacement and surgical implants; and, of course, erectile dysfunction therapies.

Just as men's health advocates try to transform negative perceptions of self-care as feminine, they must wrestle with the notion that providing care for the ill or disabled is women's "work." Women are more likely than men to practice caregiving, but as social worker Betty Kramer and sociologist Edward Thompson illustrate in their edited volume *Men as Caregivers*, many men are effective caregivers. Estimates indicate that between 14 percent and 18 percent of men informally provide various forms of caregiving for needy friends and family.

Yet mainstream cultural messages downplay fathers' caregiving capacity and ability to address children's health-care needs. Parenting magazines and books are commonly tailored to informing moms more so than dads about the newest and best ways to care for and protect their children. This gender bias has been so engrained in the public's mind that a book published in 2004, *From Boys to Men: A Woman's Guide to the Health of Husbands, Partners, Sons, Fathers, and Brothers,* seems intuitively marketable whereas serious doubts would accompany its hypothetical counterpart, *From Girls to Women: A Man's Guide to the Health of Wives, Partners, Daughters, Mothers, and Sisters.* Whether it's wiping noses in a childcare facility or wiping bottoms in a nursing home, societal images depict women as best suited for these positions, and the social networking patterns that shape fathers' everyday lives reinforce these stereotypes.

In her book *Do Men Mother?* sociologist Andrea Doucet interviewed Canadian primary-caregiving fathers, most of whom were single fathers or stay-at-home dads. She reports that even highly motivated fathers find it difficult to feel comfortable at young children's playgroups, which they perceive as dominated by suspicious, unwelcoming mothers. Men's less intimate and more competitive friendship styles may also curtail fathers' willingness to discuss with other men their insecurities about fathering or focus on children's needs. Although Doucet doesn't emphasize typical health issues, her findings (and those of others) suggest fathers are more likely to be excluded from parental networks in which social support and children's health and childcare information are meaningfully shared. Moreover, fathers are less apt than mothers to take on the "community responsibility" tasks of engaging with adults involved with caring for children. Notably, some of these adults monitor children's physical, emotional, and mental health.

promoting health-conscious fathering

For far too long, many men have been ignorant of or ignored how their poor health habits jeopardize their children's well-being. With the U.S. Department of Health and Human Services report Healthy People 2020 on the horizon, now is the time to challenge men to foster positive health outcomes for their children. So what can be done to improve these patterns?

Generally speaking, men engage in more unhealthy behaviors and are less attentive to their self-care than women. The emerging evidence tells us, too, that men's exposure to health risks prior to their children's conception can contribute to prenatal problems. Moreover, men's poor health habits are related to children being more likely to smoke, abuse drugs, and eat poorly as well as be overweight and experience other negative health outcomes.

To understand and alter these patterns we must fully grasp fathers' lives as men and the diverse decisions affecting them. In other words, as the constrained choice theory implies, choices and priorities about health exist as part of a larger context and compete with other decisions about income, work, housing, partner/family, and personal image. Thus, we must commit to a multilevel approach to promoting social change that incorporates national and state policies, community-based strategies, workplace agendas, family support, and individual commitments.

> For far too long, many men have been ignorant of or ignored how their poor health habits jeopardize their children's well-being.

Various social circumstances make it difficult for boys and men, some more than others, to forge and sustain healthy lifestyles and transmit similar values and benefits to their children. Constraints come in many forms, including conventional masculine discussion and business cultures that glorify stereotypes of the macho athlete or worker, inner-city and rural planning that limits recreational facilities for youth and adults alike, inadequate supports to educate men about reproductive health care and the consequences of paternity, workplace conditions and economic realities that expose men—especially those from economically disadvantaged backgrounds—to work-related health hazards, and peer pressure that extols a masculinity grounded in body toughness and risk-taking. Unfortunately, too many boys and men navigate their social networks, leisure, and work lives in ways that reinforce this less-than-ideal approach toward health.

Despite the constraints, men do have choices. Some recent research suggests, in fact, that men are capable of looking out for their own health and caring for others effectively if they put their minds to it. Ideally, as feminist values promoting gender equity inside the home gain wider appeal, and research accumulates to document the connections between fathers' and children's health, definitions of "good fathering" will summon fathers to pursue a healthier lifestyle while cultivating the same for their children.

Getting large numbers of men to adopt such a mindset requires broad public support and will require an intense public health service campaign—one that an Obama administration might be well suited to launch. Realistically, though, concrete progress in altering individual commitments and choices will come when men regularly encourage each other to be more attentive to their own and their children's health. The seeds for this shift can be sewn most visibly in places that traditionally have been instrumental in discouraging health consciousness: locker

Opportunities in communities, like coaching, allow fathers to be involved with kids' health. (Paul W via Creative Commons)

rooms, fraternities, many work sites, and other places where male respect holds sway. Of course, these efforts also need to be augmented by men's partners.

The harsh reality for some men is that their chances to perceive and pursue healthy choices for themselves and their children hinge on politically sponsored national and state initiatives. In other words, for many men living in poor inner cities and rural areas, structural and legislative changes are needed to improve access to fresh-food markets, healthcare facilities and substance abuse programs, recreation sites, and organized sports so that more fathers and their children have viable, healthy options. It makes sense to expand Head Start programs by providing poor fathers with information, screenings, and referrals for a broad range of father-child health matters.

A less direct but critical step is to have schools, other youth-oriented organizations, and public health programs do a better job of providing teenage and young adult males comprehensive instruction on reproductive health. Because men have the capacity to influence fetal and infant life directly via their sperm quality and indirectly by how they treat the mother, they need to be educated at a young age about how their smoking, drinking, and drug use as well as their readiness to become fathers can affect their offspring's health. Although all males deserve these services, those living in poor neighborhoods are most vulnerable because they typically are the least prepared to assume many of the responsibilities associated with providing and caring for children.

Work sites are another place where men can be afforded opportunities to make better decisions about eating, exercise, stress management, and substance use, and receive medical check-ups and education about how these experiences matter for their children's health. Workplace policies, reinforced by more father-friendly corporate cultures, can ensure fathers have increased access to flexible schedules and nonstigmatized family-leave time. These benefits can make it easier for fathers to accompany their children to medical visits as well as provide hands-on care for their sick children.

Health-care institutions, in addition to educating men, can promote men's greater participation by providing more convenient evening and weekend hours while making their operations more male-friendly. Like the decisive trend beginning in the 1970s that saw fathers participating in childbirth preparation classes and being present when their children were born, the medical community must find innovative ways to integrate more fathers into their children's pediatric care. Today's creative childbirth preparation classes might produce promising results by coordinating new fatherhood programs with interventions to curb smoking, drinking, and drug use.

Ultimately, fathers must answer the call to communicate proactively with their children and monitor their well-being in consultation with healthcare providers and others who have a vested interest. Perhaps most importantly, if men adopt healthier behaviors for themselves and reduce their stress, they can more readily model such behaviors and authentically encourage their children to do the same.

RECOMMENDED RESOURCES

C. E. Bird and P. P. Rieker. *Gender and Health: The Effects of Constrained Choices and Social Policies* (Cambridge University Press, 2008).

> An overview of how diverse layers of social life are interconnected, contributing to health disparities between men and women.

W. H. Courtenay. "Constructions of Masculinity and Their Influence on Men's Well-Being: A Theory of Gender and Health." *Social Science & Medicine* (2000) 50: 1385–1401.

> A critical review of how various conditions shape the kind of masculinity men construct and how those practices contribute to differential health risks.

A. Doucet. *Do Men Mother? Fathering, Care and Domestic Responsibility* (Toronto University Press, 2006).

> Grounded in qualitative data, this book highlights fathers' opportunities to be more nurturing and engaged parents.

C. Garfield, E. Clark-Kauffman, and M. M. Davis. "Fatherhood as a Component of Men's Health. "*Journal of the American Medical Association* (2006) 296: 2365–68.

> A thoughtful interdisciplinary essay that conceptualizes the relationship between fatherhood and men's health.

C. L. Menning and S. D. Stewart. "Nonresident Father Involvement, Social Class, and Adolescent Weight." *Journal of Family Issues* (2008) 29: 1673–1700.

> Provides a quantitative analysis of two waves of the well-respected National Longitudinal Study of Adolescent Health survey.

REVIEW QUESTIONS

1. In what ways can a father negatively affect his children's health before birth? After birth? Which mechanisms are biologically based? Which are socially based? Did any of them surprise you?

2. How can gendered expectations of masculinity affect fatherhood? Do you think ideas about masculinity would have to change in order to improve parenting by fathers?

3. List both positive and negative examples of fatherhood in the popular media. Which are more abundant? Why?

4. The author suggests several policies that would help mitigate the number of fathers having a negative effect on their children's health. Which of these policies seem most promising to you? What other ideas would you add to the list?

stephen poulson

autism, through a social lens

47

spring 2009

sociology has much to offer the parents, caregivers, and researchers who want to understand what has been called the fastest-growing developmental disability in society today.

Since the early 1990s the United States has seen a 10-fold increase in autism diagnoses. In 2007, 1 in 150 children were diagnosed with it, according to the Centers for Disease Control.

More than 40 percent of autistic children attending public school in 2006 spent their entire day in a special education classroom or attended a special school for children with disabilities, according to the U.S. Department of Education. These children have a disability severe enough that they probably have few prospects for meaningful employment after they leave school. But increasingly, many children are being identified as "high-functioning" autistics and are often mainstreamed, with significant help, into "regular" classrooms where they may not appear much different than their typical peers.

Sociologists are well positioned to weigh in on what, exactly, autism is, whether there really are more people today with autism than just a few decades ago, how autism is diagnosed and treated, and how families and other social institutions cope with the challenges associated with it. Though sometimes reluctant to study biological and genetic disabilities, sociologists—especially in Western Europe and Australia—are beginning to make important contributions to both public and medical understandings of

> Sociologists are beginning to make important contributions to both public and medical understandings of autism.

the conditions underlying autism and how to deal with them most effectively.

Although my own academic sociological expertise is in a different area entirely, over the last two years I've been observing an autistic boy, Sam [not his real name], and have come to see that sociology has so much more to offer the parents, caregivers, and researchers who want to understand what has been called the fastest-growing developmental disability in society today.

some basics

At its most basic, an autism diagnosis means an individual has an impaired ability to communicate and acquire social skills. It's usually associated with children and manifests itself initially in early stages of social development.

The severity of autism impairment varies among children, so it's characterized as a "spectrum disorder." High-functioning autistics and people with Asperger's syndrome are socially awkward and have difficulty understanding common social interactions, but they can learn to navigate the social world reasonably well. On the other end of the spectrum, people diagnosed with low-social-functioning autism may not even be able to speak.

A characteristic associated with autism is repetitive self-stimulating behavior, called stimming. The most common examples are rocking, pacing, repeating words, stacking objects, and banging one's head, among others. Of course, many people "stim" when stressed—I occasionally pace the floor—but autistic stimming seems to facilitate a deep withdrawal into the self.

The rocking, the pacing, the stacking, and the banging appears to help those with autism shut out the larger world and often provides them with great comfort. High-functioning autistics don't like change or surprises and they often develop mild stims that lower their distress when confronted with new situations.

Somewhat associated with stimming are the routines to which many autistics devote themselves. These sometimes include an unyielding abidance to "rules" that organize their lives, like a sequence of events that must be followed before going to school, before entering a room, or while riding in a car.

I believe people with autism are, for the most part, like everyone else—only quite a bit more so. Most people are nervous in new situations and when meeting new people, but many with autism find these circumstances debilitating.

When autistics are confronted with new situations, their rules often become more important. But new situations usually require that rules be broken. This paradox can result in a circle of escalating distress for many autistics, which is why many avoid new places and new people.

It seems that many, in fact, regard themselves—and other people—primarily as objects. Put another way, they regard the objects and people in their lives as not much different from one another. This isn't meant to imply that people with low-functioning autism aren't often extraordinarily attached to their primary caregivers, but rather that their emotional attachment to objects and routines is usually quite intense. These individuals are unlikely to enter the workforce as adults. They often require extraordinary care—sometimes nearly one-on-one supervision

James Vaughan, now nearly 6, was diagnosed as severely autistic just after his second birthday. (Scott Vaughan via Creative Commons)

during the day—to insure they're clothed, fed, and safe.

Most parents of autistics quickly learn the various stimuli in the world (automatic doors, for example) that are affronts to their child's sensibilities and cause meltdowns. The primary difference I associate with an autistic meltdown compared to a typical temper tantrum is that they often seem driven by extraordinary fear. They usually last until a child is successfully redirected, or perhaps decamped to a quiet place where they're given an object they love to manipulate.

Asperger's is often considered a type of autism disorder, but some argue it should be treated as distinct from autism. While "Aspies" usually have some serious social delays, they can also be verbally precocious, have average or above-average intelligence, and are usually preoccupied by a few narrow interests they're willing to talk (and talk, and talk) about to anyone vaguely interested. Sometimes they're referred to as "little professors." They usually attend regular schools where, despite some serious social and academic deficits, they may also be precocious at a few endeavors.

Tim Page, a Pulitzer Prize–winning critic diagnosed with Asperger's as an adult, wrote recently in *The New Yorker*, ". . . if we are not very, very good at something we tend to do it very poorly. Little in life comes naturally—except for our random, inexplicable, and often uncontrollable gifts—and, even more than most children, we assemble our personalities unevenly, piece by piece, almost robotically, from models we admire."

creating the autism spectrum

In medical lexicon, autism is described as "a complex syndrome without a uniform etiology." In layman's terms this means the causes of autism are diverse and unknown.

Although arguments associated with biological determinism and autism—particularly that a person's genes "cause" autism—tend to receive the significant attention in the popular media, most scholars who study autism believe social and environmental factors have contributed significantly to the increase in diagnoses in the United States and around the world.

For example, it's generally accepted among clinicians that expanded diagnostic criteria and greater screening is one reason for the increase in diagnoses. There are also indications that changes in obstetric medical technologies and practice may affect the increase. Still, these social factors probably don't account for the entire 10-fold increase. There's a strong correlation between the age of parents (particularly fathers) and the incidence of autism diagnosis among offspring. And, most experts assume biological predisposition accounts for the greater number of diagnoses among boys (although it should be noted girls are likely underdiagnosed for social reasons such as the fact that autism presents differently in girls than boys).

Sociologists and sociological thought have clearly played a role here. The few sociologists who study genetic predisposition and social life are often interested in what is commonly referred to as gene-environment interplay. This is the idea that some genes, or combinations of genes, predispose people toward certain traits and characteristics. At the same time, experiences—particularly among young children whose brains are undergoing rapid development—play a crucial role in how these behavioral predilections play out. Ultimately, it's social experience that turns on and refines a person's social capacities.

Sociologist Peter Bearman heads one such promising research program. Funded with a $2.5 million grant from the National Institutes of Health, Bearman takes the interactions between genetic predisposition and social structure seriously and investigates a wide range of social factors, including how changes in diagnostic criteria and social networks affect autism diagnosis. Bearman's research could well help us better understand how the interaction of genes and the social environment are contributing to the dramatic increase in diagnoses.

Another well-known sociological approach that may help in this regard concerns the increasing "medicalization" of society. This is primarily the idea that behaviors once considered common are now identified as disorders that require attention by professionals.

A reference point for much of this literature is David Rosenhan's now famous experiment in which sane pseudo-patients, after gaining admittance to psychiatric hospitals, were never identified as "sane" by professional staff at these hospitals. This study demonstrated the malleability of professional medical opinion when diagnosing (and creating) psychiatric disorder. Closely associated with this perspective is the work of Peter Conrad on the medicalization of attention deficit/hyperactivity disorder (ADHD). More recently, Conrad and others have argued the increase in medical disorders—such as adult ADHD—is related to the increasing influence of Western pharmaceutical companies in shaping diagnosis and treatment regimes for a whole range of physiological conditions and disorders.

It's likely the social creation of the "autism spectrum" has subsumed other types of diagnoses used in past. The more generic description of "mental retardation" was probably a common diagnosis a generation ago, for example. In this regard, one reason for the increase in autism diagnoses may simply be that the public and medical professionals are now aware of it in ways they weren't previously.

Some speech and occupational therapists I've met believe autism has become the diagnosis for children who have any measurable social or academic delay. Indeed, many therapists and medical practitioners believe the increase in autism diagnoses has resulted from the recently created and gradually expanded criteria used to evaluate a range of behaviors.

autism and self

Because their goal is to teach children with autism to better understand social life and the world around them, clinicians who treat autism draw directly (if not always consciously) upon sociological ideas. In particular, treatments for autistic children employ George Herbert Mead's insights about how we create a "self"—that we

> The creation of the "autism spectrum" has subsumed other types of diagnoses used in the past, like the more generic description "mental retardation."

begin to do so by making comparisons to others during childhood play. Children with autism are exceptions in that they aren't particularly interested in playing with, or evaluating behaviors, in the same manner as typical children.

Autistic children have considerable difficulty establishing "joint attention." Most people, when they communicate, quickly fall into sync with each other. They establish eye contact and focus their attention on each other's faces and body language. Autistic children don't do this. Indeed, one marker for the disability is that many don't understand nonverbal communication like waving hello or goodbye. When typical 2- and 3-year-old children sit in a room during story time at the library, most will intuitively be drawn to the person at the center of the room reading the story. An autistic child, assuming they aren't [sic] overwhelmed by the activity in the first place, may find something in the room to pay attention to, but it's less likely to be the storyteller.

James has had two and a half years of ABA therapy and his father Scott, who photographed him, said the results have been "amazing." (Scott Vaughan via Creative Commons)

Older autistic children, when viewing scenes from popular movies—a loud argument, a fight, a particularly passionate embrace—focus far less attention on people's faces, and particularly their eyes, than other children. They also take in the entire scene—tables, windows, doors, other objects in the room—more than typical people. As a result, many autistics can describe, sometimes in extraordinary detail, objects that appeared in the scene, but they miss much of the social interaction that takes place between the actors. Many autistics can be taught, or learn on their own, how to pay greater attention to people.

I was often alarmed when I began interacting with autistic children at just how little "self" many had constructed. I have observed one child, Sam, for nearly two years since his diagnosis with high-functioning autism at age 3. His general disposition—when not distressed—is amicable, but also very deliberate. He was far more "serious" than other toddlers. At 3 he didn't wave or say "hello" or "goodbye." He didn't point at objects he wanted. He rarely, unlike other children his age, imitated behavior. He didn't know how to ask a question, so he solved problems by using extraordinary complex methods of inductive and deductive reasoning. He had a reasonable vocabulary for his age, but he didn't understand the word "yes." He always referred to himself in the third person. In short, he had significant delays in his acquisition of symbolic language.

Moreover, the world and the people in it, particularly when he was visiting a new place or meeting new people, often overwhelmed him. When this happened he had a repertoire of relatively mild self-stimulating behaviors—he generally paced and repeated words—that he used to settle himself. The categories and rhythms Sam used to organize, navigate, and give meaning to his world—he was fascinated by shapes and colors—were so different than those of other children I thought he might not be able to form a meaningful social relationship as an adult.

treating autism

Treatments for autism are intense and expensive. At Sam's age, it's generally assumed that at least 20 to 25 hours of direct contact with a trained therapist, most often in one-on-one sessions for at least two years, is the minimum standard required. The specific approaches and therapies used to treat autism are contentious, but there's a clear record—beginning with the applied behavioral analysis (ABA) therapies conducted by Ivar Lovass in the 1980s—that treatment before age 3 can have a profound impact on an autistic's social functioning later in life.

Overall, the primary goal of all therapies, not just ABA approaches, is to teach autistics to establish joint attention. All aspire to engage autistic children in the social world, and to, in some manner or another, compel them to compare themselves to others. Often this involves teaching autistic children how to play more like typical children. Along the way, clinicians demonstrate that while social relationships can be contentious, sporadic, and random, they're satisfying, too. The most successful treatments teach, often in an intellectual manner, a sense of emotional empathy.

In the best cases, school systems have programs that provide the bulk of this therapy—in Sam's case, which is not necessarily typical, he received nearly 16 hours of therapy per week at school. Autism spectrum disorders, though, aren't covered by most health insurance providers, at least in Virginia where he lives, so the additional 10 hours of therapy each week was provided by Sam's family at a cost of $8,000 annually. Tuition at private schools in Virginia that provide ABA therapy to lower-functioning autistics with a near one-to-one student-therapist ratio cost as much as $80,000 per academic year.

(It probably doesn't take a sociologist to see these numbers and begin thinking about inequalities in access to treatment that might come into play in different communities and contexts.)

Sam was largely taught to focus on people by sitting at a table across from a therapist who demanded that he pay attention to her. She used snacks, toys, and other reinforcers to help the process along. Once he gained this skill he was largely released from the "table work" and, with the help of aides, practiced interacting with other children his age. Over time he was slowly immersed into a Head Start classroom where, with the help of aides, he learned to play with others and use the social skills he was being taught. He's still shadowed by aides, but he spends more time in the typical classroom than the special ed classroom. He also took part in a coordinated battery of other group activities—play groups, youth soccer, gymnastics, and swim lessons—to reinforce the therapy he received.

So, for the past 20 months Sam has been pushed, drilled, perhaps even coerced, into becoming a more social person. As he approaches his fifth birthday, his conversational style is different than other children's, but his social interactions are often reciprocal and, for

Scott says James enjoys the time he spends with his therapists and teachers. (Scott Vaughan via Creative Commons)

the most part, increasingly "normal." While most clinicians are careful to tell parents that children can't be "cured" of autism, there's increasing evidence some high-functioning autistic children—particularly those who receive similar interventions at an early age—do age out of many behaviors associated with autism.

how families cope

To date, some of the best sociological studies of autism have focused on how families cope with caring for autistic children. Sociologist David Gray has conducted one of the few longitudinal studies of family coping. He conducted 28 interviews with parents roughly 10 years following their children's initial diagnosis and treatment.

The highest levels of self-reported psychological and emotional distress for parents occurred when they were first identifying their child's disorder and attempting to secure treatment services. While parents, roughly 10 years later, still experienced stress because of their children's autistic behaviors, two-thirds were less so than 10 years before. Moreover, many said other family members and friends had become far more sympathetic and helpful over time. Not surprisingly, the level of an autistic child's social functioning appears related to the stress parents report experiencing. For families whose children were often violent or aggressive, their distress was still considerable.

Gray found noticeable gender differences in how parents responded to autistic children. For example, many mothers reported leaving full-time employment to care for their autistic child. No fathers (who were underrepresented in the study) had interrupted their careers. And while life gets easier for many families that raise autistic children, many parents still reported experiencing social stigma, mothers far more than fathers. Some found it difficult to go into public with their children because their child's behaviors embarrassed them. On occasion, some were rebuked by strangers for allowing their child to act out in public. Often, other family members, and even strangers in public places, attributed the cause for an autistic child's behaviors to bad parenting. Some parents reported they were excluded at times from family and social events because of their child's disability. At the same time, this was less commonly reported during follow-up interviews 10 years later.

Initially very concerned about how their typical children would be affected by having an autistic sibling, 10 years later most parents reported siblings generally experienced little social stigma from their peers and had learned to accommodate their autistic sibling's disability.

> Autism raises broader questions about fundamental assumptions of what's different and what's normal, about what's genius and what's deviance.

One other important area of concern for parents of autistic kids was their child's prospects once they became adults. In this respect, some had hoped their children with autism might be employable, but were increasingly concerned about the lack of occupational programs available to prepare their children for work. Many assumed they would continue to care for these children well into their adulthood.

other sociological dimensions

Parents have often been at the forefront of activism and organizing around issues related to autism. Similar to other disability movements (such as activism associated with securing treatment for post-traumatic stress disorder), an increasing number of social movement organizations—Autism Speaks is one—currently champion more research on autism-related causes. Some of these organizations focus on eliminating medical practices they believe contribute to autism, others primarily provide the public with information about recognizing early signs of autism, given the efficacy of early intervention programs.

More to the point of treatment, a number of autism organizations are trying to secure legislation that mandates insurance companies provide coverage for autism spectrum disorders. Some states have already mandated coverage, but the majority don't. Activists are also concerned with the "free and appropriate public education" provision of the Americans with Disabilities Act. Under this provision, beginning at age 3, autistic children (mentioned specifically in the law) should be provided with an appropriate education tailored to their specific disabilities.

Not surprisingly, given the costs of these interventions some school districts don't provide these services. In fact, it's been common for districts to simply refuse to identify children as autistic because officials regard the cost of providing services as too expensive. In other cases, autistic children are simply placed in existing programs that aren't tailored to their disabilities. As a result, many families with autistic children move to school districts that have established autism programs. Parents of autistic children are suing school boards more often now for ignoring this law, and they're often winning.

Activism like this gives rise to a whole range of questions medical and organizational sociologists are well positioned to take up: Who determines which treatments children receive in the absence of health care coverage? How we do deal with basic inequalities in access to treatment? And perhaps even more provocatively, why is it that some parents embrace the diagnosis of autism while others resist or even fight the label?

Autism raises broader questions about fundamental assumptions concerning what's different and what's normal, about what's genius and what's deviance. A common and particularly provocative debate among people with Asperger's and autism, for example, concerns the degree to which they should be forced to conform to social norms established by the "neuro-typical."

Many with high-functioning autism and Asperger's, while recognizing their differences compared to the neuro-typical, resent the specific labels associated with their conditions and argue against the characterization that they have a disability. Some individuals who self-identify as "neurologically non-typical" are becoming outspoken advocates against the use of genetic testing on fetuses on the assumption that screening for autism and Asperger's—like the current screening for Down syndrome—could become commonplace in the future. Others argue prominent scientists and innovators—Albert Einstein or Bill Gates, for example—would likely be on the autism spectrum, and insist autistic reasoning is, in some ways, superior to typical reasoning.

Here it's also interesting to point out that clinicians who treat autistic children sometimes spend time navigating the criminal justice system because of the idiosyncrasies and compulsions many autistics have. For example, some are fanatical "collectors" and when they see something they want—in a store, in a neighbor's yard—it's hard to resist adding it to their collection. Autistics are also easy marks for criminals and are sometimes unwitting accomplices to crime due to their social naiveté. Autistics are bullied more often—a neighbor of mine who once worked with autistic children received routine calls about a young man, usually mild in disposition and temperament, being constantly provoked on his bus ride home from school. When this happened he inevitably grew agitated, would scream profanities at his bus driver, and then literally force him—he grabbed the steering wheel more than once—to stop the bus. He was often miles from his house, but he would disembark and walk along the roadside while screaming profanities until someone he knew came and picked him up.

Was this young man "deviant?" Were his actions violent? It's often these types of scenarios—generally an autistic's increasing distress accompanied by an escalation of inappropriate behavior like throwing objects, hitting themselves, or screaming—occurring in a public place that cause some to end up in the courts. Given that many are sensitive to noise, public places, and crowds, otherwise simple excursions—a holiday vacation that requires air travel—can result in uneasy confrontations with security personnel. As a result, it's increasingly common that law enforcement officials are trained in how to handle disturbances created by autistics in public places.

Sociological thinking about identity underlies a great deal of autism diagnosis and treatment. Sociologists are beginning to make important contributions to autism research by situating it in broader social contexts, including the institutions that do (or do not) assist those with the condition and the inequalities that may come with access to treatment.

Still, the most basic questions about autism and the broader implications they raise are the most intriguing to sociological readers and researchers. And here, more than anything, is an opportunity to have a greater understanding of interactions between socialization and genetic heritability. Perhaps as sociologists spend more time watching how children with autism are taught to navigate the social world they'll find interesting examples that show how socialization—despite disability—still determines much of who we become.

RECOMMENDED RESOURCES

Simon Baron-Cohen. *Mindblindness: An Essay on Autism and Theory of the Mind* (MIT Press, 1997).

> An accessible book by a psychologist that explains why autism is important to understanding human psychology.

Peter S. Bearman, Molly A. Martin, and Sara Shostak, eds. "Genes and Social Structure." *American Journal of Sociology* (2008) 114 (1): 1–316.

> A collection of studies that demonstrate approaches used by sociologists who study gene-environment interplay.

Temple Grandin. *Thinking In Pictures and Other Reports from My Life with Autism* (Vintage Press, 1996).

> The first popular autobiography written by a person diagnosed with autism as a child.

David Gray. "Ten Years On: A Longitudinal Study of Families of Children with Autism." *Journal of Intellectual & Developmental Disability* (2002) 27 (3): 215–22.

> A study that investigates how living with autistic children affects family life over time.

Roy Richard Grinker. *Unstrange Minds: Remapping the World of Autism* (Basic Books, 2007).

> A broad overview, written by an anthropologist with a distinctive sociological bent.

Ami Klin, Warren Jones, Robert Schultz, Fred Volkmar, and Donald Cohen. "Visual Fixation Patterns During Viewing of Naturalistic Social Situations as Predictors of Social Competence in Individuals with Autism." *Archives of General Psychiatry* (2002) 59: 809–16.

> A study that demonstrates autistics have difficulty reading faces and understanding people's emotional states.

REVIEW QUESTIONS

1. According to the article, what are some reasons that might explain the rise in autism diagnoses?
2. What insights about diagnosis and/or treatment are revealed by viewing autism through a social lens?
3. Children with autism are often seen as abnormal or deviant. In this case, who ultimately defines what is "normal" and what is "deviant"? Why do such labels matter?

michael j. shanahan, shawn bauldry, and jason a. freeman

beyond mendel's ghost

48

fall 2010

working together, geneticists and sociologists are showing that there is a dynamic, complex relationship between genes and social behavior.

At a major conference on genetics in 2003, a team of researchers reported that the Maori, the indigenous people of New Zealand, are far more likely than Caucasians to carry a variant of the MAOA gene that has been associated with aggressive behavior. The scientists argued that the difference made sense and reflected the fact that more aggressive individuals survived the migratory journey by which the Maori originally populated Aotearoa, the islands that would later become New Zealand.

Unfortunately, it took little imagination for editorialists to deform this line of reasoning, arguing that such genetic differences would explain the Maori's higher rates of crime. Substantial segments of the New Zealander public agreed, and the "warrior gene" was born.

The media is filled with coverage of findings like this, linking genetic variation to behavioral traits such as violence, generosity, personal success, and even political beliefs. Unfortunately, these studies are often publicized by the media—and sometimes by study authors themselves—in a way that glosses over the nuances of what we know about genetics as well as sociology.

During the 20th century, sociology's relationship to genetics was frequently combative.

> If genes and environments combine in complex ways to predict behavior, who better to help map these social complexities than sociologists?

In the 1980s and 1990s, inflammatory arguments propounded by the likes of Charles Murray and Richard Herrnstein about a genetically based American underclass put sociologists in the position of arguing against the relevance of genetics for explaining social behavior. But, as the 21st century commences, sociologists are now engaging in the genetically-informed study of behavior and including molecular genetic information in their data collection efforts.

Why the sea change? Contrary to simplistic news coverage, genetic factors do not determine behaviors in any straightforward way. Rather, they combine with—and even change in response to—"environmental factors," which include everything from the mother's womb to nutrition and prescription drugs to the subject of sociology proper, social context. A person may have genetic risks for alcoholism, but whether that person becomes an alcoholic depends on a wide range of environmental experiences—including social factors—occurring over the lifecourse. People are not Mendel's famous pea plant flowers, the coloration of which was almost completely determined by genes. And if genes and environments combine in complex ways to predict behavior, who better to help map out these social complexities than sociologists, who have been developing this expertise for over a century?

As sensationalist stories about "warrior genes" jazz up the front page, an understanding of how genetics and sociology interact is increasingly necessary to make sense of research that claims to find a relationship between microscopic genes and macro-level social outcomes. While sociologists and geneticists are just beginning to flesh out this relationship between genes and social actors, a glimpse at the early results can go a long way towards helping us interpret the ongoing stream of studies trumpeting the genetic basis of our social lives.

> Differences in gene expression can help us understand *how* social contexts alter associations between genes and behaviors.

genes

Scientists have long drawn on studies of rats and mice to show that genetic and social factors combine in complex ways to predict behaviors. Decades of research in psychology showed that "creating" an aggressive mouse takes generations of selective breeding coupled with a consistently stressful environment. Neither the breeding nor the stressors by themselves reliably led to a mouse prone to attack. At the same time, studies of familial lineages suggested that specific genes are associated with specific behaviors, including aggression. So, for example, scientists observed that a risk variant (or "allele") of the MAOA gene—which metabolizes neurotransmitters like dopamine—was much more common than would be expected across several generations of a Dutch family marked by high levels of violence.

With advances in genotyping (the measurement of genes), these lines of research merged and focused on human behavior, allowing for

the study of *gene-environment interactions* (sometimes referred to as "GxE") how the effects of genes on behavior are conditioned by environmental features, or vice versa. For example, in a highly cited and replicated study in *Science,* Avshalom Caspi and his colleagues show that an MAOA allele coupled with childhood maltreatment before the age of five significantly increases the likelihood of an antisocial psychiatric disorder in young adulthood. The gene *alone,* however, had little effect.

Studies like Caspi's quickly proliferated and sociologists joined in the "GxE rush" to identify combinations of genes and environments that reliably predicted specific behaviors of longstanding interest to their discipline—physical and mental health, the stress process, indicators of status attainment, interpersonal relationships, health-related behaviors, violence, sexual behavior, and so on. It seemed to be just a matter of finding the magic genetic bullet and its appropriate environmental trigger.

Actor Elijah Wood holds a piece of artwork created from his DNA profile by a company called DNA 11. The piece was auctioned to benefit a children's charity. (DNA 11 via Creative Commons)

But such research faces challenges. Like much of sociology, gene-environment research is usually non-experimental: people are not randomly assigned to genes (like MAOA alleles) and to environments (like maltreatment), with their behaviors recorded by observers wearing white coats and safety glasses. So it's rarely clear whether a specific environmental feature's relationship to a specific gene is actually causal. Features of the environment like child maltreatment are highly correlated with other negative social experiences (e.g., parental drug use) and it is also known that genes "hunt in packs," meaning that behaviors likely reflect networks of genes that work together. For that matter, behaviors are often highly correlated. Even if MAOA and maltreatment are the real culprits, do they actually predict antisocial behaviors or something else, like substance abuse?

Also, a great deal of gene-environment research has proceeded with little reference to conceptual models. Ideally, empirical analyses are guided by prior research about how the brain works—how specific genes are related to brain structure and function and, therefore, to how people perceive and react to their experiences. A causal account can then be formulated to link chains of biological, psychological, and social processes that reliably lead to specific behaviors.

Despite these challenges, sociology has an important role to play in helping to conceptualize and measure environmental factors. Indeed, developments in genetics have only served to underscore the importance of social context and the need for a sociological presence in gene-environment research. A major theme of this new research is that the image of DNA as an unchanging set of instructions is downright inaccurate. Although it is true that the base pairs that make up a person's DNA (remember A, G, C, and T from high school biology?) never change, social experiences alter their *expres-*

sion, or how the base pairs are interpreted and translated into their "products" (typically proteins). These differences in gene expression can help us to understand *how* social contexts alter associations between genes and behaviors.

One class of expression mechanisms is *epigenetic processes,* which change how the long and spindly DNA molecule is compacted. Many scholars believe that they are a principle mechanism by which social context "turns genes on and off." Studies with mice and rats show that epigenetic changes account, to some degree, for why stress is related to depression, complex settings to intellectual development, and lack of maternal warmth to anxiety—all topics of interest to sociologists. Given close similarities between these animals and humans, scientists have little doubt such findings will inform human behavioral science.

Apparently more common are *transcriptional processes*, which alter the rate at which genes make proteins and other goodies. Recent research in humans shows that transcription accounts for why chronic stress and loneliness each lead to a heightened inflammatory response, which is in turn related to a wide range of disease states (such as depression, asthma, and cardiovascular disease). For example, even among people with high socioeconomic status (SES) in adulthood, low SES during childhood is associated with cardiovascular disease. Gregory Miller and his colleagues recently showed that low SES in childhood increases the likelihood of a heightened stress response in adulthood by way of transcription. Thus, an adverse environment early in life increases the likelihood of heightened reactions to stressors throughout later life, regardless of one's achievements and status in society, culminating in stress-related illnesses.

Although gene expression studies of social context and human behavior are still novel, they have already vividly shown that DNA is highly reactive to status, stress, and one's connectedness to other people, topics of long-standing interest in sociology. And, in a nutshell, there has never been more empirical evidence pointing to the importance of social factors in regulating genetic action. The rift between sociology and molecular genetics is, at this point in history, very narrow indeed.

actors

Perhaps the greatest benefits to sociology from paying attention to genetics are major clues about how people experience and react to their environments. As noted, most gene-environment research is premised, hopefully explicitly, on neuroscience (and increasingly the immune system, which is tightly linked to the brain): genes are related to differences in the brain, which in turn are related to how people pay attention and regulate their behaviors, learn, are motivated, and experience emotional states. And in fact, modern neuroscience is progressing by leaps and bounds in understanding these intricacies. Given the differences among individuals, what aspects of social settings matter?

Our own research has focused on one genetic variant, TaqIA, and educational continuation. The research builds on a large body of findings—many studies based on experimental designs—showing that TaqIA is associated with dopamine and how efficiently people learn from mistakes. In brief: it may be that people with TaqIA risk do not perceive adverse experiences as negatively as other people, and so they tend not to learn from their mistakes as efficiently. Because of these differences, they also tend to be more impulsive and perhaps more aggressive, prone to addictions, and distractable.

> Genetic ascription, particularly in the rough-and-tumble world of public discourse, could lead to new forms of discrimination.

Our research began with a simple question: what happens to such people in modern settings—families, workplaces, and schools? To date, we have focused exclusively on one outcome: educational attainment. Assuming that students with TaqIA risk do not learn efficiently from their mistakes, we should see differences in how far they and students without TaqIA risk continue in their schooling. In fact, the results, which are preliminary but intriguing, suggest that TaqIA has an association with whether boys graduate from high school and continue to college. We have also found that there are several combinations of social capital that can compensate for TaqIA risk. For example, TaqIA has little effect on educational continuation among male students who report having a teacher who is a mentor. Having educated parents who are highly involved in a quality high school also makes a big difference.

One of the implications of this research is that impulsive and attentional difficulties may be decisively detrimental in classrooms, a theme that has received very little attention in sociological research on education to date. That is, molecular genetics has provided a clue as to the features of social settings that might matter and that might help students, peers, and teachers find academic success in spite of some kids' diminished capacity to learn from mistakes.

Is one implication of this research that students be genotyped for TaqIA status (thereby creating new opportunities for prejudice and discrimination)? No. Although TaqIA suggests a series of behaviors that may detract from educational processes, many children with this risk *will not* exhibit them and many children without it *will* exhibit them. As we noted, there is a strong consensus that single genes do not cause complex behaviors in any straightforward way.

To name but a few biological complications: genes often work in tandem, forming networks that are presently not well understood; within these networks, single genes may be "turned on or off" based on what other genes are doing, social experiences, and other biological processes; and RNA transcription processes—how RNA "writes out" the DNA's code to make other molecules—is far more complex than was once thought. Moreover, our research shows that the connections between TaqIA and education are highly dependent on social circumstances (forms of social capital).

The big point is that the behaviors suggested by TaqIA should now be studied with great care and, should these behaviors explain the TaqIA-education association, then the focus should be on them. Impulsivity and related behaviors, Irrespective of TaqIA status, may be detrimental to educational attainment. The even bigger point is, however, that our example shows how a realistic view of the actor—one that specifies differences in how people perceive, interpret, and react to their social setting—holds the promise of enriching the study of social processes.

There is a final consideration for why sociology should engage with genetics. It's part promise of intellectual enrichment and part *realpolitik:* universities, governmental agencies, and many intellectual societies and their journals are now thoroughly interdisciplinary in their outlook. In this new intellectual environment, sociology is beginning to bring its unique expertise to a wider community of behavioral scientists who are collaboratively studying the central issues of human health and well-being. Such efforts have been and will continue to be major opportunities for Intellectual cross-fertilization. The alternative would be to insist on "sociological purity" and, in the process, run the very real risk of intellectual irrelevance.

warriors

We began by talking about the controversy over a "warrior gene" among New Zealand's Maori, in which we could see (alongside the promises just discussed) the dangerous side of research linking genetics and behavior. Two such dangers—genetic reductionism and genetic ascription—go hand-in-hand. Genetic reductionism refers to attempts to explain a phenomenon based solely on genetic factors. Genetic ascription extends these explanatory accounts, attributing a characteristic behavior to a group that is defined by genetic factors. The "warrior gene" case illustrates the "perfect storm" of these problems.

Yet, a distinction needs to be made between what the scientists claimed and how these claims were construed. The scientists reported differences in the percentages of MAOA alleles in subpopulations. This is a very common type of observation for a geneticist to make since many alleles differ in how they are distributed across sub-populations, a phenomenon called *population stratification*. The scientists also developed an argument to explain why these differences might make sense. Although their argument is

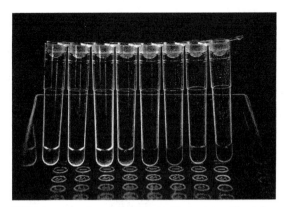

DNA samples in a lab at Duke University. (Patrick Alexander via Creative Commons)

obviously speculative, post hoc arguments of this sort—especially emphasizing migratory patterns—are also common lines of reasoning for geneticists who study population stratification.

Importantly, however, their arguments are far removed from how public discourse "processed" them: that differences in the distribution of MAOA alleles explain why the Maori commit more crimes than Caucasians. Again, genes are not related to complex behaviors in any simple way. So the vast majority of geneticists (and sociologists) are simply incredulous when confronted with reports about the "gene for X" where X refers to a complex social behavior. A gene like MAOA may indeed be related to aggressive behavior (or, for example, TaqIA to impulsivity), but these associations are highly contingent on a multitude of biological and social considerations. And of course the leap from a tendency toward aggressive impulses and committing a crime is complicated by a multitude of social factors encompassing, among other things, families, neighborhoods, and enforcement patterns. Although there is little scientific disagreement about these contingencies, such a level of nuance is difficult to convey to the public.

The warrior gene controversy is a case study in why many sociologists are (and should be) wary of genetic studies of socially-imbued behaviors: genetic reductionism and ascription, particularly in the rough-and-tumble world of public discourse, could lead to new forms of discrimination.

responsibilities

Reacting to the warrior gene controversy, bioethicists Dana Wensley and Michael King drew a useful distinction (and one that applies to all science). On the one hand, scientists are trained extensively in their "internal responsibilities"—making sure that the many steps of the scientific procedure are followed carefully. But many biological scientists may not be sufficiently aware of ideological baggage that they bring to their research because they are members of societies with histories of racism, sexism, and a host of unscientific presumptions about how groups differ. Sociology provides much-needed perspective on the social factors that influence the production of scientific knowledge. Indeed, this point has already been capably illustrated by ethnographic studies of, for example, how scientists in the lab study genetic markers for race and how teachers in medical schools teach about racial disparities in health.

On the other hand, according to Wensley and King, scientists also have "external responsibilities": with journalists, they share a responsibility for what groups in society do with their findings. As Wensley and King note, "Beyond the traditional obligation to provide reliable knowledge, science has an obligation to provide 'socially robust' knowledge, which can only be achieved through scientists being sensitive to the wide range of social implications of their research." These external responsibilities have been the subject of sociological research as well. How is genetic research reported in the mass media? And how do people interpret such reports? Much of this work is inspired by the research of Celeste Condit, who was trained as a rhetorician and studies how the public construes media reports about genetics and behavior and formulates understandings. This body of research suggests that media reports of genetics

> Sociology provides much-needed perspective on the social factors that influence the production of scientific knowledge.

and behavior tend to be technically accurate but the tone of such reports often highlights the power of genes and overstates scientific understanding of how genes are related to complex outcomes. These issues of representation and construal will require further study if science is to provide "socially robust" knowledge.

Sociology thus has many roles to play with respect to both the internal and external responsibilities that Wensley and King identify. The internal responsibility is to make sure that genetic studies of behavior adequately appreciate the role of social context. Genes are highly responsive to social experiences and their associations with behavior are highly conditioned by social factors. In contributing to this line of research, sociology will likely benefit from refined views of the actor and cross-fertilization from other, closely related fields of study. The external responsibility is to make sure that society continues to appreciate the central place of social factors in shaping behaviors. Rules, scripts, norms, small group processes, and organizational and institutional structures all influence human behavior in complex ways that have little to do with genetics. This is of course the *raison d'être* of sociology. And cutting across these internal and external responsibilities, questions inspired by a sociology of knowledge perspective must also be addressed: what social forces influence how genetic research into behavior is regulated, produced, interpreted, disseminated, and used?

In what must be one of the great intellectual ironies of the behavioral sciences, it turns out that the genetic study of behavior will be markedly incomplete without reference to social forces.

RECOMMENDED RESOURCES

Peter Bearman, Sara Shostak, and Molly Martin (eds). "Exploring Genetics and Social Structure," *American Journal of Sociology* (2008), 114 (supplement).

A collection of essays illustrating the diverse ways that sociology and genetics can be integrated.

Jeremy Freese and Sara Shostak. "Genetics and Social Inquiry," *Annual Review of Sociology* (2009), 35:107–28.

A broad examination of how social scientists are incorporating molecular genetics into their research and studying genetic research as a social phenomenon.

Kenneth S. Kendler, Sara Jaffee, and Dan Romer (eds). *The Dynamic Genome and Mental Health: The Role of Genes and Environments in Development* (Oxford University Press, 2010).

A volume of cutting-edge papers that explore how genetic and environmental factors jointly give rise to psychopathology.

Jo C. Phelan, Bruce G. Link, and Naumi M. Feldman. "The Genomic Revolution and Beliefs about Essential Racial Differences: A Backdoor to Eugenics?" *Annual Meeting of the American Sociological Association*, 2010.

An empirical study that examines how people construe the meaning of race from media reports of genetic differences.

Michael J. Shanahan and Scott Hofer. "Molecular Genetics, Aging, and Well-Being: Sensitive Period, Accumulation, and Pathway Models." In Robert H. Binstock and Linda K. George (eds), *Handbook of Aging and the Social Sciences*, 7th edition (Elsevier, 2010).

A discussion of recent epigenetic and transcription studies and their implications for lifecourse models of health.

REVIEW QUESTIONS

1. Before reading this article, did you think nature or nurture was a stronger determinant

in the lives of human beings? What about now?

2. The authors stress that sociology and genetics are more intertwined than people realize. If this is the case, should sociologists and geneticists work together? What might this partnership look like?

3. Some people think genetic research could enable parents to choose their children's genes, from preventing diseases to choosing skin color, eye color, and so on. What are the pros and cons of this possibility? What would the authors most likely say about it?

4. Activity: Pretend you have the ability to choose which genetic characteristics you can pass on to your children. List three that you would select. Why? Compare your list with your classmates'.

lisa f. berkman

the health divide

fall 2004

49

the united states is one of the world's wealthiest nations, yet the health of average americans lags behind that of citizens in other developed countries. the huge amounts we spend on health care are not buying our population good health. the reason is a widening gap between the health of rich and poor americans.

The United States spends more on health care than any other nation in the world, both in absolute dollars and as a proportion of the national economy. Yet it ranks in the bottom half of industrialized countries in life expectancy. Overall, Americans' health is worse than that of people in Japan, Sweden, and France, as well as less affluent countries like Spain, Italy, and Cyprus. While the richest and best-educated Americans are as healthy as their counterparts in other rich nations, poor and less-educated Americans have a life expectancy comparable to adults in many Third World countries. A recent study found that African-American men in Harlem were less likely to live to age 65 than were men in Bangladesh. The vast sums we spend on health care do not buy most Americans good health.

Americans' health has improved considerably over the past century. But the health gap between rich and poor persists and may have even increased over the past two decades. The gap encompasses men and women, blacks and whites, recent immigrants and those who have been here for many generations. Improving the health of the worst-off Americans remains a major challenge. Meeting that challenge depends on understanding the causes of poor health in people who are socially and economically disadvantaged and on our ability to do something about those causes.

understanding americans' ill health

One possible explanation for why the United States lags so noticeably behind other developed countries in health is that many Americans lack access to quality medical care. Some researchers believe that if all Americans received top-notch treatment, the United States would rank near the top in citizens' health. But the evidence does not support this hope. While good health care for all Americans should remain a high priority for many reasons, studies in Great Britain have found that better access to care does not necessarily reduce health disparities between the rich and poor. By the 1980s, British citizens had 30 years of experience with free and universal access through the National Health Service. But according to Mel Bartley, during the 1980s the gap in death rates between rich and poor had actually increased—in step with rising economic inequality.

Over a longer period, 1930 to 1990, the death rate for middle-aged British men with the lowest levels of education and income dropped from about 1,300 to about 900 deaths per 100,000 people, but among men with the most money and schooling death rates dropped much faster, from 920 to 310. Thus, the death rate of British men at the bottom of the social scale went from being 50 percent higher than that of men at the top to 300 percent higher. The experience of the United Kingdom suggests that improving access alone is unlikely to solve the problem. It also suggests that we should look more closely at the link between economic inequalities and health. In particular, the large health differences among groups in the United States may explain our low international ranking. For example, consider the proportion of infants who die each year. In the 1990s, about 11 of every 1,000 infants born in the United States died before the age of one, an unusually high rate. But this number masks enormous variability. White women with at least some college education lost fewer than 6 infants per 1,000 born, compared to 9 infant deaths per 1,000 births to white women who had not finished high school. Black women confront even higher infant mortality rates. Black mothers who had attended college lost 14 per 1,000 infants, while black women with less than a high school education lost 20. This compounded risk is sometimes referred to as the double jeopardy of poor black women, among whom infant mortality rates are four times higher than the best-off white women.

Even with all the neonatal technology in the United States, it ranks 25th in infant mortality among 38 developed countries. Neonatal intensive care units now regularly save small, low birth weight infants who years earlier would have died. Yet American infant mortality rates remain similar to those in the Czech Republic, Greece, Portugal, Belgium, and Cuba. Why? In the United States, less-affluent mothers are more likely to smoke, and are less likely to get prenatal care, have health insurance, or vaccinate their children. Poor American women have limited resources for housing, nutrition, and transportation. Frequently, their jobs provide no sick leave. All of these factors contribute to poor health for their infants.

American children born today can expect to live eight years longer than children born in the 1950s. But, again, aggregate statistics conceal substantial differences across socioeconomic groups. For example, the life expectancy of 45-year-old Americans, an excellent indicator of adult health, rises steadily as family income rises. This is true for men, women, and people in all racial and ethnic groups. Thus, in the 1980s, 45-year-old black and white men in families earning at least $25,000 could expect to live about seven years longer than white and black men in families earning less than $10,000. Income made less difference for black and white women—four and three years, respectively—but it mattered nonetheless.

To show this connection between social standing and health, figure 1 displays death rates from different causes—chronic diseases, injuries, and communicable diseases—for men and women, according to the level of education they attained (more education typically brings better jobs and more wealth). In all cases, as education increases, death rates drop. We see that not only do the least-educated Americans experience the worst health, but also that there is a gradient of risk—each increase in education brings better health. The same pattern holds for diabetes, homicide, suicide, and Americans' ratings of their own health.

Not every cause of death follows this pattern. For instance, lung cancer rates among older women actually increase as education rises. This is in part because affluent women started smoking in the 1950s and 60s, before less well-to-do women did, and now, decades later, they are suffering the deadly consequences. However, over the past 20 years smoking rates have remained steady for less-educated men and women while they have fallen among the better educated. Today, smoking is highest among high school dropouts. In addition, men and women with at least some college education are less likely to drink heavily and to lead sedentary lifestyles than the less educated, while poorer women are more likely to be overweight. Thus, the connection

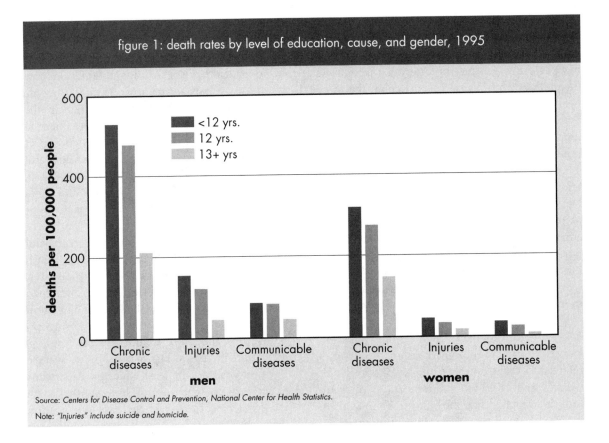

figure 1: death rates by level of education, cause, and gender, 1995

Source: Centers for Disease Control and Prevention, National Center for Health Statistics.

Note: "Injuries" include suicide and homicide.

between disease and social standing changes over time depending upon the underlying causes of those diseases and who is vulnerable. In general though, the economically better-off have significantly better odds of experiencing a long life relatively free of disability, disease, or risk of death by violence.

understanding health inequality

Some researchers argue that it is not being poor that makes people sick, but being sick that makes people poor. Sickly children have trouble learning and doing well in school, and adults who are sick miss work and lose income. While part of the connection between poverty and ill health is undoubtedly due to the debilitating effects of illness, most studies suggest that this can only partly explain the relationship between illness and income. Studies that follow children or working adults over a number of years find that where people are on the social and economic ladder affects their health in several ways. The accumulation of disadvantage over decades significantly impairs health. Also, people are particularly vulnerable to the effects of poverty and disadvantage in certain periods of life, notably early childhood. Disadvantaged people become less healthy than others both because of their living conditions and their social circumstances, such as their relationships and jobs. These situations affect people's health biologically—through exposure to toxins, increases in blood pressure, and suppressed immune responses—and psychologically—through reduced self-confidence, greater depression, and turning to potentially self-destructive behavior like smoking and drinking.

Social scientists have often distinguished between the distal and proximate causes of diseases, or to use less jargon, upstream conditions (such as people's work) and downstream conditions (such as their blood pressure). The great majority of recent health campaigns in the United States have targeted the downstream or physical conditions rather than the economic and social sources of disease (neighborhood environment, work settings, or poverty). The national institutes that fund health research, such as the National Institutes of Health and the Centers for Disease Control, spend the bulk of their funds to study the biological and behavioral risk factors for disease. Only recently have new efforts emerged in many countries, including the United States, to understand and attack the upstream social conditions that underlie and are the fundamental causes of poor health. Historically, public health interventions were very successful in reducing disease. Efforts to clean up drinking water and air and to reduce exposure to toxins in the workplace substantially improved Americans' health by changing collective conditions rather than individual behavior. For example, once scientists discovered the problem of contaminated water in the nineteenth century, officials did not simply ask people to boil their household water before drinking it. Instead, they built facilities to clean the water in each city before piping it into peoples' homes. Often, asking individuals to change their behavior is less effective than changing their environment.

Today, many public health experts contend that if we were to emphasize altering the broader, environmental conditions that lead to poor health, we would increase our chances of reducing social inequalities in health. Our historical experience suggests that environmental interventions that do not rely heavily on the actions of individuals—especially people with the fewest resources and options—are most likely to succeed. Consider two additional examples. The first deals with the physical and material environment and the second with the social environment. In both cases, the health divide is closed by maintaining the excellent health of the well-to-do while improving the health of those less well-off.

Material deprivation and exposure to toxins. Inequality manifests itself in the conditions under which people live and work; poorer people are less able to avoid harmful environments. Take lead exposure, which is among the most dangerous and yet common threats to cognitive development and health. In the United States today, young children most often absorb lead from lead-based paint in old houses. There is a clear, inverse relationship between the level of lead in the blood of young children and their family's income. Even children from middle-income families have, on average, twice the blood levels of lead as children from the highest-income families. About 12 percent of children from poor families have elevated lead levels and poor black children have rates of more than 20 percent. Researchers in the environmental justice movement also have documented the proximity of hazardous waste sites to neighborhoods of minorities and those with concentrated poverty. Studies of air pollution show that such neighborhoods have less healthy air than wealthier neighborhoods.

Poor people and ethnic minorities face greater risks of toxic poisoning and injuries at work, too. For example, agricultural work, which is done almost exclusively by Hispanic and migrant workers, accounts for 13 percent of U.S. workplace fatalities even though just 3 percent of the workforce labors in such occupations. Pesticide toxicity alone causes more than 300,000 cases of illness and 100,000 deaths annually among farm workers.

Social deprivation and stress. The social conditions of work, not just the physical conditions, pose a greater health risk for those in low-ranking as opposed to high-ranking occupations. In his study of British civil servants, Michael Marmot found that workers in lower occupational grades had less control at work, received less support, and faced greater demands than workers above them in the system. Civil servants with less control and more demands at work were also more likely than others to get sick and die. Job stress explained a large part of the link between occupational grade and poor health. Having little control over one's work—for example, not being able to take time off for personal calls and errands or not being able to manage the work pace—is a particularly important health risk. Studies of city bus drivers show how highly stressed they are as they make their rounds on a schedule that is virtually impossible to maintain. After weeks on the job, many experience increases in blood pressure, gain weight, and often become hypertensive and diabetic—results both of hard hours at work and lack of control over their circumstances.

The nature of work in the United States has changed over the past decades such that job insecurity, instability, shift-work and reduced investment in training has placed increasing stress on employees, especially those with less education and fewer opportunities to move up the job ladder. The percentage of workers who are satisfied with their jobs has dropped over the past 10 years. As one worker interviewed by Studs Terkel said, "Most of us, like the assembly line worker, have jobs that are too small for our spirit. Jobs are not big enough for people." In a recent *New York Times* editorial, Adam Cohen suggests that work today is even less likely than 30 years ago to provide meaning and a sense of accomplishment for workers. It is this social experience that translates into poor health. In addition, jobs that strain the balance between work and home by not providing adequate family and sick leave may undermine the health of entire families, not only of the employees. Imagine the stress that a young single mother working in a small business that does not allow sick leave faces when she comes to work knowing that her young child is ill. She might experience increases in blood pressure, changes in the way her body metabolizes food, changes in immune response as she worries about losing her pay or even her job if she leaves work to care for her child—or similar responses if she stays at work and worries. The long shifts that many parents work before returning to family responsibilities take a toll, especially on those with few social and economic resources. The day-to-day difficulties of juggling an insecure and inflexible job with the demands of family life is physiologically hard on many Americans.

People who are socially isolated run notably high risks for early death, according to research in the United States, the United Kingdom, and throughout Europe. In the first study I conducted on this topic, my colleagues and I suspected that one of the reasons that poor economic conditions resulted in poor health was that they disrupted the key social relationships that people depend on practically and emotionally. We found, in a sample of almost 7,000 adults in Alameda County, California, that men and women who were economically disadvantaged were more likely than others to be isolated—to lack intimate connections such as a spouse, close friends, or relatives, and ties to their communities such as club or church memberships. For example, both black and white women with less than a high school education were more likely to be single mothers than their better-educated counterparts. As part of the study, these people were followed over many years. Those who were socially isolated were much more likely to die prematurely. Many studies that track people for decades find the same outcome: people who report few close ties and community memberships are two to three times more likely to die early than those with extensive social bonds.

That poor people tend to be more isolated than others is one reason that their risks are elevated. It is true that working-class families tend to have closely knit social networks, heavily composed of kin. However, these ties may not substitute for connections that help people find jobs, get loans and obtain other practical help (see "Social Networks: The Value of Variety," *Contexts*, Winter 2003). As William Julius Wilson points out, African Americans living in poor, racially and economically segregated neighborhoods often lack access to the kinds of connections and relationships that would help them get better jobs and maintain strong families. Thus, economic inequality, especially poverty, impairs health by making it more difficult to find and maintain the kinds of social relationships that are essential to well-being.

The job stress, economic insecurity, and isolation common among the less affluent affect their health indirectly, through lack of resources, inadequate information, and harmful habits. The same social circumstances also directly affect people's physiology. When people are confronted with long-term, chronically stressful circumstances—like fearing a job layoff or being short of money at the end of the month—their bodies experience a stress reaction often called the "fight or flight" response. While adaptive in the short term, over the long run this response exhausts the body and takes a toll on many of its systems. Elevations in blood pressure, blood sugar, and other such metabolic changes increase the risk of diabetes, cardiovascular disease, and strokes. These same stress responses can also reduce immune system functions, leading to a greater risk of infectious diseases and cancer. People pay a biological price for the heightened and continued vigilance required of them in stressful social situations.

People also encounter very different social and physical circumstances in their homes, neighborhoods, schools, and workplaces. These circumstances influence their health and well-being over a lifetime, leading to more frequent sickness and earlier deaths. It is not simply that poverty leads to poor health, but each step up the economic ladder, from the bottom to the top rung, brings with it improved health and lower risks.

It is this inequality in health, derived from inequalities in economic situations, that accounts for the disappointing place of the United States in the international health rankings. If we could reduce the "health divide" between rich and poor either by improving the health of the most disadvantaged or by reducing the extent of economic disadvantage, we could remedy this national failure.

San Francisco city buses stuck in mid-day traffic. The stress on bus drivers of trying to meet unrealistic schedules—and on other workers who have little control over their work—increase their risk of being overweight, and of having high blood pressure, hypertension, and diabetes. (Courtesy of Lisa F. Berkman)

what are the policy options?

There are two general approaches to reducing inequalities in health. The first involves the use of progressive taxation, economic safety nets, or other redistributive policies to reduce economic inequality. This approach stems from the notion that inequality needs to be attacked directly. In the United States, both private and public policies—negotiated wage rates and the minimum wage, for example—affect this goal. The second approach tries to block the downstream paths by which economic inequality creates health inequality. Cleaning up the environmental dangers, improving working conditions, re-balancing work and family responsibilities, increasing access to health care, and improving nutrition are some ways to block the conversion of inequality into poor health. In the current political climate, the second approach may be the more viable alternative. However, both are worthy of more serious consideration.

These two options are not mutually exclusive and may be pursued simultaneously. Promoting healthful public and private policies at all levels requires collective effort. Most Americans are comfortable with the notion of living in a society with economic inequality. However, they are less comfortable with inequalities of death and with America's dismal ranking on health. Therein may lie some leverage.

This work is supported by the Russell Sage Foundation and Robert Wood Johnson Scholars in Health and Society Program.

RECOMMENDED RESOURCES

Donald Acheson. *Independent Inquiry into Inequalities in Health Report* (The Stationery Office, 1998).

Summarizes a governmental inquiry into health inequality in the United Kingdom.

Mel Bartley. *Health Inequality: An Introduction to Theories, Concepts and Methods* (Blackwell Publishing, 2004).

Bartley provides an introduction to assessing health inequality, especially from the American perspective, directed at both social scientists and journalists.

Lisa F. Berkman and Thomas A. Glass. "Social Integration, Networks and Health." In *Social Epidemiology*, eds. Lisa F. Berkman and Ichiro Kawachi (Oxford University Press, 2000).

Reviews the work on social networks and health.

Howard Frumkin. "Minority Workers and Communities." *Occupational Medicine: State of the Art Reviews* 14(1999): 495–517.

This excellent study details the working conditions of minority workers in the United States.

Bruce G. Link and Jo C. Phelan. "Social Conditions Are Fundamental Causes of Disease." *Journal of Health and Social Behavior*, Special Issue (1995): 80–94.

The authors review the connection between social and economic disadvantage, social networks, and health.

Michael G. Marmot. "Health Inequalities Among British Civil Servants: The Whitehall Study." *Lancet* 337 (1991): 1387–93.

This is an excellent paper on the longstanding Whitehall Study of Inequality in Health.

United States Department of Health and Human Services. *Health, United States, 1998 with Socioeconomic Status and Health Chart Book* (United States Department of Health and Human Services, 1998).

This government publication displays health statistics drawn from national surveys.

William Julius Wilson. *The Truly Disadvantaged* (University of Chicago Press, 1987).

A classic work on the influence of residential segregation in the United States.

1. What does Berkman describe as the "double risk" for black mothers?
2. How would you explain our health care system to someone who lived outside the United States? Compare our system with those of other industrialized countries. Why do you think we have kept our current health care system despite our high spending and low rankings on life expectancy and infant mortality?
3. Identify the specific factors Berkman discusses to break down health care inequality. Can you think of any she did not include?
4. Health care seems to be constantly debated. Using your school's library, find an article on the 1993–1994 Universal Health Care debate. Can you find anything in the article that is supported by the research of Berkman or Mechanic? Is there anything that is refuted by Berkman and Mechanic's research?

part **12**

Crime and Punishment

richard rosenfeld

crime decline in context

50

spring 2002

skyrocketing violent crime rates obsessed americans for decades. crime rates have now been dropping for ten years. what has happened, and how can we learn from it?

After rising to a peak in the early 1990s, crime rates in the United States have been falling for almost a decade. The turnaround was sudden, unexpected, and years later remains something of a puzzle. Some observers attribute most of the drop to tougher sentences and rising rates of imprisonment. Others believe more vigilant policing of loitering, public drunkenness, and other so-called quality-of-life offenses is responsible. Still others point to shrinking drug markets or the booming economy of the 1990s. No strong consensus exists regarding the sources of the crime drop.

Even if we cannot say with certainty what is responsible for the crime decline of the 1990s, it is possible to rule out some of the usual causes and identify some of the real factors in the crime drop. But the first step in unraveling the mystery of the crime decline is to determine whether it happened at all.

real crime decline?

Several years after the rate of crime began declining, most Americans continued to rank crime among the nation's most serious public problems and to believe that crime rates were still going up. A relatively small percentage of Americans have direct experience with serious crime. The primary source of public information about crime is the mass media. Given the constant media drumbeat of murder and may-

hem, it is not surprising that people would be unaware or skeptical of claims that crime rates were dropping. But they were and still are.

The crime decline is real, not an artifact of changes in the rate at which crimes are reported to or recorded by the police. It is significant, long, and deep enough to qualify as a trend and not just a short-run statistical anomaly. It is pervasive, cutting across major offense categories and population groups. Finally, it is time-limited. Crime rates cannot be negative, so the rate of decline curve should slow in the coming years. And it is possible, of course, that crime rates will increase, as they did in the 1980s. Predicting the future is always hazardous, but the best guesses about the next decade will be based on an informed assessment of the recent past.

documenting the decline

A "crime rate" is the number of offenses of a specified type divided by the population of some jurisdiction. By taking population size into account, crime rates can be compared across places and times with different populations. The nation has two "official" crime rates. One consists of offenses known to the police. These are compiled in the FBI's Uniform Crime Reports (UCR). The other is based on reports by victims to the Justice Department's annual National Crime Victimization Survey (NCVS). Both of the crime indicators include information on serious violent and property offenses, such as assault, rape, robbery, burglary, and auto theft. The UCR also records homicides which, of course, are not counted in victim surveys. Both the FBI report and the Justice Department survey are limited to so-called street crimes and omit serious white-collar, corporate, and governmental offenses (e.g., price-fixing, violations of workplace safety rules, pollution, corruption, antitrust violations and false advertising). National indicators for such "suite" crimes do not exist, so no one knows whether they have been rising or falling.

The FBI statistics indicate that street crime has substantially decreased over the past decade. In 1991 the FBI counted 24,700 criminal homicides in the United States, or 9.8 homicides for every 100,000 Americans. By the end of 1999, the number of homicides had dropped to 15,500, and the rate fell to 5.7 per 100,000, a 42 percent decline. The nation's robbery rate also fell by about 40 percent and the burglary rate dropped by one-third during the 1990s. The decreases were less steep, but still appreciable, for rape and aggravated assault (assaults involving serious injury or the use of a weapon), both of which declined by about 20 percent. There is some reason to believe that the declines in nonlethal violence are even sharper than those reported in the FBI report because victims became bolder about reporting such incidents to the police and the police recorded more of them. However, the drop registered in the FBI report and police statistics is mirrored in Justice Department survey results that are unaffected by patterns in reporting and recording.

So the declines in crime are real, but are they meaningful? The simple answer is yes. By the year 2000, homicide and burglary rates were lower than at any time since the mid-1960s. Victimization rates have fallen for youth, adults, blacks, whites, males, and females, in large cities and rural areas, in every region of the country. But the timing and magnitude of these changes differ across population groups, and those differences offer important clues regarding the causes of the crime decline.

> So the declines in crime are real, but are they meaningful? The simple answer is yes. By the year 2000, homicide and burglary rates were lower than at any time since the mid-1960s. Victimization rates have fallen for youth, adults, blacks, whites, males, and females, in large cities and rural areas, in every region of the country. But the timing and magnitude of these changes differ across population groups, and those differences offer important clues regarding the causes of the crime decline.

Consider the difference in the timing of the decrease in youth and adult homicide victims. The victimization rates for people over the age of 24 have fallen more or less continuously since 1980. On the other hand, youth homicide followed a more cyclical pattern, falling during the early 1980s, rising from the mid-1980s to a peak in 1993 and then falling again since then. The increase in youth homicide during the 1980s and early 1990s was so dramatic that it gave rise to concerns about a national youth violence "epidemic." The victimization rate for 14- to 17-year-olds nearly tripled, and that for 18- to 24-year-olds almost doubled between 1984 and 1993. The fall from the 1993 peak in youth homicide has been equally pronounced (figure 1). The trends in the rates at which teenagers and young adults committed homicide were almost identical to the victimization trends.

I focus on criminal homicide in this discussion because more accurate and detailed information about the characteristics of victims and offenders exists for homicide than for other crimes and because it is the most serious. How-

figure 1: homicide rates by age of victim, 1980–1998

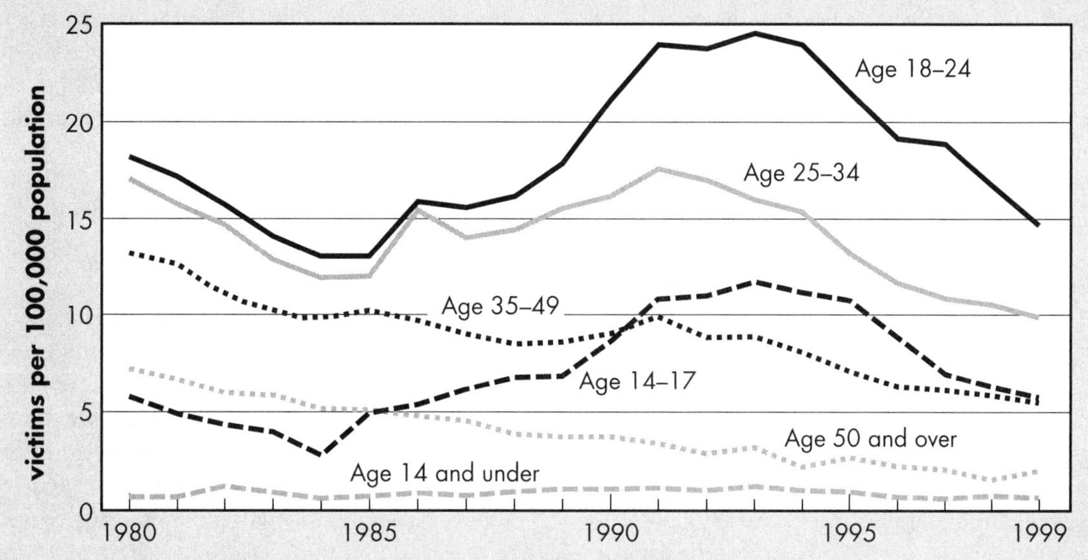

victims per 100,000 population

Age 18–24

Age 25–34

Age 35–49

Age 14–17

Age 50 and over

Age 14 and under

ever, the same basic patterns also characterize serious nonlethal criminal violence.

A credible explanation of the homicide decline, then, must explain why the time trends were different for adult and youth homicides, the first dropping steadily since 1980, the second fluctuating. Another notable pattern in the homicide drop involves the differing time trends for offenses committed with and without firearms. Roughly two-thirds of homicides in the United States are committed with a gun. Both the increase in youth homicide during the 1980s and early 1990s and the decrease over the last several years are restricted largely to the firearm category. Youth homicides involving other weapons or no weapons exhibit a gradual downward shift over the past 20 years, and adult homicide rates have decreased in

both the firearm and nonfirearm categories. The "action," then, in the national homicide rate for the last two decades is a consequence of rising and falling rates of youths killing and being killed with guns. A sufficient explanation of recent homicide trends cannot ignore the prominent role of guns in the cycle of youth violence.

The cycling up and down in youth firearm violence occurred earliest and was most pronounced in the largest cities and among young African-American males. The same changes happened in smaller cities and among white teenagers and young adults, but happened a year or two later and the fluctuations were smaller. (Persons of "other races" constitute only 2 to 3 percent of the nation's homicide victims.) A sufficient explanation of the recent homicide trends should accommodate these race, sex, and city-size differences as well.

An explanation of the crime drop should account for why the trends differ for youth and adults and why they are most evident in firearm homicides, in the large cities and among young black men. Serious explanations should account for both the rise and the decline in crime rates since the 1980s. And the best explanation will connect those recent changes to longer-term trends and to the social conditions that make the United States the murder capital of the industrial world, the crime decline notwithstanding.

drug markets and the spread of firearms

No single explanation of the crime decline has been proposed that meets all of these conditions. One of the more promising, however, attributes the increase in youth homicide rates beginning in the mid-1980s to the diffusion of violence in and around urban crack markets. The high demand for crack led drug dealers to recruit young inner-city males as sellers and arm them to fend off attacks from rival dealers and protect themselves from street robbers. A classic arms race resulted as other young people acquired guns in an increasingly threatening urban environment. The diffusion of firearms fueled escalating rates of youth homicide, with the sharpest increases occurring in the largest cities where the crack epidemic began. The increases in youth homicide, in turn, drove up the total homicide rate.

If this explanation of the increase also applies to the homicide decline, the turning point and drop in youth homicide should have been preceded by corresponding changes in the urban crack markets. That is exactly what happened. The crack epidemic crested around 1990 and the drug markets began to shrink, the process occurring first in the largest cities. The firearm-diffusion hypothesis squares with most of the basic facts underlying the crime decline. It accounts for why the drop occurred in the larger cities before the smaller ones, why it has been concentrated among young African Americans and why it has involved firearms. (Drug dealers do not use fists, sticks, or knives to settle disputes.) Most important, it highlights the changes among adolescents and young adults, and thereby situates the crime decline of the 1990s in the context of earlier increases.

what about adults?

The firearm-diffusion story does not explain everything we want to know about the crime decline. It is silent on the long-term decrease in homicide among adults. What little we know about that decline suggests it is driven in part by a marked decrease in "intimate partner" homicides—killings involving husbands, wives, boyfriends, and girlfriends—and in part by the explosive increase in incarceration since 1980. But neither of these factors explains the adult homicide decline in its entirety, and the reduction in intimate partner homicide itself requires explanation.

Recent research suggests that plummeting marriage rates and the growth of hot lines, shelters, legal advocacy, and other domestic violence prevention resources have contributed to the drop in intimate partner killings. One study found the greatest declines in intimate partner homicides over the last 25 years occurred in those cities with the largest drops in marriage rates, the largest increases in divorce rates, and the most rapid growth in shelters and legal advocacy programs for domestic violence victims. Interestingly, the largest homicide drops occurred in the rate at which women kill their husbands or boyfriends and not, as might be expected, in the rate at which women are killed by their male partners. Researchers speculate that domestic violence programs, by offering women a nonviolent means of escaping abusive relationships, make it less likely they will have to kill their way out. However, because prevention programs are designed to assist women, their growth should have little effect on male behavior. Although interesting, such speculations remain just that. In general, criminologists know even less about the causes of the 20-year adult homicide drop than about the youth homicide epidemic.

criminal justice, the economy, and firearms policy

Even allowing for some lag between shrinking drug markets and falling rates of youth firearm violence, the crime decline is far longer and deeper than can be explained by the waning of the crack epidemic alone. It seems certain that other factors are at work, and there is no lack of alternative explanations, some of which are truly inspired. For example, economists Steven Levitt and John Donahue have proposed that the drop in youth violence during the 1990s is due in large part to the legalization of abortion in the 1970s. Their logic is that the increase in abortions, especially among poor women, led to fewer births of unwanted children who, had they been born, would have contributed more than their share of criminal violence as teenagers in the 1990s. Although Levitt and Donahue offer some intriguing evidence for their thesis, proving the counterfactual—that is, demonstrating that something would have happened (more crime) had something else not happened (legal abortions)—is inherently difficult. And even if they are correct about how the increase of abortion might have led to the contraction of youth crime, their argument is silent on the long-term decline in adult crime, as well as on the abrupt increase in youth crime during the 1980s. Finally, who is to say how many children, once born, remain "unwanted"?

The "more abortions, less crime" thesis is, not surprisingly, controversial. It is also quite new, and replication studies by other researchers have not yet appeared. Several other explanations for the crime drop have received greater research attention. Four are particularly prominent in both scholarly and policy circles: better policing, growing imprisonment, the booming economy, and firearms policies.

policing

Some analysts believe that smart and tough policing is behind the crime drop. That is the reason former Mayor Rudolph Giuliani and former police commissioner William Bratton gave for the dramatic drop in New York City's homicide rate during the 1990s. However, homicide rates also have decreased sharply in cities that did not noticeably alter their policing policies, such as Los Angeles, or that instituted very different changes from those in New York, such as San Diego. Aggressive policing against minor offenses may have contributed to the crime decline in New York and elsewhere but, as Orlando Patterson and Christopher Winship have pointed out, at the price of heightened police-citizen tension and violence.

prison expansion

The other criminal justice response that has been touted as responsible for the crime drop is the massive expansion in incarceration. The prison population has quadrupled since 1980 and now numbers more than 1.3 million inmates. It would be surprising if incarceration growth of that magnitude had no effect on the crime rate. But little agreement exists on the size of that effect. Also, whatever crime suppression effects incarceration may have must be reckoned against possible crime increases resulting from the diminished economic prospects of ex-prisoners and the disruptions in the local community when so many men are away in prison.

Prison expansion has been accompanied by a growth in the number of sentenced offenders subject to the death penalty and a dramatic rise in executions since the revival of capital punishment in the United States in the 1970s. By the end of 1999, more than 3,500 inmates were on death row, and nearly 600 had been executed. However, whatever the merits of the death penalty, less violent crime does not appear to be one of them. No credible evidence supports the use of capital punishment to reduce homicide or other forms of criminal violence.

the economy

One benign alternative to expanded imprisonment is expanded employment. There seems little doubt that the record drops in unemployment rates, including those for minority teenagers, during the economic boom of the 1990s contributed in some way to the crime decline over the same period. But in what way? The relationship between employment and crime is far from simple and is the subject of ongoing debate among social scientists. Do crime rates fall during periods of economic growth because more people are working or because working people are making more money? And if people are earning more and buying more, that creates more opportunities for theft and the violence that sometimes accompanies it. Moreover, a drop in the unemployment rate or an increase in wages may reduce crime only when illegitimate opportunities for making money, such as drug dealing, are disappearing. If that is true, it is the combination of rising legitimate and falling illegitimate opportunities that has made criminal activity a less attractive alternative to legal work for many low-income youth.

A sizable fraction of teenagers, inner-city teenagers in particular, switch back and forth from low-end jobs in the legitimate and illegitimate labor markets, depending on shifts in prevailing opportunities. During periods of stagnation in the legitimate labor market and growth in illegitimate opportunities, such as the 1980s crack epidemic, we should observe increases in youth crime and violence. Likewise, we should observe drops in teenagers' criminal involvement when their legitimate opportunities are expanding and their illegitimate opportunities are shrinking, as during the economic boom and crack market crash of the 1990s. Both observations fit the temporal pattern of serious youth violence over the past two decades.

firearms policy

Given the significant role of guns in serious criminal violence, it is not surprising that the crime decline has been linked to changes in firearm regulations. Some analysts believe that granting persons permission to carry firearms in public deters violent crime by making offenders wary of armed victims. Others favor background checks and waiting periods, such as those required by the 1994 Brady Act, as a way to reduce criminal misuse of handguns. Some people think, in the words of one pro-gun enthusiast, that more guns lead to less crime, while others believe that fewer guns, or fewer guns in the "wrong" hands, will reduce serious criminal violence. Evidence regarding the effectiveness of either policy is mixed. Some firearm initiatives, such as the popular gun buyback programs that have sprung up over the past decade, clearly do not reduce levels of firearm violence. More promising strategies include longer prison sentences for using a gun in a crime and police "gun patrols" in which seizures of illegal guns are focused in high-risk areas. However, we do not know how much of the crime decline can be attributed to either of these factors.

the big picture

What is the significance of these various partial accounts of the 1990s crime decline? First, none of them is a complete explanation for the crime drop. That is not just because researchers lack sufficient evidence; more important is that major social phenomena, such as serious crime, are rarely driven by a single factor. A comprehensive explanation of the crime decline will have to encompass multiple, interacting factors. Second, we cannot create a comprehensive explanation simply by adding together the various causal factors highlighted in these partial accounts, because we lack a theory that tells us just how it is that law enforcement, imprisonment, economic expansion, drug markets, and firearm diffusion—not to mention abortion—combine to reduce crime in the context of long-term trends. We badly need such an account if we are to anticipate and prepare for, much less forestall, the next increase.

The basic function of institutions such as the family, economy, and political system is to regulate social behavior in the service of basic human needs. When institutions function properly, they enjoy high levels of legitimacy. People believe in the institutions, play by the rules, and crime rates decline.

Although such a theory has not yet been produced, productive first steps have been taken. Gary LaFree argues that changes in crime rates reflect the rise and fall of institutional legitimacy in a society. The basic function of institutions such as the family, economy, and political system is to regulate social behavior in the service of basic human needs. When institutions function properly, they enjoy high levels of legitimacy. People believe in the institutions, play by the rules, and crime rates decline. At other times, people question whether institutions are getting the job done—for example, when divorce and unemployment rates rise. Institutions lose people's allegiance and the capacity to control people's behavior, and crime rates go up. LaFree has applied his theory to the dramatic rise in crime rates that occurred during the late 1960s and in the 1970s, a period of significant social upheaval, political scandal,

and institutional challenge. Crime rates stabilized in the 1980s, in part, LaFree suggests, because some of the changes that had wrenched the family and economy slowed or reversed (divorce rates stopped climbing, the economy began to grow), and also because policy-makers responded to the increase in crime by expanding other institutions, such as the social welfare and criminal justice systems. Those expansions helped to head off further crime increases.

When LaFree published his argument, the crime decline of the 1990s had just begun, yet if the theory of institutional legitimacy is correct, crime rates will fall when the economy is booming, consumer confidence (an indicator of economic "legitimacy") is climbing, and prisons are expanding—all trademark characteristics of the roaring nineties. These changes evidently were sufficient to offset the effects of the Clinton scandals on political legitimacy and to permit a substantial downsizing of the welfare rolls.

Legitimacy theory, however, is both too broad and too narrow to fully explain the crime decline and the longer trend of which it is a part. It is too broad because it tells us little about the youth violence epidemic of the 1980s and the social conditions in the cities that nourish drug markets and high levels of firearm violence. And it is too narrow because it does not explain why, even during periods of strong institutional legitimacy such as the 1950s, rates of criminal violence in the United States remain higher than those in most other developed nations (figure 2).

The sharp increase in youth homicide rates in the late 1980s, as noted earlier, was brought about by the firearm violence emanating in and

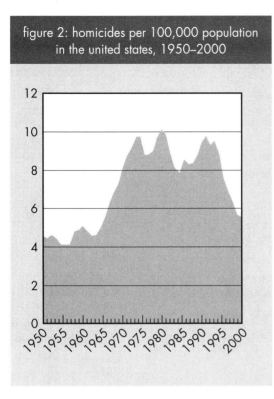

figure 2: homicides per 100,000 population in the united states, 1950–2000

around the inner-city crack markets. But why were the crack markets so heavily concentrated in already distressed urban areas, and why were they so violent? The insights of a number of sociologists shed light on these issues. Crack sellers were attracted to those neighborhoods where residents were least able to keep them out. William Julius Wilson describes such areas as being subject to multiple "dislocations" in the form of chronically high levels of joblessness, family disruption and extreme social isolation. Their residents are often unable to engage in the kind of cooperative and supervisory activities that Robert Sampson and his colleagues term "collective efficacy." Collective efficacy enables communities to contain street crime and resist the predations of drug dealers—in fact, it very

much defines what we mean by the word *community*. Along with isolation from mainstream patterns of conduct, alienation from formal institutions of justice, and diminished personal security comes the development of an alternative "code of the street" that, according to Elijah Anderson, encourages violent responses, particularly among young men, to perceived slights, insults, and disrespect.

Prolonged joblessness and reduced collective efficacy explain why illicit drug markets emerge when and where they do; isolation, alienation, and the code of the street explain why they are so violent. These ideas help to fill in the gaps in LaFree's theory, but they do not contradict its basic premise that crime rates increase with the loss of institutional legitimacy. On the contrary, it is hard to imagine a better illustration of that premise than the barren institutional landscape typical of so many high-crime inner-city neighborhoods.

how long will it last?

If the ideas of Wilson, Sampson, Anderson, and others help to narrow the focus of the legitimacy theory on the isolated ghetto poverty areas of the inner cities, we should remember that even at its low points, criminal violence in the United States remains very extensive by international standards. The U.S. homicide rate in particular—even the white homicide rate alone—is higher than that of every other developed nation. Some analysts have, reasonably enough, tied the high level of lethal violence to the limited regulation and widespread possession of firearms in the United States. Certainly firearms are deadly implements, but still we must ask why they are so unrestricted and plentiful in comparison with other nations, and more basically, why they are so often used to kill people.

An influential theory proposes that people use violence as a means of "self-help" when they lack lawful means of resolving conflicts or protecting themselves. Abused women's use of violence when they lack alternative ways to protect themselves from abusive partners is one example. Now consider the role of gun violence in illicit drug markets. Unable to use the police and courts for resolving disputes with suppliers, competitors, and customers, dealers use violence to enforce discipline, secure territory and supplies, collect debts, and protect against theft. Once guns enter the picture, the violence that begins as an enforcement code in drug markets can quickly diffuse throughout a community as people seek to protect themselves by any means necessary.

As the demand for crack diminished, so did the markets that supplied the drug and generated the violence, and the crime drop began. Multiple factors caused the crime decline of the 1990s, as well as the increase that preceded it. These factors tend to be cyclical. While cycles in the demand for particular drugs, in economic conditions, and in police aggressiveness in going after guns can reduce crime, those reductions are cyclically limited. Lasting and deeper reductions in crime will require correspondingly major reductions in the chronic economic insecurity, social isolation, and alienation found in our nation's most violent communities. The current decline in crime offers opportunities for social change that are not available when people are too afraid to participate in their communities. But time is running out.

RECOMMENDED RESOURCES

Elijah Anderson. *Code of the Street: Decency, Violence, and the Moral Life of the Inner City* (W.W. Norton, 1999).

Alfred Blumstein and Joel Wallman, eds. *The Crime Drop in America* (Cambridge University Press, 2000).

Gary LaFree. *Losing Legitimacy. Street Crime and the Decline of Social Institutions in America* (Westview, 1998).

Robert J. Sampson, Stephen W. Raudenbush, and Felton Earls. "Neighborhoods and Violent Crime: A Multilevel Study of Collective Efficacy." *Science* 277 (1997): 918–24.

William Julius Wilson. *When Work Disappears: The World of the New Urban Poor* (Alfred A. Knopf, 1996).

REVIEW QUESTIONS

1. Why are there two different crime rates? What are the differences that result in the two rates?
2. Identify the major factors that explain the drop in crime during the 1990s. While these factors undoubtedly interact with one another, which would you guess explains the greatest amount of the decrease? Explain your position.
3. As mentioned in the essay, particular types of crime are not discussed because of the way that crime rates are reported. Write two paragraphs on how these omissions might affect public opinion. Why do some types of crime evade our awareness? How do you think this might affect public perceptions of the race, class, and age of criminals?
4. William Julius Wilson describes "dislocations" and Robert Sampson mentions "collective efficacy" when discussing how the social characteristics of particular areas may facilitate crime. What do these concepts refer to? Are they related to the major facts that explain the drop in crime during the 1990s?

saundra d. westervelt and kimberly j. cook

coping with innocence after death row   **51**
fall 2008

signigicant barriers await those exonerated of capital crimes—barriers that make it hard to cope with the injustice of confinement and rebuild a life on the outside.

Kennedy Brewer spent 13 years behind bars—seven on death row—for the rape and murder of a 3-year-old girl. On February 15, 2008, he became the 127th death row inmate in the United States exonerated and released from prison.

The crime was heinous, the police needed a suspect, and Brewer was the last man known to see the girl alive. The primary evidence used against him was the testimony of a dentist, widely discredited at the time, who claimed bite marks on the girl matched Brewer's teeth.

In 2001, Brewer's appellate attorneys presented DNA evidence of an exact match to another suspect who has since confessed to the crime. Based on this evidence, the court vacated Brewer's conviction but the district attorney—the same one who presided over Brewer's initial conviction—kept him in jail for five more years, claiming he planned to retry the case.

Finally, after intervention by the Mississippi Attorney General's Office and the Innocence Project at Cardozo Law School, the charges against him were dismissed.

The enduring images of exonerees are of vindicated individuals reunited with family and friends in a moment of happiness and relief, tearful men embraced by supporters who have long fought for their release. We think of these moments as conclusions, but really they're the start of a new story, one that social science is beginning to tell about how exonerees are greeted by their communities, their homes, and

their families, and how they cope with the injustice of their confinement and rebuild their lives on the outside.

understanding exoneration

The ranks of those exonerated of crimes they didn't commit increases every year. Some sources report the number of exonerees now tops 340 for murder or sexual assault since 1989, 200 for DNA exonerations secured by the Innocence Project, and 129 for exonerees released from death row since 1973. The true number of exonerees is no doubt larger, but no system keeps an accurate count.

The swell in the ranks of the exonerated raises questions central to society's ideas about fairness, justice, and responsibility.

Studies of wrongful convictions document the scope of the problem, detail individual cases of wrongful conviction, and identify the legal and social factors leading to wrongful convictions. To date, only two have addressed the consequences of a wrongful conviction for the innocent exoneree—a study by Kathryn Campbell and Myriam Denov of the post-release experiences of five Canadian exonerees and Adrian Grounds' study of the psychiatric assessments of 18 British exonerees. Neither focuses on American exonerees or capital cases.

While the scholarly literature is scant, the struggles of exonerees receive sustained attention in the popular press. Most articles focus on individual cases, describing the numerous obstacles exonerees encounter. But a November 2007 article in *The New York Times* by Janet Roberts and Elizabeth Stanton provides an in-depth examination of the experiences of more than 100 DNA exonerees and is coupled with an online multi-media presentation that includes audio clips of exonerees discussing their experiences.

Sociological research can help us understand exonerees in ways that go beyond basic descriptive and journalistic accounts. We begin, strangely enough, with studies of responses to disasters.

> Sociological research can help us understand exonerees in ways that go beyond basic descriptive and journalistic accounts.

Robert Lifton argues that some disasters are short-lived events with a distinct beginning and end—such as floods, tornados, or bombings. Others are "sustained catastrophes" that extend over long periods, like those experienced by abuse victims or prisoners of war.

If incarceration of an innocent person can be considered a sustained catastrophe, we can understand the human suffering experienced by exonerees just as we do other trauma survivors. Models of trauma, coping, and stigma management help explain the "life after death" experiences of those we most often think of as surviving sustained catastrophes (cancer and AIDS patients, abuse victims). So, too, these ideas help us understand how death row exonerees negotiate trauma after release.

the exonerees

Since 2003, with the help of funding from the University of North Carolina at Greensboro and the American Sociological Association, we've conducted 18 life-story interviews with death row exonerees. After years of hearing their stories told by attorneys, judges, and the media, we wanted to give them a venue to speak for themselves and claim their own stories. They came from varying backgrounds and had spent anywhere from two years to 26 years in prison and one year to 18 years on death row (see table). All were convicted of heinous and stigmatizing crimes.

Kirk Bloodsworth and Charles Fain were accused of raping and killing young girls. Delbert Tibbs, Walter McMillian, and Shabaka Brown are African-American men accused of raping and/or killing white victims in the Deep South.

Four of our interviewees experienced the trauma of confronting a death in the family while being wrongfully tried, convicted, and sentenced to death for the murder. Gary Gauger was convicted of murdering his elderly parents, Sabrina Butler her 9-month-old son, Greg Wilhoit his wife, and Scott Taylor* his wife and 15-month-old son, along with five other non-family members.

Two of the exonerees we met came close to an execution date. Brown came within 15 hours of electrocution and had been measured for his burial suit. Butler expected to be executed and waited all day for someone to escort her to the execution chamber.

She recalls crying, "They gonna kill me, they gonna kill me," and thinking, "I was scared to death because I thought that they was gonna kill me for somethin' that I didn't do. And I couldn't tell nobody to help me." No one came that day—she'd received a stay of execution, but nobody told her.

---

*This exoneree prefers to remain anonymous. We have chosen this pseudonym for him.

exonerees involved in this research

Name	Sex	Race	Age at conviction	State where tried	Years in prison	Years on death row	Year of exoneration	DNA?	Actual offender[s] found
Fain	M	W	35	ID	18	18	2001	yes	no
Melendez	M	L	34	FL	17.5	17.5	2002	no	yes
Tibbs	M	B	34	FL	2	2	1977	no	no
Gauger	M	W	41	IL	3	1	1996	no	yes
Krone	M	W	35	AZ	9.5	2	2002	yes	yes
Butler	F	B	19	MS	5	2	1995	no	no
Bloodsworth	M	W	23	MD	8	1	1993	yes	yes
Brown	M	B	25	FL	14	14	1987	no	no
Wilhoit	M	W	33	OK	6	5	1993	no	no
McMillian	M	B	47	AL	6	6	1993	no	no
James	M	B	23	OH	26	1	2003	no	no
Howard	M	B	23	OH	26	1	2003	no	no
Keaton	M	B	18	FL	2	1	1973	no	yes
Gell	M	W	23	NC	8.5	5	2004	no	no
Cobb	M	B	37	IL	9	4	1987	no	no
Taylor*	M	B	29	IL	13	10	2003	no	no
Beeman	M	W	25	OH	3	2	1979	no	no
Rivera	M	L	28	NC	2	1.5	1999	no	yes

* This exoneree prefers to remain anonymous. We have chosen this pseudonym for him.

We know that, in general, survivors often feel guilty for living when others die and experience hyper-arousal, intrusive thoughts, and feelings of hopelessness and apathy. They tend to have difficulty envisioning the future and connecting to others emotionally, and struggle with feelings of fear, worthlessness, helplessness, isolation, and rejection. And we saw similar survivor's guilt among these exonerees.

Juan Melendez told us that hundreds of death row inmates applauded his departure. Yet, he couldn't bring himself to write them letters, saying, "They aren't outside, they are in there, it don't feel right."

"I can't write letters. I can't talk on the phone. I don't like to visit. I don't like to go anywhere. I don't like to leave the house. What's the point? . . . So . . . the days go by, and pretty soon it's one year, it's three years, it's five years, it's, you know? . . . Don't wanna bust out of my comfort zone. Don't wanna grow," Gauger said of the apathy he feels about maintaining relationships with those close to him.

Wilhoit puts it succinctly: "People say that I'm emotionally unavailable."

Fear of repeat accusations also curtails much of exonerees' social activity. Bloodsworth is careful to let his wife know exactly where he is at all times, refusing to be alone unless someone can verify his whereabouts.

Many exonerees simply feel helpless. Depending on their length of incarceration, they return to a world dramatically different from the one they left. Technology such as ATM machines or cell phones is confounding and many struggle just to relearn the basics of walking (for sustained periods or by negotiating space), eating with utensils, and sleeping.

"I can't really see more than two weeks in advance," said Gauger, describing his inability to envision the future. "I've lost the ability to really comprehend that. I think I got that at Statesville (prison) 'cause commissary comes every two weeks."

Learning to manage stigma is a challenge for exonerees just as it is other survivors. The debilitating effects of stigma for exonerees echo those described in the classic work by Erving Goffman, who introduced the concept of stigma and "spoiled identity" to sociologists.

Several exonerees were greeted with fear from neighbors, suspicion from family, and hate messages from others. Frequently, community members still see them as guilty criminals who "beat the system."

> Bloodsworth is careful to let his wife know exactly where he is at all times, refusing to be alone unless someone can verify his whereabouts.

Bloodsworth often found "child killer" written in the dirt on his truck, and neighbors told Butler's children their mother was a "baby killer." Because of her notoriety, Butler can't find employment in her Mississippi hometown. Rejected by her church, she still feels searing glares while grocery shopping or about town. So she rarely goes out. Some exonerees move away from the communities in which they were tried, hoping anonymity will insulate them from stigma.

Two factors affect how much stigma exonerees experience—whether they receive a public apology from legal officials upon release and whether the actual offender is identified in their case. Both profoundly impact community opinion and influence how community members view and treat exonerees.

Without an apology or formal "delabeling," exonerees struggle to reshape their identities as "innocent," especially when public officials continue to doubt them. Prosecutors, in particular, often publicly maintain exonerees' guilt, even in the face of overwhelming evidence of their innocence. Media often report these public comments but rarely provide full coverage of the evidence.

Such prosecutorial proclamations, combined with the public's general belief that officials rarely pursue cases against "good" people and the cynical barb that "everyone in prison is innocent," lead the public to believe exonerees "got out on a technicality." Thus, while family and friends partially insulate exonerees from stigma, the real power to destigmatize lies, cruelly, with those most responsible for their wrongful convictions.

negotiating exoneration

Survivors of life-threatening trauma, including exonerees, rely on multiple coping strategies that shift over time. Strategies of incorporation and rejection are chief among them.

As Dapna Oyserman and Janet Swim have noted, coping strategies can be aimed at either producing positive outcomes for survivors or avoiding the negative effects of the trauma itself. For exonerees, strategies of incorporation might include absorbing the "exoneree" identity into their self-concept and finding some good that can come from their negative experiences. Exonerees and other survivors use a variety of techniques to make sense of what happened to them, such as telling their stories openly, finding meaning in their experiences, establishing ties to other survivors, and relying on family support. Many exonerees participate in activism and education by speaking publicly about their cases. Recounting their stories helps them "normalize" the trauma and builds confidence through acknowledgment and affirmation. Some cope by seeking out other exonerees at conferences and events, finding comfort in community with those who understand their plight.

Others explore spirituality to find positive meaning in their wrongful convictions. "You

> Several exonerees were greeted with fear from neighbors, suspicion from family, and hate messages from others.

gotta make medicine from poison. . . . I believe that the Great Spirit took me to death row so that I could be a witness and a voice against [the death penalty]," Tibbs said. Butler believes her tragedy was a spiritual lesson, God's way of telling her she was on the wrong path.

Of course, some exonerees can find nothing positive in their trauma. Their strategies of rejection aim to reduce or avoid the negative consequences of their wrongful convictions and involve socially isolating or numbing themselves emotionally. This can include self-destructive behaviors like drug and alcohol abuse and violence.

"I just could not function at all. . . . The only thing I wanted to do was . . . get high and drink . . . because I wanted to forget," Bloodsworth said. As we've seen, others choose isolation, avoiding the accusatory glare of the public whenever possible.

looking ahead

The joy on exonerees' faces at their release quickly fades when they confront the challenges of managing their trauma and rebuilding their lives. Several said they needed a "decompression period" to adjust to everyday living on the outside. Their immediate physical needs involve finding housing, medical attention, employment and training, and emergency financial support. But their emotional and psychological needs also demand attention: managing anger and bitterness, reconnecting with family and children, addressing drug or alcohol dependency, and negotiating social rejection and stigma.

Their legal needs, too, continue long after the protracted court battles to gain their freedom. They need help getting their records expunged, seeking a gubernatorial pardon, filing a compensation claim or suing the state for wrongful incarceration, managing whatever media attention or offers may come their way, and negotiating bureaucracies to file for Social Security, disability, or welfare assistance.

Although exonerees consistently identify needs for services and assistance, their most pressing need, they say most often, is for an apology—something very few ever receive. This adds to their bitterness and anger, fuels public hostilities toward them, and exacerbates the trauma they've already experienced.

Very little help for those physical, emotional, and legal needs is available. Most support and assistance comes from family, friends, local advocates, and their attorneys. While the public often views compensation as the solution to most exonerees' problems, only 25 states and the District of Columbia currently have compensation statutes in place to provide financial assistance to the wrongly convicted. In many of those states the application procedures are limiting, legally complex, and costly to pursue. Only one of the 18 exonerees we interviewed was able to successfully negotiate this process to receive compensation. While the expansion of such statutes is needed in those states that don't currently have them, compensation is no panacea for the array of trauma-based challenges confronting exonerees.

Instead, exonerees need wide-ranging assistance based on their multi-dimensional needs. Only a few organizations currently exist to address those needs, including the Innocence Project, the Witness to Innocence Project, the Life After Exoneration Program, and the Darryl Hunt Project for Freedom and Justice. And despite their good work, their scope and reach are limited. Exonerations are most often local events and require services from local community groups, employers, and service agencies.

> Without an apology or formal "delabeling," exonerees struggle to reshape their identities as innocent.

It's difficult for the Life After Exoneration Program, in California, or the Darryl Hunt Project, in North Carolina, to assist exonerees in Idaho, Mississippi, Florida, or Illinois.

These local exonerations, then, are perhaps best addressed on a local level, supplemented by the experience and resources of these larger organizations. Barry Scheck and Peter Neufeld, co-founders of the Innocence Project, called for the development of a network of innocence projects in each state in the late 1990s. Now, a similar network of "reintegration programs" is needed to partner with innocence projects to assist exonerees in rebuilding their lives.

Such programs would be well-situated to provide services, legal aid, employment assistance, and transition funds by drawing on networks of lawyers, physicians, employers, counselors, and advocates. A community reintegration forum might help prepare communities to embrace exonerees. By fostering the reintegration of exonerees back into their communities, such a network of programs may ultimately complete the exoneration process.

continuing controversy

A hallmark of the U.S. legal system is its foundation on the due process rights of the accused to prevent mistakes. The conviction and incarceration of an innocent person, especially in a capital case, represents a grave failure of that process. At present, the consequences of such failures have received little informed evaluation.

Despite a decade of raised public awareness of wrongful convictions, exonerations are still rife with controversy. They provide a window into the competing value systems embedded in both the criminaljustice system and public opinion about the administration of justice.

While some recognize the mistakes and abuses in the system that lead to wrongful convictions, others remain skeptical about the true innocence of exonerees. The public is therefore torn between believing the evidence of innocence before them and a strong desire to believe in the accuracy and virtue of the system. Cynics hold that if exonerees didn't do what they were convicted of this time, no doubt they did do something along the way to merit the punishment they received. Perhaps the reality of long, painful, and undeserved punishment is too horrible for us to confront.

The U.S. legal system provides as many rights to the accused and safeguards against wrongful conviction as almost any nation in the world. In establishing the current slate of due process rights, lawmakers took to heart the adage that it's better to have 10 guilty people go free than convict one innocent person.

Yet at odds with this fundamental principle are the pressures on the criminal justice system to arrest, convict, and incarcerate in the name of public safety that we see today. Exonerations draw these competing values to the surface. While on one hand Americans want to convict the guilty and only the guilty, on the other they want to give those in the system wide latitude to arrest and convict offenders to keep us safe.

Exonerations expose these tensions by forcing us to weigh which of these competing principles is more important. Is justice best served when the system operates accurately but slowly and some guilty individuals slip through the cracks? Or when the system swiftly processes the guilty at the expense of a few—or a few hundred, or a few thousand—innocent lives along the way? Which type of error shall we tolerate?

Exonerations also raise the difficult issue of responsibility. In studies of wrongful convictions we typically ask the question of responsibility this way: if an innocent person is wrongly convicted, who is responsible—the police, prosecutor, judge, public, media, or "the system" writ large? When examining exonerations rather than wrongful convictions, however, the question of responsibility is inextricably linked to the question of "justice." If innocent people are exonerated of crimes, what is our responsibility to them? How do we create, or recreate, justice for the exonerated?

In comparison to the parolees convicted for crimes they committed, we currently provide even less help to exonerees upon release. Exonerees get no time in a halfway house; no access to drug rehabilitation; no help with job skills, housing, or employment; and no bus fare, not even pocket change to make a phone call from the prison lobby for a ride home. Exonerees rarely even get something as seemingly simple as an apology, a recognition by someone in power that the exoneree was wronged, a recognition of responsibility.

We seem unable to fully embrace the idea that justice for exonerees requires official recognition of responsibility to aid them in rebuilding a life. Our hesitancy in this regard may be entangled with our competing need to believe in the efficacy of the system. To publicly acknowledge our responsibility to exonerees is also to acknowledge a flawed system—and the other innocent people in prison awaiting vindication.

RECOMMENDED RESOURCES

Kathryn Campbell and Myriam Denov. "The Burden of Innocence: Coping with a Wrongful Imprisonment." *Canadian Journal of Criminology and Criminal Justice* (2004) 46: 139–63.

> Details the post-release experiences of five Canadian exonerees.

Erving Goffman. *Stigma: Notes on the Management of Spoiled Identities* (Prentice-Hall, 1963).

> The classic sociological analysis of stigma.

Adrian Grounds. "Psychological Consequences of Wrongful Conviction and Imprisonment." *Canadian Journal of Criminology and Criminal Justice* (2004) 46: 165–82.

> Examines psychiatric assessment information for 18 British exonerees.

Robert Jay Lifton. "History of Trauma." In *Beyond Invisible Walls*, Jacob D. Lindy and Robert Jay Lifton, eds. (Brunner-Routledge, 2001).

> Introduces Lifton's concept of "sustained catastrophe."

Michael L. Radelet, Hugo Adam Bedau, and Constance E. Putnam. *In Spite of Innocence* (Northeastern University Press, 1992).

> The seminal work on wrongful conviction of the innocent.

Janet Roberts and Elizabeth Stanton. "A Long Road Back After Exoneration, and Justice Is Slow to Make Amends." *New York Times*, November 25, 2007.

> Multi-media presentation of interviews with more than 100 DNA exonerees.

REVIEW QUESTIONS

1. Are you in favor of the death penalty? Does knowing that over one hundred people on death row have been exonerated in the United States change your opinion on this issue?
2. How does this article make you think about the criminal justice system in general? Do you have faith in the system, on the whole, to treat offenders fairly?
3. The author asks, "Is justice best served when the system operates accurately but slowly and some guilty individuals slip through the cracks? Or when the system swiftly processes the guilty at the expense of a few innocent lives along the way?" What do you think?
4. The sociological concept of *labeling* is very important to the quality of life of these exonerees. On the basis of what you know and what you learned from this article, discuss how a label can be so powerful.

robert j. sampson

rethinking crime and immigration

52

winter 2008

immigration tracks the reduction in crime in the united states since the 1990s. it thus pays to reconsider the role of immigration in crime, cities, culture, and societal change.

The summer of 2007 witnessed a perfect storm of controversy over immigration to the United States. After building for months with angry debate, a widely touted immigration reform bill supported by President George W. Bush and many leaders in Congress failed decisively. Recriminations soon followed across the political spectrum.

Just when it seemed media attention couldn't be greater, a human tragedy unfolded with the horrifying execution-style murders of three teenagers in Newark, New Jersey, attributed by authorities to illegal aliens.

Presidential candidate Rep. Tom Tancredo (R-Colorado) descended on Newark to blame city leaders for encouraging illegal immigration, while Newt Gingrich declared the "war at home" against illegal immigrants was more deadly than the battlefields of Iraq. National headlines and outrage reached a feverish pitch, with Newark offering politicians a potent new symbol and a brown face to replace the infamous Willie Horton, who committed armed robbery and rape while on a weekend furlough from his life sentence to a Massachusetts prison. Another presidential candidate, former Tennessee senator Fred Thompson, seemed to capture the mood of the times at the Prescott Bush Awards Dinner: "Twelve million illegal immigrants later, we are now living in a nation that is beset by people who are suicidal maniacs and want to kill countless innocent men, women, and children around the world."

Now imagine a nearly opposite, fact-based scenario. Consider that immigration—even if illegal—is associated with lower crime rates in most disadvantaged urban neighborhoods. Or that increasing immigration tracks with the broad reduction in crime the United States has witnessed since the 1990s.

Well before the 2007 Summer of Discontent over immigration, I proposed we take such ideas seriously. Based on hindsight I shouldn't have been surprised by the intense reaction to what I thought at the time was a rather logical reflection. From the right came loud guffaws, expletive-filled insults, angry Web postings, and not-so-thinly veiled threats. But the left wasn't so happy either, because my argument assumes racial and ethnic differences in crime not tidily attributable to material deprivation or discrimination—the canonical explanations.

Although Americans hold polarizing and conflicting views about its value, immigration is a major social force that will continue for some time. It thus pays to reconsider the role of immigration in shaping crime, cities, culture, and societal change writ large, especially in this era of social anxiety and vitriolic claims about immigration's reign of terror.

some facts

Consider first the "Latino Paradox." Hispanic Americans do better on a wide range of social indicators—including propensity to violence—than one would expect given their socioeconomic disadvantages. To assess this paradox in more depth, my colleagues and I examined violent acts committed by nearly 3,000 males and females in Chicago ranging in age from 8 to 25 between 1995 and 2003. The study selected whites, blacks, and Hispanics (primarily Mexican Americans) from 180 neighborhoods ranging from highly segregated to very integrated. We also analyzed data from police records, the U.S. Census, and a separate survey of more than 8,000 Chicago residents who were asked about the characteristics of their neighborhoods.

Notably, we found a significantly lower rate of violence among Mexican Americans compared to blacks and whites. A major reason is that more than a quarter of those of Mexican descent were born abroad and more than half lived in neighborhoods where the majority of residents were also Mexican. In particular, first-generation immigrants (those born outside the United States) were 45 percent less likely to commit violence than third-generation Americans, adjusting for individual, family, and neighborhood background. Second-generation immigrants were 22 percent less likely to commit violence than the third generation. This pattern held true for non-Hispanic whites and blacks as well. Our study further showed living in a neighborhood of concentrated immigration was directly associated with lower violence (again, after taking into account a host of correlated factors, including poverty and an individual's immigrant status). Immigration thus appeared "protective" against violence.

Consider next the implications of these findings when set against the backdrop of one of the most profound social changes to visit the United States in recent decades. Foreign immigration to the United States rose sharply in the 1990s, especially from Mexico and especially to immi-

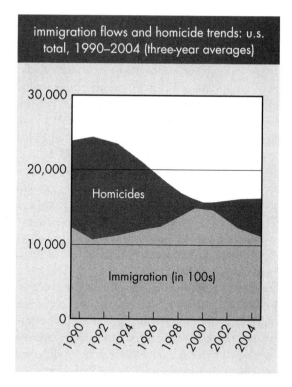

immigration flows and homicide trends: u.s. total, 1990–2004 (three-year averages)

grant enclaves in large cities. Overall, the foreign-born population increased by more than 50 percent in 10 years, to 31 million in 2000. A report by the Pew Hispanic Center found immigration grew most significantly in the mid-1990s and hit its peak at the end of the decade, when the national homicide rate plunged to levels not seen since the 1960s. Immigrant flows have receded since 2001 but remain high, while the national homicide rate leveled off and seems now to be creeping up. Both trends are compared over time in the figure "immigration flows and homicide trends."

The pattern upends popular stereotypes. Among the public, policy makers, and even many academics, a common expectation is that the concentration of immigrants and the influx of foreigners drive up crime rates because of the assumed propensities of these groups to commit crimes and settle in poor, presumably disorganized communities. This belief is so pervasive that in our Chicago study the concentration of Latinos in a neighborhood strongly predicted perceptions of disorder no matter the actual amount of disorder or rate of reported crimes. And yet immigrants appear in general to be less violent than people born in America, particularly when they live in neighborhoods with high numbers of other immigrants.

We are thus witnessing a different pattern from early 20th century America, when growth in immigration from Europe, along with ethnic diversity more generally, was linked with increasing crime and formed a building block for what became known as "social disorganization" theory. New York today is a leading magnet for immigration, yet it has for a decade ranked as one of America's safest cities. Crime in Los Angeles dropped considerably in the late 1990s (45 percent overall) as did other Hispanic influenced cities such as San Jose, Dallas, and Phoenix. The same can be said for cities smack on the border like El Paso and San Diego, which have long ranked as low-crime areas. Cities of concentrated immigration are some of the safest places around.

counterpoint

There are criticisms of these arguments, of course. To begin, the previous figure juxtaposes two trends and nothing more—correlation doesn't equal causation. But it does demonstrate the trends are opposite of what's commonly assumed, which is surely not irrelevant to the many, and strongly causal, claims that immigration increases crime. Descriptive facts are at the heart of sound social science, a first step in any causal inquiry.

Perhaps a bigger concern is that we need to distinguish illegal from legal immigration and focus on the many illegal aliens who allegedly are accounting for crime waves across the country—the "Newark phenomenon." By one argument, because of deportation risk illegal immigrants are afraid to report crimes against them to the police, resulting in artificially low official estimates in the Hispanic community. But no evidence exists that reporting biases seriously affects estimates of the homicide victimization rate—unlike other crimes, there is a body. At the national level, then, the homicides committed by illegal aliens in the United States are reflected in the data just like for everyone else. The bottom line is that as immigrants poured into the country, homicides plummeted. One could claim crime would decrease faster absent immigration inflows, but that's a different argument and concedes my basic point.

There is also little disputing that in areas and times of high legal immigration we find accompanying surges of illegal entrants. It would be odd indeed if illegal aliens descended on areas with no other immigrants or where they had no pre-existing networks. And so it is that areas of concentrated immigration are magnets for illegal concentration. Because crime tends to be negatively associated with undifferentiated immigration measures, it follows that we can disconfirm the idea that increasing illegal immigration is associated with increasing crime.

Furthermore, our Chicago study did include both legal and illegal immigrants. I would estimate the illegal status at roughly a quarter—but in any case no group was excluded from the analysis. The other important point is that the violence estimates were based on confidential self-reports and not police statistics or other official sources of crime. Therefore, police arrest biases or undercounts can't explain the fact that first generation immigrants self-report lower

Cities of concentrated immigration are some of the safest places around.

violence than the second generation, which in turn reports less than the third generation.

So let us proceed on the assumption of a substantial negative association across individuals, places, and time with respect to immigration and violence. What potential mechanisms might explain the connections and are they causal? Thinking about these questions requires attention be paid to confounding factors and competing explanations.

Social scientists worry a lot about selection bias because individuals differ in preferences and can, within means, select their environments. It has been widely hypothesized that immigrants, and Mexicans in particular, selectively migrate to the United States on characteristics that predispose them to low crime, such as motivation to work, ambition, and a desire not to be deported. Immigrants may also come from cultures where violence isn't rewarded as a strategy for establishing reputation (to which I return below).

This scenario is undoubtedly the case and central to the argument—social selection is a causal mechanism. Namely, to the extent that more people predisposed to lower crime immigrate to the United States (we now have some 35 million people of foreign-born status), they will sharply increase the denominator of the crime rate while rarely appearing in the numerator. And in the neighborhoods of U.S. cities with high concentrations of immigrants, one would expect on selection grounds alone to find lower crime rates. Selection thus favors the argument that immigration may be causally linked to lower crime.

Another concern of social scientists is common sources of causation, or "competing" explanations. One candidate is economic trends. After all, potential immigrants respond to incentives and presumably choose to relocate when times are better in their destinations. Although a legitimate concern, economics can't easily explain the story. Depending on the measure, economic trends aren't isomorphic with either immigra-

tion or crime at either the beginning or end of the time series. Real wages were declining and inequality increasing in the 1990s by most accounts, which should have produced increases in crime by the logic of relative deprivation theory, which says that income gaps, not absolute poverty, are what matters. Broad economic indicators like stock market values did skyrocket but collapsed sharply while immigration didn't.

Scholars in criminology have long searched for a sturdy link between national economic trends and violence, to little avail. The patterns just don't match up well, and often they're in the opposite direction of deprivation-based expectations. The best example is the 1960s when the economy markedly improved yet crime shot up. Don't forget, too, the concentrated immigration and crime link remains when controlling for economic indicators.

Finally, the "Latino Paradox" in itself should put to rest the idea that economics is the go-to answer: Immigrant Latinos are poor and disadvantaged but at low risk for crime. Poor immigrant neighborhoods and immigrant-tinged cities like El Paso have similarly lower crime than their economic profile would suggest.

Competing explanations also can't explain the Chicago findings. Immigrant youths committed less violence than natives after adjustment for a rich set of individual, family, and neighborhood confounders. Moreover, there's an influence of immigrant concentration beyond the effects of individual immigrant status and other individual factors, and beyond neighborhood socioeconomic status and legal cynicism—previously shown to significantly predict violence. We estimated male violence by age for three types of neighborhoods:

· "Low-risk," where a very high percentage of people work in professional and managerial occupations (90th percentile), few people hold cynical attitudes about the law and morality (10th percentile), and there are no immigrants;

· "High-risk," where professional/managerial jobs are scarce, cynicism is pervasive, and there are also no immigrants;

· "High-risk, immigrant neighborhoods," defined by similarly low shares of professional/managerial workers and high legal cynicism, but where about one-half of the people are immigrants.

The estimated probability an average male living in a high-risk neighborhood without immigrants will engage in violence is almost 25 percent higher than in the high-risk, immigrant neighborhood, a pattern again suggesting the protective, rather than crime-generating, influence of immigrant concentration.

Finally, we examined violence in Chicago neighborhoods by a foreign-born diversity index

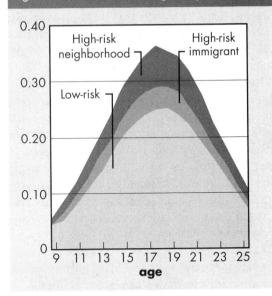

estimated probability of violence by third-generation males in chicago neighborhoods

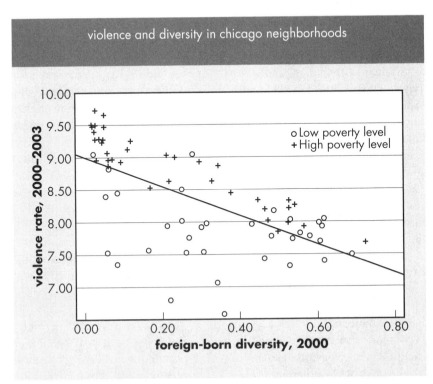

violence and diversity in chicago neighborhoods

capturing 100 countries of birth from around the world (see "violence and diversity in chicago neighborhoods"). In both high- and low-poverty communities, foreign-born diversity is clearly and strongly linked to lower violence. Concentrated poverty predicts more violence (note the high poverty areas above the prediction line) but violence is lower as diversity goes up for low- and high-poverty neighborhoods alike. Interestingly, the link between lower violence and diversity is strongest in the most disadvantaged neighborhoods.

crime declines among non-hispanics

A puzzle apparently remains in how immigration explains the crime decline among whites and blacks in the 1990s. One agitated critic, for example, charged that my thesis implies that for every Mexican entering America a black person would have to commit fewer crimes. But immigration isn't the only cause of the crime decline. There are many causes of crime—that declines ensued for blacks and whites doesn't in itself invalidate the immigration argument.

This critique also exposes a misconception about immigrant diversity. Immigration isn't just about Mexicans, it's about the influx of a wide range of different groups. The previous figure, for example, represents 100 countries, a conservative template for many places. In cities such as Los Angeles and New York, immigrant flows are erasing simple black-white-brown scenarios and replacing them with a complex mixture of immigrant diversity.

Even the traditionally black-white city of Chicago reflects evidence of immigration's broad reach. When we looked at whites and blacks we still found surprising variation in generational status, with immigration protective for all racial/ethnic groups except Puerto Ricans/other Lati-

nos. In fact, controlling for immigrant generation reduced the gap between African Americans and whites by 14 percent, implying one reason whites have lower levels of violence than African Americans is that whites are more likely to be recent immigrants. The pattern of immigrant generational status and lower crime is thus not just restricted to Latinos, and it extends to helping explain white-black differences as well.

Added to this is substantial non-Latino immigration into the United States from around the world, including Russia, Poland, India, and the Caribbean, to name just a few countries. Black and white populations are increasingly characterized by immigrants (Poles and Russians among whites in Chicago, for example, and Caribbeans and West Africans among blacks in New York). According to Census 2000, the Chicago area has more than 130,000 Polish immigrants, so we aren't talking about trivial numbers.

Perhaps more important, focusing on the "what about whites and blacks" question misses the non-selection-based component of a broader immigration argument. We're so used to thinking about immigrant adaptation (or assimilation) to the host society we've failed to fully appreciate how immigrants themselves shape the host society. Take economic revitalization and urban growth. A growing consensus argues immigration revitalizes cities around the country. Many decaying inner-city areas gained population in the 1990s and became more vital, in large part through immigration. One of the most thriving scenes of economic activity in the entire Chicagoland area, for example, second only to the famed "Miracle Mile" of Michigan Avenue, is the 26th Street corridor in Little Village. A recent analysis of New York City showed that for the first time ever, blacks' incomes in

> The pattern of immigrant generational status and lower crime isn't just restricted to Latinos, it helps explain white-black differences, too.

Queens have surpassed whites', with the surge in the black middle class driven largely by the successes of black immigrants from the West Indies. Segregation and the concentration of poverty have also decreased in many cities for the first time in decades.

Such changes are a major social force and immigrants aren't the only beneficiaries—native born blacks, whites, and other traditional groups in the United States have been exposed to the gains associated with lower crime (decreases in segregation, decreases in concentrated poverty, increases in the economic and civic health of central cities, to name just a few). There are many examples of inner-city neighborhoods rejuvenated by immigration that go well beyond Queens and the Lower West Side of Chicago. From Bushwick in Brooklyn to Miami, and from large swaths of south central Los Angeles to the rural South, immigration is reshaping America. It follows that the "externalities" associated with immigration are multiple in character and constitute a plausible mechanism explaining some of the variation in crime rates of all groups in the host society.

There are important implications for this line of argument. If it is correct, then simply adjusting for things like economic revitalization, urban change, and other seemingly confounding explanations is illegitimate from a causal explanation standpoint because they would instead be mediators or conduits of immigration effects—themselves part of the pathway of explanation. Put differently, to the extent immigration is causally bound up with major social changes that in turn are part of the explanatory process of reduced crime, estimating only the net effects of immigration will give us the wrong answer.

> We're so used to thinking about immigrant adaptation we've failed to fully appreciate how immigrants themselves shape the host society.

cultural penetration and societal renewal

A related cultural implication, while speculative and perhaps provocative, is worth considering. If immigration leads to the penetration into America of diverse and formerly external cultures, then this diffusion may contribute to less crime if these cultures don't carry the same meanings with respect to violence and crime.

It's no secret the United States has long been a high-violence society, with many scholars positing a subculture or code of the streets as its main cause. In one influential version, shared expectations for demanding respect and "saving face" lead participants in the "street culture" of poor inner cities to react violently to perceived slights, insults, and otherwise petty encounters that make up the rounds of daily life. But according to the logic of this theory, if one doesn't share the cultural attribution or perceived meaning of the event, violence is less likely. Outsiders to the culture, that is, are unlikely to be caught in the vicious cycles of interaction (and reaction) that promote violence.

The massive penetration of immigrant (particularly, but not only, Mexican) populations throughout the United States, including rural areas and the South, can properly be thought of as a diffusion-like process. One possible result is that over time American culture is being diluted. Some of the most voracious critiques of immigration have embraced this very line of argument. Samuel Huntington, in one well-known example, claims the very essence of American identity is at stake because of increasing diversity and immigration, especially from Mexico. He may well be right, but the diagnosis might not be so bad if a frontier mentality that endorses and perpetuates codes of violence is a defining feature of American culture.

A profound irony in the immigration debate concedes another point to Huntington. If immigration can be said to have brought violence to America, it most likely came with (white) Irish and Scottish immigrants whose cultural traditions emphasizing honor and respect were defended with violent means when they settled in the South in the 1700s and 1800s. Robert Nisbett and Dov Cohen have presented provocative evidence in favor of this thesis, emphasizing cultural transmission in the form of Scotch-Irish immigrants, descendants of Celtic herdsman, who developed rural herding communities in the frontier South. In areas with little state power to command compliance with the law, a tradition of frontier justice carried over from rural Europe took hold, with a heavy emphasis on retaliation and the use of violence to settle disputes, represented most clearly in the culture of dueling.

In today's society, then, I would hypothesize that immigration and the increasing cultural diversity that accompanies it generate the sort of conflicts of culture that lead not to increased crime but nearly the opposite. In other words, selective immigration in the current era may be leading to the greater visibility of competing non-violent mores that affect not just immigrant communities but diffuse and concatenate through social interactions to tamp down violent conflict in general. Recent findings showing the spread of immigration to all parts of America, including rural areas of the Midwest and South, give credence to this argument. The Willie Hortinization of illegal aliens notwithstanding, diversity and cultural conflict wrought by immigration may well prove healthy, rather than destructive, as traditionally believed.

RECOMMENDED RESOURCES

Richard Nisbett and Dov Cohen. *Culture of Honor: The Psychology of Violence in the South* (Westview, 1996).

A fascinating take on the cultural roots of violence in the United States, including the culture of honor posited to afflict the South disproportionately and traced to European immigration.

Eyal Press. "Do Immigrants Make Us Safer?" *New York Times Magazine*, December 3, 2006.

A *New York Times* writer considers the questions raised in this article, taking to the streets of Chicago.

Rubén G. Rumbaut and Walter A. Ewing. "The Myth of Immigrant Criminality and the Paradox of Assimilation: Incarceration Rates among Native and Foreign-Born Men." (Immigration Policy Center, 2007).

A recent synthesis of the empirical facts on immigration and crime, with a special focus on incarceration.

Thorsten Sellin. *Culture Conflict and Crime* (Social Science Research Council, 1938).

Widely considered the classical account of immigration, culture, and crime in the early part of the 20th century.

REVIEW QUESTIONS

1. What is the "Latino paradox"? Why is it important in the debate on immigration and crime?
2. Considering the fact that many see the United States as a country built by immigrants, why do you think that recent Latino immigrants have been so stigmatized in the United States?
3. How do you make sense of the finding that recent Latino immigrants were least likely to commit violent crimes? What do you know about crime in America that might help explain this finding?
4. We know now that immigration does not increase crime. Why do you think this cultural belief exists without evidence to back it up? What story might it tell about how immigrants are viewed in this country?

michael massoglia and jason schnittker

no real release

53

winter 2009

it's not surprising to learn that prison is bad for inmates' health, but upon release, ex-cons bring the health risks they've been exposed to back to their communities, creating health problems that threaten everyone.

Media attention to the inadequacies of the prison health care system, often reported in vivid detail, has had real implications for prison policies and management. There's now growing recognition of the role prisons play in the spread of infectious disease and serious efforts to curtail infection among prisoners.

In California, for example, a class-action lawsuit resulted in a series of measures and a $7 billion request from the governor's office to improve prison health care and the prison health-care workforce. Along similar lines, in response to heath care inadequacies uncovered during an internal evaluation, the Federal Bureau of Prisons recently made a series of recommendations to improve health care delivery to inmates.

But the health problems of prisoners extend far beyond prison walls. As former inmates return home to their families and communities, so too do the health risks to which they're exposed. Taken together, the health problems that flow between prisons and communities create an incarceration-health link that threatens inmates and non-inmates alike.

This incarceration-health connection is driven in part by the difficulties of successfully reintegrating offenders into their communities. A number of other sociological processes link incarceration to poor health and inadequate

> As former inmates return home to their families and communities, so too do the health risks to which they're exposed.

health care. Ex-prisoners have difficulty obtaining employment, for example, especially the sort of employment that provides good health insurance. Prison can also affect family relationships, disrupt educational careers, limit housing options, and compromise other social characteristics that affect health.

Given these influences, those concerned with breaking the prison-health connection need to think both within and beyond the prison walls and develop additional safety nets for prisoners, former prisoners, and the communities to which they return.

the health of inmates

At a simple descriptive level, we know that former inmates suffer from poor health. Compared to those who have never been in prison, ex-prisoners suffer from higher rates of chronic illness, disability, and psychiatric disorders.

This might seem obvious, particularly to anyone who's ever watched a movie or television drama about how violent prisons can be. It's easy to imagine such an environment leading to harm through, for example, trauma, violence, or unprotected sex. It's also easy to imagine such an environment leading to poor health through indirect pathways, including intravenous drug or alcohol abuse, which often begins well before a sentence is served.

But the incarceration-health link is actually much more complex. Some features of incarceration are actually beneficial for some prisoners. A study by researchers at the University of Pennsylvania found the health of inmates might actually improve after admission, especially among those who were severely disadvantaged beforehand. Prisons provide food, shelter, exercise, and, at least for some, protection greater than they had before. Moreover, prisons are required by law to provide free health care commensurate with that available in the community.

Many inmates take advantage of these opportunities and use their newfound access to health care for both prevention and treatment. For some, the care they receive is more thorough than what they had on the outside. For many others, it's the only care they've ever had, which means even relatively poor quality care results in improvements to their lives.

In interviews we conducted with current and former inmates, many recognized the value of prison care, regardless of its limitations. One HIV-positive ex-inmate stressed the benefits of prison care unequivocally: "I would not be alive, sitting and talking to you two right now, if I had not received the . . . medical health services, that I've got from prison."

causal relationship?

Of course, there are complexities to the claim that incarceration is causally related to health at all. Many inmates are on their way to poor health when they start their sentence, if they're not sick already. Furthermore, even if there is a causal connection, we haven't yet identified a mechanism that would explain exactly how prisons cause people to get sicker.

The clearest story would seem to be one based on the risks that put inmates in harm's way. A good deal of discussion, for example, has centered on the possibility of prisons as "breeding grounds" for infectious disease. And in these cases, unprotected sex is seen as the primary risk factor.

By the same token, some argue the connection between incarceration and health is driven almost entirely by the kinds of behaviors that put people at risk for both incarceration and poor health in the first place. Many inmates, for example, are serving time for drug-related offenses, including IV drug use, and unfortunately, many will return to drug use upon release. So, too, will some inmates return to a life of violence and crime.

We commit a serious mistake, however, if we think about the incarceration-health relationship only in terms of a narrow set of risky practices that lead to a narrow set of disease outcomes. Neither infectious disease nor drug use is the only pathway to poor health—or perhaps even the most important. Nor is it the case that incarceration is linked to health only through health-specific risks, such as smoking, alcohol abuse, or violence.

While these behaviors no doubt contribute to the problems of some former inmates, the most significant pathways to poor health are tied to more general problems of reintegration into mainstream society. Indeed, focusing on the risk or threat that infectious inmates pose to the public might very well present yet another barrier to reintegration. Nevertheless, reintegration remains the key to understanding the incarceration-health link—and the spillover effects of incarceration on families and communities.

returning home

Former inmates, who already have a diminished social position because of their past, often suffer from long periods of unemployment, poverty, and marital instability—some of the best-known risk factors for poor health.

A major contributor to the stress of incarceration is the stigma associated with it. The status of "ex-con" is highly devalued and leads to, among other things, high rates of discrimination. A number of studies link self-reports of discrimination with stress and poor health, including higher levels of major depression, anxiety, and blood pressure.

This research generally suggests discrimination is harmful irrespective of its source, but discrimination stemming from incarceration in particular might be especially harmful because not only does it increase stress, it diminishes the resources necessary for coping. The stress of discrimination can be reduced, for example, by social support or a strong sense of self-worth, but these resources aren't readily available to inmates. Indeed, some traits that might lead to successful coping while in prison—such as strong emotional control or social disengagement—may be entirely dysfunctional when it comes to coping with the stress of life on the outside.

At the same time, the psychological consequences of discrimination are greater among those who feel they have no way to redress their mistreatment. Unlike discrimination on the basis of race or gender, discrimination on the basis of a criminal record is, in some domains, legally sanctioned. At a minimum, some former inmates may be inclined to see any difficulties they encounter finding work or housing entirely in light of their verdict and sentence, rather than prejudice or a failure of the system.

The situation of former inmates is also unusually severe with respect to health care. In the United States, the single biggest barrier to receiving adequate care is being uninsured. The uninsured receive fewer preventive and diagnostic services, as well as less treatment for chronic conditions. Health insurance is usually acquired through an employer or a spouse, purchased privately, or provided through some public source, such as Medicaid.

Even if a former inmate secures some form of insurance, it's unlikely this insurance will meet his or her needs adequately. Many insurance policies don't provide full benefits for preexisting conditions, which means inmates who develop chronic conditions while in prison are unlikely to receive adequate treatment for it following release. Moreover, many former inmates suffer from multiple ailments simultaneously, which makes treatment difficult even among those with the highest quality insurance seeking care in the best facilities.

There are reasons to suspect that the negative health consequences of incarceration extend well beyond the offender.

families and communities

Our story so far is that incarceration exposes individuals to health risks, stress, and stigma that produce negative health consequences, which tend to reinforce one another in a cycle of risk exposure and social disadvantage.

It's tempting to think of this web of consequences as finite and isolated. Many of these problems are, after all, limited to former inmates. Their numbers in the United States are certainly growing, but this population remains a rather small fraction of the total. There are reasons to suspect, though, that the negative health consequences of incarceration extend well beyond the offender.

The overwhelming majority of inmates are eventually released—more than 650,000 each year—and many return home to communities as well as to families with children. Sociological research shows the families of former inmates may suffer as much as the offender, and in surprisingly similar ways.

There's remarkable overlap between the psychological symptoms experienced by ex-prisoners and those experienced by their children. At least one study finds that many children of inmates report symptoms of post-traumatic stress disorder, including hypervigilance, anxiety, and even flashbacks of their parent's arrest. Parental separation is also traumatic, for both parents and children. These spillover effects may be even more acute for the families of female prisoners because women provide the bulk of child care in many families. Moreover, many inmates were actively involved parents prior to their sentence, making their absence even more acute.

In our interviews, several inmates reflected on the trauma their arrests caused their families. Among other things, they were concerned about missing key developmental periods in the lives of their children and how, for some, incarceration severely undermined their identity as a parent.

"When I got arrested [my daughter] didn't have any teeth, she wasn't really crawling, she was just kind of getting up on all fours and rocking back and forth. When I got out she was talking, she had teeth, she was saying words," one former inmate said. Reflecting on his nine months behind bars, one father found it hard to think of himself as anything other than a "serious deadbeat dad."

The gap left by an absent parent is often filled by other influences. For example, children from single-parent households are more likely to be influenced by peers their age than adults. This has negative consequences for a number of health behaviors, including smoking. Making matters worse, when parents do eventually return, they may find themselves unable to eliminate these influences entirely. Parents with a prison record may have a hard time cultivating trust with their children, in part because they now find it difficult to place much trust in others.

Incarceration also affects a family's access to care. Because many families receive health insurance through an employer, and many women receive insurance through their spouse, it's no surprise the families of inmates are more likely to be uninsured. The children of inmates may be especially vulnerable because they're young and, by virtue of their poor socioeconomic status, more likely to suffer from chronic conditions. Left untreated, these conditions usually worsen and can lead to additional complications, including, for instance, diminished educational attainment.

For similar reasons, the health of former inmates may be linked to the health of communities. Laws in some jurisdictions limit the areas where former inmates can reside, depending on an inmate's specific offense. Because of these restrictions, ex-inmates tend to be clustered in areas of severely disadvantaged health care services compared to those available in the community as a whole.

Because they're required by law to provide emergency care regardless of a patient's ability to pay, costs at hospitals providing services to a large pool of uninsured patients tend to be higher. These issues are compounded when high numbers of uninsured people are coupled with an elevated need for care, as would be expected in communities with a concentration of unhealthy former inmates. Faced with rapidly escalating costs, such hospitals are forced to adapt, either by cutting services or charging more. In either case, the people who live in these communities, whether insured or not, suffer. Some studies, although concerned more with insurance than the situation of inmates, find that the services most likely to be cut under these conditions are psychiatric care, which is most important for former inmates specifically and the disenfranchised in general.

policies to minimize impact

Some of the options for breaking the incarceration-health connection are worthy in their own right, but may be limited in their impact. For example, judges and correctional officials could consider health more directly and tailor their sentencing and confinement decisions accordingly. This would be particularly helpful for those inmates with pre-existing conditions, who have unique health care needs and are at the greatest risk for suffering the most from their incarceration.

At the same time, the safety of the prison environment could be improved. First and foremost this would require reducing prison overcrowding. Correctional officials can do little to increase prisoner safety when resources are strained to the breaking point by serving too many inmates with too little funding. Reducing overcrowding would likely help reduce rates of disciplinary infractions, assault, and even suicide.

Although these changes would be important and beneficial, they're unlikely to alter what happens following release. Nor are they likely to diminish the consequences of incarceration for families and communities. To break the prison-health connection we must improve the transition from prison to home, which requires a multi-dimensional approach that targets prisoners themselves but also the broader social context.

One element in a broad approach could be to provide more explicit training with respect to employment and housing for the soon-to-be-released, domains in which inmates face especially strong barriers. At minimum, such instruction could assist prisoners in reentry planning and help them develop coping strategies to smooth their transition.

Another element could encourage closer and more direct supervision of former inmates' health or provide counseling on stress and coping. The United States already has a mature system for supervising ex-inmates in the parole system. Adding oversight for their health and health care would be a bold yet feasible proposition. Because providing inmates with adequate care may ease reintegration, it could also promote the system's goals of reducing recidivism and improving public safety.

Of course, improving reintegration also necessitates creating real opportunities for former inmates. One place to start is in better protecting the rights and liberties of current and former inmates. At present, former inmates are afforded few legal protections against discrimination, and their work, families, and identities suffer as a result. Additionally, many are stripped of important civil rights including, for example, the right to vote and to receive state-sponsored educational loans. In many cases, the rationale for these policies seems merely punitive. Providing more legal safeguards for prisoners could help promote the goals of the criminal justice system to facilitate reintegration and, at the same time, promote better health.

Perhaps the most compelling rationale for change, however, rests with reforming a system that has, in many respects, become cruel and unusual. Prisons are cruel in inflicting lasting damage and unusual in disadvantaging entire communities. The connections between prisons and health are matters of public health and social justice, and so may require new legal measures as much as additional services.

> To break the prison-health connection we must improve the transition from prison to home with an approach that targets prisoners themselves but also the broader social context.

Not all inmates are the same—the vast majority of inmates are men, and a disproportionate number are African American. Furthermore, a great many are young and, thus, not naturally at risk for poor health. Although most of the existing research has focused on young men, it's important to consider how demographic characteristics might shape the health effects of incarceration.

Along these lines, some suggest the incarceration-health link might be stronger or weaker for different demographic groups. For example, the stigma of incarceration may be less among African Americans simply because so many more African Americans are incarcerated. Some also speculate on gender differences, although it isn't clear who suffers most. On one hand, the stigma of incarceration could be greater for men if a history of incarceration accentuates perceptions of dangerousness. On the other, the stigma of incarceration could be worse for women precisely because incarceration for them is inconsistent with stereotypes regarding passivity and is much less prevalent.

To date, research indicates much of this speculation is incorrect, at least with respect to self-reported health and disability. Our own research finds similar health effects of incarceration for both African Americans and whites, as well as for men and women. The stigma of incarceration may be so powerful that it overwhelms many other characteristics we might typically expect to affect health.

For example, even youth is no safeguard against poor health in prison. Indeed, while adjusting to prison life might be easier for younger inmates, incarceration might have more lasting negative consequences for them if they have yet to establish the kind of mature identity that could prevent them from whole-heartedly embracing the habits and attitudes of prison life.

Of course, not everyone who goes to prison suffers lasting harm. In fact, many adjust to life behind bars quite well and many also adjust to life following release. Nevertheless, very few leave prison entirely unscathed, and any number of the pathways linking incarceration to health may be sufficient to produce poor health.

RECOMMENDED RESOURCES

National Commission on Correctional Health Care. *The Health Status of Soon-to-Be-Released Inmates* (National Commission on Correctional Health Care, 2002).

   A two-volume comprehensive assessment of the health and health care needs of inmates.

Mark V. Pauly and José A. Pagán. "Spillovers and Vulnerability: The Case of Community Uninsurance." *Health Affairs* (2007) 26: 1304–14.

Provides an empirically grounded review of spillover effects related to high levels of community uninsurance, of direct relevance to the incarceration-health literature.

Becky Pettit and Bruce Western. "Mass Imprisonment and the Life Course: Race and Class Inequality in U.S. Incarceration." *American Sociological Review* (2004) 69: 151–69.

Uses a nationally representative data set to calculate the chances of incarceration for different demographic groups, and argues incarceration is a "phase in the life course" for some disadvantaged groups in America.

Jeremy Travis. "Public Health." In *But They All Come Back: Facing the Challenges of Prisoner Reentry* (Urban Institute, 2005).

A good introduction to the health and health care needs of current and former inmates, with a particular focus on policy.

David R. Williams, Harold W. Neighbors, and James S. Jackson. "Racial/Ethnic Discrimination and Health: Findings From Community Studies." *American Journal of Public Health* (2003) 93: 200–8.

A thorough review of the discrimination–health-literature.

REVIEW QUESTIONS

1. Describe the ways that incarceration is linked to poor health and inadequate health care. In contrast, how is incarceration beneficial to the health of some prisoners?

2. This article demonstrates how the stigma of incarceration can be "contagious," affecting how the children of ex-cons are seen and see themselves. What are some other stigmas that seem to rub off on friends and family?

3. As you learned in this article, discrimination against ex-cons is legally sanctioned. Should it be? Why or why not? Who does this benefit? For whom is it a disadvantage?

4. Activity: Imagine that you are a social worker in a community where many former inmates return after leaving prison. What policies might you advocate to address the health needs of your community in light of prisoner re-entry? What resources would you need? What community leaders or organization would you need to enlist for support?

bruce western and becky pettit

beyond crime and punishment: prisons and inequality

54

fall 2002

changes in government policy on crime and punishment have put many poor minority men behind bars, more than their arrest rates would indicate. the growth of the penal system has also obscured the extent of economic inequality and sowed the seeds for greater inequality in the future.

Even during the economic boom of the 1990s, more young black men who had dropped out of school were in prison than on the job. Despite rapid growth in employment throughout the economy, released prisoners in the 1990s earned little and were often unemployed. In these two ways—high imprisonment rates among disadvantaged men and poor economic prospects for ex-inmates—the penal system affects inequality in the American society.

Inequality is disguised because data on employment often do not include the mostly poor men who are locked away behind bars. When we count prisoners among the unemployed, we find that racial inequality in employment and earnings is much greater than when we ignore them. Taking prisoners into account substantially alters our understanding of how young black men are faring, dramatically so when we focus on young black men with little education. In addition, the penal system fuels inequality by reducing the wages and employment prospects of released prisoners. The low-wage, unstable employment they experience when they return to society deepens the divisions of race and class.

For most of the twentieth century, imprisonment policies had little effect on social inequality.

Prison was reserved for the most violent or incorrigible offenders, and the inmate population was consequently small. This began to change in the early 1970s when stricter law enforcement enlarged the prison population. While incarceration once used to flag dangerousness or persistent deviance, by 2000 it had become a common event for poor minority males.

the expansion of the penal system

Between 1920 and 1970, about one-tenth of one percent of Americans were confined in prisons. The prison population increased sixfold in the three decades after 1970. By June 2000, about 1.3 million people were held in state and federal prisons, and 620,000 inmates were in local jails. This translates into a total incarceration rate of seven-tenths of one percent of the U.S. population. The current incarceration rate is five times the historical average of the 1925–70 period and six to eight times the incarceration rates in Western Europe. With the important exception of homicide, however, American levels of crime are similar to those in Western Europe.

These numbers mask the concentration of imprisonment among young black men with little schooling. Although there are no official statistics, we've calculated the proportion of penal inmates among black and white men at different ages and levels of education by combining data from labor force and correctional surveys. Incarceration rates doubled among working-age men between 1980 and 1999 but increased threefold for high school dropouts in their twenties. By 1999, fewer than one percent of working-age white men were behind bars, compared to 7.5 percent of working-age black men (figure 1). Figures for young black unskilled

men are especially striking: 41 percent of all black male high school dropouts aged 22–30 were in prison or jail at midyear in 1999.

Although 9 out of 10 inmates are male (92 percent), women represent the fastest-growing segment of the inmate population. During the recent penal expansion, the female inmate population has grown more than 60 percent faster than the male inmate population. African-American women have experienced the greatest increase in criminal justice supervision.

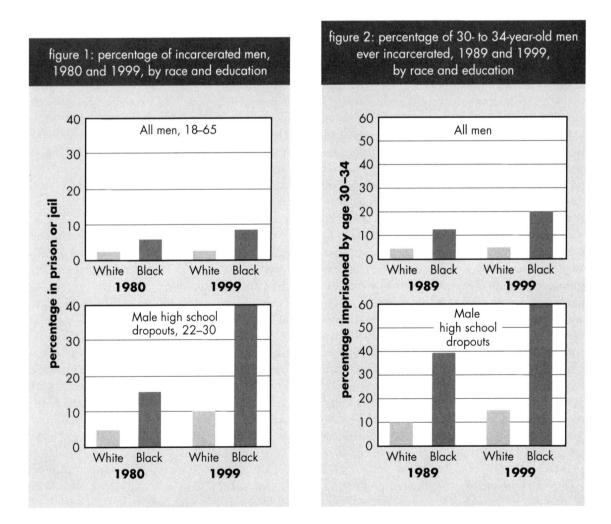

figure 1: percentage of incarcerated men, 1980 and 1999, by race and education

figure 2: percentage of 30- to 34-year-old men ever incarcerated, 1989 and 1999, by race and education

Racial disparities in incarceration are even more stark when one counts the men who have ever been incarcerated rather than just those in prison on a given day. In 1989, about 2 percent of white men in their early thirties had ever been to prison compared to 13 percent of black men of the same age (figure 2). Ten years later, these rates had increased by 50 percent. The risks of going to prison are about three times higher for high school dropouts. At the end of the 1990s, 14 percent of white and 59 percent of black male high school dropouts in their early thirties had prison records.

The high rate of imprisonment among black men is often explained by differences in patterns of arrest and criminal behavior. Blacks are eight times more likely to be incarcerated than whites. With the important exception of drug offenses, blacks are over represented among prison inmates due to race differences in crime and arrest statistics. In 1991, for instance, black men accounted for 55 percent of all homicide arrests and 47 percent of homicide offenders in prison. Drug offenses aside, about three-quarters of the racial disparity in imprisonment can be linked to racial differences in arrests and in criminal offending as reported in surveys of crime victims. Although age and educational differences in incarceration have not been studied as closely as race, crime rates are also known to be high among young, poorly educated men. In short, young, black, male high school dropouts are over represented in prison mainly because they commit a disproportionate number of crimes (or, at least, street crimes) and are arrested for them. But that is not the whole story.

The explosion of the penal population after 1970 does not reflect increasing crime rates. The prison population has grown steadily every year since 1974, but crime rates have fluctuated up and down with no clear trend. For example 13.4 million crimes were reported to the police in 1980. In that year 182,000 people were admitted to state and federal prisons. In 1998, 12.4 million crimes were reported, and 615,000 people were sent to prison. Crime had gone down (see "Crime Decline in Context," *Contexts*, Spring 2002), but the number of people going to prison had tripled.

To explain the prison boom, we need to look beyond trends in crime. The exceptional pattern of incarceration among drug offenders provides an important clue. Drug offenders account for a rapidly increasing share of the prison population and the surge in drug-related imprisonment coincides with shifts in drug policy. Beginning in the 1970s, state and federal governments increased criminal penalties and intensified law enforcement in an attempt to reduce the supply, distribution, and use of illegal narcotics. Drug arrests escalated sharply throughout the 1980s and 1990s, and drug offenders were widely sentenced to mandatory prison terms. While the total state prison population grew at about 8 percent annually between 1980 and 1996, the population of drug offenders in state prisons grew twice as quickly.

The war on drugs was just one part of a broad trend in criminal justice policy that also toughened punishment for violent and repeat offenders. For example, between 1980 and 1996, the average time served in state prison for murder increased from 5 to more than 10 years. Habitual offender provisions, such as California's three-strikes law, mandated long sentences for second and third felony convictions. Rates of parole revocation have also increased, contributing to more than a third of all prison admissions by the late 1990s.

> To explain the prison boom, we need to look beyond trends in crime. The exceptional pattern of incarceration among drug offenders provides an important clue.

Why did the punitive turn in criminal justice policy affect young male dropouts so dramatically? Consider two explanations. First, as we have seen, socially marginal men are the most likely to commit crimes and be arrested for them, so simply lowering the threshold for imprisonment—jailing offenders who in an earlier era would have just been reprimanded—will have the biggest impact on this group. Second, some legal scholars claim that policy was redrawn in a way that disproportionately affected young minority males with little schooling. Michael Tonry makes this argument in a prominent indictment of recent anti-drug policy. Street sweeps of drug dealers, mass arrests in inner cities and harsh penalties for crack cocaine were all important elements of the war on drugs. These measures spotlighted drug use among disadvantaged minorities but neglected the trade and consumption of illicit drugs in the suburbs by middle-class whites. From this perspective the drug war did not simply lower the threshold for imprisonment, it also targeted poor minority men.

Although the relative merits of these two explanations have not yet been closely studied, it is clear that going to prison is now extremely common for young black men and pervasive among young black men who have dropped out of school. Imprisonment adds to the baggage carried by poorly educated and minority men, making it harder for them to catch up economically and further widening the economic gap between these men and the rest of society.

incarceration conceals inequality

Regardless of its precise causes, the effects of high incarceration rates on inequality are now substantial. Although the 1990s was a period of economic prosperity, improved job opportunities for many young black men were strongly outweighed by this factor. The stalled economic progress of black youth is invisible in conventional labor force statistics because prison and jail inmates are excluded from standard counts of joblessness.

Employment rates that count the penal population among the jobless paint a bleak picture of trends for unskilled black men in the 1990s. Standard labor force data show that nearly two-thirds of young black male high school dropouts had jobs in 1980 compared to just half in 1999 (figure 3). When inmates are counted in the population, however, the decline in employment is even more dramatic. In 1980 55 percent of all young black dropouts had jobs. By the end of the 1990s fewer than 30 percent had jobs, despite historically low unemployment in the labor market as a whole. Incarceration now accounts for most of the joblessness among young black dropouts, and its rapid growth drove down employment rates during the 1990s economic boom.

Because black men are overrepresented in prison and jail, incarceration also affects estimates of racial inequality. A simple measure of inequality is the ratio of white to black employment rates. In 1999, standard labor force data (which do not count convicts) show that young white dropouts were about one and a half times more likely to hold a job than their black counterparts. Once prison and jail inmates are counted among the jobless, the employment rate for young white dropouts is about two and a half times larger than for blacks. If we relied just on the usual labor force surveys, we would

> The penal system not only conceals inequality, it confers stigma on ex-prisoners and reduces their readiness for the job market. Consequently, ex-convicts often live at the margins of the labor market, precariously employed in low-wage jobs.

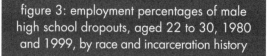

figure 3: employment percentages of male high school dropouts, aged 22 to 30, 1980 and 1999, by race and incarceration history

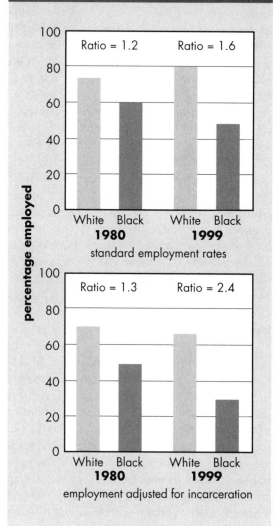

standard employment rates

Ratio = 1.2   Ratio = 1.6

White Black   White Black
1980   **1999**

employment adjusted for incarceration

Ratio = 1.3   Ratio = 2.4

White Black   White Black
1980   **1999**

percentage employed

ger counted in the wage statistics, it appears that the average wage of workers has increased. This seeming rise in average wages doesn't represent a real improvement in living standards, however. We estimate that the wage gap between young black and white men would be 20 percent wider if all those not working, including those in prison and jail, were counted.

incarceration increases inequality

The penal system not only conceals inequality, it confers stigma on ex-prisoners and reduces their readiness for the job market. Consequently, ex-convicts often live at the margins of the labor market, precariously employed in low-wage jobs. Ethnographic research paints a vivid picture. For example, in Mercer Sullivan's *Getting Paid*, delinquent youth in New York City cycled through many jobs, each held for just weeks or months at a time. One subject, after entering an ex-offender employment program at age 20, briefly held a factory job, but "he was fired for being absent and then went through three different jobs in the next four months: he tried delivering groceries, being a messenger, and doing maintenance in a nursing home." His experience was typical of Sullivan's subjects.

James Austin and John Irwin's interviews with current and former inmates in *It's About Time* reveal some of the difficulties ex-convicts have finding jobs. Released prisoners may have to disclose their criminal history or risk its discovery in a background check, or jobs may require special licenses or membership unavailable to most ex-convicts. Both may serve as substantial obstacles to employment. For example, a 38-year-old ex-convict living in the San Francisco Bay Area recalls, "I was supposed to get this light industrial job. They kept putting obstacles in front of me and I talked my way over them every time, till she brought up my

underestimate employment inequality for this marginal group by 50 percent.

Isolating many of the disadvantaged in prisons and jails also masks inequality in wages. When low earners go to prison and are no lon-

being on parole and then she went sour on me. If they catch me lying on the application about being in prison or being on parole, they will [report a violation] and give me four months [in prison]." He also was unable to get a job in dry cleaning because he lacked certification: "I had dry-cleaning training a long time ago, but this time I wasn't in long enough to go through the program. It takes several years. You have to have the paper to get a job. I could jump in and clean anything—silks, wools—remove any spot, use all the chemicals, but I don't got any paper. They won't let you start without the paper."

Statistical studies have tried to estimate the toll incarceration takes on earnings after release. Ideally, to measure the effect of prison time, we would compare the pay of groups who were the same in all respects except for their prison records. However, criminal offenders are unusual in ways that are hard to observe. They may be more impulsive or aggressive, and these sorts of characteristics aren't consistently measured by our usual surveys. Thus different studies yield different estimates.

With these caveats in mind, statistical studies suggest that serving time in prison, by itself and with other characteristics of workers accounted for, reduces wages by between 10 and 30 percent. However, this is a simplified picture of how imprisonment affects job opportunities. Research also shows that incarceration affects the growth—and not just the level—of wages. While pay usually increases as men get older, this is not so true for ex-convicts. This suggests that men with prison records find it hard to get jobs with career ladders or seniority pay. Instead, they are more likely to work in day labor or other casual jobs.

Because young black men with little education are imprisoned in such large numbers, the economic effects of incarceration on individual ex-convicts can add up to large economic disadvantages for minority communities. Neigh-borhoods with many people going to prison develop bad reputations that smear even the law abiding. In *When Work Disappears*, William Julius Wilson reports on interviews with Chicago employers which show how the stigma of criminality can attach to entire minority communities. Considering job candidates from the West Side, one employer observed, "Our black management people [would] say 'No, stay away from that area. That's a bad area . . .' And then it came out, too, that sooner or later we did terminate everybody from that area for stealing . . . [or] drinking." National statistics also show how imprisonment widens the inequality between groups. Estimates for 1998 show that the reduced earnings of ex-convicts contribute about 10 percent to the wage gap between black and white men. About 10 percent of the pay gap between all male college graduates and all high school dropouts is due to the reduced wages that inmates earn after they are released.

the price of safety

The inequalities produced by the penal system are new. The state and federal governments have never imprisoned so many people, and this increase is the result not of more crime but of new policies toward crime. This expansion of imprisonment represents a more massive intrusion of government into the lives of the poor than any employment or welfare program. Young black men's sustained contact with official authority now sets them apart from mainstream America in a novel way.

The inegalitarian effects of criminal justice policy may be justified by gains in public safety. We have in this article treated the penal population primarily as disadvantaged and not as dangerous people, but a large proportion of prisoners are violent offenders. Many commit crimes again and again. Criminals may be poor men, but they also perpetrate crime in poor neighborhoods. From this viewpoint, the proliferation of prisons represents a massive investment in the public safety of disadvantaged urban areas.

But can enduring public safety be achieved by policies that deepen social inequality? A great deal of research indicates that effective crime control depends on reducing economic divisions, not increasing them. There is a strong link between criminal behavior and economic disadvantage. To the extent that prison undermines economic opportunities, the penal boom may be doing little to discourage crime in communities where most men have prison records. If high incarceration rates add to the stigma of residence in high-crime neighborhoods, the economic penalties of imprisonment may affect ex-convicts and law-abiding citizens alike. The criminal justice system is now a newly significant part of a uniquely American system of social inequality. Under these conditions, the punitive trend in criminal justice policy may be even tougher on the poor than it is on crime.

RECOMMENDED RESOURCES

Alfred Blumstein and Allen J. Beck. "Population Growth in U.S. Prisons, 1980-1996." In *Crime and Justice: Prisons*, vol. 26, ed. Michael Tonry and Joan Petersilia (University of Chicago Press, 1999).

Mercer L. Sullivan. *"Getting Paid": Youth Crime and Work in the Inner City* (Cornell University Press, 1989).

Michael Tonry. *Malign Neglect: Race, Crime, and Punishment in America* (Oxford University Press, 1996).

Bruce Western, Jeffrey R. Kling, and David F. Weiman. "The Labor Market Consequences of Incarceration." *Crime and Delinquency* 47 (July 2001): 410–27.

Bruce Western and Becky Pettit. "Incarceration and Racial Inequality in Men's Employment." *Industrial and Labor Relations Review* 54 (October 2000): 3–16.

William Julius Wilson. *When Work Disappears: The World of the New Urban Poor* (Knopf, 1996).

REVIEW QUESTIONS

1. What do Western and Pettit mean when they state that incarceration rates "mask" other measures of inequality?
2. The authors offer two explanations for how the increasingly punitive criminal justice system has affected young male dropouts. Compare these explanations, with particular attention to the differences between the groups at risk.
3. This article ends with an important question: Should we insure short-term public safety by supporting inequalities that will assuredly bring about longer-term social ills? What do you think will be the unintended consequences of prioritizing short-term public safety?
4. Activity: Many police departments give detailed statistics online by precinct (or neighborhood or district). Find the police department Web site for two locations (e.g., your hometown and where you are going to school), and do a search for "crime statistics" for each. Compare the results. What sorts of statistics are provided (e.g., different types of crimes, changes over time)? Are you statistically safer in one of the two locations?

part **13**

Politics

andrew j. perrin

why you voted

55

fall 2008

voting is the educated, emotion-free weighing of the issues. it's a ritual in which lone citizens express personal beliefs that reflect the core of who they are and what they want for their country.

On November 4, 2008, probably 140 million Americans cast votes in the election for President of the United States. Nearly as many citizens, although eligible, chose not to vote, whether out of inertia, disgust, or apathy.

From one point of view, not voting is a rational thing to do. Political scientist Anthony Downs showed decades ago that voting costs time, energy, transportation, and more, and the chances one's own vote will actually change the election's outcome are vanishingly small. It makes sense to stay home.

And yet 140 million of us do it. We take time away from our responsibilities, travel to a place we might never otherwise go, wait in line, and emerge with nothing more than a tiny lapel sticker proclaiming "I Voted" and a feeling of superiority over our non-voting fellow citizens.

Moreover, roughly 20 percent of the eligible population will lie about voting. In an enduring puzzle of public opinion research, more people will tell survey researchers they voted in any given election than actually did so.

This happens because voting is more than straightforward choice-making. Voting is never just the educated, emotion-free weighing of issues and the subsequent casting of a ballot. Indeed, it is a ritual in which lone citizens express personal beliefs that reflect the core of who they are and what they want for their countrymen, balancing strategic behavior with the opportunity to express their inner selves to the world.

In other words, voting in America has two faces: the first, a ritualistic expression of personal belief without regard to strategy; the second, a cold, calculating form of citizenship where what anthropologist Julia Paley calls the "choice-making citizen" weighs the costs and benefits of particular policies and votes accordingly.

We can't understand who votes, and how, without understanding the two faces of voting that come together in citizens' minds and activities.

we don't vote over the phone

The standard approach to studying voting decisions generally ignores the ritualistic face of democratic decision-making.

The modern study of voting dates most prominently to *The American Voter*, a 1960 study by political scientists Angus Campbell, Philip E. Converse, Warren E. Miller, and Donald E. Stokes. Building upon earlier studies that had considered voting patterns in specific cities or regions, *The American Voter* mobilized newly available techniques of scientific public opinion research to understand how Americans made such decisions.

The authors explained voting decisions as a "funnel of causality" pushing in on individuals, a hierarchy of influences on their decisions that grew progressively stronger as the act of voting drew near. To predict whether any given individual would vote, and for whom, one only needed a few known criteria—essentially, what kind of person you were, how much you knew, what you believed, and whom you knew.

This approach was to become the gold standard of voting studies. But it's important to understand some of the decisions these innovative researchers made. First and foremost, they conceived of the voting decision as essentially an individual activity.

They mounted an extraordinary polling effort, asking a national sample of voters a series of well-crafted questions that have become the staples of the American National Election Studies (NES). These surveys, funded by the National Science Foundation and taken every two years, form an immense proportion of what we know about voting and political participation. They are, in fact, the basis of more than 5,000 articles and books published between 1960 and 2008.

Surveys of individual voters, however, as we all know from the barrage of polls we witness each election cycle, rely on contacting individual citizens by telephone and asking them a standard set of multiple choice questions. But this is a pretty poor approximation of how people actually vote, because it takes voters outside their normal social contexts—the neighborhoods, workplaces, schools, unions, clubs, and religious groups in which they actually live their lives and form their views.

As productive as the *American Voter* model of studying voting has been, conceiving of voting as decisions made by individual citizens who understand the issues, weigh them, and dispassionately select a candidate has put limits on how scholars have understood voting and how Americans have decided whether, and how, to vote.

the evolution of the modern voter

Not so long before the 1950s, voting was altogether different. In the late 1800s citizens voted in the open, their choices available for all to see. Political parties mobilized their support-ers, told them whom to vote for, got them to the polls, and even printed the ballots themselves. Voting was social, collective, exciting, and fraught with corruption (at least to our modern sensibilities), a reality illustrated by George Caleb Bingham's classic painting *The County Election* and documented in Michael Schudson's magisterial book *The Good Citizen*.

The Progressive movement of the early 20th century changed this, applying the then-overwhelming faith in scientific rationality to reforms in the political arena. Progressive reforms included the "Australian Ballot," the secret, government-provided ballot voters now see and consider utterly obvious. They prohibited personal rewards from being handed out by elected officials, substituting objective rules and expertise for the personal networks and influence of the prior era.

At the same time, progressive reforms made voting less exciting, harder to figure out, more dependent on individual rather than collective knowledge, and, certainly, more isolated. These are the characteristics voting maintains today. This was a classic case of "rationalization," the double-edged sword sociological giant Max Weber considered the centerpiece of modern life.

By the 1980s, political pundits were increasingly worried that low turnout—typically around half of registered voters in presidential elections, and much lower in local elections—was a bad omen for American democracy. The so-called me generation was chastised for caring little about the concerns of community or society, and the decline in voter turnout was a prominent symptom.

A wide variety of answers to why this happened surfaced, including the complexity of ballots, the influence of big money and special interests in politics, perceived lack of difference among the candidates, and the logistical hassles of registering and voting. A prominent set of studies found that voters were likely to be white as well as more educated and wealthier than the average population. The effects of this inequality were exacerbated by the fact that people were more likely to vote if they were contacted personally by a campaign or party—and the people most likely to be contacted were also white, wealthy, and educated.

Convinced that registration barriers were keeping particularly low-income and African-American citizens from the polls, social scientists Frances Fox Piven and Richard Cloward argued for making registration easier in their influential 1988 book *Why Americans Don't Vote*. In 1993 their campaign paid off with passage of the Motor-Voter Bill, which required states to allow citizens to register to vote when they applied for driver's licenses, thereby substantially reducing the burden of registration. The same impulse is behind recent trends to allow "no excuses" early voting, "vote by mail," "one-stop voting," and other reforms designed to make it easier for citizens to vote. Interestingly, most studies have found little evidence these reforms have, indeed, increased voter turnout.

voting and expression

Voting in America is among the most cherished ways of expressing political individuality, and in many cases it's the only way citizens actually participate in their political communities. To take part in this ritual, citizens must often decipher complicated ballots in carefully created and guarded isolation. This isolation is not just physical, it's also psychological. We work hard to give citizens the idea that the vote they will cast is their own, that the vote says something important about what they truly believe, who they are, and that it is among the most important things they can do as citizens.

And it works. Consider, for example, the candidates who periodically run for president as independents or nominees of minor parties. In virtually all such cases, the independent candidate stands no real likelihood of winning and is often accused of being a "spoiler"—a candidate who, by virtue of being in the race, distorts the outcome from what it otherwise should be. Voters are regularly implored not to "waste votes" on such candidates, since their votes would be ineffective or even counterproductive.

> Voting in America is among the most cherished ways of expressing political individuality.

Yet voters continue to cast ballots for such candidates in substantial numbers, and both the 1992 and 2000 elections were probably significantly affected by these votes. In recent elections with a significant third-party candidate, 4 million voters (about 4 percent of the total) in 2000 and a striking 20.4 million (nearly 20 percent) in 1992 "wasted" these votes. Even in the closely contested 2004 election, in which there was no serious third-party candidate, more than 1.2 million voters (about 1 percent) voted for a candidate other than George W. Bush or John Kerry. Why?

If we understand a vote as a strategic resource, something like a purchase—exchanging something of symbolic value for one selection among several—it's impossible to figure out why citizens would "throw away" their votes by casting them for a candidate with no possibility of winning. But if we instead consider voting as individuals' opportunity to express their own private, core beliefs, it is priceless.

Consider, too, the controversy over the so-called butterfly ballots in the 2000 Florida presidential election. In heavily Jewish and Democratic Palm Beach County, an unlikely proportion of citizens voted for right-wing candidate Pat Buchanan, whom many Jews considered an anti-Semite, rather than the more likely Al Gore.

In an important analysis, political scientist Henry Brady and colleagues showed that most of that vote was probably due to confusing ballot design—a conclusion shared by Buchanan himself. Apart from the strategic value of these votes, the idea that the voter's core beliefs might have been (falsely) expressed as a preference for Buchanan was the stuff of anxiety and jokes alike. A spate of humorous bumper stickers and other materials proclaimed "Jews for Buchanan" and "Don't Blame Me, I Voted for Gore . . . I Think." This anxiety persists with reformers' insistence that electronic voting machines leave a "paper trail"—a way, if all else fails, to presumably rescue future elections from technical snafus.

In both of these cases our votes are understood as expressions of who we are, our deepest ideals and values. But this presents a strange paradox. Why should such a thoroughly social behavior, a practice that expresses our core values about how society should be structured, be practiced in enforced privacy? The answer lies not only in the history of voting, but in the importance of ritual. As political theorist Danielle S. Allen writes, the ritual of voting simultaneously allows us to imagine ourselves as members of an abstract national community and as effective, thinking, competent individuals.

the ritual

Rituals like voting are the practices we use to hold society together—to help us, in the words of the anthropologist Benedict Anderson, imagine ourselves as a community. We carry with us the memories of elections past, refracted through the collective imagination provided by the news media and everyday conversations. Voting connects citizens to these memories, making us a part of them and infusing them with meaning.

When Americans went to the polls this month, we engaged in just such a public ritual. And we use electoral ritual to understand the world around us—precisely the function of ritual in society.

Nearly 50 years after *The American Voter*, a team of political scientists analyzed the 2000 version of the NES, which the original book had launched. The basic model, they found, remains unchanged. Interviewing thousands of voters in isolation (and also separate from their voting booths and their feelings on voting day), they found that the most important elements of the voting decision remained individual in character.

It still holds true that if you tell me who you are, what you know, whom you know, and what you believe, chances are good I can tell you (and the world) whether you will vote, and for whom. Who we are as citizens—our class, race, sex, region of the country, and education—does say a lot about whether we are likely to vote and for whom. Stable political identifications—particularly identification with a political party, the importance of which *The American Voter* first demonstrated and which remains crucial—tell us yet more.

But voting and citizenship are about more than who you are and whom you know (the bread-and-butter concepts of studies like these). They're about what you believe, what you can imagine, and what communities you are part of.

As we move farther away from the narrow end of *The American Voter*'s funnel, it becomes increasingly important to understand how people imagine these communities and their own interests within those communities. In essence, it becomes important to understand how we become who we are, how we learn what we

> Rituals like voting are the practices we use to imagine ourselves as a community.

know, how we meet those we know, and how we come to believe what we do.

ritual and reform

There are often calls for major reforms to fix some of the perceived problems with voting. Two of the most common are adding direct or deliberative features to our democratic practice and making it easier to vote by encouraging early voting, voting by mail, and easing registration requirements.

Americans have long been excited by the ideal of direct democracy, whether by town meeting, electronic plebiscite, or ballot initiative. What could be more democratic than bringing an issue directly to the *demos*—the people—to decide for themselves instead of relying on a clumsy, hierarchical system of representation? Similarly, the idea of some sort of national conversation—whether by town meetings, public forums, or electronic debates—sparks Americans' ambitions to improve democratic practice.

But the ritual aspect of voting complicates all these pictures.

If direct democracy allows citizens to answer questions more directly, who gets to ask the questions? How do citizens sort themselves into groups when deliberating? How do these groups help determine the outcome of deliberation?

None of this means voting reforms—whether institutional, "direct," or deliberative—should be off the table. But none will be successful unless it takes into account both faces of the curious practice of voting in America. The ritual face of American democracy is every bit as important as its procedural face.

RECOMMENDED RESOURCES

Danielle S. Allen. *Talking to Strangers: Anxieties of Citizenship since* Brown v. Board of Education (University of Chicago Press, 2004).

Discusses how Americans imagine voting and citizenship in the political culture the civil rights movement helped develop.

Benedict Anderson. *Imagined Communities.* 2nd ed. (Verso, 1991).

This classic work shows how people use everyday experience and the news media to imagine themselves as part of groups whose members they've never seen and will never meet.

Michael S. Lewis-Beck, William G. Jacoby, Helmut Norpoth, and Herbert F. Weisberg. *The American Voter Revisited* (University of Michigan Press, 2008).

In this ambitious book, the original *The American Voter* is carefully reconstructed with data from 2000 to evaluate how voting has stayed the same and how it has changed since the 1950s.

Michael Schudson. *The Good Citizen* (Harvard University Press, 1999).

This historical study details how the ideas and assumptions behind American citizenship have changed since the writing of the Constitution.

REVIEW QUESTIONS

1. Why does Perrin say that voting could be understood as an irrational act? Do you agree?
2. Did you vote in the last presidential election? Why or why not? How did you make your decision on whom to vote for?
3. Activity: Research compulsory voting in countries such as Australia. Debate the pros and cons of making voting mandatory for all eligible U.S. citizens.

katherine mccoy

uncle sam wants them

winter 2009

private companies have become major players in all types of modern warfare. the implications for fighting wars—and fighting against wars—are more complicated than you think.

Throughout most of the 20th century, warring nation-states generally had two options to increase their military strength. They could create a coalition—as the United States did in World War II—or institute a draft—as it did in Vietnam. Today, though, countries have a third option. Rent. Hiring private military corporations, sometimes called private security corporations or private security firms, has fast become a popular way for nations to fight wars.

As a result, much of today's military workforce isn't part of the military at all. These military contractors come from across the globe and challenge how we think about nations, states, citizens, and how to exercise accountability in war.

For example, when a Panamanian subsidiary of an American firm hires Colombians to fight Iraqis, which country is responsible for their welfare and answers for their crimes? Which public is likely to mount an anti-war campaign or launch a yellow ribbon drive? And whom do they target? These questions, and the answers to them, have significant consequences for how war gets waged, when it stops, and who's accountable for it.

These private companies have become major players in all types of modern warfare. Many scholars have focused on the increasing role these corporations play in weak states, especially in Africa, where they are significant domestic players in civil conflict and resource wars. Some,

like Stephen Brayton, worry that in failed states, corporations are gaining the "civic and political loyalty" that should belong to the military or police, yet are accountable only to the elites who hire them.

Military companies, though, are as much a tool of the strong as the weak.

the move to private military corporations

Scholars have long thought of fighting wars as something nation-states did through their citizens. Max Weber famously defined the modern state as holding a monopoly over the legitimate use of violence, meaning that only state agents— usually soldiers or police—were allowed to wield force. In contrast to pre-modern Europe, in which local rulers often hired mercenaries to protect their kingdoms, modern states largely put aside the mercenary option in favor of standing armies composed primarily of citizens dedicated (officially, at least) to protecting the entire nation. Throughout the 19th and 20th centuries, international law was developed based on this idea of the nation-state.

There were, of course, exceptions to this rule. In the American Revolutionary War the British hired Hessians to fight the colonists, while some mercenaries on the American side became famous war heroes. Even as late as the 1970s European colonial powers hired mercenaries to defeat African "liberation" movements, prompting the United Nations to propose an international treaty against mercenarism. Despite such exceptions, the shift from pre-modern to modern warfare was marked by the idea that, from here on out, states did—and should—fight wars with their own militaries. Mercenaries appeared as an occasional threat to governments and international order, but only a marginal threat, and one that was waning.

But just as the sun seemed to set on the individual mercenary, it rose on the era of the military corporation. Private military corporations (PMCs) are legal entities that supply governments, non-governmental organizations (NGOs), and industry with private soldiers, often referred to as guards or simply "contractors."

The ratio of military contractors to soldiers has climbed with each U.S. military intervention since the 1991 Gulf War. More private contractors work in the Iraq War than soldiers.

The first modern PMCs can be traced back to the Vietnam War. What made the rise of these organizations possible, explains the Brookings Institution's P. W. Singer in *Corporate Warriors*, is the combination of the end of the Cold War, the subsequent downsizing of armies, the availability of smaller high-tech weaponry, and the ideological trend toward outsourcing and privatizing government functions.

Some argue that PMCs are a stronger, more organized form of mercenarism, while others claim they're a natural extension of the defense industry's shift from providing goods to providing services. Contractors today provide nearly all the services previously performed by soldiers in war zones, from guarding bases to interrogating prisoners to developing military strategy.

Since the 1990s, PMCs have taken on increasingly larger roles in war and military campaigns. In fact, the ratio of military contractors to soldiers has climbed with each U.S. military intervention since the 1991 Gulf War, such that more private contractors work in the Iraq War than soldiers. And there's no reason to expect this trend to slow down. Already estimated at more than $100 billion, the PMC market is projected to be worth between $150 billion and $200 billion by 2010.

logistics of pmcs

Governments that contract PMCs have practical reasons for doing so. One is cost. Using contractors instead of public employees saves the government from paying employees' pensions or peacetime salaries, potentially producing long-term savings. In the short term, however, open-ended contracts and hefty pricetags make contractors more expensive than soldiers. Thus, the true cost of contracting remains an open debate.

Perhaps more important than cost is strategy. PMCs can be rapidly deployed in unanticipated, short-term conflicts. As such, they can free up soldiers for more sustained military work on other fronts. Moreover, outsourcing "tail-end" jobs, such as laundry and construction, to civilians reduces the demands on a stretched national army.

Many analysts argue a reliance on contractors has allowed the United States to pursue two simultaneous wars despite the 1990s military downsizing. But in countries with weak armies, PMCs can provide a decisive military boost. Sierra Leone is the classic example—it successfully used Executive Outcomes, a South African PMC, to drive back rebels from the capital city in the mid-1990s.

While most PMCs are headquartered in militarily powerful countries such as the United States, Britain, and Israel, a disproportionate number of the PMC workforce itself comes from the global South. According to a survey conducted by the PMC industry's think tank, the Peace Operations Institute, in U.S. operations only about 10 percent of contracted workers are Americans, while 60 percent belong to the country in which military operations are taking place (Iraqis in Iraq, for example) and 30 percent come from other countries. A Congressional Research Services report reveals those numbers are fairly representative of U.S. efforts in Iraq, with a slightly higher percentage of contractors (65

> In U.S. operations, about 10 percent of contracted workers are Americans, 60 percent are from the country in which military operations are taking place, and 30 percent come from other countries.

percent) being Iraqi and about one-quarter being other foreigners.

That last group, called "third-country nationals" (TCNs), is made up of workers from around the world. They are routinely paid about one-tenth of what their American counterparts earn. Host-country nationals (HCNs) tend to be paid wages commensurate with local jobs.

The international composition of the PMC workforce is notable. Former Haliburton subsidiary KBR alone has employees from 38 different countries working in Iraq. Some third-country nationals—Filipinos and Indians, for example—perform the bulk of support work on American military bases, such as laundry and food service, while others—especially Nepalese, South

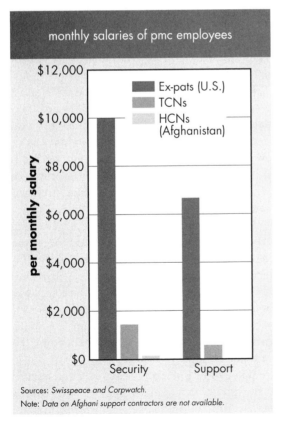

monthly salaries of pmc employees

Legend:
- Ex-pats (U.S.)
- TCNs
- HCNs (Afghanistan)

per monthly salary

Sources: *Swisspeace and Corpwatch.*
Note: *Data on Afghani support contractors are not available.*

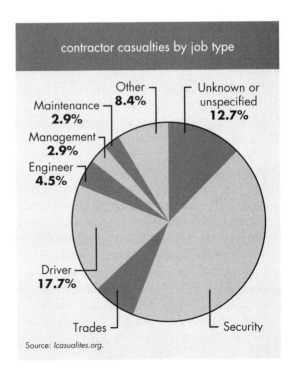

contractor casualties by job type

Other **8.4%**
Maintenance **2.9%**
Management **2.9%**
Engineer **4.5%**
Unknown or unspecified **12.7%**
Driver **17.7%**
Trades
Security

Source: *Icasualites.org.*

Africans, and Latin Americans—are hired for security work. The latter usually come from countries with a recent history of counterinsurgency or other claims to military expertise.

Despite the division between those performing more "tooth-end" and "tail-end" jobs, in war all are vulnerable to attack. The chart "contractor casualties by job type" shows the breakdown in Iraq.

consequences of contractors

The move to PMCs changes the entire spectrum of military labor. It marks a dual shift in the way we think of a military labor force: from public to private, and from domestic to international. This shift affects more than the clothes people wear in war or the languages they speak on base. It undermines old lines of accountability. Military historian Martin van Crevald argues the monopoly over force meant that in war, "it is the government that directs, the army that fights, and the people who suffer." This may be a dysfunctional relationship, but one with the potential to curb violence nonetheless.

To the extent that the state, the army, and the people all represent the same nation, their fates are interconnected. In democratic countries, "the people" must approve the government's decision to send the military, and they might retract that approval as military casualties start mounting. Having public, national forces fight wars helps the whole nation experience and internalize their costs. Citizens see "our men and women in uniform" being shipped off to war and the flag-draped coffins when those same soldiers don't make it home alive. This helps bring the costs of war home to the voting public.

In contrast, using PMCs externalizes the costs of war and outsources accountability. As private

employees, contractors don't leave the same impression on public consciousness that soldiers do, and they're less amenable to public oversight.

This is truer for some contractors than others. Recent history shows deaths or disappearances of American contractors do make political waves in the United States. Military analysts James Manker and Kent Williams point out that, "Regardless of where the responsibility is placed contractually, [when American contractors are involved] the media [sic] reports it as a U.S. casualty, a U.S. captive, or a U.S. wounded without respect to who is at fault." Indeed, author Jeremy Scahill points out that the 2004 deaths of four Americans working for Blackwater in Fallujah made

> Deaths or disappearances of American contactors do make political waves in the United States. Captured or killed foreign contractors don't receive such treatment.

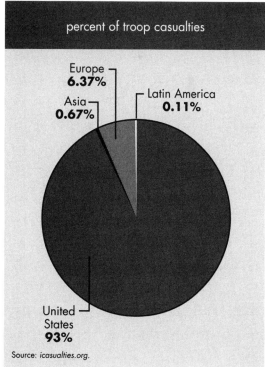

percent of troop casualties

Europe **6.37%**

Asia **0.67%**

Latin America **0.11%**

United States **93%**

Source: icasualties.org.

headlines in the United States for days, and the 2003 capture of three American contractors by FARC guerrillas in Colombia led to ongoing Congressional inquiries throughout their five years of captivity.

Captured or killed foreign contractors don't receive such treatment. For instance, there was limited political response in the United States when insurgents captured and beheaded 12 Nepalese contractors working in conjunction with the U.S. mission in Iraq. For this very reason, companies sometimes enlist foreign contractors for high-risk or high-visibility roles, such as gunners or pilots. This first became evident to me during my fieldwork on PMCs in Colombia, when I asked a State Department employee why Central Americans were flying U.S.-sponsored counter-drug and counter-insurgency missions there.

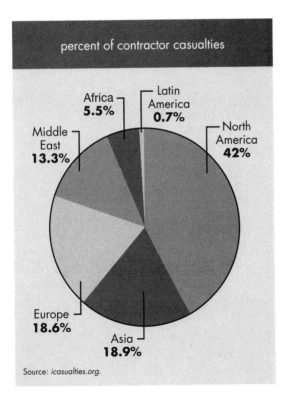

percent of contractor casualties

Latin America 0.7%
Africa 5.5%
Middle East 13.3%
North America 42%
Europe 18.6%
Asia 18.9%

Source: icasualties.org.

"Since these are combat missions, [the U.S. government] didn't want American pilots flying because of risk and liability," he responded.

The pattern seems to hold in some other contexts. A Swisspeace report notes that in Afghanistan, security-heavy PMCs such as Blackwater, Dyncorp, and ArmorGroup have some of the highest ratios of third-country nationals. Indeed, some military analysts consider the relative invisibility of foreign contractors to be one of privatization's key benefits. As a 2005 Rand report notes, the advantages of PMCs are greatest "when policymakers worry less about the safety of non-American contract personnel than about American lives."

In Iraq, non-American contractors are the hidden casualties of war. Among state-supported coalition troops, Americans make up 93 percent of the casualties. Among contractors, they represent only 43 percent (North America plus Latin America) of casualties. The rest are third-country nationals from Europe, Asia, and the Middle East. This percentage would be even smaller if Iraqi contractor deaths were included, but such data are not currently available. Because they aren't Americans, Iraqi and third-country contractor deaths generally aren't reported in U.S. newspapers, even though contractors work side by side with coalition troops.

Using contractors—especially foreigners—also makes it difficult to determine who's legally responsible when something goes wrong. This is a problem both for protecting contractors' welfare and for holding them accountable for crimes. For example, in Iraq there have been widespread reports of PMCs confiscating foreign contractors' passports and keeping contractors against their will. This led the Defense Department to issue a memorandum in 2006 calling on the companies to clean up their act, but little seems to have changed.

One likely explanation for this inertia is that the foreign contractors are hired through an international web of subcontractors and subsidiaries, effectively deflecting responsibility from any one company. A *Washington Post* article from 2004 outlined the contract chain for a group of Indian support contractors: "[The Indian company] Subhash Vijay had hired them to work for Gulf Catering Co. of Riyadh, Saudi Arabia, which was subcontracted to Alargan Group of Kuwait City, which was subcontracted to the Event Source of Salt Lake City, which in turn was subcontracted to KBR of Houston."

Having such a multinational, highly subcontracted workforce further complicates the already difficult task of holding security contractors legally accountable when they commit crimes. Moreover, without knowing who contractors are or how many are out there, it's hard even for the state to exercise accountability over them—numerous government reports acknowledge the lack of an accurate count of the number of contractors and subcontractors involved in U.S. military operations.

In some cases, PMCs offer governments strategic flexibility at the expense of full political accountability. For instance, the Defense Department and State Department have effectively used foreign contractors to exceed Congress's limits on the number of troops involved in a military campaign. (In an effort to contain certain military operations, Congress may place a ceiling, or cap, on the number of soldiers that can be deployed on a mission. But caps generally don't apply to contractors.)

Congress has tried at times to close this loophole by capping the number of contractors as well, but these caps apply only to Americans, not foreigners. This is the case in Colombia, where the use of foreign military contractors allows U.S. companies to deploy more than the 600-person cap imposed by Congress. This official invisibility of foreign, private participants in such military campaigns makes the conflicts seem smaller and more controllable.

A few groups have tried to increase accountability by reinforcing the political relationships between states and their contractor citizens. In the United States, human rights organizations are advocating for Defense Department contractors to be brought under the military chain of command; this will probably come before the U.S. Supreme Court later this year. The UN's Working Group on the Use of Mercenaries has pushed PMC recruitment countries to enact stricter domestic legislation to control the flow of their citizens to the PMC market abroad. Some countries see legislation as a way to help their governments control potentially violent citizens. For example, South Africa has enacted strict, but arguably ineffective, laws intended to stop Apartheid-era shock troops from selling their services on the international market.

On the other hand, some developing nations see this market as a solution to the problems of insecurity. For countries like Colombia, the international war market provides a way to employ demobilized paramilitaries and retired soldiers. Whether this is an effective way to reintegrate ex-combatants remains to be seen.

What is clear, however, is that governments currently have neither the authority nor the responsibility over private employees that they have for their own citizen-soldiers operating abroad. The triple challenges of a lucrative international market, weak government controls, and lack of political will to control contractors all lead contractors to operate as free agents. The Blackwater armed guard in Iraq has no more ties to his home state than his compatriot who works at a hotel in Jordan. From the perspective of their governments and their fellow citizens, both are simply international labor migrants.

the rub of controlling pmcs

The Heritage Foundation's James Carafano argues that nations do have the tools to hold today's private soldiers, and those who hire them, accountable. In *Private Sector, Public Wars*, he argues that "Unlike medieval kings [who used mercenaries], modern nations can use the instruments of good governance to control the role of the private sector in military competition." Among those instruments he lists "[a]n enabled citizenry with ready access to a vast amount of public information."

But there's the rub. Which citizenry is he talking about? Under Weber's ideal, this was never a question—those who fought, those who ordered them into battle, and those who elected the decision-makers were all citizens of the same country. But with privatization and internationalization, there's no national constituency that automatically identifies with contractors, or with the wars they fight. This poses its own security risk. Privatization removes war one step away from the country that orders it, and internationalization removes it yet another. When the workers of war become more remote and more invisible, the entry barriers to war are lowered. It's easier to wage war with anonymous soldiers.

Any serious attempts to regulate PMCs will have to deal with this issue. There are many proposals for making the industry cleaner, such as increasing contractor professionalism and creating greater transparency in bids for government contracts. These steps are important for increasing what political scientist Deborah Avant calls "functional control" of the PMC industry, but they do nothing to increase what she calls "political control." That will only come through laws that help people feel some sense of ownership over the PMC world. Our ability to re-create that sense of public empowerment in this new world will help determine what military privatization means in the long run. It may make the difference between the state hiring out some of the functions of war, and having a private shadow army.

RECOMMENDED RESOURCES

Deborah Avant. *The Market for Force* (Cambridge University Press, 2005).

> A political scientist takes on the question of what political and security tradeoffs we can expect with military privatization.

James Jay Carafano. *Private Sector, Public Wars: Contractors in Combat—Afghanistan, Iraq, and Future Conflicts* (Praeger Security International, 2008).

> This security analyst believes PMCs are an important military tool that can be adequately controlled by improving the existing system of government contracting.

Jennifer K. Elsea and Nina M. Serafino. "Private Security Contractors in Iraq: Background, Legal Status, and Other Issues." Congressional Resource Service Report for Congress, July 11, 2007.

> This report discusses the role and status of third-country nationals, as well as Americans and Iraqis, in the current Iraq campaign.

P. W. Singer. *Corporate Warriors: The Rise of the Privatized Military Industry* (Cornell University Press, 2003).

> The author introduces the wide variety of contexts in which PMCs operate and develops a framework for dividing the industry between security and support functions.

United Nations Working Group on the Use of Mercenaries as a Means of Violating Human Rights and Impeding the Exercise of the Rights of People to Self-Determination. Annual Reports.

> The UN group charged with studying PMCs releases annual reports detailing the labor violations against third-country national contractors and the human rights violations committed by contractors.

REVIEW QUESTIONS

1. How are contracted troops different from military troops? What do you think are contract troops' reasons for joining a war? How might they compare with the reasons that military troops usually cite?

2. Were you aware that of the large number of PMCs who participated in the war in Iraq? What are you reactions to this article?

3. Do you think it is ethical to hire contracted troops to fight wars? Why or why not?

4. Why do you think deaths of foreign contractors are not usually covered in the U.S. media? What is your reaction to this? Is the idea of dying while fighting a war different for foreigners than for citizens?

5. Activity: Research the Geneva Conventions that govern international wars. What complications to these agreements arise from using PMCs in international wars?

the social significance of barack obama   **57**

fall 2008

*in 2008, contexts convened a panel of esteemed sociologists at contexts.org and asked them to discuss the
social significance of barack obama's campaign for president of the united states and what it might mean,
sociologically speaking, were he to win the office.*

*here we provide an abridged version of that discussion (you can read each commentator's prepared opening
statement online). to continue the conversation online—especially now that you know the outcome of the
election, which none of us did when this issue went to press—visit contexts.org/obama.*

Doug Hartmann, *Contexts* co-editor: *When
we first put out the call for this roundtable,
we got a number of responses to the Obama
candidacy that were quite critical and pessimistic, far more so than we might have expected,
given both the popular and intellectual enthusiasm for the Obama campaign. Why do you think
this is? And what does it suggest about sociologists and their orientation to politics, American
society, and/or social change more broadly?*

Josh Pacewicz: I think there's . . . something
particular about the Obama campaign that
draws out cynicism [for us]. Thirty years ago,
I'm sure nearly everyone in the United States
would have understood Obama's success similarly to his more progressive supporters today
(i.e., as a victory for historically marginalized
groups). But that is not how many of Obama's
other supporters seemed to understand his
campaign, nor do I think Obama would have
been as successful if he had been universally
understood this way. I think this says something fundamental about our time: if we chalk
Obama's success up to a progressive shift in the

electorate (i.e., in the way many of us and our
colleagues understand progressivism) we might
miss an important piece of a developing story.

Eduardo Bonilla-Silva: My reaction to
Obama reflects my background as a sociologist
of color from the Caribbean as well as a person
who has been involved in left-wing politics for
almost 30 years. I have seen many black politicians in the Caribbean not deliver on their promises once they reach the post of premier, governor,
or president. The best predictors for this outcome, in my view, are leaders who are wishy-
washy, not clearly connected to social
movements, and who in the course of their electoral campaign "compromise" on almost anything to get elected. That has helped me, as most
folks in the Caribbean, to develop a healthy
skepticism on all mainstream politicians and
realize that leaders must be, paraphrasing Dr.
King, "judged by the content of their politics and
not by the color of their skin." But I realize that
for Americans, Obama and his promise seems
like a unique moment in their history. They have
never seen or experienced something like this.

Hence, few dare break the spell and question things.

Joe Feagin: The real question is about Obama's electability. It is not so easily dismissed as some suggest. First, keep in mind that of all whites who have voted so far in all Republican and Democratic primaries, only 25 percent have voted for Obama. Some 75 percent of all whites who have so far voted only for whites. In addition, the *New York Times* July poll that asked whites about whether most acquaintances would vote for a black man found that 19 percent said no. The figure was this high for white independents and Republicans and fairly near that for Democrats.

Assuming this is a sizable group of white acquaintances, then this is a chilling finding. The 19 percent is higher than the percentage of young people who are voters, or the percentage of blacks who are voters. Candidates win presidential elections by a few percentage points, and how can Obama win in a situation of white racist thinking and framing? Whites lie in polls, and yet almost everything we think we "know" about this election comes from polls.

The data are why I am pessimistic about his chances, and no other reason. I remain amazed that the social science data on whites' racist views are largely ignored in almost all commentary, left and right, on this election. The coming attacks, I predict, will successfully play into the old white racial frame and peel off numerous whites who now "support" or "lean to" Obama.

Jeff Manza: Obama's electability speaks to other questions about race and political change in America. I think Joe is right to point out that there are good reasons to think that enough white Democratic voters may end up voting for McCain to tip the election his way. But, we would have to think that the swing based on "race" is very large indeed to permit a McCain victory. If Joe is right, it would require that Obama would "underperform" by something like 5 percent to 7 percent to lose this election. That is an awful lot of old-fashioned racism among normal Democratic and independent voters (noting that old fashioned racists who always vote Republican anyway are irrelevant).

I think the Democratic campaign is going to benefit from a number of things that polls do not always pick up, some of which might offset whites lying to pollsters about their Obama preference. There is a huge reserve of anger and high motivation among activists and rank-and-file Democrats that will push up turnout among likely Democratic voters. I see nothing like that among Republicans; indeed, the religious right is divided and the Republican "base" is not excited about McCain, only fearing a large Democratic sweep, and that is a much weaker motivation for action. Cell-phone-only users are out of the sample in polls, and are likely to be Obama voters. And, we have every reason to expect significantly increased turnout among minority voters that is, again, not necessarily being picked up.

Gianpaolo Baiocchi: When we talk about optimism and excitement surrounding Obama, let's also consider the international context. There is a joke that if Barack Obama loses the general election he should run for President of Brazil, given the fascination with his campaign there, as in many other nations around the world.

U.S. racial structures are often the subject of discussion in the public sphere in a surprising number of places around the world; traditionally in Brazil, the discussion had to do with the visible aspects of racism in the United States (lynching, Jim Crow, ghettoes) to reaffirm that Brazil's supposedly fluid system of racial categories is less racist and more democratic. More recently it has had to do with affirmative action tentatively implemented in some universities: in the absence of U.S.-style racism, the argument goes, Brazil should not need U.S.-style solutions. But now the discussion, not always polite, has turned indignant. "How can it be that a more racist country like the United States can have a black presidential candidate?"

His very presence on the national stage in the United States seems to speak to the successes of U.S.-style multiculturalism and affirmative policies (strategies that are racially explicit but work within structures) to publics around the world, despite his actual biography.

Certainly some of the social significance of Obama's campaign and eventual presidency has to do with these types of global implications.

Hartmann: Where do you stand on the sources of enthusiasm and support for Obama, what they reveal about his significance, and what they might suggest about his ability to lead and govern?

Enid Logan: My reading of the situation is that the progressive coalition that is backing, or potentially backing, Obama is in fact quite fractured. Though my initial comments focused primarily on conflicts among women, Obama's recent movement to the right has also vexed many of his lefty/liberal white male supporters, who had formerly endorsed him almost uncritically. While there is much enthusiasm for Obama among different sectors of the electorate, I am not at all sure there is a great deal of consensus about the direction he should take the country, or the significance of his candidacy. As Obama has not emerged from a social movement, there are many serious questions arising from his candidacy—concerning racial justice, gender equality, poverty, elitism, religion, patriotism, and nation—that progressives have not had the chance to hash out together collectively. And there is much work to be done by those of us who care passionately about these issues to

make sure the kind of change Obama might bring about is, in fact, change we can live with.

Bonilla-Silva: Doug is right about the huge level of enthusiasm for Obama. Americans are truly sick and tired of "politics and usual" and this national mood opened the door for Obama to emerge and tell Americans what they longed to hear—a message of unity, hope, the end of partisanship, and "change." But enthusiasm for a candidate does not a social movement make. John F. Kennedy and Robert Kennedy generated a lot of enthusiasm, but we would not say they created a social movement. But the question is, why is a black man generating so much enthusiasm among a large segment of the white electorate? This new political landscape does not reflect the "declining," but rather the "changing," significance of race.

I have argued that Obama is the product of 40 years of racial transition from Jim Crow to what I have labeled as the "new racism," which includes incorporating anti-minority minority leaders in the Republican Party (e.g., Clarence Thomas, Linda Chavez, Bobby [Jindal], etc.) and of post-racial sanitized minority leaders in the Democratic Party (Andrew Young, Bill Richardson, Harold Ford, etc.). All these leaders do not pose a challenge to the socio-political order and teach the "wretched of the earth" the wrong political lesson: that electoral, rather than social movement, politics is the way to affect change.

Sociologists—and the immense majority of sociologists in America are white—are not cynical or pessimistic about Obama. In fact, they are as much caught up in the "Obama craze" as the average American. Most sociologists are indeed happy, happy, happy about the prospects of having a black president and I dare suggest for the same reasons as the average white Obama supporter.

Manza: Let me offer a slight dissenting note here. It strikes me that worrying about how "progressive" Obama will be once in office—if he wins—based on what happens or is said during the campaign is off base. You run for office to win, and doing so sometimes requires rhetoric that narrows the perceived differences between you and your opponent in areas where the other party is historically stronger. This is exactly what the Obama campaign has done. It makes him look a good deal less progressive than in late 2007 when he was speaking to progressive Democratic voters. We should keep in mind that the disconnect between campaign rhetoric and policy initiatives once in office can be enormous.

Baiocchi: Obama is no social movement candidate—that is, he does not come from social movements and his candidacy (energizing as it is to many) is not a social movement. However, there is much in his campaign that alludes to the rhetoric and style of social movements. "Si se puede," etc. And I think some of the appeal of his candidacy has to do with that. There is a profound asymmetry between the Republicans and Democrats when it comes to their relationships to their putative "bases." Maybe it is because, as Domhoff and others have suggested, liberals lost the post–World War II war of ideas in the United States.

Pacewicz: I feel part of the issue with progressive politics is also related to the "institutionalization/integration into the political realm" aspects of political power, in addition to "civil society/voluntary mobilization." Based on what I have seen, the Democratic Party still gets a rush of volunteers around election time or in connection with a particularly contentious issue; many of these folks are spillovers from other local and national movements. What has really

declined is long-term organizational capacity. I think this has almost everything to do with the decline of organized labor.

Hartmann: *One question that has been talked about a lot: Is Obama black enough?*

Bonilla-Silva: The question of Obama's blackness makes sense if we understand that historically there has always been a "black majority" that has shared a similar set of life chances. By this standard, Obama is not Jesse, or Al, or Farrakhan, or Maxine Waters, or any other black leader with roots in the poor and working-class segment of the black community. The question of his blackness then is not about his skin color, but about his life experiences and how his different experiences and background may affect his politics. Obama is black lite not because he is half-white, but because he has taken an almost raceless political stand and persona. This said, the legitimacy of Obama's blackness should be judged by his politics and, in my view, his are "neo-mulatto" politics.

Baiocchi: I think it is telling that we as a group have hesitated to get to the question of Obama's blackness. It's almost as if we played by the rules of acceptable discourse around his post-racial candidacy.

Obama himself, as we've all noted, avoids the language of racial injustice and doesn't dwell on the question of his own blackness. It's almost left largely to others to identify him. Post-racial politeness, though, calls for us to not to speak of the thorny issue.

But Obama's post-racial discourse is almost like a fiction that no one buys but everyone is supposed to pretend is believable. African Americans don't, and whites don't either. But decorum calls for avoidance of the issue, especially by the candidate himself. His campaign has tried to avoid leaking to the press the stories of threats and burnings of campaign offices in the heartland. And remember how everyone pounced on Obama for "playing the race card from the bottom of the deck" for the innocent statement that he didn't look like the presidents on dollar bills?

These rules speak profoundly to how things work in the current juncture of race relations, as discussed by both Eduardo and Joe. One way to interpret it is that the price a candidate of color must pay for mainstream respectability is the abandonment of racial discourse. Certainly something else going on is the "generational" effect that has had play in the media as well. I think it is correct to say there is a newer generation of African-American leadership that has come of age after the civil rights movement, with a different relationship to racial discourse, having lived much or most of their lives in the era of polite racism as opposed to overt Jim Crow. I think it is also a generation that has seen the erosion of civil rights victories but had in some way a different horizon of possibilities because every civil rights era victory reversed (busing, affirmative action, and so on) has been justified as no longer being necessary since racism officially became "a thing of the past."

Logan: On the issue of racial identity, I believe Obama is opening up the space for new, expanded notions of blackness. The more time he spends in the national spotlight, the choices will, hopefully, no longer only be to be seen as either a) "authentically black," i.e., in all ways identified with "the hood," poor blacks, and the "urban experience," or as b) "not really black," "honorary white," "black lite" (to use Eduardo's phrase), or "not black enough."

While I realize a number of progressive scholars and activists (from Jesse Jackson to Ralph Nader) disagree, for many members of the black professional classes I have interviewed, Barack

Obama is not simply a "whitewashed" black man. He is, rather, someone who represents the increasing diversity of the black community. Not all of us are from the hood. Some of us are biracial. Increasing numbers have parents from the Caribbean or Africa.

Obama seems to represent a blackness that is cosmopolitan, global, progressive, multifaceted, and forward-looking, rather than primarily referencing slavery, the Civil Rights Movement, and our glorious past as Kings and Queens in Africa. We are more diverse, complex, and dynamic than previously assumed, no longer so easily stereotyped or pigeonholed. We may not want to be asked to speak only about "black issues" or on behalf of the entire black community. We may sip a latte and shop at Whole Foods from time to time, but we can still drop a three-pointer on cue, listen to Jay-Z on our iPods, and give our significant others a fist-pound as they go off to face the day.

The problem with all this is that I'm not sure many of Obama's black middle-class supporters are clear enough about the bargain Obama is implicitly making in our names. While they may differ on the ways and extent to which race shapes their lives, none of the people I have spoken to thinks of themselves as "post-racial," believes the United States to be a "magical place," or thinks racism in America is dead (to quote African-American commentator Tavis Smiley, "I love America . . . but this ain't Disneyland").

We must listen carefully to what Obama is saying, and ask ourselves if he is agreeing to too much. For one, he has conceded that the children of the black professional classes should probably be excluded from affirmative action policies. And while robust debates about personal responsibility have been taking place among black people for years, there is a degree to which Obama sometimes seems to be airing dirty laundry in public and scolding black people in order to score points with whites (yes, I'm agreeing with

Jesse here). That should make more of us uncomfortable. The undertones of the new politics of race that may come to characterize the Age of Obama thus sometimes seem rather sinister. The crux of the subtext I read is that it is time for us all to get past race, especially blacks.

Hartmann: *We've covered a lot of ground, more than we'll be able to print. Any final thoughts? Things we've missed? Overwhelming points you need to bring home?*

Bonilla-Silva: I want to wrap up in a provocative fashion by daring to make some bold predictions. So as I look into my sociological crystal ball, here is what I see. Barring some John Edwards–like scandal or a tragedy, Obama will be elected President of the United States. After Obama is elected President, the United States will experience a brief "We shall overcome" period of euphoria, a "Yes we can" frenzy. However, we will soon return to the politics of "America the Brutiful." On the home front, President Obama will talk about unity and about how we are one indivisible nation under (his) God, but most of his policies will do little to challenge the capitalist, gendered, and racial character of the polity. President Obama will not dare intervene with the "invisible hand of the market" that has been slapping all of us quite hard as of late. President Obama will not make a priority of crafting policies to reduce the 25 percent difference in earnings between men and women with similar qualifications. And, President Obama will take a middle-of-the-road, post-racial stand on race matters that will maintain the racial status quo. On the crucial symbolic issue of affirmative action, he will reaffirm Bubba's mended but not ended stand.

America will remain Amerika, but will have a brown person in charge of keeping the White House white. Whites, whether they supported Obama or not, will rejoice and postulate a sotto voce that Obama's election demonstrates the nation has finally moved "beyond race" and, accordingly, will object more vociferously than ever before to anyone who dares speak about racism. Blacks and other racial minorities, after their little intoxication with Obama's hope liquor, will sober up and realize having a black man in "charge" does not necessarily put food on their tables. And in a short time, we will all see the curious spectacle of white folks fanatically supporting a black president while black folks ask "their" president, "Damn, where did the change we could believe in go?"

Hartmann: *Anybody else?*

Logan: I think Obama's probable election (I agree that support for him among black and under-25 cell-phone-only users is likely greatly underestimated and very important) will accelerate certain trends in American racial politics that began to germinate long before he declared his candidacy last February.

One major trend I see coming ever more to the forefront is the importance, or visibility, of the class divide in the black community, both in terms of the discussions that take place among African Americans, and in terms of how blacks are seen by non-blacks in the wider world. As recent sociological research has emphasized, black experiences of race and racism in the United States today differ tremendously depending upon social class.

REVIEW QUESTIONS

1. Why were many of the commentators in this panel highly skeptical of Obama's being elected? What do you think their skepticism might say about cultural beliefs about race at the time?

2. Do you think any of these commentators changed their views once the election was over? Why or why not?
3. Imagine that Hillary Clinton had won the Democratic nomination for president. Do you think she would have been questioned about being "woman enough" to be president? Why or why not? And what does this tell us about how race and gender operate in contemporary America?
4. Do you think Obama's election opened the door for other racial minorities to become president? Why or why not?

jeffrey c. dixon

turkey, islam, and the eu

58

fall 2009

a close examination of theological, historical, and contemporary evidence reveals the limits of civilization clash arguments for understanding islam, turkey, and the place of both in europe.

After the September 11th attacks on the United States, more than a few Americans came to believe that Islam and Western Christianity were embroiled in a battle over fundamental differences—a "clash of civilizations," so to speak. But this rhetoric was neither new nor particular to the United States. Across the Atlantic for some time, in fact, it has been used in the debate over the proposed entry of Turkey, a Muslim country, into the European Union (EU).

Mainly Sunni and officially a secular country, Turkey geographically straddles Europe and Asia. It applied for full membership into (what is now) the EU in 1987, much to the displeasure of some European politicians.

Turkey's application to the EU remains controversial for many reasons—its economy, its human rights policies, and the possibility of massive out-migration among them. But prominent opposition in Europe centers around issues of culture.

Former French president Giscard d'Estaing famously said, "[Turkey's] capital is not in Europe . . . and 95 per cent of its population is outside Europe. [It has] a different culture, a different approach, and a different way of life. It is not a European country." The *New York Sun* reported former French president Jacques Chirac said that Turkey will need to undergo a "major cultural revolution" to join the EU. Former German chancellor Helmut Schmidt said there are "great cultural differences" between Turkey and the EU, according to Deutsche Press. And the former president of the European Union of Christian Democrats, Wim van Velzen, said the EU had "cultural, humanitarian and Christian values different to Turkey's," the *Financial Times* reported. Even Pope Benedict XVI has weighed in, saying, "The roots that have formed Europe . . . are those of Christianity. . . . Turkey is founded on Islam. . . . Thus the entry of Turkey into the EU would be anti-historical," the *Christian Science Monitor* reported.

At the core of these beliefs about cultural differences between Turkey and Europe is the perception that Islam and liberal democracy are incompatible, a view popularized by the late Samuel P. Huntington in his book *The Clash of Civilizations*.

But claims of cultural and civilization differences between Turkey and the EU are exaggerated. Where liberal-democratic value differences exist, in contrast to the "clash" thesis, they're generally not patterned according to religious "civilizations." A closer examination of theological, historical, and contemporary evidence reveals the limits of civilization clash arguments for understanding Islam, the diversity of Muslim nations, and Turkey's place among them.

> Claims of cultural and civilization differences between Turkey and the EU are exaggerated.

Samuel P. Huntington, the author of Clash of Civilizations. *(World Economic Forum/Peter Lauth via Creative Commons)*

the thesis

Samuel Huntington popularized the "clash of civilizations" in a highly influential *Foreign Affairs* article published in 1993 and later in a *New York Times* best-selling book. In the latter, he writes, "[T]he most important distinctions among people [today] are not ideological, political, or economic. They are cultural. . . . The most important groupings of states are no longer the three blocs of the Cold War, but rather the world's seven or eight civilizations." These civilizations contain all the elements of culture, including identity, values, and history, but the clash of civilizations thesis holds that historical religious traditions are the major "fault lines."

The civilizations that have received the most attention are Western Christian, which includes Protestantism and Catholicism and thus most of Europe, and Islam, which includes Turkey and Middle Eastern and North African countries, according to Huntington's classification of civilizations.

Democratic pluralism, separation of church and state, and rule of law are hallmarks of Western Christian civilization, Huntington writes.

Islamic civilization, on the other hand, is characterized by the ideas that God rules the universe, law reflects God's—not humans'—wishes, and there are no social divisions among people because Muslims are seen as part of a single community, or *ummah*.

In Huntington's view, Western Christian and Islamic civilizations are also distinct from an Orthodox Christian civilization, which includes Greece, Cyprus, Bulgaria, Romania, and is especially prominent in Eastern Europe. Whereas Western Christianity emphasizes separation of church and state, God is Caesar's junior partner in Orthodoxy and God is Caesar in Islam, as Huntington puts it.

Because of these differences, he writes, Western Christian countries are most likely to accept liberal democracy and its values, such as rule of law (especially versus rule of God), and recognize minority rights; Orthodox Christian countries are somewhat less likely and Islamic countries are least likely.

Although Huntington hedges somewhat in calling Turkey a "torn country" because the elite and masses support "Western" and "Islamic" values, respectively, he nevertheless locates Turkey in the Islamic civilization. He points to evidence suggesting that Turkey had retreated to its Islamic roots in the 1980s and 1990s, specifically with the religious-based Welfare Party's political victories in the 1990s. After the publication of Huntington's major works on this topic, the religious-based Justice and Development Party was elected in 2002 and re-elected in 2007, seemingly confirming Huntington's thesis as it applies to Turkey and the EU.

criticism of "the clash"

Despite its popular appeal, social scientists have criticized the clash of civilizations thesis on numerous grounds. To begin, it assumes Islam is inherently anti-democratic, which overlooks theological and historical evidence to the contrary. Sociologist Mansoor Moaddel, for example, notes similarities between concepts in Islamic scripture and democratic political arrangements. "Such concepts as *shura* (consultative body), *ijma* (consensus), and *masliha* (utility) pointed to an affinity between Islam and democracy," he wrote.

Moreover, the Caliphate—the basis of Muslim political authority and another reason Huntington sees Islam as anti-democratic—"disappeared as an actual imperial system with the Mongol conquest of Baghdad in 1258," wrote Islamic studies expert John Esposito and historian John Voll in their book *Islam and Democracy*. Although the Caliphate remained important in the Ottoman Empire, from 1299 through 1923, various democratic and modernization reforms were enacted under that rein, and later under the Committee of Union and Progress. Just some of the reforms, according to Turkish studies expert Erik Zurcher in *Turkey: A Modern History*, included a French-based penal code ensuring equality under the law, a Belgian- and Prussian-inspired constitution, further *laic* (the French model of religion-state relations) reforms, and an expansion of women's rights. While democracy has been difficult to achieve in Turkey and other Muslim countries, these facts call into question the notion that Islam is inherently or automatically anti-democratic.

The clash of civilizations thesis also overlooks the variation within Islamic civilization, including Muslim countries' unique histories and processes of democratization. Many of these countries' histories are described in detail in *The History of Islamic Societies*, and Turkey emerges here as exemplary. Historian Ira Lapidus writes, "Turkey alone of the Muslim-populated regions of the Middle East emerged

> The culture clash thesis assumes Islam is inherently anti-democratic, which overlooks theological and historical evidence to the contrary.

from the First World War as a fully independent country." Among the many continued changes with the establishment of the Republic of Turkey in 1923 were the formal abolition of the Sultanate and the Caliphate, and giving women the right to vote, which occurred before 1935. In Turkey's first free, multiparty general election in 1950, the incumbent Republican People's Party was defeated by the oppositional Democratic Party—an unprecedented event in Muslim countries at the time. "Indeed of the 53 [Organization of the Islamic Conference] states, only Turkey can pass Huntington's test of democracy . . . [and] . . . Turkey alone has formally enacted the separation of religion and the state," wrote Bernard Lewis, an expert on Near Eastern studies, in the 1990s. While the extent to which contemporary Turkish democracy is untroubled or unique among Muslim countries is debatable, as Lewis and others acknowledge, the historical record and case studies at least indicate that Islamic civilization is more heterogeneous than Huntington assumes.

The clash thesis is premised on the fundamental notion that religion is important (and more important) today, but the evidence indicates that there is variation within civilizations and Turkey is again on the periphery of "Islamic" civilization. For instance, data from the Pew Global Attitudes Survey—a 44-nation survey conducted in 2002—reveal that only between 11 percent and 36 percent of people in the eight current EU member states surveyed (Great Britain, Italy, Germany, France, Poland, Slovakia, Bulgaria, and Czech) think religion is "very important." In Turkey, 65 percent of people say religion is "very important." Yet, this is much less than in many other majority-Muslim countries, such as Pakistan (91 percent), Indonesia (95 percent),

Bangladesh (88 percent), Senegal (97 percent), and Mali (90 percent). Interestingly, too, Turkey is most similar to the (Western Christian) United States in which 59 percent of people say that religion is "very important."

Contemporary evidence of liberal-democratic policies and values also calls into question the assumptions that civiliations are homogeneous and that they divide over religion. Muslim countries—defined here as independent countries with a population of more than 50 percent Muslim—are indeed considered to be less free

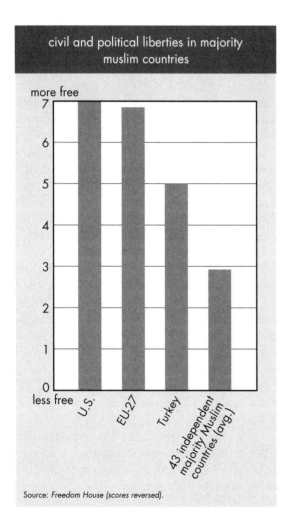

civil and political liberties in majority muslim countries

more free

7

6

5

4

3

2

1

0

less free

U.S.

EU-27

Turkey

43 independent majority Muslim countries (avg.)

Source: *Freedom House (scores reversed).*

than the United States and the 27 EU members, for example, as judged by Freedom House's combined civil liberties and political rights ratings (where 1 = not free and 7 = free: see "civil and political liberties in majority muslim countries"). However, there is a great deal of variation in freedom in these countries, and Turkey is among the most free Muslim countries.

Perhaps most importantly, none of this means Muslims don't want democracy. On the contrary, people in Muslim countries prize democracy to the same extent as their counterparts in other countries, according to research on World Values Survey data by political scientists Ronald Inglehart and Pippa Norris. And where there are differences in liberal-democratic values (such as "secularism"), these authors have found, they are best explained by their lack of economic development—not religious civilizations, as Huntington suggests.

additional data and support

My analysis of World and European Values Survey data from 1999 to 2002 aims to understand whether Turkey is culturally different from the EU, perhaps due to its "Islamic" religious tradition. Except for Cyprus, this survey covers all the now- 27 EU member states (12 of which were candidates at the time), plus Turkey. These individual-level survey data are just one way of measuring cultural values. It's also possible to gauge liberal-democratic values through content analyses of media, policies, or law, for example.

With these data, I constructed five separate scales measuring elements of people's liberal-democratic values that resemble the values Huntington discusses and are promoted by the EU: democracy, rule of law, and respect for human and minority rights.

The first, "global democracy," is a scale that measures the extent to which people think democracy is a better system than alternatives and a "good" system overall. Questions about people's evaluations of a democracy's economy, decision--making process, and ability to maintain order constitute a second scale called "specific democracy." "Religion and state" is a third scale that taps people's values about whether or not nonbelievers or religious politicians should hold office. People's values about the extent to which strong leaders, experts, and the army should run the country constitute a fourth scale, called "anti-authoritarian" values. "Ethnic tolerance" is the final scale and includes questions about people's willingness to have those of a different race and immigrants as neighbors.

For all the scales, higher scores indicate more agreement with liberal-democratic values (100 is the potential maximum).

The graph "liberal-democratic values in the eu" displays these values by broad civilizational groupings: The pattern in liberal-democratic values Huntington would suggest is only evident and statistically significant with respect to ethnic tolerance values (the last set of bars). Only here do we find that Western Christian countries are most tolerant, followed by Orthodox countries, and then Turkey. Contrary to the clash of civilizations thesis, there are no "civilizational differences" in global or

---

Other social issues stand in the way of Turkey's integration into the EU.

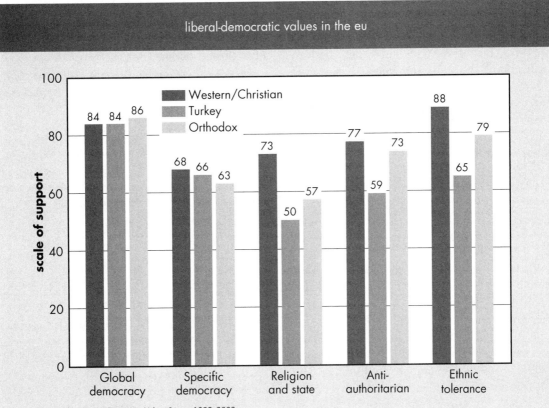

Source: World Values Survey/European Values Survey 1999–2002.

specific evaluations of democracy, as the first two sets of bars indicate. That is, people in Turkey hold similarly (positive) evaluations of democracy and its specific workings as people in the Western Christian and Orthodox EU countries. While separation of religion and state and anti-authoritarian values receive significantly less support in Turkey than in Western Christian EU states, my statistical analyses reveal that these and other differences are best explained by Turkey's relative poverty in the EU—it was the third poorest EU member or candidate state as of 1999, following only Bulgaria and Romania.

Turkey is similar to Orthodox Christian countries in its people's (relative lack of) support for separation of religion and state and anti-authoritarian values. When I look at data by country, people in Turkey express the same level of support for these values in particular as people in Romania, which entered the EU in 2007. This further undermines the "clash of civilizations" thesis in explaining values as well as calls into question the sincerity of cultural difference arguments as a means of excluding a country from the EU.

culture and integration

Claims that contemporary Turkey is a "model Muslim democracy" shouldn't be overblown, nor should they obscure all the other social issues that stand in the way of Turkey's integration into the EU.

Turkey's large population, for example, would grant it great political power in the EU Council and would likely encourage immigration, and is thus a large stumbling block in itself. At the formal policy level, there are concerns Turkey doesn't meet the democratic and human and minority rights conditions for EU entry. The Turkish state's conflict with its Kurdish citizens, as well as its refusal (until recently) to grant some minority rights (such as the right to broad-

cast in Kurdish), constitute still other policy obstacles. (Though to be fair, democratic deficits didn't preclude others' EU entries, including the post-Communist countries that entered in 2004 and 2007, such as Romania.)

The questions that remain are by what standards Turkey's EU application will eventually be judged and to what extent perceptions—inaccurate though they may be—of Turkish-EU cultural differences color future EU policy decisions. And in this context the fact remains that Turkey is more similar to Europe than the clash of civilizations thesis implies or than European publics and politicians assume.

RECOMMENDED RESOURCES

Larry Diamond, Marc F. Plattner, and Daniel Brumberg, eds. *Islam and Democracy in the Middle East* (Johns Hopkins University Press, 2003).

> A collection of articles from *Journal of Democracy* that describe the contemporary political situation of Muslim countries.

John L. Esposito and John O. Voll. *Islam and Democracy* (Oxford University Press, 1996).

> An overview of the theological and political aspects of Islam and democracy in the Ottoman Empire and Turkey set in a comparative context.

Ira M. Lapidus. *A History of Islamic Societies* (Cambridge University Press, 1988).

> A 1,000-page opus that provides historical comparisons of empires and modern Muslim states.

Mansoor Moaddel. "The Study of Islamic Culture and Politics: An Overview and Assessment." *Annual Review of Sociology* (2002) 28: 359–86.

> A comprehensive review of Islamic theology and history that outlines the theoretical and empirical difficulties of studying contemporary Muslim countries.

Pippa Norris and Ronald Inglehart. "Islamic Culture and Democracy: Testing the 'Clash of Civilizations' Thesis." *Comparative Sociology* (2002) 3–4: 235–63.

An analysis that puts Huntington's claims to test using World Values Survey data from a modernization perspective.

Erik J. Zurcher. *Turkey: A Modern History* (I. B. Tauris, 2004).

A detailed treatment of contemporary Turkey set in the context of the late Ottoman Empire. Includes controversial Committee of Union and Progress and Armenian issues.

REVIEW QUESTIONS

1. Describe the "clash of civilizations" theory of relations between Islam and the Christian West. How does Turkey challenge this theory?
2. How is Turkey socially different than other Islamic countries? Can Turkey be seen as more than just a geographic "bridge" between Europe and the Middle East?
3. What political or economic factors (other than Islamic culture) are involved in the debate about Turkey's admittance into the EU?
4. Activity: Why would a country want to be a member of an organization such as the EU? Visit the European Union Web site to research stated benefits of membership. What else can you add to the list based on your sociological knowledge about groups, culture, and international relations? Do you see any drawbacks?

randy stoecker

community organizing and social change

winter 2009

community organizing became a lightning rod in the 2008 political campaign. its foundations in sociology are part of the reason why.

It was 2008, early in the presidential campaign season. Everyone was talking about whether a woman or an African American would be the Democratic party nominee for president. And then they began talking about community organizing.

In the early days of the Democratic primary we learned that both Hillary Clinton and Barack Obama had connections to it. Clinton had written her undergraduate thesis on the famous community organizer Saul Alinsky. Obama had actually done it in Chicago through the Gamaliel Foundation, one of the national faith-based community organizing networks.

Obama's community organizing experience, described in his autobiography *Dreams from My Father*, became a lightning rod at the 2008 Republican National Convention where former New York City Mayor Rudolph Giuliani and Governor Sarah Palin mocked Obama and community organizing.

Community organizers responded—within days you could buy a t-shirt saying "Jesus was a community organizer. Pontius Pilate was a Governor." (Pontius Pilate, of course, was the public official said to have ordered the crucifixion of Jesus.) Networks grew across the country as community organizers and community organizing groups initiated a massive media strategy and registered voters by the hundreds of thousands. The Association of Community Organizations for Reform Now (ACORN) alone

registered more than 400,000 new voters and nearly 1 million others who had fallen off the rolls. Local community organizing groups in major cities each registered sometimes tens of thousands of voters.

Then came the Republican attacks on ACORN, one of the country's largest community organizing networks. ACORN's success at voter registration drives in swing states brought out the worst anti-democracy impulses from conservatives. In more than a dozen states right-wing politicians accused ACORN of voter registration fraud. Republican presidential candidate John McCain, in an impossibly bizarre attempt at misdirection, even charged ACORN with causing the global financial meltdown (ACORN had, in fact, identified predatory lending as a problem and began organizing against it more than a decade earlier).

ACORN fought back, and the GOP went down in defeat in virtually every battle, with their attempts to thwart voter registration turned back by courts, attorneys general and, increasingly, popular opinion.

And now, we have a president who is a community organizer. We could, perhaps, say "former" community organizer. But once you learn the craft of community organizing, and witness its ability to empower people, its spirit stays with you. It certainly has for Obama. Community organizing's democratic, and fundamentally sociological, impulses—understanding how power works and using that understanding to build the power of all the people—bring a sense of reward and satisfaction unmatched by other forms of political practice.

There's a great deal more to community organizing than Barack Obama and ACORN, however. At its root, community organizing isn't about big organizations or charismatic leaders, or even about specific political agendas or ideologies. Rather, it's about activating people at a local, neighborhood level to claim power and make change for themselves. It's the process by which grassroots organizations form and grow, their members develop leadership skills, and ordinary people learn to change social policy.

Community organizing's democratic, and fundamentally sociological, impulses bring a sense of reward and satisfaction unmatched by other forms of political practice.

The belief is that poor and working class people have been shut out from access to political and economic power because they haven't organized themselves in this way. Once they're organized, the theory goes, they'll have a voice in policy issues. Without community organizing, there are only fleeting demonstrations, isolated spokespeople, and top-down social policy.

the origins of organizing

Community organizing has been unique to the United States until recently when U.S.-style global capitalism downsized and eliminated government services in nation after nation and forced community-level responses. But in this country, Alexis de Tocqueville documented our foreparents' willingness to form voluntary organizations two centuries ago.

The founding of this country in opposition to central government and collective tax redistribution, by a relatively small group of people with exclusionary religious and cultural beliefs, in a very big space, provided fertile ground for a form of political action that focused on smaller community-based interest groups. The idea of bringing together like-minded neighbors to defend local space has remained ever since. And while the participatory impulses of community organizing now push it to be inclusive and democratic, its original populist underpinnings mean the craft is more anti-elitist than either conservative or progressive.

The power and presence of community organizing varies over time, as urban historian Robert Fisher explored in his book *Let the People Decide*. Working-class people forced to stand in bread lines during the Great Depression, African Americans responding to the ravages of segregation while their white neighbors enjoyed the expanding wealth of the late 1950s and 1960s, and urban neighborhood residents realizing that corporations and governments were disinvesting from their communities in the 1970s and 1980s were the source of the most powerful community organizing periods in the past century. But even during historical periods when not much appeared to be happening on the surface, community organizers were working behind the scenes in rural and urban communities across the nation.

The person most clearly associated with community organizing is Saul Alinsky, who helped build powerful neighborhood organizations, first in Chicago in 1939 and then across the nation into the 1970s. His influence extends to many of the community organizers working today, and he influenced the development of many of the community organizing networks—national organizations that support the development of thousands of neighborhood and community organizations across the country.

Those networks include Alinsky's own Industrial Areas Foundation (IAF), the Gamaliel Foundation, the PICO National Network, the Direct Action Research and Training Center (DART), the Midwest Academy, National People's Action (NPA), ACORN, and others. The list is split about evenly between those networks that are faith-based—relying on religious principles for their motivation and congregations for their participants—and secular networks such as ACORN, NPA, and the Midwest Academy.

In ACORN we see the other foundation of community organizing—the civil rights movement. While we best know the civil rights movement because of its large national events and its religious leaders, the movement was built by African American community organizers such as Ella Baker in rural communities and urban neighborhoods across the southern United States. Myles Horton, the long-time leader and co-founder of the Highlander Folk School in Tennessee, was perhaps the crossing point between the Chicago influences that guided Alinsky and the southern civil rights movement.

Until today, the most successful recent community organizing period was in the 1970s when small neighborhood groups across the country began realizing banks weren't making loans in their communities. As they studied and fought against this practice of "redlining" they built a national movement that produced the federal Community Reinvestment Act. The result, by some estimates, was as much as $1 trillion of investment into poor and working class communities across the country.

Today, there are community organizing groups in every state and every large city. Perhaps because of its local scale and methodological process, most scholars never judged community organizing interesting enough for serious study. So no one has counted all the groups, some of which come and go with the ebb and flow of issues and funding.

We know even less about the numbers of lives touched by those organizations. Many groups are part of one of the national community organizing networks, others operate independently. Many are informal groups composed of community members who have maybe never heard the term community organizing. We suspect the organizations number in the thousands and have hundreds of thousands, possibly millions, of members.

Despite these large numbers, community organizing didn't get the attention it deserved until the practice elected a community organizer as President of the United States. While nearly everyone knows something about the civil rights movement, and many have heard of Alinsky, few of us knew of any of the major community organizing networks until ACORN became so prominent this past election season.

Now we're finally understanding how powerful community organizing can be. Indeed, in many ways community organizing is the foundation of social change.

how it works

You may have encountered community organizers knocking on your door. They aren't the ones trying to convince you to adopt their religion, or give money and sign a petition, or vote for their candidate. They're the ones asking you about the most important issues in the community, and encouraging you to come to a meeting to talk about those issues. They want to know what you think and what issues you're willing to work on. They will definitely twist your arm—hard—to get you to contribute at least your time and maybe your money, too. But their main focus will be in getting you to work on issues you already care about. Of course, if you want to discriminate against gays and lesbians, oppose equal rights for all, or limit democracy to only the rich or educated, they won't work with you. Their commitment, first and foremost, is to the expansion of democracy, and that's what leads those on the extreme right to fear them so much.

Consequently, individual community organizers are more likely to identify with the political left, because that's where they find the most sympathy for expanding democracy. But they also find themselves organizing in white working-class communities, where injecting progressive ideology into the process might get them booted from the neighborhood, and where community members often support discrimination. One of Alinsky's greatest disappointments was the racism practiced by his first, and most successful, community organizing effort in Chicago's Back of the Yards community. And community organizers today, such as Rinku Sen in her book *Stir It Up*, are asking whether some degree of ideology should help guide organizing.

But because community organizing groups focus on issues generated by their members from the ground up, they typically don't affiliate with political parties or strict ideological platforms that impose issues on them from the top down. Two slogans of community organizing show just how embedded the culture of populism is in the practice.

The first says "no permanent friends, no permanent enemies." In contrast to Giuliani's bluster at the Republican National Convention, in the documentary *The Democratic Promise* we see him promoting the efforts of East Brooklyn Congregations—a faith-based community organizing group—after the same film showed the previous Democratic mayor, Ed Koch, mocking them. The second slogan is "never do for anyone what they can do for themselves," which sounds as much like "pull yourselves up by your own bootstraps" as any conservative should want. The difference, of course, is that the organizer is there to help people develop their own strategy to demand and get boots.

In most cases, implementing these principles follows a common path. The community organizer enters the neighborhood and gets to know people. Some networks have a special name for this process—the one-to-one. In a one-to-one, the organizer talks with individuals in the community, learning how they feel about it, what issues they're passionate about, and what skills and resources they could contribute to an organizing effort. Sometimes the organizer also visits existing civic organizations and congregations.

At this point, they're organizing what historian Mary Beth Rogers described as cold anger in her book of the same name. This is the process of taking unfocused frustration and channeling it into social change strategy. Hot anger is the anger of riots. Cold anger is rational anger, the anger of organizing.

Eventually, this process gives the organizer a sense of who the community leaders are—not the official leaders, but the actual leaders—and what the important issues are. Then they start organizing meetings in people's homes, church basements, or other places people gather. It's these places where most of the work of community organizing is actually done.

Those meetings lead to the selection of issues for the group to work on and the development of a strategy to work on them. In some communities that may be about trying to rid a park of gang violence, in others it may be about getting rid of an unwanted developer. The organizer's job is to help the group pick an issue they actually have some hope of winning, and then helping them develop a strategy for doing so. The group then initiates a campaign strategy around that issue, often involving some form of confrontation such as a large public meeting with a

You may have encountered community organizers knocking on your door. They're the ones asking you about the most important issues in the community.

targeted corporate or public official. The group insists on a yes or no answer to very specific demands.

The goal is not just to win on the issue, but to build an organization that can win on other issues as well and become an institutionalized force in the political system. To this end, some community organizing groups hold large annual celebrations where they promote their past victories and prioritize their current issues.

organizing in action

Community organizing is guided by the principle "the people shall rule," and its task is to help the people not only gain power, but the skill to grow and use that power. Community organizers, with some exceptions, don't lead, they propel. The organizer is, in the best case, the expert who knows how to get people to a meeting, develop a strategy, and win a policy battle. But it's the people who come to that meeting who are supposed to choose the issue, develop a position on that issue, design a strategy, and lead the public effort.

An action training event led by Bertha Lewis, now ACORN's chief organizer, illustrates this process. Lewis and other ACORN organizers were part of a three-year project to build community organizing capacity in Toledo, Ohio, and they held monthly trainings the first year.

The day before this particular training she met with the leaders of two neighborhood organizations. Together they decided to focus the training around how to do a public action, and chose a local slumlord operating in both neighborhoods as the target.

The morning of the training Lewis brought together the neighborhood organizations' two dozen members to talk about the issue, come up with a position statement, and develop an action strategy—picketing the slumlord's sub-

urban home. Then, everyone made signs and Lewis trained neighborhood people to lead all the important parts of the action. Someone would speak to the media, someone would lead the chants, someone would negotiate with the police if they came.

When the group left for the action, you could almost taste the tension and worry—it was the first time most of them had participated in a public action. Would they get arrested? Would they be slandered in the news? But they started picketing, negotiated the rules of peaceful protest with the police who arrived on the scene, were interviewed by the TV news, and they left with a new sense of power. It started out as just a training, but it launched a multi-year campaign that eventually helped shut down the slumlord's company.

In the early days of a community organizing effort like this one, the residents often don't know enough to sustain it without the organizer's help, just like they may not know enough to replace the shingles on their roof or repair their pipes without an expert to help. The organizer plays a much more prominent role in those early days. But unlike the roofer or plumber who does the work for you, the best organizers help you learn to do it yourself. In the best community organizing, it's the leaders—community residents—who give the news interviews, do the public speaking, and yell "Charge!" in the campaign.

building on the foundation

It's possible community organizing's new visibility will result in new resources, energy, and initiatives. There are now efforts through the National Organizers Alliance to channel former campaign organizers into community organizing. A newly revitalized community organizing practice may help turn the tide of a decaying polity and a corrupt economy, focusing especially on the poor and working class who lack access to the fundamentals of life itself—a living wage, an affordable mortgage, and health care.

These possibilities come with risks. Politicians don't necessarily have ideals and goals compatible with community organizing, and we don't know whether the office of president will influence Obama more than he can influence it.

Adding to this uncertainty, new initiatives have emerged posing as community organizing under labels such as consensus organizing, community building, or asset-based community development. Promoted by academics, foundation officials, and government officials, these models replace an understanding of oppressive social structures that divide the haves and have-nots with an assumption of common interests between them that will allow for conflict-free social change. Such an approach contains within it the threat of a renewed backlash against community organizing.

For community organizing to continue making meaningful contributions to broad-based empowerment and bottom-up social change, education about the realities of oppression and training in power-based community organizing strategies will be crucial. Most community organizing networks have to support their own organizer education programs, and in some cases that can mean only 10 days of training and an apprenticeship.

Our universities and colleges—and sociology departments—haven't been helpful in this regard. Community organizing courses don't exist on many college campuses, and the number of degree programs that focus on community organizing can be counted on two hands. This has long been the case. In fact, three main historical heroes of community organizing—

Alinsky, Horton, and Jane Addams (who co-founded with Ellen Gates Starr the famous settlement house Hull House in Chicago)—studied with or were colleagues of the famous University of Chicago sociologists of their time. But none of them ever felt welcomed enough to make a career out of sociology or academia.

Perhaps now is the time to finally make that right. In the process, academics can begin to combine their efforts with community organizers and their grass-roots leaders, replacing higher education's charity-based approach to service learning and civic engagement with a social justice approach that supports community organizing groups and helps secure the foundation for social change.

> A newly revitalized community organizing practice may help turn the tide of a decaying polity and a corrupt economy.

RECOMMENDED RESOURCES

COMM-ORG (Online Conference on Community Organizing). http://comm-org.wisc.edu

> A Web site that assembles key works on community organizing from academics and practitioners, and offers a discussion list with more than 1,200 members.

Peter Dreier. "Shifting Gears: Transforming Obama's Campaign into a Movement for Change." *Huffington Post*, November 6, 2008.

> A sociological reflection on the role of community organizing in the Obama presidency by a prolific writer.

Robert Fisher. *Let the People Decide: Neighborhood Organizing in America*. Updated ed. (Twayne Publishers, 1997).

> A social history of community organizing in the United States.

Robert Kleidman. "Community Organizing and Regionalism." *City and Community* (2004) 3(4): 403–21.

> An analysis of the challenges of moving community organizing beyond local issues.

Aldon Morris. *The Origins of the Civil Rights Movement* (Free Press, 1984).

> One of the few sociological studies of the civil rights movement from a community organizing point of view, focusing on the network of local organizations and strategies at the foundation of the movement.

Rinku Sen. *Stir It Up* (Jossey-Bass, 2003).

> Explores how to integrate racial/ethnic identity and ideology into community organizing, and move from local to larger issues.

REVIEW QUESTIONS

1. What is community organizing? How does it compare with other efforts to make social change in the world?
2. Several large companies and corporations have begun to use the grassroots organizing tactics often seen in community organizing. Why do you think this is the case?
3. Activity: Understanding power—its uses and abuses—is essential to community organizing. Form small groups and discuss your opinions on the following statements:
   - Power corrupts.
   - You can't get anything done without power.
   - Money is power.
   - Organizations that want to change things in their community should seek power.

part 14

Global to Local Connections

syed ali

permanent impermanence

60

spring 2010

dubai's expatriates have long out-numbered its citizens. ali explains why and speculates on what it means for the rest of the world.

was standing on the helipad of a new, swanky highrise apartment building in the Dubai Marina with my friend Vishul in the summer of 2006. We took in the panoramic, nighttime view of skyscrapers in the making, each capped with cranes lit red and white like so many giant *Transformer* action figures. Vishul, who'd grown up in Dubai, turned three hundred and sixty degrees and jokingly exclaimed, "*This* is the future!" And, until the global economic meltdown hit in late 2008, it probably was.

Dubai has been lauded by Western statesmen and the media as a model for the rest of the Muslim world to follow—a capitalist, consumerist paradise tolerant of alternative (read: Western) lifestyles and undisturbed by terrorism. This city of the future is ruled over by a benign autocrat, Sheikh Mohammed bin Rashid Al Maktoum, and is populated mainly by foreigners. These expatriates, who comprise over 90 percent of the population, account for 99 percent of the private sector workforce and 90 percent of the public sector workforce in jobs ranging from construction workers and maids to engineers, architects, and bankers. Because Dubai has been a migrant-receiving city since the early 1900s, its massive foreign population is nothing new. In fact, even

> Dubai has been lauded as a model for the rest of the Muslim world—a capitalist, consumerist paradise tolerant of alternative lifestyles and undisturbed by terrorism.

before the United Arab Emirates (of which Dubai is a semi-autonomous member) received independence in 1971, Dubai's migrant population exceeded its native citizen population.

What's astounding, though, is that all expatriates are in Dubai on short-term visas. Unlike immigrant-receiving countries such as the United States, United Kingdom, France, and Germany, Dubai has no form of permanent immigrant incorporation. Even in countries as strict as Switzerland, migrants, including lower-skilled "guest workers," can find roads to permanent settlement and family reunification. So while guest workers and their children throughout Europe may find it varyingly difficult to acquire citizenship, they often have the legal right to stay permanently.

In Dubai, expatriates willingly give up political rights such as free speech and due process, and they live precariously on short-term visas that can be revoked at any time for any reason. In exchange, they earn tax-free wages as "economic mercenaries," fully aware that they are there solely to work. For lower-level workers from developing countries, the trade-off includes the unstated promise that they will live and toil in harsh conditions in Dubai so they can send remittances and make a better life for themselves back home. The middle class, mainly South Asians and Arabs from outside the Arabian Gulf who fill the bulk of lower and middle white-collar positions, find better occupational possibilities, better schools, more comfortable family living, and a largely crime-free environment enticing. And for upper-class professionals (Westerners, but also South Asians, Arabs, and others) there is the lure of the "good life"— comprised of cheap household help (maids alone form ten percent of the population), luxury accommodations, spas, clubs, bars, restaurants, outdoor sports, and prostitution—that has made Dubai so famous in the West.

> Even before the United Arab Emirates received independence, Dubai's migrant population exceeded its native citizen population.

On its surface, the case of Dubai and its permanently impermanent workforce seems singular. But, as many Western countries implement restrictive guest worker programs that limit immigrants' ability to stay and circumscribe many of their rights, the case of Dubai's expatriates may actually be a harbinger of the future of global migration.

a mercenary life

All expatriates in Dubai, even those born in Dubai, are on short-term, renewable visas, regulated through the *kafala,* or sponsorship, system. Expatriates' residence visas are, as in the rest of the Arabian Gulf countries, tied to their sponsors, usually their employers. Changing jobs is virtually out of the question, and any expatriates who quit or are fired, with some exceptions for professionals, have to leave the country for a six-month period before they can return to take another job. So long as expatriates in Dubai hold on to their jobs and don't bring negative attention to themselves, though, they can stay until the retirement age of 60, at which point, unless they own a business or

receive permission on a case-by-case basis, they must leave.

Not unexpectedly, laborers, the middle class, and professionals experience their temporariness differently. Laborers including construction workers, maids, cab drivers, and lower-level service workers (who generally earn slightly better than third-world-level wages) constitute the vast majority of Dubai's population and are highly regulated in their working and social lives. Their passports are confiscated upon arrival (an illegal practice that even government ministries engage in), their wages are often withheld for months at a time to prevent them from quitting (a practice the government tolerates), and unions and strikes are illegal. Workers who have participated in strikes or protests have been immediately deported without a trial or due process of any kind. Many men (especially construction workers) are housed in remote, overcrowded, filthy labor camps, and most of the rest of the working class shares rooms in overcrowded, filthy, and dilapidated villas or apartment buildings. Socially, they fare no better: construction workers, for example, are often denied entry to the shopping malls they build.

(Stephan Geyer via Creative Commons)

Where laborers' lives are largely regulated by this series of "sticks," the middle class and professionals' lives are regulated mostly with "carrots" like high salaries, fast professional advancement, and luxury living. The government doesn't need to enforce discipline, as these expatriates essentially live in a "gilded cage," willingly trading political rights for economic possibilities. And the government is more than happy to allow these expatriates wide latitude in their social behaviors (they're free to worship as they like, drink, and openly visit prostitutes, for instance) so long as none of those behaviors looks remotely political.

While professionals, and to a lesser extent the middle class, find a great degree of social freedom, in the end they too, like laborers, are simply factors of production, there to create wealth for the ruler, the government, and the national citizen population. The *kafala* system essentially defines the bulk of the population as disposable and temporary. It is not incidental that the government insists expatriates are "guest workers."

The transience of expatriates is underscored by the fact that citizenship is basically unattainable and there is no such category as permanent residence. The most commonly stated reasons given by government officials for denying citizenship or permanent residence are the threats of cultural extinction and demographic imbalance posed by the possibility of absorbing so many expatriates into the pool of citizens. These twin arguments are repeated time and time again. However, there are two critical but unstated factors that are central to the management of expatriates in Dubai and the government's stance on naturalization. First, the government's legitimacy depends to a great degree on its ability to guarantee a high standard of living to national citizens. Allowing expatriates to naturalize might lead to the state having to spread its welfare largesse among a much larger pool of recipients. Second, the *kafala* system provides a simple and effective mechanism of social control. As expatriates are in Dubai primarily to work, the mere possibility of deportation is enough to stifle any kind of threat they may pose to the political-economic order.

Many scholars argue that formal, legal citizenship is becoming less important in an increasingly globalized world. As money, goods, ideas, and people move further and faster than ever before, legal and social barriers to movement have weakened. The idea of dual citizenship is more widely accepted than it ever has been, further eroding the historical notion that citizens should have loyalty to only one place. Even illegal migrants can often become legal by proving that they have conducted themselves like "good citizens" in their new land.

The literature on citizenship has expanded the concept to take into consideration how the boundaries of the nation-state have become, literally and figuratively, more permeable and, in some ways, less relevant over time. International treaties and institutions (especially those making human rights universal) and the free movement of people and capital greatly affect the sovereignty of states and how they relate to both citizens and noncitizens living within their borders. In the past 20 years, terms such as "flexible citizenship," "post-national citizenship" and "denationalized citizenship" have gained currency. And while there are major differences between these influential concepts and other ideas that expand upon the notion of what is and who is a citizen, taken together they announce that "citizen" is more than simply a legal category and that people can claim to "belong" to a place without legally belonging to that place.

> Laborers' lives are regulated by a series of "sticks," while middle class and professionals' lives are regulated mostly with "carrots."

But legal citizenship and the realistic possibility of obtaining it remains important—you simply cannot legally and securely live somewhere without a proper visa or citizenship. The non-legal dimensions of citizenship, including the cultural, economic, consumer, and psychological angles, are largely meaningless without formal legal standing. Consider one of the most basic factors of citizenship: generally, you cannot be deported—and if you are deported, the other forms of citizenship become moot. For non-citizens, these other forms of citizenship can only be meaningful if the threat of deportation is minimal.

Dubai's expatriates live in a "gilded cage," willingly trading political rights for economic possibilities.

These are things that expatriates in Dubai, most of whom are from the developing world, understand all too well. While there are no publicly available data on the numbers of deportations, they occur frequently enough that stories of deportees serve as widely known cautionary tales that help keep laborers, the middle class, and professional expatriates in line. These nonnatives are careful to stay out of trouble with the police, they make certain not to engage in behavior that might look political, and they avoid criticizing the ruling family or national citizens in general. At any point and for practically any reason, the government or an employer may arbitrarily cancel a worker's visa and trigger immediate deportation.

The threat of deportation and the lack of any legal recourse is one reason why so many expatriates would welcome the possibility of naturalization or, at least, permanent residence. Without these possibilities, expatriates understand that their stay in Dubai, no matter how long-term, is by definition temporary. They plan accordingly: Westerners know they will return to the West. Laborers know they will also go back home. South Asian and Arab middle-class and professional expatriates must either go home (an undesirable outcome for many) or attempt to go to the West seeking new professional opportunities for themselves or education for their children.

Expatriates born in Dubai also understand that they are temporary residents. Of the forty-five South Asian and Arab second-generation expatriates I interviewed, more than half had acquired permanent residence or citizenship in Western countries, and most of the rest were trying to do the same. Hardly anyone I interviewed intended to return to their legal home in their parents' third-world country of origin, but few had any illusions of calling Dubai home. I was stunned to hear one young, Indian corporate headhunter say bluntly, "Dubai is a pitstop, a place where you come, make a good amount of money and you get out." Why was this so shocking? The young man in question had been born and raised in this "pitstop." Until just before we met, he'd never even been outside the U.A.E.

In response to recent international pressure and spiraling unemployment among national

Construction workers from Pakistan and Afghanistan on a site in Dubai. (Paul Keller via Creative Commons)

citizens, some Arabian Gulf states have begun to rethink the *kafala* system. Bahrain was the first to initiate radical change, discarding the sponsorship system altogether in August 2009. Its expatriates will now be "sponsored" directly by the government, and their visas will no longer be tied to a particular job. Following Bahrain, Kuwait took a first step toward abolishing the *kafala* system when it announced that its expatriates would be able to change jobs after three years without sponsor approval or after one year if the sponsor doesn't object. Using language that Human Rights Watch would approve of, a Kuwaiti minister lauded the change and called the *kafala* system "modern-day slavery."

The abolition of the *kafala* system could lead to higher wages, especially at the middle and lower ends of the job market, where most workers are from the developing world and paid accordingly. Bahrain and Kuwait also hope that the current high unemployment rates among national citizens will be reduced, as the financial costs of hiring and training nationals become more attractive to private-sector firms. Conspicuously though, officials in Dubai have remained mum on any similar changes. Their silence is deafening—and unsurprising, given that Dubai's government-owned companies in construction, hospitality, and other sectors employ tens of thousands of workers at all levels, and government coffers are enriched through those depressed wages.

These policy changes represent a monumental shift for the region. The basic premise of my

Outside Dubai's airport. (Nico Crosafilli via Creative Commons)

research has been that the *kafala* system colors every aspect of life in Dubai. If similar, radical changes were undertaken in Dubai, the way of life for expatriates and national citizens alike would be drastically altered. Expatriates would have freedom of mobility in the labor market and would no longer have to fear deportation should they lose or quit their jobs. This is a particularly important issue today, as Dubai is in the middle of a recession, with megaprojects at a standstill and many completed highrises standing empty. Workers are being laid off in such large numbers that some estimate Dubai's population may have shrunk by an incredible 17 percent in 2009.

> Economist Paul Krugman writes that a guest worker program could amount to a dangerous betrayal of the United States' democratic ideals.

the "dubai effect"

The story of Dubai's expatriate population feels, at first, like an outlier. But it may end up being replicated beyond Dubai and the Arabian Gulf countries. While Bahrain and Kuwait are in the process of abandoning the *kafala* system, Western countries are increasingly adopting labor policies similar to those of Dubai and the other Gulf countries. These policies mainly concern working-class laborers, but as in the Gulf, professionals may find themselves living under similar visa regimes. For example, more than half of skilled workers from non–European Union countries arrive in the United Kingdom on "intra-company" transfers. As of a 2008 overhaul, the United Kingdom's visa system is largely grounded through employers. While Tier 1 visas, issued for highly skilled professional migrants, do not require a sponsor, Tier 2 employees applying for permanent status must be sponsored or they'll be forced to leave. Further, in 2009, the government was considering banning transferred, "intra-company" workers from citizenship altogether, a move that could conceivably turn them into Dubai-like expatriates: legal, but impermanent.

Similarly, the United States has programs limiting the ability of professionals from overseas to stay, most notably the H-1B program. The H-1B program is mostly for IT professionals, whose visas are tied to their employers. They can stay up to six years, so long as they are employed, and they are allowed to apply for permanent residency. There is, however, no guarantee that it will be granted; my friend Vishul tried, but failed, to adjust his own H-1B status and had to leave the country. At its peak, the H-1B program covered roughly 200,000 people a year, but the number of these visas being issued yearly has since dropped to its original 1999 level of 65,000.

The United States has also toyed with the idea of a wide-ranging guest worker program for lower-skilled workers. This would echo the Bracero Program, which brought temporary Mexican agricultural laborers to the United States from 1942–1964, but ended in part because of widespread abuse of workers. In 2006, Congress proposed a plan to create a permanent guest worker program that would admit 400,000 more workers a year. While it was not enacted, many in Congress made it clear that when immigration reform is eventually addressed it must include some kind of temporary guest worker program.

Recognizing aspects of the *kafala* system creeping into national policy debates, the Nobel Prize–winning economist Paul Krugman mused on what he called "the Dubai Effect" in the *New York Times*. Writing in 2006, Krugman said that a guest worker program could amount

Indian workers stroll past some of Dubai's enormous—and mostly empty—skyscrapers. (Paul Keller via Creative Commons)

to a dangerous betrayal of the United States' democratic ideals. It would, he wrote, basically form an entrenched caste system of temporary workers whose interests would largely be ignored and whose rights would be circumscribed. Further, their wages would undoubtedly be less than those of people with greater labor market mobility, though the ripple effects of a glut of guest workers would be expected to lower wages for all workers in sectors where guest workers are "bonded" to their employers, Dubai-style.

Following Krugman, I wonder if Western states increasingly adopt policies like those in the Arabian Gulf countries, they will see situations of non-assimilation similar to those played out among expatriates in Dubai. Of course, unlike in Dubai, any children born in the United States acquire citizenship by birth, but there would still be a sizeable community of adults who were essentially in the country, but not of it. If that's the case, Dubai and its permanently impermanent population would look less like a unique example and more like a prescient harbinger of the future experience of incorporation—or lack thereof.

RECOMMENDED RESOURCES

Human Rights Watch. Building Towers, Cheating Workers: Exploitation of Migrant Construction Workers in the United Arab Emirates (November 2006).

> Examines government collusion in employers' exploitation of workers in the UAE.

Andrzej Kapiszewski. *Nationals and Expatriates: Population and Labour Dilemmas of the Gulf Cooperation Council States* (Ithaca Press, 2001).

> Explores how Arabian Gulf countries controlled their expatriate labor force and kept their citizens happy before the latest economic boom.

Aihwa Ong. *Flexible Citizenship: The Cultural Logics of Transnationality* (Duke University Press, 1999).

> Details how globalization and transnational behavior have changed the meaning of citizenship.

Yasemin Soysal. *Limits of Citizenship: Migrants and Postnational Membership in Europe* (University of Chicago Press, 1994).

> Shows how formal citizenship declines as states, influenced by the global discourse of human rights, increasingly grant rights and benefits to non-citizens.

REVIEW QUESTIONS

1. What are the strengths and weaknesses of Dubai's immigration policies? What are the intended and unintended consequences?
2. Who makes immigration policy in Dubai? Who benefits because of it? Who doesn't?
3. How is the situation of migrant workers in Dubai similar to those in the United States? How is it different?
4. Do you agree with the author's conclusion that Dubai policy may be the future of global migration? Why or why not? Would this be desirable?

michael goldman and wesley longhofer

making world cities

61

winter 2009

not all world cities are alike and they can't be built the same way, as a case study of bangalore illustrates.

n the spring of 2007, someone moved to a city. The move was a momentous one in terms of its demographic implications—it marked the tipping point of a new urban century in which more than half the world's population now lives in cities.

Most metropolitan growth is occurring in cities of the global South, such as Guangzhou in China and Johannesburg in South Africa, where the populations are expected to double over the next three decades. It's imagined these "world cities" will be the spark-plug needed to kickstart national economies and catapult them into the global marketplace.

How things have changed. Back in the 1980s, scholars and analysts considered these cities too chaotic and a drag on national economic growth. There was too much overcrowding, too much violence, and too many public health crises. International finance institutions portrayed these places as "mega-cities" that posed megaproblems for the economic potential of poorer countries. Hence, the World Bank and the regional development banks directed their loans and policies away from cities and toward specific industries and infrastructure such as dams, power plants, and highways.

Since the early 1990s, though, beginning with sociologist Saskia Sassen's *The Global City*, we've witnessed a substantial "urban turn" in scholarly and policy emphasis. Global or world cities are now believed to be key sites from which the global economy will derive its ingenuity and energy.

In the global South, select cities promise to be catalysts for their national economies, too. Indeed, many scholars and analysts envision the Bangalores and Shanghais to be globally competitive in their own rights, propelling their slower-moving countries to the top of the global economy. And the World Bank leads the way, shifting its lending priorities toward these cities and priming them for an economic boom by financing various global-city solutions.

> Global or world cities are now believed to be key sites from which the global economy will derive its ingenuity and energy.

Although cities in India and China have become pivotal players in the global economy, issues and problems abound. For one thing, world-class airports and cutting-edge architecture aren't tides that lift all boats. Projects like these often lead to mass displacement and mounting inequality. For example, the "Shanghai miracle," according to geographer Fulong Wu, occurred on the backs of millions of urban residents forced off their land and out of their social and economic networks.

What's more, judging Shanghai or Jakarta by the same criteria as New York and London underplays the complexities of world-city making in the global South. In many of these cities, urban dwellers are struggling to make cities for themselves through transnational circuits of capital, labor, and ideas that connect diverse cities across countries and regions. These processes reveal not so much a singular set of world cities, but a diverse "world of cities" that includes London and Tokyo, but also Kampala, Istanbul, and others.

Take, for instance, the city of Bangalore in southern India. Over the past two years we've conducted fieldwork on how world-city projects take shape in this hotspot of globalization. We've found that making world cities involves much more than turning Bangalore into the next Singapore. Rather, Bangalore is part of a circuitry of world city–making processes that determine the contours of the city. From real estate speculators in Dubai to Muslim traders on the Indian coast, these "worlding" processes transcend the limits of any single city.

the (re)making of bangalore

World-city boosters and poverty-fighting experts have converged in Bangalore hoping to capitalize on its booming software industry to drive the Indian economy. The "Silicon Valley of Asia" boasts the highest growth rate in India, with some of its most profitable software companies recording 40 percent growth and profit rates in recent years. Famously, it was on a Bangalore golf course overlooking the offices of Microsoft and IBM that author and *New York Times* columnist Thomas Friedman discovered the "world is flat."

No longer is Bangalore known merely for its outsourcing and call centers—it's imagined to be a glimpse into India's plug-n'-play future. Its iconic image as a new "world city" has attracted worldwide acclaim. Professional circles from China to Scotland have adopted the "Bangalore model" of urban planning in an effort to hitch their own national economies to key cities like Dalian and Glasgow.

However, to elevate Bangalore into the elite club of world cities like London and New York, the local city must be upended. Meeting the demands of the Microsofts and Googles of the world has required billions of dollars in loans from international banks to transform its feeble infrastructure so it can provide world-class services. Doing so also requires thousands of acres of land on the city's periphery currently occupied by hundreds of thousands of villagers and farmers.

And the challenges facing urban planners and development professionals in Bangalore are great. Big-city traffic clogs its small town roads. Water and power shortages occur daily, and waterborne illnesses due to overflowing sewers happen all too frequently. (The average citizen receives water from the city for a few hours every third day.) Inequality between the rich and poor has risen five-fold since the software boom began in the early 1990s. Local activists and researchers claim that anywhere from 25 percent to 45 percent of its population (now nearing 7 million) lives in informal, slum-like settlements.

To overcome these problems, Bangalore has undergone the financing and construction of "world class" infrastructure that will attract foreign investment, as well as keep Indian companies in town. One illustrative example is the highly anticipated international airport that opened last spring (the previous airport—the third busiest in India—was an old military airbase). The government granted enough subsidized land to the Siemens and Unique Zurich-led consortium to build an airport one and a half times the size of Heathrow in London. Yet the airport opened with only one runway. The remaining land is being acquired to transform the surrounding area into high-value gated residential communities, seven-star hotel complexes, medical tourism hospitals, and business centers.

From the airport, consultants and investors will (eventually) hop on a state-of-the-art monorail system and zip down to the IT corridor, a parcel of land the size of Paris that houses Indian and foreign call centers and software firms. Throughout the expanding metropolitan area, the World Bank and Asian Development Bank are lending for major water and sanitation improvements, road upgrades and expansions, and overhauls of the government sector with new laws and regulatory bodies.

Overcoming rising congestion and a lack of space has led to greater spatial expansion as well, making Bangalore one of the fastest growing metropolitan areas in the world. Part of this expansion has been the construction of a six-lane expressway connecting Bangalore to the second-largest city in the state, Mysore. The Pennsylvania-based firm in charge of constructing the expressway has planned five privately owned townships alongside it, complete with shopping malls, tourist attractions, and corporate campuses. Yet, such world-city-making projects are only possible by paving over vibrant rural economies and livelihoods.

sidewalks of resistance

As billions of dollars are poured into highways, private townships, and the new airport, resistance from local Bangaloreans continues to mount. On a sunny Sunday this past November, hundreds of residents marched to protest the widening of streets and felling of trees for the new elevated Metro system. Bicyclists claimed that tearing down more than 90,000 beautiful shade-producing trees ruined the appeal of what was once known as India's "garden city." Shop owners and concerned citizens pushed for

the Metro to be built underground so businesses wouldn't be shuttered to make way for it. Advocates for the poor argued that widening roads would turn sidewalks, where so much daily commerce and social interaction occurs, into prime real estate. Purge the city of its street vendors and sidewalks, and you've stripped the life out of the Indian city.

Widening the streets to make room for a world-class Metro system is one of the many consequences of lifting Bangalore to its high expectations as a world city. The six-lane Mysore expressway is expected to displace 200,000 rural denizens alone, according to local activists. Consequently, activists and neighborhood groups have staged protests and demonstrations to protect their city from the growing inequality and mass displacement associated with world-city projects.

On some level, such resistance is familiar given the history of displacement and gentrification that made way for city-making in other parts of the world, including top-tier cities like Paris and New York. Yet, not all resistance is "local." For example, a mostly Muslim trading community in Kerala, where similar projects are taking place, has quietly "occupied" urban plots cleared for real estate speculation. By setting up their own relationships with small commodity-producing towns in eastern China, the traders sell goods to people who can't afford to shop in the luxury malls sweeping across the cities. In doing so, urban residents have made their own versions of a "world city."

This network of traders selling goods made in China points to a complex global circuitry of world-city making that also includes banks, real estate developers, migrant workers, and software companies. To examine one world city in isolation overlooks these interurban connec-

> As billions of dollars are poured into highways, private townships, and the new airport, resistance from local Bangaloreans continues to mount.

tions from which world cities are made and resisted. And thus, to better understand Bangalore, observers and scholars, including us, inevitably follow the connections to other cities such as Singapore, Dubai, and Shanghai, to name a few.

world city circuits

Scholars of global or world cities have often highlighted their similarities and connections to one another. Cities like London and Tokyo comprise key nodes in an emergent global economy, particularly as centers of financial capital and high-end services. This has led to a hierarchical view of global cities that defines lower-tiered cities by the absence of qualities found in the first tier. As geographer Jennifer Robinson points out, such a framework pushes most cities "off the map" that many sociologists use to make sense of urban life.

Rather than thinking of cities in terms of hierarchies, or within what scholars call a core-periphery model, cultural anthropologist Aihwa Ong suggests it's better to think of them as parts of lateral circuits that move across national boundaries. These circuits include high-end financial transactions, such as those between Wall Street and London, as well as interurban networks of labor and resistance that are particularly emblematic of city making in the global South.

Much of the research on world cities continues to focus on elite financial circuits, such as those that run through India's software sector. As one project manager at Infosys—the second largest software company in India—told us, today 98 percent of the company's work is business from outside India, and 65 percent is from the United States.

"Let's just say, when you buy a book online, we do it," he joked.

In a fascinating bit of role reversal, the chairman of Wipro, another successful Bangalore-based IT company, recently told the *Wall Street Journal* he was looking to set up hubs in American "states which are less developed," such as Idaho and Virginia.

However, the currents and circuits of these global cities run well beyond software and finance. Many of the farmers and workers displaced by world-city projects like the airport or expressway end up in the city's growing slums. But some others take up low-wage construction jobs overseas, typically in Dubai, under what Human Rights Watch calls indentured and slave-like conditions.

Ironically, people displaced by real estate speculation at home end up producing wealth for real estate firms in Dubai, which in turn is invested back in Bangalore, only to displace more people like them. The overflowing market of construction workers keeps wages down and profits up in Dubai, while back in India, surpluses from real estate investments are financing other world-city projects in Shanghai and Singapore.

Not coincidentally, many people who live in these cities have begun to challenge these "worlding processes" through their own interurban circuits, in order to reclaim and remake their city in their own image rather than the imagined one of world-city boosters. In his work on African cities, urban scholar AbdouMaliq Simone argues it's actually the Africans marginalized by failed world-city projects who mobilize "the city as a resource for reaching and operating at the level of the world." We find the same thing happening in Bangalore and across India where elite world-city policies have catalyzed alternative sets of social relations for the poor majorities

> Rather than thinking of cities in terms of hierarchies, it's better to think of them as parts of lateral circuits.

struggling for sustenance within these rapidly changing urban environments.

One of the most effective responses to such widespread dispossession is the National Alliance of People's Movements (NAPM), the largest grassroots social movement in India today. NAPM has tapped into the collective ire fomenting across villages and cities where vulnerable communities are being swept aside in the tide of world-city projects and special export zones. As the power of Indian trade unions, farmers' organizations, and progressive political parties have weakened considerably over the past decade, NAPM is organizing the dispossessed and forcing the public to reconsider the allure of real estate speculation as the driving force of city planning.

cities that thrive

In other words, the making of a world city like Bangalore entails a variety of interurban connections, ranging from real estate speculation to labor migration to "world-city" models to social-movement organizing. However, to rationalize the world-city imperative in order to build more gated communities and elite transport systems only focuses on one of these circuits—the most visible and expensive one that connects Bangalore to the top-tier cities through real estate and capital. It entails seeing Bangalore or Lagos or Jakarta through the lens of an imaginary European metropolis and not through the eyes and lives of their rural and urban denizens.

As long as we perpetuate old myths about the "mega-cities" of the global South as stagnant and helpless, and frame the rise of stellar industries such as IT as "saviors," we risk being blinded by their fleeting glimmer. Cities like Bangalore have always been more vibrant and complex than we've assumed. And it's their vibrancy that's challenging the displacement and inequality that comes with billion-dollar loans and world-class infrastructure.

Perhaps a world city could be one that takes care of its non-elite inhabitants first, and refuses to unbundle itself so that every burst of human energy, parcel of land, and urban space gets diverted to global circuits of capital. The potential consequences of the big move in 2007 extend far beyond its demography—remaking the new urban century around elite-based "world cities" paves over the importance of urban life that actually sustains the majority. When the imagined sparkplugs of the "new" global economy overshadow lived urban experiences, city leaders risk planning an urban landscape devoid of a place people can call home.

RECOMMENDED RESOURCES

David Harvey. *The New Imperialism* (Oxford University Press, 2005).

   A collection of incisive essays from one of the foremost theorists on cities, politics, and capital.

Aihwa Ong and Ananya Roy. *Worlding Cities: Asian Experiments and the Art of Being Global* (Basil Blackwell, forthcoming).

   An edited volume that innovatively thinks through recent trends in world-city making across Asia.

Jennifer Robinson. *Ordinary Cities: Between Modernity and Development* (Routledge, 2006).

   An engaging call for a cosmopolitan urban studies that takes seriously the dynamics of a "world of ordinary cities" rather than just world cities.

AbdouMaliq Simone. *For the City Yet to Come* (Duke University Press, 2004).

   A beautifully written set of essays on how marginalized Africans "make" their cities.

REVIEW QUESTIONS

1. Development is often seen in a positive light. What are possible negative consequences? Think of an example from your own city or town.
2. With these negative implications of global cities in mind, why do these cities and communities continue to pursue growth? In other words, what are common reasons in support of world cities?
3. The article claims that inequality in Bangalore has increased five-fold since the software boom of the 1990s. What might be some factors leading to the increase in inequality? Include examples from the article and others you think the article may have overlooked.
4. Activity: The article mentions that the World Bank funds many projects related to the expansion and infrastructure of global cities. Go online to find out more about the World Bank and its projects.

ching kwan lee

rights activism in china

62

summer 2008

the 2008 olympics turned the world's attention to china. in this essay, ching kwan lee introduces readers to the weiquan *social movement within china, which has brought chinese citizens together to demand labor rights, property rights, and land rights.*

If the Beijing Olympic Games are the coming-out party for a Chinese Communist leadership eager to showcase the country's achievement and aspirations, many zealous party crashers have announced their early arrival.

From the usual suspects like Reporters Without Borders and Human Rights Watch to the unusual alliance of Nobel laureates, U.S. lawmakers, and Hollywood celebrities, the rallying cry for detractors has been China's human rights violations at home and abroad.

For the better part of the past year, most of the international media attention and political debate has focused on high-profile, highly charged cases involving Sudan, Tibet, and the torch relay itself. Less visible to international audiences (and, likely, to future Olympic visitors), however, is another kind of rights activism.

Without any national organizations or charismatic public leaders, a quiet "rights revolution" is taking shape among ordinary Chinese people whose everyday lives have been radically, and in many cases adversely, transformed by three decades of market reform. What the Chinese call *weiquan*, meaning "the protection of lawful rights," has become a generalized social movement commanding intense passion in many quarters of Chinese society.

Weiquan is invoked constantly in different kinds of public discussions, including newspaper headlines, academic writings, and everyday conversations. Rather than appealing to the purportedly universal notion of human rights, Chinese citizens demand the specific rights—labor rights, property rights, and land rights—enshrined in various Chinese laws.

The rights activism of *weiquan* is profoundly transforming Chinese society, the Chinese state, and the relationships between them. With the state simultaneously promoting rights and restricting them (if not violating them altogether), and with society itself deeply contentious and in constant change, the outcomes of all this are far from clear. But a better understanding of how rights—and the law itself—are being constructed and struggled over provides a fascinating window into contemporary China.

> Understanding the struggles over rights and the law itself provides a fascinating window into contemporary China.

the challenges of legal revolution

The Chinese leadership has repeatedly insisted that "ruling the country according to the law" (*yifazhiguo*) is a key principle of government in the reform era. Written into the constitution in 1999, all major party announcements and government reports invoke the "rule of law," and in the past 25 years, more than 400 pieces of legislation, 1,000 administrative acts, 10,000 local rules and regulations, and 30,000 administrative procedures have been enacted or amended. To appreciate just how phenomenal this legislative explosion has been, consider that during the Cultural Revolution from 1966 to 1976 the government passed only nine laws.

That this legal proliferation has occurred alongside China's spectacular economic development is not coincidental. But more than just the imperative of the market economy motivates the turn to the law. The legitimation of one-party authoritarianism is another major concern for the Chinese Communist government.

> The central government now emphasizes legality and a wide range of "rights" for citizens to ensure a harmonious and just society.

Popular support for the ruling regime was strong in the first two decades of market reform, but in recent years discontent about social injustice, wealth, and power gaps has fueled social unrest. The central government therefore now emphasizes legality and a wide range of "rights" for citizens as a means of ensuring a harmonious and just society. This new configuration has been the basis of rights claims made by aggrieved Chinese citizens. Outside China, globalization of legal norms and practices has also reinforced the practical need for and the legitimating functions of Chinese law reform.

If the central government in Beijing pursues legal reform to bolster its authoritarian rule, however, the implementation of law and protection of actual citizens' rights face formidable obstacles at the local level.

The top priority of local governments—those at or below the provincial levels—is accumulation of revenue and resources rather than legal reform. Partly this is the result of the central government's strategy of economic and fiscal decentralization. By allowing revenue retention at the provincial and local levels, the central leadership has prodded entrenched vested interests among provincial officials to promote and sustain the reform drive. But fiscal decentralization has also generated powerful financial incentives for local governments and government officials to collude with employers, investors, and land developers in violation of citizens' lawful rights. Since the Chinese judiciary is also decentralized, with local governments funding and employing court personnel, local courts are often beholden to the capricious dictates and interventions of local officials.

Filling the gap between laws promulgated by Beijing and lawlessness at the local level is the precarious crucible of rights activism being forged by Chinese citizens. Navigating fluid political spaces, Chinese workers, homeowners, and farmers are using strategies ranging from petitions to government bureaucracies, new civil associations, and public protests to work both within and against emerging systems of law and legality in contemporary Chinese society.

labor rights activism

A series of labor laws have been passed since the early 1990s, and more are expected. The National Labor Law (1994), the Trade Union Law (1992 and 2002), and most recently the Labor Contract Law (2007) and the Law on the Mediation and Arbitration of Employment Disputes (2007) have replaced "policies" and the elusive socialist social contract in regulating employment relations. These laws explicitly define such workers' rights as hours, compensation, wage rates, and social insurance. At the same time, in an effort to contain labor activism within institutional channels, the law lays down a set of bureaucratic procedures for labor dispute resolution and prohibits independent unionism.

In spite of all this legislation, labor standards in China have remained abysmal over the 30-year period since economic reform began. Chinese labor problems have been so obvious and unsettling that the central government felt compelled to commission a multi-ministry survey in 2006 on the conditions of the country's 130 million migrant workers. These workers are largely from the countryside and provide the main source of labor for manufacturing, construction, and services in the country. The survey gave an authoritative and shocking portrait: only 12.5 percent of workers have a signed labor contract and only 48 percent are paid regularly. Most work every day of the week and are seldom paid the legal overtime wage.

Lacking the ability to form independent unions, aggrieved workers find the National Labor Law and the legalized labor arbitration systems—flawed as they are—their most important institutional sources of leverage. In their attempt to claim legal rights, workers are also assisted by numerous (their ephemeral and ambiguous legal status makes it almost impossible, not to mention undesirable, to count them) non-governmental organizations focused on labor. Many major cities have non-governmental organizations (NGOs) that specialize in offering legal advice or other assistance to migrant or female workers.

Under the influence and guidance of transnational or international labor advocacy groups, Chinese NGOs adopt standard features resembling those in other countries: legal counseling sessions, hot lines, and labor-law classes. The protocols of internationally funded projects often require an annual quota of labor lawsuits for which these organizations must provide representation. They usually choose cases with "paradigmatic" significance and wide demon-strative effects, either for the court or for workers.

For example, a popular NGO servicing women workers, well funded by international foundations and visited by prominent female political figures including Hillary Clinton and Cherie Blair, eagerly took up a domestic worker's complaint about wage arrears and lack of rest days. The goal was to stir public debate about the lack of legal protection for the large number of women working in private middle-class homes in the cities.

Another NGO sued the American fast-food giant Kentucky Fried Chicken, which employed mostly dispatched (or subcontracted) workers and allegedly denied them severance payments when workers left the firm. This case became a cause célèbre for Chinese NGOs when the fast-food giant stopped hiring subcontracted workers altogether.

The idea of "labor rule of law" is universally embraced, a common denominator among the international labor community, the Chinese government, and Chinese NGOs. Its utility for workers and labor activists in China is apparent in the newly established national network of Working Stations for Migrant Workers Legal Aid, a joint effort between the United Nations Development Programme, the All China Lawyers' Association, and the China International Center of Economic and Technical Exchange under the Ministry of Commerce. This project aims to train a nationwide network of qualified lawyers dedicated to working full time for migrant workers in 20 provinces.

The growth of the Chinese bar has also, perhaps inadvertently, contributed. Denounced as "rightists" in the Mao era and numbering only 3,000 at the beginning of reform, there are now some 150,000 attorneys in China and another 100,000 "barefoot lawyers" working without formal certification. Since labor cases aren't economically attractive, bigger law firms and more established lawyers shun them in favor of lucrative corporate and criminal cases. Yet, younger and newly minted lawyers without established clients, as well as lawyers without official registration, take up labor rights cases out of moral and civic obligation, or simply to fill an emerging market niche. Regardless of their motivation, the growth of the legal profession has channeled labor grievances into the legal system.

With legal assistance, many workers are now filing labor dispute arbitration claims and lawsuits, while others take their grievances to the street by blocking traffic, holding managers hostage, or threatening to commit collective suicide. Labor unrest even prompted Beijing to pass (against very vocal and public opposition from foreign investors) a controversial Labor Contract Law in 2007 that required employers to sign labor contracts with employees and "restricted" the practice of casual employment. However, the institutional dependence of the Chinese judiciary on local governments seriously undermines the legal system's capacity to resolve the mounting pressures generated by rising legal rights consciousness, labor unrest, and persistent violation of labor laws by employers.

property rights activism

Housing stock in urban China has been almost totally privatized since 1998, when the government overhauled the public housing system previously organized by socialist work units and local governments. And while private residential neighborhoods have since mushroomed in major cities, violence by thugs has become a serious challenge for urban homeowners.

Thugs are routinely hired by land developers and their subsidiary property management companies to silence and intimate homeowner activists or elected members of the homeowners' associations who dare challenge their interests. A Renmin University study of 100 residential neighborhoods in Beijing found that from 2001 to 2005, 80 percent experienced serious conflicts between property management companies and homeowners and 37 percent witnessed physical violence and bodily injuries in these disputes. Hence the term "property management terrorism."

The root cause of property rights violations is the enormous financial interests at stake for both local governments and their allied land developers in China's housing market.

The incentive for local governments to protect the interests of land developers and their subsidiary property management companies can be traced to fiscal decentralization, especially fiscal reform in 1994. At that time, the central government regained budgetary control over a range of taxation revenues from local governments. As a consequence, local administrations become ever more eager to locate or create sources of revenue that could be kept at the local level. Land lease sales and urban redevelopment projects emerged as the two main revenue streams for local governments under this fiscal regime.

This tendency was exacerbated when the former premier Zhu Rongji targeted the housing market as a way to stimulate domestic consumption after the 1997 Asian financial crisis dampened external growth. Since the late 1990s, in fact, construction and real estate have become the pillars of local state finance, accounting for 50 percent or more of budgetary income in many localities and jurisdictions. Moreover, many land development companies are owned by municipal agencies, state-owned companies, or official acquaintances. In Shanghai, a newspaper report found 60 percent of real estate developers in 2006 were "red-hat merchants," or private businessmen backed by the government.

As in the case of labor rights, the collusion of local officials and property capital has created major obstacles for property owners seeking to enact and ensure their lawful rights as stipulated in the 2007 Property Rights Law. This landmark piece of legislation, crafted explicitly for the rapidly growing Chinese middle class, calls for the establishment of homeowners' associations and stipulates the rights and responsibilities of homeowners' congresses over a wide range of community affairs, including sanitation, security, and environmental protection.

Thanks to their intricate and intimate ties with the local government (especially the Ministry of Construction) land developers and their affiliated management companies encroach on homeowners' rights in numerous ways. They have been known to, among other things, convert green areas into additional housing units, overcharge management fees and parking rentals, misappropriate income generated by advertisements on bulletin boards, intimidate homeowners who want to change property management companies, and obstruct the formation of homeowners' associations.

Aided by their relatively privileged social backgrounds and technical and legal knowledge, homeowners have been able to resist these practices in a wide array of ways. They have filed lawsuits and made extensive use of neighborhood Web sites. Some homeowners have staged hunger strikes for collective ownership of hot water furnaces, used motorcade protests against property management companies overcharging for parking spaces, and refused to pay management fees. Others collectively petition the Ministry of Construction or the local government when the local authorities refuse to register newly formed homeowners' associations, or stage mass occupations of property management company offices. Leveraging the media has also helped augment the social impact of homeowner activism.

Property rights activism has a tendency to evolve from concrete issues concerning daily community services to more general demands for power and autonomy in running their communities. Activism sharpens homeowners' collective awareness of the power imbalance that belies the ideals of equality inscribed in the law. This direct confrontation between local state interests and their agents on the one hand, and homeowners organized as neighborhood communities on the other, is producing an awakening among homeowners as "citizens" in relation to the state and not just as owners of material objects.

Whereas labor NGOs are vulnerable both financially and organizationally, the legality of homeowners' associations is enshrined in the Property Rights Law. They're also "organic" in the sense that they're organized and staffed by homeowners themselves and based in their communities, unlike labor NGOs that are organized by professionals, academics, or transnational advocacy groups. In major cities, including Guangzhou, Shenzhen, Chongqing, Shanghai, and Beijing, federations of homeowners' associations have formed and pledged support for each others' work. To date, only a minority of commercial housing neighborhoods have elected a homeowners' association. The Ministry of Construction announced that 18 percent of Beijing's commercial residential neighborhoods have homeowners' associations. The legal right to form their own associations isn't used widely yet, but the trend is unmistakable.

Finally, as in the case of labor rights activism, lawyers play a central role. Many are attracted to the large and lucrative market property rights lawsuits offer. Others are motivated by political idealism and civic consciousness. Seeing property rights The rising volumes of property-related civil lawsuits and administrative litigation lawsuits against the Ministry of Construction, which oversees the governance of commercial residential communities, attests to the intensifying conflicts over property rights.

rural land rights activism

In December 2007, tens of thousands of farmers in 150 villages in three provinces (Tianjin, Heilongjiang, and Shaanxi) made a highly unusual political move: they issued three separate statements to the entire country that they were retaking their land, which had been illegally requisitioned by local officials. It was an act they characterized as their collective right under rural land use rights regulated by the Land Management Law, most recently revised in 1998, and the Rural Land Contracting Law (2003).

One public announcement asserted that "rural collective land should be owned by all the villagers . . . Officials and their powerful allies abused the authority of the state and the village collective to usurp our rights as land owners. While they turned themselves into landlords, we villagers become their serfs. We have decided to change this form of land ownership . . . Land is farmers' life blood and their most important human right."

Extraordinarily bold moves like these are part of a rising tide of rural struggles over land use rights. Coercive expropriation, withholding of farmer compensations, and lack of job replacement for those whose land has been taken—each now trigger several thousand land-related conflicts in the Chinese countryside every year. These protests often turn violent and see paramilitary troops, armed police, and hired thugs clashing with villagers who resisted illegal land grabs by local officials. Protesters have been shot dead and villagers have taken local officials hostage.

As in the case of labor and property rights activism, the source of land rights protests is the institutional conflict between decentralized accumulation and legalistic legitimation—in other words, between the interest in revenue and growth of the local government and the central government's concern for maintaining stability and equity through law.

The Land Administration Law and the Law on Rural Land Contracting stipulates that rural land is owned by "village collectives," while individual households retain land use rights by contracting plots of land from these village collectives, initially for 15, and later 30, years. But these collectives are vulnerable to the decisions of local governments.

Under the pretext of "urban development," the establishment of high-tech zones and university cities, or simply "public interests," local governments can ignore the negotiation procedures and compensations stipulated by law and transfer—for a fee—the farmers' land to state-owned land. The land-use right can then be sold to private developers. Local governments stand to reap a windfall of profits from such land seizures. Indeed, an estimated 34 million to 40 million farmers have lost some or all of their land since 1987.

Like aggrieved workers and homeowners, villagers vent their discontent by petitioning, filing lawsuits, eliciting media attention, and organizing collective protests. Since land grabs often involve local (township and county) governments or the "high-tech zone committee" under them, the Administrative Litigation Law provides the legal basis for farmers to complain about official abuse of power. Again, since the authority of the judiciary is partial and subordinated to the local government, many of these lawsuits have been dismissed by the court.

Blocked by local judiciary, enraged farmers often resort to petitioning Beijing or the provincial government. These long distance "appeals" are increasingly becoming a hide-and-seek game wherein local police and monitors attempt to intercept, arrest, and detain petitioners heading

> These struggles will define China long after the Olympic Games depart.

to the national or provincial capital. Mass petitioning and violent confrontations have increased in tandem with farmers' use of national laws to fight local infractions of land-use laws.

In these legal mobilizations, farmers implicitly or explicitly assert the right to be treated as equal citizens with access to the protection of the law, in addition to insisting on the right to subsistence. Compared to workers, farmers fighting for their land rights command very little organizational or financial support from either international associations or the domestic NGO sector. Compared to homeowners in cities, farmers are also more financially constrained and have less access to professional legal knowledge and services.

An intriguing development in this arena that could have repercussions in others in coming years is the rise of barefoot lawyers. The Chinese legal system allows citizens the right to enlist the legal representation of other ordinary citizens, so long as no fee is charged. These volunteer lawyers are self-taught legal workers motivated by a sense of justice, righteousness, and local heroism to protect fellow villagers and farmers against all kinds of local official abuses.

beyond beijing

The fact that the fights over everyday rights described here have escaped international headlines is perhaps not surprising given media conventions and conventional biases and assumptions about China and the Olympic Games themselves. But it's nonetheless disappointing. A real opportunity lost.

This is not only because an understanding of rights activism affords such a rich perspective on Chinese culture and society and all the forces driving the near-total transformation of the most [populous] nation in the world. It's also because of the tensions between economic growth and social stability, between authoritarian rule and a more responsive state and involved citizenry; the problematic relationships between state and local government; and the more grounded and specific cultural conceptions of rights and the law itself. And perhaps most importantly, it's because these are the struggles that will linger and define China long after the spectators and the spectacle of the Olympic Games depart.

RECOMMENDED RESOURCES

Neil J. Diamant, Stanley Lubman, and Kevin J. O'Brien, eds. *Engaging the Law in China: State, Society and Possibilities for Justice* (Stanford University Press, 2005).

> This reviews a range of legal rights struggles in China.

Ching Kwan Lee. *Against the Law: Labor Protests in China's Rustbelt and Sunbelt* (University of California Press, 2007).

> The author's work explores the politics of labor rights involving migrant workers and state-sector workers.

Elizabeth J. Perry. "The Chinese Conceptions of 'Rights': From Mencius to Mao and Now." *Perspectives on Politics* (2008) 6(1): 37–50.

> The author argues that there are fundamental differences between Chinese and American conceptions of rights.

REVIEW QUESTIONS

1. How would you define human rights? Compare and contrast your definition with the one used in this article.
2. How do conflicts between local and central governments affect labor, property, and land rights?
3. Why do lawyers play a central role in rights activism in China? What else might influence

whether or not people seek legal remedies for rights violations?

4. The author laments that fights over "everyday rights" do not make headlines. How might things change if they did?

5. Activity: Find a copy of the Universal Declaration of Human Rights. Are you surprised by any of the 30 items on the list? Do any seem more or less important to you? Why?

peggy levitt

salsa and ketchup: transnational migrants straddle two worlds   **63**

spring 2004

transnational immigration will continue to increase during the twenty-first century. though newcomers strive to assimilate, they often retain strong ties to their native land. living across borders poses challenges for both the country immigrants come from and the new nation they adopt.

The suburb, with its expensive homes with neatly trimmed lawns and sport-utility vehicles, seems like any other well-to-do American community. But the mailboxes reveal a difference: almost all are labeled "Patel" or "Bhagat." Over the past two decades, these families moved from the small towns and villages of Gujarat State on the west coast of India, first to rental apartments in northeastern Massachusetts and then to their own homes in subdivisions outside Boston. Casual observers watching these suburban dwellers work, attend school, and build religious congregations might conclude that yet another wave of immigrants is successfully pursuing the American dream. A closer look, however, reveals that they are pursuing Gujarati dreams as well. They send money back to India to open businesses or improve family homes and farms. They work closely with religious leaders to establish Hindu communities in the United States, and also to strengthen religious life in their homeland. Indian politicians at the state and national level court these emigrants' contributions to India's political and economic development.

The Gujarati experience illustrates a growing trend among immigrants to the United States and Europe. In the twenty-first century, many people will belong to two societies at the same time. Researchers call those who maintain strong, regular ties to their homelands and who organize aspects of their lives across national borders "transnational migrants." They assimilate into the country that receives them, while sustaining strong ties to their homeland. Assimilation and transnational relations are not mutually exclusive; they happen simultaneously and influence each other. More and more, people earn their living, raise their family, participate in religious communities, and express their political views across national borders.

Social scientists have long been interested in how newcomers become American. Most used to argue that to move up the ladder, immigrants would have to abandon their unique customs, language, and values. Even when it became acceptable to retain some ethnic customs, most researchers still assumed that connections to homelands would eventually wither. To be Italian American or Irish American would ultimately have much more to do with the immigrant experience in America than with what was happening back in Italy or Ireland. Social scientists increasingly recognize that the host-country experiences of some migrants remain strongly influenced by continuing ties to their country of origin and its fate.

These transnational lives raise fundamental issues about twenty-first-century society. What are the rights and responsibilities of people who belong to two nations? Both home- and host-country governments must decide whether and how they will represent and protect migrants and what they can demand from them in return. They may have to revise their understandings of "class" or "race" because these terms mean such different things in each country. For example, expectations about how women should balance work and family vary considerably in Latin America and in the United States. Both home- and host-country social programs may have to be reformulated, taking into account new challenges and new opportunities that arise when migrants keep one foot in each of two worlds.

two cases: dominicans and gujaratis in boston

My research among the Dominican Republic and Gujarati immigrants who have moved to Massachusetts over the past three decades illustrates the changes that result in their origin and host communities. Migration to Boston from the Dominican village of Miraflores began in the late 1960s. By the early 1990s, nearly two-thirds of the 550 households in Miraflores had relatives in the Boston area, most around the neighborhood of Jamaica Plain, a few minutes from downtown. Migration has transformed Miraflores into a transnational village. Community members, wherever they are, maintain such strong ties to each other that the life of this community occurs almost simultaneously in two places. When someone is ill, cheating on their spouse, or finally granted a visa, the news spreads as fast on the streets of Jamaica Plain,

Boston, as it does in Miraflores, Dominican Republic.

Residents of Miraflores began to migrate because it became too hard to make a living at farming. As more and more people left the fields of the Dominican Republic for the factories of Boston, Miraflores suffered economically. But as more and more families began to receive money from relatives in the United States (often called "remittances"), their standard of living improved. Most households can now afford the food, clothing, and medicine for which previous generations struggled. Their homes are filled with the TVs, VCRs, and other appliances their migrant relatives bring them. Many have been able to renovate their houses, install indoor plumbing, even afford air conditioning. With money donated in Boston and labor donated in Miraflores, the community built an aqueduct and baseball stadium, and renovated the local school and health clinic. In short, most families live better since migration began, but they depend on money earned in the United States to do so.

Many of the Miraflorenos in Boston live near and work with one another, often at factories and office-cleaning companies where Spanish is the predominant language. They live in a small neighborhood, nestled within the broader Dominican and Latino communities. They participate in the PTA and in the neighborhood organizations of Boston, but feel a greater commitment toward community development in Miraflores. They are starting to pay attention to elections in the United States, but it is still Dominican politics that inspires their greatest passion. When they take stock of their life's accomplishments, it is the Dominican yardstick that matters most.

The transnational character of Miraflorenos' lives is reinforced by connections between the Dominican Republic and the United States. The Catholic Church in Boston and the Church on the island cooperate because each feels responsible for migrant care. All three principal Dominican political parties campaign in the United States because migrants make large contributions and also influence how relatives back home vote. No one can run for president in the Dominican Republic, most Miraflorenos agree, if he or she does not campaign in New York. Conversely, mayoral and gubernatorial candidates in the northeastern United States now make obligatory pilgrimages to Santo Domingo. Since remittances are one of the most important sources of foreign currency, the Dominican government instituted policies to encourage migrants' long-term participation without residence. For example, under the administration of President Leonel Fernandez (1996–2000), the government set aside a certain number of apartments for Dominican emigrants in every new construction project it supported. When they come back to visit, those of Dominican origin, regardless of their passport, go through the customs line for Dominican nationals at the airport and are not required to pay a tourist entry fee.

religious ties

The people from Miraflores illustrate one way migrants balance transnational ties and assimilation, with most of their effort focused on their homeland. The Udah Bhagats, a subcaste from Gujarat State, make a different set of choices. They are more fully integrated into certain parts of American life, and their homeland ties tend to be religious and cultural rather than political. Like Gujaratis in general, the Udah Bhagats have a long history of transnational migration. Some left their homes over a century ago to work as traders throughout East Africa. Many of those who were forced out of Africa in the 1960s by local nationalist movements moved on to the United Kingdom and the United States instead of moving back to India.

Nearly 600 families now live in the greater Boston region.

The Udah Bhagats are more socially and economically diverse than the Miraflorenos. Some migrants came from small villages where it is still possible to make a good living by farming. Other families, who had moved to Gujarati towns a generation ago, owned or were employed by small businesses there. Still others, from the city of Baroda, worked in engineering and finance before migrating. About half of the Udah Bhagats now in Massachusetts work in factories or warehouses, while the other half work as engineers, computer programmers, or at the small grocery stores they have purchased. Udah Bhagats in Boston also send remittances home, but for special occasions or when a particular need arises, and the recipients do not depend on them. Some still own a share in the family farm or have invested in Gujarati businesses, like one man who is a partner in a computer school. Electronics, clothing, and appliances from the United States line the shelves of homes in India, but the residents have not adopted Western lifestyles as much as the Miraflorenos. The Gujarati state government has launched several initiatives to stimulate investment by "Non-Resident Gujaratis," but these are not central to state economic development policy.

In the United States, both professional and blue-collar Gujaratis work alongside native-born Americans; it is their family and religious life that is still tied to India. Some Bhagat families have purchased houses next door to each other. In an American version of the Gujarati extended family household, women still spend long hours preparing food and sending it across the street to friends and relatives. Families gather in one home to do puja, or prayers, in the evenings. Other families live in mixed neighborhoods, but they too spend much of their free time with other Gujaratis. Almost everyone still speaks Gujarati at home. While they are deeply grateful for the economic opportunities that America offers, they firmly reject certain American values and want to hold fast to Indian culture.

As a result, Udah Bhagats spend evenings and weekends at weddings and holiday celebrations, prayer meetings, study sessions, doing charitable work, or trying to recruit new members. Bhagat families conduct these activities within religious organizations that now operate across borders. Rituals, as well as charitable obligations, have been redefined so they can be fulfilled in the United States but directly supervised by leaders back in India. For example, the Devotional Associates of Yogeshwar or the Swadhyaya movement requires followers back in Gujarat to dedicate time each month to collective farming and fishing activities; their earnings are then donated to the poor. An example of such charitable work in Boston is families meeting on weekends to assemble circuit boards on subcontract for a computer company. For the Udah Bhagats, religious life not only reaffirms their homeland ties but also erects clear barriers against aspects of American life they want to avoid. Not all Indians are pleased that Hindu migrants are so religious in America. While some view the faithful as important guardians of the religious flame, others claim that emigrants abroad are the principal underwriters of the recent wave of Hindu nationalism plaguing India, including the Hindu-Muslim riots that took place in Ahmedabad in 2002.

the rise of transnational migration

Not all migrants are transnational migrants, and not all who take part in transnational practices do so all the time. Studies by Alejandro Portes and his colleagues reveal that fewer than 10 percent of the Dominican, Salvadoran, and Colombian migrants they surveyed regularly participated in transnational economic and political activities. But most migrants do have occasional transnational contacts. At some stages in their lives, they are more focused on their country of origin, and at other times more committed to their host nation. Similarly, they climb two different social ladders. Their social status may improve in one country and decline in the other.

Transnational migration is not new. In the early 1900s, some European immigrants also returned to live in their home countries or stayed in America while being active in economic and political affairs at home. But improvements in telecommunications and travel make it cheaper and easier to remain in touch than ever before. Some migrants stay connected to their homelands daily through e-mail or phone calls. They keep their fingers on the pulse of everyday life and weigh in on family affairs in a much more direct way than their earlier counterparts. Instead of threatening the disobedient grandchild with the age-old refrain, "wait until your father comes home," the grandmother says, "wait until we call your mother in Boston."

The U.S. economy welcomes highly educated, professional workers from abroad, but in contrast to the early twentieth cetury, is less hospitable to low-skilled industrial workers or those not proficient in English. Because of poverty in their country of origin and insecurity in the United States, living across borders has become a financial necessity for many less-skilled migrant workers. At the same time, many highly skilled, professional migrants choose to live transnational lives; they have the money and know-how to take advantage of economic and political opportunities in both settings. These days, America tolerates and even celebrates ethnic diversity—indeed, for some people, remaining "ethnic" is part of being a true American, which also makes long-term participation in the homeland and putting down roots in the United States easier.

Nations of origin are also increasingly supportive of long-distance citizenship, especially countries that depend on the remittances and political clout of migrants. Immigrants are no longer forced to choose between their old and new countries as they had to in the past. Economic self-sufficiency remains elusive for small, nonindustrialized countries and renders them dependent on foreign currency, much of it generated by migrants. Some national governments actually factor emigrant remittances into their macro-economic policies and use them to prove credit-worthiness. Others, such as the Philippines, actively promote their citizens as good workers to countries around the world. Transnational migrants become a key export and their country of origin's main connection to the world economy. By footing the bill for school and road construction back home, transnational migrants meet goals that weak home governments cannot. The increasingly interdependent global economy requires developing nations to tie themselves more closely to trade partners. Emigrant communities are also potential ambassadors who can foster closer political and economic relations.

the american dream goes transnational

Although few immigrants are regularly active in two nations, their efforts, combined with those of immigrants who participate occasionally, add up. They can transform the economy, culture, and everyday life of whole regions in their countries of origin. They transform notions about gender relations, democracy, and what governments should and should not do. For instance, many young women in Miraflores, Dominican Republic, no longer want to marry men who have not migrated because they want husbands who will share the housework and take care of the children as the men who have been to the United States do. Other community members argue that Dominican politicians should be held accountable just like Bill Clinton was when he was censured for

his questionable real estate dealings and extra-marital affairs.

Transnational migration is therefore not just about the people who move. Those who stay behind are also changed. The American-born children of migrants are also shaped by ideas, people, goods, and practices from outside—in their case, from the country of origin—that they may identify with during particular periods in their lives. Although the second generation will not be involved with their ancestral homes in the same ways and with the same intensity as their parents, even those who express little interest in their roots know how to activate these connections if and when they decide to do so. Some children of Gujaratis go back to India to find marriage partners and many second-generation Pakistanis begin to study Islam when they have children. Children of Miraflorenos born in the United States participate actively in fundraising efforts for Miraflores. Even Dominican political parties have established chapters of second-generation supporters in the United States.

Transnational migrants like the Miraflorenos and the Udah Bhagats in Boston challenge both the host and the origin nations' understanding of citizenship, democracy, and economic development. When individuals belong to two countries, even informally, are they protected by two sets of rights and subject to two sets of responsibilities? Which states are ultimately responsible for which aspects of their lives? The Paraguayan government recently tried to intercede on behalf of a dual national sentenced to death in the United States, arguing that capital punishment is illegal in Paraguay. The Mexican government recently issued a special consular ID card to all Mexican emigrants, including those living without formal authorization in the United States. More than 100 cities, 900 police departments, 100 financial institutions, and 13 states accept the cards as proof of identity for obtaining a drivers' license or opening a bank account.

These examples illustrate the ways in which countries of origin assume partial responsibility for emigrants and act on their behalf.

Transnational migration also raises questions about how the United States and other host nations should address immigrant poverty. For example, should transnationals qualify for housing assistance in the United States at the same time that they are building houses back home? What about those who cannot fully support themselves here because they continue to support families in their homelands? Transnational migration also challenges policies of the nations of origin. For example, should social-welfare and community-development programs discriminate between those who are supported by remittances from the United States and those who have no such outside support? Ideally, social programs in the two nations should address issues of common concern in coordination with one another.

There are also larger concerns about the tension between transnational ties and local loyalties. Some outside observers worry when they see both home-country and U.S. flags at a political rally. They fear that immigrants' involvement in homeland politics means that they are less loyal to the United States. Assimilation and transnational connections, however, do not have to conflict. The challenge is to find ways to use the resources and skills that migrants acquire in one context to address issues in the other. For example, Portes and his colleagues find that transnational entrepreneurs are more likely to be U.S. citizens, suggesting that becoming full members of their new land helped them run successful businesses in their countries of origin. Similarly, some Latino activists use the same organizations to promote participation in American politics that they use to mobilize people around homeland issues. Some of the associations created to promote Dominican businesses in New York also played a major role in securing the approval of dual citizenship on the island.

These are difficult issues and some of our old solutions no longer work. Community development efforts directed only at Boston will be inadequate if they do not take into account that Miraflores encompasses Boston and the island, and that significant energy and resources are still directed toward Miraflores. Education and health outcomes will suffer if policy makers do not consider the many users who circulate in and out of two medical and school systems. As belonging to two places becomes increasingly common, we need approaches to social issues that not only recognize, but also take advantage of, these transnational connections.

RECOMMENDED RESOURCES

Luis Guarnizo, Alejandro Portes, and William Haller. "Assimilation and Transnationalism: Determinants of Transnational Political Action among Contemporary Migrants." *American Journal of Sociology* 108 (2003): 1211–48.

> The authors report on a survey of the political activism among Salvadoran, Colombian, and Dominican transnational migrants.

Peggy Levitt. *The Transnational Villagers* (University of California Press, 2001).

> A study of the social, political, and religious life of a transnational community conducted in Boston and in the Dominican Republic.

Peggy Levitt, Josh DeWind, and Steven Vertovec, eds. Special Volume on Transnational Migration. *International Migration Review* 37 (2003).

> A synthesis of research to date on transnational migration, including articles by European and U.S. scholars.

Alejandro Portes, William Haller, and Luis Guarnizo. "Transnational Entrepreneurs: The

Emergence and Determinants of an Alternative Form of Immigrant Economic Adaptation." *American Sociological Review* 67 (2002): 278–98.

Summarizes results from a survey of transnational economic activity by Dominican, Salvadoran, and Colombian migrants.

Glick Schiller and Georges Fouron. *Georges Woke Up Laughing: Long-Distance Nationalism and the Search for Home* (Duke University Press, 2001).

This study of Haitian transnational migration emphasizes its effects on citizenship and national sovereignty.

Michael Peter Smith and Luis Gurnizo, eds. *Transnationalism from Below: Comparative Urban and Community Research.* Vol. 6. (Transaction Publishers, 1998).

The editors introduce the field and present articles on selected topics.

REVIEW QUESTIONS

1. Identify and define the key terms used in this essay. For example, what are "remittances"? What is "transnational migration"?
2. Of the two groups Levitt mentions, one appears to have their "salsa and ketchup" a little more mixed. Which one do you think best fits this description? Which measures support your answer?
3. The essay details important differences between the transnational migrants of a century ago and today. What are these differences?
4. The notion of America as a "melting pot" is pervasive. Canadians, on the other hand, tend to describe their diversity as a cultural "mosaic." What metaphor would you use to describe the cultural phenomenon described in this essay, and why?

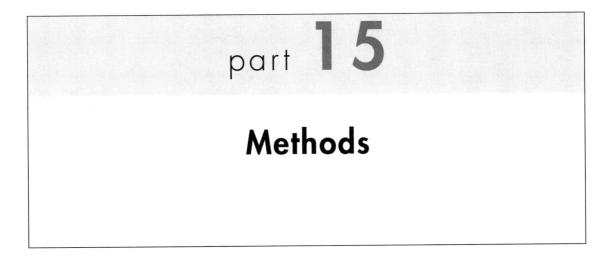

part **15**

Methods

howard schuman

sense and nonsense about surveys

64

summer 2002

understanding surveys is critical to being an informed citizen, but popular media often report surveys without any guidance on how to interpret and evaluate the results. some basic guidelines can promote more sophisticated readings of survey results and help teach when to trust the polls.

Surveys draw on two human propensities that have served us well from ancient times. One is to gather information by asking questions. The first use of language around 100,000 years ago may have been to utter commands such as "Come here!" or "Wait!" Questions must have followed soon after: "Why?" or "What for?" From that point, it would have been only a short step to the use of interrogatives to learn where a fellow hominid had seen potential food, a dangerous animal, or something else of importance. Asking questions continues to be an effective way of acquiring information of all kinds, assuming of course that the person answering is able and willing to respond accurately.

The other inclination, learning about one's environment by examining a small part of it, is the sampling aspect of surveys. A taste of something may or may not point to appetizing food. A first inquiry to a stranger, a first glance around a room, a first date—each is a sample of sorts, often used to decide whether it is wise to proceed further. As with questions, however, one must always be aware of the possibility that the sample may not prove adequate to the task.

> The percentage of people who refuse to take part in a survey is particularly important. In some federal surveys, the percentage is small, within the range of 5 to 10 percent. For even the best nongovernment surveys, the refusal rate can reach 25 percent or more, and it can be far larger in the case of poorly executed surveys.

sampling: how gallup achieved fame

Only within the past century—and especially in the 1930s and 1940s—were major improvements made in the sampling process that allowed the modern survey to develop and flourish. A crucial change involved recognition that the value of a sample comes not simply from its size but also from the way it is obtained. Every serious pursuit likes to have a morality tale that supports its basic beliefs: witness Eve and the apple in the Bible or Newton and his apple in legends about scientific discovery. Representative sampling has a marvelous morality tale also, with the additional advantage of its being true.

The story concerns the infamous *Literary Digest* poll prediction—based on 10 million questionnaires sent out and more than two million received back—that Roosevelt would lose decisively in the 1936 presidential election. At the same time, George Gallup, using many fewer cases but a much better method, made the more accurate prediction that FDR would win. Gallup used quotas in choosing respondents in order to represent different economic strata, whereas the *Literary Digest* had worked mainly from telephone and automobile ownership lists, which in 1936 were biased toward wealthy people apt to be opposed to Roosevelt. (There were other sources of bias as well.) As a result, the *Literary Digest* poll disappeared from the scene, and Gallup was on his way to becoming a household name.

Yet despite their intuitive grasp of the importance of representing the electorate accurately, Gallup and other commercial pollsters did not use the probability sampling methods that were being developed in the same decades and that are fundamental to social science surveys today. Probability sampling in its simplest form calls for each person in the population to have an equal chance of being selected. It can also be used in more complex applications where the chances are deliberately made to be unequal, for example, when oversampling a minority group in order to study it more closely; however, the chances of being selected must still be known so that they can later be equalized when considering the entire population.

intuitions and counterintuitions about sample size

Probability sampling theory reveals a crucial but counterintuitive point about sample size: the size of a sample needed to accurately estimate a value for a population depends very little on the size of the population. For example, almost the same size sample is needed to estimate, with a given degree of precision, the proportion of left-handed people in the United States as is needed to make the same estimate for, say, Peoria, Illinois. In both cases a reasonably accurate estimate can be obtained with a sample size of around 1,000. (More cases are needed when extraordinary precision is called for, for example, in calculating unemployment

rates, where even a tenth of a percent change may be regarded as important.)

The link between population size and sample size cuts both ways. Although huge samples are not needed for huge populations like those of the United States or China, a handful of cases is not sufficient simply because one's interest is limited to Peoria. This implication is often missed by those trying to save time and money when sampling a small community.

Moreover, all of these statements depend on restricting your interest to overall population values. If you are concerned about, say, left-handedness among African Americans, then African Americans become your population, and you need much the same sample size as for Peoria or the United States.

who is missing?

A good sample depends on more than probability sampling theory. Surveys vary greatly in their quality of implementation, and this variation is not captured by the "margin of error" plus/minus percentage figures that accompany most media reports of polls. Such percentages reflect the size of the final sample, but they do not reveal the sampling method or the extent to which the targeted individuals or households were actually included in the final sample. These details are at least as important as the sample size.

When targeted members of a population are not interviewed or do not respond to particular questions, the omissions are a serious problem if they are numerous and if those missed differ from those who are interviewed on the matters being studied. The latter difference can seldom be known with great confidence, so it is usually desirable to keep omissions to a minimum. For example, sampling from telephone directories is undesirable because it leaves out those with unlisted telephones, as well as those with no telephones at all. Many survey reports are based on such poor sampling procedures that they may not deserve to be taken seriously. This is especially true of reports based on "focus groups," which offer lots of human interest but are subject to vast amounts of error. Internet surveys also cannot represent the general population adequately at present, though this is an area where some serious attempts are being made to compensate for the inherent difficulties.

The percentage of people who refuse to take part in a survey is particularly important. In some federal surveys, the percentage is small, within the range of 5 to 10 percent. For even the best nongovernment surveys, the refusal rate can reach 25 percent or more, and it can be far larger in the case of poorly executed surveys. Refusals have risen substantially from earlier days, becoming a major cause for concern among serious survey practitioners. Fortunately, in recent years research has shown that moderate amounts of nonresponse in an otherwise careful survey seem in most cases not to have a major effect on results. Indeed, even the *Literary Digest,* with its abysmal sampling and massive nonresponse rate, did well predicting elections before the dramatic realignment of the electorate in 1936. The problem is that one can never be certain as to the effects of refusals and other forms of nonresponse, so obtaining a high response rate remains an important goal.

questions about questions

Since survey questions resemble the questions we ask in ordinary social interaction, they may seem less problematic than the counterintuitive and technical aspects of sampling. Yet survey results are every bit as dependent on the form, wording, and context of the questions asked as they are on the sample of people who answer them.

No classic morality tale like the *Literary Digest* fiasco highlights the question-answer process, but an example from the early days of surveys illustrates both the potential challenges of question writing and the practical solutions.

In 1940 Donald Rugg asked two slightly different questions to equivalent national samples about the general issue of freedom of speech:

· Do you think the United States should forbid public speeches against democracy?
· Do you think the United States should allow public speeches against democracy?

Taken literally, forbidding something and not allowing something have the same effect, but clearly the public did not view the questions as identical. Whereas 75 percent of the public would not allow such speeches, only 54 percent would forbid them, a difference of 21 percentage points. This finding was replicated several times in later years, not only in the United States but also (with appropriate translations) in Ger-

many and the Netherlands. Such "survey-based experiments" call for administering different versions of a question to random subsamples of a larger sample. If the results between the subsamples differ by more than can be easily explained by chance, we infer that the difference is due to the variation in wording.

In addition, answers to survey questions always depend on the form in which a question is asked. If the interviewer presents a limited set of alternatives, most respondents will choose one, rather than offering a different alternative of their own. In one survey-based experiment, for example, we asked a national sample of Americans to name the most important problem facing the country. Then we asked a comparable sample a parallel question that provided a list of four problems from which to choose the most important; this list included none of the four problems mentioned most often by the first sample but instead provided four problems that had been mentioned by fewer than 3 percent of the earlier respondents. The list question also invited respondents to substitute a different problem if they wished (see table 1). Despite the invitation, the majority of respondents (60 percent) chose one of the rare problems offered, reflecting their reluctance to go outside the frame of reference provided by the question. The form of a question provides the "rules of the game" for respondents, and this must always be kept in mind when interpreting results.

Other difficulties occur with survey questions when issues are discussed quite generally, as though there is a single way of framing them and just two sides to the debate. For example, what is called "the abortion issue" really consists of different issues: the reasons for an abortion, the trimester involved, and so forth. In a recent General Social Survey, nearly 80 percent of the national sample supported legal abortion in the case of "a serious defect in the baby," but only 44 percent supported it "if the family has a

A. Open question	B. Closed question
"What do you think is the most important problem facing this country today [1986]?"	"Which of the following do you think is the most important problem facing this country today [1986]—the energy shortage, the quality of public schools, legalized abortion, or pollution—or, if you prefer, you may name a different problem as most important." 1. Energy shortage 2. Quality of public schools 3. Legalized abortion 4. Pollution

Source: *Adapted from H. Schuman and I. Scott, "Problems in the Use of Survey Questions to Measure Public Opinion," Science v. 236, pp. 957–59, May 22, 1987.*

In a survey experiment, less than 3 percent of the 171 respondents asked the question on the left volunteered one of the four problems listed on the right. Yet 60 percent of the 178 respondents asked the question on the right picked one of those four answers.

low income and cannot afford any more children." Often what is thought to be a conflict in findings between two surveys is actually a difference in the aspects of the general issue that they queried. In still other cases an inconsistency reflects a type of illogical wish fulfillment in the public itself, as when majorities favor both a decrease in taxes and an increase in government services if the questions are asked separately.

solutions to the question wording problem

All these and still other difficulties (including the order in which questions are asked) suggest that responses to single survey questions on complex issues should be viewed with considerable skepticism. What to do then, other than to reject all survey data as unusable for serious pur-

poses? One answer can be found from the replications of the forbid/allow experiment above: Although there was a 21 percentage points difference based on question wording in 1940 and a slightly larger difference (24 percentage points) when the experiment was repeated some 35 years later, both the forbid and the allow wordings registered similar declines in Americans' intolerance of speeches against democracy (see figure 1). No matter which question was used—as long as it was the same one at both times—the conclusion about the increase in civil libertarian sentiments was the same.

More generally, what has been called the "principle of form-resistant correlations" holds in most cases: if question wording (and meaning) is kept constant, differences over time, differences across educational levels, and most other careful comparisons are not seriously affected by specific question wording. Indeed, the distinction between results for single questions and results based on comparisons or associations holds even for simple factual inquiries. Consider, for example, a study of the number of rooms in American houses. No God-given rule states what to include when counting the rooms in a house (bathrooms? basements? hallways?); hence the average number reported for a particular place and time should not be treated as an absolute truth. What we can do, however, is try to apply the same definitions over time, across social divisions, even across nations. That way, we gain confidence in the comparisons we make—who has more rooms than who, for example.

We still face the task of interpreting the meaning of questions and of associations among ques-

tions, but that is true in all types of research. Even an index constructed from a large number of questions on the basis of a sophisticated statistical calculation called factor analysis inevitably requires the investigator to interpret what it is that he or she has measured. There is no escaping this theoretical challenge, fundamental to all research, whether using surveys or other methods such as field observations.

Survey researchers should also ask several different questions about any important issue. In addition to combining questions to increase reliability, the different answers can be synthesized rather than depending on the angle of vision provided by any single question. A further safeguard is to carry out frequent experiments like that on the forbid/allow wordings. By varying the form, wording, and context of questions, researchers can gain insight into both the questions and the relevant issues. Sometimes variations turn out to make no difference, and that is also useful to learn. For example, I once expected support for legalized abortion to increase when a question substituted *end pregnancy* for the word *abortion* in the phrasing. Yet no difference was found. Today, more and more researchers include survey-based experiments as part of their investigations, and readers should look for these sorts of safeguards when evaluating survey results.

the need for comparisons

To interpret surveys accurately, it's important to use a framework of comparative data in evaluating the results. For example, teachers know that course evaluations can be interpreted best against the backdrop of evaluations from other similar courses: a 75 percent rating of lectures as "excellent" takes on a quite different meaning depending on whether the average for other lecture courses is 50 percent or 90 percent. Such comparisons are fundamental for all survey results, yet they are easily overlooked

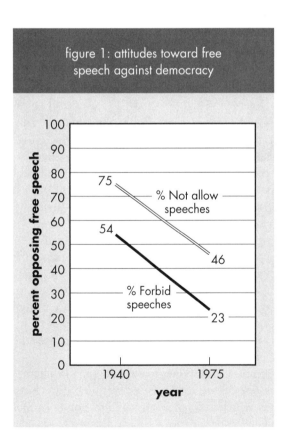

figure 1: attitudes toward free speech against democracy

A2. We are interested in how people are getting along financially these days. Would you say that you (and your family living there) are *better off* or *worse off* financially than you were *a year ago?*

1. BETTER NOW   3. SAME   5. WORSE   8. DON'T KNOW

A3. Now looking ahead—do you think that *a year from now* you (and your family living there) will be *better off* financially, or *worse off*, or just about the same as now?

1. WILL BE BETTER OFF   3. SAME   5. WILL BE WORSE OFF   8. DON'T KNOW

A4. Now turning to business conditions in the country as a whole—do you think that during the next 12 months we'll have *good* times financially, or *bad* times, or what?

1. GOOD TIMES   2. GOOD WITH QUALIFICATIONS   3. PRO-CON

4. BAD WITH QUALIFICATIONS   5. BAD TIMES   8. DON'T KNOW

A8. Looking ahead, which would you say is more likely—that in the country as a whole we'll have continuous good times *during the next 5 years* or so, or that we will have periods of widespread *unemployment* or depression, or what?

_____

_____

A18. About the big things people buy for their homes—such as furniture, a refrigerator, stove, television, and things like that. Generally speaking, do you think that now is a good or a bad time for people to buy major household items?

1. GOOD   3. PRO-CON   5. BAD   8. DON'T KNOW

Section of interview form used in the Survey of Consumers conducted by the Survey Research Center, University of Michigan. Courtesy of Survey Research Center, University of Michigan.

when one feels the urge to speak definitively about public reactions to a unique event.

Comparative analysis over time, along with survey-based experiments, can also help us understand responses to questions about socially sensitive subjects. Experiments have shown that expressions of racial attitudes can change substantially for both black and white Americans depending on the interviewer's race. White respondents, for instance, are more likely to support racial intermarriage when speaking to a black than to a white interviewer. Such self-censoring mirrors variations in cross-race conversations outside of surveys, reflecting not a methodological artifact of surveys but rather a fact of life about race relations in America. Still, if we consider time trends, with the race of interviewer kept constant, we can also see that white responses supporting intermarriage have clearly increased over the past half century (see table 2), that actual intermarriage rates have also risen (though from a much lower level) over recent years, and that the public visibility of cross-race marriage and dating has also increased. It would be foolish to assume that the survey data on racial attitudes reflect actions in any literal sense, but they do capture important *trends* in both norms and behavior.

Surveys remain our best tool for learning about large populations. One remarkable advantage surveys have over some other methods is the ability to identify their own limitations, as illustrated by the development of both probability theory in sampling and experiments in questioning. In the end, however, with surveys as with all research methods, there is no substitute for both care and intelligence in the way evidence is gathered and interpreted. What we learn about society is always mediated by the instruments we use, including our own eyes and ears. As Isaac Newton wrote long ago, error is not in the art but in the artificers.

table 2: percent of white americans approving or disapproving of racial intermarriage, 1958–1997		
"Do you approve or disapprove of marriage between blacks and whites?"		
Year	Approve	Disapprove
1958	4	96
1978	34	66
1997	67	33
Source: *Gallup Poll.*		

RECOMMENDED RESOURCES

Philip E. Converse. "The Nature of Belief Systems in Mass Publics." In *Ideology and Discontent*, ed. D. E. Apter (The Free Press, 1964).

A profound and skeptical exploration of the nature of public attitudes.

Robert M. Groves. *Survey Errors and Survey Costs* (Wiley, 1989).

A sophisticated consideration of the sources of error in surveys.

Graham Kalton. *Introduction to Survey Sampling* (Sage Publications [Quantitative Applications in the Social Sciences], 1983).

A brief and lucid introduction to sampling.

Benjamin I. Page and Robert Y. Shapiro. *The Rational Public: Fifty Years of Trends in Americans' Policy Preferences* (University of Chicago Press, 1992).

In part, a persuasive reply to Converse's skepticism.

Howard Schuman and Stanley Presser. *Questions and Answers in Attitude Surveys: Experiments on Question Form, Wording, and Context* (Academic Press, 1981) (Reprint edition with new preface, Sage Publications, 1996).

Several experiments discussed in the present article are drawn from this volume.

Samuel A. Stouffer. *Communism, Conformity, and Civil Liberties*, with introduction by James A. Davis (Doubleday, 1955; Transaction Publishers, 1992).

Stouffer's keen awareness of both the possibilities and the limitations of survey data is reflected in this classic investigation. Also relevant to today's political climate.

Seymour Sudman, Norman M. Bradburn, and Norbert Schwarz. *Thinking About Answers: The Application of Cognitive Process to Survey Methodology* (Jossey-Bass, 1996).

A clear discussion of survey questioning by three well-known researchers.

Roger Tourangeau, Lance J. Rips, and Kenneth Rasinski. *The Psychology of Survey Response* (Cambridge University Press, 2000).

A comprehensive account of response effects, drawing especially on ideas from cognitive psychology.

REVIEW QUESTIONS

1. Schuman suggests that telephone directories do not provide an adequate listing of possible survey respondents. Why? Is there another reason, one that might be in your pocket or purse?

2. Table 1 offers a good example of how a respondent can be asked an open or closed question. What are the advantages and disadvantages of both? Try constructing two questions, one open and one closed, on the same topic, selected from an earlier essay.

3. In the final section of his essay, Schuman describes how many researchers now try to use multiple methodologies (e.g., participant observation, survey data, longitudinal studies, case studies). Write a paragraph reflecting on what you think the benefits of such an approach would be.

patricia a. adler and peter adler

the promise and pitfalls of going into the field

65

spring 2003

firsthand reports from the field comprise some of the most valuable work in the social sciences. but findings are often controversial. understanding how fieldwork is carried out can help readers assess ethnographic research.

Barbara Ehrenreich, a white, divorced Ph.D. in her 50s, spent a year working low-wage jobs as a waitress in Florida, a housecleaner in Maine, and a Wal-Mart sales clerk in Minnesota. Her detailed ethnography, the best-selling *Nickel and Dimed,* reveals how physically demanding and personally demeaning these jobs are, and how workers are trapped in them. Ehrenreich's book has received wide critical acclaim, a typical book review in the *Minneapolis Star Tribune* calling it "piercing social criticism backed by first-rate reporting."

Some ethnographies are, however, more controversial. William Foote Whyte, then a young, Protestant graduate student at Harvard, wrote a classic ethnography of Italian-American youth in the early 1940s, *Street Corner Society*, describing the "corner boys" who hung around the neighborhood and participated in illegal activities. He described them as a "gang." Yet Marianne Boelen, an Italian immigrant to America who years later revisited his setting and re-interviewed his subjects, asserted that Whyte had made methodological and substantive errors in his work. These boys were not a gang, she claimed, but rather followed a typical Italian pattern: women occupied indoor space and men claimed the outdoors. He might have realized this had he paid greater attention to gender. His errors also resulted, she

alleged, from relying too closely on one key informant, "Doc," whose role he exaggerated.

That two important ethnographies can produce such different reactions, from critical acclaim to academic controversy, raises several questions about ethnographic methods. How can readers know if researchers have gotten the evidence and its interpretation right? What kinds of stories should we believe? We need to be able to assess the validity and value of ethnographic work, just as we do with other methods. Herbert Gans, in *The Urban Villagers*, notes that "every social research method is a mixture of art and science," but that participant observation is the best empirical research method available because it allows us to study, firsthand, what people do, think, and believe, in their own groups. While all methods may be subject to problems such as shaping findings to fit preconceptions, Gans continues, "ethnography is most successful when it becomes an all encompassing 14- to 16-hours a day experience, with at least a year's full-time fieldwork, and a good deal of additional time to analyze and think about the data."

Ethnography, as we defined it when we edited the *Journal of Contemporary Ethnography,* includes observing social activities as an outsider, observing while participating in the activities, and conducting intensive interviews. Considered

Philippe Bourgois during his study of a homeless encampment in San Francisco, 1994. (Courtesy of Jeff Schonberg)

the ethnographic genre

Ethnography can be divided into three crucial stages: data gathering, data analysis, and data presentation. One might be an exemplary field researcher, able to fit into myriad social settings and to elicit the insiders' view from a variety of people, but this is not enough. Ethnographers need to step back as well, to take a detached look at people's worlds so they can analyze underlying patterns of behavior. These careful observations and astute interpretations must be backed up by prose that brings readers into people's complex lives. We will see how exemplary researchers optimize the rewards of fieldwork while avoiding its pitfalls.

data gathering

Good ethnography takes time. The strength of ethnographers' data depends on the quality and depth of the relationships they forge and the rapport and trust they establish with the people they study. Superficial relationships yield superficial insights. Researchers sometimes spend up to several years in the field, as we did in our studies of drug dealers and smugglers in *Wheeling and Dealing* and elite college athletes in *Backboards & Blackboards*.

Ethnographers, in having to gain people's trust, require highly developed social skills. They must be able to get along with all sorts of people, from powerful managers to weak employees. For instance, in an outstanding ethnography of the homeless, *Down on Their Luck*, Leon Anderson and David Snow spent parts of two years under bridges, in Salvation Army shelters and plasma centers, at the city hospital and police department, and on the streets of Austin, Texas. Ethnography also requires intimacy and commitment. For example, in studying drug traffickers, our long-term relationships with central figures were often tested by crises or suspicions

the most accessible to readers of all the social scientific methods, ethnography draws on the language and perspective of everyday members of society, and is often written like investigative journalism. A successful ethnography captures readers' fancies, bringing them closer to the lives of others, and, like a good movie or book, offers insight into people's ordinary worlds. Literally translated as a "portrait of the people," ethnography describes and analyzes the beliefs, motivations, and rationales of a people in a particular setting or subculture. It makes the familiar distant and the distant familiar.

Although ethnography resembles journalism, it differs by requiring the systematic, long-term gathering of data and by engaging general theories of human behavior rather than simply reporting the news. Ethnography resembles literature as well, but differs in focusing on social trends and patterns rather than character development. Finally, ethnography differs from commonsense interpretations by drawing on meticulous field research rather than popular stereotypes. But as the controversy around Whyte's classic ethnography teaches us, it is not always obvious which ethnographic reports are sufficiently systematic, sufficiently accurate or sufficiently useful.

Ethnography's vitality and breadth is shown by the number of awards given to books employing this approach in the past decade. Some recent titles have garnered special attention:

Anderson, Elijah. *Code of the Street*. New York: Norton, 1999. An examination of inner-city black America, this book describes the complex code of rules governing violence in urban areas.

Bourgois, Philippe. *In Search of Respect*. New York: Cambridge University Press, 1995. A provocative account of crack dealing in Spanish Harlem.

Casper, Monica. *The Making of the Unborn Patient*. New Brunswick, NJ: Rutgers University Press, 1998. Discusses controversies in biomedical experimentation by looking at doctors who perform surgeries on unborn babies.

Duneier, Mitchell. *Sidewalk*. New York: Farrar, Straus, and Giroux, 1999. An ethnography of poor black men who make their living selling magazines and secondhand goods on the streets of Greenwich Village.

Fine, Gary Alan. *Morel Tales*. Cambridge, MA: Harvard University Press, 1998. An insider's look at the subculture of mushroom collectors.

Hondagneu-Sotelo, Pierrette, *Domestica*. Berkeley: University of California Press, 2001. An excellent portrayal of the new immigrant women in Los Angeles who serve as housecleaners, nannies, and domestics.

Karp, David. *Speaking of Sadness*. New York: Oxford University Press, 1996. Using autobiographical and participant observation data, this book examines the lives of people who live with depression.

Miller, Jody. *One of the Guys*. New York: Oxford University Press, 2001. Drawing on comparative research in two Midwestern cities, this book looks at the underlying causes and meanings of female gang membership.

Mitchell, Richard. *Dancing at Armageddon: Survivalism and Chaos in Modern Times*. Chicago: University of Chicago Press, 2002. A rare look at a secretive group, survivalists, who inhabit the backwoods of America and prepare themselves for civilization's collapse.

Sanders, Clinton. *Understanding Dogs*. Philadelphia: Temple University Press, 1999. Explores the everyday experiences of living with canine companions.

Snow, David, and Leon Anderson. *Down on Their Luck*. Berkeley: University of California Press, 1993. Provides one of the most trenchant accounts of the problems involved with living on the streets of America today.

of betrayal, and loyalty was expected on both sides during the six years of explicit research and for many years afterwards.

According to current thinking, ethnographers should get as near to the people they are studying as possible. Even studying one's self (auto-ethnography), as Carolyn Ellis did in *Final Negotiations*, where she documented the changing emotions she and her partner experienced as he was dying of emphysema, or as Carol Rambo Ronai did in her writings on incest, has become acceptable. Some ethnographers combine the intimacy of autobiography with the more general approach of talking to others who have gone through similar traumas or events. Best illustrated by David Karp in *Speaking of Sadness*, a study of manic-depressives, the author recounts his own bouts with depression as well as data gleaned from numerous observations and interviews with self-help groups for this illness. Karp's own experiences helped him gain participants' trust and gave him a deeper understanding of the emotional complexity of mood fluctuation. In evaluating ethnography, then, readers should pay attention to not only the length of time researchers spent in the field (a year or two tends to be the minimum depending upon the locale and topic of study), but also the depth of involvement they established with their subjects.

Sometimes problems arise when researchers are either too close or similar to their subjects or too distant or different from them. Researchers who are too close may "go native," uncritically accepting their subjects' perspectives. Researchers too distant may fail to penetrate beyond the fronts people design for public presentation. For example, Richard Mitchell, in *Dancing at Armageddon*, a study of survivalists, became involved with people whose behaviors evoked some repugnance. To forge the necessary rapport, he had to overcome his initial feelings of alienation, to spend time getting to know participants, and to establish friendship and trust on other planes. Readers who suspect ethnographers may have such problems should look for frank and personal methodological discussions that specifically address how they encountered and dealt with these issues.

Good ethnography is systematic, rigorous, and scientific. One of the chief criticisms leveled at ethnography is that it is anecdotal, careless, and casual, depending too much on researchers' subjectivity. Poor ethnography may result when researchers are biased by their own opinions or history, or when they carry their preconceived attitudes, either personal or professional, into the field and cannot transcend them. Derek Freeman aimed this charge against Margaret Mead, claiming that in *Coming of Age in Samoa* she uncritically accepted the assertions of a few adolescent girls about their uninhibited sexuality to support her mentor's views that nurture trumped nature. Bias may also result from researchers' poor location or sponsorship in the field, where their access to the group is somehow impeded. And researchers can generate problems when they fail to gather multiple perspectives or prefer their own beliefs to the beliefs of others. (Recently, some "postmodern" ethnographers have concluded that the process is so idiosyncratic that there should be no claims to describe the world, only to describe researchers' reactions to the world.)

To overcome these problems, ethnographers should include the voices of a full spectrum of participants, not just the ones they can easily reach. Generally, it is easier for researchers to "study down," looking at the downtrodden, the powerless, and the underclass, who, unlike the powerful, do not have the ability to insulate themselves. Researchers may also more easily gather data from people like themselves, overlooking members of dissimilar groups. Part of Boelen's allegation against Whyte was that his perspective was skewed toward "Doc," his key informant, a man much like himself. Good ethnography gains the perspectives of all involved, so that the ultimate portrait is rounded and thorough. In Jack Douglas and Paul Rasmussen's study, *The Nude Beach*, the voices of the nudists, other beachgoers, residents, and police are all heard, providing this sort of completeness. An ethnography that only privileges some voices and perspectives to the exclusion of others may not be as representative.

An array of methodological tactics may help to generate the multiple perspectives required. Ethnographers may combine direct observation, participation, interviewing, and casual conversation to triangulate their findings. For instance, in researching drug traffickers, we cross-checked our observations against our own common sense and general knowledge of the scene, against a variety of reliable, independent sources, and against hard evidence such as newspaper and magazine reports, arrest records, and material possessions. Similarly, Judith Rollins, in her study of domestics and their employers, *Between Women*, worked as a domestic for ten employers. In studying human-canine relationships for *Understanding Dogs*, Clinton Sanders not only drew on his own love of dogs and experiences as a dog owner, but also participated in the training of guide dogs and their owners, a "puppy kindergarten," observations of dogs and their owners in public settings, participant observation at a veterinary hospital for 14 months, and formal interviews with dog owners, veterinarians, and trainers.

To help readers assess what role the researchers' personal views played in their reports, an ethnographic report should include methodological reflections. Researchers use these "confessional tales" to explain problems, and then describe the ways they overcame them. Alan Peshkin confessed the problems he faced studying Bethany, a Christian fundamentalist community and school, for *God's Choice*: "I discovered, so to speak, that being Jewish would be the personal fact bearing most on my research . . . They taught their children never to be close friends, marry, or to go into business with someone like me. What they were expected to do with someone like me was to proselytize . . . To repeat, Bethany gored me." Yet, Peshkin was able to surmount his role as "odd man out" and to forge close research ties by living in the community for 18 months, attending all regular church and school activities, dressing and speaking as a member, and interviewing a significant portion of the school's teachers, students, and parents.

Ethical concerns are often raised about ethnography, since researchers interact so closely with their subjects and could potentially deceive or harm them. A maelstrom of controversy surrounded Laud Humphreys' *Tearoom Trade*, a study of impersonal homosexual encounters in public restrooms, partly because he was covert, observing without telling the men he watched that he was a researcher. Humphreys rejoined that he caused no harm to his subjects, and would not have been able to conduct the research under the strictures of "informed consent," rules that require the permission of those studied. New "Institutional Review Board" regulations at universities now require researchers to relinquish their data to the authorities, often raising conflicts between their loyalty to the people they studied and to the government. When faced with this dilemma, Rik Scarce went to jail for six months rather than turn over his field notes on environmental activists in the state of Washington to the police. Not everyone will take such drastic steps, though, and recent guidelines have been designed to safeguard subjects from their researchers by making sure people know that what they say cannot be protected.

Some feminist and "activist" ethnographers believe researchers improve their ethical stance by eschewing the traditional "value neutral" position and openly aligning themselves with their subjects, "making the personal political" and working for social change. Others seek an ethical stance in "taking their findings back to the field," showing their writings to subjects and asking for feedback. At the same time, however, some ethnographers believe this leads researchers to censor themselves from writing things their subjects might interpret as too critical, pushing them toward "going native" in the field.

Perhaps most importantly, good ethnography conveys what it is like to "walk in the shoes" of the people being studied. No other method lets researchers adequately study hidden, secretive, and sensitive groups, since deviants, criminals, and others with something to hide are unlikely to talk to strangers. Jeffrey Ferrell's work on illegal graffiti artists and Jeffrey Sluka's investigation of violent political combatants in Ireland, for example, provide insightful ethnographic research into subterranean worlds. Readers should understand people's joys, feel their frustrations and sorrows, and know their problematic, complex, and contradictory worlds. For instance, Karp's *Speaking of Sadness* delves deeply into the poignant fears and frustrations experienced by people who suffer from depression. One person Karp interviewed described the way depression stole away who she was and replaced her life with a black hole: "Depression is an insidious vacuum that crawls into your brain and pushes your mind out of the way. It is the complete absence of rational thought. It is freezing cold, with a dangerous, horrifying, terrifying fog wafting through whatever is left of your mind." In *Sidewalk*, Mitchell Duneier explains some of the practical problems that Greenwich Village African-American street vendors encounter in doing what we all take for granted: going to the bathroom. In the words of one of his informants: "I gotta get me a paper cup and I'm gonna be all right. . . . Now everybody out here gets a cup. You can't go to the bathroom in the stores and restaurants, because they don't want you in there if you ain't got no money to spend. So how you gonna piss? You gotta get a cup." Thus, we learn about not only the vernacular of the men themselves, but also the everyday turmoil that they encounter.

data analysis

Ethnographers begin forming their analyses early in their fieldwork, testing and refining them over time. Researchers usually remain near, or connected to their settings throughout the time they write up their data, to fill in holes they discover and to check their interpretations against their informants'. Yet their observations about the specifics of a particular time and place must be joined by more far-reaching, general analyses. They want, for example, to speak about not just a poor neighborhood, but poor neighborhoods in general. One test of how well ethnographers have succeeded in capturing more general patterns comes when people in comparable settings recognize the descriptions they read. For instance, in our college athlete study, we were frequently satisfied when we gave lectures at universities and athletes in the audience came up afterwards to say that we "got it right."

Good ethnography generates, modifies, extends, or challenges existing understandings of social life. For instance, Pierrette Hondagneu-Sotelo's study of immigrant domestic workers in Los Angeles, *Doméstica*, is powerful because it shows that American husbands' failures to share household duties and the influx of immigrant workers have combined to create a pattern in which housekeepers work in affluence but live in poverty.

data presentation

Ethnographers must write clearly and actively, avoiding jargon, highly technical terms, or obscure phrases. Ethnography also should "give voice" to participants, enabling readers to get a sense of how people converse and what language they use. In *Code of the Streets*, Elijah Anderson uses a voice from the neighborhood to explain why low-income African-American girls in vulnerable situations may become pregnant early: "I done see where four girls grow up under their mama . . . Mama working three to eleven o'clock at night . . . Can't nobody else tell 'em what to do. Hey, all of 'em pregnant by age sixteen. They can get they own baby, they get they own [welfare] check, they get they own apartment. They wanna get away from Mama."

What anthropologist Clifford Geertz called "thick description" is another hallmark of ethnography. Good ethnographies vividly present participants' stories, using colorful words, adjectives, or other literary devices to highlight the vibrancy of group culture. With sounds and action, Philippe Bourgois brings readers into the midst of the scene in this excerpt from *In Search of Respect*, his ethnography of Puerto Rican crack dealers in East Harlem: "But then when we stepped out of the room, she turns to me and whispers [snarling], 'You motherfucker.' She like turns on me again. And then I went [burying his head in his hands], 'Oh, my God.' And I got mad [making exaggerated whole-body wrestling motions], and I grabbed her by the neck, and I threw her to the sofa. [pounding fist to palm] BOOM . . . and I WHAAAAM, POOM [pounding again], smacked her in the face with all my might." Even when the subject matter is disturbing, it should be easy, not hard, to read this type of social science.

Successful ethnography elicits the "uh-huh" effect in readers, presenting subjects' everyday behavior in ways that people can recognize. Lyn Lofland, an observer of public places, succinctly summarized behavior that we all do, but rarely acknowledge. She described how people get ready to enter a public space: they "check for readiness" (clothes, grooming, mirror glances),

"take a personal reading" (pause, scan the area, check the layout), and "reach a position" (find a secure location or niche). These sorts of rich and resonating descriptions serve to authenticate ethnographic presentations.

the contributions of ethnography

In making the familiar distant, researchers find new ways of looking at what we think we know and bringing the unknown to light. Weak ethnography runs the risk of rediscovering the obvious. Poorly presented ethnography may stop at subjects' understandings of their worlds, or may analyze these in mundane, trivial or superficial ways. Gary Alan Fine's work is notable for introducing readers to the nuances of unusual subcultures, such as mushroom collecting, or taking familiar worlds, such as the Little League, and providing a framework for a much broader understanding of children's culture.

Good ethnography may also be socially influential. It may speak to social policy and public awareness as well as to scholarly knowledge and theoretical understanding. For example, Arlie Hochschild brought recognition to contemporary working women—who still do most of the housework and child care—with her research on *The Second Shift*. What seemed to be individuals' personal problems, she showed, emerged from social changes affecting many families. In the 1990s, government agencies implemented programs to distribute condoms, clean needles, and bleach after ethnographies of the drug world exposed the HIV dangers in the practices of street people. Whether or how ethnographic findings are used depends on the administration in power and the tenor of the times, however. The traditionally liberal leanings of sociologists have made their suggestions more appealing to Democratic politicians. Others believe, however, that ethnography should take theory-building, not political activism, as its goal. As famed ethnographer Erving Goffman put it: "I can only suggest that he who would combat false consciousness and awaken people to their true interests has much to do, because the sleep is very deep. And I do not intend to provide a lullaby, but merely to sneak in and watch the people snore."

Ethnography has the power to incite, infuriate, enthrall, and excite. Ethnographers need to be careful in their representation of others, scrupulous in how they relate to informants in order to obtain data, and true to their own integrity in not violating others' privacy. However, their stories are vital, allowing readers insight into worlds to which they will never be privy or to ones that they would otherwise never understand. The great ethnographies endure for decades because the evidence is accessible, the messages remain critical, and the stories of people's complex worlds continue to be fresh and insightful.

RECOMMENDED RESOURCES

Paul Atkinson, Amanda Coffey, Sara Delamont, John Lofland, and Lyn Lofland. *Handbook of Ethnography* (Sage, 2001).

A useful resource on the history of ethnography, its current disciplinary borders, substantive foci, and methodological advances.

Norman K. Denzin and Yvonna Lincoln. *Handbook of Qualitative Research*, 2nd ed. (Sage, 2000).

A definitive source on controversies, nuances, and new directions for all qualitative research, but particularly focused on ethnography.

Randy Hodson. Workplace Ethnography File. www.soc.sbs.ohio-state.edu/rdh/welist.htm

A comprehensive Web site that lists workplace ethnographies. This inventory of articles and books includes ethnographic research on organizations, cutting across a wide variety of disciplines.

John Lofland and Lyn Lofland. *Analyzing Social Settings*, 3rd ed. (Wadsworth, 1995).

First published in 1971, this is the longest standing primer on doing ethnography, covering data gathering, data analysis, and data presentation.

REVIEW QUESTIONS

1. Define "ethnography." How does it differ from journalism?

2. One of the most challenging aspects of ethnography is also one of its main benefits: The close, personal contact with respondents and the rich, meaningful tales that intimacy provides may come into conflict with a felt need for "objectivity." Write two paragraphs on the challenge of being both "participant" and "observer." How do the costs and benefits of this approach resonate with your own notions of sociology and science?

3. From class readings and your own understanding of sociological research, discuss what you think the role of theory should be in ethnography. Should one keep theory out of the process of data collection and analysis? Is this possible? Should theory be established at the outset, as something to be proved or disproved? Should it be "built" from the "ground up"?

4. Activity: Pick a social setting. Write two paragraphs describing the character of the place, the people one finds there, and the activities that take place within it. Try to evoke the "feel" of this setting as much as possible for the reader. Now write a third paragraph attempting to generalize from your description to a broader social issue raised somewhere within this *Reader* (e.g., power, racism, sexuality, inequality).

robert s. weiss

in their own words: making the most of qualitative interviews

66

fall 2004

successfully conducting in-depth interviews requires much more than being a good listener. researchers must choose interview subjects carefully, push for concrete details, and pore over reams of transcripts to develop their stories. but the result can be a rich and compelling understanding of people's lives.

In the 1840s, British sociologist-journalist Henry Mayhew sought to learn about the lives of London's seamstresses—how they did their work and managed to survive on so little income. He found his answers by asking the women themselves and his interviews made vivid the dismal conditions of their lives. One young woman, after describing how little she was paid for long hours of work, said: "I was single. . . . I had a child, and he used to cry for food. So, as I could not get a living for him myself by my needle, I went into the streets and made out a living that way." The novels of Charles Dickens captured readers' sympathies, but they were only fiction. Mayhew presented the experiences of real people.

Such "qualitative interviews" are now so common that it is easy to forget how radical Henry Mayhew's procedure—which assumes that ordinary people can provide valid accounts of their own lives—was in his day. Indeed, qualitative interviewing was considered by many researchers so simple that it required no special techniques; listening attentively and respectfully was enough. More recently, practitioners have recognized that training is needed to make the most of interviewing and to avoid its pitfalls.

Studies based on in-depth interviews illuminate the social world. They describe the survival struggles of families on welfare, the ups and downs of physicists' careers and the tendency of two-job couples to assign homemaking to the wives. They reveal the emotional and social implications of organizational charts, from prisons to medical schools. Diane Vaughan's interview study of the bureaucratic processes that led to the disastrous 1986 *Challenger* launch has become an important reference for institutions—medical schools as well as NASA—trying to reduce catastrophic errors.

The type of interview used in these studies is often called "qualitative" to distinguish it from an interview done for a survey. Qualitative interviews ask about the details of what happened: what was done and said, what the respondent thought and felt. The aim is to come as close as possible to capturing in full the processes that led to an event or experience. The researchers' report will likely be a densely detailed description of what happened, but it may also provide a basis for a theory of why it happened. In contrast, surveys ask well-crafted questions that elicit brief answers. The answers are then added up and expressed as numbers or percentages. Surveys are quantitative; they report the distribution of people's actions or opinions in tables or statistics (see "sense and nonsense about surveys"). In-depth interviews yield descriptions of experiences, processes, and events.

More than any other technique social scientists use, in-depth interviewing can shed light on events that would otherwise remain unknown because they happened in the past or out of public sight. In-depth interviews can provide vivid descriptions of personal experience—for example, what it feels like to succeed or to fail at an undertaking, or the emotional consequences of a new child or a death in the family. They are the best source of information about people's thoughts and feelings and the motives and emotions that lead them to act as they do.

but can we trust what we are told?

For her study of religiously inspired terrorism, national security expert Jessica Stern interviewed leaders of terrorist groups. They seemed entirely truthful when they told her about their commitment to producing a better world, but when she asked about the sources of their funds, they exaggerated the importance of small gifts and minimized contributions from wealthy donors. Most of those who were widely known to have received funds from governments simply lied. The adequacy and accuracy of interview data depends on what respondents are willing to report.

Lies or evasions such as these are not the only way interview findings can be compromised. Even respondents who want to be accurate may distort. Memory of an event is never simply a replay of a mental videotape. It is a reconstruction, an integration of fragments of stored knowledge, perceptions, and emotions. From these elements people build a coherent story, perhaps accompanied by visualized scenes

of the event. The account and its accompanying images may be close to what happened, but inevitably there will be omissions, distortions, and additions.

Psychologist Elizabeth Loftus and her students have repeatedly demonstrated that memory is vulnerable to false associations. In one study, they showed subjects who lived in the Disneyland area advertisements in which Bugs Bunny appeared as a member of the Disneyland staff. Actually, Bugs Bunny has never entered Disneyland; he is a Warner Brothers property. But nearly a quarter of the subjects who read the false advertisements later reported meeting Bugs Bunny at Disneyland. They seemed to have put together memories of an actual visit to Disneyland with awareness of a link between Disneyland and Bugs Bunny, forgetting that the awareness stemmed from the advertisements. How can sociologists depend on data that are so fallible? And how can readers assess the trustworthiness of their reports?

To begin with, things are not so bad; it is easy to exaggerate the unreliability of interview data. Loftus and her students found that when her subjects reported a false memory, they tended to be less confident than when they reported something that had actually happened. Other indicators of the trustworthiness of a report include the density of detail the respondent provides, the apparent vividness of recall, and the extent to which the respondent's description makes sense in the context of his or her life.

Reports based mainly on interviews are often strengthened by the inclusion of other kinds of information. Jessica Stern, in her report on terrorism, provided a context for her interviews by describing the settings in which the interviews were held: homes, hotel rooms, restaurants, house trailers, and isolated terrorist camps. She also described the dress, manner, and facial features of the terror group members she interviewed and her own reactions of sympathy, repugnance, and fear. In her *Challenger* report, Diane Vaughan relied on interviews to explain what could not be understood from NASA's internal memos, but she reported the memos as well. Often a survey can strengthen arguments based primarily on qualitative interviews, by showing how one person's story or opinion fits into larger patterns.

The interviewer's direct observations can also help readers judge whether skepticism is appropriate. Did a respondent seem to be straightforward or evasive? The interviewer's observations of settings can corroborate what respondents say, as when a view of spacious grounds supports a respondent's claim that an organization is successful, but it can also contradict their claims, as when someone professing asceticism is interviewed in an opulent setting.

doing it right

The cooperation of the respondent is of paramount importance to the success of an interview. While full cooperation cannot always be achieved, cooperation is likely to be maximized by an interviewer who is respectful and friendly, yet task-focused. In my own research, I bring two copies of consent forms describing the study to my interviewees, both copies bearing my signature. After briefly explaining the study, I give both forms to the respondent, ask him or her to read one and, if comfortable with it, to sign one of the copies and keep the other. I usually have a tape recorder and ask if it is all right to turn it on. My aim is to establish that the respondent and I are coworkers in producing information the study requires.

A good research partnership is more important to the quality of the interview than the phrasing of specific questions. If the respondent and I get along well, he or she will accept that the detailed accounts I request are important for the study and will tolerate any fumbling or uncertainty in my questions.

In qualitative interviewing, questions are usually formulated during the interview rather than written out beforehand. There are no magic phrasings which will reliably elicit illuminating responses. However, there are several principles that are helpful. Concrete observations are almost always more useful than a respondent's generalizations. It is hard to guess from generalizations what underlying events the respondent is drawing on, or even whether the generalizations are based on specific events at all. So if a respondent says, "We got along fine," the interviewer should ask something like, "When you say that, what are you thinking of?" or "Can you tell me the last time that happened?" or "Can you think of a time that really showed that happening?" It can sometimes help for an interviewer to add, "The more concrete you can be, the better."

Respondents can provide fuller and more accurate reports if they are asked about events that happened recently. To know about the respondent's use of time, it makes sense to ask about yesterday; to learn about an event that occurs frequently, it makes sense to ask about the last time it happened. Should the respondent object that yesterday or the most recent event was not typical, it is then possible to ask what made it unusual, and then to ask for a description of an earlier day or event that was more nearly typical.

When a respondent is describing an important sequence of events, the interviewer might mentally check that the description contains adequate detail. In a study of work stress in an organization, a respondent might say, "I knew I was in trouble so I looked up this vice president and asked him for help." The interviewer might then have the respondent fill in what happened between when he recognized that he had a problem and when he asked for help from a particular

from interview to report

The following excerpts are from a study of retirement. The first part illustrates the sort of specific interview material a researcher might obtain. It is drawn from one of about a dozen interviews that address "puttering." The second part illustrates how such data are integrated into a general report.

Excerpts

Interviewer: What are your days like?

Respondent: Very quiet and uneventful.

Interviewer: Like yesterday, what, how did yesterday work? Maybe start in the morning.

Respondent: Well, I, I got up, had some breakfast I went out, ah, went out for about three or four hours and did a little bit of window shopping, a little Christmas shopping. I got back around noontime or so. Ah, I had lunch, watched the news . . . then just puttered around the house. Then I usually go to bed around 9 or 10 o'clock. Last night it was 10 o'clock. I had supper and watched television for a while and then I usually go to bed. But, like I said, very unexciting, very uneventful.

Interviewer: If you wanted to describe a really boring hour and get across what it felt like and what was going on. . . .

Respondent: Well I don't have a problem with that. I, ah, I can sit down and do absolutely nothing for an hour. And it doesn't bother me. I enjoy a chance to relax and not have the pressure of having to do something.

Report

Puttering is a relaxed way of moving through a day, engaging in activities as they attract one's attention, undertaking nothing that demands energy and concentration. The dishes need doing, so why not do them now? It's nice out, and a bit of gardening might be enjoyable. It's noontime, time for a sandwich and the news on television. Later, magazines need to be picked up and a room straightened. There is time for a bit of reading. E-mail may be checked, or an hour taken to organize the attic. Nothing has special urgency.

Retirees seem not to be bored by puttering. There is always something to fill time with, and the puttering is regularly interrupted by an activity to attend to, a hobby to pursue, a walk, or a bit of shopping or coffee with a friend. Mr. Oldsten was among the many respondents who liked taking it easy. He had been the purchasing director for a high-tech company, a job that was frequently stressful. His wife was still employed and so he spent most of the day alone.

Yesterday, I got up, had some breakfast, I went out for about three or four hours and did a little bit of window shopping. I got back around noontime or so. I had lunch, watched the news, then just puttered around the house. I had supper and watched television for a while. I usually go to bed around 9 or 10 o'clock, last night it was 10 o'clock. Very unexciting, very uneventful. I can sit down and do absolutely nothing for an hour. And it doesn't bother me. I enjoy a chance to relax and not have the pressure of having to do something.

executive. So, the interviewer might ask, "Could you start with when you realized you were in trouble and walk me through what happened next? How did the thought of going to the vice president come to you and what happened then?"

Although qualitative interviews are sometimes called conversational, they are not. Imagine a conversation in which a retiree, asked by a friend whether he had gone back to the office to see the people he had worked with, had replied, "People who come back after they've retired, the people who're there are nice, but there's nothing to talk about." The friend would hardly press the retiree for details he had not volunteered by asking, "Is there a specific time you're thinking of? Can you walk me through what happened?" But those are the questions an interviewer would ask.

shaping the study

Good interviews are windows into people's lives. Researchers can often edit the transcripts to cut out the questions and rearrange respondents' answers into engrossing first-person stories. Anthropologist Oscar Lewis, in his book *Children of Sanchez*, painted a compelling portrait of the lives of people in an impoverished Mexican family by presenting edited transcripts of qualitative interviews with the family's father and his four adult children. Journalist Studs Terkel has used excerpts from qualitative interviews as the entire content of books such as *Working*, in which his respondents discuss their jobs.

Both Lewis and Terkel focused on the stories of particular individuals, but many social scientists want to generalize about people's experiences and so want the breadth of information that multiple cases can provide. They want to be able to report not only about one particular retiree's experience, but about the experience of a population of retirees. That requires a sample of cases that includes the full range of important differences in the population. For example, an investigator studying the experience of retiring would want to talk with retirees from a range of occupations, both men and women, the married and unmarried, and people who liked their work and those who hated it.

Sometimes the topic makes it difficult to obtain a good sample. For example, in a study of active drug users an investigator may be restricted to a small group within which he or she finds acceptance. Investigators in such situations must make do, but they must also be aware of the limitations of their sample. They may learn how their respondents are distinct, but in any case, generalizations from unsystematic "convenience samples" have to be treated with caution.

Several factors must be taken into account when determining how many people should be interviewed. The more varied the population, the larger the sample needs to be to cover an adequate range. A study of retired executives requires a broader sample than one of retired bankers. Also important is the extent to which the investigator wants more than one respondent from the same category—for example, how many retired bankers? Redundancy can compensate for omissions and distortions, and can also uncover important variations among people who are apparently similar.

If there seem to be between a half dozen and a dozen important types of respondents, and if the investigator would like five instances of each variation, a sample size of between 30 and 60 is a rough ideal. The larger the sample, the more confidence the investigator will have that there is adequate range and enough redundancy to make other important, perhaps unsuspected, differences apparent.

Most investigators find that the amount of data produced by qualitative interviewing sets an upper limit on the number of respondents. One and a half hours of interviewing can produce 40 single-spaced pages of typescript. A study with 80 respondents might come close to filling a file drawer. Follow-up interviews with each respondent can double the volume. In my experience, 100 respondents are the most that can be dealt with comfortably, and so large a sample will almost surely provide enough material to yield an adequate basis for trustworthy generalization.

what to do with the data

Analyzing interview data can be daunting. There is likely to be a great deal of it, and no obvious place to start. Researchers may read through a few transcripts and feel excited by what is there, yet wonder how they can ever extract the essential message of those few transcripts, let alone the entire set. But there are fairly systematic ways of proceeding.

Just as in solving a jigsaw puzzle, the analysis of qualitative interview material requires sorting and integrating. For a study on retirement, one might begin by separating out the materials that deal with the decision to retire, with retirement parties, with the immediate reaction to being retired and so on. Within each of the sorted sets of materials, the investigator will identify "meaning units"—passages that deal with the same issue. A respondent's description of being urged to retire by a boss can be a single meaning unit, whether it was a brief comment or a full story. The investigator then summarizes all the meaning units dealing with an issue. That summary, perhaps augmented by interpretations or explanations, constitutes a report on the particular sector. The final study is then produced by integrating all of the sector reports into a single coherent story.

Before computers, researchers made marginal notes on interview transcripts, cut out passages with scissors, and sorted the resulting slips of paper into physical file folders. Computers have changed all this into virtual cutting and sorting. Some investigators use one of several computer programs designed specifically to assist in analyzing interview materials.

Investigators sometimes want to do more than use responses to narrate a subject, they want to explain what they have found. Developing an explanatory theory is a task that inevitably challenges the investigator's knowledge, insight, and creativity. But researchers have the ability to return to their interview transcripts to assess the validity of their conclusions in light of everything they were told.

rooting out bias

In recent years, social scientists who do qualitative interview studies have questioned some of the assumptions that underlie this method. Two

These audio tapes and written transcripts provide a durable record of in-depth interviews with teachers from two different schools about recent school reforms. The transcripts were subsequently coded and imported into a computer database so that passages from different interviewees addressing the same issue could be compared systematically. (Courtesy of Robert S. Weiss)

lines of critique have been especially important. The feminist critique focuses primarily on the relationship of interviewer and respondent, while the constructivist approach is more concerned with interpretation of interview materials.

The feminist critique arose from the experiences female investigators had while interviewing other women. The researchers were struck by the difference between their relationships with respondents and the sort of relationships that had been taken for granted in earlier studies. Previously, rapport was recognized as important, but respondents were largely related to only as providers of data, people whose words would be taken down, analyzed, and interpreted. Feminist scholars feel that this approach dehumanizes respondents and requires researchers to deny any identification with the interviewees. They feel it is essential to acknowledge their kinship with respondents. After all, the researchers were themselves insiders in their respondents' worlds: they too have families and family problems, work to which they are committed and priorities to juggle. It is more in keeping with this reality to replace inquiring with sharing.

Feminist investigators, among whom Ann Oakley has been a leading figure, also dislike the idea that after extracting information from respondents, they have nothing further to do with them. They want to acknowledge that interviewing establishes a relationship and that gaining access to someone's private life brings with it responsibilities. They feel it important to be of help to those respondents who are doing badly or, at the least, to accurately represent their plight. They also dislike the idea of owning the data drawn from respondents' lives. Some discuss their reports with their respondents and modify statements with which respondents disagree.

Constructivist investigators, such as Kathy Charmaz, were worried by investigators' insufficiently reflective leap from the reports of respondents to more general conclusions. They recognize that interpretations are not implicit in the data, but rather are influenced by the ideas and concerns that investigators bring to the data. In their view, investigators should acknowledge explicitly that their conclusions do not capture reality in the way that one might capture a butterfly. Instead, investigators shape respondents' reports in many possible ways. For example, a respondent's description of a problem with a boss may be classified as an instance of organizational friction rather than as a cause of work stress.

The constructivist perspective recasts the question of how close to reality an investigator can really get by talking to people. It argues that there is no single clear-cut reality to be located by means of interviews. Rather, what an investigator makes of interview information depends on his or her preconceptions and concerns. The interviews themselves may provide a basis for a number of interpretations, each of them consistent with the interview information.

The feminist and constructivist critiques draw attention to problems of ethics and interpretation that are implicit in the conduct of qualitative interview studies. When judging the credibility of a report these issues should be considered alongside other possible challenges, such as respondent credibility and the potential for investigator bias.

Perhaps the major threat to the validity of qualitative interviewing studies, more than distortions during the interview, is investigator bias. An investigator who is determined, consciously or unconsciously, to have a particular theme emerge from his or her study can choose respondents whose interviews are likely to produce that picture, encourage the respondents to give answers consistent with it, and write a report that neglects whatever might disconfirm it. Only a small minority of qualitative interview studies are significantly biased and these can usually be recognized easily.

reading interview studies

How can a reader evaluate a qualitative interview study? A good place to begin is with the sample. If the study was of people in a similar situation, did the sample have adequate range and redundancy? Did the interviews take place in a setting that encouraged respondents to provide full and accurate reports? If an event was witnessed by a number of people, are all relevant perspectives represented? And did the interview guide cover the full range of relevant issues? (Reports will often include an "interview guide," a list of the topics covered in the interviews, in an appendix.)

The trustworthiness of the data interpretation also can be judged by how closely it seems to be linked to the interviews, whether it appears to take all the interviews into consideration and the extent to which key points are buttressed by convincing quotations. Also worth considering is the investigator's use of supporting data from quantitative studies or from interviewers' observations. Finally, the investigator's conclusions could be matched against the conclusions of other studies and evaluated for their consistency with everything else the reader knows.

More than 150 years after Mayhew's groundbreaking work, qualitative interviewing is and will remain a fundamental method of social science. Even if other sources of information exist in archives or are accessible to observation, only qualitative interviewing can provide firsthand access to the experience of others. An oft-repeated joke describes a drunk searching for a lost wallet under a streetlight. "Did you drop it here?" someone asks. "Nope," he replies. "Dropped it in the alley. But the light's better here." Qualitative interviewing is looking in the dark alley, whatever might be the problems of doing so. If we want to learn from the experiences of other people, we must ask them to inform us. Although we are much more knowledgeable about how to conduct an interview than was Mayhew, and more aware of the difficulties that can arise as we try to achieve understanding from the information we obtain, fundamentally our approach remains the same.

RECOMMENDED RESOURCES

Kathy Charmaz. "Grounded Theory: Objectivist and Constructivist Methods." In *Handbook of Qualitative Research*, eds. Norman Denzin and Yvonna Lincoln (Sage Publications, 2000).

> This is both a brief exposition of how to do a qualitative study and a discussion of constructivist ideas.

Joseph C. Hermanowicz. *The Stars Are Not Enough: Scientists—Their Passions and Professions* (University of Chicago Press, 1998).

> Describes the interplay of ambition, career, and self-appraisal among physicists.

Arlie Russell Hochschild, with Anne Machung. *The Second Shift: Working Parents and the Revolution at Home* (Viking, 1989).

> Describes the unequal distribution of familial responsibilities in two-job families.

Oscar Lewis. *The Children of Sanchez, Autobiography of a Mexican Family* (Random House, 1961).

> In this classic study, Lewis recounts the life stories of a Mexican worker and his children.

Ann Oakley. "Interviewing Women: A Contradiction in Terms." In *The American Tradition in Qualitative Research* Vol. III, eds. Norman Denzin and Yvonna S. Lincoln (Sage Publications, 2001).

> An influential feminist critique of traditional approaches to interviewing.

Jessica Stern. *Terror in the Name of God: Why Religious Militants Kill* (HarperCollins, 2003).

Uncovers the aims, strategies, and motives of terrorists who believe they are doing God's work.

Diane Vaughan. *The* Challenger *Launch Decision: Risky Technology, Culture, and Deviance at NASA* (University of Chicago Press, 1996).

Describes the rational decision making that led to the tragically mistaken *Challenger* launch.

Robert S. Weiss. *Learning from Strangers: The Art and Method of Qualitative Interview Studies* (Free Press, 1994).

A text on qualitative interview methods.

REVIEW QUESTIONS

1. What are some reasons for being careful about trusting interviewees? How can such problems be minimized?

2. Why is cooperation important in qualitative interviews?

3. What are the feminist and "constructivist" critiques of qualitative interviews? How do these critiques recast the relationship between interviewer and respondent?

4. Activity: Develop a 15-question interview to administer to one of your classmates. Prepare both closed and open questions (see "sense and nonsense about surveys"), and be ready to improvise during the interview session. Afterwards, drawing on the "from interview to report" sidebar, prepare your own report of the interview. Which questions elicited the most interesting or unexpected answers, and why?

michael j. lovaglia

from summer camps to glass ceilings: the power of experiments

67

fall 2003

social science experiments on a few individuals from similar backgrounds can give rise to strategies for coping with social problems, ranging from intergroup conflict to women's inequality in the workplace. how does research on such narrow groups contribute to broad social understanding and insight?

A man in torn clothes sprawls across an urban sidewalk. He moans softly. Pedestrians hurry by with no more than a worried glance. No one stops to help. Someone watching from afar might wonder at such uncaring behavior; surely some conscientious person would stop. Moreover, these pedestrians are all young adults wearing clerical garb, seminarians studying for the ministry. They are hurrying to the church to deliver sermons on the Good Samaritan. Why did they not stop? Researchers who staged this test found that seminary students did not stop because they worried about being late. Their personal obligation to keeping an appointment outweighed their general commitment to helping others.

Experiments such as this one startle us into new ways of understanding people. Although we tend to explain why people do what they do—or, in this case, not do—as an expression of personal character, experiments show that the context of events determines behavior to a significant extent. Experimental studies carry great weight in the social sciences, gaining acceptance in prestigious journals and, in a high-profile example, last year's Nobel Prize in Economics. Some experiment results also get exposure in popular media, generating prime-time news coverage and Hollywood films.

Many people who hear about these experiments—and some social scientists, too—wonder how experiments achieve their power to convince, especially when their results often defy common sense. Experiments usually feature contrived conditions and record the behavior of at most a few hundred participants, many of whom are college students. Yet the results can tell us a lot about society.

the robbers cave experiment and summer camp movies

A sociological experiment in the 1950s demonstrated the effectiveness of a now common strategy in which competing corporations form joint ventures that would appear to prevent one firm from gaining advantage over the other (much like the United States and Russia cooperating on the space station). In 1954, Muzafer Sherif, an early proponent of social science experiments, set up a summer camp near Robbers Cave State Park in Oklahoma to test theories about group conflict and how to avoid it. He believed that individuals develop a group identity when they work together toward a common goal. Groups become more cohesive and rigid when faced with competition from another group. This competition creates frustration, triggering hostility and conflict between the groups. Sherif thought a solution to the conflict might be found in the same process by which groups form: working toward a common goal. If hostile groups have to work together, then members might learn to see each other as part of a combined larger group, which would reduce their conflict.

A group of 22 boys—all white, middle-class and close to their 12th birthdays—came to the Robbers Cave summer camp. Sherif and his colleagues divided them into two teams, the Eagles and the Rattlers. Each team completed projects requiring the cooperation of members, such as building a diving platform at a swimming hole. In the second phase of camp activities, the two teams competed against each other in various contests. The results are familiar. Rivalry between teams generated hostility and even a little mayhem (exaggerated in subsequent summer camp movies), and threatened to spin out of control. Hostility emerged during the first contest—a baseball game. Boys in each group cursed members of the opposing group and called them names. At dinner, Eagles refused to eat with Rattlers. Later, the Eagles tore down the Rattlers' flag and burned it. The Rattlers retaliated by vandalizing the Eagles' cabin. A food fight erupted in the mess hall.

The experiment showed that hostility between groups develops spontaneously when individuals within a group work together and then compete as a team against another group. The final phase of the experiment showed how to reduce conflict. On a hot summer day, researchers disabled the water supply and asked volunteers to find the problem. Boys from both groups stepped forward, located the problem, and worked together to solve it. Afterward, they all shared the water in a friendly manner. Finding water was important enough that it neutralized the groups' mutual antipathy, fostering cooperation and the beginning of trust.

An overarching cooperative task that requires the contributions of both groups for success reduced intergroup conflict. This principle is widely applied today, in contexts as distant as international relations, even though the experiment had nothing directly to do with such serious settings.

describing the world or testing theories

The logic of social experiments differs from that of other social research. Survey researchers, for example, try to describe a population of people by selecting a large, representative sample and then asking questions to determine respondents' attitudes and other characteristics. In contrast, experiments test theories rather than describe a population. That is, they test for evidence of a specific social process in a small sample of people, chosen to be as similar as possible. If a theory predicts a particular result under certain conditions, experimenters then set up only those conditions. In this way, researchers can tell whether the predicted differences in behavior are produced by the conditions of the experiment instead of by individual differences among the participants.

Psychologist Philip Zimbardo's prison experiment at Stanford University is another famous example. He tested the theory that the brutal behavior of guards in prison camps (such as those in Nazi Germany) was a result of their being guards, rather than a result of their being individuals psychologically prone to act brutally. Zimbardo predicted that normal, mentally healthy, American men would become brutal or be brutalized simply because they became either prison guards or prisoners.

In the early 1970s, Zimbardo created a "prison" in the basement of the psychology

The hallmarks of good experimental research:

- A comparison between two groups as similar as possible but for one theoretically important difference (for example, undergraduate women assigned by coin flip to be team leaders or followers).
- Controlled conditions that allow the experiment to be repeated by other researchers.
- Follow-up studies that confirm the initial results and rule out competing explanations.
- A theory supported by experimental results that makes valid predictions in other contexts, spawning new research that reinforces the theory.

Pitfalls to avoid:

- Experimental results in one context cannot be simply exported to other contexts or cultures; they can support theories, which may then be used to make predictions for findings in other contexts.
- Ethical problems must be carefully considered. What effect might the research have on the lives of experiment participants?

building at Stanford. He selected only male Stanford undergraduates to participate, ruling out those with any prior psychological problems. He then randomly assigned the participants to be either prisoners or prison guards. The procedure is like flipping a coin. Heads and the participant becomes a guard, tails and he gets arrested. Random assignment helped to ensure that the two groups in the experiment—guards and prisoners—would be similar in other ways. Within a day of the prisoners' arrival, guards began acting brutally and prisoners showed signs of anxiety. Conditions rapidly deteriorated until the experiment had to be stopped. (Because social experiments directly change people's lives, extraordinary care must be taken to avoid causing harm. Some social experiments have the potential to be as dangerous as a clinical trial testing a new drug. Today, universities' Institutional Review Boards review proposed social experiments as stringently as they do medical and other scientific studies on people.)

The Stanford prison experiment helped shift thinking away from blaming German culture for the Holocaust and toward the social conditions that promote brutal behavior. The study received much media attention and was made into a popular German movie, *Das Experiment*. Ironically, the film version concluded that the solution to brutality is for individuals to take personal responsibility for their actions. But a solution that follows more consistently from the study itself is to construct social situations that discourage brutality.

Why was this experiment so influential? It said nothing directly about German behavior during the Holocaust. Rather, it tested a theoretical prediction that a coercive setting can induce brutal behavior. A good experiment subtly shifts the burden of scientific proof, challenging other researchers to show whether a social process demonstrated in the experiment operates differently in a complex, naturally occurring setting. Simple experiments are convincing in part because they demonstrate a difference in the behavior of people in contrasting situations. Simplicity helps build agreement; most people observing the results of the Stanford and Robbers Cave experiments would interpret their meanings similarly. Controlled conditions also allow other researchers to repeat the experiments to see if the same results occur, perhaps using slightly different procedures. Good experiments can in these ways extend theories and produce new knowledge.

Of course, no single study, theory, or method, no matter how good, establishes a scientific fact. Instead, science synthesizes different kinds of research from a variety of researchers to reach its conclusions. An experiment such as Zimbardo's Stanford prison makes a simple yet forceful statement that builds on earlier and inspires later research pointing to a conclusion. Eventually, we better understand the social processes underlying a problem and can attempt a practical intervention. Experiments also can be used to directly assess the effectiveness of alternative social policies.

arresting domestic violence: experimenting with social policy

In 1981, police in Minneapolis changed the way they responded to reports of domestic violence. Before 1981, police officers had the discretion to arrest the person who committed the assault, order him (or her) to leave the home for a short period or provide on-site counseling. Advocates expressed concern that police were treating episodes of domestic violence too leniently, thereby failing to deter future assaults. Lawrence Sherman and Richard Berk designed an experiment to test whether making an arrest in a domestic violence case deterred future assaults better than the other two options of separating the couple and counseling.

The experiment had important implications for public policy, but it also addressed a longstanding dispute between two theoretical traditions in criminology. Deterrence theory holds that punishment discourages future criminal behavior. This school of thought maintains that suspects who are arrested will be less likely to commit another assault than those who are separated or counseled. A second theoretical tradition, known as labeling theory, suggests that when individuals are arrested, they become stigmatized as criminals by both society and in their own eyes. Their new self-image as a criminal then increases the likelihood of subsequent criminal behavior. (Labeling theory is the reason that names of juvenile offenders are kept out of the media except for serious offenses.) If labeling theory is valid, then those arrested for domestic violence actually would be more likely to commit another assault.

During the Sherman-Berk experiment, whenever Minneapolis police officers responded to a domestic violence call, they determined which procedure—arrest, separation, or counseling—to follow by random assignment. Researchers tracked the behavior of suspects in the study for six months following the domestic violence incident. Results showed a deterrent effect for arrest and no evidence for labeling theory. That is, suspects who had been arrested were slightly less likely to commit another assault during the subsequent six months than were those who had been separated or counseled.

Although the deterrence effect of arrest was small, the experiment had a large effect on public policy. Arrest in domestic violence cases became the preferred procedure in many police departments and 15 states passed mandatory arrest laws. Meanwhile, debate over implications for social theory continued. During the next decade, other researchers repeated the experiment in several other police jurisdictions. The new results were more complicated. Arrest deterred suspects who were employed, perhaps because arrest is more serious for those who have a lot to lose. For unemployed suspects, arrest had the opposite effect, as predicted by labeling theory. They were more likely to commit a subsequent assault than the unemployed men who had been separated or counseled. The theoretical advance was exciting, but it left policy implications unresolved. In practice, police officers are still uncertain whether making an arrest will be beneficial in a domestic violence case. More systematic research could better equip police and judges to make such critical, sometimes life-and-death decisions.

We may need a system that produces public policies in a way similar to the system of clinical trials that produces new medical drugs. None of the alternatives available to the police in the Minneapolis experiment was new. But we do not have an organized system to formulate new policies, test them, and then compare them to alternative policies in controlled experiments. Such a system is worth considering. It might lead to more effective public policy the way that our system of developing new drugs has led to more effective medicine.

why do some groups score low on standardized tests?

Low intelligence seems the obvious explanation for low scores on a mental ability test. But what if something besides intelligence determines test scores? In the 1990s, psychologist Claude Steele's experiments yielded the startling discovery that scores on standardized tests depend not only on students' ability to answer, but also on what they expect the consequences of their test scores to be. Students who are stereotyped as having low ability may underperform when they are apprehensive about getting a low score.

Steele and his colleagues conducted a simple experiment. They gave a difficult standardized test—like the college SAT but harder—to a group of Stanford students. Instructions for taking the test varied. Some students, selected at random, were told the test results could be used to compare their performance to that of other students. Some students were told the test was only to familiarize them with similar tests they would encounter at the university. When students were told the tests were just for familiarization, black students scored about the same as white students of similar academic attainment. But when students thought they were going to be compared, black students scored lower than did comparable white students—as is common on standardized tests.

My colleagues and I conducted subsequent experiments showing that Steele's theory was not limited to particular racial groups, but applied to any stigmatized group. We randomly assigned white university undergraduates to be treated as an advantaged "majority" or disadvantaged "minority," by telling some students that their left- or right-handedness made it unlikely that they would be able to contribute to a group project, and also that other group members might resent their inability to contribute. Then, we gave the students a standard test of mental ability, explaining that the results of the test would be used to assign them to group positions such as "supervisor," "analyst," or "menial" in the group project. We found that students' test scores were substantially lower if they were treated as a disadvantaged "minority" for as little as 20 minutes.

The line of research begun by Claude Steele now includes many studies by different researchers. They show that when black and white students take the same standardized test, different expectations for the consequences of the test—not differences in mental ability—determine whether white students have an advantage. That is, while the best mental ability tests do a fair job of determining differences in cognitive skills among otherwise similar individuals, differences in test scores between racial and ethnic groups are created by social conditions rather than by the groups' mental abilities.

Applied programs based on this research show promise for increasing the academic performance of disadvantaged students. One surprising detail is that the performances of the best black students suffer the most. The threat of fulfilling a negative stereotype is felt most keenly by black students with the potential to excel; it is they who worry most about the potential backlash from their competition with white students. This may explain why remedial programs to improve academic performance of weaker students have not closed the gap between blacks and whites generally. Honors programs that encourage black students to undertake accelerated studies may have more effect, because promising black students have more academic ability than their grades and test scores suggest. Claude Steele helped develop a successful program to improve the performance of incoming minority students at the University of Michigan that emphasizes high academic standards, affirming students' ability to achieve those standards, and building trust that successful minority students can be accepted in the academic community.

how can women attain status equal to men at work?

Social experiments can also suggest strategies individuals can use to improve their lives. Status Characteristics Theory explains how individuals attain influence in work groups: people who are expected to contribute more to the group gain more influence in the group and receive greater rewards from the group. That is,

expected contributions often count more than actual contributions. Individuals expected to perform well are more often followed by the group and rewarded accordingly. For example, a woman may make a brilliant suggestion that guarantees a successful project, but her suggestion may be ignored until a respected male co-worker endorses it. He then gets the credit.

Research using the theory confirms that people expect men to contribute more to group success than women and that men do have more influence in decision making. Men get more credit for the group's successes and less blame for the group's failures. And when group members are evaluated, men get higher performance ratings and bigger rewards. To achieve the same level of rewards, women must work harder and contribute more than men. Status Characteristics Theory can also explain the familiar strategies women have used to break through to positions of influence in the workplace. Traditionally, they have out-competed men, following a masculine model that includes demonstrating competence through hard work and aggressive, even ruthless, competition. Successful women sometimes feel that they have sacrificed too much of themselves by following "male" strategies.

In the early 1980s, Cecilia Ridgeway conducted experiments using this theory that produced remarkable results for professional women struggling for career advancement under a glass ceiling. Ridgeway realized that people value not only the ability of a person to contribute, but also whether that person is motivated by a desire to help the group; they would not expect a person who is competent but selfish to contribute much of value. Ridgeway proposed that, because of gender stereotypes, however, people expect that even selfishly motivated men will contribute to the group, but expect contributions from women only when women demonstrate that they care about the group.

the hawthorne experiment

In the late 1920s and early 1930s, a Western Electric Company assembly plant near Chicago was the site of a series of studies aimed at developing scientifically based strategies for increasing worker productivity.

One experiment led to a concept called the "Hawthorne Effect." The researchers took a small group of female workers away from their peers, and placed them in a separate room so the experimenters could study the effect of changes in lighting, work procedures, and break times on their productivity. It came as no surprise that improved lighting increased the workers' productivity, at least at first. But when the experimenters lowered the lighting to earlier levels, productivity continued to increase. Similar results after changing other aspects of the workers' environment led researchers to a conclusion that has since become known as the Hawthorne Effect: Workers increased their efforts because they were getting attention from the researchers, and because they bonded together as members of a prestigious "special" group.

Though legendary in its implications, the experiment has been criticized for design flaws and for confounding key variables, for example, two members of the study group were replaced mid-experiment with two new workers selected for their industriousness and cooperativeness. Simultaneous investigations by other sociologists revealed that workers who bonded strongly could unite to suppress work effort as well as speed it up.

Despite such shortcomings, reports of the Hawthorne experiment were used with enthusiasm by advocates of the human relations approach to workplace management. They felt that the results of the experiment challenged the scientific management perspectives that had shaped the Hawthorne studies in the first place. As a concept, the Hawthorne Effect—which posits that many interventions work, whatever they are, simply because people respond to being studied—also has been applied to a range of situations, such as student achievement in experimental schools, community organizing, and military campaigns. Such applications confirm the power of relatively small experiments to stimulate thinking about issues of great importance, both for sociologists and for the larger public.

Ridgeway conducted an experiment to test this theory. Four team members worked together to reach a decision. One of the team members—secretly collaborating with the experimenters—made comments that were either group-motivated ("It is important that we cooperate") or self-motivated ("I want to win points for myself"). As predicted, in the self-motivated condition, male collaborators had more influence over the groups' decisions than female collaborators.

In the group-motivated conditions, however, women collaborators' influence increased while the men's stayed at about the same high level as when they appeared selfish. Put another way, group-motivated women had as much influence as equally competent men regardless of the males' motivations.

The results suggest a strategy to succeed at work that women could use as an alternative to the competitive male one. Demonstrated competence is primary. Assertiveness also helps, but the focus on ruthless competition may be unnecessary for women's success. Instead, emphasizing a concern for other group members and the importance of working together to accomplish group goals can help competent women achieve recognition for their contributions. Future research in actual workplaces will help refine an effective strategy.

from theory to practice

The power of experiments flows from their use to test general theories. Sherif's Robbers Cave experiment tested a theory that explains how cooperation forms within groups and competition develops between them. Ridgeway tested her theory that influence in groups flows from the expectations people have about the ability and motivation of group members to contribute to group success.

Alone, a social experiment only demonstrates some phenomenon in one restricted context. But when experiments test theories, and their results lead to more tests in wider contexts, as well as other research with other methods, then we gain knowledge capable of transforming society. The experiments described have inspired lines of research with the potential to increase cooperation among competing organizations, decrease domestic violence, reduce the racial gap in academic success, and remove the glass ceiling limiting women in business. They successfully made the leap from small groups to helping us understand society at large.

RECOMMENDED RESOURCES

American Sociological Review. "Employment, Marriage, and the Deterrent Effect of Arrest for Domestic Violence: Replications and Re-Analyses," 57 (1992): 679–708.

Three research articles analyze followup studies to the original Sherman and Berk experiment on police responses to domestic violence.

Joseph Berger and Morris Zelditch, Jr., eds. *Status, Rewards and Influence* (Jossey-Bass, 1985).

An overview of research on status processes in task groups.

Bernard P. Cohen. *Developing Sociological Knowledge: Theory and Method* (Nelson Hall, 1989).

A classic text that describes social science as a reciprocal process in which research tests theory and theory develops through the interpretation of research.

Michael J. Lovaglia. *Knowing People: The Personal Use of Social Psychology* (McGraw-Hill, 2000).

An accessible overview of social psychological research useful for individuals in their personal lives.

Michael J. Lovaglia, Jeffery W. Lucas, Jeffrey A. Houser, Shane R. Thye, and Barry Markovsky. "Status Processes and Mental Ability Test Scores." *American Journal of Sociology* 104 (1998): 195–228.

A research article demonstrating the adverse effect of a negative stereotype on the standardized test scores of white students.

Cecilia Ridgeway. "Status in Groups: The Importance of Motivation." *American Sociological Review* 47 (1982): 76–88.

An important research article that suggests a way for women to achieve equal status in the workplace.

Muzafer Sherif, O. J. Harvey, B. Jack White, William R. Hood, and Carolyn W. Sherif. *The Robbers Cave Experiment: Intergroup Conflict and Cooperation* (Wesleyan University Press, [1961] 1988).

The classic study on the origins of conflict between groups and a method for bringing together competing groups.

Claude M. Steele. "Thin Ice: 'Stereotype Threat' and Black College Students." *Atlantic Monthly*. August, 1999.

> An accessible overview of research and applied programs for reducing the disadvantage of black college students.

REVIEW QUESTIONS

1. In what ways might experiments on only a few individuals potentially contribute to sociological knowledge?
2. Muzafer Sherif conducted an experiment with 22 boys at a summer camp, separated into two groups, "Eagles" and "Rattlers." Explain why hostility developed between the two groups and the circumstances in which intergroup hostility could be reduced.
3. Describe the Hawthorne study, and explain what the "Hawthorne Effect" is. On what methodological grounds has this experiment been criticized?
4. The author mentions the ethical challenges posed by social science experiments. If some experiments can offer a richer understanding of intergroup conflict and help explain surprisingly brutal behavior, why should Institutional Review Boards (IRBs) be involved in the research process?

editors and contributors

Douglas Hartmann is in the sociology department at the University of Minnesota. He is the author of *Race, Culture, and the Revolt of the Black Athlete: The 1968 Olympic Protests and their Aftermath.*

Christopher Uggen is in the sociology department at the University of Minnesota. He is the author (with Jeff Manza) of *Locked Out: Felon Disenfranchisement and American Democracy.*

Patricia A. Adler is in the department of sociology at the University of Colorado at Boulder. She is the editor (with Peter Adler) of *Constructions of Deviance: Social Power, Context, and Interaction.*

Peter Adler is in the department of sociology and criminology at the University of Denver. He is the editor (with Patricia A. Adler) of *Constructions of Deviance: Social Power, Context, and Interaction.*

Syed Ali is in the sociology/anthropology department at Long Island University in Brooklyn, New York. He is the author of *Dubai: Gilded Cage.*

Elizabeth A. Armstrong is in the department of sociology at the University of Michigan. She studies how social class shapes women's academic, social, and romantic paths.

Javier Auyero is in the sociology department at the University of Texas at Austin. He is the author (with Debora Swistun) of *Flammable: Environmental Suffering in an Argentine Shantytown.*

Gianpaolo Baiocchi is in the sociology department and the Watson Institute for International Studies at Brown University. He is the author (with Patrick Heller and Marcelo Kunrath Silva) of *Bootstrapping Democracy: Transforming Local Governance and Civil Society in Brazil.*

Shawn Bauldry is in the sociology department at the University of North Carolina–Chapel Hill. He is interested in research methods and educational attainment.

William Beaver is in the social science department at Robert Morris University. He studies educational issues.

Lisa F. Berkman is the epidemiology director of the Harvard Center for Population and Development Studies. She is the author (with Ichiro Kawachi) of *Neighborhoods and Health.*

Ellen Berrey is in the sociology department at the University at Buffalo, The State University of New York. She studies political rhetoric on diversity and employment discrimination.

Joel Best is in the sociology and criminal justice department at the University of Delaware. He is the author of *Stat-Spotting: A Field Guide to Identifying Dubious Data.*

Eduardo Bonilla-Silva is in the sociology department at Duke University. He is the author (with Moon Kie Jung and Joao Vargas) of *The State of White Supremacy: Racisms, Governance, and the USA.*

Robert J. Brym is in the department of sociology at the University of Toronto. He is the author of *Sociology as a Life or Death Issue.*

Jess Butler is in the sociology department at the University of Southern California. She studies cultural practices, post-feminist sexualities, and racial politics.

Deborah Carr is the trends editor of *Contexts* and is in the department of sociology at Rutgers University. She is the co-author of *Essentials of Sociology.*

Bruce G. Carruthers is in the sociology department at Northwestern University. He is the author (with Terence Halliday) of *Bankrupt: Global Lawmaking and Systemic Financial Crisis.*

Mark Chaves is in the department of sociology at Duke University. He is the author of *Congregations in America.*

Kimberly J. Cook is in the department of sociology and criminology at the University of North Carolina–Wilmington. She is the author of *Divided Passions: Public Opinions on Abortion and the Death Penalty.*

Jeffrey C. Dixon is in the department of sociology and anthropology at the College of the

Holy Cross. He studies political sociology and race and ethnicity.

F. Nii-Amoo Dodoo is in the department of sociology at Pennsylvania State University and is the director of the Regional Institute for Population Studies at the University of Ghana. He studies the intersections of gender and power in fertility decisions.

Douglas B. Downey is in the sociology department at the Ohio State University. He studies schools and inequality.

Elaine Howard Ecklund is in the department of sociology at Rice University. She is the author of *Science vs. Religion: What Scientists Really Think.*

Kathryn Edin is in the department of sociology at Harvard University. She is the author (with Maria Kefalas) of *Promises I Can Keep: Why Poor Women Put Motherhood before Marriage.*

Paula England is in the department of sociology at Stanford University. Her research focuses on gender inequality in labor markets and how gender and class affect family life.

Bonnie Erickson is in the department of sociology at the University of Toronto. She studies social networks, inequality, work, and gender.

George Farkas is in the department of education at the University of California–Irvine. His research focuses on reducing inequality in education.

Joe Feagin is in the department of sociology at Texas A&M University. He is the author (with L. Houts) of *Backstage Racism.*

Jason A. Freeman is in the department of sociology at the University of North Carolina–Chapel

Hill. He studies religion and its role in genetics and health.

Ashley E. Frost is in the sociology department at Penn State University. She studies gender inequality, men's attitudes, and population issues in sub-Saharan Africa.

Frank F. Furstenberg, Jr. is in the sociology department and Population Studies Center at the University of Pennsylvania. He studies the family in disadvantaged urban neighborhoods, adolescent sexual behavior, and children's well-being.

Joshua Gamson is in the sociology department at the University of San Francisco. He is the author of *Claims to Fame: Celebrity in Contemporary America*.

Herbert J. Gans is a professor emeritus in the department of sociology at Columbia University. He is the author of *Imagining America in 2033*.

Kathleen Gerson is in the department of sociology at New York University. She is the author (with Jerry A. Jacobs) of *The Time Divide*.

Benjamin G. Gibbs is in the sociology department at Brigham Young University. He studies the origins of social stratification.

Michael Goldman is in the sociology department and the Institute for Global Studies at the University of Minnesota. He is the author of *Imperial Nature: The World Bank and the Struggle for Social Justice in the Age of Globalization*.

Laura Hamilton is in the department of sociology at the University of California, Merced. She studies how social class shapes women's academic, social, and romantic paths.

Geoff Harkness is in the liberal arts departments at Northwestern University and Carnegie Mellon University in Qatar. He studies visual ethnography, race and ethnicity, and culture.

Sharon Hays is in the gender studies and sociology departments at the University of Southern California. She studies gender, culture, and social inequality.

Cedric Herring is in the department of sociology and the Institute of Government and Public Affairs at the University of Illinois at Chicago. He studies stratification, social policies, and labor force issues.

Kathleen E. Hull is in the department of sociology at the University of Minnesota. She is the author of *Same-Sex Marriage: The Cultural Politics of Love and Law*.

Jerry A. Jacobs is in the sociology department at the University of Pennsylvania. He is the author (with Ann Boulis) of *The Changing Face of Medicine*.

J. Craig Jenkins is in the department of sociology and the Mershon Center for International Security Studies at the Ohio State University. He is the editor (with Bert Klandermans) of *The Politics of Social Protest: Comparative Perspectives on States and Social Movements*.

Maria Kefalas is in the department of sociology and the Institute for Violence Research and Prevention at St. Joseph's University. She is the author (with Patrick Carr) of *Hollowing Out the Middle: The Rural Brain Drain and What it Means for America*.

Sheela Kennedy is in the Minnesota Population Center at the University of Minnesota. She studies family, children, and economics.

Lane Kenworthy is in the sociology and political science departments at the University of Arizona. He is the author of *Progress for the Poor*.

Pearl Latteier holds a Ph.D. in communication arts from the University of Wisconsin-Madison. Her dissertation was about Hollywood's social-problem films.

Kate Ledger is a freelance writer in St. Paul, Minnesota. She is the author of the novel *Remedies*.

Ching Kwan Lee is in the department of sociology at the University of California, Los Angeles. She is the author of *Against the Law: Labor Protests in China's Rustbelt and Sunbelt*.

Stephen Lerner is the architect of the SEIU's Justice for Janitors campaign and has served as the director of the union's Property Services Division for two decades.

Peggy Levitt is in the sociology department at Wellesley College and the Transnational Studies Initiative at Harvard University. She is the author of *God Needs No Passport: Immigrants and the Changing American Religious Landscape*.

Andrew M. Lindner is in the sociology department at Concordia College, Moorhead. He studies the intersection of media and politics.

Meika Loe is in sociology and women's studies at Colgate University. She is the author of *The Rise of Viagra: How the Little Blue Pill Changed Sex in America*.

Enid Logan is in the sociology department at the University of Minnesota. She is the author of *At this Defining Moment: Barack Obama's Presidential Candidacy and the New Politics of Race*.

Wesley Longhofer is in the department of organization and management at Emory University.

He studies comparative political sociology, philanthropy and non-profits, and globalization.

Michael J. Lovaglia is in the department of sociology at the University of Iowa. He is the author of *Knowing People: The Personal Use of Social Psychology*.

The MacArthur Foundation Research Network on an Aging Society consists of John W. Rowe, Lisa F. Berkman, Robert Binstock, Axel Boersch-Supan, John Cacioppo, Laura Carstensen, Dana Goldman, Linda Fried, James Jackson, Martin Kohli, Jay Olshansky, and John Rother.

Jeff Manza is in the department of sociology at New York University. He is the author (with Christopher Uggen) of *Locked Out: Felon Disenfranchisement and American Democracy*.

William Marsiglio is in the sociology, criminology, and law department at the University of Florida. He is the author of *Men on a Mission: Valuing Youth Work in our Communities*.

Nicole MartinRogers is a sociologist with Wilder Research, a non-profit health and human services organization in St. Paul, Minnesota.

Michael Massoglia is in the department of sociology and crime, law, and justice at Pennsylvania State University. He studies crime and health.

Paul Mattessich is a sociologist with Wilder Research, a non-profit health and human services organization in St. Paul, Minnesota.

Katherine McCoy is in the sociology department at Bucknell University. She studies the use of private military corporations in war and conflict.

Vonnie C. McLoyd is in the psychology department and the Center for Human Growth and

Development at the University of Michigan. She studies the effects of economic disadvantage and work-related transitions on family life.

Ann Meier is in the department of sociology at the University of Minnesota. She studies the form, character, and consequences of adolescent relationships.

Timothy Ortyl is in the sociology program at the University of Minnesota. He studies gender, sexuality, and non-traditional families.

Josh Pacewicz is an ASA post-doctoral fellow at Stanford University. He studies political preference formation in the United States.

Andrew J. Perrin is in the sociology department at the University of North Carolia, Chapel Hill. He is the author of *Citizen Speak: The Democratic Imagination in American Life.*

Lindsey Peterson is in the sociology department at the Ohio State University. She studies stratification, movements, and political sociology.

Becky Pettit is in the department of sociology at the University of Washington. She is the author (with Jennifer Hook) of *Gendered Tradeoffs: Family, Social Policy, and Economic Inequality in Twenty-One Countries.*

Stephen Poulson is in the sociology department at James Madison University. He is the author of *Social Movements in Twentieth-Century Iran: Culture, Ideology, and Mobilizing Frameworks.*

Mark R. Rank is in the George Warren Brown School of Social Work at Washington University in St. Louis. He is the author of *One Nation, Underprivileged: Why American Poverty Affects Us All.*

Ela Rausch is a sociologist with Wilder Research, a non-profit health and human services organization in St. Paul, Minnesota.

Jen'nan Ghazal Read is in the sociology department and global health institute at Duke University. She studies the social integration of Muslim Americans and Arab Americans.

Vincent J. Roscigno is in the sociology department and the Criminal Justice Research Center at the Ohio State University. He is the author of *The Face of Discrimination: How Race and Gender Impact Work and Home Lives.*

Richard Rosenfeld is in criminology and criminal justice at the University of Missouri-St. Louis. He is the author (with Steven Messner) of *Crime and the American Dream.*

Ruben Rumbaut is in the sociology department at the University of California, Irvine. He is the author (with Alejandro Portes) of *Immigrant America: A Portrait.*

Robert J. Sampson is in the department of social sciences and the Radcliffe Institute for Advanced Study at Harvard University. He is the author of *Great American City: Chicago and the Enduring Neighborhood Effect.*

Stephen J. Scanlan is in the department of sociology and anthropology at Ohio University. He studies comparative social change with an emphasis on food insecurity and development.

Jason Schnittker is in the sociology department at the University of Pennsylvania. He studies how social and genetic factors interact to produce physical and mental health outcomes.

Howard Schuman is an emeritus professor of sociology at the University of Michigan. He is the author of *Meaning and Method in Polls and Surveys*.

Richard Settersten, Jr., is in human development and family sciences and the Hallie Ford Research Center at Oregon State University. He is the author (with Barbara E. Ray) of *Not Quite Adults: Why 20-Somethings Are Choosing a Slower Path to Adulthood, and Why It's Good for Everyone*.

Michael J. Shanahan is in the department of sociology at the University of North Carolina–Chapel Hill. He studies links among genetic factors, status attainment processes, and health.

Robin W. Simon is in the sociology department at Florida State University. She studies gender and other social factors in the experiences and expression of emotion.

Randy Stoecker is in community and environmental sociology at the University of Wisconsin–Madison. He is the author of *Research Methods for Community Change*.

Pamela Stone is in the sociology department at Hunter College and the Graduate Center of the City University of New York. She is the author of *Opting Out? Why Women Really Quit Careers and Head Home*.

Debora Swistun is an anthropologist at the Universidad Nacional de la Plata (Argentina). She is the author (with Javier Auyero) of *Flammable: Environmental Suffering in an Argentine Shantytown*.

Edward E. Telles is in the sociology department at Princeton University. He is the author (with Vilma Ortiz) of *Generations of Exclusion: Mexican Americans, Assimilation, and Race*.

Donald Tomaskovic-Devey is in the department of sociology at the University of Massachusetts–Amherst. He studies racial and gender inequality.

Patricia Warren is in the college of criminology and criminal justice at Florida State University. She studies racial disparities in crime and justice outcomes.

Robert S. Weiss is an emeritus professor of sociology and is in the Gerontology Institute at the University of Massachusetts–Boston. He is the author of *Staying the Course*.

Ronald Weitzer is in the sociology department at George Washington University. He is the author of *Sex for Sale: Prostitution, Pornography, and the Sex Industry*.

Barry Wellman is a sociologist at the University of Toronto and the Centre for Urban and Community Studies. He studies social communication, information, and computer networks.

Bruce Western is in the department of sociology at Harvard University. He is the author of *Punishment and Inequality in America*.

Saundra D. Westervelt is in the department of sociology at the University of North Carolina–Greensboro. She is the author of *Wrongly Convicted: Perspectives on Failed Justice*.

W. Bradford Wilcox is in the sociology department at the University of Virginia. He studies how gender, religion, and race influence marriage, parenthood, and cohabitation.

Min Zhou is in the departments of sociology and Asian American studies at the University of California, Los Angeles. She is the author of *Contemporary Chinese America: Immigration, Ethnicity, and Community Transformation*.